THE PROSPECTS OF COMMON CONCERN OF HUMANKIND IN INTERNATIONAL LAW

The Common Concern of Humankind today is central to efforts to bring about enhanced international cooperation in fields including, but not limited to, climate change. This book explores the expression's potential as a legal concept and a future legal principle. It sets out the origins of Common Concern, its differences to other common interest legal principles, and expounds the potential normative structure and effects of the principle, applying an approach of carrots and sticks in realising goals defined as a Common Concern. Individual chapters test the principle in different legal fields, including climate technology diffusion, marine plastic pollution, human rights enforcement, economic inequality, migration, and monetary and financial stability. They confirm that basic obligations under the principle of Common Concern of Humankind comprise not only that of international cooperation and duties to negotiate, but also of unilateral duties to act to enhance the potential of public international law to produce appropriate public goods.

THOMAS COTTIER, former managing director of the World Trade Institute, is Professor Emeritus of European and International Economic Law at the University of Bern and an adjunct professor of law at the University of Ottawa. He has published widely in the field of international economic law, with a particular focus on constitutional theory and general principles of law, trade regulation and intellectual property.

ZAKER AHMAD, former student and researcher at the World Trade Institute, received his PhD from the Faculty of Law of the University of Bern. He is an Assistant Professor of law at the University of Chittagong in Bangladesh.

THE PROSPECTS OF COMMON CONCERN OF HUMANKIND IN INTERNATIONAL LAW

Edited by

THOMAS COTTIER
World Trade Institute

In association with

ZAKER AHMAD
World Trade Institute

CAMBRIDGE
UNIVERSITY PRESS

University Printing House, Cambridge CB2 8BS, United Kingdom

One Liberty Plaza, 20th Floor, New York, NY 10006, USA

477 Williamstown Road, Port Melbourne, VIC 3207, Australia

314–321, 3rd Floor, Plot 3, Splendor Forum, Jasola District Centre, New Delhi – 110025, India

79 Anson Road, #06–04/06, Singapore 079906

Cambridge University Press is part of the University of Cambridge.

It furthers the University's mission by disseminating knowledge in the pursuit of education, learning, and research at the highest international levels of excellence.

www.cambridge.org
Information on this title: www.cambridge.org/9781108840088
DOI: 10.1017/9781108878739

© Cambridge University Press 2021

This publication is in copyright. Subject to statutory exception and to the provisions of relevant collective licensing agreements, no reproduction of any part may take place without the written permission of Cambridge University Press.

First published 2021

A catalogue record for this publication is available from the British Library.

ISBN 978-1-108-84008-8 Hardback

Cambridge University Press has no responsibility for the persistence or accuracy of URLs for external or third-party internet websites referred to in this publication and does not guarantee that any content on such websites is, or will remain, accurate or appropriate.

CONTENTS

List of Figures   *page* vii
Notes on Contributors   ix
Preface   xiii
Acknowledgements   xvii
List of Abbreviations   xix

PART I   Theory

1   The Principle of Common Concern of Humankind   3
THOMAS COTTIER

PART II   Case Studies

2   Trade-Related Measures to Spread Low-Carbon
Technologies: A Common Concern–Based Approach   95
ZAKER AHMAD

3   Marine Plastic Pollution as a Common Concern
of Humankind   153
JUDITH SCHÄLI

4   Exploring the Recognition of New Common Concerns
of Humankind: The Example of the Distribution
of Income and Wealth within States   199
ALEXANDER BEYLEVELD

5   Reshaping the Law of Economic Sanctions
for Human Rights Enforcement: The Potential
of Common Concern of Humankind   247
IRYNA BOGDANOVA

6   Migration as a Common Concern of Humankind   292
THOMAS COTTIER AND ROSA MARIA LOSADA

vi   CONTENTS

7   International Monetary Stability as a Common Concern of Humankind   347

LUCIA SATRAGNO

8   Financial Stability as a Common Concern of Humankind   400

FEDERICO LUPO-PASINI

PART III   Epilogue

9   Comments: The Doctrinal Approach of Common Concern   431

PETER-TOBIAS STOLL, DUNCAN FRENCH AND OISIN SUTTLE

10   Comments: Extraterritoriality and Common Concern   447

CEDRIC RYNGAERT, CLAUS ZIMMERMANN AND KRISTA NADAKAVUKAREN SCHEFER

Index   461

FIGURES

2.1 Innovation cycle *page* 98
2.2 Complementarities in trade-related technology diffusion 116
3.1 Approximate positions of open-ocean plastic accumulation zones 161

CONTRIBUTORS

ZAKER AHMAD earned his PhD from the Faculty of Law of the Unversity of Berne in 2020. The focus of his research is on using the doctrine of Common Concern in the field of international trade to facilitate diffusion of low-carbon technologies. He is Assistant Professor at the University of Chittagong in Bangladesh. Apart from teaching, Zaker has some experience of consultancy in trade policy matters. He holds a MILE degree from the WTI and an LLM from the University of Chittagong.

ALEXANDER BEYLEVELD is a senior researcher at the Mandela Institute, University of the Witwatersrand and was awarded a PhD in Law by the Faculty of Law of the University of Bern in 2020. Prior to holding his current position, Alex worked at Webber Wentzel, a corporate law firm in Johannesburg. He has also spent time as a doctoral fellow and teaching assistant at the World Trade Institute (WTI) in Bern, as well as at the World Trade Organization (WTO) as an intern, first in its Market Access Division and then with its Appellate Body Secretariat. Prior to his time at the WTI and WTO, Alex was a legal researcher and clerk to Justice Sisi Khampepe of the Constitutional Court of South Africa.

IRYNA BOGDANOVA was awarded her PhD by the Faculty of Law of the University of Bern in 2020. In 2015 she graduated from the Master of International Law and Economics Program at the World Trade Institute, University of Bern. Iryna received her bachelor's and master's diplomas with honours from the National University of Kyiv-Mohyla Academy, Ukraine. In 2016 Iryna worked as an intern at the Appellate Body Secretariat of the World Trade Organization. Previously, she worked as a consultant at one of the leading European law firms in Brussels. Prior to that, Iryna worked as a legal and corporate affairs manager for a multinational corporation in Ukraine.

THOMAS COTTIER is Emeritus Professor of European and International Economic Law and senior research fellow. He was a founder and former managing director of the World Trade Institute, University of Bern, Switzerland. He has a long-standing interest in squaring general principles of law, human rights and sustainability with international economic law, in particular in the field of international trade regulation, and to contribute to the doctrine of multilevel governance harnessing globalisation. He taught and published widely in the field, was a former trade negotiator for Switzerland and has been a member and chair of several GATT and WTO dispute settlement panels.

DUNCAN FRENCH is Pro Vice Chancellor and Professor of International Law at the University of Lincoln, United Kingdom. He specialises in international environmental law and law of the sea, inter alia, having written widely on sustainable development, common concern and differentiated responsibilities. His most recent work has been on the draft Global Pact for the Environment, the International Seabed Authority, and international environment dispute settlement.

ROSA MARIA LOSADA obtained her PhD from the Faculty of Law of the University of Bern in 2020. She worked as deputy head and head ad interim of the Third-State Nationals Unit in the Swiss Federal Office for Migration (FOM) – now the State Secretariat for Migration. She worked previously as a legal counsellor in the same unit, as well as in the unit responsible for visa affairs in the FOM. Prior to this she was a legal adviser to the Swiss Federal Department of Finance and the Swiss State Secretariat for Economic Affairs. She was also a legal counsellor working on issues of Galician migrant return, for the Spanish regional government of Galicia.

FEDERICO LUPO-PASINI is Associate Professor in Corporate and Commercial Law at Durham Law School, UK. His research focuses on international financial law and financial regulation. In particular, he is interested in the role of legal institutions in the development of the international financial system and the emerging digital financial ecosystem. He also maintains a lively interest in international economic law, especially international trade law. He obtained his PhD from the National University of Singapore, and a master's in international law and economics from the World Trade Institute. In addition to his academic work, Dr Lupo-Pasini is also active as a consultant on international trade and international finance law for various international organisations and governments. Since 2017, he has been an adviser to the government of Northern Ireland on the trade implications of Brexit.

LIST OF CONTRIBUTORS xi

KRISTA NADAKAVUKAREN SCHEFER is a vice director of the Swiss Institute of Comparative Law. She is also on the faculty of the World Trade Institute in Bern and is an adjunct instructor at the universities of Basel and Bern. Krista teaches international investment law and World Trade Organization law courses at several law faculties in Switzerland. She is the author of a textbook on international investment law and has published numerous articles on investment and trade topics. Dr Nadakavukaren gained a *juris doctor* from Georgetown University Law School, and her doctorate and *habilitation* from the University of Bern. She is a member of the Executive Council of the Society of International Economic Law, an editor of Hart Publishing's series Studies in International Trade and Investment Law, and is on the editorial board of the Brill series World Trade Institute Advanced Studies.

CEDRIC RYNGAERT is Chair of Public International Law at Utrecht University (Netherlands) and Head of the Department of International and European Law of the University's Law School. Among other publications, he authored *Jurisdiction in International Law* (2nd ed., Oxford University Press, 2015), *Jurisdiction over Antitrust Violations in International Law* (Intersentia, 2008) and *Selfless Intervention: The Exercise of Jurisdiction in the Common Interest* (Oxford University Press, 2020). In 2012, Professor Ryngaert obtained the Prix Henri Rolin, a five-yearly prize for international law and international relations for his work on jurisdiction.

LUCIA SATRAGNO obtained her PhD from the Faculty of Law of the University of Bern in 2020. She is a research fellow at the Centre for Banking and Finance Law, National University of Singapore. She obtained the prestigious Van Calker scholarship from the Swiss Institute of Comparative Law in 2014 and the Spark of Hope Foundation scholarship in 2015. Previously, Lucia worked as a research fellow (2012–14), and before that as a legal counsel (2004–10). Lucia holds a law degree with honours from the University of Buenos Aires (2003) and an LLM with distinction from the Queen Mary University of London (2010–11).

JUDITH SCHÄLI holds a PhD from the Faculty of Law of the University of Bern in 2020. She works in the Legal Affairs Division of the Swiss Federal Office for the Environment. As a member of the Advisory Group, she has contributed to two studies on marine plastic litter and microplastics commissioned by the UN Environment Executive Director for his reports to the UN Environment Assembly in 2016 and 2017. Judith studied international relations and international and European law at the universities of Geneva and Bern. Her research focuses on international environmental governance and the law of the sea, with a particular focus on plastics. She has authored several publications in these fields.

PETER-TOBIAS STOLL is a professor of public law and public international law at Göttingen University and the Executive Director of the Institute for International Law and European Law, where he heads the Department for International Economic and Environmental Law. He co-chairs the European Society of International Law Interest Group on International Economic Law and the Study Group on Preferential Trade Agreements of the International Law Association.

OISIN SUTTLE is Assistant Professor of Law at Maynooth University. He previously taught at Queens University Belfast, Sheffield University and University College London, where he earned his PhD. He teaches and writes principally on international economic law and legal and political theory, including in particular problems of justice, legitimacy and interpretation in international economic law. He is the author of *Distributive Justice and World Trade Law: A Political Theory of International Trade Regulation* (Cambridge University Press, 2018). Other research has been published in leading journals including *European Journal of International Law, International and Comparative Law Quarterly*, and the *Modern Law Review*.

CLAUS ZIMMERMANN is an Associated Partner with Noerr in Brussels. He advises governments and private stakeholders on international and EU trade and investment matters, with a particular emphasis on litigation under the auspices of the WTO, the EU courts and at the member state level. Before entering private practice in 2011, he worked for, inter alia, the WTO Appellate Body Secretariat and the IMF Legal Department. He holds a DPhil in public international law from the University of Oxford and a PhD in economics from the University Paris 1 Panthéon-Sorbonne. His research on international economic law has been published in leading journals and his monograph *A Contemporary Concept of Monetary Sovereignty* was published by Oxford University Press (2013).

PREFACE

International law, as we know it, increasingly fails to deal with contemporary global challenges. Power relations prevail in this multipolar world. Disciplines on climate change under the UNFCCC and the 2015 Paris Accord remain weak; multilateral rules on migration beyond refugee law are virtually non-existent. Combating global pollution in effective ways, in particular of the global commons and protecting biodiversity, has been failing. Developing countries often pay the price and are not sufficiently supported in the process of climate adaptation. The financial crisis and the great recession have brought about a widespread renaissance of nationalism. The same holds true for the global coronavirus (Covid-19) pandemic in 2020, despite the fact that it is recognised as a *public health emergency of international concern* under WHO international health regulations. Remedies to challenges, if at all, are primarily sought on the level of the nation state or regional integration in Europe, often without much success due to extensive interdependence of value chains in a globalised economy. Trade sanctions are being unilaterally imposed in trade war disrespecting all legal disciplines of the multilateral trading system of the World Trade Organization, much to the detriment of consumers who pay additional and penalising taxes on products. Income disparities continue to increase within societies. Ever since, compliance and enforcement of human rights have remained weak in international law. Central banks, operating without close cooperation and formal integration fail to provide adequate responses in the context of a globalised economy, denying decent returns on hard-won savings.

Against this backdrop, this book examines the potential of the doctrine of Common Concern of Humankind. While it remains extremely difficult to achieve progress in policy and treaty-making, given the predominance of nationalist sentiments, our hope is that the doctrine of Common Concern of Humankind may offer an avenue for progress in further developing the arsenal of legal principles of law and of international law. We argue in this book that a proper legal principle of Common Concern

xiv   PREFACE

of Humankind (CCH) may emerge, comparable to the doctrine and principle of sustainability, as a means to address these pressing transnational and transboundary issues and problems. The principle has the potential to reinforce international cooperation, compliance, and enforcement of international law in an increasingly smaller and interdependent world. It can make a difference to multilevel, global or earth governance. The principle offers the possibility to the legal profession and courts of law to gradually develop its contours and to make a difference in addressing pressing global needs in future case law within the existing framework of international law. Common Concern of Humankind will bring about a new perspective and narrative.

Common concern of humankind, while recognised in the fields of climate change and preservation of biodiversity, has not been sufficiently explored in legal theory and practice so far. Its contours have remained unclear beyond the call for enhanced international cooperation in the production of global public goods and community interests. Yet, common concern bears the potential to develop into a legal principle in a process of claims and responses. It is able to enhance cooperation, legitimise, but also limit, extraterritorial state action as an incentive to bring about appropriate responses addressing common and shared problems threatening world peace and stability.

This volume discusses the potential of such a principle, its relationship to global public goods governance, as well as links to the doctrine of multilevel governance and constitutionalisation of law, as public goods need to be produced on appropriate levels of governance. Such linkages offer the basis for new insights into the potential and operation of a legal principle of Common Concern applicable not only in international law, but also in European and national law. The book explores how the legal principle of Common Concern may evolve in a process of claims and responses, how it can be operationalised and its implications for vertical allocation of powers and checks and balances within the system, as well as for installing appropriate incentives for states to engage in enhanced international cooperation and to comply with international obligations incurred. Once recognised for a particular issue and area, the principle triggers obligations and consultation, negotiations and cooperation. It entails obligations to undertake related homework. It is subject to enhanced compliance and duties to act vis-à-vis non-complying entities.

Part I of the volume expounds the history and theoretical and legal implications, conceptualising duties to cooperate in solving shared problems, obligations to undertake homework and implications or

PREFACE

compliance and enforcement. Part II reaches beyond the classical fields of environmental law, in particular climate change, and examines the potential in several and diverse case studies relating to the diffusion and transfer of low-carbon technology, marine plastic pollution, income inequality, the protection of human rights, migration, and monetary and financial stability. These case studies are partly extractions from more extensive PhD research efforts undertaken in these fields. As they are addressed to different communities, they explore the doctrine of Common Concern of Humankind from their respective angle. Diverse as these areas are, they were chosen on purpose to examine to what extent Common Concern of Humankind can deploy normative effects beyond climate change and biodiversity. They show the potential in terms of conceptualising Common Concern of Humankind in international law. They show that the impact of an emerging principle of Common Concern of Humankind will not be uniform and vary from field to field. The emphasis changes. In areas devoid of substantive rules, such as migration or inequality, Common Concern initiates conceptual avenues. In other areas, such as climate change, marine pollution or monetary and financial law, the focus is on homework and compliance. Finally, in mature areas, such as human rights, the principle of Common Concern brings stronger enforcement by its duty to act subject to the principle of proportionality. Part III of the book finally reproduces feedback offered by renowned scholars in the field. Discussions and the published literature by summer 2019 were taken into account in preparing this volume. One key positive development since then has been the multiple requests received from different governments to re-frame protection of atmosphere as a "common concern of humankind", instead of the previously agreed "pressing concern of the international community as a whole", in the context of the ongoing work at the International Law Commission. We hope that the book may serve as a source of inspiration and hope for this and future generations.

Thomas Cottier & Zaker Ahmad

ACKNOWLEDGEMENTS

This book is based upon a research project generously funded by the Swiss National Science Foundation (SNF) from 2015 to 2019 in forming a research team and supporting five competitively appointed PhD positions, two of them funded by another SNF envelope and a scholarship of the Swiss State Secretariat for Economic Affairs (SECO), respectively. We all are grateful for entrusting this task to the principal investigator and these and two additional, self-funded contributors. All have been based, or are related to, the family of the World Trade Institute (WTI) of the University of Bern, Switzerland. We thank colleagues at Division I of the SNF, staff and anonymous reviewers of the project for assessing the project and their support. We thank the group of colleagues who attended workshops and advised on particular aspects of the problem, in particular Professor Duncan French (Lincoln, UK), Professor Dr Krista Nadakavukaren Schefer (Lausanne); Professor Cedric Ryngaert and Dr Natalie Dobson (Utrecht), Professor Peter-Tobias Stoll (Göttingen), Dr Oisin Suttle (Maynooth) and Dr Claus Zimmermann (Brussels). We are grateful for their willingness to have their comments published in the final chapters of this book. I am most grateful to Zaker Ahmad for valuable and careful assistance in reviewing chapters and preparing the typescript of the book.

We should like to thank the staff and colleagues at the WTI, for hosting the project and making available the valuable infrastructure of the Institute. We are grateful for support and encouragement to Professors Joseph Francois, Peter van den Bossche and Michael Hahn, to Margrit Vetter, the administrative director, to Markus Obi, financial officer and accountant, to Yvonne Motzer, librarian, and to Dr Doris Oberdabernig for heading the doctoral programme and organising interesting workshops. At the WTI, researchers and PhD students found an appropriate biotope to exchange views, test ideas and providing mutual support in advancing, step by step, the research agenda of this project and forming a small community of like-minded colleagues and friends.

Other than the lonely business of legal research, this project was truly collaborative and subject to mutual support, review and improvement.

We are grateful to Cambridge University Press and anonymous reviewers for assessing and accepting the manuscript in 2019 and producing it professionally. In particular, we extend our gratitude to Finola O'Sullivan and Robert Judkins for overseeing the progress, to Martin Barr for copy-editing support, and to Maheen Neena for facilitating the publication process.

Thomas Cottier
Bern, February 2021

ABBREVIATIONS

AB	Appellate Body
BCBS	Basel Committee on Banking Supervision
BIS	Bank for International Settlements
CBD	Convention on Biological Diversity
CBDR	common but differentiated responsibility
CCH	Common Concern of Humankind
CIRR	Commercial Interest Reference Rates
CJEU	Court of Justice of the European Union
COP	Conference of Parties
CO_2	carbon dioxide
CPD	International Conference on Population
CVD	countervailing duty
DSU	Understanding on Rules and Procedures Governing the Settlement of Disputes
ECA	export credit agency
ECB	European Central Bank
ESCB	European System of Central Banks
ESF	Exchange Stabilisation Fund
EST	environmentally sound technologies
FDI	foreign direct investment
FSB	Financial Stability Board
GATS	General Agreement on Trade in Services
GATT	General Agreement on Tariffs and Trade
GCM	Global Compact for Safe, Orderly and Regular Migration
GFC	global financial crisis
GFMD	Global Forum on Migration and Development
GFSN	global financial safety net
GHG	greenhouse gas
GMG	global migration group
GPG	global public goods
GVC	global value chain
HIs	horizontal inequalities

LIST OF ABBREVIATIONS

ICAO	International Civil Aviation Organization
ICJ	International Court of Justice
ICP	United Nations Open-Ended Consultative Process on Oceans and the Law of the Sea
ICT	information and communications technology
IFDP	International Finance Discussion Papers
ILA	International Law Association
ILC	International Law Commission
ILO	International Labour Organization
IMF	International Monetary Fund
IMS	International Monetary System
IOM	International Organization for Migration
IPCC	Intergovernmental Panel on Climate Change
IUCN	International Union for Conservation of Nature
LCT	low-carbon technology
LDC	least-developed country
MBI	market-based instruments
MEA	multilateral environmental agreement
MFN	most-favoured-nation
NDC	nationally determined contribution
NPA	non-physical attributes
NT	national treatment
OECD	Organisation for Economic Co-operation and Development
ODA	official development assistance
PPM	process and production measures
QE	quantitative easing
R2P	responsibility to protect
RCP	regional consultative processes on migration
RFA	regional financing arrangements
SCM	subsidies and countervailing measures
SDGs	sustainable development goals
TBT	Agreement on Technical Barriers to Trade
TFEU	Treaty on the Functioning of the European Union
TNA	technology needs assessment
TRIPS	Trade-Related Aspects of Intellectual Property Rights
TRN	transnational regulatory network
SWIFT	Society for Worldwide Interbank Financial Telecommunication
UN	United Nations
UNCLOS	United Nations Convention for the Law of the Sea
UNCSD	United Nations Conference on Sustainable Development
UNEA	United Nations Environment Assembly
UNEP	United Nations Environment Programme

UNFCCC	United Nations Framework Convention on Climate Change
UNHCR	United Nations High Commissioner for Refugees
USD	United States Dollars
UNSC	United Nations Security Council
VIs	vertical inequalities
WTO	World Trade Organization

PART I

Theory

1

The Principle of Common Concern of Humankind

THOMAS COTTIER

International law is the art of creating normativity out of reality.

James Crawford[1]

1.1 Introduction

Collective action problems occurring in the process of globalisation are mainly caused by a lack of appropriate and effective global institutions able to ensure the sustainable production of global public goods.[2] States are inherently preoccupied with the pursuit of their own interests defined by domestic political processes.[3] Global society is left without swift and adequate solutions to its most grave problems. International cooperation frequently fails in such configurations as countries and governments

---

The author is truly indebted to Peter-Tobias Stoll, Cédric Ryngaert, Duncan French, Roland Portmann and other participants of the workshop on common concern held at WTI in Bern on 22 June 2018, and in particular members of the research team Zaker Ahmad, Alexander Beyleveld, Lucia Satragno and Iryna Bogdanova for comments on a previous draft and suggestions made, as well Mira Burri for inputs in designing the research project.

[1] 'Foundations of International Law', lecture, University of Cambridge (autumn 2003), cited in N. Stürchler, *The Threat of Use of Force in International Law* (Cambridge: Cambridge University Press, 2007), p. 125.

[2] This chapter partly draws and builds on T. Cottier, P. Aerni, B. Karapınar, S. Matteotti, J. de Sépibus and A. Shingal, 'The Principle of Common Concern and Climate Change', *Archiv des Völkerrechts*, 52 (2014), 293–324. All URLs cited were accessed between August and October 2018.

[3] E. Brousseau *et al.* (eds.), *Global Environmental Commons: Analytical and Political Challenges in Building Governance Mechanisms* (Oxford: Oxford University Press, 2012); E. Brousseau, T. Dedeurwaerdere and B. Siebenhüner, Cambridge, MA: MIT Press, 2012); E. Brousseau *et al.* (eds.), *Reflexive Governance for Global Public Goods* (Cambridge, MA: MIT Press, 2012); I. Kaul 'Rethinking Public Goods and Global Public Goods', ibid. at 37–54; I. Kaul 'Global Public Goods: Explaining Their Underprovision', *Journal of International Economic Law*, 15 (2012), 729–50.

are not able and willing to define long-term goals to the detriment of short-term advantages.[4] The United Nations and other international organisations, given their present structure, are not in a position to offset such priorities. The same holds true for regional and even domestic law. The European Union is not sufficiently empowered and equipped to effectively contain vested interests; and within nations, powerful local interests tend to undermine the pursuit of global public goods by central government – or the other way round. This is particularly evident in, but not limited to, the problem of global warming and climate change. Despite strong empirical evidence and scientific studies provided by the United Nations Intergovernmental Panel on Climate Change (IPCC) in an unprecedented scientific effort and coordination,[5] most countries fall short of taking up the challenge in an effective and efficient manner due to sectoral vested interests in the energy sector and elsewhere. There clearly is a need to strengthen mutual commitments in addressing these issues.

The 1992 United Nations Framework Convention on Climate Change (UNFCCC) recognised in its preamble that the adverse effects of climate change amount to a common concern of humankind.[6] This statement is not further qualified. It would seem limited to a factual observation of the obvious, as all humans, present and future, are affected by climatic changes one way or the other. But it also recognises the claim that climate change is partly human-made and thus a responsibility to be taken seriously.

In the field of climate change, the statement of common concern of humankind in the UNFCCC supported, and perhaps triggered, an initial commitment to cooperate in climate change mitigation and adaptation, taking into account the shared but differentiated responsibility of industrialised and developing countries alike. This led to the 1997 Kyoto Protocol, which defined broad goals for reducing carbon emissions.[7] The initial commitment period of the Kyoto Protocol expired in 2012, and subsequent negotiations have had limited success. They have failed

---

[4] See N. Krisch, 'The Decay of Consent: International Law in an Age of Global Public Goods', *American Journal of International Law*, 108 (2014), 1–40.

[5] www.ipcc.ch (accessed 28 Aug. 2018).

[6] United Nations Framework Convention on Climate Change, 9 May 1992, 31 ILM 849, 851, https://unfccc.int/resource/docs/convkp/conveng.pdf.

[7] D. Bodansky, 'The History of the Global Climate Regime', in U. Luterbacher and D. Sprinz (eds.), *International Relations and Global Climate Change* (Cambridge, MA: MIT Press, 2001), pp. 23–40.

THE PRINCIPLE OF COMMON CONCERN OF HUMANKIND   5

to bring about more precise terms and commitments beyond the target of limiting average increases of global temperature to no more than 2 °C (today 1.5°C) by the end of this century[8] – a goal perhaps already unachievable, even with aggressive mitigation measures.[9] Subsequently, the Conferences of Copenhagen, Cancún, Durban and Doha failed to make substantial progress except for long-term political commitments. Despite the acknowledgement of climate change as a common concern, this acknowledgement could not be in any distinct way successfully implemented to address the evident collective action problem.

The 2015 Paris Agreement reiterated climate change as a common concern.[10] It brought about progress as it extended responsibilities to all nations. This was a major political achievement. Moreover, its adoption and entry into force provide strong signals to the private sector, encouraging long-term investment in renewable energy and sustainable construction policies on local levels. Whatever the commitment of governments, sustainability has become an important consideration in business and finance. Yet, and despite reiterated acknowledgement of climate change as a common concern of humankind, the agreement still falls short of prescribing more precise obligations at abatement. The model adopted essentially leaves the matter to unilateral commitment, and it has remained controversial to what extent such commitments amount to obligations under international law. Moreover, the United States announced on 1 June 2017 its intention to withdraw from the 2015 Paris Agreement by 2020, substantially undermining on the federal level the effort to address collective action problems in a successful manner.[11]

---

[8] UNEP, 'The Emissions Gap Report: Are the Copenhagen Accord Pledges Sufficient to Limit Global Warming to 2 °C or 1.5 °C?', *United Nations Environmental Programme* (2010). In 2018, the IPCC issued a report calling for a maximum of 1.5 °C, IPPC, *Global Warming of 1.5 °C*, http://report.ipcc.ch/sr15/pdf/sr15_spm_final.pdf.

[9] V. Ramanathan and Y. Xu, 'The Copenhagen Accord for Limiting Global Warming: Criteria, Constraints, and Available Avenues', *Proceedings of the National Academy of Sciences*, 107 (2010), 8055–62.

[10] UNTS 1760, p. 79, https://unfccc.int/process/conferences/pastconferences/paris-climate-change-conference-november-2015/paris-agreement (containing all six official languages of the text). See text accompanying *infra* n. 46.

[11] 'Trump Administration Delivers Notice U.S. Intends to Withdraw from Paris Climate Deal', *Politico*, 4 Aug. 2017; www.politico.com/story/2017/08/04/trump-notice-withdraw-from-paris-climate-deal-241331 (accessed 28 Aug. 2018). The Biden Administration rejoined the Paris Accord in January 2021. 'Biden returns US to Paris climate accord hours after becoming president', *The Guardian*, 20 Jan. 2021; https://www.theguardian.com/environment/2021/jan/20/paris-climate-accord-joe-biden-returns-us.

6   THOMAS COTTIER

Under the 1992 United Nations Convention on Biodiversity (CBD), the recognition and commitment to common concern of humankind led to the adoption of national policies on preserving biodiversity, and also to the Bonn Guidelines on access and benefit sharing, which resulted in the Nagoya Protocol on Access to Genetic Resources.[12] As with climate change mitigation, efforts at combating the loss of biodiversity have not yet yielded the expected results. Erosion continues despite the political endorsement of common concern, and benefit sharing is still in its infancy.

The 2001 international Treaty on Plant Genetic Resources for Food and Agriculture (ITPGRFA) equally recognises genetic resources as a common concern of humankind.[13] It developed a sophisticated system of plant conservation, registration and open exchange for a list of crops. The treaty currently applies to only 64 crops and forages, while the majority of crops have been left under the permanent sovereignty of states over natural resources, at their free disposition in terms of trade and conservation.[14]

Finally, the Convention for the Safeguarding of the Intangible Cultural Heritage of 17 October 2003 invokes the will and common concern to safeguard intangible cultural heritage.[15] It focuses on international cooperation to bring about transparency and in the identification of the heritage of intangible cultural goods. The convention includes an

[12] Convention on Biological Diversity, UNTS vol. 1760 p. 79; 31 ILM 818, 822 (see www.cbd .int/convention); Nagoya Protocol on Access to Genetic Resources and the Fair and Equitable Sharing of Benefits Arising from Their Utilisation to the Convention on Biological Diversity, opened for signature 2 Feb. 2011, XXVII.8.b UNTC (not yet in force), www.cbd.int/abs/text/default.shtml; Bonn Guidelines on Access to Genetic Resources and Fair and Equitable Sharing of the Benefits Arising out of Their Utilisation, COP Dec VI/24, Item A, 6th mtg, UNEP Doc. UNEP/CBD/COP/6/20 (7–19 Apr. 2002), www.cbd.int/doc/decisions/COP-06-dec-en.pdf.

[13] "Cognizant that plant genetic resources for food and agriculture are a common concern of all countries, in that all countries depend very largely on plant genetic resources for food and agriculture that originated elsewhere;" www.fao.org/plant-treaty/overview/ texts-treaty/en.

[14] See M. Halewood, I. Isabel, Lépez Noreiga and S. Louafi (eds.), *Crop Genetic Resources as a Global Commons* (Abingdon, UK: Routledge, 2013) (interestingly not addressing the notion of common concern despite reference to it in the preamble of the treaty).

[15] 'Being aware of the universal will and the common concern to safeguard the intangible cultural heritage of humanity', http://portal.unesco.org/en/ev.php-URL_ID=17716& URL_DO=DO_TOPIC&URL_SECTION=201.html.

THE PRINCIPLE OF COMMON CONCERN OF HUMANKIND   7

international fund through which activities in Member States are supported. Common concern is not used in an operational manner in the convention and does not entail a normative dimension.

The reasons for such failures and very limited success in addressing common concerns by means of international cooperation are manifold. Most of them are well known.[16] Some are of an economic nature and some are political, but a prime culprit certainly relates to the predominant basic concepts of the Westphalian system of coexistence, which are firmly centred on permanent sovereignty of the nation state over natural resources, as well as on the principle of territoriality. These inherent reasons prompt fierce competition among domestic industries on the world market, free-riding and mercantilist and protectionist beggar-thy-neighbour policies. They render governments largely unwilling to lose competitive advantages by adopting measures of climate change mitigation or effective protection of biodiversity which could affect the level playing field. International cooperation has been largely successful in areas of mutual interest and reciprocity which amounts to a fundamental tenet of contractual international law and perhaps, at the end of the day, of all law successfully addressing human interaction.[17] Law is mainly successful and voluntarily complied with where it is based upon mutual interest, on give and take of benefits and advantages in a balanced manner.

On such foundations based upon mutual interests and reciprocity, the General Agreement on Tariffs and Trade (GATT) evolved in a comprehensive system of multilateral agreements within which countries are able to pursue and defend their interests, including a strong, albeit lately challenged, system of judicial dispute settlement in the WTO.[18] The law of the sea provided the foundations for the successful evolution of case law on maritime boundary delimitation led by the International Court of

---

[16] For climate change mitigation, see D. C. Esty and A. L. I Moffa, 'Why Climate Change Collective Action Has Failed and What Needs to Be Done within and without the Trade Regime', *Journal of International Economic Law*, 15 (2012), 777–9; for conservation through use of plant genetic resources, see Halewood *et al.*, *supra* n. 14, pp. 16–17.

[17] B. Simma, *Das Reziprozitätselement im Zustandekommen völkerrechtlicher Verträge. Gedanken zu einem Bauprinzip der internationalen Rechtsbeziehungen* (Berlin: Dunker & Humblodt, 1972).

[18] See generally P. van den Bossche and W. Zdouc, *The Law and Policy of the World Trade Organization* (4th ed., Cambridge: Cambridge University Press, 2017).

8   THOMAS COTTIER

Justice.[19] The law of investment protection, enshrined in hundreds of bilateral investment protection agreements produced a substantial body of case law. Finally, the process of nuclear disarmament was able, for a long time, to reduce the risk of warfare.[20] All these areas are strongly based upon the pursuit of national interests and political reciprocity which can best be pursued by way of international cooperation and commitments, rather than unilateral action. Other than environmental law, these areas did not call upon common concern of humankind, but are rooted in traditional realism, the pursuit of national interests based upon reciprocity.

In areas such as climate change, protection of biodiversity, marine pollution, genetic resources and cultural diversity, the essential element of reciprocity in terms of interests and benefits is lacking. Other than in trade and market access rights or international investment, benefits are not directly mutual; obligations incurred are essentially one-sided. Benefits produced are not limited to states incurring obligations but are to the advantage of all humankind in creating and enhancing global public goods. They are not necessarily reciprocated by commitments taken by others. Equally, reciprocity is largely lacking in untapped areas of common concern, such as migration, human rights or monetary and financial stability or food security. Home countries of migrants are not genuinely interested in cooperating with host countries. Human rights policies abroad benefit the people, but do not directly create reciprocal advantages for the state incurring obligations. Traditional monetary and financial policies, including banking regulations, are conducted unilaterally in the pursuit of national or federal EU interests. They do not depend upon reciprocity, and international cooperation traditionally has been limited among central banks.[21] Food security is perceived and conceptualised as a matter of national interest and not in terms of reciprocal advantages. All this in return incentivises unilateral policies of free riding, attitudes of wait and see and leaving burdens to others, while seeking to enhance individual competitiveness in international coexistence.

---

[19] See generally T. Cottier, *Equitable Principles of Maritime Boundary Delimitation: The Quest for Distributive Justice in International Law* (Cambridge: Cambridge University Press, 2015).

[20] R. Greenspan Bell and M. Ziegler (eds.), *Building International Climate Cooperation. Lessons from the Weapons and Trade Regimes for Achieving International Climate Goals* (Washington, DC: World Resources Institute, 2012).

[21] See Chapter 7 in this volume.

One is therefore – perhaps too readily – tempted to put the idea and concept of common concern of humankind aside as a piece of wishful thinking. Yet, the world today faces unprecedented problems which no longer can be framed in terms of short-term national interests and reciprocity in a traditional manner and way. Conventional wisdom in international law and relations and statism simply do not produce critical results. Today's and future collective action problems in a highly integrated and interdependent world call for new foundations in defining rights and obligations in key areas riddled with unresolved major problems which are able to address long-term interests in a reciprocal manner. They need to secure that all countries alike are engaged in making contributions and commitments to their mutual benefit, commensurate with their levels of social and economic development and powers they may exert. Efforts to this effect are made by stressing the importance of community interests in the theory of international law, by framing constitutionalisation of international law and by focusing on global governance and public trusteeship. These ambitious efforts at restructuring international law and relations in a comprehensive manner, stressing the need for cooperation, are general and partly elusive, while common concern of humankind builds upon the existing framework with effects limited to, and focused upon, particular areas identified in a process of claims and responses in international relations.

Common concern of humankind thus bears the potential to be further developed beyond a political commitment to international obligations of cooperation within the United Nations and other international organisations, going beyond the legal disciplines of Article 56 of the United Nations Charter. A new principle of Common Concern of Humankind (CCH) may serve as a foundation to define, legitimise and assess domestic measures addressing shared problems of humankind.[22] It may offer guidance in revisiting the doctrine of cooperation, compliance and extraterritorial effects of domestic law and duties to act. It may thus help to improve compliance with international obligations incurred. It may help to revisit and reshape traditional precepts of national sovereignty.

---

[22] Henceforth, upper case will be used to depict Common Concern as a doctrine and emerging principle, other than descriptions of common concern of humankind used so far in international instruments and most of the literature in lower case.

In this context, the extension of emissions trading to all civil air traffic to and from the European Union under the umbrella of the UNFCCC is an encouraging example in point. The imposition of the measure was highly controversial, but was successful in eventually bringing governments to the negotiating table within the International Civil Aviation Organization (ICAO). While justified by the Court of Justice of the European Union (CJEU) in terms of extraterritorial application,[23] a future legal principle of Common Concern may further contribute to justifying, clarifying and defining the scope and the limitations of such actions in addressing climate change mitigation as a matter of international law. It may assist in compliance, defining the law of sanctions and countermeasures addressing free riding and failure to act in support of addressing collective action problems in the pursuit of creating global public goods.

While climate change is the most prominent example, the potential of a future principle of CCH is equally suitable to address and structure other major global problems. It bears the potential to address collective action and governance problems in a wide variation of different fields, for example the field of marine pollution, the enforcement of protection of human rights, the fields of migration, monetary and financial stability, and grossly uneven distributions of wealth and income in the context of investment protection and international trade. Within projects funded mainly by the Swiss National Science Foundations and the Swiss State Secretariat for the Economy (SECO), six PhD projects are dedicated to exploring such wider recourse and are discussed in subsequent chapters of this book. Other areas yet untapped here relate to food security, cyberspace, information technology and big data which no longer can be addressed and regulated within the bounds of nation states.

This chapter briefly explores the historical foundations of common concern of humankind. It expounds, as a doctrine, its potential to emerge as a principle of international law, shaping rights and obligations in international cooperation, domestic commitments, possibilities and limits of extraterritorial effect and its impact on the law of sanctions and countermeasures in seeking compliance with international obligations incurred. It expounds the process of the principle of Common Concern, defines thresholds and addresses the relationship to other and

---

[23] C-366/10, *Air Transport Association of America and others* v. *Secretary of State for Energy and Climate Change*, judgment of 21 Dec. 2011.

THE PRINCIPLE OF COMMON CONCERN OF HUMANKIND   11

related legal concepts. It discusses the particular role of non-state actors and domestic courts in compensating the lack of reciprocity often found on the international level. It expounds the added value beyond existing law which Common Concern brings to the table and to international law of the twenty-first century. It provides the basis upon which the doctrine is tested in different regulatory areas, while equally taking into account feedback from the other studies included in this volume.

We submit in concluding that common concern indeed has the potential for a structural principle of CCH which not only could deploy effects on the global level affecting all humankind, but as a general principle of law operating within today's realities and multilevel governance. Thus, it could also operate within states, interfacing different communities. It provides important foundations in addressing collective actions problems which cannot be solved independently but at least require cooperation and interaction of two jurisdictions. It provides inspiration and guidance in treaty negotiations in different sectors and may eventually apply as a legal principle in its own right.

1.2   History, Evolution and Main Issues

1.2.1   Expression in Treaties

In 1988, based on a proposal tabled by Malta,[24] the UN General Assembly adopted Resolution 43/53, Protection of Global Climate for Present and Future Generations of Mankind, recognising 'that climate change is a common concern of mankind, since climate is an essential condition which sustains life on earth'.[25]

This was not an entirely new way of defining the shared and common character of a specific area which is of significant importance to the entire international community.[26] The idea of common concern was referred to in international law, prior to the debate on climate change, in the context

---

[24] Malta though insisted that conservation of climate should be considered as a part of the common heritage of humankind.

[25] Protection of Global Climate for Present and Future Generations of Mankind, GA Res. 43/53, UN Doc. A/RES/43/53 (6 Dec. 1988), www.un.org/documents/ga/res/43/a43r053.htm.

[26] P. Sands, Symposium: 'The Globalization of Law, Politics, and Markets: Implications for Domestic Law Reform, the "Greening" of International Law: Emerging Principles and Rules', *Indiana Journal of Global Legal Studies*, 1 (1994), 293.

12 THOMAS COTTIER

of addressing shared problems relating to shared jurisdiction and resources.[27] It has its roots in the allocation of a joint protective zone in the high seas, restricting the hunt of fur seals in the Bering Sea in response by the tribunal to US claims of exclusive jurisdiction in the 1893 fur seal arbitration.[28] As early as 1949, tuna and other fish were considered to be 'of common concern' to the parties to certain treaties by reason of their continued use by those parties.[29] Invoking humankind depicts the commonality and collective responsibility of states equally found in other areas of international law. Outer space and the moon, on the other hand, are the 'province of all mankind';[30] waterfowl habitats are regarded as 'an international resource';[31] the natural and cultural heritage are 'part of the world heritage of mankind as a whole';[32] the conservation of wild animals is for the good of mankind[33] the resources of the seabed, ocean floor and subsoil are 'the common heritage of mankind';[34] and plant genetic resources are 'a heritage of mankind'.[35]

[27] The author is indebted to Eva Köhler for insights into the historical development of Common Concern in her student paper entitled 'Common Concern of Mankind – Die historischen Entwicklungen des Konzepts und seine inhaltliche Bedeutung', master's thesis (University of Bern, Switzerland, 30 Dec. 2012) (on file with author).

[28] Award between the United States and the United Kingdom relating to the rights of jurisdiction of United States in the Bering Sea and the preservation of fur seals, 15 Aug. 1893, Reports of International Arbitral Awards vol. XXVIII 263–76, http://legal.un.org/riaa/cases/vol_XXVIII/263-276.pdf. The summary award does not discuss the notion of common interests, but mainly sets out the parameter of the protective zone while recognising freedom of the high seas and declaring unilateral claims by the United States unlawful. See M. Hoepfner, 'Behring Sea Arbitration', in R. Bernhardt (ed.), *Encyclopedia of Public International Law* (Amsterdam: North-Holland, 1981), pp. 36–7.

[29] Convention for the Establishment of an Inter-American Tropical Tuna Commission, 31 May 1949, 80 UNTS 3, 3 (entered into force 3 Mar. 1950).

[30] Treaty on Principles Governing the Activities of States in the Exploration and Use of Outer Space, Including the Moon and Other Celestial Bodies, 27 Jan. 1967, art. 1, 610 UNTS 205, 207 (entered into force 10 Oct. 1967).

[31] Convention on Wetlands of International Importance Especially as Waterfowl Habitat, 2 Feb. 1971, 996 UNTS 245, 246 (entered into force 21 Dec. 1975).

[32] UNESCO Convention on the Protection of the World Cultural and Natural Heritage, 16 Nov. 1972, 27 UST 37, 40, 11 ILM 1358, 1358 (entered into force 15 July 1975).

[33] Convention on the Conservation of Migratory Species of Wild Animals, 23 June 1979, 19 ILM 11, 15–16 (entered into force 1 Nov. 1985).

[34] United Nations Convention on the Law of the Sea. Adopted 10 Dec. 1982, www.un.org/depts/los/convention_agreements/convention_overview_convention.htm.

[35] United Nations Food and Agriculture Organization Plant Genetics Undertaking, Art. 1, UN FAO, 37th sess., UN Doc. C/83/Rep. (1983).

THE PRINCIPLE OF COMMON CONCERN OF HUMANKIND   13

These notions are not clearly distinguished. Some scholars suggested that other areas such as fresh water[36] or rainforests,[37] deforestation[38] and desertification[39] and marine biological diversity[40] should be under the umbrella of either common heritage of humankind or common concern of mankind concepts. The same could be said for soil in the context of food security as soil quality not only affects local populations but also feeds people abroad, dependent upon the importation of agricultural products of good quality.[41]

Eventually, the concept of 'common concern of humankind' was developed and applied as a treaty-based notion: the 1992 UNFCCC states that 'change in the earth's climate and its adverse effects are a common concern of humankind'.[42] The French text says: 'conscientes que les changements du climat de la planète et leurs effets néfastes sont un sujet de préoccupation pour l'humanité tout entière'.[43] The Spanish text reads:

---

[36] E. Brown Weiss, 'The Coming Water Crisis: A Common Concern of Humankind', *Transnational Environmental Law*, 1 (2012), 153–68; Brown Weiss, *International Law for a Water-Scarce World* (Leiden: Martinus Nijhoff, 2013); P. Cullet, 'Water Law in a Globalised World: The Need for a New Conceptual Framework', *Journal of Environmental Law*, 23 (2011), 233–54. The author notes that at present, the proposal to consider water as part of the common heritage of humankind sounds like wishful thinking in a context where states have not even managed to agree on a progressive international treaty for transboundary watercourses. Yet, the idea has already progressed. This is confirmed, for instance, by recent developments in Quebec where water is now legally considered common heritage.

[37] D. Humphreys, 'The Elusive Quest for a Global Forest Convention', *Review of European Community and International Environmental Law*, 14(1) (2005), 1–10; P. Mason, 'Inadequacies of the Amazon Fund: Evaluating Brazil's Sovereignty in the Context of Promising Market Mechanisms and the Need for International Oversight to Protect the Amazon Rainforest', *Touro International Law Review*, 13(116) (2010).

[38] J. Brunée and A. Noellkaemper, 'Between Forests and the Trees: The Emerging International Forest Law', *Environmental Conservation*, 23(309) (1996), 207–314.

[39] D. French, 'Common Concern, Common Heritage and Other Global(ising) Concepts: Rhetorical Devices, Legal Principles or a Fundamental Challenge?', in M. J. Bowman, P. G. G. Davies and E. J. Goodwin (eds.), *Research Handbook on Biodiversity and Law* (Cheltenham, UK: Edward Elgar, 2016), pp. 334–60.

[40] C. Bowling, E. Pierson and S. Ratté, 'The Common Concern of Humankind: A Potential Framework for a New International Legally Binding Instrument on the Conservation and Sustainable Use of Marine Biological Diversity in the High Seas', www.un.org/depts/los/biodiversity/prepcom_files/BowlingPiersonandRatte_Common_Concern.pdf.

[41] S. T. Cottier and E. Bürgi Bonanomi, 'Soil as a Common Concern: Towards Disciplines on Sustainable Land Management', in T. Cottier and K. Nadakavukaren Schefer, *Encylopedia of International Economic Law* (Cheltenham, UK: Edward Elgar, 2017), p. 627.

[42] UNFCCC, *supra* n. 6.

[43] www.admin.ch/opc/fr/classified-compilation/19920113/index.html.

'Reconociendo que los cambios del clima de la Tierra y sus efectos adversos son una preocupación común de toda la humanidad'.[44] (In the 2015 Paris Accord the term problem is used: 'Reconociendo que el cambio climático es un problema de toda la humanidad'; subsequent texts again use the term *preoccupation*.) The German translation reads: 'in der Erkenntnis, dass Änderungen des Erdklimas und ihre nachteiligen Auswirkungen die ganze Menschheit mit Sorge erfüllen'.[45]

These terms were reproduced in the preamble of the 2015 Paris Agreement and newly linked to a multitude of aspirations essentially related to human rights and intergenerational equity:[46]

> Acknowledging that climate change is a common concern of humankind, Parties should, when taking action to address climate change, respect, promote and consider their respective obligations on human rights, the right to health, the rights of indigenous peoples, local communities, migrants, children, persons with disabilities and people in vulnerable situations and the right to development, as well as gender equality, empowerment of women and intergenerational equity.

The 2017 Declaration of Ethical Principles in relation to Climate Change of 13 November 2017 restates climate change as a common concern but adds new and important elements to the effect that the task is one of multilevel governance:[47]

> *Also recognizing* that climate change is a common concern for all humankind, and convinced that the global and local challenges of climate change cannot be met without the participation of all people at all levels of society including States, international organizations, sub-national entities, local authorities, indigenous peoples, local communities, the private sector, civil society organizations, and individuals.

In French, the texts reads:

> *Reconnaissant également* que le changement climatique est une préoccupation commune de l'humanité, et convaincus que les défis mondiaux et locaux ne peuvent être relevés sans la participation de tous, à tous

---

[44] https://unfccc.int/process/conferences/pastconferences/paris-climate-change-conference-november-2015/paris-agreement.

[45] www.admin.ch/opc/de/classified-compilation/19920113/index.html.

[46] https://unfccc.int/process/conferences/pastconferences/paris-climate-change-conference-november-2015/paris-agreement (containing all six official languages of the text).

[47] http://portal.unesco.org/en/ev.php-URL_ID=49457&URL_DO=DO_TOPIC&URL_SECTION=201.html (accessed 28 Aug. 2018).

THE PRINCIPLE OF COMMON CONCERN OF HUMANKIND 15

les niveaux de la société, y compris les États, les organisations internatio-
nales, les entités infranationales, les peuples autochtones, les
communautés locales, le secteur privé, les organisations de la société civile
et les individus.

In Spanish, the text reads:

Reconociendo también que el cambio climático es una preocupación
común de toda la humanidad, y convencidos de que no hay posibilidad
de responder a los problemas mundiales y locales que plantea el cambio
climático sin la participación de todas las personas y todos los estratos de
la sociedad, desde Estados y organizaciones internacionales hasta enti-
dades subnacionales, autoridades locales, poblaciones indígenas, comuni-
dades locales, sector privado, organizaciones de la sociedad civil
y particulares.

The 1992 Biodiversity Convention (CBD) equally affirms that 'conservation of biological diversity is a common concern of humankind'.[48] The
2001 International Treaty on Plant Genetic Resources for Food and
Agriculture (ITPGRFA) states 'that plant genetic resources for food and
agriculture are a common concern of all countries, in that all countries
depend very largely on plant genetic resources for food and agriculture
that originated elsewhere'.[49] This term, however, is also used for cultural
goods in a broad sense. In the preamble of the 2003 UNESCO
Convention for the Safeguarding of the Intangible Cultural Heritage, it
is referred to as follows: 'Being aware of the universal will and the
common concern to safeguard the intangible cultural heritage of
humanity'.[50]

As of 2018, these are the main references to common concern that
currently exist in international treaty language. Sometimes, related
terms are used. The preamble of the 1992 UN Convention on
Desertification uses the following terms: 'Reflecting the urgent concern

---

[48] Convention on Biological Diversity, 5 June 1992, *supra* n. 12.

[49] International Treaty on Plant Genetic Resources for Food and Agriculture, preamble,
para. 3, adopted by consensus at the 31st session of the Conference of the FAO of 3
Nov. 2001 (see *supra* n. 13); the preceding instrument, the non-binding International
Undertaking on Plant Genetic Resources for Food and Agriculture proclaimed the
'universally accepted principle that plant genetic resources are a heritage of mankind
and consequently should be available without restriction' (Halewood *et al.*, *supra* n. 14,
p. 12).

[50] Convention for the Safeguarding of the Intangible Cultural Heritage adopted 17
Oct. 2003 (*supra* n. 15).

of the international community, including States and international organizations, about the adverse impacts of desertification and drought'.[51] The International Law Commission (ILC) states that it is a '[p]ressing concern of the international community as a whole', albeit in a different context, merely as a criterion to select its topics.[52]

Recourse to the notion of concern has been limited to, or related to, regulatory areas of natural resource management and efforts to protect them from overexploitation and degradation. This is also true for using the concept for the protection of cultural diversity as it is considered of vital importance to the conservation of biodiversity and thus the preservation of a multitude of generic resources. Common concern, however, has not been employed in other areas indicated above of public international law, so far. It has been highly path dependent within the environmental and ecological legal community so far and does not potentially encompass all of international law.

Neither human rights, nor compliance with basic standards, nor *jus cogens* are expressed in terms of common concern. The central focal point here has been human dignity and less so the dimension of international cooperation and compliance. The same holds true in international economic law. Neither trade law nor investment law, nor monetary, financial and tax law have recourse to common concern. Also, the doctrine and principles of sustainable development goals (SDGs) do not conceptualise common concern of humankind, albeit the fact that it is at the heart of the matter.[53] Finally, on the procedural side, duties to consult, to negotiate and to cooperate often have not had recourse to common concern of humankind and seek to evolve without the support of it. This leads to the question whether CHH has a life and standing on its own, or whether it merely captures what the law, in other forms and content, already entails. Can it go beyond rhetoric and political appeal?

---

[51] United Nations Convention to Combat Desertification in those Countries Experiencing Serious Drought and/or Desertification, particularly in Africa, UN GA A/CC/241/27 (12 Sept. 1994), www.unccd.int/sites/default/files/relevant-links/2017-01/English_0.pdf.

[52] G. Nolte, 'The International Law Commission and Community Interests', in E. Benevisti and G. Nolte (eds.), *Community Interests across International Law* (Oxford: Oxford University Press, 2018), pp. 101–17, 114.

[53] www.un.org/sustainabledevelopment/sustainable-development-goals.

THE PRINCIPLE OF COMMON CONCERN OF HUMANKIND   17

1.2.2   What Is CCH?

1.2.2.1   Scholarly Work

It does not come as a surprise that in the literature common concern of humankind is a notion originally and mainly dealt with in the context of international environmental law. It was alluded to, but not further developed, in the 1987 *Brundtland Report*[54] and eventually discussed mainly in relation to the concept of common heritage of mankind[55] – avoiding property allocations.[56] The latter essentially emerged in support to claims by developing countries relating to marine resources in the context of UNCLOS III and the Area, preventing the appropriation of manganese nodules in the high seas by states. Through collaborative efforts, developing countries sought to obtain access to advanced technology and shared exploitation by invoking common heritage.[57] At the same time, these countries reiterated the principle of permanent sovereignty over natural resources, denying the concept of shared resources within national territories. Common heritage of mankind constrained both national sovereignty of industrialised and developing countries and eventually failed to materialise in result except for the 1979 Agreement

---

[54] United Nations, *Our Common Future: Report of the World Commission on Environment* (New York: United Nations, 1987), www.un-documents.net/our-common-future.pdf (accessed 28 Aug. 2018). The first part of the report was entitled 'Common Concerns'.

[55] W. Stocker, *Das Prinzip des Common Heritage of Mankind als Ausdruck des Staatengemeinschaftsinteresses im Völkerrecht* (Zurich: Schulthess, 1983); K. Baslar, *The Concept of Common Heritage of Mankind in International Law* (Leiden: Brill, 1998); R. Wolfrum, 'The Principle of Common Heritage of Mankind', *Zeitschrift für ausländisches öffentliches Recht und Völkerrecht (ZaöRV)*, 43 (1983), 312–37.

[56] M. Tolba, 'The Implications of the "Common Concern of Mankind Concept" on Global Environmental Issues', *Revista IIDH*, 13 (1991), 237–46; A. Kiss, 'International Trade and the Common Concern of Humankind', in K. Bosselmann and B. J. Richardson (eds.), *Environmental Justice and Market Mechanisms: Key Challenges for Environmental Law and Policy* (Leiden: Kluwer Law International, 1999); J. Brunnée, 'Common Areas, Common Heritage and Common Concern', in D. Bodansky, J. Brunnée and E. Hey (eds.), *The Oxford Handbook of International Environmental Law* (Oxford: Oxford University Press, 2007), pp. 550–73; J. Murillo, 'Common Concern of Humankind and Its Implications in International Environmental Law', *Macquarie Journal of International and Comparative Environmental Law*, 5 (2008), 133–47.

[57] Cottier, *supra* n. 19, pp. 50–9.

Governing the Activities of States on the Moon and Other Celestial Bodies (Moon Treaty)[58] and the 1959 Antarctic Treaty.[59]

Common concern of humankind was a response to the rejection of common heritage of mankind as it did not question the principle of permanent sovereignty over natural resources. Scholars expounded possible legal implications, from soft law to customary international law, even ascribing effects of *jus cogens*, prohibiting severe environmental harm as a community interest.

A group of legal experts was convened by UNEP in 1990 to lay down the normative foundations in preparation for the 1992 Rio Conference. In its report, it stressed the importance to balance the rights of states with the interests of the international community. To this effect, the group invoked the concept of common concern of mankind, transgressing the notion of international concern. Referring to climate change, it found that the concept is 'focusing on issues which were truly fundamental to all mankind'.[60] Brunnée considers common concern to amount to a facet of the doctrine of common interest and thus taking up an existing tradition in international law.[61] Nolte seems to understand it as a specific subset of community interests inherent to international law.[62] Others relate the roots to the public trust doctrine.[63] Judge Cançado Trindade considers common concern of humankind to be a derivative concept of common heritage of mankind, devoid of controversial proprietary features, rooted in natural law and subject to further elaboration. He stresses the importance of commonness in both concepts and argues that it

---

[58] UNTS 1363, p. 3; https://treaties.un.org/Pages/ViewDetails.aspx?src=IND&mtdsg_no=XXIV-2&chapter=24&clang=_en (accessed 28 Aug. 2018).

[59] UNTS 402 I 5778 https://treaties.un.org/pages/showDetails.aspx?objid=0800000280136dbc (accessed 28 Aug. 2018).

[60] 'Report on the Proceedings of the Meeting, Prepared by Co-Rapporteurs A. A. Cançado Trindade and D. J. Attard', in D. J. Attard (ed.), *The Meeting of the Group of Legal Experts to Examine the Concept of the Common Concern of Mankind in Relation to the Global Environmental Issues*, Malta, 13–15 Dec. 1990 (Nairobi: UNEP, 1991), pp. 19–47, 20. For a summary, see A. A. Cançado Trindade, *infra* n. 64, at 344–5.

[61] J. Brunnée, '"Common Interest": Echoes from an Empty Shell? Some Thoughts on Common Interest and International Environmental Law', *ZaöRV*, 49 (2008), 791–808.

[62] Nolte, *supra* n. 52, at 114.

[63] V. P. Nado and K. R. William, 'The Public Trust Doctrine: A Viable Approach to International Environmental Protection', *Ecology Law Quarterly*, 5 (271) (1976). Today, the doctrine will be of particular interest to implement CCH in domestic law (K. King, 'Redefining the Common Concern Principle: The Public Trust Doctrine as the Domestic Component to Common Concern', student paper, Faculty of Law, University of Ottawa, 22 Jan. 2015 (on file with author)).

THE PRINCIPLE OF COMMON CONCERN OF HUMANKIND   19

would have been better if common concern of humankind – to be further developed – had preceded the proprietary doctrine of common heritage of mankind. Both are mutually supportive and stress 'universally shared values'.[64] Cottier *et al.* expounded the role of a principle of Common Concern of Humankind (CCH) (in capital letters) in climate change mitigation and adaptation, in particular addressing the relationship to public goods.[65] Horn discussed common concern of humankind as a potential foundation to a human right to the environment, to environmental human rights and to intergenerational equity.[66] Soltau, in an effort to unpack common concern of humankind, identifies the following fundamental characteristics essentially based on community interests: (a) the interests concerned extend beyond those of individual states and touch on values or ethics of global significance; (b) threats to the interests concerned are marked by their gravity and potential irreversibility of impacts and (c) safeguarding the interests involved requires collective action and entails collective responsibility.[67] Kirgis discusses common concern as a foundation for action *erga omnes* and a standing of states in environmental affairs affecting all states.[68]

As to normativity, Dobson ascribes to the principle an important 'signalling function'.[69] Brown Weiss emphasises the importance of values and considers common concern as an important emerging principle as a legal basis for new commitments to sustainability.[70] Brunnée recognises

---

[64] A. A. Cançado Trindade, *International Law for Humankind: Towards a New Jus Gentium* (2nd ed., Leiden: Martinus Nijhoff, 2013), pp. 344, 348, 352.

[65] T. Cottier, P. Aerni, B. Karapınar, S. Matteotti, J. de Sépibus and A. Shingal, 'The Principle of Common Concern and Climate Change', *Archiv des Völkerrechts (AVR)*, 52 (2014), 293–324.

[66] For detailed and extensive discussion, see L. S. Horn, 'The Common Concern of Humankind and Legal Protection of the Global Environment', PhD (University of Sydney, 2000) (on file with author).

[67] F. Soltau, 'Common Concern of Humankind', in C. P. Carlane, K. R. Gray and R. G. Tarasofsky (eds.), *The Oxford Handbook of International Climate Change Law* (New York: Oxford University Press, 2016), pp. 202–13, at pp. 207–8.

[68] F. L. Kirgis. 'Standing to Challenge Human Endeavours that Could Change the Climate', *American Journal of International Law*, 84 (1990), 525–30; L. Horn, 'The Implications of the Concept of Common Concern of a Human Kind on a Human Right to a Healthy Environment', *Macquarie Journal of International and Comparative Environmental Law*, 1 (2004), 233–69.

[69] N. L. Dobson, 'Extraterritoriality in International Law: The Case of EU Climate Protection', PhD (University of Utrecht, 2018), p. 43.

[70] E. Brown Weiss, 'Nature and the Law: The Global Commons and the Common Concern of Humankind', *Sustainable Humanity, Sustainable Nature: Our Responsibility*, Political

the potential for common concern to evolve by consensus in treaty and customary law.[71]

While mainly limited to environmental law, Beitz alludes to common concern as a foundation for international human rights protection in general.[72] Nadakavukaren Schefer and Cottier develop the relationship of a principle of Common Concern to the emerging Responsibility to Protect (R2P) in international humanitarian law. They suggest that R2P amounts to perhaps the most advanced area of Common Concern, as it not only entails a right, but also an obligation to act abroad.[73] Cottier submits that *jus cogens* – and the difficulties in implementing the concept – could be conceptualised in terms of a principle of CCH.[74] Kontolemis suggests it as relevant to the more concrete case of exchange rate policies.[75] Finally, Cottier and Matteotti-Berkutova analyse the relation of WTO law to and limitations imposed on the principle of Common Concern by the disciplines of the law of the World Trade Organization (WTO), for example in referring to border tax adjustment or subsidies.[76]

In all these works, it is generally recognised that common concern of humankind entails a normative potential, but the contours have largely remained vague, undefined, not agreed and so far not accepted in state practice and international law beyond preambular treaty texts. Up to present date, it has remained unclear whether common concern of humankind goes beyond the concept of common interests in natural resource law, dating back to the nineteenth-century discussions on global

---

Academy of Sciences, Extra Series 41 (Vatican City, 2014); www.pas.va/content/dam/accademia/pdf/es41/es41-brownweiss.pdf (accessed 15 Sept. 2018).

[71] Brunée, *supra* n. 56, at 564–7.

[72] C. Beitz, C., 'Human Rights as a Common Concern', *American Political Science Review*, 95 (2001), 269–81.

[73] K. Nadakavuaren Schefer and T. Cottier, 'Responsibility to Protect (R2P) and the Emerging Principle of Common Concern', in P. Hilpold (ed.), *Die Schutzverantwortung (R2P). Ein Paradigmenwechsel in der Entwicklung des Internationalen Rechts?* (Leiden: Martinus Nijhoff, 2013), pp 123–42; see Section 1.7.3.

[74] T. Cottier, 'Improving Compliance: *Jus Cogens* and International Economic Law', *Netherlands Yearbook of International Law*, 46 (2017), 329–56; see Section 1.7.2.

[75] Z. Kontolemis, 'Exchange Rates Are a Matter of Common Concern: Policies in the Run-up to the Euro?', *Directorate General Economic and Monetary Affairs Papers*, 191 (2003); see Chapter 7 in this volume.

[76] T. Cottier and S. Matteotti-Berkutova, 'International Environmental Law and the Evolving Concept of Common Concern of Mankind', in T. Cottier, O. Nartova and Z. Bigdeli Sadeq (eds.), *International Trade Regulation and the Mitigation of Climate Change* (Cambridge: Cambridge University Press, 2009), pp. 21–47.

THE PRINCIPLE OF COMMON CONCERN OF HUMANKIND   21

commons, in particular those of the high seas.[77] Equally, the relationship to community interests, recently attracting much attention, has remained unclear and was only marginally touched upon.[78] The relationship to community interests and to other legal principles, except for the principle of common heritage of mankind, and other areas of public international law has not been sufficiently explored; neither has there been an attempt to move towards a broader and admittedly more ambitious exercise of conceptualising common concern as a matter of a fundamental legal principle, albeit a promising potential has been recognised.[79]

Overall, the content and implications of common concern of humankind are not settled and need further work. French aptly summarises the current state of play: either it is possible to conceptualise common concern of humankind and bring about normative coherence, or there is 'a real risk that the discussion descends into little more than retrospective realpolitik'.[80]

1.2.2.2   Work of the ILC

The International Law Commission of the United Nations (ILC) addressed common concern of humankind in its discussion on the legal protection of the atmosphere. In his second report, rapporteur Shinya Murase carefully elaborated on the emerging concept of common concern of humankind and suggested, in light of existing references in international agreements, to deploy the concept in the present context

---

[77] *Supra* n. 28; J. Brunnée, 'Common Interest – Echoes from an Empty Shell', *Zeitschrift für ausländisches öffentliches Recht und Völkerrecht (ZaöRV)*, 49 (1989), 791–808; A. Pardoand and C. Q. Christol, 'The Common Interest: Tension between the Whole and the Parts', in R. Macdonald and D. Johnston (eds.), *The Structure and Process of International Law* (The Hague: Kluwer, 1993), pp. 643–60.

[78] See E. Benvenisti and G. Nolte (eds.), *Community Interests across International Law* (Oxford: Oxford University Press, 2018); W. Benedek, K. de Feyter, M. C. Kettemann and Ch. Voigt, *The Common Interest in International Law* (Cambridge: Intersentia, 2014).

[79] Horn, *supra* n. 66.

[80] French, *supra* n. 39, pp. 334–59, 344. See also F. Biermann, 'Common Concern of Humankind: The Emergence of a New Concept of a New Concept of International Environmental Law', *Archiv des Völkerrechts (AVR)*, 34 (1996), 426–81; E. Brown Weiss, 'The Coming Water Crisis: A Common Concern of Humankind', *Transnational Environmental Law*, 1 (2012), 153–68; Brunée, *supra* n. 56, at 564–67, yet allowing for consensus-based developments of common concern doctrine in treaty and customary law.

22 THOMAS COTTIER

and to recognise that the degradation of the atmosphere is a common concern of humankind:[81]

> Draft Guideline 3: Common concern of humankind
>
> The atmosphere is a natural resource essential for sustaining life on Earth, human health and welfare, and aquatic and terrestrial ecosystems, and hence the degradation of atmospheric conditions is a common concern of humankind.

The second report on the protection of the atmosphere amounts, as of today, to the most extensive official document on common concern within the United Nations. The rapporteur carefully reviews existing treaties and the literature, its relationship to common heritage, duties to cooperate and community obligations *erga omnes*. He recognises the emerging but unsettled status of common concern of humankind. He no longer suggests it in terms of a normative concept to protect. Instead he proposed, in parallel and line with the UNFCCC, to include the finding that the degradation of the atmosphere is a common concern of humankind.[82] The suggestion was met with opposition in the Commission. Mr Murphy argued that the concept has not been known in the present context and that there is no evidence in state practice. It therefore should not be used. Moreover, it has remained undefined:

> There was no need to continue the list to make it clear that States did not find the concept helpful when developing treaty regimes. The Special Rapporteur seemed to think that the presence of the simple word 'concern' in some of those instruments was sufficient to support the concept

---

[81] International Law Commission, 67th sess., Geneva, 4 May–5 June and 6 July–7 Aug. 2015, second report on the protection of the atmosphere by Shinya Murase, Special Rapporteur, A/CN.4.681 (2 Mar. 2015), at 25, 49. The first report suggested in more normative terms that protection of the atmosphere is a common concern of humankind:

Draft Guideline 3: Legal Status of the atmosphere

(a) The atmosphere is a natural resource essential for sustaining life on earth, human health and welfare, and aquatic and terrestrial ecosystems; hence, its protection is a common concern of humankind.
(b) Nothing in the present draft guidelines is intended to affect the legal status of airspace under applicable international law.

[82] Ibid., 17–25.

THE PRINCIPLE OF COMMON CONCERN OF HUMANKIND 23

of common concern of humankind, but that logic was both untenable and unpersuasive. The reality was that States were perfectly well aware of the concept and had pointedly and repeatedly chosen not to use it . . .

Of the 10 States that had, in autumn 2014, commented on the concept of common concern of humankind as it had appeared in the Special Rapporteur's first report, 8 had expressed serious concerns about using the phrase. The most common objection had been the undefined character of the concept and the uncertainty as to what legal obligations flowed from it. He therefore considered that using the concept of common concern in the face of rather extensive contrary State practice would be unjustified and inappropriate, and hence a poor decision. As such, he did not think that draft guideline 3 should be sent to the Drafting Committee.[83]

Mr Nolte equally emphasised that the implications of the common concern of humankind are not established to be taken up as a principle and should be restrained to preambular language.

[H]e had expressed doubts about the wisdom of recognizing a principle of common concern of humankind, as he considered that the implications of such an approach should be established first. Although he was somewhat reassured by the Special Rapporteur's report, which clearly excluded the expansive interpretations of the concept proposed by certain academics, he was still not convinced that recognizing the protection of the atmosphere as a common concern of humankind should take the form of a principle, as proposed in draft guideline 3. The fact that States had been reluctant to use the phrase 'common concern of humankind' was not a reason for the Commission not to use it. However, rather than being recognized as a principle, it could be mentioned in the preamble, as was the case in the United Nations Framework Convention on Climate Change, along with any explanation necessary to avoid the risk of too broad an interpretation.[84]

In light of these comments, reference to common concern of humankind was deleted in subsequent work on the protection of the atmosphere, reflecting the conservative mandate of the ILC in codifying international law and contributing to its development. Even a factual statement that degradation of the atmosphere was considered too extensive.

The renewed recognition of common concern of humankind in the 2015 Paris Agreement renders some of the objections made in the ILC

---

[83] ILC, 67th sess. (first part), Provisional summary record of the 3246th meeting, 6 May 2015, A/CN.4/SR.3246 (11 Jan. 2016), at 4–5.

[84] Ibid., at 9. But see also n. 85.

obsolete.[85] The problem of lacking precision and undefined and vagueness remains and needs to be addressed. Yet, rejecting common concern as a potential principle for such reasons reflects a strong positivist tradition which ignores the function of the ILC to contribute to the evolution of international law in addressing real-life problems of the international community. It fails to recognise that principles emerge and gain contours through conceptual work, practice and application. It is in the nature of a principle that it cannot be set out in terms of a precise rule at the outset but bears the potential to grow and develop in time, as it could, for example, be observed in the field of maritime boundary delimitation based upon equitable principles fully undefined at the outset.[86] While some restraint may be justified in terms of a narrowly understood mandate of the ILC, rejecting the concept is regrettably an opportunity missed. The finding does not dispense international lawyers, negotiators and courts of law from seeking to identify its place and role in international law in light of contemporary challenges. It does not dispense from addressing the problem of sovereignty and its impact on the failure to address pressing issues and challenges.

1.2.2.3 Open Questions and Agenda

We can readily see from the scholarly debate that common concern of humankind implies some kind of enhanced commitment and obligations to international cooperation, reinforcing the shift of classical international law from coexistence to cooperation[87], and ultimately perhaps even to integration and legal harmonisation in specific regulatory areas. Yet, as confirmed and observed by the ILC, the normative impact of common concern of humankind, failing effective cooperation, has remained unclear. Many issues remain open and there are fears that the concept is too intrusive and hostile to self-determination.

Does a future principle of CCH, alter the rules on, and the quality of, international cooperation, unilateral application of domestic law and recourse to sanctions and countermeasures? Does CCH alter, or impact upon, the existing principles defining the boundaries of extraterritorial application of domestic law as they can most clearly be observed in the

---

[85] See also Nolte *supra* n. 52, at 114–15, noting that the ILC underestimated the normative potential of the principle in light of its restatement in the 2015 Paris Accord on climate change.

[86] See Cottier, *supra* n. 19.

[87] W. Friedmann, *The Chancing Structure of International Law* (London: Stevens, 1964).

THE PRINCIPLE OF COMMON CONCERN OF HUMANKIND   25

application of domestic competition law.[88] What is the role of unilateral measures addressing free riding? How does it relate to shared but differentiated responsibility? What is the role of responsibility and liability in the context of CCH? Does the principle go beyond existing obligations to avoid transboundary harm in international environmental law?[89] Does it assume responsibilities of states in responding to developments of potentially global impact which take place in other jurisdictions? Finally, what is the relationship to community interests and public goods, in particular global public goods?

In asking these questions, recall that the notion of common concern of humankind – other than common heritage of mankind – does not fundamentally alter the paradigms of permanent sovereignty over natural resources and of territoriality.[90] But, as a legal principle, it may modify jurisdictional boundaries in assuming enhanced and shared responsibilities among states. The responsibility of each state to prevent harm, in particular by the adoption of national environmental standards and international environmental obligations, will also differ based on the extent of its development.[91] As reflected in Principle 7 of the 1992 Rio Declaration, states are required to cooperate to assume differential responsibilities and to take into account the needs of all members of the international community in developing and applying policies and laws previously thought to be solely a matter of domestic jurisdiction.[92]

Developing a normative principle of Common Concern seeks to structure the interactive process of producing public goods by defining duties to negotiate and cooperate, the obligations to do homework, and the

---

[88] See leading cases: *A. Ahlstöm Oy* v. *Commission*, Case 114/85, [1988] ECR 5193; *United States* v. *Aluminum Company of America*, 148 F 2d 416 (2nd Cir. 1945); cf. R. Wish and D. Bailey, *Competition Law* (7th ed., Oxford: Oxford University Press, 2011), pp. 191, 297.

[89] *Trail Smelter Case* (Decision of 11 Mar. 1941) (*United States* v. *Canada*) 3 RIAA 1938.

[90] See also. French, *supra* n. 39, pp. 334–60.

[91] See P. Sands, *Principles of International Environmental Law* (Cambridge: Cambridge University Press, 2004).

[92] Rio Declaration on Environment and Development, A/Conf. 15/26 (Vol. I) Annex I, Principle 7 states: 'States shall cooperate in a spirit of global partnership to conserve, protect and restore the health and integrity of the Earth's ecosystem. In view of the different contributions to global environmental degradation, States have common but differentiated responsibilities. The developed countries acknowledge the responsibility that they bear in the international pursuit of sustainable development in view of the pressures their societies place on the global environment and of the technologies and financial resources they command.'

scope of second-best unilateral action of states or of the EU, furthering solutions to the problem identified.

The distinction of principle and rules offers the foundation of analysis as to whether Common Concern is a suitable legal concept.[93] A comparison with established foundations and principles of public international law will be necessary, in particular sovereignty, permanent sovereignty over natural resources, non-interference and self-determination, equality of states, shared interests and public trust, UN principles of cooperation, emerging principles relating to sustainable development,[94] shared responsibility,[95] and traditional legal principles in particular human rights, the protection of legitimate expectations, equity and proportionality. The relationship to existing treaty obligations, in particular in the field of international trade, need to be further discussed. What is the impact of a principle of CCH on treaty interpretation? What is its impact in the context of sanctions and countermeasures addressing failures to honour the principle of Common Concern?[96] Finally, we ask what role the principle of Common Concern can play beyond international law. To what extent can it be employed, within a system of multilevel governance, to address shared problems within unions and states as well?.

1.3 Foundations and Prospects of CCH

1.3.1 A Process of Claims and Responses

Common concern of humankind, so far, has mainly been a source of inspiration. It encourages and stimulates taking up responsibilities and to reflect and to develop appropriate policy instruments in addressing a challenge of magnitude. As a source of inspiration, it assists in developing new forms of cooperation, funding and interaction emerging in state practice and treaty-making. It thus is able to influence, as a powerful message, the evolution of international law in the age of globalisation facing new types of challenges beyond long-standing threats to international peace and security addressed in the United Nations Charter.

---

[93] R. Dworkin, *Taking Rights Seriously* (Cambridge, MA: Harvard University Press, 1978).

[94] K. Gehne, *Nachhaltige Entwicklung als Rechtsprinzip* (Tübingen: Mohr Siebeck, 2011).

[95] P. A. Nollkaemper, 'Issues of Shared Responsibility before the International Court of Justice', in E. Rieter and H. de Waele (eds.), *Evolving Principles of International Law, Studies in Honour of Karel C. Wellens* (Leiden: Martinus Nijhoff, 2012), pp. 199–237.

[96] Cottier and Matteotti-Berkutova, *supra* n. 76.

It assists shaping new approaches to different regulatory areas addressed in this project and book and beyond.

At the same time, and given the undefined and elusive shape of common concern of humankind, it can be objected that the notion is devoid of a normative concept and thus part of hortatory treaty language of no legal consequence. It may deploy symbolic and psychological effects. It may stimulate debate and action, emphasising the seriousness of a problem. Indeed, the description of common concern in the 2015 Paris Agreement encompasses all kinds of inflationary aspirations which render meaning difficult beyond existing normative concepts in public international law. Moreover, it can be easily objected that the scope is limited to specific declarations and treaties calling upon common concern in specific areas of environmental law; it therefore cannot be applied in terms of a general principle. Finally, it may be argued that common concern does not and cannot amount to a general principle of law. Unlike equity, proportionality, good faith and the protection of legitimate expectations (such as acquiescence and estoppel), or the prohibition of the retroactive effect of law, common concern is not known in domestic legal systems, unless disguised in other principles such as solidarity (*Bundestreue*) within federations. At any rate, it is interesting to observe that in 2019 the most comprehensive and modern encyclopaedia of public international law did not include an entry on common concern on humankind.[97] To the best of our knowledge, it has not played a role in international adjudication as of today. It need not stay like that.

While the legal nature of common concern of humankind so far has been elusive and in very early stages of inception, we submit that this source of inspiration should be further developed and recognised as a principle of law based upon which legal effects in terms of rights and obligations shall be broadly defined. Beyond recognition in the field of international environmental law, it bears the potential to emerge into a legal discipline of its own in the process of claims, responses, debate and recognition addressed. Likewise, and inspired by processes in international law, common concern may eventually evolve in a principle of law applicable to multilevel governance within states. Sub-federal levels face the same challenges. Within the European Union and regional integration, transboundary problems may amount to common concerns. Within federate states, common concerns arise among and between

---

[97] See *Max Planck Encyclopedia of Public International Law* (Oxford: Oxford University Press, 2012), vol. III.

28   THOMAS COTTIER

states, provinces, *Bundesländer* and cantons. And within these, common concerns arise among districts and communes on the local level.

Indeed, established legal principles at the outset often find their roots in broad moral, philosophical and scholarly argument and claims. They eventually find recognition in case law, international declarations and, perhaps, eventually in treaty law. We recall the advent of the principle of non-intervention in the nineteenth and twentieth centuries, until its full and formal recognition and the prohibition of warfare in Article 2(4) of the UN Charter.[98] We recall that the principle of human dignity entered international law and informed the body of human rights. We recall the evolution and recognition of the Continental Shelf doctrine and subsequently of the exclusive economic zone (EEZ), and of equitable principles in maritime boundary delimitation, based upon the unilateral 1945 Truman Proclamation. They were eventually shaped judge-made law.[99] We recall the advent of the principle of common heritage of mankind, and more recently of the principle of sustainable development, the discussion of which was launched in the *Brundtland Report* in 1987. Today, the latter forms part of the mainstream of international law. It led to the recognition of the principle of sustainable development and the SDGs. Other principles have remained contested as of today, such as the precautionary principle, as opposed to a precautionary approach. Others again are inherently limited to reciprocal treaty relations, in particular the principles of most-favoured-nation treatment and national treatment in international economic law.

The recognition of these principles depends upon an international process of claims by states, the economy, non-state actors including businesses, non-governmental organisations (NGOs), political parties and civil society, and upon responses to such claims in the international political and legal process. They are not objectively existing or part of natural law.[100] Responses may accept, qualify or reject claims made, and

---

[98] See N. Stürchler, *The Threat of Use of Force in International Law* (Cambridge: Cambridge University Press, 2007), pp. 7–28.

[99] For a detailed account and analysis, see Cottier, *supra* n. 19.

[100] See also Nolte, *supra* n. 52, at 103:

> A community interest is not something which exists objectively, but needs to be socially established (constructed, recognized). The establishment of a community interest in international law usually begins with a claim by a certain actor which then becomes politically more widely accepted, by persuasion or by different forms of pressure. The process by which a community interest is established is usually fed by many informal (political

depending upon consent or acquiescence eventually may find entry into treaty law or be recognised as customary international law by courts of law, essentially as a matter of judge-made law. The history and formation of public international law has been shaped over the last three centuries by such processes, from the early days of the Westphalian system confronted with claims of sovereignty, developed in the scholarship of Bodin and Hobbes, the principles of *mare clausum* expounded by Selden and of freedom of the high seas argued by Grotius, or the principles of sovereign equality of states, of self-determination and of independence. What today we take for granted as well-established principles of public international law found its inception in scholarly writings and the process of claims and responses of states. Each period in history faces its own challenges, bringing about new principles. It is difficult to see why this should be different in today's interdependent world for a principle of CCH.

1.3.2   Towards a Principle of Law

CCH may thus evolve into a general principle, structuring the governance of serious transboundary problems. Claims and responses will define its contours and normative contents beyond elusive aspirations. Claims and responses will also control the recognition of fields of law to which the principle of CCH applies. Today, global warming is the prime example in point. While the contours remain vague, we recalled above that the international community agreed to rate global warming and the challenges of climate change mitigation and adaptation as a common concern of humankind in the 1988 United Nations General Assembly Resolution upon the motion of Malta who introduced the idea – after pioneering the concept of common heritage of mankind. It was adopted in the 1992 Framework Convention and restated in the 2015 Paris

> or other) impulses whose legal relevance is determined by secondary rules of international law. Secondary rules determine how a political process can result in a legal rule. The process by which an international legal rule may emerge is usually determined by an international organization, or by a conference of states parties, or by the conclusion of a treaty, or by the formation of a rule of customary international law.

> Nolte is referring to J. Klabbers, 'What Role for international Organizations in the Promotion of Community Interests?', in E. Benvenisti and G. Nolte (eds.), *Community Interests in International Law* (Oxford: Oxford University Press, 2018), pp. 86, 92. The distinction of secondary and primary rules draws upon H. L. A. Hart, *The Concept of Law* (Oxford: Clarendon Press, 1961).

30 THOMAS COTTIER

Agreement.[101] Other areas may witness a similar process in future days. Whether or not a matter is deemed a common concern is open to initiatives, to debate, approval or rejection in the diplomatic and legal process of lawmaking. In addition to treaty-making, specific areas of common concern may emerge in the process of customary lawmaking, argued and finally determined in case law on the basis of the evidence of *opinio juris sive necessitates*. There is no difference to other principles recognised in such processes. Finally, they may flow from recognising existing legal concepts as a common concern, such as *jus cogens* and the existence of peremptory norms, or the doctrine of Responsibility to Protect (R2P), the law of sanctions and countermeasures, and of extra-territorial effect of domestic law.[102] Subsequent chapters of the book will address whether and why the principle of CCH can and should apply to a particular transboundary problem. In this chapter, we focus on the principle as such.

The principle of CCH, as applied to a specific sector and issue, may thus eventually be recognised in treaty law, based upon agreement, consensus or majority rule. It may modulate and find specific expression, suitable to particular fields of law. It will be a matter of international and domestic courts to decide whether the principle has achieved a status in customary international law or as a general principle of law in relation to particular regulatory areas, or in general. It is likely that they will play a leading role in shaping the general principle beyond politics and international diplomacy. The authority of it will essentially depend upon how the inspirational force and power of common concern is creatively taken up by scholars, legal counsels, advocates and judges sitting over unresolved issues in this process of claims, responses, debate and recognition. As in history, courts of law and the way they operate in an organised adversarial manner is the most suitable branch of governance to make these determinations in general law.

In the process of law, legal principles provide fundamental guidance and directions; they differ from specific rules and the standard dichotomy of making and applying such rules. Conceptualising CCH as a principle thus seeks to expound underlying values, broadly defined rights and obligations the application of which depends upon a particular context. Accordingly, results may vary within the broad framework of the principle. We thus should not expect a detailed set of rules

---

[101] See Section 1.2.1.
[102] See Sections 1.7.2–1.7.3.

THE PRINCIPLE OF COMMON CONCERN OF HUMANKIND 31

commensurate with the principle. This does not exclude that the principle and its components eventually will produce more detailed and specific rules which may further refine its contents and provide enhanced legal security in different fields of the law. Common Concern thus may translate in specific regimes in treaties, legislation and case law, comparable to the evolution of English equity which brought about particular legal institutions in the course of time.[103] Or, it may be comparable to modern developments in human rights practice or practice relating to the principles of non-discrimination in the case law of the WTO, refining the scope of protection and exceptions thereof. At this stage, the inquiry is limited to expound the fundamental tenets of Common Concern and to demonstrate that it basically is suitable for a legal principle in international law and a legal principle in a domestic and federal context. It may provide guidance to take up shared problems within sub-federal entities under constitutional law.

In doing so, Common Concern is able to borrow from existing legal disciplines and ideas, shaping them in a new context of transboundary problems. It does not start from scratch, but builds upon the traditions of equity, the doctrine of public trust and the fundamental idea of law in preserving peace and stability in society.

1.3.2.1 Recourse to Equity

Equity has played an important role in addressing problems unsettled in positive law. It is present in all legal systems and offers a door of entry for emerging societal, moral and economic concerns to be taken into account in the legal process. This equally applies to the issue of common concern.[104] The law, by its nature, falls behind the realities and equity has, throughout history, served as an instrument to realign the law with changing needs and perceptions of justice.[105] It builds bridges between law and changing realities. It is not a coincidence that new challenges in law have been addressed by recourse to equity, in particular in inter-

---

[103] See, e.g., Jill E. Martin (ed.), *Hanbury & Martin: Modern Equity* (15th ed., London: Sweet & Maxwell, 1997).

[104] I am indebted to Duncan French for his encouraging me to examine the role of equity in providing foundations for the principle of Common Concern.

[105] R. A. Newman (ed.), *Equity in the World's Legal Systems: A Comparative Study* (Brussels: Brylant, 1972).

national law.[106] While fundamental rights have largely assumed previous functions of equity in domestic and constitutional law, equity emerged as a main driver in the law of international resource management. We recall the role of equity in maritime boundary delimitation, providing the basis for a proper topical methodology developed by the International Court of Justice and courts of arbitration.[107] The approach was transported also into the field of international water allocation and management in the 1997 Convention on the Law of the Non-Navigational Uses of International Watercourses, expounding topical criteria for reasonable and equitable use of water.[108] We recall the inception of intergenerational equity, proposed by Edith Brown Weiss, underpinning environmental concerns and of sustainable development.[109] Equity evolves in a series of equitable principles relating to a particular field and context. These principles in turn, provided the basis for more detailed rules often developed in treaty law. Seen through the lenses of equity and its functions, the advent of CCH heralds a new era of legal developments, transgressing and partly correcting positive law in the process of claims and responses. Importantly, a principle of Common Concern, based upon equity, will allow taking it into account in the process of legal interpretation and the shaping of new rules, legitimising the effort.

1.3.2.2   Recourse to Public Trust Doctrine

Another ancillary foundation of the principle of CCH can be located in the public trust doctrine, found in the traditions of Roman law and of common law. Essential public goods are entrusted to government and defined territorially. The protection of natural resources, watercourses, the sea and landscapes are key responsibilities of government and entail obligations to protect and take action in preserving these goods. To the extent that they reach beyond territorial allocation, transnational, but also transregional or transcontinental goods can be addressed in terms of

---

[106]   Cottier, *supra* n. 19, pp. 1–41; T. Cottier, 'Equity in International Law', in T. Cottier, S. Lalani and C. Siziba (eds.), *Intergenerational Equity: Environmental and Cultural Concerns* (Leiden: Brill/Nijhoff, 2019), pp. 11–32.

[107]   Cottier, *supra* n. 19, pp. 271–644.

[108]   http://legal.un.org/ilc/texts/instruments/english/conventions/8_3_1997.pdf.

[109]   E. Brown Weiss, 'Our Rights and Obligations to Future Generations in International Law', *American Journal of International Law*, 84 (1984), 198; Brown Weiss, *In Fairness to Future Generations: Common Patrimony and Intergenerational Equity* (Tokyo: United Nations University, 1989).

THE PRINCIPLE OF COMMON CONCERN OF HUMANKIND   33

common concerns.[110] Building upon public trust, obligations to protect and act are extended to the realm of international, interregional or intercontinental cooperation and duties to act. Edith Brown Weiss developed the concept of global trust and fiduciary obligations which support, and largely overlap with, the idea and doctrine of common concern.[111] Klaus Bosselmann subsequently builds upon the concept of trusteeship in developing far-reaching changes in global governance.[112] Today, climate change mitigation and partly climate change adaptation are a case in point. The same holds true for the management of soil, forests, deserts and mountains, and of international watercourses and the sea. Addressing marine pollution, in particular the problem of amassing plastic residues in the high seas thus amounts to a CCH and will be dealt with accordingly in the chapter authored by Judith Schäli.[113] Public trust provides a powerful foundation to address transnational problems relating to natural resources. The question arises whether it may also reach other public goods beyond natural resources, such as monetary stability, or the problem of migration, or the protection of fundamental human rights. Public trust doctrine has not been applied to such areas so far, and additional foundations of common concern may be necessary.

1.3.2.3   Recourse to Community Interests

Building upon the doctrine of common interests, the doctrine community interests emerged as an important foundation to justify taking into account the interest of others, beyond bilateral relations among states. It is fair to say that the general concept has been recognised today in a world increasingly interdependent and economically integrated. It mainly stands for the proposition of enhanced international cooperation.[114] Community interests influence the application and interpretation of international law, in particular in applying and concretising broad notions of law. They provide the basis for obligations *ergo omnes*.

Community interests, however, cannot be readily defined; often they overlap and concur with national interests. and are not necessarily

---

[110] *Supra* n. 63.

[111] E. Brown Weiss, 'The Planetary Trust: Conservation and Intergenerational Equity', *Ecology Quarterly*, 11 (1984), 495.

[112] K. Bosselmann, *Earth Governance: Trusteeship of the Global Commons* (Cheltenham, UK: Edward Elgar, 2015).

[113] See Chapter 3 in this volume.

[114] See Benevisti and Nolte, *supra* n. 78; Benedek *et al.*, *supra* n. 78.

juxtaposed to bilateral relations.[115] For example, a bilateral agreement on climate change between two major emitters is both in the national interest and a community interest of the international community at large. Community interests therefore often crystallise in particular legal principles, such as common heritage of mankind, or the Area in the law of the sea, or the principle of sustainable development or the few rights and obligations under *jus cogens*. In fact, many legal principles of international law, or recognised in international law, express community interests as much as national interests, such as the principle of most-favoured nation treatment in WTO and investment law, *pacta sunt servanda*, the protection of legitimate expectations and estoppel. These interests, as much as the legal order as such, are general in nature, and of interest independently of the particular relationship of states at hand. They represent public interests broadly speaking and seek to realise and protect public goods in the international realm, as much as public interests protect and represent public goods in domestic law.[116]

Perhaps, the particular nature of community interests in a narrower sense and of interest in the present context can best be identified in areas where reciprocity of interests is lacking, and thus of frequent free riding among states which need to be compensated for, and balanced with, by recourse to the interests of the international community of non-state actors and humans in general. States tend to refrain from entering into agreements or to fully implement them if they cannot directly benefit from advantages incurred in the bargain. Rather they seek to engage in beggar-thy-neighbour policies and profit from contributions of third states without impairing own competitive advantages. Climate change, erosion of biodiversity and marine pollution are examples in point. The lack of enforcement of human rights is yet another one. The same holds true for national migration policies. It is here that international law needs to recognise community interests which can be protected by third countries and international organisations even in the absence of international agreements. In this context, the guarantees under *jus cogens* amount to the main achievement of protecting community interests, obliging states to comply and enabling third states to protect them even in absence of

---

[115] S. Besson, 'Community Interests in International Law: Whose Interests Are They and How Should We Best Identify Them?', in Benevisti and Nolte, *supra* n. 78, at 37–49.

[116] Community interests clearly relate to public goods and multilevel governance, discussed in Sections 1.4.1–1.4.2.

THE PRINCIPLE OF COMMON CONCERN OF HUMANKIND   35

treaty obligations.[117] The evolving doctrine of R2P is based upon and expresses community interests in the same way.[118]

Invoking such interests in the operation of law extends jurisdiction to states not directly involved and establishes international responsibilities and rights and even obligations to act. The crucial test of a community interest thus rests upon extended jurisdiction to invoke and defend such interests on behalf of humans and resources affected outside of national jurisdiction.

Given the indeterminacy of community interests in general, crystallisations in legal principles and even rules define the content and scope of community interests more precisely in a particular context. They offer legal security and predictability. But rather than identifying community interest, the principle of CCH addresses a particular and unresolved problem and subjects it to a set of normative effects. In this way, the recognised but vague doctrine of community interests is able to provide a basis and foundation for the crystallisation of more specific rights and obligations under a principle of CCH, bundling and expressing community interests in well-defined parameters and areas of international law and relations. *Jus cogens* thus can be conceptualised as a common concern of humankind.[119]

1.3.2.4 Preserving Peace and Security

Finally, we refer to the essential function of law and legal principles to preserve peace and stability in society. In international relations, the essence of international law ultimately is dedicated to this task and function. The principle of common heritage of humankind is fully in line with obligations and rights of states under the UN Charter and the Friendly Relations Declaration.[120] Preserving and promoting peace and stability amounts to a key foundation and rationale of international law and thus also provides an important foundation for the doctrine of CCH. It will assist in shaping its contours, boundaries and thresholds.[121]

Threats to peace and stability are not limited to impending aggression and warfare for which domestic law and international law is essentially

---

[117] See Section 1.4.3.2.
[118] See Section 1.4.3.3.
[119] Cottier, *supra* n. 74. See Section 1.7.3.
[120] 2625 (XXV). Declaration on Principles of International Law concerning Friendly Relations and Co-operation among States in accordance with the Charter of the United Nations, 24 Oct. 1970, A/Red/25/2625; www.un-documents.net/a25r2625.htm (accessed 28 Aug. 2018).
[121] See Section 1.3.3.

settled. The prohibition of aggressive warfare and the principle of friendly relations among nations do not call upon additional support by the doctrine of common concern. However, other threats to peace and stability are not sufficiently encapsulated in law and prevention and remedies remain unclear. It is here that the doctrine of CCH is able to provide appropriate answers in addressing threats which, for example, are caused and created by systemic and serious violations of human rights in a particular community. Such violations may lead to threats to peace and security not only within that community, but also for neighbours, regions and sometimes the world at large. Some of these threats are dealt with in the case studies included in the volume. Human dignity and the protection of fundamental rights thus offer an important foundation of, and rationale for, the principle of Common Concern to the extent that persistent disrespect of these values threatens peace and stability and establish linkages to the emerging doctrine of R2P. Likewise, threats to peace and security may results from economic imbalances caused by monetary crisis. It may be caused by failure to properly manage international migration flows, causing unrest and upheaval. Threats to international peace and security may be caused by gross inequalities, in particular inequality of income within a community, affecting human dignity. These imbalances may affect neighbours and the international community at large and thus amount to a common concern. Finally, threats to peace and international stability no longer are limited to homocentric concerns, but also entail ecological and environmental concerns, affecting long-term livelihoods of humans, plant and animal life on the globe. They are long-term threats to international peace and security if not properly recognised and addressed in time.

1.3.3 Addressing Shared Problems and Transboundary Preoccupations

Recourse to common concern both in literature in treaty language suggests that it stands for the proposition of an important shared problem and shared responsibility, and for an issue which reaches beyond the bounds of a single community and state as a subject of international law. Shelton aptly expresses it: 'Issues of common concern are those that inevitably transcend the boundaries of a single state and require collective action in response.'[122] This understanding has a factual and normative component, different from community interests.

---

[122] D. Shelton, 'Common Concern and Humanity', *Environmental Law and Policy*, 39 (2009), 83.

Much of the literature reviewed defines common concern in terms of common interests and values, rather than a shared problem. There are important overlaps. Common interests often amount to, and result in, a shared problem and thus a common concern. This is particularly true in relation to the preservation and management of natural resources. Shared problems, common interests and values, however, do not necessarily coincide. Countries may not be interested in solving or contributing to the resolution of a particular transboundary problem. Shared interests do not necessarily exist and still give rise to a shared problem and common concern. As discussed above, free-riding states do not share the same interest as states seeking to address the issue. It is for such reasons that common concern goes beyond shared interests and international cooperation and needs to address and include mechanisms securing compliance.

It is therefore important to adopt a more factual basis in the first place, independently of common interests, and to define common concern as a starting point in terms of a shared problem which exists in the real world. The existence of threat of a real transboundary problem, the resolution or prevention of which requires collective action and cooperation among two or more states provides the essential starting point.

This understanding is confirmed by the terms used. The term *common* not merely depicts the ordinary, but also something 'shared by, coming from, or done by two or more people, groups, or things', or 'belonging to or "make it clear that the concern affects all of humanity and thus is of a global dimension in all languages alike.

According to the *Oxford Dictionary*, the noun *concern* means '*anxiety, worry*', but also '*a matter of interest or importance to someone*'.[123] The French texts use the term *préoccupation*.[124] In Spanish, the terms *problema* and *preocupatión* are similar to the French meanings.[125] The German translations use the term *Sorge*.[126] In the Russian language, the

---

[123] https://en.oxforddictionaries.com/definition/concern.

[124] 'Souci vif et constant qui absorbe l'esprit au point de le détourner d'autres objets', www.larousse.fr/dictionnaires/francais/pr%c3%a9occupation/63589?q=pr%c3%a9occupation#62873.

[125] Intranquilidad, inquietud o temor que produce alguna cosa, and Lo que provoca interés o atención, www.wordreference.com/definicion/preocupaci%C3%B3n.

[126] (durch eine unangenehme, schwierige, gefahrvolle Situation hervorgerufene quälende Gedanken; bedrückendes Gefühl der Unruhe und Angst(gehoben); but also: Bemühen um jemandes Wohlergehen, um etwas; Fürsorge), www.duden.de/rechtschreibung/Sorge.

term *общая озабоченность* is used for the UNFCCC and the Paris Agreement as well as the Convention for the Safeguarding of intangible Cultural Heritage. It translates into common concern, while the term *общая задача* is used in the Convention on Biological Diversity, meaning a common goal. In Chinese, the term for common concern 人类的共同关切 (Chinese Pinyin *Renlei Gongtong Guanqie*) means 'a common problem and task which needs to be taken up jointly by whole humankind.[127]

It seems fair to say that these terms also share an understanding that the matter at hand is worrying, but at the same of great interest or importance and to be taken care of. Concern not merely describes a fact, a problem or adverse effects, but equally entails a normative component that there is a problem which needs to be addressed. Common concerns in terms of preoccupations and goals call for joint action. This is the very normative dimension marking and establishing the principle of CCH. In French, it could be termed *principe de préoccupation commune de l'humanité*, in Spanish *principe de preocupación común* de toda la humanidad, in German perhaps *Prinzip des gemeinsamen Anliegens der Menschheit*.

Importantly, common concern of humankind does not depict a particular natural feature and condition, such as climate, biodiversity, desserts, forests, but relates to changes and adverse effects in these areas, potentially harmful to the human condition and life.[128] In climate change, it is the problem of warming (and not the climate). In biodiversity and culture, it is insufficient conservation and erosion of diversity (and not diversity as such). The problem to be addressed thus relates to the management of change and of adverse and harmful effects. The latter also opens the concept to configurations rooted beyond natural features and human-made legal institutions, such as human rights, migration, or monetary and financial stability in the field of economic relations all discussed in this volume. It is not possible to define common concerns once and for all and in advance. Many of them are known; new problems and challenges may yet arise in the course of globalisation and technological change and progress. The terms also indicate that common concern of humankind cannot be limited to environmental preoccupations. It essentially encompasses all transboundary problems of similar magnitude, thus affecting all areas of international law and relations.

---

[127] I am indebted to Iryna Bogdanova for the Russian, and to Jiangiang Nie for Chinese translations.
[128] Brunnée, *supra* n. 56, at 565.

Finally, the term common concern as a transboundary problem is not limited to international law. It bears the potential to play an important role in domestic law, interfacing different constituencies and territories within domestic law. Shared problems between two local communities equally amount to a common concern and call for cooperation. It may play a role in interfacing international and domestic law and thus become relevant for the doctrine of multilevel governance. In the following chapters, we focus on international law and how it may impact domestic law and multilevel governance. Insights on thresholds, related concepts and rights and obligations may, however, be extended in analogy and accordingly to other layers of governance, including shared problems on the regional, national and local levels. They may provide the basis for common concern as a future principle of law recognised by nations.

1.3.4 Defining Thresholds: Threats to Peace and Stability

The recognition of global warming and the loss of biological and cultural diversity as common concerns of humankind by the international community imply that common concern depicts serious problems of major magnitude. There is a multitude of shared problems in international relations which states cannot successfully solve on their own and depend upon transboundary cooperation. Yet, the doctrine and principle of CCH cannot successfully apply to all collective action problems without risking inflationary effects and being watered down. It is important to limit the concept, in international law, to serious and pressing problems in view of the legal obligations and rights attached to the principle discussed below. A threshold level has to be reached which calls for mobilisation of public opinion and action taken on all levels of governance. Climate change and the loss of biological diversity prove the point that the gravest long-term threats are being envisaged. The recognition of common concern of humankind in these particular areas sets the standard and threshold in international relations.

In assessing serious problems of major magnitude, we recall the foundation of common concern of humankind in keeping peaceful relations and stability. We turn to the very essence of public international law, in fact all of law, which seeks to preserve peaceful relations among humans and support and promote welfare of humanity. The threshold of threats to peace and stability and welfare goes to the very foundations and heart of public international law and the legitimacy to limit traditional perceptions of independence, sovereignty and self-determination of states. The benchmark to be considered for the principle of CCH should be problems threatening and undermining this very basic function of the law. To the extent that a shared problem threatens these goals, it becomes a matter of common concern and should be addressed accordingly. At the same time, the threshold limits the principle of Common Concern to problems of utmost importance. They avoid minor problems to be exposed to enhanced legal obligations incurred under the principle.

It is therefore submitted that the principle of CCH is limited to problems in the various fields of public international law which could potentially threaten international stability, peace and welfare. As discussed, such threats are not limited to aggression and warfare, as the potential and disastrous implications of climate change and the loss of biodiversity recall. They are not limited to the classical homocentric notions and threats of war and peace, but equally entail threats caused by excessive exploitation of natural resources threating foundations of livelihood.

Traditionally and classically, international peace and security is dealt with by states around the powers of the Security Council of the United Nations.[129] It comprises disarmament, international humanitarian law, use and threat of force, international peace and security, including economic sanctions and perhaps anti-terrorism.[130] Given that the prohibition of threat and use of force in international relations under Article 2(4) of the UN Charter and the limitation to self-defence in Article 51 thereof, the main collective action problems in law and challenges to peace and stability today lie elsewhere beyond the realm of open aggression. Peace, stability and welfare within societies and political systems in particular are threatened today next to ecological degradation, economic instabilities, erratic trade policies and crisis, monetary and financial instability, mismanagement of migration flows, by systemic violations of human rights and depletion of natural resources affecting the very foundations of human life and society.

Such problems may eventually lead to civil unrest, civil war, revolution and international conflict. Yet, unlike in classical areas of peace and war,

---

[129] See UN website Peace and security; www.un.org/en/sections/what-we-do/maintain-inter national-peace-and-security (accessed 10 May 2018).

[130] See e.g. R. Higgins, P. Webb, D. Akande, S. Sivakumaran and S. Sloan, *Oppenheim's International Law United Nations* (Oxford: Oxford University Press, 2017), vol. I, pp. 95–6.

THE PRINCIPLE OF COMMON CONCERN OF HUMANKIND 41

there are no comparable legal thresholds in place as to where and when they produce a threat to international peace, stability and human welfare. It hardly can be said that proper thresholds are only reached when open international conflict threatens international peace and security in the traditional sense are imminent. This point in time is too late. Thresholds to trigger enhanced obligations and commitments must be found in a preventive manner before such stages are reached.

It is submitted that the doctrine and the emerging principle of CCH allow defining appropriate thresholds, calling for commitment and action in other forums and international organisations, and unilaterally if need be. We propose that the threshold should be comparable to, and commensurate with, the one recognised in international law for threats to peace and security as defined by the UN Security Council and state practice.

The threshold of threat to international peace, stability and welfare is highly contextual and it is difficult to provide specific general criteria. The main emphasis lies upon threats, and addressing those amounts to the main function of CCH. Historical experience offers important guidance in assessing whether developments may lead to civil disruptions and even war. Beyleveld for example shows in his contribution that gross income inequality triggered international conflict and strive in the past and thus potentially amounts to a CCH.[131] Satragno recalls the disruptions to peace called by monetary instability and crisis.[132] Lupo-Pasini argues, on the basis of financial crisis, along the same lines for financial stability.[133] Cottier and Losada show that migration badly managed may threaten not only peace and democracy within society, but lead to international tensions, threatening peace and welfare.[134]

In assessing whether a problem is a common concern, the views of scholarship and science should be taken into account in order to make informed fact-based and informed decisions. Scientific evidence, as ably demonstrated in the case of climate change or in monetary affairs, may offer guidance in other areas, such as marine pollution as Schäli shows.[135] Factual evidence should inform the debate whether an issue falls under the principle of Common Concern,. It will always be a topic of reasonable disagreement and political debate which is essentially interest driven. At

---

[131] Chapter 4 in this volume.
[132] Chapter 7 in this volume.
[133] Chapter 8 in this volume.
[134] Chapter 6 in this volume.
[135] Chapter 3 in this volume.

42 THOMAS COTTIER

the end of the day, it will often be matter for judges to assess whether an issue lawfully is dealt with as Common Concern and measures and steps taken jointly or unilaterally can, or cannot, be justified accordingly.

Unilateral claims, responses and debate as to whether a particular issue amounts to a common concern of humankind should be voiced by governments and civil society and take place in appropriate international forums and organisations functionally assigned to a particular regulatory area. They assume the role which the United Nations Security Council cannot play in addressing the causes of major crises as it is limited to deal with short-term symptoms. We see a particular role for the UN General Assembly, for G20 to address horizontal issues and to decide whether a particular economic issue falls under the principle of CCH and should be dealt with accordingly. The Bretton Woods institutions, specialised organisations of the UN, the WTO all may invoke the principle in response to challenges threating world peace and stability in order to take and legitimise appropriate action addressing the issue. These processes of claims and responses always will be contentious, messy and difficult. Hearings with scholars, experts and interest groups should be held. Consensus will not come easily, but may eventually forge as existing treaty texts demonstrate.

1.3.5   Areas of Application in International Law

While common concern emerged in the field of natural resources and environmental law, it is clear by now that the doctrine and emerging principle of CCH is suitable for applications across the board of public international law. Studies undertaken within the present project and book relate to shared problems in monetary law, the issue of massive and increasing income inequality, the realisation of the core and undeniable essence human rights, the duty to protect (R2P), the problem of migration, all beyond the fields of climate change and transfer of technology and problems relating to pollution of the high seas. Other areas may eventually be explored: for example, core areas of sustainable development expressed today in terms of SDGs, food security and soil quality, international trade and investment law, navigation, or telecommunications, big data and cybercrime. The principle of Common Concern can be used to reconceptualise the concept of *erga omnes* obligations, of community rights and *jus cogens*.[136] It will influence

---

[136] *Barcelona Traction Case*, ICJ Rep. 1970, p. 32, para. 33; see C. Annacker, 'The Legal Regime of *Erga Omnes* Obligations in International Law', *Austrian Journal of Public*

THE PRINCIPLE OF COMMON CONCERN OF HUMANKIND   43

the doctrine of extraterritorial application of domestic laws and the law of countermeasures and sanctions in international economic law, including trade regulation.

In conclusion, the principle of CCH may play a decisive and positive role in all areas, where there still is a lack of appropriate institutions at the global or regional level offsetting and compensating for the lack of reciprocal interests of states, where collective action fails and leadership is needed to generate appropriate incentives for others to join an international effort of cooperation in the long run. It is in this function that the relationship of Common Concern to equity as a motor of legal developments in the face of a changing world is apparent. The principle of Common Concern offers a basic structure. It seeks to delineate obligations to act, and rights to act beyond the scope of territorial application of laws of the nation states and of the European Union. The understanding is informed by the experience made in trade policy where unilateral action, or the threat of it, triggered cooperation, and permitted the institutionalisation of economic globalisation[137] and the building of the multilateral trading system of the GATT and the WTO over decades with a bottom-up approach.[138]

1.4   Related Concepts in Context

Before developing the normative contents of the principle of common heritage of humankind, it is useful to delineate it from related concepts in context beyond those already discussed in terms of foundations above. They partly influence the shapes of the duties discussed in Sections 1.5–1.7 on cooperation, homework and compliance. And some may be partly integrated into the principle.

International Law, 46 (1994), 131–66; B. Simma, 'From Bilateralism to Community Interests in International Law', *Recueil des cours*, 250 (1994), 217–384; C. Tomuschat, 'International Law, Ensuring the Survival of Mankind on the Eve of a New Century', *Recueil des cours*, 281 (1999), 9–438. See also ILC report (*supra* n. 81), paras. 43–51.

[137] J. Braithwaite and P. Drahos, *Global Business Regulation* (Cambridge: Cambridge University Press, 2010).

[138] T. Cottier, 'Confidence-Building for Global Challenges: The Experience of International Economic Law and Relations', in R. Greenspan *et al.* (eds.), *Building International Climate Cooperation* (World Resources Institute, 2012), pp. 117–76.

44   THOMAS COTTIER

1.4.1   The Relationship to Public Goods

The doctrine of CCH is aligned in many ways with the notion of global public goods and the effective management of the global commons.[139] However, the two concepts are not identical and need to be distinguished. While Common Concern depicts an unsolved transnational problem, public goods stand for the proposition of non-rivalrous and non-excludable goods.[140] One describes issues, the other solutions, outcomes and products which are aimed to be achieved in the public, as opposed to private, spheres. Depicting an issue as a common concern ideally leads to solving underlying problems in producing appropriate public goods.

Paul A. Samuelson was the first economist to develop the theory of public goods. He defined a public good (or 'collective consumption good' as he called it) in his classic 1954 paper 'The Pure Theory of Public Expenditure', as follows:

> [goods] which all enjoy in common in the sense that each individual's consumption of such a good leads to no subtractions from any other individual's consumption of that good.[141]

This essentially is the property of non-rivalry. In addition, a *pure public good* exhibits a second property called non-excludability, defined as the impossibility to exclude any individual from consuming the good. The essential characteristic of a public good is that its consumption by one individual does not actually or potentially limit actual and potential consumption by others.

While the theoretical concept of public goods does not distinguish with regard to the geographical region in which a good may be produced or consumed, some theorists use the term 'global public good' to mean a public good which is non-rival and non-excludable throughout the whole

---

[139] I. Kaul, Isabelle Grunberg and M. A. Stern (eds.), *Global Public Goods – International Cooperation in the 21st Century*, published for the United Nations Development Programme (New York: Oxford University Press 1999); E. Brousseau *et al.* (eds.), *Global Environmental Commons: Analytical and Political Challenges in Building Governance Mechanisms* (Oxford: Oxford University Press, 2012); E. U. Petersmann (ed.), *Multilevel Governance of Interdependent Public Goods: Theories, Rules and Institutions for the Central Policy Challenge in the 21st Century*, 18 EUI Working Papers RSCAS (Florence: Robert Schuman Centre for Advanced Studies, 2012–13).

[140] Brousseau *et al.*, *supra* n. 139, at 23.

[141] P. A. Samuelson, 'The Pure Theory of Public Expenditure', *Review of Economics and Statistics*, 36 (1954), 387–89.

THE PRINCIPLE OF COMMON CONCERN OF HUMANKIND   45

world, as opposed to a public good which exists in just one national area.[142] Knowledge can be cited as an example of a global public good. It does not diminish by those using it.

Global public goods must meet two criteria: one, their benefits must possess strong qualities of 'publicness' (i.e. be marked by non-rivalry in consumption and non-excludability); and two, their benefits must be quasi-universal in terms of countries, people and generations. This last property in particular makes humanity as a whole the beneficiary of a global public good. In keeping with this definition, sustainable climatic conditions clearly are a global public good.

While climate change is undeniably a global concern, other concerns may be regional, national or even local, correlating to a regional, national or local public good. Public goods in fact correlate with perceptions of multilevel governance seeking to appropriately allocate regulatory powers with a view to producing public goods commensurate with the level of governance.[143] Common Concern and public goods therefore correlate with each other on different levels. They both contribute important building blocks to the doctrine of multilevel governance. As much as it is the essence of governance to produce appropriate public goods – local, national regional or global – common concerns relating to these different spheres call for appropriate responses by appropriate governance. It is important to keep in mind these layers and differences. Local common concerns call for different answers from global common concerns. What they share is that a problem is grave and exceeds a single community. It should ideally be addressed with a cooperative effort. In both cases the law needs to answer the question of what to do if such cooperation fails to materialise.

Looking at natural resources, few goods are purely public or purely private. Most possess mixed characteristics and benefits. Goods that only partly meet either or both of the defining criteria are called impure public goods. Because impure goods are more common than the pure type, the term 'public good' is used to encompass both pure and impure public goods. Natural resources may be termed impure public goods as consumption is limited in the long run. The examples of clean air, global warming or fish stocks at the high seas make the point.

Proper public goods, on the other hand, essentially are human institutions of governance, in particular the law, government and

[142] Kaul *et al.*, *supra* n. 139.
[143] Petersmann, *supra* n. 139.

international organisations. They are human-made. They essentially result from addressing and solving, albeit often imperfectly, shared problems, i.e. common concerns in a broad sense. Legal institutions, in particular are proper public goods, such as the Constitution, human rights, contract law, property, torts, all laws and regulations of a general nature. The law as a public good, however, also deals with private goods, regulating them. Common Concern seeking to create appropriate public goods and regulation includes problems relating to private goods and property rights. Institutions of public international law, such as the multilateral trading system of the WTO, or the European Union, are public goods of immense importance. Peace and security, the absence of violence, are public goods, which law and policy are bound to protect and promote to the benefit of all in a non-rivalrous and non-excludable manner. Recent scholarship increasingly extended the doctrine of public goods to legal institutions and the need to protect them in a pluralist world. International law plays an important role in producing and protecting such goods using different forms of international cooperation.[144]

The scope of public goods therefore is broader and different from Common Concerns of Humankind, properly speaking. The latter, as a concern, focuses on a number of serious problems threating peace, stability and welfare in the long run where public goods need to be created and protected while appropriate structures to this effect are not yet properly in place. In other words, CCH depicts common and shared important problems and failures of governance in producing these public goods. The quest for CCH is motivated by the need to remedy such configurations and deficiencies and bring about the production of these public goods to the benefit of humankind. The legal qualities of the concept therefore should be shaped accordingly.

1.4.2   The Relationship to Multilevel Governance

Common concerns, defined as problems transgressing a particular jurisdiction, are not per se limited to global concerns, but can equally be found like public goods on local, national or regional levels. While CCH

---

[144] G. Shaffer, 'International Law and Global Public Goods in a Legal Pluralist World', *European Journal of International Law*, 23 (2012), 669–39, essentially relying upon S. Barret, *Why Cooperate: The Incentive to Supply Global Public Goods* (Oxford: Oxford University, 2007) who differentiates between different types of public goods and argues that so-called aggregate public goods render international cooperation indispensable.

inherently affects the globe or continents, we can equally conceive of understanding serious local problems as a matter of common concern if they inherently are transboundary and call for mutual cooperation and interaction. These concerns should be addressed properly in the context of constitutional law. It is here that insights from substantive and procedural rules to sustaining public goods can also be applied and further developed in responding to the problem of common concern, such as the doctrine of public trusts. With regard to proper Common Concerns of Humankind, however, the question arises on what level of governance they should best be addressed. For example, climate change mitigation and adaptation, while a global common concern, calls for appropriate action on all levels of governance, from multilateral to local levels.

The 2017 Declaration of Ethical Principles in relation to Climate Change of 13 November 2017 restated climate change as a common concern but added new and important elements to the effect that the task is one of multilevel governance:[145]

> *Also recognizing* that climate change is a common concern for all humankind, and convinced that the global and local challenges of climate change cannot be met without the participation of all people at all levels of society including States, international organizations, sub-national entities, local authorities, indigenous peoples, local communities, the private sector, civil society organizations, and individuals,

The United Nations Convention to Combat Desertification in Countries Experiencing Serious Drought and/or Desertification, Particularly in Africa not only stresses a particular region it its title, but also emphasises in its preamble the dimension of multilevel governance and the need to take action on the local level:[146]

> Recognizing that national Governments play a critical role in combating desertification and mitigating the effects of drought and that progress in that respect depends on local implementation of action programmes in affected areas.

The emerging doctrines of multilevel governance assist in optimal allocation and assignments of tasks on different layers of governance in the production of public goods relating to the Common Concern at hand.

---

[145] http://portal.unesco.org/en/ev.php-URL_ID=49457&URL_DO=DO_TOPIC&URL_SECTION=201.html.

[146] *Supra* n. 51.

48 THOMAS COTTIER

The advent of the European Union has largely contributed to conceptually overcoming the fundamental divide between domestic and international law in the long run. Its evolution contributed to an understanding of law in terms of different interactive layers of governance, from local to global dimensions. The limitation of international law to interstate law at the exclusion of individuals has been challenged and gradually changed by the advent of human rights protection. Research and doctrine have been addressing the interaction of different layers of government, their legitimacy and the interaction of different sources of law in an environment of ever-increasing fragmentation of law.[147]

The field shows a variety of different constitutional theories, including, on the one hand, the doctrine of sovereignty-modern (John Jackson) and a human rights–based approach (Petersmann),[148] regimes based upon mutual recognition (Joerges),[149] compensatory constitutionalism (Peters),[150] constitutional pluralism (Walker),[151] global administrative law (Kingsbury, Krisch, Steward and Wiener)[152] or the model of a five-storey house discussed below, taking into account cosmopolitan political theory (Cottier). On the other hand, theories advocating inherent fragmentation and pluralism (Koskenniemi, Teubner, Joerges) reject the idea of seeking coherence but consider fragmentation inherent to the complexities of life and the world.[153]

---

[147] For international trade, see T. Cottier and P. Delimatsis (eds.), *The Prospects of International Trade Regulation: From Fragmentation to Coherence* (Cambridge: Cambridge University Press, 2011).

[148] See J. H. Jackson, *Sovereignty, the WTO, and Changing Fundamentals of International Law* (Cambridge: Cambridge University Press, 2006); E. U. Petersmann, *International Economic Law in the 21st Century: Constitutional Pluralism and Multilevel Governance of Interdependent Public Goods* (Oxford: Hart, 2012).

[149] C. Joerges, 'The Idea of a Three-Dimensional Conflicts Law as Constitutional Form', in C. Joerges and E. U. Petersmann (eds.), *Constitutionalism, Multilevel Trade Governance and International Economic Law* (Oxford: Hart, 2011), pp. 413–55.

[150] A. Peters, 'Compensatory Constitutionalism: The Function and Potential of Fundamental International Norms and Structures', *Leiden Journal of International Law*, 19 (2006), 579–620. See also J. Klabbers, A. Peters and G. Ulfstein, *The Constitutionalization of International Law* (Oxford: Oxford University Press, 2009).

[151] N. Walker, 'The Idea of Constitutional Pluralism', *Modern Law Review*, 65 (2002), 317–59.

[152] B. Kingsbury, N. Krisch, R. B. Stewart and J. B. Wiener (eds.), 'The Emergence of Global Administrative Law', *Law and Contemporary Problems*, 68 (2005), 1–356. See also S. Cassese (ed.), *Research Handbook on Global Administrative Law* (Cheltenham, UK: Edward Elgar, 2016).

[153] M. Koskenniemi and P. Leino 'Fragmentation of International Law? Postmodern Anxieties', *Leiden Journal of International Law*, 15 (2002), 553–79; G. Teubner,

THE PRINCIPLE OF COMMON CONCERN OF HUMANKIND   49

The doctrine of a five-storey house essentially argues that all levels of governance, from local to global, entail human conduct and behaviour, and share basic traits in terms of legal foundations and sources, albeit in very different constellations and compositions.[154] It no longer makes a fundamental difference between domestic and international law in terms of allocating powers to regulate and enforce. It is similar to the perception of sovereignty-modern developed by the late John H. Jackson. It helps identifying the allocation of common concerns and public goods to different layers of government, and where they best should be addressed. In particular, it assists in distinguishing global, regional, national and local concerns and corresponding public goods. It also helps allocating powers in terms of power-sharing among different layers beyond federalism.[155]

The five-storey house, informed by the idea that all layers of governance are of equal importance and reflect human interaction, does not have a preference for one layer over the other, but recognises the international level as equally importance and valuable, often indispensable in the pursuit of CCH, playing an important part next to domestic layers. For example, climate change as a CCH is not confined to global efforts of the international community, but bears out on all layers of government, including local rules on construction or traffic. Preferences in the political process, informed by ideologies, accordingly will be shaped accordingly and play out in a plurality of view. Legal theory and the five-storey house, however, offer a framework which allows structuring this process and debate in a rational manner. Common Concern will help refining jurisdiction in matters, which no longer can be dealt with on the basis of strict territorial application of domestic law.

'Societal Constitutionalism: Alternatives to State-Centred Constitutional Theory', in C. Joerges, I.-J. Sand and G. Teubner (eds.), *Transnational Governance and Constitutionalism* (Oxford: Hart, 2004), pp. 3–28; G. Teubner, *Constitutional Fragments: Societal Constitutionalism and Globalization* (Oxford: Oxford University Press, 2012); G. Shaffer, 'International Law and Global Public Goods in a Legal Pluralist World', *European Journal of International Law*, 23 (2012), 667.

[154] T. Cottier and M. Hertig, 'The Prospects of 21st Century Constitutionalism', in A. von Bogdandy and R. Wolfrum (eds.), 7*Max Planck Yearbook of United Nations Law* (2003), pp. 261–328; T. Cottier, 'Multilayered Governance, Pluralism, and Moral Conflict', *Indiana Journal of Global Legal Studies*, 16 (2009), 647–79; T. Cottier, 'Towards a Five Storey House', in Joerges and Petersmann, *supra* n. 149, pp. 495–532.

[155] B. Geys and K. A. Konrad, 'Federalism and Optimal Allocation across Levels of Governance', in H. Enderlein, S. Wälti and M. Zürn (eds.), *Handbook on Multi-level Governance* (Cheltenham, UK: Edward Elgar, 2010), pp. 32–46.

The different case studies in this volume explore channels of mobilising non-state actor action to resolve Common Concern issues through participation and deliberation in the broader and more transformative sense of reinvention of governance..

There is, of course, substantial reasonable disagreement in terms of the role of states and international cooperation in the pursuit of Common Concerns of Humankind.[156] This issue is at the heart of politics and theoretical debate. To the extent that the existence of a CCH is not denied, statist theories will stress the importance of the state and a corresponding weakness of international law and organisations.[157] On the other side of the spectrum, cosmopolitan political theory[158] is likely to actively embrace Common Concerns of Humankind, stressing the importance of international cooperation and the role of international organisation. There will be no agreement on multilevel governance and where common concerns are best taken up. The work of the ILC reported above makes the point. These matters need to be sorted out in the process of politics and international diplomacy.

Multilevel governance also provides a suitable foundation to come to terms with the role and impact of private actors in the reflexive process of producing public goods in addressing common concerns.[159] It takes into account that the private sector, civil society and NGOs play an important role. Increasingly, there is agreement in the literature that contemporary governance is fluid and in its very essence an adaptive process, even if the momentary snapshot conveys stability. Key in this fluidity and continuous transformation is the understanding that state sovereignty is fragmented and there is a multiplicity of actors and forms of power driving the management of social systems. The state is no longer the monopolist of power, both domestically and on the international scene.[160] Yet, the state has not disappeared and some have even argued that the role states

---

[156] For the theory of reasonable disagreement and political discourse in democracy, see S. Besson, *The Morality of Conflict: Reasonable Disagreement and the Law* (Oxford: Hart, 2005).

[157] J. L. Goldsmith and E. A. Posner, *The Limits of International Law* (New York: Oxford University Press, 2005).

[158] S. Caney, *Justice beyond Borders: A Global Political Theory* (Oxford: Oxford University Press, 2005); K. A. Appiah, *Cosmopolitanism: Ethics in a World of Strangers* (London: Norton, 2006).

[159] Brousseau *et al.*, *supra* n. 139.

[160] J. Black, 'Enrolling Actors in Regulatory Systems: Examples from UK Financial Services', *Public Law* (2003), 63–91; O. Lobel, 'The Renew Deal: The Fall of Regulation and the Rise of Governance in Contemporary Legal Thought', *Minnesota Law Review*, 89 (2004),

THE PRINCIPLE OF COMMON CONCERN OF HUMANKIND   51

play may have been augmented, precisely because of the increased complexity and fuzziness[161] – a hypothesis, which needs to be assessed individually for different regulatory domains.

The multitude of actors in the process of claims and responses to common concern and implementing policies enriches but confirms the concept of multilevel governance and the appropriate allocation of powers of between different layers of governance. In doing so, the principle of Common Concern will help refining jurisdiction in matters, which no longer can be dealt with on the basis of strict territorial application of domestic law; it will explore channels of mobilising non-state actor action to resolve common concern issues through participation and deliberation in the broader and more transformative sense of reinvention of governance.[162] Yet, states and government continue to play a key role. The multitude of actors does not undermine the structure of multilayered governance.

1.4.3   The Relationship to Other Legal Principles

The doctrine of CCH and a future legal principle does not undermine existing foundations of public international law. It squarely fits into the Westphalian system of nation states, relying up sovereign equality, the prohibition of use and treat of force and of occupation and appropriation of territory. It does not question the principle of permanent sovereignty over natural resources. Other than the principle of common heritage of mankind, Common Concern does not challenge national jurisdictions to legislate, adjudicate and enforce. While they share the component of commonality, the two concepts need to be clearly distinguished. More

---

262–390. I am indebted to Mira Burri for drawing attention to these and the following aspects of governance.

[161] C. Shearing, 'Reflections on the Refusal to Acknowledge Private Governments', in J. Wood and B. Dupont (eds.), *Democracy, Society and the Governance of Security* (Cambridge: Cambridge University Press, 2006), pp. 11–32; D. W. Drezner, *All Politics Is Global: Explaining International Regulatory Regimes* (Princeton, NJ: Princeton University Press, 2007); S. P. Croley, *Regulation and Public Interests: The Possibility of Good Regulatory Government* (Princeton, NJ: Princeton University Press, 2008).

[162] C. Sabel and J. Cohen, 'Directly-Deliberative Polyarchy', *European Law Journal*, 4 (1997), 313–40; S. Burris, M. Kempa and C. Shearing, 'Changes in Governance: A Cross-Disciplinary Review of Current Scholarship', *Akron Law Review*, 41 (2008), 1–66; J. N. Rosenau, 'Governing the Ungovernable: The Challenge of a Global Disaggregation of Authority', 1 *Regulation and Governance* 88–97 (2007).

52   THOMAS COTTIER

complicated is the relationship to *jus cogens* and peremptory norms and the emerging doctrine of R2P.

1.4.3.1   Common Heritage of Mankind

Common Concern grew out of rejected implications of common heritage of humankind[163] and operates in line with existing public international law. Under the concept of CCH, international interest in the conservation and use of the resource is legitimised without challenging the territorial sovereignty of the state where the resource is located.[164] It will be seen that these principles are partly modulated as the principle of Common Concern inherently reinforces cooperation and compliance beyond the law of coexistence. But it essentially continues to respect the tradition of national sovereignty and existing power structures to regulate, adjudicate and enforce.

The principle of common heritage of humankind, often described, is based on the idea that there should be no individual ownership claims over the matter covered. It recognises that all states have a stake in its conservation and sustainable use and seeks to ensure joint management to the broadest possible extent. The terms of the original UNCLOS determined that the principle of common heritage refers to ensuring that exploitation is equitable. The principle of common heritage entails shared ownership and control no longer subject to permanent sovereignty of nation states. The resource is 'shared, under the control of no state, or under the sovereign control of a state, but subject to a common legal interest'.[165] It primarily relates to the exploitation of natural resources and is limited to those.

Cullet explains the difficulties associated with moving away from a legal concept based on sovereignty in the context of biodiversity or climate change regimes because there is a lot at stake for states in terms of immediate control over natural resources and economic development.[166] In the context of the law of the sea, a qualitatively much bigger step was taken when states negotiated a new legal regime for resources of

---

[163] *Supra* n. 55.

[164] J. Blake, 'On Defining the Cultural Heritage', ICLQ, 49 (2000), 61–85.

[165] Centre for International Sustainable Development Law, 'The Principle of Common but Differentiated Responsibilities: Origins and Scope' (Centre for International Sustainable Development Working Paper and Legal Brief Series, 2002), https://cisdl.org/public/docs/news/brief_common.pdf.

[166] P. Cullet, 'Water Law in a Globalised World: The Need for a New Conceptual Framework', *Journal of Environmental Law*, 23(2011), 233–54.

the ocean floor beyond 200–350 nautical miles; that is, beyond the boundaries of established continental shelf limits, which had never been previously claimed by any state.[167] The underlying philosophy was based upon common ownership and translated into the concept of the Area and a common enterprise. These institutions would secure shared and common terms of exploitation, preventing appropriations of the seabed by single nation states. The concept was eventually suspended due to pressures from the United States and led to less interventionist changes to the UNCLOS Agreement.

Common Concern takes these difficulties into account. It operates within the principle of permanent sovereignty of states over natural resources. Resource management primarily remains the responsibility of individual states. Yet, as embedded in the UNFCCC and the CBD or the ITPGRFA, it is premised on a common and shared R2P, and a shared legal interest in not harming, a particular environmental resource. It inherently embodies international cooperation. Common Heritage, on the other hand, reflects a further step of legal integration and sharing of resources transgressing national sovereignty. The scope of CCH, and its operative parts of the principles, however, thus will strongly depend upon the notion and understanding of sovereignty. We return to this issue below.

1.4.3.2 *Jus cogens*

Jus cogens stands for the proposition of community norms which all states are obliged to respect, but also entitled to enforce independently to whom harm is done. The few minimal standards, in particular the prohibition of torture, of apartheid, of refoulement, of genocide and potentially core labour and the prohibition of child labour (short of schooling) amount to recognised core values of humankind which must not be violated and can be enforced by all states alike.[168] Whether Common Concern deploys similar legal effects remains to be assessed. The two do not necessarily coincide, and *jus cogens* and peremptory norms have a life of their own. Much depends upon the legal effects assigned to the principle of Common Concern as to whether they overlap

---

[167] See Agreement Relating to the Implementation of Part XI of the United Nations Convention on the Law of the Sea (adopted 28 July 1994, came into force 28 July 1996) UN Doc. A/RES/48/263.

[168] See M. den Heijer and H. van der Wilt (eds.), '*Jus Cogens*: Quo Vadis?', *Netherlands Yearbook of International Law* (Leiden: Springer, 2015).

54   THOMAS COTTIER

or even form part of the emerging principle. We return to the issue below.[169]

1.4.3.3   R2P

R2P emerged as a doctrine addressing the dilemma created by prohibiting the use of force short of United Nations Security Council approval or self-defence and the need to avoid genocide and systemic violations of human rights abroad. It essentially stipulates and entails an obligation to intervene in such cases by appropriate means. The doctrine emerged independently of Common Concern and relates to national security and human right protection, rather than to natural resources and environmental law. The question arises to what extent R2P – like *jus cogens* – can and should be expressed in terms of CCH. Again, much depends upon the legal effects assigned to the principle, in particular whether in certain circumstances it also entails obligations to act as opposed to the authority to act. We return to the relationship of Common Concern and R2P below.[170]

1.4.4   *Common Concern and National Sovereignty*

Since the Westphalian Peace of 1648, the American Revolution and the process of decolonisation in nineteenth-century Latin America and after the Second World War in the twentieth century, national sovereignty stands for the proposition of liberty, independence and self-determination. Principles of non-intervention and the prohibition of war and aggression are essentially built upon this trait and tradition. Common Concern, as a principle and however shaped, affects these basic tenets of statehood. It inevitably, in its different components, affects and restricts sovereignty, in particular when commitments are based upon customary law and do not form part of a treaty committed to. Opponents will argue against the doctrine of Common Concern invoking national sovereignty, self-determination and liberty as it potentially restricts sovereignty in terms of obligations to cooperate. Yet, we cannot see a fundamental conflict here.

First, commitments made under international law are per se restrictions incurred upon unfettered sovereignty in return of benefits

---

[169] See Section 1.7.2.
[170] See Section 1.7.3.

otherwise foregone. The essence of consent consists of self-limitation. Acceptance of a grave and shared problem as a CCH in the process of claims and responses reflects the contractual nature of international law. It is not precluded by traditional precepts of sovereignty.

Claims, responses and debate clarify the relationship of Common Concern to self-determination, independence and sovereignty. There is no contradiction. As states need to agree to an emerging principle in treaty law and in the formation of customary law, these principles are respected. It is subject to consent and thus not different from other principles of international law. States are not obliged to sign and ratify treaties relating to Common Concern. They may persistently object to legal recognition in customary law.

Provided the principle is widely recognised and applied throughout multilevel governance, it may finally achieve the status of a general principle of law applicable, like equity, to all legal systems alike. The process of claims and responses is not driven by force, but by the better argument and the prospects of solving impending problems to which responsible and accountable governments and citizens cannot reasonably object. Tension with self-determination, independence and conflicting interests may arise in recourse to extraterritorial application and compliance. Yet, these tensions take place within the overall accepted and agreed umbrella of the agreed principle which inherently limits the exercise of self-determination in the pursuit of addressing shared problems and creating appropriate public goods.

Second, we recall at this point that sovereignty, in its beginning, was about enabling and preserving peace and security within states. It was not motivated by independence and self-determination, but to enhance welfare in society. Jean Bodin was motivated to write about sovereignty as the ultimate power of the state (rather than the emperor) by internal strife and religious wars. In *Les six livres de la République*, published in 1583 he placed the welfare of individuals at the heart of the concept:

> Or, si la vraie félicité d'une République et d'un homme seul est tout un, et que le souverain bien de la République en général, aussi bien que d'un chacun en particulier, gît [dans les] vertus intellectuelles et contemplatives, comme les mieux entendus ont résolu, il faut aussi accorder que ce peuple-là jouit du souverain bien, quand il a ce but devant les yeux, de s'exercer en la contemplation des choses naturelles, humaines, et divines, en rapportant la louange du tout au grand Prince de nature. Si donc nous confessons que cela est le but principal de la vie bienheureuse d'un chacun

en particulier, nous concluons aussi que c'est la fin et félicité d'une République.[171]

Thomas Hobbes in *Leviathan*, published in 1651 in the middle of the English Revolution, conceived of the transfer of sovereign powers from a human to a central authority primarily in order to keep peace at home and to allow individuals to have a more contented life:

> The final Cause, End, or Designe of men (who naturally love Liberty, and Dominion over others,) in the introduction of that restraint upon themselves, (in which wee see them live in Commonwealths,) is the foresight of their own preservation, and of a more contended life thereby; that is to say, of getting themselves out from that miserable condition of Warre, which is necessarily consequent (as hath been shwen) to the naturell Passons of men, when there is no visible Power to keep them in awe, and tye them by feare of punishment to the performance of the Covenants, and observation of those Lawes of Nature set down in the fourtheenth and fiftheenth Chapters.[172]

The purpose to appoint a sovereign is 'to the end he may use the strength and means of them all, as he shall think expedient, for their Peace and Common Defence'.[173] Sovereignty thus is not limited to independence and defence, but essentially comprises peaceful relations within society.

Jean-Jacques Rousseau developed the idea of people's sovereignty as a means to enable democracy; sovereignty being the exercise of the *volonté génerale* created by social contract to defend the community.[174] All these theorists share in common that sovereignty serves the purpose of creating peaceful conditions and thus prosperity and welfare within society and subsequently serving the purpose of creating essential public goods. It is not an end it its own; neither is self-determination and independence.

---

[171] J. Bodin, *Les six livres de la République*: *Un abrégé du texte de l'édition de Paris de 1583* (édition et présentation de Gérard Mairet, Paris: Librairie générale française, 1993), p. 46; fn. omitted, referring to Cicero and Aristotle; http://classiques.uqac.ca/classiques/bodin_jean/six_livres_republique/bodin_six_livres_republique.pdf (accessed 28 Aug. 2018).

[172] T. Hobbes, *Leviathan*, repr. of 1651 ed. (Oxford: Clarendon Press, 1909), ch. XVII, http://files.libertyfund.org/pll/pdf/Hobbes_0161_EBk_v7.0.pdf.

[173] Ibid., p. 134.

[174] 'On voit par cette formule que l'acte d'association renferme un engagement réciproque du public avec les particuliers, & que chaque individu contractant, pour ainsi dire, avec lui-même, se trouve engagé sous un double rapport; savoir, comme membre du Souverain envers les particuliers, & comme membre de l'Etat envers le Souverain' (Jean-Jacques Rousseau, *Du contract social, ou principes du droit politiques* (1780–89), ch. VII); www.rousseauonline.ch/pdf/rousseauonline-0004.pdf.

THE PRINCIPLE OF COMMON CONCERN OF HUMANKIND   57

These are legitimate only to the extent that they are able to create essential public goods.

Current debates depict sovereignty as an essentially contested concept coined by disagreement not only relating to normative contents but also the correct application (i.e. the concept of sovereignty itself).[175] Zimmermann, in the analysis of monetary sovereignty, stresses the goals of monetary and financial stability, while independence or the lack of independence of monetary policy in a globalised world remains the main preoccupation and cause to study the problem of contemporary sovereignty.[176] In an oral statement during the 2018 conference he forcefully made the point that the legitimacy of sovereignty entirely depends upon the purpose and goals assigned, and that these goals need to serve peace, prosperity and public welfare and the creation of appropriate public goods, going back to the original precepts when statal sovereignty was introduced to restore peaceful relations:

> The contemporary mainstream view of states being instruments at the service of their peoples as true holders of sovereignty may be regarded as a corollary of the fundamental idea of popular sovereignty or sovereignty of the people. As was first explained by Samantha Besson, this form of sovereignty triggers duties of cooperation, on the part of the entities which cannot ensure the protection of all the values they should protect, or, translated into the concept we are discussing here, which cannot ensure that the common concerns of humankind are properly addressed.[177]

Where these public goods cannot be achieved independently, sovereignty inherently is bound to be shared and exercised jointly as cooperative sovereignty. Self-determination and public welfare goals need to be balanced properly. Modern theories relating to sovereignty thus stress the concept and idea of shared and cooperative sovereignty, the

---

[175] S. Besson, 'Sovereignty in Conflict', in C. Warbrick and S. Tierney (eds.), *Toward an International Legal Community? The Sovereignty of States and the Sovereignty of International Law* (London: BIILC, 2006), pp. 168–171; also, 8(15) *European Integration Online Papers (Elop)* (2004); https://papers.ssrn.com/sol3/papers.cfm?abstract_id=594942 (accessed 31 Aug. 2018). See also D. Sarooshi, 'The Essentially Contested Nature of the Concept of Sovereignty: Implications for the Exercise of by International Organizations of Delegated Powers of Government', *Michigan Journal of International Law*, 25 (2004), 1107; Sarooshi, *International Organizations and their Exercise of Sovereign Powers* (Oxford: Oxford University Press, 2005), pp. 3–11.

[176] K. D. Zimmermann, *A Contemporary Concept of Monetary Sovereignty* (Oxford: Oxford University Press, 2013), pp. 24–36; Zimmermann, 'The Concept of Monetary Sovereignty Revisited', *European Journal of International Law*, 24 (2013), 797–818.

[177] Zimmermann, Chapter 10 in this volume.

allocation of powers among different layers of government as the essence of modern sovereignty within an overall global legal system.[178] As the principle of Common Concern seeks to prevent or remedy threats to international peace, security and welfare in a broader sense, the purpose is in line with the original goals of sovereignty enabling to maintain law and order, provide peace and welfare and prosperity in society. The principle of CCH thus complements the same goals aspired to by self-determination and enters the stage where these very goals cannot be secured by states alone but depend upon international cooperation. Common Concern helps us to reshape and understand the proper functions of contemporary modern sovereignty. We can perceive it as a dialogue between the two concepts, influencing each other in shaping and coordinating their respective contours.

The principle of Common Concern thus is compatible with modern doctrines of cooperative sovereignty depicted in particular by Besson.[179] It also is compatible with the doctrine of sovereignty modern expounded by the late John Jackson. According to him, sovereignty is a matter of properly allocating powers to regulate, adjudicate and enforce to appropriate levels of governance in line and accordance with the basic tenets of doctrine of multilevel governance discussed. The principle of Common Concern brings us back to the original goals of sovereignty, supporting people, families and children in their life in the pursuit of happiness and to contribute to intergenerational equity. We may conclude by saying that CCH amounts to an important ingredient of modern sovereignty and its limitation in international relations.

This also applies to the principle of permanent sovereignty over resources. Exploitation and control needs to respect welfare functions and today in particular sustainable development and resource management. It is an obligation in line with Common Concerns of Humankind and cannot be invoked to deny the existence of shared problems and free riding. For example, the recognition of climate change as CCH bars governments from justifying unfettered exploitation of coal and gas by invoking permanent sovereignty over natural resources. Sovereignty must be exercised and deployed in line with climate goals agreed to. Beyleveld further develops this idea in the context of addressing income inequality within states – a completely new topic exposed and tested under the doctrine of CCH. In addressing such novel issues, it is

---

[178] See *supra* n. 148 and n. 154.
[179] Besson, *supra* n. 175.

THE PRINCIPLE OF COMMON CONCERN OF HUMANKIND   59

necessary to reconceptualise sovereignty and go back to the roots and original rationale of sovereignty in creating peaceful order and welfare.[180]

Based upon these foundations, and taking into account related concepts, we now turn to the legal effects and implications of CCH suggested. We propose the following blueprint entailing three fundamental components: duties to cooperate consult and negotiate; duties to assume responsibilities in domestic law and undertake what we call homework; and finally to contribute by appropriate measures to international compliance with international commitments made. They go beyond existing rights and obligations under international law and compound the essence of the legal principle of CCH. In analogy, these rights and obligations also apply *mutatis mutandis* to other layers of multilevel governance, subject to more specific rules which may exist on the regional and federal levels of domestic governance.

1.5   The Duty to Cooperate

The principle of equality of states per se does not entail an obligation to cooperate. States are free to choose their friends and foes, to engage or not in international cooperation, or to refrain from it. Duties to cooperate are nevertheless frequent within the framework of the United Nations and other international organisations. Article 56 of the United Nations Charter sets out obligations to cooperate in seeking the goals in Article 55 which relate to enhancing standards of living, social and health conditions, culture, education and the respect of human rights. These duties induced what Friedmann called the changing structure of public international law after the Second World War.[181] Partly, and in addition, duties to cooperate are based upon customary international law. Again, these do not rely upon a general principle of cooperate but focus on particular fields of the law. Overall, duties to cooperate have remained specific and limited to particular areas. They do not establish general obligations across the board of international law. Importantly, they do not extend to problems depicted under the doctrine of CCH.

Likewise, international law does not know a general duty to consult and to negotiate. These obligations, where they exist, are equally treaty-based and sometimes based upon customary international law. They were pioneered in the emerging field of natural resources and

---

[180] See Chapter 4 in this volume, pp. 220, 227, 229.
[181] *Supra* n. 87.

international environmental law.[182] Duties to cooperate and negotiate were recognised by the International Court of Justice in the 1974 *Fisheries Jurisdiction Case* as a matter of compensating for the absence of well-defined rules in allocating marine resources to competing interests.[183] They can also be extensively found in the multilateral trading system. Members are obliged to negotiate within trade rounds. Obligations to negotiate require good faith efforts to seek results and agreement, but they do not oblige states to do so. Finally, states are obliged under universal standards of UN law and the Friendly Relations Declaration to settle their disputes by peaceful means in light of the prohibition to use or threaten to use force.[184] This entails, in a case of dispute to consult, to negotiate, to seek conciliation or legal dispute settlement.

It is submitted that in matters recognised by the international community to amount to a Common Concern of Mankind, by the very nature of the problems identified, international cooperation is required and logically indispensable as the shared problem inherently can only be addressed and solved by joint efforts. International cooperation thus is at the heart of mitigation and adaptation of climate change, albeit states are reluctant to enter into binding agreements, instruments and detailed targets. The very point of recognising a matter to amount to a CCH is to recognise the essential need to cooperate in the field concerned. In that regard, the principle is fully in line with the doctrine of community interests.

Such cooperation primarily requires the building of mutual trust. It therefore calls for transparency and joint efforts in fact-finding. It calls for consultations, concertation and negotiations, and cooperation in law enforcement in matters pertaining to Common Concerns of Humankind. It eventually leads to building appropriate institutions by which decisions are being taken and funding is being organised and dispensed. In the various fields recognised as Common Concerns of Humankind, detailed rules may evolve which differ, depending on the particular nature of the subject and diverging needs. This is particularly true for financial implications and support. Yet, they all would share the following minimal

---

[182] See F. L. Kirgis, *Prior Consultation in International Law* (Charlottesville: University Press of Virginia, 1983).

[183] *Fisheries Jurisdiction Case* (*United Kingdom* v. *Iceland*) Merits, Judgement, ICJ Rep. 1974, p. 3.

[184] Declaration on Principles of International Law concerning Friendly Relations and Co-operation Among States in Accordance with the Charter of the United Nations, UNGA Res. 2625 (XXV) (24 Oct. 1970) GAOR 25th sess. supp. 28, 121; see H. Keller, 'Friendly Relations Declaration (1970)', IX MPEPIL 250 (2012).

THE PRINCIPLE OF COMMON CONCERN OF HUMANKIND   61

standards which could and should eventually be recognised within a general principle of CCH.

1.5.1   Transparency

The importance of transparency has been increasingly recognised generally and in different field of international law.[185] It is prominent in international economic law and the multilateral trading system of the WTO. Members are obliged to publish their laws, regulations and precedents and engage in periodical notifications of data and practices and reply to request for information. Regular trade policy reviews allow identifying potential problems and shortcomings.[186]

It is submitted that states in matters pertaining to CCH should be under a general obligation to grant access to information required, to publish pertinent laws, regulations and precedents in the field. It is a matter of negotiations to define such obligations in greater detail; a general principle of common concern would entail minimal standards to grant access to information upon request, and to publish relevant information, legislation, practices and precedents.

1.5.2   Duty to Consult and Negotiate

At the heart of cooperation lies the duty to consult in building mutual trust, and the obligation to negotiate upon request. The duty implies seeking agreement, but does not oblige to agree commensurate and in line with the very nature of negotiating processes. Parties disagreeing should be under the obligation to state the reasons why agreement failed. Inherently, countries and authorities claiming a matter to pertain to a common concern imply the willingness and readiness to consult and to negotiate in addressing the transboundary problem. Likewise, the acceptance by the addressee to take the matter up in consultations and negotiations implies recognition as a common concern unless explicitly stated otherwise.

1.5.3   Burden-sharing and Differentiated Responsibility

Matters pertaining to Common Concerns of Humankind may entail difficult and contentious issues of financial support and of making

---

[185] See A. Bianchi and A. Peters, *Transparency in International Law* (Cambridge: Cambridge University Press, 2013).

[186] See M. Kende, *The Trade Policy Review Mechanism: A Critical Analysis* (Cambridge: Cambridge University Press, 2018).

available appropriate technologies and market access to address the common concern and to produce appropriate public goods. Recognition of a Common Concern will often depend upon complex and contentious arrangements of burden-sharing, commensurate with the economic performance and levels of social and economic development of states. The principle of shared and differentiated responsibility in climate change adaptation and mitigation under the 1992 Framework Convention and the 2015 Paris Agreement is an example in point. It is submitted, and following climate change as a Common Concern, that the recognition of a problem as a Common Concern always entails the basic obligation to make contributions by states commensurate with historical performance in creating the problem at hand, existing levels of GDP and other accepted indices, such as the Global Development Index (GDI), or specific indicators applicable to a particular policy area falling under the principle Common Concern. It strongly depends upon the subject matter. The study on the implications of Common Concern on transfer of technology of renewable energy will particularly elaborate on this point.[187]

Recourse to equity and distributive justice help to define specifically and contextually commitments commensurate with the ability to afford contributions to the global effort in solving and settling a problem identified. Financial contributions and contributions in kind and the law – for example in the field trade, investment and technology transfers of relevance and importance to the preoccupation addressed – provide essential incentives and carrots to engage and support the recognition of a problem as a Common Concern on the part of countries depending upon cooperation and technical assistance. Likewise, such contributions are key incentives for donor countries to achieve recognition of Common Concern and to secure compliance with commitments made in accordance with the principle of shared and differentiated responsibility in the field.

1.5.4 Cooperation in Implementation and Compliance

CCH calls for cooperation in implementing and realising international commitments in domestic policy and law. Countries should cooperate in designing policies and instruments of implementation in accordance with commitments made. Regulatory agencies assigned to comparable tasks in different countries shall exchange information, consult and work

---

[187] See Chapter 2 in this volume.

THE PRINCIPLE OF COMMON CONCERN OF HUMANKIND   63

together with a view to prepare the ground for regulatory convergence and cooperation and implementation relating to the problem recognised as a CCH. These activities also prepare the ground to foster cooperation in law enforcement, requiring specific rules to define jurisdiction and powers of authorities and courts of law in engaging in transboundary law enforcement and recognition of foreign legal acts and judgments. An area recognised as a Common Concern thus should entail mutual assistance by administrative bodies and judicial assistance by legal authorities. Common Concern entails an advanced level of cooperation and thus of legal integration.

1.6   Obligation to Do Homework

Next to cooperation, CCH calls for action in domestic law and policy. It is at the heart of the principle and amounts to a key obligation under the doctrine of CCH in order to offset the lack of reciprocity, to avoid free riding and the endemic tragedy of the global commons (Hardin). The recognition of a problem as a common preoccupation entails the need to engage appropriate domestic resources and activities, again in accordance with equity and distributional justice and shared responsibility, to address the challenge. *Think globally – act locally* translates into domestic homework. We introduce the term 'homework' as a legal denomination to address a bulk of obligations under the principle of CCH. We consider the term suitable to convey a commitment in colloquial terms.

CCH is not limited to implementing international obligations by central government and institutions. Often, the main thrust will be measures undertaken upon own initiatives and bottom up. Depending on the problem and the public goods which need to be produced in response to the challenge, all layers of government may be involved. For example, the abatement of CO_2 emissions calls for action on all layers in accordance with regulatory powers assigned. The doctrine of multilevel governance and the five-storey house seeks to identify appropriate levels to take up an issue; these theories are not limited to international relations but also entail the structure and devolution in domestic constitutional law.

1.6.1   *Implementing International Obligations*

From the point of view of international law, homework entails the realisation and implementation of task and obligations assumed in customary international law and in international agreements, commensurate with the principle *pacta sunt servanda*. CCH as a concept and principle does not alter existing obligations of general international law. It does not affect the modes of implementation which differ under constitutional law oscillating between dualist and monist theories. However, given the need to address the shared problem, it gives priority in allocating resources and effort to the task over other ones of less pressing needs. It influences the interpretation of existing agreements, rights and obligations and calls for an understanding of norms in conformity with the principle of CCH. It is part of the context in the process of construing international law in accordance with the principles set out in Article 31 of the Vienna Convention on the Law of Treaties.

1.6.2 Adopting Autonomous Measures

The impact of CCH in a particular area goes beyond commitments made in international treaties. It deploys a profound and inspiring impact in autonomous domestic policymaking, comparable to the respect of civil and political rights, and the progressive implementation of social and economic rights and of SDGs. While the pace is defined by domestic political processes and debate, the principle of CCH stimulates programmes and legal developments at all levels of government commensurate with public goods to be created in addressing the common problem at hand. For example, countries adopt unilateral measures relating to climate change mitigation and adaptation, the administration of migration flows, the reduction of pollution, or shaping tax laws with a view to addressing pressing income inequality. Common Concern may reinforce rights and obligations incurred under already existing domestic constitutions and law. As in international law, it may influence the interpretation and implementation of domestic law. Indeed, the principle of CCH may eventually be recognised as a maxim and principle in constitutional law, emphasising the need to address complex transboundary problems in cooperation with other countries.

Importantly, unilateral promises made under domestic law may have international legal implications. Measures promised to be undertaken at home may amount to a unilateral promise which is binding under international law and good faith doctrines of estoppel. Other countries and jurisdictions may rely upon the realisation of such measures. Failure to implement or withdrawal of such measures may induce international

THE PRINCIPLE OF COMMON CONCERN OF HUMANKIND   65

responsibility,[188] which the principle of CCH further reinforces. For example, unilateral commitments made under the Paris Agreement deploy effects in international law. The recognition of climate change as a CCH implies that they are subject to a ratcheting mechanism and no longer, once adopted, can be unilaterally withdrawn without consulting affecting parties to the Agreement. Homework thus is not undertaken in isolation. Efforts made cannot be isolated by invoking self-determination and independence. It is part of a larger effort under the umbrella of the principle of Common Concern and thus needs to take into account the needs and preoccupations of others.

1.6.3 Extraterritorial Effects of Domestic Law

Domestic measures, in line with the principle of territoriality, normally deploy effects within a particular jurisdiction. They do not apply outside of it. Such containment, however, will often be difficult to align in addressing issues under the auspices of Common Concern of Humankind, given their nature as a shared, transboundary problem, often of global reach. Measures adopted in implementing international law obligations or of domestic measures may often deploy effects beyond the boundaries of the particular jurisdiction. International law does not exclude such effects, but seeks a careful balance between the interests of different jurisdiction. States are free to adopt measures having extraterritorial effect unless prohibited by international law. Extraterritorial jurisdiction of states, under the traditional international law as established in the 1927 *Lotus* rule and mainly expounded in international criminal law and in competition law and policy, requires sufficient attachment to the territory of the state.[189] Competition law and policy and the enforcement of foreign judgments today are the main traditional areas of extraterritorial application. To the extent that domestic market structures are affected, conduct deployed abroad may fall under the domestic jurisdiction and anti-trust rules are enforced irrespective of the geographical origin of causing conduct. Expansive jurisdiction is often considered intrusive and sometimes combated by blocking statutes, rejecting

---

[188] *Nuclear Tests Case (Australia v. France)*, ICJ Rep. 1974 253; *Legal Status of Eastern Greenland (Norway v. Denmark)* [1933] PCIJ Ser. A/B No. 53, 71 (Ihlen Declaration).

[189] C. Ryngaert, *Jurisdiction in International Law* (Oxford: Oxford University Press, 2008); Dobson, *supra* n. 69, discussing common concern but not extending particular weight to assessing interests for and against extraterritorial application.

recognition of foreign acts and rulings. Doctrine and case law suggest balancing diverging interests. In the field of international trade, extraterritorial effects of product standards are recognised; countries are free to determine non-discriminatory levels of protections required for like-imported products sold on their markets and the consumers subject to their jurisdiction. Such requirements indirectly impact the modes of production in exporting countries. Likewise, the imposition of labels and of private standards deploys similar effects.

More and more, product standards do not relate to the physical characteristics of a product, but the modes of production. In the field of international trade, it is largely due to the implementation of global value chains which call for shared or unilaterally defined standards in respect of product quality, but also of environmental, labour and human rights standards.

Extraterritorial effects of so-called non-product-related production and process methods (PPMs) have been controversial.[190] Some argue that they do not affect the likeness of products as countries are free to define the conditions for sale and distribution on their own territory. Others emphasise the trade-restrictive effects of such measures. PPMs impose on the modes of production in exporting countries. Without compliance, such products cannot be imported. Likewise, PPM-related labels reduce equality of opportunity on markets. Even if voluntary, producers are practically required to adopt and implement them. Moreover, these measures imply extensive monitoring of production which further imposes on national sovereignty and regulatory autonomy.

Given the increasing importance of PPMs in different policy areas, including climate change, the law is increasingly accommodating them. CCH will further support this evolution. For example, border tax adjustments in climate change mitigation, neutralising carbon leakage and restoring equal conditions of competition for domestic producers essentially rely upon modes of production, capturing carbon-intensive modes while exempting sustainable modes of production. To the extent that they result in lower taxes for domestic production, exceptions made under Article XX GATT will be supported by the principle of Common Concern of Mankind. The same holds true for carbon tariffs imposed on

---

[190] For a detailed analysis, see K. Holzer, *Carbon-related Border Adjustment and WTO Law* (Cheltenham, UK: Edward Elgar, 2014); C. R. Conrad, *Process and Production Methods (PPMs) in WTO Law: Interfacing Trade and Social Goals* (Cambridge: Cambridge University Press, 2014).

THE PRINCIPLE OF COMMON CONCERN OF HUMANKIND   67

highly polluting products.[191] Common Concern justifies the introduction of differential tariffs and additional tariff lines for sustainable modes of production of the product at hand. WTO case law relating to environmental concerns and animal protection indicates that in result they are justified under exception clauses, provided all the conditions of Article XX GATT are met.[192] Likewise, labels linked to certain production methods are, in principle, accepted under the Agreement on Technical Barriers to Trade (TBT).[193] The same is likely to apply to prescriptions as to how particular services need to be generated and provided. They eventually will support the implementation of minimal labour standards and human right in international economic law beyond business-driven initiatives to improve conditions of production in response to corporate social responsibility. [194]

CCH supports recourse to PPMs and impacts on the balance of interests in extraterritorial application of laws. While today action can be defended if the nexus to the own territory is sufficient, Common Concern would not require such linkages but depend upon examination whether the measure and action is able to support the attainment of a Common Concern as defined by the international community. For example, governments are authorised to take appropriate action against highly polluting means of production abroad, bluntly ignoring the Common Concern of global warming. Likewise, governments can be authorised to take action in response to blatant and systematic neglect of the Common Concern of protecting fundamental human rights and lives. At the same time, territoriality often will remain a matter of practical expediency, as states are largely dependent upon attachment to their territory one way or the other in implementing laws and measures. The obligation to cooperate and negotiate, inherent to Common

---

[191] T. Cottier, O. Nartova and A. Shingal, 'The Potential of Tariff Policy for Climate Change Mitigation: Legal and Economic Analysis', *Journal of World Trade*, 48 (2014), 1007–37.

[192] *European Communities – Measures Prohibiting the Importation and Marketing of Seal Products*, WT/DS400/AB/R (22 May 2014). In principle, the case accepted import restrictions based upon methods of killing baby seals, subject to exceptions of Inuit products essential to preserve their livelihood in the Arctic.

[193] *United States – Measures Concerning the Importation, Marketing and Sale of Tuna and Tuna Products (Art. 21.5 DSU)*, WT/DS381/28 (4 Dec. 2015). The panel and AB in principle endorsed the possibility to regulate by law production methods by means of non-mandatory labels.

[194] T. Cottier, 'The Implications of *EC–Seal Products* for the Protection of Core Labour Standards in WTO Law', in H. Gött (ed.), *Labour Standards in International Economic Law* (Leiden: Springer, 2018), pp. 69–92.

68   THOMAS COTTIER

Concern, allows addressing practical problems and mitigating negative effects of PPMs. Regulatory cooperation and convergence, strongly encouraged by Common Concern under duties to cooperate and negotiate, eventually will eliminate such problems to the extent that common and shared PPM standards in particular regulatory fields.

1.7   Securing Compliance

In the decentralised system of international law, securing compliance with obligations incurred and relating to Common Concern is of utmost importance. It is a corollary to enhanced cooperation, funding, training, technology transfer and market access rights. To this effect, the principle of CCH essentially relies upon the established mechanism of international law which entitles states to act in terms of sanctions and countermeasures. The critical question is whether the principle also entails a new obligation to act. We think so as this essentially marks the main difference, innovation and essential feature of a fully fledged principle of CCH.

1.7.1   Sanctions and Countermeasures

In general, voluntary compliance is widespread in international relations. As Henkin recalled, most countries comply in self-interest with international obligations almost all of the time.[195] Compliance in the daily operation of international law normally does not depend upon enforcement as it mostly is in the interest of the state concerned. It is mostly based upon reciprocal interests. Questioning the legal nature of the field in the Austinian tradition,[196] relies upon a perceived misperception of the operation of law in international relations. We would argue that failures to comply are not more frequent than in domestic law despite its policing powers. Just compare existing crime rates or widespread speeding on roads and frequently lacking respect for traffic rules. However, the lack of reciprocity in critical areas call for additional

---

[195] L. Henkin, *How Nations Behave: Law and Foreign Policy* (Council of Foreign Relations, 1979). See also E. Brown Weiss, 'Rethinking Compliance with International Law' and M. Hirsch, 'Compliance with International Norms in the Age of Globalization', in E. Benvenisti and M. Hirsch, *The Impact of International Law on International Cooperation* (Cambridge: Cambridge University Press, 2004), pp. 134–65, 165–93 respectively.

[196] Goldsmith and Posner, *supra* n. 157.

THE PRINCIPLE OF COMMON CONCERN OF HUMANKIND   69

disciplines securing compliance. It is here that the principle of Common Concern makes a difference.

Other than in international trade and investment, which relies upon immediate mutual benefits, compliance is tempered by temptations to opt out and let other assume main responsibilities to produce global public goods. Free riding in climate change or the protection of biodiversity, or in migration are examples in point where reciprocity is lacking. The same is true in the field of human rights. Failures to comply and lack of enforcement mechanism are endemic in this field as Iryna Bogdanova's chapter in this volume shows. She particularly focuses on this aspect of the principle of Common Concern.[197] While the duty to cooperation offers carrots to comply, sticks are equally required to address free-riding and failing full compliance with duties incurred and promises made. Incentives supporting international compliance and securing that recognised Common Concerns of Humankind are dealt with in priority at home and in international relations, call for tools backing up these obligations.

These tools are essentially based upon established disciplines of state responsibility in international law. States affected by violations of law are entitled to engage in countermeasures, subject to the prerogatives of the UN Security Council under Chapter VII of the UN Charter in response to threats to the peace and to mandatory obligations of dispute settlement in the field of international trade regulation. States are entitled to the re-establishment of lawful conditions (*restitutio in integrum*), but normally adopt sanctions or countermeasures (in trade the withdrawal of market access concessions) in order to remedy the violation and injury imposed.[198] Such measures are subject to the principle of proportionality and must not exceed what is required to achieve compensation for damage and losses incurred.

---

[197] See Chapter 5 in this volume.

[198] The traditional term reprisal today is essentially limited to armed conflict, and was generally replaced by the term countermeasures, while retorsions react to lawful, but unfriendly conduct of another state (M. Ruffert, 'Reprisals', VIII MPEPIL 929 (2012)). The term sanctions generally applies to collective measures adopted under Chapter VII of the UN Charter, but today is also used for measures adopted by other international organisations or single states in response to violations of international law, in accordance with Article 54 ILC Draft Articles on Responsibility of States for Internationally Wrong Acts (2001) GAOR 56th sess., supp. 10, 43, allowing states to 'invoke the responsibility of another State, to take lawful measures against that State in order to ensure cessation of the breach and reparation in the interest of the injured State or of the beneficiaries of the obligations breached' (A. Pellet and A. Miron, 'Sanctions', IX MPEPIL 1, 11 (2012)).

A recognised common concern would logically require all states involved and affected to take appropriate countermeasures, offsetting free riding and non-compliance. CCH accordingly calls for a multilateral system and appropriate international institutions securing compliance. While we defined CCH pertaining to serious problems potentially threating peace and stability, it must be noted that the main system addressing such threats often is not suitable to address Common Concerns. The task of the Security Council of the United Nations is essentially limited to combat impending use of force and immediate threats to peace, including systemic human rights violations and terrorism. However, it does not address underlying causes and creeping developments. The Security Council has no mandate to address climate change mitigation or adaptation, or the loss of biodiversity or cultural heritage. It does not address gross inequality of wealth and income and act upon it despite the fact that it bears the potential of aggression and warfare, both internally and internationally. It does not address issues of massive land and marine pollution and other common concerns. These matters are left to specialised international organisations and other forums such as G20 (or previously G7 and G8) where enforcement and sanctions generally do not formally exist. They thus essentially depend upon individual states, or groups of states such as the European Union, to be addressed in terms of unilateral and concerted measures until appropriate tools and instrument are developed in the global level.

The doctrine and principle of CCH thus could stimulate a reform of the United Nations sanction system and review the task of the Security Council to collectively address failing states in areas recognised to amount to a CCH, unless the matter is assigned to specialised international organisations empowered to act against violations of the principle. Endemic problems of vetoing decisions in the Security Council and frequent reliance upon consensus diplomacy in international organisations would require seriously reviewing the existing system and moving towards majority decisions in areas other than the use of force.

Given the difficulties to achieve such a goal, it remains imperative that individual states, and groups of states, for the time being, remain free to take recourse to unilateral economic measures on behalf of the international community in areas governed by the principle of CCH.

1.7.2 The Right to Act

In the absence of a multilateral system, the principle of Common Concern supports and reinforces existing, but still controversial, powers, expressed in Article 54 of the ILC draft article on state responsibility to equally act on behalf of the international community and affected states. The doctrine of *jus cogens* and peremptory norms, entitling all states to take action, can be conceptualised as an expression of the principle of CCH. Systemic violations of *jus cogens* not only harm individuals when states disregard human rights. The special status of *jus cogens* and peremptory norms in international law addresses fundamental threats to peace and stability. Experience shows that endemic violations of norms protected by *jus cogens* entail major risks not only for individuals, but society and international relations at large. These potential implications justify assigning special legal effects and recognising them as community norms. Much the same underlines the doctrine and principle of CCH. We argued elsewhere that for such reasons *jus cogens* can and should be conceptualised in terms of CCH.[199]

From here, it may be argued that norms of international law pertaining to problems and preoccupations of CCH per se are community norms, beyond the rules of *jus cogens*. As the problem affects all, directly or indirectly, such as global warming, monetary instability, massive pollution, gross violations of human rights or mishandling of migration, tolerance of gross inequality of wealth and income, rules pertaining to these fields, to the extent they exist, can be invoked by all states irrespective of direct injury or harm. The principle of CCH thus entails obligations *erga omnes*.

State responsibility normally is invoked to address and remedy harm and injury done by violating international obligations. Violations of norms relating to problems recognised as CCH often will not entail direct injury to other states but rather to the international community at large. The principle reinforces calling upon state responsibility in the case of violation of community norms and call for cessation or assurances of non-repetition in accordance with Article 48(2) ILC Draft.[200] Injury and harm thus is no longer a prerequisite to invoke state responsibility.

Enforcing compliance will require large markets with bargaining powers to take action and exert pressures to comply. Smaller countries often do not have the leverage, unless measures are taken jointly or within an international organisation. Economic and trade sanctions are of utmost importance. Remedies available today within the system of the

---

[199] Cottier, *supra* n. 74.
[200] See J. Crawford, 'State Responsibility', IX MPEPIL 527 (2012).

WTO do not live up to these expectations. Countermeasures in terms of withdrawal of concession can only take place if violations pertain to the production and export of specific goods and services. Article XX GATT requires a close linkage between measures taken and the products at stake. Restrictions can be justified in response not only to the physical characteristics of the product, but also in response to PPMs which are much more important from the point of view of the principle of Common Concern relating to environmental standards, human rights and labour standards.[201] However, restrictions cannot be used under this provision law in support of CCH independently of such a connection. Such measures today are exclusively left to retaliations following the lack of implementation of WTO rulings, adopted by the Dispute Settlement Body under Article 16 of the Dispute Settlement Understanding (DSU) and to the Security Council and collective sanctions the adoption of which, however, is often blocked. It therefore will be necessary to expand trade measures within the WTO at the outset in order to address recognised Common Concerns of Humankind and to explore the impact of national security exceptions and to reform trade rules in order to render them compatible with the principle of CCH. Iryna Bogdanova particularly addresses these issues on compliance in her contribution.[202] For example, failures to comply with obligations incurred in the field of climate change mitigation should be open to responses in targeting and restricting market access rights for exported goods and services. Potential restriction of market access rights amount to the most important incentives to prevent and avoid free riding in areas recognised and protected by the principle of CCH. Potential recourse to such measures brings the field into the realm of reciprocity. It offers a stick which will enhance compliance at the outset. It is difficult to argue against these propositions if CCH and the pressing problems which they express and entail are taken seriously. Such action, or the threat to take action, brings reluctant governments to the table.[203]

It will be argued that Common Concern thus will foster powerful states and reinforce the balance of power in international relations. Enforcement of international law should not be left to powerful markets and actors, such as the European Union, the United States and China. These concerns are legitimate and give rise to the argument that the

---

[201] Cottier, *supra* n. 194.
[202] See Chapter 5 in this volume.
[203] For a leading example, see n. 23.

principle of CCH, in the final analysis, is an imperial concept. In response, it can be argued that the recognition of the principle of CCH and its application to different areas is subject to the process of claims and responses outlined above. This secures potential participation of all states in treaty negotiations and the process of forming customary international law. Moreover, actors taking unilateral measures are subject to the rule of law and to the principle of proportionality in shaping countermeasures. Finally, they can be addressed by fostering the role of international organisations and courts of law in collectively enforcing obligations incurred. It is a matter of creating appropriate checks and balances within the system of multilevel governance.

1.7.3 The Duty to Act

While Common Concern provides the foundations of authorisation to act, the most difficult and controversial question relates to the problem of to what extent the principle also entails obligations to act. The main deficiencies of state responsibility, *jus cogens* and obligations *erga omnes* is that states in international relations are most reluctant to take action where not directly affected, despite global public goods and community rights being at risk. Again, the lack of reciprocity deters from assuming responsibilities. Moreover, as indicated, smaller states do not have adequate means to do so.

The question arises whether a basic duty can and should be assigned to the principle of CCH. We think so in light of existing structural weaknesses of international law addressing a common concern. A fully fledged principle should entail duties to act. It only applies to recognised common concerns and does not allow for action outside of areas of grave concern to peace and security in accordance with the threshold defined. It will be subject to modulations, in accordance with specific needs and may not apply in all areas. Importantly it will not trigger automatic action but is subject to the principles of proportionality and accountability.

There is a fundamental difference between authorisation and obligation to act. While the former leaves the matter in the discretion of government, the latter compels to engage and take necessary steps. Such obligations are gradually emerging in the area of R2P, which is of key importance to Common Concern. This doctrine was developed and submitted by Canada to close the gap between the prohibition of use of force and the frequent impossibility to obtain clearance by the Security

74   THOMAS COTTIER

Council even in case of impending massive violations of human rights, including genocide.[204] It was inspired by unsatisfactory legal assessment of the NATO intervention in the Balkans. States are in principle obliged to intervene in preventing and remedying such action.

In 2001 the Canadian government created the International Commission on Intervention and State Sovereignty (ICISS), the Commission released an extensive report entitled *The Responsibility to Protect*. The report introduced the concept of R2P, which emerged as a viable alternative to the idea of humanitarian intervention, as it was known before. The further developments of R2P were strongly supported by the Secretary-General Kofi Annan. Subsequently, UN member states formally accepted the responsibility of each state to protect its population from genocide, war crimes, ethnic cleansing and crimes against humanity. Such formal recognition was enshrined in paragraphs. 138 and 139 of the 2005 *World Summit Outcome Document:*[205]

> Responsibility to protect populations from genocide, war crimes, ethnic cleansing and crimes against humanity
>
> 138. Each individual State has the responsibility to protect its populations from genocide, war crimes, ethnic cleansing and crimes against humanity. This responsibility entails the prevention of such crimes, including their incitement, through appropriate and necessary means. We accept that responsibility and will act in accordance with it. The international community should, as appropriate, encourage and help States to exercise this responsibility and support the United Nations in establishing an early warning capability.
>
> 139. The international community, through the United Nations, also has the responsibility to use appropriate diplomatic, humanitarian and other peaceful means, in accordance with Chapters VI and VIII of the Charter, to help to protect populations from genocide, war crimes, ethnic cleansing and crimes against humanity. In this context, we are prepared to take collective action, in a timely and decisive manner, through the Security Council, in accordance with the Charter, including Chapter VII, on a case-by-case basis and in cooperation with relevant regional organizations as appropriate, should peaceful means be inadequate and national authorities are manifestly failing to protect their populations from genocide, war

---

[204] For a historical account, see E. Gilligan, 'Redefining Humanitarian Intervention: The Historical Challenge of R2P', *Human Rights Journal*, 12 (2013), 21–39.

[205] United Nations, World Summit Outcome Document, paras. 138–9 (2005); https://documents-dds-ny.un.org/doc/UNDOC/GEN/N05/487/60/PDF/N0548760.pdf?OpenElement.

THE PRINCIPLE OF COMMON CONCERN OF HUMANKIND   75

crimes, ethnic cleansing and crimes against humanity. We stress the need for the General Assembly to continue consideration of the responsibility to protect populations from genocide, war crimes, ethnic cleansing and crimes against humanity and its implications, bearing in mind the principles of the Charter and international law. We also intend to commit ourselves, as necessary and appropriate, to helping States build capacity to protect their populations from genocide, war crimes, ethnic cleansing and crimes against humanity and to assisting those which are under stress before crises and conflicts break out.

Several resolutions of the Security Council include references to R2P: Resolution 1674 on the Protection of Civilians in Armed Conflict that includes the first official Security Council reference to R2P, and Resolution 1706, which authorised the deployment of UN peacekeeping troops in Darfur, which referred to Resolution 1674 and paragraphs 138 and 139 on the Responsibility to Protect in the 2005 *World Summit Outcome Document*. R2P supports the emerging doctrine and principle of Common Concern. It can be conceptualised and understood as an emanation of the overarching principle addressing joint problems threatening stability and peaceful relations. It is clearly focused on the violation of core human rights and their essence.[206] At the same time, the doctrine of Common Concern also may assist in further developing R2P which today is limited to action taken within the United Nations security system. The issue of unilateral or collective action taken up by states or alliances outside the United Nations has remained unresolved. It is highly controversial. The doctrine and principle of CCH may assist in defining the foundations and boundaries of unilateral und plurilateral action in cases where collective security measures remain blocked and vetoed by single members of the Security Council.

The principle of Common Concern may also assist in further defining the scope of gross violations of human rights, in particular the right to life and the prohibition of torture. It is difficult to see why R2P should not also extend, as originally suggested, to encompass all gross and systemic violations of human rights, beyond the protection of populations from genocide, war crimes, ethnic cleansing and crimes against humanity. Legal security and prevention of unlawful intervention can equally be achieved by deploying criteria proposed under the doctrine and principle of CCH.

---

[206] See Chapter 5 in this volume.

To be sure, the move towards an obligation, as opposed to a right to intervene, is a major step. Intervention is notoriously controversial in politics and international relations. It will be objected that an expansive understanding of extraterritorial reach is inconsistent with national sovereignty. R2P itself is most controversial, let alone an extension of pertaining to Common Concerns of Humankind and unilateral and plurilateral action. However, a basic obligation to intervene in the realm of Common Concern facilitates and structures decision-making at home in light of violations of international law faced and an obligation to address such violations. It facilitates coordination among states in bringing about concerted responses and international relief operations. The main challenge amounts to equal treatment of comparable constellations. It will be argued that an obligation to act needs to be applied consistently, and cannot be subject to opportunism and unequal treatment. Yet, the impossibility to save lives in one instance should not imply that lives in other instances cannot be saved. It will be a matter of taking into account all pertinent factors in assessing the obligation and making a determination on a case-by-case basis.

In many instances, proactive and preventive action and intervention will not be possible, entailing disproportionate risks, tensions and costs. Often, means required to act successively exceed what can be reasonably achieved in remedying the situation. The principle of proportionality, central to sanctions and countermeasures, tempers the obligation to act and in many instances will reduce it to provide reasons why action was not possible and feasible to be taken. The principle is well established. It applies across the board of all disciplines of international law while varying before different courts of law due to varying functions in the context.[207] It certainly applies to the doctrine and principle of Common Concern.

Measures contemplated to be taken must be suitable to achieve the goal. They must be necessary; not exceeding what is required to this purpose. They must be well calibrated. As the case of gross and persistent violations of the essence of human rights indicated, proactive intervention may be called upon to prevent immediate harm and injury from being produced. Duties to protect exist in preventing massive harm to

---

[207] For a comprehensive study of the implications of the principle in international law, see T. Cottier, R. Echandi, R. Liechti-McKee, T. Payosova and C. Sieber, 'The Principle of Proportionality in International Law: Foundations and Variations', *Journal of World Investment & Trade*, 18 (2017), 628–72.

THE PRINCIPLE OF COMMON CONCERN OF HUMANKIND 77

ecology and the environment, in particular marine environment not limited to national zones of jurisdiction, massive harm produced to the quality of air by continued massive emissions of CO_2 emissions. Given the seriousness of the problems, the ultimate yardstick for duties to act is whether it makes an appropriate contribution, respecting proportionality, to accelerate the solution of the impending problem recognised as a CCH.

The obligation to state the reasons why measures are taken, or not taken, increases accountability of governments and transparency and inform domestic debate on foreign policy. Accountability is understood with Boven 'as a relationship between an actor and a forum, in which the actor has an obligation to explain and to justify his or her conduct, the forum can pose questions and pass judgment, and the actor may face consequences'.[208] One of the main effects of the duty to act therefore lies in greater transparency and accountability in foreign affairs.

It is obvious that such legal effects attached to the principle of CCH will increase opposition to the concept, going beyond international cooperation. The more the principle of Common Concern takes shape and entails specific duties, the more difficult it will be to have it accepted as a legal principle. States will fear that it serves an undue instrument of intervention and limitation of self-determination, and thus finally being a threat to national sovereignty. Yet, if the problems addressed are recognised and taken seriously, nobody should object to a system not only of effective incentives and carrots to cooperate internationally and fund appropriate policy measures, but also to sticks attached in order to secure compliance in a field considered to be of utmost importance to the international community and humankind. If sovereignty, as discussed, is understood and legitimised as a concept enabling peace for, and welfare of, individual members of society, measured intervention to bring about welfare effects in a field recognised as a CCH cannot be opposed by invoking self-determination. Finally, such measures are and will be subject to judicial review. States affected can defend themselves before international tribunals, challenging sanctions and countermeasures taken, in particular questioning proportionality of the measures. The experience of WTO dispute settlement shows that such defences are effective and provide important safeguards against abuse of powers.

---

[208] M. Bovens, 'Analyzing and Assessing Accountability: A Conceptual Framework', *European Law Journal*, 13 (2007), 447–68, at 450.

The basic duty to act emerges at the heart of the principle of Common Concern, subject to the principles of proportionality and accountability. It amounts to an essential and defining ingredient of the principle. It is here that it transgresses traditional domains and disciplines of international law. It profoundly adds a new dimension in general international law, calling for a reasoned response to violations of community rights. In many instances, action will not be suitable and possible. But the mere fact that such action needs to be considered and options examined renders states accountable towards the principle of Common Concern and thus enhanced compliance with international law.

1.8   The Application of CCH

1.8.1   Treaty Interpretation

Upon completing the normative dimensions suggested to form the essence of CCH, we turn to its role as a potential principle of law in the process of applying and interpreting the law.

Principles of law, along with human rights and principles of non-discrimination, play a crucial role in adjudicating complex problems for which positive law and treaty texts do not provide clear answers. Principles of law guide judges and courts of arbitration in the process of law. The principle of CCH, once recognised in the process of claims and responses in customary international law and treaty law, offers guidance similar to other principles such as equity, good faith and the protection of legitimate expectations, in particular estoppel, and proportionality, all with a view to serve justice. Likewise, general principles recognised in customary international law, in particular the principles of the prohibition of use of force, equality of states, the principle of sustainability inform the process of interpretation of particular rules and treaty text within Article 31(3)(1)(c) of the Vienna Convention of the Law of Treaties. International courts of law are obliged to take such principles into account. The principle of CCH thus is able to inform the interpretation and application of rules, on a case-by-case basis, relating to duties to cooperate, to comply with obligations incurred and in assessing countermeasures taken seeking to secure compliance, taking into account the thresholds threats to international peace and security. The potential of CCH as a tool of interpretation is of utmost importance in all areas subject to the principle. Zaker Ahmad particularly addresses this potential in interpreting WTO rules in the context of dissemination of

THE PRINCIPLE OF COMMON CONCERN OF HUMANKIND 79

technology related to renewable energy.[209] Iryna Bogdanova explores the impact of it on enhancing compliance fundamental rights.[210]

1.8.2 The Role of Non-State Actors and Domestic Courts of Law

Neither the right to act, nor the basic duty to act is able to fundamentally remedy the lack of reciprocity of interests inherent to collective action problems and free riding in many areas susceptible to quality as a CCH. Governments and politicians are generally reluctant to engage beyond the spheres where own and proper, narrowly defined interests are directly affected. Up to this point, we dealt with the problem as an international and intergovernmental affair, leaving civil society and domestic courts aside. It is time to frame the role of non-state actors and domestic courts in the process of compliance with international obligations, homework and the rights and duties assigned to the principle of Common Concern.

1.8.2.1 Non-State Actors

Non-state actors, in particular political parties, NGOs, but also business associations, multinational corporations and media have voice and play an important role shaping public opinion whether or not a particular problem should be considered to amount to a common concern and thus be dealt in accordance with the principle of CCH. Frequently, initial claims will originate from NGOs dedicated to a particular cause and campaigning to create awareness and generate governmental response and action. Non-state actors today play a significant role in foreign policymaking and international relations in informing and shaping political processes, setting trends and shaping the law and standards.[211] These activities mainly focus on the political process, entailing lobbying and campaigning. It is less developed in the field of compliance and securing accountability by governments. Obligations of international cooperation, the duty to do homework, the right to act and in particular the basic duty to act under the principle of CCH all bear the potential to strongly foster these functions under the influence and work of non-state actors. Political science research has shown that governments effectively

---

[209] See Chapter 2 in this volume pp. 124–32, 142–3.
[210] See Chapter 5 in this volume, pp. 289–90.
[211] See generally A. Peters, L. Koechlin, T. Förster and G. Fenner Zinkernagel (eds.), *Non-State Actors as Standard Setters* (Cambridge: Cambridge University Press, 2009).

respond and act to non-state actors' activities and interventions, in particular in the field of human rights protection.[212]

Non-state actors are well placed to monitor whether governments implement and comply with international obligations incurred. National players monitor homework to be undertaken in implementing legislation and unilateral voluntary measures. They encourage governments to act internationally in response to violations of international obligations. Foremost, states' basic duty to act against violations of the law in the realm of a recognised common concern entitles non-state actors to hold governments accountable in discharging these duties.

Accountability in compliance with obligations will mainly be a matter of political and public discourse. However, since legal obligations are at stake and allegedly violated, non-state actors should be entitled under the principle of Common Concern to file lawsuits in domestic courts assessing whether the homework is properly undertaken and whether the basic duty to act and to take appropriate and reasonable measures against failing states is being honoured.

1.8.2.2   Domestic Courts of Law

The principle of CCH also informs the work of domestic courts in applying international law or in respecting the doctrine of consistent interpretation of domestic law in accordance with international law. To the extent that Common Concern evolves into a legal principle applicable to all layers of governance, it will join the canon of general principles of law and may be directly applied as a matter of domestic constitutional law, informing the interpretation of legislation and regulations in various and often complex technical fields. This latter function is likely to be of significant importance, as domestic courts are likely to play an important role in redressing the lack of reciprocity of interests identified, jointly

---

[212] Research conducted by political scientists confirms that demands of the electorate can influence policymakers to respond to grave human rights violations taking place elsewhere in the world (E. V. McLean and T. Whang, 'Designing Foreign Policy: Voters, Special Interest Groups, and Economic Sanctions', *Journal of Peace Research* 51(589) (2014); St. Chan, 'Principle versus Profit: Debating Human Rights Sanctions', *Human Rights Review*, 19(45) (2018)). Scholars have demonstrated a positive correlation between coverage of human suffering in the US media and a government's response in the form of economic sanctions (D. Pekson, T. M. Peterson and A. Cooper Drury, 'Media-Driven Humanitarianism? News Media Coverage of Human Rights Abuses and the Use of Economic Sanctions', *International Studies Quarterly*, 58(855) (2014)). I am indebted to Iryna Bogdanova for these references.

THE PRINCIPLE OF COMMON CONCERN OF HUMANKIND 81

with the influence and impact of non-state actors in domestic forums, impacting on domestic political process in addressing common concerns.

Recent times have witnessed increased recourse to domestic courts in areas pertaining to common concerns of humankind. The University of Colombia Climate Change Litigation Databases[213] documents an increasing number of cases brought against governments for failing to honour obligations incurred in climate change mitigation. In 2015, a Dutch court ordered the government to reduce CO_2 emissions by 25 per cent on the basis of human rights and tort claims, the court recognised that the government has a duty independent of international commitments to undertake abatement to achieve the goals of the 2015 Paris Agreement.[214] The landmark decision was eventually appealed by the government arguing that the court sidelined democracy it its ruling.[215] Cases against governments are brought on the basis of tort law, human rights, constitutional provisions and the public trust doctrine. They relate to natural resources, including climate change and biodiversity, and human rights violations. At the same time, there is a significant movement in establishing jurisdiction of home courts of companies operating abroad for human rights violations on the basis of tort law, filling what was properly called the governance gap in judicial protection of victims in developing countries lacking appropriate protection of the rule of law.[216] The foundations of claims in areas pertaining to common concern, or potentially pertaining to it, have remained unclear. Most of the cases filed have not been ruled on. Courts face complex challenges and the evolution in the field will be shaped by trial and error. It is submitted that the principle of CCH, recalling its foundations in equity and the public trust doctrine, with recognition of a basic duty to act will assist in clarifying jurisdictions of courts and foundations of claims against government, in particular for failure to act appropriately. Courts of law

---

[213] http://climatecasechart.com/ (accessed 28 Aug. 2018).

[214] *The Guardian*, 24 June 2016, 'Dutch Government Ordered to Cut Carbon Emissions in Land-mark Ruling'; www.theguardian.com/environment/2015/jun/24/dutch-government-ordered-cut-carbon-emissions-landmark-ruling (accessed 28 Aug. 2018).

[215] *The Guardian*, 28 May 2018, 'Dutch Government Appeals against Court Ruling over Emissions Cuts'; www.theguardian.com/environment/2018/may/28/dutch-government-appeals-against-court-ruling-over-emissions-cuts.

[216] See P. Simons and A. Macklin, *The Governance Gap: Extractive Industries, Human Rights, and the Home State Advantage* (New York: Routledge, 2014). See in particular *Garcia* v. *Tahoe Resources Inc.*, 2017 British Columbia Court of Appeals (BCCA) 39; www.canlii.org/en/bc/bcca/doc/2017/2017bcca39/2017bcca39.html.

hereby are able to play an important role in redressing the lack of reciprocity in international relations and to compel governments to act accordingly, taking into account broad margins of political discretion. Independent domestic courts are able to substantially enhance accountability and rationality of policymaking in areas of pressing problems under the doctrine of Common Concern of Mankind. The doctrine and principle will assist in defining more precisely the role of domestic courts in the process of globalisation as to when they should and can intervene within the domestic balance of powers.

1.9 Summary and Conclusions

The doctrine of CCH reflects a highly interdependent globe. Communications, technology, international trade, foreign direct investment and civilisational evolution enhance convergence among countries. At the same time, divergences and differences remain substantial, in terms of income and GDP, economic opportunities, culture, lifestyles and political system. Independence and self-determination, today often cloaked in nationalism and sovereignty, loom large. The world is far from being a village. Yet, the world shares a number of serious problems, preoccupations and challenges which countries cannot solve on their own and are exposed to free riding due to lack of reciprocal interests. Solutions depend upon enhanced international cooperation and effective compliance; failing that, international stability, peace and welfare are at risk and may lead to warfare and destruction in the long run. Climate change is the main paradigm. The issue was legally recognised as a common concern of humankind. So was the problem of eroding biodiversity. Additional ones may be added in a process of claims of responses within the international community. They are discussed in subsequent chapters. The principle of CCH can potentially be applied across all international law.

While the principle of cooperation will be paramount, mechanisms of cooperation, procedures, decision-making, funding schemes, rules and sanctions and countermeasures and the role of unilateral responses may find specific expressions and safeguards in appropriate treaty regimes. The status of the principle will vary among different fields. While recognised in environmental law, it has a long way to go in other areas. Equally, the emphasis will vary among different areas. While cooperation and homework prevail, for example in the field of climate change and dissemination of technology or monetary and financial law, the emphasis

THE PRINCIPLE OF COMMON CONCERN OF HUMANKIND   83

will be on compliance in the field of human rights or combating marine pollution. The problem of income inequality will mainly pertain to homework. In other areas, such as migration, strong cooperation, homework and compliance all are required in tandem will take a long time to build. The duty to act will remain most controversial. Each of the areas examined and discussed in this book shows particular problems, calling upon particular regulations which are inspired by the tenets of the outlined principle of CCH. Treaty negotiations on specific issues may be informed and inspired by the principle, but will settle down with tailor-made solutions in shaping appropriate institutions and mechanisms.

A fully fledged principle of CCH may eventually emerge in customary law as an amalgamation of all these efforts. Courts of law may shape it one way or the other. It may evolve as a legal principle of multilevel governance equally applying within regional integration and federal and subfederal levels in addressing shared pressing problems. The general principle, once recognised, will then apply by default. But even before that state is reached, the blueprint of CCH inspires and gives directions, showing the way forward. It expounds what at the end of the day should be achieved in order to redress fundamental deficiencies in addressing collective action problems and the lack of reciprocal interests of states in areas of vital importance to humanity and future generations.

1.9.1 Structural Effects on International Law

CCH, as a source of inspiration, direction and eventually a legal principle of international law recognised by the international community deploys, while building upon the existing framework, significant long-term structural effect on international law. It will move it from coexistence and cooperation to integration in the long run. In reality, this blueprint is likely to materialise piecemeal in a gradual process of claims and responses, trial and error. In the long run, it will develop and foster a new understanding of sovereignty of states and the realisation of multilevel governance with a view to producing appropriate public goods on appropriate levels of governance.

Relating to serious problems threatening peace and stability, where it may eventually and fully apply as a result of a process of claims and responses, the principle of CCH brings about a new combination of duties to cooperate and to negotiate, of funding and of measures seeking enhanced compliance with commitments made also with the support of domestic courts. It offers a new equation of carrots and sticks which addresses and remedies the fundamental problems of lack of reciprocal interests and frequent free riding by states. Main tenets can be summarised as follows.

1.9.1.1 From Cooperation to Integration

CCH, if taken seriously, bears the potential to introduce a new era and phase of international law, moving in the final analysis from coexistence and cooperation to integration in key areas dependent on close interaction. These processes are framed by duties to work together. Long-term solutions of common concern problems depend upon regulatory convergence and cooperation essentially relying upon mutual trust and confidence. The duty to negotiate establishes a first mainstay of the principle. Structures required to successfully do so will often call for new joint bodies and institutions. They call for close interaction with domestic law. Clear lines between domestic and international law will blur in shaping overall multi-level governance and integrating international law in an overall constitutional structure. From here, the principle of Common Concern may develop into a constitutional principle shaping multilevel governance within regions, regional integration federal and even unitary states.

1.9.1.2 Responsibilities at Home

Common Concern primarily entails responsibilities to act within a given jurisdiction. *Think globally – act locally* will be translated into legal terms. States are entitled, but also obliged, to address common concerns as defined by the international community within their own boundaries. In contrast to the principle of permanent sovereignty over natural resources, the principle of Common Concern not only authorises but obliges governments to take action in addressing the Common Concern within their own jurisdictions and territories. This is the second mainstay of the principle of CCH. National efforts at abating global warming therefore emanate from this principle independently of treaty obligations, as much as efforts to stop depletion of fisheries within their own territorial waters and the EEZ. The same holds true for all other areas potentially recognised as a CCH, for example in the field of migration or monetary affairs, and the protection of the essence of human rights against systemic and persistent violations or in addressing gross income inequalities destabilising society. Common Concern stresses the importance of the topic concerned and assists in defining priorities in domestic policymaking. The duty to do one's homework, finally, strengthens the role of non-state actors and domestic courts in the process of compliance.

THE PRINCIPLE OF COMMON CONCERN OF HUMANKIND 85

1.9.1.3 Enhanced Extraterritorial Effects

The principle of CCH authorises taking action in relation to facts relating to the Common Concern produced outside the proper jurisdiction of a state to the extent that this is required for the proper and effective implementation of domestic policies. Rights and obligations relating to Common Concerns go beyond the traditional precepts of territoriality. While today action can be defended if the nexus to a state's own territory is sufficient, Common Concern would not require such linkages but depend upon examination of whether the measure and action is able to support the attainment of a Common Concern as defined and recognised by the international community. Countries will be entitled to prescribe PPMs in support of domestic policies. This is the third mainstay. Imports may be depended upon compliance with such rules. For example, governments are authorised to take appropriate action against highly polluting means of production which bluntly ignore the Common Concern of global warming by means of adopting appropriate production and process standards. Likewise, governments are authorised to take action in response to blatant and systematic neglect of the Common Concern of preserving the essence of fundamental human rights and labour standards, combating systematic violations thereof in shaping market access for goods and services originating in that jurisdiction.

1.9.1.4 Improving Compliance

Next to enhancing extraterritorial effects of domestic law, CCH reinforces the law of state responsibility. Norms pertaining to areas recognised as a CCH are community norms in nature and can be enforced by all states in appropriate forums and in bilateral relations as expounded in Article 48 ILC draft on state responsibility. There is no need to be exposed to direct harm and injury which normally brings about claims to state responsibility and reparation of injury. Harm is established by undermining measures adopted in addressing the CCH at stake. This is the fourth mainstay.

1.9.1.5 Obligations to Act

While Common Concern provides the foundations of authorisation to act, the most controversial question relates to the problem as to what extent the principle also entails obligations to act. There is a fundamental difference between authorisation and obligation to act. While the former leaves the decision to the discretion of government, the latter compels it

86 THOMAS COTTIER

to engage and take necessary steps. Such obligations are gradually emerging in the area of R2P, which is of key importance to Common Concern. It only applies to shared problems threatening peace, stability and welfare. We submit that the basic obligation to act amounts to the fifth mainstay of the principle of Common Concern. It essentially defines its particular feature as a legal principle going beyond established principles and rules of international law. Importantly, this obligation is subject to proportionality and imposes, at a minimum, an explanation and justification why no action has been taken. The requirement contributes to creating awareness and enhancing transparency and internal accountability of governments. The obligation to act is monitored by non-state actors and subject to judicial review by domestic courts of law.

1.9.2 A New and Different Realism

It will be objected that the prospects of such a principle, even as a source of inspiration, are antithetical to national sovereignty and self-determination. They ignore the prerogatives of government in foreign affairs and seek to establish new functions for domestic courts which they are not able to discharge. It will be deemed to be too intrusive. Governments will refrain from accepting a principle of CCH if rights and obligations as outlined are attached, in particular basic duties to act. From a statist point of view, it is not realistic and amounts to cosmopolitan daydreaming. Arguably, it stretches international law, based upon national sovereignty, beyond its limits. Also, it will be objected that it results in new imperialism and hegemony as it empowers strong actors more than weaker ones. All this creates anxieties. It therefore was suggested leaving the concept vague and open-ended, short of legal rigour, and to rather build it gradually in state practice without defining the concept.

The question, indeed, is exactly about realism. It is a fact of life that the existing system and traditional precepts of sovereignty of nation states fail to produce adequate results to protect the expectations of future generations. They fail to produce the public goods essential to preserve peace and stability and legal security. Since serious problems recognised under the principle of CCH are inevitably shared and cannot be solved independently, and since failure to solve the problems potentially leads to crisis and destruction, it is in our view utterly realistic to face the challenge and assume appropriate responsibilities in the interest of future generations. Everything else simply is irresponsible and morally unsound and incompatible with the functions of sovereignty to secure welfare and peace for the population. Instead, we submit six arguments addressing these weaknesses, and in support of the principle of CCH.

First, the principle of Common Concern of Mankind and its obligations and effects is limited to shared, serious problems. It does not apply across the board. States face enhanced rights and obligations only in areas structurally perilous to peace, stability and welfare. The acceptance of the principle and its extension to particular collective action problems is subject to claims and responses and thus acceptance in treaty law or customary international law. It cannot be unilaterally imposed but is achieved due to persuasion in addressing pressing needs.

Second, the principle of CCH with its obligations to cooperate, homework, compliance and duties to act addresses the lack of reciprocal interests and free-riding inherent to many collective action problems. It introduces appropriate carrots and sticks to foster mutual interests of states and communities to take up a problem, framing also the roles of non-state actors and courts of law. The costs of abstaining and free riding exceed the benefits of cooperation.

Third, the principle of CCH domestically supports governments in taking appropriate measures and in convincing electorates and over-coming populist resistance and nationalism vis-à-vis collective action problems at stake. Recourse to international law obligations to act, and accountability, structures the debate and facilitates positive outcomes.

Fourth, the principle of CCH facilitates and supports the adoption of appropriate domestic policy measures. This is of great importance for large markets and powerful states and entities. The extension of extraterritorial application of domestic law pertaining to areas falling under the principle of Common Concern facilitates the adoption of measures and policies which otherwise are opposed due to impending losses of comparative advantage and competitiveness. Such incentives are of paramount importance as the resolution of main collective action problems, in particular climate change, loss of biological diversity, monetary stability, migration, human rights compliance, corporate taxation and the avoidance of profit-shifting, essentially depends upon homework undertaken in large markets and how they treat imported products (goods and services) and immigration. Medium and smaller markets and countries tend to follow these policies in securing access to larger markets. It is therefore essential that the principle of Common Concern of Mankind primarily facilitates action by large markets and powerful states in addressing collective action problems.

Fifth, the principle of CCH does not leave medium and small states powerless once they have agreed to assume responsibility and to take a problem on board. They can form flexible coalitions in supporting the principle and its application of severe problems. They can develop initiatives on the international level at cooperation and harmonisation of standards and rules. They can shape appropriate procedures of participation and decision-making in international organisations by adopting majority rulings. They can offset passivity and even resistance by large markets and powers, and develop joint leadership under the principle of CCH.

Sixth, the principle of CCH is subject to judicial control in international courts and arbitration. Measures taken and having extraterritorial effect, as well as countermeasures and sanctions imposed are subject to the principle of proportionality. They need to pass a necessity test. Should countries, in particular large markets, adopt measures not suitable to address the collective action problem in a conducive manner, such measures can be challenged in court, subject to single or collective countermeasures.

In conclusion, we submit that the principle of Common Concern takes into account existing power structures and offers adequate checks and balances in addressing anxieties voiced. The principle, essentially based upon traditional functions of equity, assist international law to find appropriate responses to globalisation. There are no viable alternatives in addressing pressing collective action problems and the lack of reciprocal interests. We need to move international and domestic law, in such areas, towards enhanced legal integration and to developing the five mainstays of the principle of CCH in scholarship and beyond.

On these foundations, Part II of this book turns to exploring the prospects of CCH in different and diverse areas of public international law. The following chapters show that challenges vary in different fields. While some need to focus on developing new concepts and rules at the outset, such as in transfer of technology of renewable energy in the context of climate change or in addressing inequality of income and wealth distribution – an entirely new topic in international law and relations. In other areas, the principle bundles already existing or emerging norms to render cooperation more visible. This in particular is the case in the fields of marine pollution and of monetary and financial law. In the field of human rights, the emphasis is on compliance and enforcement of existing obligations and in fostering linkages to international economic law. All areas show in their own way that the principle of CCH makes a valuable contribution in addressing contemporary challenges. It strengthens international law and global governance.

***

Select Bibliography

Beitz, C. (2001). 'Human Rights as a Common Concern', 95 *American Political Science Review* 269–81.

Benedek, W., de Feyter, K., Kettemann, C. and Voigt, Ch. (2014). *The Common Interest in International Law* (Cambridge: Intersentia).

Benvenisti, E. and Nolte, G. (eds.) (2018). *Community Interests across International Law* (Oxford: Oxford University Press).

Biermann, F. (1996). '"Common Concern of Humankind": The Emergence of a New Concept of International Environmental Law', 34(4) *Archiv des Völkerrechts* 426– 81.

Bowling, C., Pierson, E. and Ratté, S. (2018). 'The Common Concern of Humankind: A Potential Framework for a New International Legally Binding Instrument on the Conservation and Sustainable Use of Marine Biological Diversity in the High Seas'; www.un.org/depts/los/biodiversity/prepcom_files/BowlingPiersonandRatte_Common_Concern.pdf.

Brown Weiss, E. (2012). 'The Coming Water Crisis: A Common Concern of Humankind', 1 *Transnational Environmental Law* 153–68.

(2014). 'Nature and the Law: The Global Commons and the Common Concern of Humankind', in *Sustainable Humanity, Sustainable Nature: Our Responsibility*, Political Academy of Sciences, Extra Series 41 (Vatican City); www.pas.va/content/dam/accademia/pdf/es41/es41-brownweiss.pdf.

Brunnée, J. (2007). 'Common Areas, Common Heritage and Common Concern', in D. Bodansky, J. Brunnée and E. Hey (eds.) *The Oxford Handbook of International Environmental Law* (Oxford: Oxford University Press), pp. 550–73.

(2008). 'Common Interest: Echoes from an Empty Shell? Some Thoughts on Common Interest and International Environmental Law', 49 *ZaöRV* 791–808.

Castillo-Winckels, N. S. (2016). 'Why "Common Concern of Humankind" Should Return to the Work of the International Law Commission on the Atmosphere', 29 *Georgetown International Environmental Law Review* 131–52.

Conçado Trindade, A. A. (2013). International Law for Humankind: Towards a New *Jus Gentium* (2nd ed., Leiden: Martinus Nijhoff).

Cottier, T., Aerni, Ph., Karapınar, B., Matteotti, S., de Sépibus, J. and Shingal, A. (2014). 'The Principle of Common Concern and Climate Change', 52 *Archiv des Völkerrechts (AVR)* 293–324.

90 THOMAS COTTIER

Cottier, T., Bürgi Bonanomi, E. (2017). 'Soil as a Common Concern: Towards Disciplines on Sustainable Land Management', in T. Cottier and K. Nadavukaren Schefer (eds.), *Encylopedia of International Economic Law* (Cheltenham, UK: Edward Elgar), p. 627.

Cottier, T., Matteotti-Berkutova, S. (2009). 'International Environmental Law and the Evolving Concept of Common Concern of Mankind', in T. Cottier, O. Nartova and Z. Bigdeli Sadeq (eds.), *International Trade Regulation and the Mitigation of Climate Change* (Cambridge: Cambridge University Press), pp. 21–47.

French, D. (2015). 'Common Concern, Common Heritage and Other Global(-ising) Concepts: Rhetorical Devices, Legal Principles or a Fundamental Challenge?', in M. J. Bowman, P. G. G. Davies and E. J. Goodwin (eds.), *Research Handbook on Biodiversity and Law* (Cheltenham, UK: Edward Elgar), pp. 334–60.

Horn, L. S. (2000). 'The Common Concern of Humankind and Legal Protection of the Global Environment', PhD (University of Sydney).

  (2004). 'The Implications of the Concept of Common Concern of a Human Kind on a Human Right to a Healthy Environment', 1 *Macquarie Journal of International and Comparative Environmental Law* 233–69.

International Law Commission (2015). Sixty-seventh session, Geneva, 4 May–5 June and 6 July–7 Aug. 2015, Second report on the protection of the atmosphere by Shinya Murase, Special Rapporteur, A/CN.4.681 (2 Mar. 2015).

Kontolemis, Z. (2003). 'Exchange Rates Are a Matter of Common Concern: Policies in the Run-up to the Euro?', 191 *Directorate General Economic and Monetary Affairs Papers.*

Murillo J. (2008). 'Common Concern of Humankind and Its Implications in International Environmental Law', 5 *Macquarie Journal of International and Comparative Environmental Law* 133–47.

Nadakavuaren Schefer, K. and Cottier, T.(2013). 'Responsibility to Protect (R2P) and the Emerging Principle of Common Concern', in P. Hilpold (ed.), *Die Schutzverantwortung (R2P). Ein Paradigmenwechsel in der Entwicklung des Internationalen Rechts?* (Leiden: Martinus Nijhoff), pp. 123–42.

Nado, V. P., William, K. R.(1976). 'The Public Trust Doctrine: A Viable Approach to International Environmental Protection', 5 *Ecology Law Quarterly* 271.

Shaffer, G. (2012). 'International Law and Global Public Goods in a Legal Pluralist World', 23 *European Journal of International Law* 669–93.

Shelton, D. (2009). 'Common Concern and Humanity', 39 *Environmental Law and Policy* 83.

Soltau, F. (2016). 'Common Concern of Humankind', in C. P. Carlane, K. R. Gray and R. G. Tarasofsky (eds.), *The Oxford Handbook of International Climate Change Law* (New York: Oxford University Press), pp. 202–13.

Stec, S. (2010). 'Humanitarian Limits to Sovereignty: Common Concern and Common Heritage Approaches to Natural Resources and Environment', 12 *International Community Law Review* 361–89.

Tolba, M. K. (1991). 'The Implications of the "Common Concern of Mankind Concept" on Global Environmental Issues', 13 *Revista IIDH* 237–46.

UNEP (1990). 'Report on the Proceedings of the Meeting, Prepared by Co-Rapporteurs A. A. Cançado Trindade and D. J. Attard', in D. J. Attard (ed.), *The Meeting of the Group of Legal Experts to Examine the Concept of the Common Concern of Mankind in Relation to the Global Environmental Issues*, Malta, 13–15 Dec. 1990 (Nairobi: UNEP), pp. 19–47.

PART II

Case Studies

2

Trade-Related Measures to Spread Low-Carbon Technologies

A Common Concern–Based Approach

ZAKER AHMAD

2.1 Introduction

Effective and immediate response to the well-documented hazard of anthropogenic climate change calls for immediate and drastic reduction of greenhouse gas (GHG) emission,[1] which, in turn, requires dissemination (or 'diffusion') of the technologies necessary to such end (hereafter 'low-carbon technologies' (LCTs) or 'clean technologies'). Formally recognised as a common concern of humankind, anthropogenic climate change is a truly complex transboundary problem.[2] This chapter showcases the practical utility of the proposed Common Concern doc-

---

This chapter is a partial summary of the author's doctoral thesis entitled 'WTO Law and Trade Policy Reform for Low-Carbon Technology Diffusion'. Special thanks go to Professors Thomas Cottier, Gabrielle Marceau, and Michael Hahn for comments on the draft version; to Professors Peter-Tobias Stoll and Cedric Ryngaert for their thoughtful critique, and suggestions. All remaining shortcomings are to be attributed only to the author.

[1] This chapter's focus on the mitigation aspect of the climate change problem is without any prejudice to the equally important need to enhance climate adaptation efforts.

[2] For an account of the 'complexity' and the 'super wicked' nature of the problem, see H. van Asselt, 'Introduction', *The Fragmentation of Global Climate Governance: Consequences and Management of Regime Interactions* (Cheltenham, UK: Edward Elgar, 2014), pp. 3–4; K. Levin, B. Cashore, S. Bernstein, and G. Auld, 'Overcoming the Tragedy of Super Wicked Problems: Constraining Our Future Selves to Ameliorate Global Climate Change', *Policy Sciences*, 45(123) (2012), 126–30. For a brief account of the key attributes of climate cooperation challenge, see S. Barrett, 'Aggregate Efforts: Global Public Goods That Depend on the Combined Efforts of All States', *Why Cooperate? The Incentive to Supply Global Public Goods* (Oxford: Oxford University Press, 2010), pp. 84–91; R. O. Keohane and M. Oppenheimer, 'Paris: Beyond the Climate Dead End through Pledge and Review?', *Politics and Governance*, 4(142) (2016), 143–5.

trine[3] in the area of international trade regulation to attain the goal of wider diffusion of LCTs. It contains two principal messages. One is that climate mitigation efforts can be magnified by, inter alia, mutually beneficial trade measures that will help to spread the necessary technology-embedded goods and related services from one country to another. Another is that the proposed doctrine of Common Concern supplies the rationale and also lends itself as a normative framework to respectively inspire and structure the trade-related response measures in this regard.

The chapter begins with a brief conceptual and factual background. It then weighs in on the avenues and implications of introducing the Common Concern doctrine to the body of trade rules, with respect to diffusion of LCTs in particular. It is proposed that based on this doctrine, the narrative of trade and technology diffusion issues be framed anew, in a way that underscores the urgency of action, highlighting a range of possible options in parallel. With regard to the various ways in which such actions may be challenged at the World Trade Organization (WTO), the utility of the doctrine is further contemplated – as an aid to treaty interpretation, or inspiring reform of the rules. The concluding section puts together the overall assessment to serve as a summary, also as a future outlook.

2.1.1 Key Concepts

The term 'low-carbon technologies' (LCTs), is used here to mean 'technologies that aim to minimize GHG emissions, especially carbon dioxide emissions, relative to those technologies currently in use in a particular context'.[4] This and similar terms (e.g. cleaner technology) are in use to indicate emission reduction technologies. In this sense, the LCTs would only form a subset of the generic terms, such as technology,[5] climate

---

[3] To distinguish the proposed aspects from the traditional understanding of common concern, a terminological convention is used. When referring to its accepted meaning in the treaty context, small letters are used, e.g. 'common concern' or 'common concern of humankind'. The proposed enhanced attributes of the concept are referred to as a doctrine, using capital letters, e.g. 'Common Concern'.

[4] D. Ockwell and A. Mallett (eds.), *Low-Carbon Technology Transfer: From Rhetoric to Reality* (London: Routledge, 2012), p. 3.

[5] Technology as a concept is very expansive. It includes embodied and non-embodied (e.g. patent) technologies, as well as organisational know-how. Intergovernmental Panel on

technology, or the treaty term 'environmentally sound technologies'. The 1992 Framework Convention (UNFCCC) used the term environmentally sound technologies (EST)[6] – a notion that potentially comprises any technologies beneficial for the environment at large.[7] Although a meticulous listing of all possible LCTs is beyond the scope of this chapter, it should be mentioned that there exist opportunities for improvement across all GHG emitting sectors. In the energy sector, apart from engaging more renewable sources, smart and long-distance electricity grids and power storage technologies are important. Industries ought to make efficient use of lighting and power, as well as deploy energy-efficient capital machinery (e.g. motors, furnaces, dryers). In buildings, better insulation, heating, and air-conditioning is important. In the transportation sector, better engines, better transport management infrastructure, as well as better fuel can reduce emissions. The list could go on.[8]

Instead of technology 'transfer',[9] the current chapter uses the notion of technology 'diffusion' due to an accepted limitation of the trade rules to influence technology transfer beyond being the best possible conduit of spreading LCTs from one jurisdiction to another. To spell out: successful

---

Climate Change (IPCC), *Methodological and Technological Issues in Technology Transfer* (Cambridge: Cambridge University Press, 2000), p. 54; J. Boldt, I. Nygaard, U. E. Hansen, and S. Traerup, *Overcoming Barriers to the Transfer and Diffusion of Climate Technologies* (Roskilde: UNEP Risø Centre, 2012), p. 7; I. Nygaard and U. E. Hansen, 'The Conceptual and Practical Challenges to Technology Categorisation in the Preparation of Technology Needs Assessments', *Climatic Change*, 131(3) (2015), s. 3.

[6] Art. 4.5, United Nations Framework Convention on Climate Change (UNFCCC), 1771 UNTS 107 (1992).

[7] Agenda 21: Programme of Action for Sustainable Development 1993, UN Doc A/Conf. 151/26 (1992), s. 34.1.

[8] For an overview, see H. de Coninck and others, 'Strengthening and Implementing the Global Response', in Valerie Masson-Delmotte *et al.* (eds.), *Special Report: Global Warming of 1.5 °C* (Geneva: World Meteorological Organization, 2018), pp. 323–36, www.ipcc.ch/report/sr15 (accessed 19 Sept. 2019); C. Gandenberger, 'Theoretical Perspectives on the International Transfer and Diffusion of Climate Technologies', *Working Paper Sustainability and Innovation S 12/2015* (Karlsruhe: Fraunhofer ISI, 2015), p. 38; International Renewable Energy Agency and International Energy Agency, *Perspectives for the Energy Transition: Investment Needs for a Low-Carbon Energy System* (2017), p. 55.

[9] Taking the IPCC definition, technology transfer is understood as 'a broad set of processes covering the flows of know-how, experience and equipment for mitigating and adapting to climate change amongst different stakeholders such as governments, private sector entities, financial institutions, NGOs and research/education institutions' (IPCC, *supra* n. 5, p. 3).

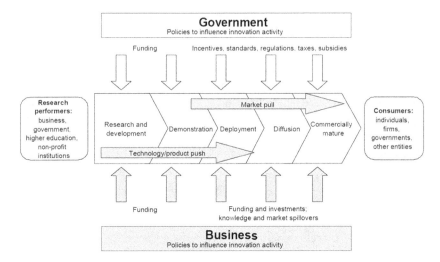

Figure 2.1 Innovation cycle
Source: Expert Group on Technology Transfer (EGTT), Recommendations on Future Financing Options for Enhancing the Development, Deployment, Diffusion and Transfer of Technologies under the Convention (2009), FCCC/SB/2009/2 8, http://unfccc.int/resource/docs/2009/sb/eng/02.pdf (accessed 19 Sept. 2019)

technology transfer requires complementarity between a range of actions[10] at home and beyond, only a part of which falls within the domain of trade rules. This is also clear from the illustration of an innovation cycle above (Figure 2.1). It indicates 'deployment' and 'diffusion' to be the stages where market pull policies are relevant to enable new technologies to gain footing. The argument, therefore, is that trade rules should contribute to creating appropriate enabling conditions for the LCTs to commercially mature worldwide.

2.1.2 Factual Context

The need to discuss diffusion of LCTs gains special prominence when seen in the context of its inextricable linkage with climate mitigation

---

[10] Especially, among others, making available adequate finance for technology innovation and capacity building (ibid., 4–5); J. Atik, 'Technology Transfer', in T. Cottier and K. N. Schefer (eds.), *Elgar Encyclopedia of International Economic Law* (Cheltenham, UK: Edward Elgar, 2017), p. 606.

action and the inadequacy of the latter worldwide. If current patterns of production and consumption continue, in next three decades the rising global mean temperature would in all probability exceed any limit[11] currently set by law.[12] The growing levels of GHG emission not only intensify the induced risks[13] and increase the cost of adaptation, but also require steeper subsequent decarbonisation efforts,[14] at the same time exponentially driving up the costs of doing so. Scientists calculate different mitigation pathways by modelling alternative scenarios. Pathways that reduce emission in line with the target enshrined in the Paris Agreement with limited or no overshoot would require 'rapid and far-reaching transitions in energy, land, urban and infrastructure (including transport and buildings), and industrial systems'.[15] Such massive-scale systemic shift is impossible without the diffusion of available appropriate technologies, especially with regard to energy systems, industries, transport systems, and buildings.[16] For example, to remain within the 1.5 degrees target, by 2050 the industrial emissions should be 75–90 per cent lower compared to the 2010 levels. According to the IPCC:

> Such reductions can be achieved through combinations of new and existing technologies and practices, including electrification, hydrogen, sustainable bio-based feedstocks, product substitution, and carbon capture, utilization and storage (CCUS). These options are technically proven at various scales but their large-scale deployment may be limited by economic, financial, human capacity and institutional constraints in

---

[11] IPCC, 'Summary for Policymakers', in Masson-Delmotte *et al.*, *supra* n. 8, p. 4.

[12] Paris Agreement, 'Report of the Conference of the Parties on Its Twenty-First Session', Decision 1/CP 21 Annex, FCCC/CP/2015/10/Add.1 (2015). Article 1(a) declares the global target as 'Holding the increase in the global average temperature to well below 2 °C above pre-industrial levels and to pursue efforts to limit the temperature increase to 1.5 °C above pre-industrial levels'.

[13] IPCC, *supra* n. 11, p. 11.

[14] Remaining within the Paris target already would require 40–70 per cent emission cuts by 2050, compared to the 2010 levels, ultimately reaching to almost zero or negative emission levels by 2100. See, IPCC, 'Summary for Policymakers', in O. Edenhofer, R. Pichs-Madruga, and Y. Sokona (eds.), *Climate Change 2014: Mitigation of Climate Change. Working Group III Contribution to the Fifth Assessment Report of the Intergovernmental Panel on Climate Change* (Cambridge: Cambridge University Press, 2014), pp. 10–12.

[15] IPCC, *supra* n. 11, p. 21.

[16] It is not intended to mean that technology diffusion is the exclusive solution. Appropriate planning and governance would play a big role in reducing emission through urban infrastructural transition, reduction in consumer demands, and land use changes for instance. Also, innovation, especially with regard to carbon-dioxide removal technologies is also of crucial complementary importance.

specific contexts, and specific characteristics of large-scale industrial installations.[17]

This chapter's particular focus on the role of trade rules in spreading LCTs is motivated in part by the need to increase future mitigation capabilities as portrayed above. It is also motivated by the positive role technology diffusion or support to that end plays in realising existing mitigation commitments as found in the nationally determined contributions (NDCs). According to one estimate,[18] 63 per cent of the NDCs commitments received in relation to the new pledge and review process established under the Paris Agreement is either fully or partially conditional upon technology support. Taking further into account that existing level of mitigation commitments are despairingly little,[19] and needs to be raised sharply as soon as possible, the need for technology diffusion becomes even more obvious.

The central assumption in this chapter can, therefore, be put as follows. As the trade rules govern the markets and transactions therein, these rules must, at the domestic and international level, play the necessary role to dismantle any market-related barriers preventing the diffusion of clean technologies. The question would nevertheless be how an empirically manifest necessity should find expression within the body of trade rules. Here lies the relevance of the doctrine of Common Concern. The following section contemplates how the doctrine can make inroads into the regime of trade law building upon the complementarity between trade and environment issues.

2.2 Climate Change as a Common Concern: Influencing Trade Rules

This section elaborates on the potential influence of the Common Concern doctrine to deepen the existing relationship between the legal regimes of climate and trade. This will then serve as the basis for a new technology diffusion narrative in the following section. Two important

---

[17] IPCC, *supra* n. 11, p. 21.

[18] C. Brandi, *Trade Elements in Countries' Climate Contributions under the Paris Agreement* (Geneva: International Centre for Trade and Sustainable Development, 2017), pp. 16–17.

[19] J. Nieto, Ó. Carpintero, and L. J. Miguel, 'Less than 2 °C? An Economic–Environmental Evaluation of the Paris Agreement', *Ecological Economics*, 146(69) (2018); IPCC, *supra* n. 11, p. 24. The IPCC calls for enhancing the scale and ambition of mitigation efforts before 2030.

factors that define the contours of this relationship ought to be kept in mind. First, and on a positive note, unlike the other issue areas covered in this volume, common concern is not an altogether novel notion in this study area. The climate change treaty regime in particular is a cradle of common concern[20] – wherein the notion is now regarded as entailing a 'common responsibility to take measures to address the concern'.[21] Together with the common subscription to sustainable development in both regimes, it can be said that there already exists sufficient common ground to attain greater synergy between the two legal frameworks. Second, and on a cautious note, it is unclear how much the traditional understanding of common concern can exert influence upon the trade regime. This is where the proposed doctrine comes in. While elaborating on these two issues in the following paragraphs, the focus will narrow down to the specific concern of low-carbon technology (LCT) diffusion.

2.2.1 Trade and Climate Cooperation at Present

At least since the establishment of the WTO, the trade regime has not been inimical to the accommodation of environmental concerns. This has been manifested in the negotiation activities to further develop new rules in the evolving institutional structure, also in the key dispute settlement jurisprudence. Due to the principle of sustainable development being accepted as one of the goals in the Marrakesh Agreement,[22] it has since been agreed that the interest of economic growth and environmental protection should go hand in hand. This notion of mutual supportiveness also applies with respect to climate change concerns.[23]

---

[20] Chapter 1 in this volume, pp. 11–5.

[21] Commentary to the Draft Article 2, International Law Association, 'Washington Conference: Legal Principles Relating to Climate Change' (2014), p. 4, https://papers .ssrn.com/sol3/papers.cfm?abstract_id=2461556 (accessed 16 Sept. 2019).

[22] Preamble, Marrakesh Agreement Establishing the World Trade Organization (WTO), 1867 UNTS 154; 33 ILM 1144 (1994). The Preamble opens with a recognition that trade and economic endeavours should be conducted 'while allowing for the optimal use of the world's resources in accordance with the objective of sustainable development, seeking both to protect and preserve the environment and to enhance the means for doing so in a manner consistent with their respective needs and concerns at different levels of economic development'.

[23] Agenda 21: Programme of Action for Sustainable Development, *supra* n. 7, s. 2.3(b); Rio Declaration on Environment and Development, UN Doc A/Conf. 151/26 (vol. I) 31 ILM 874 (1992), Principle 12; M. Cossy and G. Marceau, 'Institutional Challenges to Enhance Policy Co-Ordination – How WTO Rules Could Be Utilised to Meet Climate Objective?',

ZAKER AHMAD

The same also found expression in the operative part of the UNFCCC in the following terms:

> The Parties should cooperate to promote a supportive and open international economic system that would lead to sustainable economic growth and development in all Parties ... Measures taken to combat climate change, including unilateral ones, should not constitute a means of arbitrary or unjustifiable discrimination or a disguised restriction on international trade.[24]

Although a coherence building rule-making agenda has been put in place since 2001,[25] actual achievements remain meagre. The work initiated by the mandates granted in the Doha Ministerial Declaration, saw to some successful technical cooperation, information sharing, and mutual granting of observer status.[26] Such institutional cooperation only attained passive participation without any influence in agenda-setting.[27] The more important negotiation agenda of sketching out the relationship between the WTO and the multilateral environmental agreements (MEAs) has been in the doldrums, due to differences of views among the members.[28] Lack of alignment in members' interests also stalled the

---

in T. Cottier, O. Nartova, and S. Z. Bigdeli (eds.), *International Trade Regulation and the Mitigation of Climate Change: World Trade Forum* (Cambridge: Cambridge University Press, 2009), p. 372; L. Tamiotti and D. Ramos, 'Climate Change Mitigation and the WTO Framework', in P. Delimatsis (ed.), *Research Handbook on Climate Change and Trade Law* (Cheltenham, UK: Edward Elgar, 2016), pp. 508–9; Principles 3, 8, and 10, ILA, Washington Conference, *supra* n. 21; Principle 10 of the ILA report especially highlights the interrelationship of climate action with other regimes and therefore the need for mutually supportive development of all relevant international law.

[24] Art. 3.5, UNFCCC, *supra* n. 6.

[25] WTO, *Doha Ministerial Declaration*, WT/MIN(01)/DEC/1 (2001) para. 31. Paragraph 6 says that, 'the aims of upholding and safeguarding an open and non-discriminatory multilateral trading system, and acting for the protection of the environment and the promotion of sustainable development can and must be mutually supportive'.

[26] See generally, WTO, *Existing Forms of Cooperation and Information Exchange between UNEP/MEAs and the WTO*, TN/TE/S/2/Rev.2 (Geneva: WTO, 2007); WTO, *Matrix on Trade-Related Measures Pursuant to Selected Multilateral Environmental Agreements*, WT/CTE/W/160/Rev.8; TN/TE/S/5/Rev.6 (Geneva: WTO, 2017), pp. 134–50.

[27] The reason being that, as Marceau and Cossy identify, the institutions are a reflection of the members' common intent (*supra* n. 23, p. 376).

[28] To note the progress made so far, see Committee on Trade and Environment in Special Session, *Report by the Chairman, Ambassador Manuel A. J. Teehankee, to the Trade Negotiations Committee*, TN/TE/20 (Geneva: WTO, 2011); Cossy and Marceau, *supra* n. 23, pp. 389–92; H. Horn and P. C. Mavroidis, 'Multilateral Environmental Agreements in the WTO: Silence Speaks Volumes: MEAs in the WTO', *International Journal of Economic Theory*, 10(147) (2014), 148–50. These authors also see a 'strategic benefit' in

negotiations on an Environmental Goods Agreement.[29] Agreement on regulating illegal fisheries subsidies also remains forthcoming.[30]

In stark contrast, the dispute settlement arm of the WTO has steadily contributed to an understanding of the corpus of trade regulation in harmony with the environmental concerns. In earlier landmark cases like the *US–Gasoline* [31] and the *US–Shrimp*,[32] the Appellate Body (AB) has shown that the existing policy space in WTO can cover environmental protection interests.[33] In the *US–Gasoline* dispute, the AB did not reject the Panel's finding of clean air as an exhaustible natural resource within the meaning of Article XX(g) of GATT.[34] In the *US–Shrimp*, the AB's evolutionary interpretation of the same provision in the light of the goal of sustainable development and 'contemporary concerns facing the community of nations' solidified the mutual supportiveness standard in WTO jurisprudence.[35] In a later dispute, it was agreed that a country has a legitimate interest in not allowing its market to be used to sell

---

the negotiation deadlock. W. T. Douma, 'The WTO and Climate Change', in D. A. Farber and M. Peeters (eds.), *Climate Change Law* (Cheltenham, UK: Edward Elgar, 2016), p. 305.

[29] WTO, *Progress Made on Environmental Goods Agreement, Setting Stage for Further Talks*, www.wto.org/english/news_e/news16_e/ega_04dec16_e.htm (accessed 30 Dec. 2018). M. Wu, 'The WTO Environmental Goods Agreement: From Multilateralism to Plurilateralism', in Delimatsis, *supra* n. 23, p. 279.

[30] WTO, *Fisheries Subsidies: Ministerial Decision*, WT/MIN(17)/64 (2017).

[31] Appellate Body Report, *United States–Standards for Reformulated and Conventional Gasoline (US–Gasoline)*, adopted 20 May 1996, WT/DS2/AB/R. At page 17 of this report, the AB famously said, following Art. 3.2 of the Dispute Settlement Understanding, that the WTO rules do not stand in 'clinical isolation' from the public international law.

[32] Appellate Body Report, *United States–Import Prohibition of Certain Shrimp and Shrimp Products (US–Shrimp)*, adopted 6 Nov. 1998, WT/DS58/AB/R.

[33] See, for example, the treatment of the AB's interpretation of the covered agreements in the light of environmental commitments in the famous fragmentation report, Study Group of the International Law Commission, 'Fragmentation of International Law: Difficulties Arising from the Diversification and Expansion of International Law – Finalized by Martti Koskenniemi' (UNGA 2006) A/CN.4/L.682; A/CN.4/L.702, pp. 223–8.

[34] Panel Report, *United States–Standards for Reformulated and Conventional Gasoline (US–Gasoline)*, adopted 20 May 1996, WT/DS2/R, paras. 6.36–6.37; Appellate Body Report, *US–Gasoline, supra* n. 31, p. 14.

[35] Appellate Body Report, *US–Shrimp, supra* n. 32, paras. 128–34. The AB drew support from, among others, the Brundtland commission report, the Law of the Sea Convention, the Rio Declaration, the Convention of Biological Diversity, as well as a resolution on development assistance adopted in relation to conservation of migratory species.

104   ZAKER AHMAD

products that adversely affected dolphins beyond its territory.[36] In that
dispute, parties did not even contest that dolphins are exhaustible natural
resources.[37] More recently, the *Canada–Renewable Energy* dispute has
also seen some degree of deference being paid to a member's policy
choice to internalise climate change-related externalities.[38]

This brief account suffices to show that far from being an isolated part
of public international law, the WTO laws are dynamic and capable of
change. It is submitted that to the extent new rules are needed to entwine
the interests of free trade, climate mitigation, and technology diffusion,
the biggest challenge is to find a path that accommodates different
members' interests. Furthermore, to the extent the understanding of
current rules can be adapted to the concern of LCT diffusion, existing
jurisprudence welcomes such an approach. It remains to be seen whether
or how the doctrine of Common Concern actually fits into these two
areas. Towards that end, it is first of all necessary to specify what the
concept entails in the trade context – and the following paragraphs focus
on this.

2.2.2   The Doctrine of Common Concern as a Guide to Enhance Climate Action

2.2.2.1   Meaning of Common Concern as a Treaty Expression

As a legal expression, though the meaning of common concern is not yet
entirely settled, it repeatedly finds itself in the treaty vernacular and is a
frequent subject of scholarly contemplation.[39] With respect to the climate
law, common concern of humankind is indeed a global rallying call for
cooperation and common responsibility. One prevailing view treats this norm
as a structural vessel that allows mingling of several notions like sustainable

---

[36] Appellate Body Report, *United States–Measures Concerning the Importation, Marketing and Sale of Tuna and Tuna Products (US–Tuna II)*, adopted 16 May 2012, WT/DS381/AB/RW, pp. 95–96, 116–18.

[37] Appellate Body Report, *United States–Measures Concerning the Importation, Marketing and Sale of Tuna and Tuna Products–Recourse to Article 21.5 of the DSU by Mexico (US–Tuna II (21.5))*, adopted 20 Nov. 2015, WT/DS381/AB/RW, p. 120.

[38] Appellate Body Report, *Canada–Certain Measures Affecting the Renewable Energy Generation Sector/Canada–Measures Relating to the Feed-in Tariff Program (Canada–Renewable Energy)*, adopted 24 May 2013, WT/DS412/AB/R; WT/DS426/AB/R, paras. 5.174–5.179, 5.185–5.186, 5.189.

[39] For a general exposition, see Chapter 1 in this volume, pp. 11–24; S. Murase, *Second Report on the Protection of the Atmosphere*, A/CN.4/681 (Geneva: International Law Commission, 2015), pp. 17–24.

development, duty to cooperate, and equity.[40] This may fuel contemplation as to whether any normative content is exclusively attributable to this norm in isolation from the mix. Nevertheless, the iconic significance and the perceived utility of the expression to the state parties with regard to climate change were reconfirmed in 2015 when both the Paris Agreement and the conference of parties (COP) decision adopting the same alluded to it.[41]

Of course, the core meaning of common concern has seen some, if not universal agreement,[42] over the past thirty years. Three elements of the significance of common concern are particularly relevant for this chapter, namely: a general albeit unallocated responsibility upon all; a call to cooperate between actors at different levels; a moderate intrusion into the sovereign domain of the state, in the sense of a commitment not to worsen the concern.[43] This cautiously optimistic theme is repeated in most scholarly deliberations.[44] For example, the wording of the pre-ambular reference in the Paris Agreement reads as if parties' acknowledgement of the common concern has a sort of triggering effect to taking action.[45] Similarly, the ILA, while consolidating applicable legal principles of climate change law, accords the notion a meta-normative status – invocation of which is not itself consequential, but draws other consequential norms into action. Eventually, common concern influences all states' responsibility to take action to develop an effective and equitable cooperative regime.[46] The ILA envisages a harmonious

---

[40] See Chapter 9 in this volume, p. 436. Also, see the position of the International Law Association (ILA) as detailed in the next paragraph.

[41] See Chapter 1 in this volume, pp. 14, 23–4.

[42] Qualification in the statement is due to the debate in the International Law Commission in this regard. For details, see Chapter 1 in this volume, pp. 14–5, 23–4.

[43] M. K. Tolba, 'The Implications of the "Common Concern of Mankind" Concept on Global Environmental Issues', *Revista IIDH*, 13(1) (1991). For a related and thought-provoking discussion on the limits of the distributive autonomy of a sovereign, see Chapter 4 in this volume, pp. 218–22.

[44] Chapter 1 in this volume addresses it comprehensively (see pp. 17–24); cf. Chapter 9, pp. 435–6, 438.

[45] The relevant part of the recitals in the Preamble of the Paris Agreement, as well as the COP 21 decision adopting the Agreement, go like this: '[a]cknowledging that climate change is a common concern of humankind, Parties should, when taking action to climate change', and continues highlighting additional obligations that should also be taken into account. The novel part that is worth noting here is that the mention of common concern and climate action serves as a contextual part in the sentence, in a way that one flows out of the other.

[46] Draft Art. 2, ILA, Washington Conference, *supra* n. 21. See also paras. 3–4 of commentary to the Draft Art. 3 (Sustainable Development), paras. 2–3 of commentary to the Draft Art. 5 (Common but Differentiated Responsibility and Respective Capabilities). Draft Arts. 8 and

interaction between the common concern and sustainable development by suggesting that although the expression of common concern indicates the additional urgency of action, such actions need to take place within the broader context of sustainable development.[47]

The argument here is that there is a strong case for assigning to common concern a meaning which is at least capable of generating the legal push required to resolve the problem in question effectively. Otherwise, functionally, one risks translating the international community's repeated plea to this concept as a futile endeavour. One should recall that the avoidance of inutility is a key tenet of treaty interpretation.[48] Especially with regard to issues touching upon climate change, the accepted general and so far unallocated responsibility to address a concern should be further strengthened to match the level of ambition and action required to solve the crisis. This is the role of the proposed doctrine of Common Concern of Humankind as laid out in the opening contribution.[49] Instead of refusing to signify a normative import to the notion, the doctrine of Common Concern does exactly the opposite. It proposes a framework of responsibility that could usefully be read into the notion, potentially to resolve not only the climate inaction problem but also other cooperation failures of comparable significance. It is agreed that even within the accepted domain of common concern, the doctrine is aspirational to a degree. But such aspiration is legitimate due to its effectiveness in bridging the gap between the positive and the normative,[50] in a fact-based, objective fashion.

This chapter understands the expression of Common Concern in a way that combines positive and normative elements. It is well agreed that the expression itself is a call for climate action through effective and

---

10 further spell out the dimensions of cooperation, especially the interconnections between trade and investment regimes.

[47] Para. 5 of the commentary to Draft Art. 3 (ibid.).

[48] One iteration of the principle, i.e. *effet utile*, calls for consideration of all the terms of the treaty, as a whole, having meaning and effect. Richard K. Gardiner, *Treaty Interpretation* (2nd ed., Oxford: Oxford University Press, 2015), pp. 66, 179–80; Isabelle Van Damme, *Treaty Interpretation by the WTO Appellate Body* (Oxford: Oxford University Press 2009), pp. 278–81.

[49] See Chapter 1 in this volume, pp. 24–6.

[50] A. Vermeule, 'Connecting Positive and Normative Legal Theory', *University of Pennsylvania Journal of Constitutional Law*, 10(387) (2007), 390. Vermeule describes this approach as a 'prescriptive' theory, i.e. a claim about the best means to adopt, given a stipulated end. The doctrine of Common Concern takes a normatively agreed goal (e.g. limiting global temperature rise within acceptable level) and suggests a suitable legal framework to attain it.

equitable cooperation guided by the commitment to sustainable development. In addition, the doctrine individualises some aspects of the common responsibility in the form of duties at the domestic level, implementable, in extreme circumstances, by threat or application of economic force. This is the gist of the tripartite normative consequences: (1) cooperation, (2) homework, and (3) compliance through counter-measures. Indeed, the doctrine would find acceptance over time through a process of claims and responses.[51] To that end, the current exercise is but one small step.

2.2.2.2   Effect of the Doctrine in the Trade Regime

The recognition and acceptance of the doctrinal proposition of Common Concern are of particular relevance to clarify, as well as improve, the terms on which the trade and the climate legal regimes will attain deeper integration.[52] Active persuasion of such an agenda is important; because, despite trade being an important conveyor of LCTs and recognition that trade rules do not stand in 'clinical isolation', it is true nonetheless that these treaty-based regimes are characteristically different in terms of interests pursued, priorities maintained, and the underlying assumptions they are built upon. The extent to which the climate legal regime may strengthen its influence upon the trade regime via 'Common Concern', is related to a clear perception of the scope of trade-related actions the doctrine calls for. The latter is an exercise in elucidation, undertaken below, to outline the shared domain of Common Concern and trade.[53] Only within that space, would the proposed normative consequences operate.

Clean Technology Diffusion as a Common Concern in Trade Law   While scoping the domain of Common Concern and trade from a technology diffusion perspective, it ought to be noted that the treaty regimes in

---

[51] See Chapter 1 in this volume, pp. 26–9; G. Nolte, 'The International Law Commission and Community Interests', in Eyal Benvenisti and Georg Nolte (eds.), *Community Interests Across International Law* (Oxford: Oxford University Press, 2018), p. 103.

[52] An example on point is the way principle of sustainable development has integrated economic growth and environmental protection concerns.

[53] See Chapter 9 in this volume. The authors of the chapter emphasise the importance of delineation of the scope of special legal consequences. In addition, they warn that, absent such clarity, state consent to international rule making may be trivialised (p. 434).

question operate under different default perceptions of the market.[54] The non-reciprocal regime[55] of climate change is premised upon the shared value of climate as a global public good (GPG).[56] This is further coupled with the understanding that the collective action failure[57] to maintain the optimal climatic standards is contributed to by, inter alia, market failures, especially in not being able to control emission-intensive productions, processes, and consumption. From the climate point of view, therefore, the private market status quo is in an imperfect equilibrium, deserving correction through intervention.

In contrast, the underlying assumption in international trade law is a liberal one. As a reciprocal regime, it assumes, and reasonably so, that unfettered markets are most often the best tool for optimal allocation of resources. This is manifested in the strict prohibition of protectionist non-tariff barriers, promotion of tariff liberalisation and non-discrimination, with limited policy-motivated and prior agreed carve-outs.

Magnifying the import of the climate protection motivation in trade law through the lens of Common Concern would, therefore, require updating of the abovementioned foundational assumptions. It would be as follows. While most often free markets are optimal, cases truly involving the concern of climate change would require positive interventions to correct market failures and attain comparable levels of optimality.

The Common Concern doctrine will demand that the rules of international trade have a safe space for such interventions so that those are not perceived as distorting the free market. Scope of such a safe space would be determined by twofold criteria. First, any measure falling within that space must bear a direct linkage with the normative propositions of the Common Concern doctrine. Second, and obviously, the measures ought to be trade-related to come within the jurisdictional

---

[54] J. N. Bhagwati, 'Reflections on Climate Change and Trade', *Brookings Trade Forum* (2008), 171; A. Porges and T. L. Brewer, *Climate Change and a Renewable Energy Scale-Up: Responding to Challenges Posed to the WTO* (Geneva: ICTSD/WEF, 2013), p. 2.

[55] See Chapter 1 in this volume, p. 8.

[56] I. Kaul, I. Grunberg, and M. A. Stern, 'Defining Global Public Goods', in I. Kaul, I. Grunberg and M. A. Stern (eds.), *Global Public Goods: International Cooperation in the 21st Century* (Oxford: Oxford University Press, 1999), p. 2. A GPG differs from a global common in that it requires positive effort to produce and maintain a GPG, due to its dual characteristics of non-excludability and non-rivalry.; E. B. Weiss, *The Commons, Public Goods and International Law* (UN Web TV, 2017), http://webtv.un.org/search/edith-brown-weiss-on-the-commons-public-goods-and-international-law/5768442393001/?term=edith brown weiss&sort=date (accessed 23 May 2018).

[57] See Chapter 1 in this volume, pp. 44–6.

scope of the WTO. Together it would operate as a double-threshold gateway. To illustrate, contribution to international institutional finance for technology diffusion is a common concern, but it is not trade-related and so falls outside the scope. However, carbon pricing through a tax has a positive implication on the diffusion of LCT and it is trade-related – therefore falling within the scope of Common Concern in the trade regime.

In sum, the Common Concern doctrine places the urgency of trade-related climate action under special attention. The specific contribution of the doctrine with respect to trade law would be to develop an exclusive dialogue focusing on trade and climate change, marked not only by the urgency but also a perception of shared benefit. Such a narrative would call for effective measures to be taken to resolve the market-related problems regarding the diffusion of LCTs, among others. The contours of such actions are discussed in the next paragraphs.

Normative Influence on Domestic and International Trade Policy   It is undeniable that the legal consequence of the doctrine of Common Concern of Humankind can only ensue following a wide acceptance of the norm along the proposed lines and its internalisation at different levels of governance. This is the necessary process of claims and responses, as mentioned. However, even during the maturing process, the doctrine has important utility as an analytical and framing tool; one that supplies metrics for conceptualising important but unresolved shared problems and also suggests avenues of response.

Upon recognition, Common Concern would be able to nudge WTO members' domestic actions to facilitate diffusion of LCTs. It can also inform legal interpretations in settlements of disputes and inspire trade rules conducive to the diffusion of climate technology. As a substantive legal norm, the Common Concern–based framework is proposed to operate in a prescriptive fashion; implementing a three-pronged, inter-dependent set of desired actions – namely to cooperate, to resolve the concern domestically, and also to enforce the same across borders in deserving situations.[58]

As part of the Common Concern–based approach, cooperation to facilitate climate technology diffusion ought to take place between relevant actors, and institutions. The immediate and commonly agreed

---

[58] Ibid., pp. 59–78.

consequence of the recognition of a 'Concern' is an emergence of collective responsibility to cooperate, as well as coordination within and across institutions.[59] A common responsibility to cooperate is important as it does not yet independently exist in international law.[60] Regarding climate technology diffusion and WTO law, cooperation can be fruitful to cement the position of the doctrine within the body of WTO law, creation of a new negotiation mandate, or to develop a stronger normative justification to take domestic action.

Influencing states' adoption of domestic trade policy actions for clean technology diffusion would be the most consequential implication of the doctrine's implementation. As the next section illustrates, there exist untapped opportunities to take situation-specific trade policy measures that would greatly facilitate the flow of technology-embedded trade between countries. It has been so far agreed that there is a limitation upon states' exercise of authority in a way that aggravates a common concern. The imposition of a positive duty upon states in pursuance of the concern is, therefore, more aspirational, and so better achieved when such actions are framed in a way that is mutually beneficial. The limitation upon permanent sovereignty[61] in relation to common concern would also prohibit states from taking climate worsening measures where better alternatives would be available.

Within a well-recognised and strongly established framework of Common Concern, non-cooperation, or a wilful absence of diligent behaviour from the stakeholders can be lawfully met with unilateral countermeasures. In the domain of international trade, this translates to unilateral trade measures to enforce compliance with the Common

---

[59] T. Cottier, P. Aerni, B. Karapinar, S. Matteotti, J. de Sépibus, and A. Shingal, 'The Principle of Common Concern and Climate Change', *Archiv des Völkerrechts*, 52(3) (2014), 316–18; D. French, 'Common Concern, Common Heritage and Other Global(-Ising) Concepts: Rhetorical Devices, Legal Principles or a Fundamental Challenge?', in M. Bowman, P. Davies, and E. Goodwin (eds.), *Research Handbook on Biodiversity and Law* (Cheltenham, UK: Edward Elgar, 2016), pp. 351–2; Murase, *supra* n. 39, paras. 37–40; Chapter 1 in this volume, pp. 18–20.

[60] See Chapter 1 in this volume, pp. 59–60.

[61] Weiss, *supra* n. 56; French, ibid., pp. 340, 342; J. Brunnée, 'Common Areas, Common Heritage, and Common Concern', in D. Bodansky, J. Brunnée, and E. Hey (eds.), *The Oxford Handbook of International Environmental Law* (Oxford: Oxford University Press, 2007), p. 566; D. French, 'A Reappraisal of Sovereignty in the Light of Global Environmental Concerns', *Legal Studies*, 21 (2001), 376, 398–9; F. Biermann, '"Common Concern of Humankind": The Emergence of a New Concept of International Environmental Law', *Archiv des Völkerrechts*, 34 (1996), 430–1.

Concern doctrine. Though promising, this aspect of the doctrine deserves deeper analysis, as well as careful design before becoming effective. While this chapter does not take up this issue at length, the expert comments at the end of the volume, as well as the contribution by Iryna Bogdanova (Chapter 5) are illuminating in this regard.

Like sustainable development, Common Concern can also 'add colour and texture' to the commitments of the covered agreements.[62] Serving as a contextual norm in the climate regime, the common concern of humankind indeed will supply interpretive context[63] in case the WTO consistency of any trade-related technology diffusion measure is put to question. When used as an aid to interpretation, the doctrine can be expected to help identify the really deserving settings where trade measures should positively intervene to facilitate technology diffusion, as distinct from measures guided by protectionist intent. Use of the notion during interpretation would also help ensure and deepen the sustainable development-focused mutually supportive understanding of the trade and the climate legal regimes. The concepts of common concern and sustainable development could, therefore, be understood in a mutually congruent fashion.

2.3 Outline of a Common Concern–Based Technology Diffusion Narrative

Pursuing a trade policy agenda for the diffusion of LCT powered by the doctrine of Common Concern would require a substantial revision (hence, a new narrative) of the current approach to technology diffusion in the trade field. This section highlights that not only is it important to address market-related barriers through trade policy actions but also that it is best done accommodating the interests of the involved stakeholders in a mutually beneficial fashion. Therefore, going beyond the traditional focus on intellectual property (IP) rights, it is important to look at the opportunities to address price competitiveness issues, supply appropriate incentives, and ensure easier access to finance regarding the LCTs.

---

[62] Appellate Body Report, *US–Shrimp*, *supra* n. 32, para. 153.

[63] Pursuant to Art. 3.2, Understanding on Rules and Procedures Governing the Settlement of Disputes (DSU), in Marrakesh Agreement Establishing the World Trade Organization, Annex 2, 1869 UNTS 401 (1994); Art. 31, Vienna Convention on the Law of Treaties (VCLT), 1155 UNTS 331 (1969).

2.3.1 Trade-Related Barriers to LCT Diffusion

Despite the growing evidence on the need of market reforms for clean technology diffusion, the issue has not successfully been taken up by either the trade or the climate regime. Technology transfer is hotly debated in both institutions, but the approach to it is markedly different.[64] Even after being one of the core building blocks in the climate regime,[65] technology development and transfer discussions have never spilt over into related trade issues. It is true that early on, there were some movements in this regard, underscoring the beneficial role of fair-trade policies and market-based positive incentives (e.g. tax preferences, export credits) creating enabling environments for technology transfer.[66] But the prioritised need to ensure adequate finance for technology support activities and a lingering scepticism towards market-based approaches[67] has stemmed progress along that avenue. Enabling environment and addressing market barriers, however, found its way back to the new Technology Framework in the Paris Agreement.[68] In the trade regime, technology transfer has remained a very general and politically contested theme between the developed and the developing members, adding very little benefit overall.[69] However, there are indeed some opinions

---

[64] The differences between and the resulting misalignment of trade and climate regime is under-researched in literature. One exception is S. Humphreys, 'Structural Ambiguity: Technology Transfer in Three Regimes', in M. A. Young (ed.), *Regime Interaction in International Law* (Cambridge: Cambridge University Press, 2012), p. 175.

[65] Decision 1/CP13 'Report of the Conference of the Parties on Its Thirteenth Session' (2007) FCCC/CP/2007/6/Add.1 para. 1, 1(d), 1(e); Decision 1/CP21 Report of the Conference of the Parties on Its Twenty-First Session (2015) FCCC/CP/2015/10/Add.2, paras. 66–71; Art. 10, Paris Agreement, *supra* n. 12.

[66] Annex to Decision 4/CP7 'Report of the Conference of the Parties on Its Seventh Session' (2001) FCCC/CP/2001/13/Add.1, para. 14.

[67] H. de Coninck and A. Sagar, 'Technology Development and Transfer (Article 10)', in D. Klein, M. P. Carazo, M. Doelle, J. Bulmer, and A. Higham (eds.), *The Paris Agreement on Climate Change: Analysis and Commentary* (Oxford: Oxford University Press, 2017), pp. 262–3.

[68] Technology framework under Art. 10, para. 4, of the Paris Agreement, *Meeting of the Parties to the Paris Agreement on the Third Part of Its First Session*, Decision 15/CMA1, Annex, FCCC/PA/CMA/2018/3/Add2 (2019). As a key theme of the Technology Framework, creating enabling environment would entail, among others, '[a]ssisting governments in playing a key role in fostering private sector involvement by designing and implementing policies, regulations and standards that create enabling environments and favourable market conditions for climate technologies'.

[69] S. Moon, *Does TRIPS Art. 66.2 Encourage Technology Transfer to LDCs?* (Geneva: ICTSD, 2008), p. 2; S. Moon, *Meaningful Technology Transfer to the LDCs: A Proposal for a*

TRADE-RELATED MEASURES AND LCTS 113

calling for reform beyond the TRIPS Agreement to facilitate the flow of LCTs.[70]

A long-term trade policy agenda for removing technology diffusion barriers must take existing empirical insights into account. For example, market-related barriers are found to be the most dominant group of obstacle in the developing countries' self-assessment of mitigation technology needs completed under the UNFCCC framework.[71] This is followed by the problem of capacity and skills shortage. The identified market-related barriers most often include high cost of the technology and availability of cheaper but more polluting alternatives, affordability problems, difficulty in finding finance due to lack of interest shown by the private sectors (e.g. banks and other financiers), underdeveloped markets, irregularity of supply, etc.[72] Independent scholarly research regarding specific LCTs or sectors also come to similar findings. Policy measures in the form of feed-in tariff (FIT) schemes, tax breaks, subsidisation, sourcing commitments, and standardisation schemes have been found to be very effective to expand renewable energy markets.[73] Easy availability of finance to acquire new technologies has also been found to be very helpful.[74] Based on the clean energy technology diffusion

---

Monitoring Mechanism for TRIPS Article 66.2 (Geneva: ICTSD, 2011), p. 9; Atik, *supra* n. 10, p. 608.

[70] T. L. Brewer and A. Falke, 'International Transfers of Climate-Friendly Technologies: How the World Trade System Matters', in Ockwell and Mallett, *supra* n. 4, p. 288; R. Melendez-Ortiz and M. Sugathan, 'Enabling the Energy Transition and Scale-up of Clean Energy Technologies: Options for the Global Trade System – Synthesis of the Policy Options', *Journal of World Trade*, 51(6) (2017) 933.

[71] UNFCCC Secretariat, *Third Synthesis Report on Technology Needs Identified by Parties Not Included in Annex I to the Convention*, FCCC/SBSTA/2013/INF.7 (2013), pp. 25–8; S. Traerup, L. Greersen, and C. Kundsen, 'Mapping Barriers and Enabling Environments in Technology Needs Assessments, Nationally Determined Contributions, and Technical Assistance of the Climate Technology Centre and Network', background paper TEC/2018/17/4 (2018), https://orbit.dtu.dk/files/164669703/Barriers_and_Enablers_to_tt_25Sept.pdf (accessed 16 Sept. 2019)

[72] Traerup et al., *supra* n. 71.

[73] J. I. Lewis, 'Technology Acquisition and Innovation in the Developing World: Wind Turbine Development in China and India', *Studies in Comparative International Development*, 42(3–4) (2007), 208; J. H. Barton, *Intellectual Property and Access to Clean Energy Technologies in Developing Countries* (Geneva: ICTSD, 2007), www.iprsonline.org/New%202009/CC%20Barton.pdf (accessed 19 Sept. 2019).

[74] P. Pal and G. Sethi, 'Case Study: Technology Transfer of Energy-Efficient Technologies among Small and Medium Sized Enterprises in India', in Ockwell and Mallett, *supra* n. 4.

experience in China, Gallagher argued for market formation policies[75] to resolve economy-wide market failures in the forms of higher cost, lack of access to capital, and careless business practice. Such policies are necessary because the market does not value the benefits of the technologies into costs.[76] Economic measures with trade impact are relevant to the extent those can be put to work for attaining the market reform goals.

Studies do not find a consistent relation between patent protection flexibilities and the diffusion of LCTs. This goes against a general conviction held in the trade field, enforced by examples from the pharmaceuticals sector, that technology transfer is to do primarily with flexible IP rights, especially access to patents, and related measures of support from North to South. Studies on different clean energy technologies suggest that exponential rise[77] in research and innovation in this area has also brought high competition and anti-monopolistic market structure within the sectors.[78] Moreover, some recent studies show that firms from developing countries (e.g. Chinese and South Korean) are successfully taking the lead in certain clean technology sectors.[79] Nevertheless, in a handful of cutting-edge technologies (e.g. hybrid electric vehicles, latest generation gas turbines), patent protections can prevent access to technology by interested firms.[80] That apart, legal security of IP rights domestically is a contributing factor influencing the willingness of technology owners to out-license the

---

[75] According to Gallagher, market formation policies are predictable and stable, medium to long terms policy measures to support markets for clean technologies. Although it is difficult to say exactly which exact policy should work best, the author proposes a range of possible measures, including research development and demonstration support, carbon tax, a low-interest loan fund. K. S. Gallagher, *The Globalization of Clean Energy Technology: Lessons from China* (Cambridge, MA: MIT Press, 2014), pp. 97–101, 172–3.

[76] Ibid., pp. 167–75.

[77] A. Dechezleprêtre, M. Glachant, I. Haščič, N. Johnston, and Y. Ménière, 'Invention and Transfer of Climate Change-Mitigation Technologies: A Global Analysis', *Review of Environmental Economics and Policy*, 5(1) (2011), 109; B. Lee, I. Iliev, and F. Preston, *Who Owns Our Low Carbon Future?: Intellectual Property and Energy Technologies* (London: Chatham House, 2009).

[78] Barton, *supra* n. 73; UNEP, EPO, and ICTSD, 'Patents and Clean Energy: Bridging the Gap between Evidence and Policy' (Geneva: EPO/ICTSD/UNEP, 2010). It should be noted that the findings are limited to sectors. These technologies are not market dominant when compared to non-renewable technologies.

[79] S. Helm, Q. Tannock, and I. Iliev, 'Renewable Energy Technology: Evolution and Policy Implications – Evidence from Patent Literature', *Global Challenges Report* (Geneva: WIPO, 2014).

[80] J. Watson and R. Byrne, 'Low-Carbon Innovation in China: The Role of International Technology Transfer', Ockwell and Mallett, *supra* n. 4, pp. 79–80; Gallagher, *supra* n. 75, pp. 57, 76.

same.[81] Barton explains that unlike the pharmaceuticals sector, which influences developing countries attitude towards IP, the clean energy sector is not amenable to patent-based competition.[82] Therefore access to patents in most cases is not a great hindrance to access the technology, though of course, more clarification is required.[83]

2.3.2   The Fundamentals of a New Narrative

Based on the brief empirical observation, it is submitted that a trade regime moved by the Common Concern doctrine, should address the market barriers that prevent the diffusion of LCT. The doctrine would call for concrete action to tackle negative externality related price differences between similar traded goods and also to curb emission-intensive production processes in the global manufacturing hubs. As flanking measures, such approach would also, among others, promote policies that reform the markets for the benefit of clean technologies, attract investments in relevant sectors, supply incentives, as well as support technology exports. Simply put, the goal would be to shape the markets in a way that innovation in or adoption of LCTs makes more commercial sense everywhere in the world.[84]

Improvement of the cross-border flows of LCTs while averting the possible onset of any significant trade displacement resulting therefrom would require effective cooperation between the developed and developing stakeholders. The new narrative of the role of trade for clean technology diffusion is proposed to contain three key features. First is complementarity. For domestic trade policy actions to have an impact on the diffusion of technologies across the border, it is necessary that the measures taken complement each other. Second is ensuring mutual benefit. The stakeholders would be motivated to cooperate and take action when the common agenda reflect their respective interests (e.g. expansion of domestic technology export). Lastly, there must be an adequate reflection of the common but differentiated responsibility (CBDR) principle in the agenda, especially in the form of non-reciprocal support to the developing countries in need.

In practice, it is possible to envisage such a scheme as interactions between roughly four categories of stakeholder countries with

---

[81]   UNEP, EPO, and ICTSD, *supra* n. 78, pp. 58–60.

[82]   Barton, *supra* n. 73, pp. 4–5.

[83]   A. Abdel-Latif, 'Intellectual Property Rights and the Transfer of Climate Change Technologies: Issues, Challenges, and Way Forward', *Climate Policy*, 15 (2015).

[84]   Atik, *supra* n. 10, pp. 608–9.

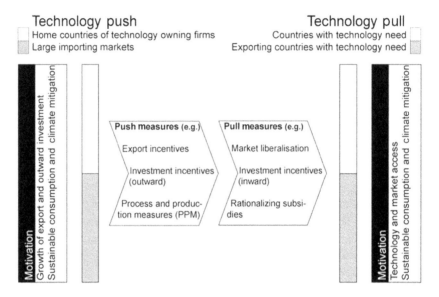

Figure 2.2 Complementarities in trade-related technology diffusion

corresponding sets of interests. Stakeholders who are technology receivers (right-hand side of Figure 2.2) can be of two kinds. The common identity between them would be that both have firms that need technology upgrades. These countries may as well be participants of the Technology Framework under the Paris Agreement. However, the key difference between these countries is that some operate as global manufacturing sources and therefore can be further influenced by process and production measures (PPMs) adopted by the importing countries. The others are countries that are less integrated into the global trading system. Depending on how much dependent on trade the technology receiving countries are, use of PPMs may even adversely affect them. Domestically, these categories of countries can engage in 'technology pull' measures (i.e. creating economic conditions that are especially inviting for the LCTs).

The other two categories of stakeholders are countries where the technology-leading firms belong and countries that have strong market power to influence technology receivers. In many cases, there will be an overlap between these groups. What is common for these two groups is that they can employ trade-related policies that would create a 'technology push', either through measures that incentivise export of LCTs or through PPM measures. This is the left-hand side Figure 2.2.

Figure 2.2 also illustrates the need for policy complementarity for effective diffusion of LCTs. To give a simple example, promoting technology exports and investment outflows as a push policy would not be effective if the receiving country heavily subsidises fossil fuels. The figure also shows how trade measures, even when taken to facilitate LCT diffusion would also serve other domestic economic interests. As it would not be realistic to assume that states would be guided by purely altruistic motives while employing push-or-pull measures, it is important that economic benefits arising therefrom are evenly distributed.

Putting the outlined narrative into effect within the WTO would first of all require a platform for cooperation and exchange of information between members. This would then facilitate the adoption of complementary and mutually beneficial trade measures. Though measures that would eventually fit this bill would depend to a degree on specific country contexts, some indications could be provided already. For example, countries leading in technology can promote out-licensing and investment outflows through providing export credits,[85] or export-based tax rebates.[86] Such promotion measures should also be complemented with facilitative steps in the technology destination markets (e.g. special price support schemes like FITs). Lowering barriers on goods and services trade that relate to the spread of LCTs makes sense across the board. So does rationalisation of domestic subsidies (i.e. while promoting climate mitigation sectors, supports to fossil-fuel-based activities should be gradually phased out). Carbon pricing, in particular, is a sensible instrument for all countries.[87] For some very specific technologies, patent protection related flexibilities (e.g. compulsory licence), or other feasible ways to access modern technologies could be explored. All these different sets of measures together can help grow and sustain the market of LCTs globally. Green government procurement can play a beneficial role in

---

[85] R. Stavins, J. Zou, T. Brewer, et al., 'International Cooperation: Agreements and Instruments', in Climate Change 2014: Mitigation of Climate Change: Working Group III Contribution to the Fifth Assessment Report of the Intergovernmental Panel on Climate Change (Cambridge: Cambridge University Press, 2014), pp. 1035–6; C. T. Less and S. McMillan, Achieving the Successful Transfer of Environmentally Sound Technologies: Trade-Related Aspects, Working Paper 2005–2 (2005), pp. 27–8, www.oecd.org/trade/envtrade/35837552.pdf (accessed 23 Apr. 2018).

[86] B. Hoekman, K. E. Maskus, and K. Saggi, 'Transfer of Technology to Developing Countries: Unilateral and Multilateral Policy Options', World Bank Policy Research Working Paper (2004), pp. 21–2, http://papers.ssrn.com/sol3/papers.cfm?abstract_id=610377 (accessed 19 Sept. 2019).

[87] Further analysis of this measure is carried out in the next section.

LCT acquisition. With respect to issues where the WTO is not the primary forum, it would be necessary that the organisation has an appropriate mandate to coordinate across institutions.

2.4 WTO Law and Common Concern Motivated Measures: A Closer Look

This section serves to take the argument a level deeper on select issues. Assuming that states may face WTO-inconsistency-related challenge while taking measures to pursue the Common Concern-inspired technology diffusion agenda; the target here is to provide a pre-indication of the possible fault lines. The utility of this exercise lies in bringing more clarity to the abstract contours of trade and technology diffusion mismatches. This, in turn, would allow pondering over an additional question – that is, what value would the Common Concern doctrine be to resolve any legal inconsistency with WTO law?

In specific terms, the current section selects two measures from the repertory of possible Common Concern-inspired trade action and analyses their WTO-consistency. One chosen measure is trade restrictive (i.e. carbon pricing) and the other is an incentive measure (export credits). The analyses are important not only for their intrinsic merit but also for their illustration of the normative import of Common Concern in practical settings.

2.4.1 The Case of Carbon Pricing with Revenue Recycling

2.4.1.1 Description

Pricing of the GHG emission is probably the single most effective step for climate mitigation. Keeping LCT diffusion as the focus, what is proposed here is a twofold step. One is to introduce a price for GHG emission occurring due to production and the other is the utilisation of the revenue earned for technology upgrades. Importantly, the latter part should not only apply domestically but also across borders – with respect to developing countries having a manifested need for technology support.[88] The proposition is based on the assumption that as emission

---

[88] There are many instances worldwide where carbon tax revenue is used domestically for technology upgrade, climate finance, or energy efficiency. See Partnership for Market Readiness, *Carbon Tax Guide: A Handbook for Policy Makers* (Washington, DC: World Bank, 2017), p. 126; K. Holzer, *Carbon-Related Border Adjustment and WTO Law* (Cheltenham, UK: Edward Elgar, 2014), pp. 236–8. This chapter does not deal with the

pricing would help trigger effective demand for less polluting technologies, related revenue recycle would also facilitate meeting the same. The overall results should be increased flow and uptake of LCTs.

An optimal carbon price can be implemented through a tax, or a tariff. While traditionally a tax or a permit trading system is considered fit for the purpose, the former is indeed more straightforward than the latter.[89] Also, a carbon tax is more certain to generate revenue than a cap-and-trade system. This section also showcases the opportunity of using tariffs as a pricing tool instead of a tax.[90] In both cases, compliance with trade rules become a relevant concern when emission pricing allegedly affect imports. With respect to tariffs, impact on imports is the essential characteristic of the measure. With respect to a carbon tax, imports can be brought under the coverage through border adjustment. In literature, border adjustment of a carbon tax has received greater attention[91] compared to the idea of introducing a carbon tariff measure.[92]

Between the options of tariff and tax, there are shared characteristics, also key differences that merit consideration to make an appropriate

---

ways in which such revenue recycling should take place, but it is nonetheless possible to think of a scheme with involvement of the relevant entities, e.g. the Green Climate Fund. A country's LCT-related needs are discernible from its economic position, as well as the technology needs assessments (TNAs) reports, when existing.

[89] Partnership for Market Readiness, *supra* n. 88, pp. 27–33; P. C. Cramton, D. J. C. MacKay, and A. Ockenfels (eds.), *Global Carbon Pricing: The Path to Climate Cooperation* (Cambridge, MA: MIT Press, 2017).

[90] A carbon tariff would operate as a differential tariff scheme for designated product categories, based on the emission footprints. Imposition of carbon tariff would call for either further deconsolidation of tariff lines, or a cooperative negotiation on deconsolidating the relevant tariff lines (T. Cottier, O. Nartova, and A. Shingal, 'The Potential of Tariff Policy for Climate Change Mitigation: Legal and Economic Analysis', *Journal of World Trade*, 48(5) (2014), 1020–1).

[91] To mention just a few from the vast literature: J. S. Odell, *Our Alarming Climate Crisis Demands Border Adjustments Now* (Geneva: ICTSD, 2018); J. P. Trachtman, *WTO Law Constraints on Border Tax Adjustment and Tax Credit Mechanisms to Reduce the Competitive Effects of Carbon Taxes* (Washington, DC: Resources for the Future, 2016); Holzer, *supra* n. 88; J. Pauwelyn, 'Carbon Leakage Measures and Border Tax Adjustments under WTO Law', in G. Van Calster and D. Prevost (eds.), *Research Handbook on Environment, Health and the WTO* (Cheltenham, UK: Edward Elgar, 2013); G. C. Hufbauer, S. Charnovitz, and J. Kim, *Global Warming and the World Trading System* (Washington, DC: Peterson Institute for International Economics, 2009), chs. 1–2; R. Howse and A. Eliason, 'Domestic and International Strategies to Address Climate Change: An Overview of the WTO Legal Issues', in T. Cottier, O. Nartova, and S. Z. Bigdeli (eds.), *International Trade Regulation and the Mitigation of Climate Change: World Trade Forum* (Cambridge: Cambridge University Press, 2009), pp. 60–9.

[92] Cottier *et al.*, *supra* n. 90; Holzer, *supra* n. 88, pp. 205–7.

choice. Both can be implemented in ways that internalise the emission-related cost of imports into the price, thereby potentially serving as an incentive to make technological upgrade along different stages of electricity production and use in the products' locations of origin. However, intuitively enough, the issue of following uniform pricing for any unit of emission at home and abroad is much more crucial for taxation-based approach than a tariff-based one. In trade law parlance, measures as such would potentially fall under the umbrella term PPMs.[93] The characteristic differences between the two approaches relate to their practical implications. A border-adjusted carbon tax can be the better choice when the sort of emission sought to be regulated exist domestically and across border. Whereas treatment of exclusively foreign-sourced emissions is easier tackled through tariffs. Compared to internal taxes, tariffs can be less prone to legal challenge. Under certain circumstances, tariffs may also offer room to vary the applied rate of duties. However, over the long-run, tariff rates are supposed to move downwards, whereas carbon prices need to rise exponentially in the opposite direction. From this perspective, in the long term, the taxation approach indeed makes better sense.[94]

Cross-border recycling of import revenue generated through the tax or the tariff is a novel proposition. The suggestion is made for several reasons. Such revenue recycling would make carbon pricing mutually beneficial, as well as shield it from being dubbed as 'green protectionism'. It would further work as an additional incentive to nudge exporters in making technology upgrades. Revenue transfers would also assist to take account of differentiated responsibility concerns. Also, as will be shown later, the differentiated support would be useful to justify adoption of a carbon pricing measure, if found to be discriminatory according to the standard of the WTO laws.

2.4.1.2 Issues in Brief

With respect to import adjustment of a domestic carbon tax, several GATT compliance issues arise.[95] One is whether a carbon tax, which is

---

[93] K. Holzer, 'Process and Production Methods (PPMs)', in Cottier and Schefer, *supra* n. 10, p. 189.

[94] For many other design considerations regarding carbon pricing policies, see I. W. H. Parry, R. Mooij, and M. Keen (eds.), *Fiscal Policy to Mitigate Climate Change: A Guide to Policymakers* (Washington, DC: International Monetary Fund, 2012); OECD, *Effective Carbon Rates* (Paris: OECD Publishing, 2016), www.oecd-ilibrary.org/taxation/effective-carbon-rates_9789264260115-en (accessed 24 Sept. 2018).

[95] General Agreement on Tariffs and Trade (1994). On a deeper level, it may be possible that a carbon tax or regulations related to it attracts breach of other covered agreements

TRADE-RELATED MEASURES AND LCTS 121

neither a customs duty nor an other duty or charge, can be imposed at the border. To do so, the tax has to fall under the scope of Article II:2(a) of GATT, which allows a charge to be levelled on a product given it is equivalent to an internal tax on the domestic like product or input – one that falls under and complies with the standard of GATT Article III.[96] The standard of equivalence between the border charge and the internal tax, guided by Article III:2 of GATT, is where the other compliance issues remain. The issue of 'likeness' requires a determination of whether products with different levels of embedded emission are comparable with each other or not. If yes, next is the question of discrimination – that is, whether a different final tax burden should be seen as a distortion of competition under the legal standard of Article III:2. Although these questions are much analysed in scholarly literature, a possible influence of the doctrine of Common Concern in finding different conclusions remains as yet unexplored.[97]

A tariff-based approach to carbon pricing would also raise similar issues to a degree. Although states have more liberty to shape their respective tariff policies, rules at the multilateral level require transparent scheduling of all tariff lines and binding them to a maximum threshold level.[98] Leaving aside the design problem of further classification of a tariff line based on carbon footprint, to the extent an applied tariff would exceed the bound levels, compliance with the GATT rules would call for cooperation and exchange of concessions between designated parties in accordance with Article XXVIII. In the absence of a positive outcome, unilateral classification and imposition of tariffs would be prone to

---

as well. One example would be if the pricing mechanism is somehow a part of the technical specification of the product, there may be a breach of the TBT Agreement. Although a possibility, the current discussion focuses exclusively on GATT.

[96] The issue of 'eligibility' is not straightforward. Although a formal settlement of the issue through dispute settlement is still to happen, scholarly opinions diverge. For the partial position of the AB, see Appellate Body Report, *India–Additional and Extra-Additional Duties on Imports from the United States (India–Additional Duties)*, adopted 30 Oct. 2008, WT/DS360/AB/R, paras. 153, 170, 172, 180; for an account of the literature, see H. Horn and P. C. Mavroidis, 'Climate Change and the WTO: Legal Issues Concerning Border Tax Adjustments', *Japanese Yearbook of International Law*, 53 (2010), 31–2; Holzer, *supra* n. 88, pp. 98–103. The position maintained here is that a carbon tax comes under the purview of Art. III:2 as it is applied to a product and by dint of that also falls under the scope of Art. II:2(a).

[97] With the exception of some preliminary conclusion presented by Cottier and Payosova (T. Cottier and T. Payosova, 'Common Concern and the Legitimacy of the WTO in Dealing with Climate Change', in Delimatsis, *supra* n. 23, pp. 26–8).

[98] Art. II:1, General Agreement on Tariffs and Trade; Cottier *et al.*, *supra* n. 90, pp. 1020–4.

attract claim of discrimination, as well as a breach of the scheduling commitment. The discrimination claim would raise issues akin to those mentioned in the previous paragraph but on a different legal context.[99]

It is commonly believed that even though a carbon pricing policy may initially be found as discriminatory, there is sufficient room to maintain a climate mitigation-minded measure under the allowance of general exceptions (Article XX). But it is not at all clear whether an emission price, applicable equally across the board, would be eventually justifiable, given the fact that arguably Article XX of GATT also calls for adjusting the treatment of countries depending on the prevailing conditions. Not only one of the foundational tenets of the climate regime is differentiated responsibility, but also the current set of rules allows parties to plan emission mitigation in a voluntary and nationally determined fashion. Where and how the balance is to be found is an open question. It would be examined whether the revenue recycling component can bolster the justifiability of a carbon pricing measure.

2.4.1.3 Possible Legal Outcome and Role of Common Concern

Existing jurisprudence on non-discrimination tilts more towards a possible finding that products differing only in emission footprints are 'like' nevertheless – leading to a probable conclusion that fiscal burdens corresponding to such footprints are discriminatory.[100] The analysis here takes a different approach to the problem. One of the arguments made is that whether or not a tax or tariff is discriminatory should also depend on whether it distorts the market or corrects the same. The Common Concern doctrine can contribute to establishing this approach. Alternatively, a carbon pricing measure is justifiable under the cover of general exception when the application of the measure is adjusted to differently situated developing countries. In that regard, it is argued that technology upgrade support to the developing countries out of carbon pricing income is an essential part of the scheme. Revenue recycling can

---

[99] It would be a claim of the breach of most-favoured-nation as laid down in Art. I of the GATT.

[100] G. Marceau, 'The Interface between the Trade Rules and Climate Change Actions', in D. Park (ed.), *Legal Issues on Climate Change and International Trade Law* (Berlin: Springer, 2016), pp. 8–13; P. Low, G. Marceau, and J. Reinaud, 'The Interface between the Trade and Climate Change Regimes: Scoping the Issues', *Journal of World Trade*, 46 (3) (2012) 485; Trachtman, *supra* n. 91.

further pre-empt from raising otherwise plausible claims of green protectionism.

Product Comparability: The Test of 'Likeness'   The determination of comparability between two sets of products (i.e. the 'like products' analysis) as a part of discrimination analysis has evolved into a case-specific[101] examination of comparing a range of attributes between the product groups.[102] The current legal standard calls for taking into consideration all the relevant properties of the products under comparison across four categories, namely (i) physical properties, (ii) end uses, (iii) consumer perception, and (iv) their classification under the Harmonized System (HS) for tariff purposes.[103] From a legal interpretation perspective, the journey to unearth the meaning of 'like products' starts from conceding the inadequacy of literal meaning and different language version of the treaty texts.[104] Then in absence of clarificatory support from the texts, the exercise proceeds to draws upon the subsequent practice,[105] namely the 1970 report on border tax adjustment.[106] The legal context in which the term appears is important to determine the subject matter scope of the analysis.[107] Overall, a decision on product likeness calls for a holistic assessment of all available evidence relating to

---

[101] Appellate Body Report, *Japan–Taxes on Alcoholic Beverages (Japan–Alcohol II)*, adopted 1 Nov. 1996, WT/DS8/AB/R, WT/DS10/AB/R, WT/DS11/AB/R, pp. 21–2; Appellate Body Report, *European Communities–Measures Affecting Asbestos and Asbestos Containing Products (EC–Asbestos)*, adopted 5 Apr. 2001, WT/DS135/AB/R, para. 99.

[102] Appellate Body Report, *EC–Asbestos*, *supra* n. 101, para. 103.

[103] Ibid., para. 101.

[104] GATT Panel Report, *Japan–Customs Duties, Taxes and Labelling Practices on Imported Wines and Alcoholic Beverages (Japan–Alcohol I)*, adopted 10 Nov. 1987, BISD 34S/83, para. 5.5; Appellate Body Report, *EC–Asbestos*, *supra* n. 101, paras. 91–2.

[105] This is done pursuant to Art. 31(3)(b), VCLT, *supra* n. 63; See Panel Report, *US–Gasoline*, *supra* n. 34, para. 6.8.

[106] GATT, *Report by the Working Party on Border Tax Adjustments*, L/3464 (1970). Especially this excerpt from paragraph 18 of the report has been the key foundation of interpreting 'like product': 'problems arising from the interpretation of the term should be examined on a case-by-case basis. This would allow a fair assessment in each case of the different elements that constitute a "similar" product. Some criteria were suggested for determining, on a case-by-case basis, whether a product is "similar"; the product's end-uses in a given market; consumers tastes and habits, which change from country to country; the product's properties, nature and quality.'

[107] 'The concept of "likeness" is a relative one that evokes the image of an accordion. The accordion of "likeness" stretches and squeezes in different places as different provisions of the WTO Agreement are applied' (Appellate Body Report, *Japan–Alcohol II*, *supra* n. 101, p. 22).

the above four categories, weighing each, to conclude upon the competitive relationship among products compared.[108]

The test of 'likeness', though very sophisticated and relatively open-ended, leaves one issue unresolved. It would seem that the non-physical attributes (NPAs) are a considerable factor not per se, but through influencing the other criteria (e.g. physical attributes, or consumer choice).[109] One can read a measure of pragmatism into this conclusion, as otherwise, the margins of discretion accorded at this stage would be too wide to prevent protectionist abuse. But the implementation of a carbon tax or tariff partially hinges upon being able to make a distinction based on the NPAs (emission footprint, for example). Hence there may be a plausible case for a controlled, case-by-case admission of the NPAs, with support from the doctrine of Common Concern. To that effect, it is emphasised that there is so far no prohibition on considering NPAs, in addition to physical properties, to determine likeness. It is also emphasised that to the extent consumers have a special preference for climate safe production; it should be given careful consideration during the analysis.

With respect to granting admittance to the NPAs, especially products' emission footprints, in likeness analysis, the doctrine of Common Concern can serve as an identifier of deserving cases. Given that climate change is a recognised common concern of humankind, a product that adds to the global emission cannot be considered as the same as one that does not, if the doctrine is taken into account. Furthermore, there is no legal obstacle in considering NPAs. The standard recourse to 'physical' properties as a criterion of consideration during dispute settlement is more of a methodological construct for structured analysis.[110] Neither the legal text nor other sources of interpretation explicitly call for the sole consideration of physical properties. Also, mere physical similarity, in itself, is not probative of likeness.[111]

---

[108] Appellate Body Report, *EC–Asbestos*, *supra* n. 101, paras. 102–3, 109.

[109] Although in *EC–Asbestos*, the AB emphasised the need to take into account 'all' the evidence, it also limited the product characteristics category to 'physical' properties (ibid., paras. 101–2). In a later dispute, the Panel held that when different production processes are used to create closely resembling final product, '[t]he difference in raw materials would only be relevant to the extent that it results in final products that are not similar' (Panel Report, *Philippines – Taxes on Distilled Spirits (Philippines–Distilled Spirits)*, adopted 20 Jan. 2012, WT/DS396/R, WT/DS403/R, para. 7.37).

[110] Appellate Body Report, *EC–Asbestos*, *supra* n. 101, para. 101.

[111] Appellate Body Report, *Philippines–Taxes on Distilled Spirits (Philippines–Distilled Spirits)*, adopted 20 Jan. 2012, WT/DS396/AB/R, WT/DS403/AB/R, paras. 112–28.

To add to the above argument, it is submitted that while construing the meaning of 'like product', not only the meaning of 'like' but also the meaning of the term product should be taken into account. Even literally, the word 'product'[112] means something coming out of a 'production'. Production is a process of resource usage and conversion, and optimal resource use along with sustainable development[113] are the cornerstones of the WTO. Keeping this preambular context in mind, it would be unreasonable to make a comparison between products without taking into account relevant differences in production processes, resource usage and emissions therefrom. Coming back to the Common Concern doctrine, relation between a product's properties to a prevalent common concern attaches special value to that attribute, thereby making it a distinguishable one.

With respect to the evaluation of climate sensitiveness of the consumers, the suggestion is for the Panels to attach varying weight from case to case. It is submitted that while making a choice between two products, whether a consumer will be guided by the price or the non-price attributes of that product, is a question that may meet varied responses based on the social context. Often consumers will be guided by price, which, in cases of a lingering Common Concern, create opportunities to be misguided. To elaborate, a general manifestation of the problem of climate change is price distortion due to uninternalised externalities of the GHG emissions.[114] A consumer is biased when she is solely guided by the price, as the latter is not reflective of all the crucial product attributes. By taking account of a situation of Common Concern, a dispute settlement Panel can make itself aware of that bias, which would enable it to make further careful assessment of the situation before attaching weight to such evidence. Although such application of discretion is consistent with the case-by-case approach of likeness determination, there so far exists no metric which can be used to guide the application of the discretion. Common Concern doctrine is poised to fill that gap.

---

[112] '[T]hing produced by an action, operation, or natural process; a result, a consequence; spec. that which is produced commercially for sale' (*New Shorter Oxford English Dictionary* (Oxford: Clarendon Press, 1993), vol. 2).

[113] Preamble of the Marrakesh Agreement refers to '*optimal* use [of resources] in accordance with the objective of sustainable development' (see *supra* n. 22).

[114] See pp. 107–9.

Nevertheless, bringing the doctrine of Common Concern into play does not at all imply that products differing in emission footprints would be automatically found as not 'like'. It should be kept in mind that the exercise of likeness analysis is to determine the nature and extent of the competitive relationship between products. Realistically, and also depending on the extent of variation in emission footprints between comparable products, recourse to the doctrine of Common Concern and consideration of NPAs may in most cases add to the degree of difference between products, but not conclude that such products do not compete at all in the market. However, acceptance of the degree of difference between products, although competing, should have an impact on how the discrimination test is carried out, as we see in the following paragraphs.

Standard of Discrimination: Change in Conditions of Competition
Adjusting carbon taxes on imports or imposing carbon tariffs can draw non-discrimination challenge in two ways. Different levels of tariffs or taxes imposed on imports from different origins might be considered as a violation of the most-favoured-nation (MFN) obligation. Whereas the difference in overall carbon tax burden between domestic and imported product group can be seen as incompatible with the national treatment (NT) obligation. In both instances of discrimination challenges, the outcome of the legal analysis would hinge upon finding distortion of the conditions of competition in the market.[115] A violation is found when such distortion is induced benefiting some imports against others (MFN), or domestic products against imports (NT).

The purpose of protecting the expectation of equal competitive opportunities guides the interpretation of Article I:1 of GATT.[116] So far, it has been found that apart from import duty exemption, access to tariff quota,

---

[115] Panel Report, *United States–Measures Concerning the Importation, Marketing and Sale of Tuna and Tuna Products (US–Tuna II)*, adopted 16 May 2012, WT/DS381/RW, para. 7.278.

[116] Following elaboration by the AB is of note, 'as Article I:1 is concerned, fundamentally, with protecting expectations of equal competitive opportunities for like imported products from all Members, it does not follow that Article I:1 prohibits a Member from attaching any conditions to the granting of an "advantage" within the meaning of Article I:1. Instead, it prohibits those conditions that have a detrimental impact on the competitive opportunities for like imported products from any Member. Conversely, Article I:1 permits regulatory distinctions to be drawn between like imported products, provided that such distinctions do not result in a detrimental impact on the competitive opportunities for like imported products from any Member' (Appellate Body Report, *European Communities–Measures Prohibiting the Importation and Marketing of Seal*

certification procedure, flexible import procedures, inter alia, can trigger such distortion of competition when not accorded to all. Similarly, under Article III:2, which exclusively deals with internal tax measures, finding of discrimination essentially requires looking at the actual market and assessing the impact of the questioned measure on changing the effective conditions of competition against some or all non-domestic like products.[117] With respect to taxation of directly competitive and substitutable products, it calls for a case-by-case inspection of the design, structure, and operation of the measure, as well as a comprehensive and objective analysis of its structure.[118]

It may seem very straightforward that a carbon tariff or a carbon tax would violate the non-discrimination rule. Within the like product group, differential carbon tariffs would indeed have a varied impact on product prices and therefore be considered distortive and discriminatory. Similarly, regarding an internal carbon tax, if the overall tax burden is higher on imports compared to domestic comparable products, it may as well be considered discriminatory. However, an alternate position could possibly be taken that if the pre-existing market distortions were taken into account and the relevant legal analysis was carried, the outcome would not be as straightforward. Such an argument could be fleshed out based on the Common Concern doctrine and the recent AB position in the *Canada–Renewable Energy* dispute.

While applying the legal standard of non-discrimination in any specific case with a view to maintaining equal competitive opportunities for actors in the market, a distinction can be made between government interventions in undistorted markets and the situations of market failure. The doctrine of Common Concern can assist in making this distinction. As the theoretical exposition in the previous section portrayed, the existence of a Common Concern has an impact on the market, inter alia,

---

Products (EC–Seals), adopted 18 June 2014, WT/DS400/AB/R, WT/DS401/AB/R, para. 5.88).

[117] We agree that although this is the general purpose of Art. III of GATT, under the first sentence of Art. III:2, the analysis is rather straightforward, i.e. evidence of dissimilar taxation among like product becomes automatically probative of discrimination. Based on our previous arguments regarding 'like products', we rather focus on the relatively probable situation of dealing with the question under the second sentence of Art. III:2 of GATT.

[118] GATT Panel Report, *United States–Section 337 of the Tariff Act of 1930 (US–Section 337)*, BISD 36S/345, para. 5.2.2; Appellate Body Report, *Philippines–Distilled Spirits*, *supra* n. 111, para. 250; Appellate Body Report, *Japan–Alcohol II*, *supra* n. 101, p. 29.

in the form of creating wrong price signals, which on their own results in suboptimal resource allocation, and thereby prolongation of the Concern. Furthermore, having recourse to the Common Concern doctrine in assessing the market condition also would indicate that governments have a role to play (responsibility to act, or 'homework' responsibility) in correcting the existing distortion. In situations as such, a dispute settlement panel can assess the problem at hand in terms of its connection to an established common concern, and analyse the impact of the intervention favourably to the extent it tends to correct the existing failure. This way, the conditions deserving interventions can be distinguished from purely protectionist moves.

The analysis set out by the AB in *Canada–Renewable Energy* dispute regarding characterisations of a market, and necessary interventions therein puts the argument above in a favourable light.[119] In that dispute, the AB expressed the view that a market is not only defined by the demand side characteristics, but also supply-side factors (e.g. production processes, and cost structures).[120] Despite the final product being identical, in case the process of production and costs faced by producers are so fundamentally different that certain methods of production would not take place in absence of government support; the support should not per se be considered distortive.[121] The argument is identical to the market failure argument made above. The analysis by the AB in this dispute indicates the need for a more nuanced and disaggregated understanding of the market and analysing the impact of government intervention in the context of the policy goal. Putting the doctrine of Common Concern into use would enable the undertaking of such analysis in a more structured fashion.

General Exception   The general exception provision of the GATT (i.e. Article XX), works as a balancing measure; one through which equilibrium is maintained between a WTO member's domestic policy-driven trade distortion and others' benefit guaranteed under the General Agreement.[122] Not only that, the provision further allows the

---

[119] It is conceded that the decision of the AB was in the legal context of the Subsidies Agreement, which indeed has a different structure and operation. However, to the extent the key concept like that of a 'market' is concerned, it is submitted that it should have the same meaning across the covered agreement.

[120] Appellate Body Report, *Canada–Renewable Energy*, *supra* n. 38, para. 5.174.

[121] Ibid., paras. 5.175, 5.177, 5.190.

[122] Appellate Body Report, *EC–Seals*, *supra* n. 116, para. 5.301.

understanding of the trade-related commitments to evolve in light of the changing global concerns.[123] For any trade measure with a declared non-trade policy motivation, securing the shelter of Article XX is a two-step process.[124] The first requirement is that the policy goal must be one endorsed by at least one of the subparagraphs of the Article. The second is operational fairness, as required under the introductory lines (the *chapeau*).

Following up, the climate mitigation and LCT diffusion objective of a revenue recycled carbon pricing measure can be argued to fall under paragraphs (b) or (g) of Article XX,[125] the latter probably being the more plausible option. As is well known, compliance with any of the subparagraph is again a two-step process. First, the measure must fall under the enshrined policy goal in particular. Second, the level of relationship with the policy goal must pass the required threshold. We focus on the possible value addition by the Common Concern doctrine in satisfying these requirements.

Arguably, the easiest avenue for the justification of carbon pricing will be to hold that, in line with the paragraph (g), the measure is 'relating to'[126] the conservation of 'exhaustible natural resources', and that similar controls have been put in place regulating domestic productions and consumptions. With support from the Common Concern doctrine, it can be convincingly shown that a stable climate is indeed an exhaustible natural resource. It has already been noted in dispute settlement juris-prudence that exhaustible natural resources are not only limited to mineral resources.[127] Furthermore, what renders climate change a

---

[123] Appellate Body Report, *US–Shrimp*, *supra* n. 32, para. 129; Study Group of the International Law Commission, *supra* n. 33, pp. 223–8.

[124] Appellate Body Report, *US–Gasoline*, n. 31, p. 22; Appellate Body Report, *US–Shrimp*, n. 32, paras. 119–21.

[125] Marceau, *supra* n. 100, pp. 13–15; Trachtman, *supra* n. 91, p. 17; Holzer, *supra* n. 89, pp. 149–57. The public morals carve-out in Art. XX(a) could possibly be used as well. For a treatment of that provision from a Common Concern viewpoint, see Chapter 5 in this volume, pp. 265–74.

[126] 'Relating to' test, which is a laxer version of the necessity test detailed later, calls for a 'close and genuine relationship of ends and means' between the policy goal and the measure itself. Appellate Body Report, *US–Shrimp*, *supra* n. 32, para. 136. As we discuss the necessity test requirement, we do not duplicate by also enlarging upon the related to test.

[127] Panel Report, *US–Gasoline*, *supra* n. 34, para. 6.37; Appellate Body Report, *US–Shrimp*, *supra* n. 32, paras. 130–1; Panel Report, *United States–Measures Concerning the Importation, Marketing and Sale of Tuna and Tuna Products–Recourse to Article 21.5 of the DSU by Mexico (US–Tuna II (21.5))*, adopted 20 Nov. 2015, WT/DS381/RW, para. 7.512.

Common Concern is, in essence, the exhaustibility factor; as it will worsen beyond recovery over the long run if anthropogenic interference is kept unchecked. Carbon pricing, either through a tax or a tariff maintains a close relationship to conservation of climatic stability as it is well agreed to be the best economic tool of emission mitigation.

One point to be carefully noted however is that apart from being related to conservation, the measure in question needs to regulate domestic activities the same way it regulates imports. Although border-adjusted carbon taxes can satisfy this requirement, a carbon tariff cannot be defended in case domestic enterprises equivalent to those under the tariff coverage remain unregulated.

With respect to paragraph (b), the crucial question would be whether emission pricing for climate mitigation and technology diffusion would be considered as 'necessary' for the protection of human, animal, or plant life. The necessity will be determined 'weighing and balancing' all the relevant factors.[128] Under this approach, the apparent trade restrictiveness of a measure would be balanced against the extent to which it is apt to make a material contribution over time to the policy goal as well as the importance of the policy goal itself.[129] Overall, it remains a holistic exercise of qualitative and quantitative analysis of three categories of factors, that is (i) relative importance of the goal; (ii) potential contribution of the measure to the goal; (iii) trade distortive impact and reasonable availability of less distorting alternatives.[130]

In the context of necessity determination, the Common Concern doctrine would contribute to establish the importance of climate mitigation as a policy objective. Recognition of climate change as a Common Concern of not only one member but of humankind undoubtedly attaches very high importance to the goal of emission mitigation.

---

[128] Appellate Body Report, *Korea–Measures Affecting Imports of Fresh, Chilled and Frozen Beef (Korea–Beef)*, adopted 10 Jan. 2001, WT/DS161/AB/R, WT/DS169/AB/R, paras. 159–62.

[129] Appellate Body Report, *Canada–Measures Affecting the Export of Civilian Aircraft–Recourse by Brazil to Article 21.5 of the DSU (Canada–Aircraft (21.5))*, adopted 4 Aug. 2000, WT/DS70/AB/RW, paras. 150–1; Appellate Body Report, *EC–Seals, supra* n. 116, para. 5.209. In both disputes, it was recognised by the AB that it is possible to qualitatively assess what a measure is apt to contribute, in the long run.

[130] Appellate Body Report, *Korea–Beef, supra* n. 128, para. 164; Panel Report, *European Communities–Measures Prohibiting the Importation and Marketing of Seal Products (EC–Seals)*, adopted 18 June 2014, WT/DS400/R, WT/DS401/R, para. 7.630; Appellate Body Report, *United States–Measures Affecting the Cross Border Supply of Gambling and Betting Services (US–Gambling)*, adopted 20 Apr. 2005, WT/DS285/AB/R, paras. 309–11.

Moreover, the potential of carbon pricing to reduce emission domestically as well as abroad would vouch for its aptness to contribute to the climate mitigation goal.

Apart from the above, finding the overall balance to determine the necessity of a carbon tariff or tax may still pose difficult questions. Assessing the possible contribution of the measure in inducing adoption of cleaner technology across the border and therefore contribute to emission mitigation may be difficult to compute. Also, mitigation can be pursued in different forms, including ways that do or do not impact the market (e.g. a carbon tax, or afforestation). The Paris Climate Agreement leaves the parties free to determine the appropriate means of mitigation, while leaving open the opportunity to develop cooperation-based market measures for the purposes of mitigation.[131] Although a complainant can always show alternative means of emission reduction, it is not clear whether different means should be considered as alternates to each other, given the fact that the more emission is reduced, the better it is for the planet in the long run.

The final *chapeau* test of Article XX is poised to prevent misuse of the carve-out.[132] It serves that goal by preventing the application of the scrutinised measure in a way that: (i) causes 'arbitrary or unjustifiable discrimination between countries where the same conditions prevail'; or (ii) acts as 'disguised restriction on international trade'. Discussion of the implications of the *chapeau* requirement for carbon pricing measures is important because of the preponderance of instances where provisionally justified trade measures were found to be inconsistent with the requirements under the *chapeau*.[133] In relation to carbon pricing, the crucial question would be whether a single price rate for carbon emission would constitute arbitrary or unjustifiable discrimination if applied to countries in different conditions.[134]

---

[131] Arts. 4 and 6 respectively, Paris Agreement, *supra* n. 12.

[132] Appellate Body Report, *US–Gasoline*, *supra* n. 31, p. 22.

[133] For example, *US–Gasoline*, *US–Shrimp*, *US–Gambling*, *Brazil–Tyres*, and lately the *EC–Seals*. In all these disputes, the measure in question failed to pass the *chapeau* test.

[134] We do not venture into interpretation of 'disguised restriction on international trade', although it is accepted that it could also be useful. For what the phrase may come to mean, see L. Bartels, 'The Chapeau of the General Exceptions in the WTO GATT and GATS Agreements: A Reconstruction', *American Journal of International Law*, 109(1) (2015), 123.

To answer the above, it is highly probable that with respect to climate mitigation-minded trade measures, treating differently situated countries with the same action would be deemed as arbitrary or unjustifiable.[135] According to the AB, whether 'same conditions prevail' between countries ought to be examined with reference to policy objective pursued by a measure.[136] Although there has never been a finding of different prevailing conditions, it would be so with respect to a climate change-related measure. It is because inherent differentiation between countries in terms of climate responsibility is an entrenched principle (known as the CBDR) of the climate regime.[137] Therefore, both to justify the *chapeau* requirement, as well as to reflect the differentiated responsibility principle of the climate law, it will be important that the implementation of a carbon pricing scheme is tailored to the specific country situations. This position is also supported by the Common Concern doctrine, as it emphasises equitable implementation.[138]

With respect to the above, it is submitted that an appropriately designed mechanism to recycle carbon pricing revenue can serve the purpose of introducing differentiation in treatment between countries while not compromising the overall mitigation opportunity. A support mechanism as such would be an essential part of a pricing scheme, especially in cases when such a measure is implemented by a developed country. Factors that may be taken into account while developing such a scheme would include the economic position of the exporting country, its technology needs as communicated under the climate framework (i.e. technology needs assessments or TNAs) and the extent to which such pricing scheme results in additional mitigation effort beyond its communicated position under the Paris Agreement (i.e. the NDC commitments).

---

[135] Appellate Body Report, *US–Shrimp*, *supra* n. 32, paras. 165, 177.

[136] Appellate Body Report, *EC–Seals*, *supra* n. 116, paras. 5.299–5.303.

[137] Known as the principle of common but differentiated responsibility and respective capabilities (CBDRRC, or CBDR), differentiation has been an evolving metric in the climate regime. While a strict dichotomy between developed and developing countries has been a hallmark of the past systems, the new Paris Agreement framework dissolves some of the distinctions (e.g. in terms of mitigation action), while maintaining others (e.g. financial support and contribution). For more, see L. Rajamani, 'Ambition and Differentiation in the 2015 Paris Agreement: Interpretative Possibilities and Underlying Politics', *International and Comparative Law Quarterly*, 65(2) (2016).

[138] See Chapter 1 in this volume, pp. 31–2.

2.4.2 *Official Export Credit Support for LCTs*

2.4.2.1 Description

Within the Common Concern-motivated narrative, one option for the promotion of LCT export can be through better engagement of government export credit agencies (ECAs). The proposition advanced here is that the government ECAs, especially those in the technology-rich jurisdictions, should extensively engage in export credit supports regarding LCTs while scaling down the same for the polluting activities. The reasons for proposing export credit activities are several. Official export credit supports are win–win deals that benefit both the technology exporting and purchasing entities. Such support schemes contribute to addressing one of the key technology diffusion barriers (i.e. a weak capital market in the technology poor destinations).[139] It can also legitimise the existence of government export finance systems parallel to the private entities.[140] From the trade law perspective, export credits can be a form of export subsidy that remains justifiable to a degree, due to the peculiarities of the subsidies regulation.

Conceptually, official export credit support forms part of a wider gamut of trade finance activities. The term 'export credit' is used here to generally indicate available forms of trade finance (i.e. by way of extending a loan – credit) with interest, or a loan guarantee, or insuring commercial and political risks involved. Export credits allow bridging the finance gap between the seller and the buyer, by allowing the buyer flexibility in terms of payment, and allowing the seller to timely recoup the investment.[141] Export credit activities are undertaken by private commercial entities, international financial institutions, as well as the government. Government involvement in export credit support, through the ECAs, known as official export credit, is generally motivated by the dual argument of export promotion and correction of market failure.[142] The market failure occurs due to the reluctance of private lending entities

---

[139] See pp. 113–4.

[140] Facing increasing competition from private financiers in short-term and low-risk markets, the authors suggest that the ECAs should focus on medium- and long-term finances, finance of large projects, developing country markets, small and medium-sized enterprises (J. Wang, M. Mansilla, Y. Kikuchi, and S. Choudhury, *Officially Supported Export Credits in a Changing World* (Washington, DC: IMF, 2005), p. 22).

[141] M. Auboin, 'Improving the Availability of Trade Finance in Developing Countries: An Assessment of Remaining Gaps', *Staff Working Paper*, ERSD-2015–06 (WTO 2015), p. 3.

[142] Wang *et al.*, *supra* n. 140, p. 5.

to be involved in transactions involving relatively high risks (e.g. new markets), or of medium to long term duration. Therefore the public fund is employed to complement the private sector activities, as well as to boost exports.[143] In OECD parlance, official export credit support can be either 'pure cover support' (e.g. guarantees and insurances), or 'official financing support' by way of extending direct credit.[144]

It should, however, be noted that official export credit support for LCTs would be most beneficial in the context of a complementary policy environment. Availability of trade finance would result in actual export transaction growth only when there is effective demand from the other side. Demand for LCT would require, inter alia, removal of counter-productive subsidies in the technology destinations (e.g. support for fossil fuel). Further, there is a need for transparency on the sending side, as very little data exist on global export credit flows. Available figures for the OECD member countries indicate that a large portion of official support goes on financing various fossil-fuel projects.[145] Also, relatively very little official export credit support currently goes into supporting transactions involving partners from low-income countries. According to OECD, in 2015, only about 5 per cent of the overall official non-ODA (Official Development Assistance) finance support went to LDCs and low-income countries.[146]

2.4.2.2   Issues of Compliance

The issue of the compliance of official export credit supports with the WTO laws harkens back to some lingering and unresolved issues involving the Subsidies Agreement (ASCM, or SCM Agreement).[147] As the

---

[143]   Ibid.

[144]   OECD, 'Arrangement on Officially Supported Export Credits' (OECD 2018) TAD/PG (2018)1, www.oecd.org/officialdocuments/publicdisplaydocumentpdf/?cote=TAD/PG(2018)1&docLanguage=En (accessed 19 Sept. 2019); D. Coppens, 'Export Credit Support', *WTO Disciplines on Subsidies and Countervailing Measures: Balancing Policy Space and Legal Constraints* (Cambridge: Cambridge University Press, 2014), pp. 338–9.

[145]   OECD, 'Statistics on Arrangement Official Export Credit Support for Electric Power Generation Projects' TAD/ECG(2015)10/FINAL.

[146]   OECD, *Non-ODA Flows to Developing Countries: Export Credits*, www.oecd.org/dac/stats/beyond-oda-export-credits.htm (accessed 7 June 2018).

[147]   Agreement on Subsidies and Countervailing Measures (SCM Agreement), in Marrakesh Agreement Establishing the World Trade Organization, Annex 1A, 1869 UNTS 14 (1994). It is of course conceded that depending on the nature of the credit support activities, the Agreement on Agriculture may come into play. However, space constraints only allows exploration of the SCM-related issues.

SCM Agreement regulates market-distorting subsidisation by the members, the issue here is whether official export credits can be termed as such. In that regard, the question of particular interest would be whether such supports result in a benefit to the recipient. If found as falling within the regulatory purview of the Subsidies Agreement, official export credit support for LCTs fall foul of Article 3's prohibition, as the purported subsidies will boost domestic export opportunity vis-à-vis other international competitors.[148] However, some forms of official credit support can avoid being outright illegal by ensuring compliance with the interest rate provisions of the OECD Arrangement[149] – a point that itself raises potential systemic objections. The meanings of some of the relevant legal provisions[150] of the SCM Agreement in this respect remain unclear.

Even if not found to be illegal per se, official export credit supports may nonetheless be vulnerable to challenges by third countries claiming price distortions, or displacement of market share in the receiving country market.[151] In the end, what may eventually emerge as a key point from the discussion is that it is necessary to revisit the legal form and application of the ASCM in light of changing global circumstances. This provides an opportunity to speculate on the relevance of the Common Concern doctrine in that particular context.

2.4.2.3   Analysis

Official Export Credit and the Scope of the ASCM   Given the fact that official export credit programmes have been successfully challenged in WTO disputes in the past, it is quite plausible that similar supports, even though climate action inspired, would be seen as subsidies under the SCM Agreement. However, the usual jurisprudential viewpoint on whether the financial contribution results in a benefit has become more

---

[148] Panel Report, *Canada–Measures Affecting the Export of Civilian Aircraft-Recourse by Brazil to Article 21.5 of the DSU (Canada–Aircraft (21.5))*, adopted 4 Aug. 2000, WT/DS70/RW, para. 5.137; Coppens, *supra* n. 144, p. 340; J. J. Nedumpara, 'Export Credits and "Safe Haven" Provisions under the WTO SCM Agreement: A Case of False Safety?', *Global Trade and Customs Journal*, 8(3) (2013), 81.

[149] OECD, *supra* n. 144. The Arrangement is an informal (non-OECD act) pact between some participants to prevent competition on export support. For a concise description, see Wang *et al.*, *supra* n. 140, appendix III.

[150] Paras. 'j' and 'k', Annex I, SCM Agreement, *supra* n. 147. It is so especially regarding the *a contrario* use of the provisions.

[151] These are different manifestations of 'serious prejudice', see SCM Agreement, *supra* n. 147, Art. 5.

136   ZAKER AHMAD

nuanced since the AB's position taken in the *Canada–Renewable Energy*
dispute.

According to Article 1 of the ASCM, a subsidy exists when there is a
'financial contribution' by the government or any public body, provided
in a way that results in 'benefit'. Except for the outright illegal ones, a
subsidy is also required to be 'specific',[152] that is, focused on specific
entities or groups thereof. Official export credit support cannot but be
considered as a financial contribution, as it is an actual (e.g. direct credit)
or potential transfer of funds (e.g. insurance),[153] extended by the government. Next, finding of benefit in case of export credits traditionally
required examination of whether the ultimate domestic recipient of the
credit, as apart from the intermediaries,[154] are better off than they
otherwise would have been in case they had to obtain the credit from
the commercial market.[155] Benefit is established prima facie when a
foreign buyer can be offered terms of payment that is not possible in
the relevant market.[156] From this point of view, finding of benefit would
appear to be very straightforward, especially in cases where there is a
capital market failure; because of the official support being extended in a
situation where the transaction would not otherwise take place under
private market conditions.

However, finding benefit in cases related to a public policy decision,
especially climate action, has become more nuanced than the straightforward conclusion portrayed above since the WTO AB decision in the
Canada–Renewable Energy dispute. In many ways, as mentioned earlier,
the approach appears to be an exercise to validate government interventions to address market failures.[157] First, the AB clarified that while

---

[152] Ibid., Art. 2.

[153] Ibid., Art. 1.1(a)(1)(i).

[154] Panel Report, *Brazil–Export Financing Programme for Aircraft–Second Recourse by
Canada to Article 21.5 of the DSU (Brazil–Aircraft (21.5) II)*, adopted 4 Aug. 2001,
WT/DS46/RW/2, p. 41; D. Coppens, 'Disciplines on Export Credit Support for Non-
Agricultural Products', Coppens, *supra* n. 144, p. 363.

[155] Appellate Body Report, *Canada–Measures Affecting the Export of Civilian Aircraft
(Canada–Aircraft)*, adopted 20 Aug. 1999, WT/DS70/AB/R, para. 157. The standard
latter became known as the 'private market test'.

[156] Panel Report, *Brazil–Aircraft (21.5) II*, *supra* n. 154, p. 15, fn. 42.

[157] The AB, while quoting the Panel, held that '[c]onsideration related to [the] externalities
will often [...] be the reason why governments intervene to create markets [...]. On this
point, we agree with the Panel's statement that, where government intervention that
internalizes social costs and benefits is limited to defining the broad parameters of the
market, "significant scope will remain for private actors to operate within those

defining the scope of the relevant market to find a benchmark of support beyond which it would be considered as benefit, one ought to take into account all available evidence, including supply-side considerations, and government demand preference, if any.[158] Following the same line of argumentation, it could be proposed that benefit analysis of official export credit support should consider climate technology-related exports as the relevant market, as apart from the market of all export transactions. The AB further mentioned that finding the appropriate benchmark in the relevant market should not be considered as thwarted by government intervention, more so in situations where the market itself is an outcome of such intervention.[159] The AB also proposed for distinctions to be made between the scenarios of creation of a new market or distortion of an existing one when benefit due to government intervention is examined.[160] Where a new market is created, the benchmark of benefit ought to be found in that market or by creating a proxy.[161]

The doctrine of Common Concern could be of use to further structure the reconciling position taken by the AB with respect to subsidy determination and overriding public policy interests. Although the deference to public policy guided interventions in the form of creation of a new market argument is welcome so far as it reflects market failure situations, it is nevertheless true that without any limits imposed, such an argument could fall prey to arbitrary designations of policy goals and result in unabated subsidisation. If the overriding policy reason to intervene in the existing market is examined with respect to the level of contribution to a Common Concern, a reasonable control could be exercised as to when government intervention should be viewed favourably and when not.

With respect to official export credit support, a benefit benchmark would then be the terms that markets would offer for export transaction, given a fixed domestic policy imperative of LCT diffusion in the relevant market. If the official export credit support is related to the Common Concern of emission mitigation and diffusion of LCT, the support itself should not be found as conferment of benefit as long as it does not exceed the level necessary to cover the risk incurred by the exporter. In other

---

parameters on the basis of commercial considerations.'" (Appellate Body Report, *Canada–Renewable Energy*, *supra* n. 38, para. 5.189).

[158] Ibid., paras. 5.171–5.178.
[159] Ibid., para. 5.182.
[160] Ibid., para. 5.188.
[161] Ibid., paras. 5.184, 5.227–5.228.

138 ZAKER AHMAD

words, the benchmark of the benefit analysis should not be the default market rates.

Official Export Credits as Prohibited Subsidies   The rules that apply to official export credit schemes are a patchwork of GATT-era provisions and subsequent development. This mix is a key reason for lingering ambiguities. The pre-WTO subsidies code is the source of the designations of cost threshold levels beyond which export credits, credit guarantees and insurances extended by the government are prohibited. These rules were appended[162] (i.e. the illustrative list) to the SCM Agreement, and are now read in combination with the export subsidy prohibition rule therein (i.e. Article 3.1). This Article itself prohibits subsidies that are export contingent, either de jure or de facto. Serving as a bridge between the Article and the illustrative list is footnote 5, holding that subsidies not prohibited under the list will not be prohibited under any other provisions.

In very simple terms, the illustrative list rules lay down that with respect to export credit guarantees and insurances, governments shall refrain from offering terms that are inadequate to cover long-term costs of such a programme (paragraph j). With respect to the grant of export credit by governments (paragraph k), the prohibition is on offering credit rates that are below their own cost of capital or on paying for the cost incurred by an entity in obtaining credits. This prohibition only operates in so far as the grant is to secure 'a material advantage in the field of export credit terms'. The second part of paragraph k, known as the safe-haven clause, in seemingly innocuous words creates a carve-out which saves from challenge any official export credit transaction in line with the interest rate provisions (essentially the CIRR)[163] of the OECD Arrangement on export credits. Overall, this applicable body of rules does not create sufficient coverage to save LCT export supports. They also raise some democratic legitimacy issues.

The safe-haven clause creating an exception for some OECD Arrangement-compliant export credits is undemocratic in nature and

---

[162] Attached as Annex I to the ASCM, the illustrative list is a non-exhaustive account of subsidies related to exportation, including thresholds beyond which such practices are prohibited.

[163] Commercial interest reference rates (CIRR) are the minimum interest rates to be charged when fixed rate export credit is granted. As part of the OECD Arrangement, the rates are revised monthly in respect of the currencies of all the members participating in the OECD Arrangement (OECD, *supra* n. 144, ss. 19–22).

of very limited utility. The carve-out can be used by the participants to the Arrangement, as well as by non-participants, so long as they comply with the interest rates and related provisions of the Arrangement. However, the fact nevertheless remains that the interest rates are periodically determined in the currencies of the participants, based on the rate of return of their respectively issued bonds.[164] Even though a non-participant can use a designated currency and the interest rates for finance activities, the rates themselves are not adjusted to the cost of capital that the country would actually face.[165] Moreover, though the wording appears as the provision is extended to all types of trade finance practice within the arrangement, the reference to interest rates makes it applicable only to actual financing supports extended at fixed rates and having repayment durations of more than two years.[166] In reality, most trade finance support nowadays takes the form of pure cover support or support at a floating interest rate. One welcome addition in the OECD Arrangement is the special set of rules applicable to climate mitigation and renewable energy export finance, where special interest rates are suggested to facilitate some relevant sectors. However, the coverage of these provisions remain wanting: for example, while a fossil-fuel power plant with carbon capture technology falls under mitigation project, industrial energy-efficiency technologies are not covered by the rules.

For official export credit schemes that are non-compliant with the OECD Arrangement or other finance approaches (i.e. credit guarantees or insurances), the illustrative list provides no saving space. Official finance support for LCT export in breach of the cost threshold suggested in the respective paragraphs would automatically be considered as an export subsidy. Compliance with the OECD Arrangement provisions will not save such finance measures.[167] Even if such support remains below

---

[164] Ibid., s. 20.

[165] Hypothetically speaking, if Brazil intends to finance aircraft export in US dollars, it has to comply with the CIRR constructed for that currency to be WTO compliant. Whereas the actual cost of raising that capital for Brazil may be much higher or lower than that faced by the USA. The safe haven in this situation would only be useful to save the USA from facing competition from Brazil. But it would not have any bearing on prohibition of subsidies, which may nonetheless take place.

[166] Coppens, *supra* n. 144, p. 380.

[167] For example, like the CIRR mentioned above, the OECD Arrangement also provides for minimum premium rates (MPRs) to be complied with when providing pure cover support. But, as said, compliance with the MPR provisions does not automatically provide any safeguard from being considered as prohibited subsidies (OECD, *supra* n. 144, ss. 23–24).

140   ZAKER AHMAD

suggested thresholds, it does not save the measure from being amenable to challenge as *de facto* or *de jure* export contingent subsidy under Article 3.1 of the ASCM.[168] Under the legal standard of Article 3.1 of the Subsidies Agreement, export contingency, when not legally explicit, can still be found if the impact of a measure is a relative increase in the ratio of export transaction compared to domestic transactions.[169] According to that standard, it can hardly be contested that official export finance LCTs do not breach Article 3.1.

Export Credit as Non-Prohibited Subsidies   Even when a technology export credit is saved by the safe-haven clause, it is not saved from challenges under other parts of the SCM Agreement. This is despite the mention in the Agreement that illustrative list measures declared as not constituting prohibited subsidy shall also not be so construed elsewhere.[170] The AB chose to read the provision narrowly, construing that the expression only related to the determination of the prohibited nature of the subsidy and not the determination of the subsidy itself.[171] The reading opens the possibility that even the Arrangement-compliant official export credit supports can be challenged multilaterally as an actionable subsidy or unilaterally countervailed.

As technology export credits would benefit the country that receives the new technology, it would be less plausible that the recipient would launch an investigation followed by a unilateral imposition of countervailing duty. However, it remains probable that a WTO member having a competing industry in the technology sector in question may bring a

---

[168] The Panels repeatedly refused to read the phrase in paragraph k 'in so far as they are used to secure material advantage' as an affirmative defence available to the respondent. Panel Report, *Brazil–Aircraft (21.5) II, supra* n. 154, paras. 5.271–5.275. While the Panel's argument is logically sound, the issue is not fully settled: in the initial appeal, the AB did not categorically reject the merit in Brazil's argument to the above effect. The AB only refrained from addressing the matter on the excuse that Brazil had not satisfied the burden of proof. This leaves room for speculation whether the AB would have accepted the argument, had the burden of proof been met. Appellate Body Report, *Brazil–Export Financing Programme for Aircraft (Brazil–Aircraft)*, adopted 20 Aug. 1999, WT/DS46/AB/R, paras. 183, 186–7.

[169] Appellate Body Report, *European Communities and Certain Member States–Measures Affecting Trade in Large Civil Aircraft (EC–Large Civil Aircraft)*, adopted 1 June 2011, WT/DS316/AB/R, paras. 1044, 1045, 1053.

[170] SCM Agreement, *supra* n. 147, fn. 5.

[171] Appellate Body Report, *United States–Tax Treatment for 'Foreign Sales Corporations' (US–FSC)*, adopted 20 Mar. 2000, WT/DS108/AB/R, para. 93; Coppens, *supra* n. 144, p. 387.

dispute against the member extending the export credit on account of 'serious prejudice'.[172] According to Article 6.3, a member can be seriously prejudiced if, inter alia, subsidies displace or impede its exports in a third-country market; or if the subsidy results in significant price undercutting. So, in cases where export credit support assists foreign firms in sectors that are also subject to export interest (e.g. export of solar panels) from elsewhere, it can plausibly draw complaints from the competitors.

Key Unresolved Issues Export credit measure to address the failure of the capital market to finance technology import would face several challenges under the SCM Agreement. The greatest probability is for such measures to fall under prohibited export subsidy as mentioned in the corresponding illustrative lists – for the safe-haven provisions are not expansive or updated to cover the range of credit measures. Moreover, subsidies compliant with the list requirements still suffer the possibility of causing serious prejudice against third-country exports in the market of the recipient of credit.

Since the AB decision in *Canada–Renewable Energy*, the finding of official export credit supports through the ECAs as a conferment benefit is not a straightforward 'but for'[173] argument anymore. It is because governments, arguably, by intervention through the ECAs may actually create markets for environmental export credit that were not previously in existence. Under such circumstance, it would be up for speculation as to what credit terms and rates offered by an ECA could avoid being characterised as a subsidy.[174]

A seemingly simple way of boosting export credit support without getting into a conflict with the SCM Agreement would be through international institutional finance. As shown above, if the granting of credit takes place by entities other than governments or public bodies, it falls outside the scope of the ASCM. However, under such a scenario, the availability of additional finance would become a key question to resolve. The history of climate finance shows us that this is not an easy question to answer.

---

[172] SCM Agreement, *supra* n. 147, Art. 5(c) read with Art. 6.3.
[173] That is, such export transactions would not take place 'but for' the support provided by an ECA.
[174] S. Charnovitz, 'Green Subsidies and the WTO', *World Bank Policy Research Working Paper* (2014), p. 54, http://documents.worldbank.org/curated/en/2014/10/20290817/green-subsidies-wto (accessed 19 Sept. 2019).

Another long-standing issue that also surfaces in the paragraphs above is that the SCM Agreement currently operates without any escape clause for legitimate policy measures. This drawback itself is a plausible reason for the recent emergence of the AB jurisprudence accommodating the possibility of market failure curing interventions. One of two equally challenging options to resolve the drawback is through interpretation; the other is through legislation. The interpretive avenue is to expand the application of the GATT Article XX to the ASCM – on which scholarly opinions vary from sceptic[175] to cautious[176] to optimistic.[177] The optimistic account is based on the role of GATT as the umbrella agreement of Annex 1A, to which the ASCM belongs, as well as the express reference to GATT in Article 32.1 of the SCM Agreement – readable as allowing the exception provision to be extended to the latter.[178] Not only does such an extension require an interpretive leap, made even more difficult due to the political turmoil at the WTO, but the overall implications of such extension is also unpredictable.[179]

The alternative, a carve-out in the ASCM, can be guided by the notions of sustainable development and Common Concern. The case for legitimising strong policy imperative backed subsidies in general and official export credit practices in particular, can be argued by either calling for the reinstatement of non-actionable subsidies provision (Article 8) or by proposing an entirely new formulation. For good reasons, the latter is a better option to pursue. The textual formulation of Article 8 is dated and focused more upon developed country interests.[180] Also, actual revival of the provision would not save the official export credit supports when

---

[175] B. J. Condon, 'Disciplining Clean Energy Subsidies to Speed the Transition to a Low-Carbon World', *Journal of World Trade*, 51(4) (2017), 685–90.

[176] B. J. Condon, 'Climate Change and Unresolved Issues in WTO Law', *Journal of International Economic Law*, 12(4) (2009), 903–6; I. Espa and G. Marín Durán, 'Renewable Energy Subsidies and WTO Law: Time to Rethink the Case for Reform Beyond Canada – Renewable Energy/Fit Program', *Journal of International Economic Law* (2018), 23–7. The authors in the latter paper share the view that even though Art. XX's scope is extended to the ASCM, it would not be of much practical use.

[177] L. Rubini, 'Ain't Wastin' Time No More: Subsidies for Renewable Energy, the SCM Agreement, Policy Space, and Law Reform', *Journal of International Economic Law*, 15 (2) (2012), 559–70.

[178] Ibid., 562–6. The author's analysis is based on the AB decisions in *China–Periodicals* (DS31) and *China–Raw Materials* (DS394, DS395, DS 398).

[179] Ibid., 570; Condon, *supra* n. 175, 686, 690; Espa and Marín Durán, *supra* n. 176, 26–7.

[180] G. Marceau, comment made at the conference where the chapter was initially presented. For different perspectives on reforming Art. 8, see Charnovitz, *supra* n. 174, pp. 60–9; S. Z. Bigdeli, 'Resurrecting the Dead – The Expired Non-Actionable Subsidies and the

found as prohibited export subsidies.[181] In this regard, a balance needs to be found between allowing climate technology-related export incentives, and imposition of safeguards to prevent unnecessary disruption of the world market. Any new carve-out to legitimise export incentives, especially official export credit support should require consideration of a number of factors. First and foremost, the policy objective must be broadly in line with the goal of sustainable development and within that paradigm, may contribute to a common concern of humankind. Second, a form of necessity test must be included. Trade distortion resulted from an export incentive should be balanced with the level of its contribution in addressing a concern. The necessity test should also take into account, inter alia, the appropriateness of the technology in question, and the manifested technology need of the recipient (e.g. the TNAs done under the climate framework). Lastly, resorting to the legitimate exception should only be available as long as such incentives are provided in a fair and transparent manner.

2.5 Common Concern as an Emerging Doctrine: Promises, Challenges, and Outlook

Following the doctrine of Common Concern as laid out in the first chapter of this book, the current chapter carried out an analysis of the possible contribution of the doctrine in addressing the absence of adequate LCT diffusion from the trade angle. Based on that, the conclusion is that the doctrine of Common Concern offers opportunities to forward the agenda of climate technology diffusion and trade along two paths. First, the doctrine is a useful framework to assess and respond to protection and production challenges regarding transboundary public goods. With regard to the WTO laws and mitigation of climate change, particularly diffusion of LCT, the doctrine of Common Concern of Humankind attaches merit to sharpen the focus on the pertinent trade-related issues while remaining within the bounds of sustainable development. Second, as a legal interpretation aid, Common Concern can further inform the understanding of the existing trade-related commitments of countries.

Lingering Question of Green Space', *Manchester Journal of International Economic Law*, 8 (2011), 2; Rubini, *supra* n. 176, 570–6.

[181] It is targeted only to save actionable subsidies (Part III of the SCM Agreement) from litigation challenges and unilateral countervailing measures (Part IV).

144   ZAKER AHMAD

The first point, that is, use of Common Concern as a conceptual framing tool, is of important analytical and strategic utility. As has been shown in this chapter, the doctrine can help build a new, broader, fact-based, and mutually beneficial narrative for LCT diffusion in trade law. Not only is such a narrative important to facilitate technology diffusion and boost overall mitigation of climate change, but it also plays a role in highlighting the useful interdependence between countries and regimes. In doing so, Common Concern–based framework can better integrate WTO in the climate 'regime complex',[182] also moving international rules from the level of ensuring cooperation to affirming integration of countries.[183]

The second point of use, that is, informing existing trade rules, is of legal importance. Going back to the fact that the doctrine of Common Concern supplies an enhanced meaning to this notion, use of the same for treaty interpretation has to fulfil two key prerequisites. First, Common Concern must have a precise legal standing as a source of law that can be resorted to during interpretive analysis. This is already possible to a degree due to the well-established position of the norm in the climate regime and a harmonious approach to treaty interpretation in WTO dispute settlement. However, formal internalisation of the concept within the body of the trade treaty regime would solidify the process, as explained later. Second, it is important that the shared understanding of the meaning of the notion moves beyond being a passing reference,[184] and develops further along the lines suggested in this volume. Although the legal discipline is not inimical to normative claims, interpretation of laws is about finding and implementing the intent of the stakeholders (i.e. states) and not about supplying the same based on normative assumptions. While the common concern of humankind remains a contextual norm capable of being invoked in the trade regime, the meaning and use of the concept would hardly go beyond establishing a shared responsibility unless the proposed deeper formulation is increasingly shared. This is the process of 'claims and responses' as mentioned by Professor Cottier.[185] A similar normative evolution is traceable in the

---

[182] R. O. Keohane and D. G. Victor, 'The Regime Complex for Climate Change', *Perspectives on Politics*, 9(1) (2011), 7.

[183] See Chapter 1 in this volume, p. 84.

[184] See Chapter 9 in this volume, pp. 435, 438.

[185] See Chapter 1 in this volume, pp. 26–9.

history of the growth of 'sustainable development' as a legal norm.[186] As the doctrine of Common Concern continues this journey, trade measures to facilitate technology diffusion would remain an inviting setting to benefit from its growing salience.

The rest of this section is an account of the possible next steps for a progressive realisation of the trade and LCT diffusion along the Common Concern frame. We highlight the areas of cooperation, domestic action, and further enforcement measures across borders.

2.5.1 Building the Foundation for Cooperation

The obligation to cooperate that arises out of a formally internalised doctrine of Common Concern in trade law goes towards filling the absence of a manifest duty to cooperate on tackling trade and climate change issues in WTO law[187] – of which trade-related LCT diffusion measures are a part. The cooperation mandate in relation to common concern should be able to kick-start the new narrative on technology diffusion,[188] by obliging states to engage in good-faith discussions focusing on trade-related barriers as well as mutually beneficial ways of overcoming the same. In practical terms, this is possible through a ministerial declaration where endorsement of climate change as a common concern of humankind is followed by the establishment of a working group mandated to take account of the range of trade-related technology diffusion barriers and make specific recommendations. Until such recommendations are acted upon, a waiver could be put in place to safeguard actions that would be WTO-inconsistent for lack of policy space (e.g. official credit support for technology-embedded exports). The cooperation dimension should also be extended to cover institutional coordination.[189] To the extent the diffusion of clean technologies is concerned, a formal liaison should exist between the proposed WTO working group and the Technology Framework under the Paris Agreement. This would ensure that steps taken across regimes are

---

[186] E. Bürgi Bonanomi, 'History of the Concept of Sustainable Development', *Sustainable Development in International Law Making and Trade: International Food Governance and Trade in Agriculture* (Cheltenham, UK: Edward Elgar, 2015), p. 9.

[187] See Chapter 1 in this volume, pp. 59–60.

[188] See, pp. 115-7.

[189] French, *supra* n. 59, 351.

integrated and geared towards an overall beneficial outcome regarding necessary technology development and transfer.

As explained in the first chapter of this book, transparency and attention to the differentiated responsibilities are also important components to ensure sustainable cooperation.[190] Transparency in imposing trade-related restrictions and incentives for technology diffusion would pave the path for prior consultations in good faith and avoid recourse to an adversarial process.[191] Transparency is especially important with respect to notifying the exact amount of subsidisation supports. Similarly, differentiation is also important not only to be compliant with the climate change regime principle but also to ensure that a justifiable trade measure is implemented in a fair manner.

It need not be that cooperation must take place multilaterally and within the WTO. It is possible that it takes place in other constellations, for example, in plurilateral settings within the WTO or under regional constellations. The considerations would generally remain the same except that significant outcome of cooperation would depend on the size of the markets of the parties as well as skill endowments.

Beyond the climate technology diffusion narrative, the responsibility to cooperate arising out of the doctrine of Common Concern can also positively influence the integration of the trade and the climate regimes. Current proposals[192] of strengthening trade and climate change relationship, for example, reform of subsidy rules,[193] settlement of the PPM debate,[194] promoting trade in sustainable electricity,[195] and other clean energy technologies[196] could all benefit from a synergistic relationship with the Common Concern doctrine. While on one hand, such broader

---

[190] See Chapter 1 in this volume, pp. 60–2.

[191] Avoiding adversarial processes would also be in line with the spirit of the Paris Agreement.

[192] Melendez-Ortiz and Sugathan, *supra* n. 70; J. Bacchus, *Global Rules for Mutually Supportive and Reinforcing Trade and Climate Regimes* (Geneva: ICTSD, 2017).

[193] I. Espa and S. E. Rolland, *Subsidies, Clean Energy, and Climate Change* (Geneva: ICTSD, 2015); L. Rubini, *Rethinking International Subsidies Disciplines: Rationale and Possible Avenues for Reform* (Geneva: ICTSD, 2015).

[194] T. Cottier, *Renewable Energy and Process and Production Methods* (Geneva: ICTSD, 2015); Holzer, *supra* n. 93.

[195] T. Cottier and I. Espa (eds.), *International Trade in Sustainable Electricity: Regulatory Challenges in International Economic Law* (Cambridge: Cambridge University Press, 2017).

[196] M. Sugathan, *Winds of Change and Rays of Hope: How Can the Multilateral Trading System Facilitate Trade in Clean Energy Technologies and Services* (Geneva: ICTSD, 2013).

recourse would bring greater acceptability for the doctrine, on the other hand, a common framing approach would generate harmony between the reform initiatives. Eventually, it might be possible to envisage a trade and climate code[197] based on the principle of Common Concern of Humankind.

2.5.2 Urging Action at the Domestic Level

Actions at the domestic level are most important, because international commitments only get translated into concrete measures through steps taken domestically. It is more so in the field of trade policy, as trade measures that will facilitate diffusion of technology are essentially domestic. As the proposed Common Concern–based narrative also highlights, domestic actions lie at the heart of everything. In that regard, the role of the doctrine is not only suggesting a range of actions, but also guiding the sovereign policy prerogatives[198] away from worsening the concerns and towards addressing the same. The priority areas in this regard should be diverting subsidies from polluting to green sectors, putting a price on carbon emissions, higher adoption of emission and efficiency standards, green public procurement, and clarification of the linkage between intellectual property rights and LCT diffusion.

Although arguably homework actions are easy to take in the context of a cooperative framework, initially the opposite may hold true. It is the unilateral actions of one or more states that initiate cooperation.[199] States are not precluded from advancing the Common Concern agenda by self-motivated measures.[200] The doctrine of Common Concern will inspire, guide, and legitimise trade measures for LCT diffusion. The inspiration will come from the enhanced importance attached to the concern on one hand, and helpful clarification of the extent of the available range of policy measures due to cooperation efforts on the other. The legitimation will arise from the support domestic measures can draw from being linked to the Common Concern–based agenda.

The compliance-related assistance from Common Concern is context-dependent. First and foremost, it can guide states to find a strategy that

---

[197] Hufbauer *et al.*, *supra* n. 91, ch. 5.

[198] See Chapter 1 in this volume, pp. 57–8, 64–5.

[199] See Chapter 10 in this volume, pp. 456, 459.

[200] These two options are proposed by Cottier as implementation of international obligation and adoption of autonomous measures (see Chapter 1 in this volume, pp. 63–4).

serves multiple purposes (e.g. technology diffusion), while pursuing domestic economic interests. It is possible to find avenues that lead to a convergence of multiple state interests, as shown before. The role of the Common Concern doctrine is to create the ground for such convergence to take place. It is also possible to use Common Concern as a rallying point to mobilise the non-state actors (e.g. NGOs, activists) to eventually put pressure on the government. Both can lead to the outcome of formal recognition and acceptance of the notion, which then further serves as the launchpad for greater recognition. When recognised, it may attach a cost to non-compliance, making compliance the feasible option.

Beyond developing a well-defined policy space to adopt domestic measures and also supplying justification when challenged, it would be difficult to argue that the framework of common concern would impose a strict duty to act for several reasons briefly mentioned here. First, it would be necessary to specify whether the obligation would be one of conduct or one of the result. Second, in the case of an obligation of result, the contours need to be specified. This in itself is a difficult exercise because of the differential context of each of the countries – an issue which was resolved in the Paris Agreement by adopting the obligation of conduct approach when it comes to mitigation action. Lastly, specification of a strict duty also brings the possibility of lodging a claim upon breach of the same, an event which potentially may have a backlash that would make states reluctant to accept Common Concern as a beneficial norm in the first place.

Trade measures naturally impose extraterritorial effects, as the measures are often applied in respect of the transactions across borders. The success of the trade measures deployed for diffusion of LCTs depends on their imposition of cross-border effect; by restricting GHG emitting technologies through PPMs, and by promoting LCTs through incentives. Extraterritorial effects are a fact and not a problem per se in WTO law, as long there is a 'sufficient nexus' between the measure itself and the domestic territory.[201] Extraterritorial effects would only be challenged in cases they are negative, in which cases their justification would depend upon available policy room and fair implementation. In both aspects, the discussion has shown that connection with a Common Concern can prove to be beneficial.

---

[201] Appellate Body Report, *US–Shrimp, supra* n. 32, para. 133.

TRADE-RELATED MEASURES AND LCTS   149

2.5.3 Inducing Compliance through Trade Countermeasures

Although this chapter has not dealt in-depth with this part of the doctrine, it nonetheless is of important value. Here we briefly summarise some of the pertinent issues involving climate technology diffusion and trade countermeasures that are worth pondering upon.

Structuring the sphere of states' unilateral actions to ensure compliance with the collective interests of the international community would be an important contribution of the Common Concern doctrine. Due to the absence of clear law,[202] unilateral action to defend common interest is largely undisciplined. As far as trade-related unilateral compliance measures are concerned, they remain the prerogative of large and powerful states, often used to further parochial rather than common interests.[203] With regard to climate mitigation, scholars have pointed out the potential benefit of using trade restriction to prevent inaction,[204] but no actual progress has been made. This is why compliance securing obligation upon states by the doctrine of Common Concern is welcome.

With respect to the diffusion of LCTs and trade, it would first of all be important to specify what may amount to non-compliance that may trigger countermeasures. It is in itself a second-order question, dependent upon the nature of primary rules developed in the first place. But, whatever exact nature the primary rules may have, the direct result of non-compliance with technology diffusion arrangements would be a potential technology recipient's inability to curb emissions to the desired level over time. To the extent such inability rises from weak primary rules (e.g. absence of assistance), countermeasures would not resolve the situation. But if such a situation arises from wilful neglect towards meaningful cooperation, or non-cooperation despite adequate support, countermeasures in the form of trade restriction would indeed be a useful tool.

---

[202] It has been well noted that the state practice of third-party countermeasures have long existed, despite a lack of clear applicable rules of international law (A. Cassese, *International Law* (Oxford: Oxford University Press, 2005), p. 271); see also Chapter 5 in this volume, pp. 252–5.

[203] Chapter 5 in this volume.

[204] A. Benjamin, M. Gerrard, T. Huydecoper, M. Kirby, M. C. Mehta, T. Pogge, Q. Tianbao, D. Shelton, J. Silk, J. Simor, J. Spier, E. Steiner, and P. Sutherland, *Oslo Principles on Global Climate Change Obligations* (2015), https://law.yale.edu/system/files/area/center/schell/oslo_principles.pdf (accessed 1 Jan. 2019). Paragraph 20 of the Oslo Principles holds that '[s]tates must make their best efforts to bring about lawful and appropriate trade consequences for States that fail to comply with the obligations set out in these Principles'.

Well-calibrated and proportionate trade countermeasures, taken in good faith by large markets can induce enough pressure upon the recalcitrant states to engage in adoption and upgrade of mitigation technologies.

2.6 Conclusion

It is important that in an interdependent global legal system, the trade rules evolve in a way that accommodates the interests of preserving and promoting public goods. To reverse the imminent and worsening hazards of anthropogenic climate change, the economic system must be redesigned and reformed in a sustainable fashion. In practical terms, it requires shifts in the patterns of production, processing, and consumptions towards low-emission growth. Rules of trade must be framed and understood in a way that brings this change. The AB once held that 'WTO rules are not so rigid or so inflexible as not to leave room for reasoned judgements in confronting the endless and ever-changing ebb and flow of real facts in real cases in the real world'.[205]

This chapter has shown that the doctrine of Common Concern of Humankind can serve as a framework to realise the progressive development of WTO law. As a legal notion, Common Concern can advance the mutually beneficial relationship between trade and climate regime. With respect to the diffusion of LCTs, the doctrine can form the basis of a new narrative involving new rule development through cooperation, inspire adoption of facilitative trade measures that internalises emission externalities, as well as contribute to a more facilitative and integrated understanding of the WTO laws.

***

Select Bibliography

Abdel-Latif, A. (2015). 'Intellectual Property Rights and the Transfer of Climate Technologies: Issues, Challenges and Way Forward', *Climate Policy* 15(1) pp. 103–26.

Atik, J. (2017). 'Technology Transfer', in Thomas Cottier *et al.* (eds.), *Elgar Encyclopedia of International Economic Law* (Cheltenham, UK: Edward Elgar), pp. 606–9.

---

[205] Appellate Body Report, *Japan–Alcohol II, supra* n. 101, p. 32.

Boldt, J., Nygaard, I., Hansen, Ulrich E., and Trærup, S. (2012). *Overcoming Barriers to the Transfer and Diffusion of Climate Technologies* (2nd ed., UNEP Risø Centre).

Brandi, C. (2017). *Trade Elements in Countries' Climate Contributions under the Paris Agreement* (Geneva: ICTSD), www.ictsd.org/sites/default/files/research/trade_elements_in_countries _climate_contributions.pdf (accessed 19 Sept. 2019).

Charnovitz, S. (2014). 'Green Subsidies and the WTO', World Bank policy research working paper, http://documents.worldbank.org/curated/en/2014/10/20290817/green-subsidies-wto (accessed 19 Sept. 2019).

Coppens, D. (2014). *WTO Disciplines on Subsidies and Countervailing Measures: Balancing Policy Space and Legal Constraints* (Cambridge: Cambridge University Press).

Cottier, T., Nartova, O., and Bigdeli, S. Z. (eds.) (2009). *International Trade Regulation and the Mitigation of Climate Change: World Trade Forum* (Cambridge: Cambridge University Press) pp. 1007–37.

Cottier, T., Nartova, O., and Shingal, A. (2014). 'The Potential of Tariff Policy for Climate Change Mitigation', *Legal and Economic Analysis, Journal of World Trade* 48.

Cramton, P. C., MacKay, D. J. C., and Ockenfels, A. (eds.) (2017). *Global Carbon Pricing: The Path to Climate Cooperation* (Cambridge, MA: MIT Press).

de Coninck, H. and Sagar, A. (2017). 'Technology Development and Transfer (Article 10)', in Daniel Klein *et al.* (eds.), *The Paris Agreement on Climate Change: Analysis and Commentary* (Oxford: Oxford University Press), pp. 258–76.

de Coninck, H. *et al.* (2018). 'Strengthening and Implementing the Global Response', in Valerie Masson-Delmotte *et al.* (eds.), *Special Report: Global Warming of 1.5 °C* (Geneva: World Meteorological Organization), pp. 313–443.

Gallagher, K. S. (2014). *The Globalization of Clean Energy Technology: Lessons from China* (Cambridge, Massachusetts: MIT Press).

Holzer, K. (2014). *Carbon-Related Border Adjustment and WTO Law* (Cheltenham, UK: Edward Elgar).

Humphreys, S. (2012). 'Structural Ambiguity: Technology Transfer in Three Regimes', in Margaret A. Young (ed.), *Regime Interaction in International Law* (Cambridge: Cambridge University Press), pp. 175–98.

Keohane, R. O. and Victor, D. G. (2011). 'The Regime Complex for Climate Change', *Perspectives on Politics* 9 pp. 7–23.

Marceau, G. (2016). 'The Interface between the Trade Rules and Climate Change Actions', in Deok-Young Park (ed.), *Legal Issues on Climate Change and International Trade Law* (Berlin: Springer), pp. 3–39.

Ockwell, D. and Mallett, A. (eds.) (2012). *Low-Carbon Technology Transfer: From Rhetoric to Reality* (London: Routledge).

Trærup, S., Greersen, L., and Kundsen, C. (2018) *Mapping Barriers and Enabling Environments in Technology Needs Assessments, Nationally Determined Contributions, and Technical Assistance of the Climate Technology Centre and Network*, background paper TEC/2018/17/4, https://orbit.dtu.dk/files/164669703/Barriers_and_Enablers_to _tt_25Sept.pdf (accessed 16 Sept. 2019).

UNEP, EPO, and ICTSD (2010). *Patents and Clean Energy: Bridging the Gap between Evidence and Policy* (Geneva: UNEP, EPO, ICTSD).

3

Marine Plastic Pollution as a Common Concern of Humankind

JUDITH SCHÄLI

3.1 Introduction

During the last couple of years, the problem of marine plastic pollution has been receiving wide attention by policymakers, media and the civil society. Awareness of the problem and of the scale and severity of its consequences is rapidly raising. The present chapter shows that there is a process underway towards recognition of marine pollution, and plastic pollution in particular, as a common concern of humankind. It aims at exploring the potentials of the doctrine suggested by the project to further reinforce global efforts to mitigate marine plastic pollution.

The chapter starts with a short analysis of the factual, political and legal dimensions of the problem of marine plastic pollution (Section 3.2). It depicts the main facts and figures (Section 3.2.1), including with regard to sources, distribution and impacts of marine plastic litter, and describes the reception of the subject in international policy (Section 3.2.2), as well as the main obligations of states under the United Nations Convention of the Law of the Sea (UNCLOS) relevant to marine litter mitigation (Section 3.2.3). Section 3.2 shows that massive accumulation of marine litter is internationally recognized as one of the most pressing environmental concerns of our time. Interestingly, the existing international legal regime stipulates several obligations of states that widely correspond to the cooperation and homework pillars of the Concept of Common Concern of Humankind as defined in this book.

The chapter builds on the author's dissertation and has thematic overlaps: J. Schäli, *The Mitigation of Marine Plastic Pollution in International Law: Facts, Policy and Legal Implications*, as approved by the University of Bern on 28 May 2020, publication forthcoming. A draft version of the chapter was presented at the conference 'Towards a Principle of Common Concern in Global Law', World Trade Institute, University of Bern, 22–23 June 2018. The author would like to thank Thomas Cottier and the members of our research team for their valuable feedback on previous drafts. She also thanks all conference participants, especially Oisin Suttle, Duncan French and Peter-Tobias Stoll, as well as the external reviewers for their helpful comments and suggestions.

154   JUDITH SCHÄLI

A short overview of the Concept of Common Concern of Humankind will be given in the subsequent section (Section 3.3). Section 3.3 will also analyse possible implications of the concept studied in this book and explore respective potentials of the concept with a view to strengthening the regime applying to marine litter mitigation. The chapter concludes that the concept indeed may complement and supplement ongoing efforts currently undertaken under the auspices of the UN Environment Assembly (UNEA) to enhance and strengthen the existing regime on marine plastic mitigation.

3.2 A Global Concern Calling for a Global Response

3.2.1 Plastics in the Marine Environment

The history of fully synthetic plastics is still young. My grandparents barely knew of them when they were children. Today's commodity plastics were developed only in the 1920s and 1930s – not even a century ago. Even after the 1950s, plastics were almost exclusively used in durable goods, such as telephones and cable insulations. Today, global annual production of plastics is at about 340 million metric tonnes and is rapidly increasing.[1] The bulk of it is no longer used for durable goods. Because of their low price and high availability, plastics have considerably influenced our production and consumption patterns and have promoted a throw-away lifestyle. Packaging accounts for 40 per cent of plastics used. Disposable bags, cups, cutlery and similar single-use items are also usually made from plastics. They have a very short average service life and soon turn into waste. When compared to their time of use, the end-of-life stage of plastics can be extremely long, as most plastics are highly bioinert and do not biodegrade. This means that, with the exception of incinerated plastics, almost every piece of plastic ever made and landfilled or released into the environment is still there – probably fragmentized into tiny pieces referred to as microplastics – and poses a potential risk to the environment and to human health.[2] About 10 per cent of an estimated amount of 2 billion metric tonnes of municipal solid waste that are

---

[1] See PlasticsEurope, 'Plastics – the Facts 2017: An Analysis of European Plastics Production, Demand and Waste Data' (PlasticsEurope Market Research Group (PEMRG) 2017), 16.

[2] David K. A. Barnes *et al.*, 'Accumulation and Fragmentation of Plastic Debris in Global Environments', *Philosophical Transactions of the Royal Society B: Biological Sciences*, 364 (2009), 1985, 1993.

generated worldwide each year[3] are plastics. As of 2015, approximately 6.3 billion metric tonnes of plastic wastes had been generated, almost 80 per cent of which was accumulated in landfills or the natural environment. By 2050, about 12 billion metric tonnes of plastic wastes will be in landfills or the natural environment if no significant changes in production and waste management trends are undertaken.[4]

About 10 per cent of all plastic wastes end up in the sea.[5] According to a study presented at the World Economic Forum in 2016, oceans are expected to contain more plastics than fish (by weight) by 2050 in a business-as-usual scenario.[6] Plastics make up 60–90 per cent of wastes that are accumulated in marine environments, including beaches and coastal waters, ocean water columns and the seabed.[7] They are

---

[3] See 'Global Waste Management Market Assessment 2007' (Key Note Publications Ltd, 2007), as cited in Anne Scheinberg, David C. Wilson and Ljiljana Rodic, *Solid Waste Management in the World's Cities: Water and Sanitation in the World's Cities 2010* (Earthscan for UN-HABITAT, 2010), p. 13. Waste Atlas, an interactive map with visualized waste management data from 162 countries, estimates global municipal solid waste generation to 1.9 billion tonnes with almost 30 percent of it to remain uncollected: 'Waste Atlas – Interactive Map with Visualized Waste Management Data', www.atlas.d-waste .com/ (accessed 20 Sept. 2019). Gupta assumes that alone in the United States, over one billion tonnes of municipal solid waste is generated annually (Ashwani K. Gupta and David G. Lilley, 'Thermal Destruction of Wastes and Plastics', in A. L. Andrady (ed.), *Plastics and the Environment* (Hoboken, NJ: Wiley-Interscience, 2003), pp. 630–1). See also Daniel Hoornweg and Perinaz Bhata-Tata, 'What a Waste: A Global Review of Solid Waste Management' (Washington, DC: World Bank, 2012), No. 15, 2.

[4] Roland Geyer, Jenna R. Jambeck and Kara Lavender Law, 'Production, Use, and Fate of All Plastics Ever Made', *Science Advances*, 3 (2017), e1700782.

[5] Richard C. Thompson, 'Plastic Debris in the Marine Environment: Consequences and Solutions', in Jochen C Krause, Henning von Nordheim and Stefan Bräger (eds.), *Marine Nature Conservation in Europe 2006: Proceedings of the Symposium Held in Stralsund, Germany, 8th–12th May 2006* (German Federal Agency for Nature Conservation, 2007), p. 108.

[6] World Economic Forum, 'The New Plastics Economy: Rethinking the Future of Plastics' (2016), 7, www3.weforum.org/docs/WEF_The_New_Plastics_Economy.pdf (accessed 20 Sept. 2019).

[7] See David K. A. Barnes, 'Remote Islands Reveal Rapid Rise of Southern Hemisphere Sea Debris', *Scientific World Journal*, 5 (2005), 915, 918; Barnes *et al.*, *supra* n. 2, 1987; José G. B. Derraik, 'The Pollution of the Marine Environment by Plastic Debris: A Review', *Marine Pollution Bulletin*, 44 (2002), 842, 843; Murray R. Gregory and Anthony L. Andrady, 'Plastics in the Marine Environment', in Andrady, *supra* n. 3, p. 380; M. R. Gregory and P. G. Ryan, 'Pelagic Plastics and Other Seaborne Persistent Synthetic Debris: A Review of Southern Hemisphere Perspectives', in James M. Coe and Donald B. Rogers (eds.), *Marine Debris: Sources, Impacts and Solutions* (New York: Springer, 1997), p. 63; Carey Morishige *et al.*, 'Factors Affecting Marine Debris Deposition at French Frigate Shoals, Northwestern Hawaiian Islands Marine National Monument, 1990–2006', *Marine*

ubiquitous in the oceans and do not only occur close to population centres, but also in polar regions, open oceans, remote islands and the deep seabed.[8] Based on twenty-four expeditions across the oceans and semi-enclosed seas between 2007 and 2013, it has been estimated that there are more than 5.25 trillion pelagic plastic particles floating in the oceans, with a total weight of almost 270,000 metric tonnes.[9] Another sampling study, published in 2018, predicted about 1.8 trillion pieces of floating plastic debris with a total weight of at least 79,000 metric tonnes inside an area of 1.6 million km^2. The study suggests that prior sampling studies greatly underestimated plastic quantities in the marine environment.[10] Considering past and current input rates of plastics from land-based and sea-based sources, as well as the high durability of plastic materials and their inability to biodegrade, especially in the marine environment, actual concentration levels of marine plastics should be two orders of magnitude higher than are observed and reported levels.[11] Most plastics in the oceans thus vanish from our view and are unaccounted for in the surveys. They are consumed by marine organisms, fragment into pieces small enough to escape sampling methods, sink to lower oceanic levels, including the ocean floor, beach along coasts or are conserved in pack ice. However, whether seen or not, they persist in the environment. And so does their impact.

More than 800 different marine species have been shown to be directly affected through ingestion of plastics and microplastic particles, entanglement in marine debris, ghost fishing by derelict fishing nets or ropes, dispersal by rafting on marine plastic debris, and provision of new

---

Pollution Bulletin, 54 (2007), 1162, 1167; Boyan Slat *et al.*, *How the Oceans Can Clean Themselves: A Feasibility Study* (2.0, Ocean Cleanup, 2014), p. 38.

[8] Gregory and Andrady, *supra* n. 7, 384; Jort Hammer, Michiel H. S. Kraak and John R. Parsons, 'Plastics in the Marine Environment: The Dark Side of a Modern Gift', in David M. Whitacre (ed.), *Reviews of Environmental Contamination and Toxicology*, vol. 220 (New York: Springer, 2012), p. 13; UNEP, *Marine Litter: An Analytical Overview* (UNEP, 2005), p. ii; UNEP, *UNEP Year Book 2014: Emerging Issues in Our Global Environment* (UNEP, 2014) 49.

[9] Marcus Eriksen *et al.*, 'Plastic Pollution in the World's Oceans: More than 5 Trillion Plastic Pieces Weighing over 250,000 Tons Afloat at Sea', *PLoS ONE*, 9 (2014), e111913, 7; cf. Andrés Cózar *et al.*, 'Plastic Debris in the Open Ocean', *Proceedings of the National Academy of Sciences*, 111 (2014), 10239.

[10] L. Lebreton *et al.*, 'Evidence that the Great Pacific Garbage Patch Is Rapidly Accumulating Plastic', *Scientific Reports*, 8 (2018), www.nature.com/articles/s41598-018-22939-w (accessed 20 Sept. 2019).

[11] Ibid., 12. See also Eriksen *et al.*, *supra* n. 9, 10.

habitats due to marine littering.[12] Affected species include all trophic levels from small filter feeding organisms at the bottom of the food chain to marine mammals, including whales.[13] In some species, ingestion is reported in over 80 per cent of a population sampled.[14] Both, entanglement and ingestion, can have lethal effects. In addition, marine plastic debris has toxicological impacts on marine ecosystems and marine biodiversity. Plastics can leach chemicals, some of which have potential negative health effects.[15] Plastic particles also tend to accumulate persistent, bioaccumulative and toxic substances from the surrounding seawater. Concentrations of such substances are several orders of magnitude higher on the surface of plastic debris than in the surrounding seawater.[16] When ingested, plastics transfer the pollutants to the tissues of organisms.[17] The chemicals penetrate cells, where they have a broad range of disrupting effects.[18] They bioaccumulate and are biomagnified throughout the food chain. Bioaccumulation of such chemicals has been

[12] CBD Secretariat, *Marine Debris: Understanding, Preventing and Mitigating the Significant Adverse Impacts on Marine and Coastal Biodiversity* (New York: McGraw-Hill Education, 2016), p. 16.

[13] Matthew Cole *et al.*, 'Microplastics as Contaminants in the Marine Environment: A Review', *Marine Pollution Bulletin*, 62 (2011), 2588, 2593; David W. Laist, 'Impacts of Marine Debris: Entanglement of Marine Life in Marine Debris Including a Comprehensive List of Species with Entanglement and Ingestion Records', in Coe and Rogers, *supra* n. 7, pp. 99–137. See also Susanne Kühn, Elisa L. Bravo Rebolledo and Jan A. van Franeker, 'Deleterious Effects of Litter on Marine Life', in Melanie Bergmann, Lars Gutow and Michael Klages (eds.), *Marine Anthropogenic Litter* (New York: Springer, 2015), pp. 75–105, with references; UNEP and GRID-Arendal, *Marine Litter: Vital Graphics* (2016) 15, with references.

[14] Chelsea M. Rochman *et al.*, 'The Ecological Impacts of Marine Debris: Unraveling the Demonstrated Evidence from What Is Perceived', *Ecology*, 97 (2016), 302, 303.

[15] Released substances include phthalates, brominated flame retardants, bisphenol A, formaldehyde, acetaldehyde, 4-nonylphenol and possibly polyfluoronated compounds, triclosan, phthalate plasticizers and lead heat stabilizers (Chelsea M. Rochman, 'The Complex Mixture, Fate and Toxicity of Chemicals Associated with Plastic Debris in the Marine Environment', in Bergmann *et al.*, *supra* n. 13, p. 131, with references).

[16] See Barnes *et al.*, *supra* n. 2, 1995.

[17] Rochman *et al.*, 'The Ecological Impacts of Marine Debris', *supra* n. 14, 303. See also Anthony L. Andrady, 'Microplastics in the Marine Environment', *Marine Pollution Bulletin*, 62 (2011), 1596, 1601–2; Emma L. Teuten *et al.*, 'Transport and Release of Chemicals from Plastics to the Environment and to Wildlife', *Philosophical Transactions of the Royal Society B: Biological Sciences*, 364 (2009), 2027.

[18] See Mark Anthony Browne *et al.*, 'Microplastic Moves Pollutants and Additives to Worms, Reducing Functions Linked to Health and Biodiversity', *Current Biology*, 23 (2013), 2388, 2388; Chelsea M. Rochman *et al.*, 'Ingested Plastic Transfers Hazardous Chemicals to Fish and Induces Hepatic Stress', *Scientific Reports*, 3 (2013), 3263, 3–4; Chelsea M. Rochman *et al.*, 'Early Warning Signs of Endocrine Disruption in Adult Fish

shown in a range of commercially important fish and shellfish.[19] Floating plastics also serve as a vector for contaminants and pathogenic micro-organisms, helping them to spread, and facilitate transport of invasive species to sensible ecosystems.

Social and economic consequences of marine plastic debris are just as severe as its ecological impacts. Marine plastic pollution poses a threat to human health and affects national economies. It impedes legitimate uses of the sea, including marine transportation, fishing and recreation. Global costs related to marine litter have been estimated at US\$13 billion per year. A part of these costs is borne by the shipping and fishing industries, tourism, aquaculture and agriculture. Another part is borne by municipalities and the public at large.[20]

Little has to be said about the utmost significance of the oceans and the services they provide. The oceans cover about 70 per cent of the earth's surface. With an average depth of 4 kilometres and a maximal depth of 11 kilometres, they constitute some 99 per cent of the living space on earth, hold 97 per cent of the planet's water and embrace 97 per cent of the biosphere.[21] An estimated ten million to a hundred million species live in marine environments, most of which are endemic to the oceans and have not yet been discovered or explored.[22] With their incredible variety of living species, oceans provide an important source of food and generate more than half of the atmosphere's oxygen.[23] At the same time, they play an important role in climate change mitigation, as they absorb

---

from the Ingestion of Polyethylene with and without Sorbed Chemical Pollutants from the Marine Environment', *Science of the Total Environment*, 493 (2014), 656.

[19] See Mark A. Browne *et al.*, 'Ingested Microscopic Plastic Translocates to the Circulatory System of the Mussel, Mytilus Edulis (L)', *Environmental Science & Technology*, 42 (2008), 5026.

[20] See, in general, Alistair McIlgorm, Harry F. Campbell and Michael J. Rule, 'The Economic Cost and Control of Marine Debris Damage in the Asia-Pacific Region', *Ocean & Coastal Management*, 54 (2011), 643; John Mouat, Rebeca Lopez Lozano and Hannah Bateson, 'Economic Impacts of Marine Litter' (KIMO International, 2010); UNEP, 'Valuing Plastic: The Business Case for Measuring, Managing and Disclosing Plastic Use in the Consumer Goods Industry' (UNEP, 2014).

[21] See Ted Danson, *Oceana: Our Endangered Oceans and What We Can Do to Save Them* (Rodale Books, 2011) 2; Sylvia A. Earle, *The World Is Blue: How Our Fate and the Ocean's Are One* (Washington, DC: National Geographic, 2010), p. 127.

[22] See Michelle Allsopp *et al.*, *World Watch Report 174: Oceans in Peril: Protecting Marine Biodiversity* (Worldwatch Institute, 2007) 7; Earle, *supra* n. 21, pp. 131–2.

[23] For more information on human fish consumption, see, for instance, Tim Schröder (ed.), 'Fish – a Prized Commodity', *World Ocean Review 2: The Future of Fish – The Fisheries of the Future* (2013), p. 32.

huge quantities of carbon dioxide.[24] Oceans generally regulate climate and temperature and degrade pollutants. They include some of the most important transportation routes for world trade[25] and are an important source of income, as well as of medicine, energy, water and mineral resources.[26] Oceans have therefore been referred to as the 'life-support system' of our planet.[27] Their cultural, recreational and aesthetic value is not quantifiable.[28]

Marine life is threatened by a wide range of human-made challenges, including overfishing, the destruction of habitats, oil pollution, eutrophication, ocean acidification due to climate change, or nuclear testing.[29] The stresses and strains we are putting on the oceans and on marine biodiversity have reached a level at which the marine environment may lose its capacity to provide food or other services and not be able to regenerate.[30] Marine plastic pollution is an additional stressor, the dimension and implications of which have long been underestimated.

---

[24] See United Nations General Assembly (UNGA), 'Report of the Secretary-General: Oceans and the Law of the Sea' (2007) UN Doc. A/62/66, para. 158; Judith Wehrli and Thomas Cottier, 'Towards a Treaty Instrument on Marine Genetic Resources', in Marta Chantal Ribeiro (ed.), *30 Years after the Signature of the United Nations Convention on the Law of the Sea: The Protection of the Environment and the Future of the Law of the Sea* (Coimbra Editora, 2014), pp. 518–51.

[25] Of volume of global trade, 80 per cent is seaborne, representing 70 per cent of its value (United Nations, 'UNCLOS at 30' (United Nations, 2012), 2, www.un.org/depts/los/ convention_agreements/pamphlet_unclos_at_30.pdf (accessed 20 Sept. 2019)). See also Earle, *supra* n. 21, 17; UNGA, 'Report of the Secretary-General: Oceans and the Law of the Sea', *supra* n. 24 , para. 158.

[26] According to the United Nations, 'the potential energy output derived from oceans well exceeds current and future human energy needs' (United Nations, *supra* n. 25, 2).

[27] Astronaut Joe Allen, as cited by Earle, *supra* n. 21, p. 265.

[28] Judith Schäli, 'Intergenerational Justice and the Concept of Common Concern in Marine Resource Allocation and Ocean Governance', in Thomas Cottier, Shaheeza Lalani and Clarence Sibiza (eds.), *Intergenerational Equity: Environmental and Cultural Concerns* (Leiden: Brill Nijhoff, 2019), pp. 70ff.

[29] According to a study on the anthropogenic impact on different marine ecosystems, no area is unaffected by human influence. A large fraction (41 per cent) is strongly affected by multiple drivers: see Benjamin S. Halpern *et al.*, 'A Global Map of Human Impact on Marine Ecosystems', *Science* 319(5865) (2008), 948, doi:10.1126/science.1149345.

[30] See United Nations, *supra* n. 25, 6; Tullio Treves, 'Principles and Objectives of the Legal Regime Governing Areas Beyond National Jurisdiction', in A. G. Oude Elferink and E. J. Molenaar (eds.), *The International Legal Regime of Areas beyond National Jurisdiction: Current and Future Developments* (Leiden: Brill, 2010), p. 22.

Sixty-four per cent of the ocean surface and about 95 per cent of its volume do not fall under national jurisdiction of a single state, but need to be jointly managed by the international community or unilateral policies and the law of states. Areas beyond national jurisdiction notably include the high seas and the deep seabed.[31] Their degradation due to human impacts follows the pattern of the tragedy of the commons as described by Hardin.[32] As most of plastic objects are buoyant and travel long distances on ocean currents, including to remote places, the problem is inherently transboundary in nature.[33] Ocean currents tend to accumulate the debris in five different subtropical convergence zones or gyres in the North and South Atlantic Ocean, the North and South Pacific and the Indian Ocean (see Figure 3.1).[34] Open-ocean accumulation zones mostly lie in areas beyond national jurisdiction and are to be considered as damaging to the global commons to which nearly all the countries contribute in a continuous way.

In coastal waters and beaches, most plastics stem from land-based sources. They mainly include mismanaged waste from urban centres and coastal dumping sites or from touristic beaches. The most commonly found plastic litter items in the marine environment, especially beaches, include cigarette butts, plastic beverage bottles and bottle caps, food wrappers, plastic grocery bags and other bags, plastic lids, straws and stirrers, foam take-away containers, and plastic cups and plates.[35]

---

[31] United Nations Convention on the Law of the Sea (UNCLOS) (opened for signature on 10 Dec. 1982, entered into force on 16 Nov. 1994) 1833 UNTS 397, 21 ILM 1261 (1982) Parts VII and XI. According to UNCLOS, areas under national jurisdiction include internal waters, the territorial sea, the continental shelf and the exclusive economic zone (EEZ).

[32] Garrett Hardin, 'The Tragedy of the Commons', *Science*, 162 (1968), 1243.

[33] Hammer *et al.*, *supra* n. 8, 5; Lebreton *et al.*, *supra* n. 10, 12.

[34] Plastic accumulation in the gyres has recently received wide media attention. The zones have been referred to as 'plastic garbage patches', 'plastic soup', 'trash vortexes' or 'plastic islands'. Yet, the zones are not comparable to solid islands and are not distinguishable on satellite images. Average particle sizes are too small for this, and many fragments are submerged. Fragments that are not washed ashore or consumed by animals will foul and eventually sink to the ground (Barnes *et al.*, *supra* n. 2, 1988; Hammer *et al.*, *supra* n. 8, 13). Plastic fragments may also sink if their density changes due to the leaching of additives (Francois Galgani, Georg Hanke and Thomas Maes, 'Global Distribution, Composition and Abundance of Marine Litter', in Bergmann *et al.*, *supra* n. 13, p. 36).

[35] See Ocean Conservancy, 'International Coastal Cleanup 2017 Report' (2017) 13 https://oceanconservancy.org/wp-content/uploads/2017/04/2017-Ocean-Conservancy-ICC-Report.pdf (accessed 20 Sept. 2019). The 2016 International Coastal Cleanup involved 504,583 volunteers in 112 countries around the world, who removed 8,346 tonnes of debris (13,840,398 items) from 24,136 km of beaches and inland waterways.

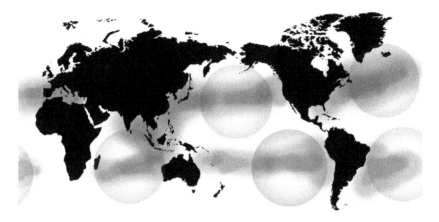

Figure 3.1 Approximate positions of open-ocean plastic accumulation zones

Primary microplastic particles are commonly found on beaches and water surfaces all over the world in form of preproduction pellets[36] or plastic microbeads as used in cosmetic products and abrasives. Secondary microplastics stem from different sources, such as laundering (textile fibres) or tyre wear. A 2017 study by the International Union for Conservation of Nature (IUCN) suggests that in some countries, more plastic is released from driving and washing activities than from the mismanagement of our waste.[37] In offshore places, about 60 per cent of marine debris is from sea-based sources, including, among other things, lost cargo from vessels and abandoned, discarded or lost fishing gear.[38] Abandoned fishing nets and ropes are particularly problematic as they continue fishing for an indefinite period of time.

Accumulation and distribution of marine plastics depend on ocean currents, winds and other natural factors, but also on a broad range of social and behavioural factors, including shore use, available waste

---

[36] Hammer et al., supra n. 8, 6, with references.
[37] See, in general, Julien Boucher and Damien Friot, 'Primary Microplastics in the Oceans: A Global Evaluation of Sources' (IUCN, 2017). See also Edgar Hernandez, Bernd Nowack and Denise M. Mitrano, 'Polyester Textiles as a Source of Microplastics from Households: A Mechanistic Study to Understand Microfiber Release During Washing', Environmental Science & Technology, 51 (2017), 7036; Sandra Schöttner, 'Vom Waschbecken ins Meer: Zu den Umweltfolgen von Mikrokuststoffen in Kosmetik- und Körperpflegeprodukten' (Greenpeace, 2017).
[38] See Hammer et al., supra n. 8, 18; Galgani et al., supra n. 34, 39.

management infrastructure and proximity to urban settlements.[39] Costal zones close to river mouths and urban centres generally experience the highest accumulation rates. As many of them are considered as biodiversity hotspots, they are particularly vulnerable to the negative impacts of plastic pollution. Also, coastal plastic pollution poses a great problem to local families and communities who bear the costs. They have to pay for the clean-ups and have a potential loss of income or additional expenditures due to the negative effects of plastic pollution on tourism, fisheries and shipping. Hence, costs related to marine plastic pollution are regularly not borne by the ones who are responsible for them in the first place.[40] Especially producers and users of plastic goods do not usually have to pay the full costs related to these products and the damage they cause when released into the environment. Such a pattern of negative externalities and equity concerns is also reflected at an international level: countries are very unevenly affected by the issue, depending on their geographic location, national economy and level of income. Developing countries, and especially small island developing countries, are generally most affected, even though their contribution to the problem may be negligible.

Equity concerns related to marine plastic pollution also have an intergenerational dimension. The full scale of the problem is still unknown and some consequences may only be revealed in the future.[41] Future generations will possibly have to bear even greater costs related to plastics that have been produced, used and discarded into the environment in the past. Also, they might not benefit from the same services that oceans provide to us, partially because marine plastic pollution inhibits oceans from providing such services.

Apart from cumbersome beach clean-ups, which are reminiscent of a Sisyphean task, there are currently no valuable clean-up technologies available for widespread marine plastic debris.[42] Especially once plastic

---

[39] See Barnes *et al.*, *supra* n. 2, 1989 and 1995; C. J. Moore *et al.*, 'A Comparison of Plastic and Plankton in the North Pacific Central Gyre', *Marine Pollution Bulletin*, 42 (2001), 1297, 1299; Peter Kershaw *et al.*, 'Plastic Debris in the Ocean', *UNEP Year Book 2011: Emerging Issues in Our Global Environment* (UNEP, 2011), p. 22.

[40] See P. Ten Brink *et al.*, *Guidelines on the Use of Market-Based Instruments to Address the Problem of Marine Litter* (UNEP, 2009), p. 22.

[41] See Gregory and Andrady, *supra* n. 7, p. 380.

[42] Different models of marine garbage collectors are currently under development or in early testing phases. However, they almost exclusively target surface plastics of a certain size, but no smaller parts, such as microplastic particles, nor submerged plastics or

objects have fragmentized into microplastic particles or have sunk to lower oceanic levels, their fate largely remains beyond human hands. With continuously rising production levels of plastics and a decreasing average service life of plastic products, plastic waste generation is rocketing. As a consequence, the abundance of marine plastic debris is also exponentially rising.[43] Plastic accumulation in the oceans will not slow down until there is a significant change in our production and consumption patterns and global waste management, including in low-income countries with weak waste infrastructures. Such a change necessarily involves all countries and all different kind of actors, including governments, producers, consumers and waste management operators. Given our incapacity of cleaning up the oceans from plastics, our only way to encounter the problem is to address it at source. Even if we succeed in doing so, existing quantities of marine debris are likely to persist for many centuries.[44]

Marine plastic pollution thus poses a long-term threat to several global public goods, such as a clean marine environment and the ecosystem services it provides, or public health. It potentially affects all of humanity and poses a threat to global welfare. Given the severity of the problem and the long-term threats it poses to the planet and to humankind, marine plastic pollution should be recognized as a matter of common concern, such as conservation of biodiversity and climate change have been recognized as common concerns.[45]

Marine plastic pollution is comparable to the loss of biodiversity or to the emission of greenhouse gases and the related impact of global warming in that the release of plastic particles into the environment is continuous, dispersed and diffuse in character. Accordingly, the risk associated with plastics is of a cumulative and indirect nature. A causal link between the production, use and disposal of plastic products and any

---

benthic plastics. Impacts by large-scale garbage collectors on marine living organisms are disputed. In spite of these uncertainties, large promotion campaigns have been nourishing the misconception that thanks to new technology, marine plastic pollution can be easily dealt with after all.

[43] See Barnes *et al.*, *supra* n. 2, 1995.

[44] Ibid., 1985; UNEP, *Marine Litter*, *supra* n. 8, 1.

[45] United Nations Convention on Biological Diversity (CBD) (opened for signature on 5 June 1992, entered into force on 29 Dec. 1993) 1760 UNTS 79, preamble; United Nations Framework Convention on Climate Change (UNFCCC) (opened for signature on 9 May 1992, entered into force on 21 Mars 1994) 1771 UNTS 107, preamble. With regard to the threshold of a common concern of humankind, See Chapter 1 in this volume (Section 1.3.4).

consequential loss or damage that may occur in the marine environment is not necessarily straightforward. Many different actors are involved in the complex life cycle of plastic products and thus share a responsibility, including producers, compounders, converters, retailers, consumers, governments, and waste management and recycling operators. Once in the marine environment, wide dispersal, complicated distribution patterns and continuous fragmentation processes of marine plastic debris make it difficult to trace it back to its source when harm occurs. Yet, while individual contribution is difficult to quantify, a collective responsibility is incontrovertible.

Nearly all the countries, even land-locked states, contribute to the problem, and all nations suffer from the consequences, even though the patterns of contribution and consequences are not necessarily congruent. Marine plastic pollution is an inherently global issue, a common action problem, calling for responses at various levels of governance, from local to global. It is a responsibility which should be shared by all the states. From an international law perspective, an appropriate response to the problem of marine plastic pollution thus involves the whole international community. Cooperation among all countries, including both technologically advanced nations and countries with weak waste management infrastructures, is absolutely necessary. Technological and financial support of countries in need seems an essential feature for any common response to the problem.

3.2.2   A Rising Issue on the Global Political Agenda

Although there is, so far, no reference in an international convention to marine plastic pollution as a common concern of humankind, a process towards such recognition is well underway. Marine plastic pollution is, indeed, an illustrative example of such a recognition process, starting with awareness creation on a global scale and a call for international cooperation.

At the sixth meeting of the United Nations Open-Ended Informal Consultative Process on Oceans and the Law of the Sea (ICP) in 2005, marine debris was identified as 'a global transboundary pollution problem that constitutes a serious threat to human health and safety, endangers fish stocks, marine biodiversity and marine habitats and has significant costs to local and national economies'.[46] At its seventeenth

---

[46] UNGA, 'Report on the Work of the United Nations Open-Ended Informal Consultative Process on Oceans and the Law of the Sea at Its Sixth Meeting' (2005) UN Doc. A/60/99, para. 14.

meeting in 2016, the ICP again focused on the theme 'Marine debris, plastics and microplastics' and highlighted that the size of the problem had increased exponentially since the topic of marine debris was addressed at the sixth meeting in 2005. It moreover noted that marine debris in general, and plastics in particular, were some of the greatest environmental concerns of our time, along with climate change, ocean acidification and loss of biodiversity. The ICP emphasized the need to address the issue, both downstream, through improved mechanisms for waste management, disposal and recycling, and upstream, by addressing consumption and production patterns, including through awareness-raising campaigns.[47]

The UN General Assembly took up on the issue after the sixth meeting of the ICP in 2005: it urged states to integrate the issue of marine debris into national strategies dealing with waste management and to adopt appropriate economic incentives to address the problem. It also encouraged states to cooperate and to develop and implement joint prevention and recovery programmes for marine debris, and recognized the need to build the capacity of developing states for a more sustainable waste management.[48] It has repeated such calls with increasing emphasis in its annual resolution on oceans and the law of the sea ever since. Also, marine debris and marine plastics have occupied an increasingly prominent place on the global political agenda during the last decades, both under the auspices of the UN and beyond. UN Environment played a central role in awareness-raising activities and the introduction of the topic in global political discussions and processes.[49] They issued a series

---

[47] UNGA, 'Report on the Work of the United Nations Open-Ended Informal Consultative Process on Oceans and the Law of the Sea at Its Seventeenth Meeting' (2016), para. 12; UNGA Res. 72/73 (2017), 'Oceans and the Law of the Sea', para. 188.

[48] UNGA Res. 60/30 (2005), 'Oceans and the Law of the Sea', paras. 12 and 65–71.

[49] A milestone in this regard was the adoption of the *Global Programme of Action for the Protection of the Marine Environment from Land-based Activities* (GPA) at the 1995 Washington Conference. The GPA is a guidance document for the implementation of existing obligations and commitments with regard to the protection of the marine environment from land-based pollution sources. It suggests actions to be taken at the national, regional and international levels and addresses litter as a source of marine pollution (UNEP, 'Global Programme of Action for the Protection of the Marine Environment from Land-Based Activities' (1995) UN Doc. UNEP(OCA)/LBA/IG.2/7, paras. 140–8). In 1997, the UN General Assembly adopted a resolution on institutional arrangements of the GPA and designated UN Environment as the lead agency in the implementation of the GPA (UNGA Res. 51/189 (1996), 'Institutional Arrangements for the Implementation of the Global Programme of Action for the Protection of the Marine Environment from Land-Based Activities'). Since 2001, the UN General Assembly has

166   JUDITH SCHÄLI

of documents and guidelines on marine litter and plastics[50] and co-organized a series of events, including the Fifth and Sixth International Marine Debris Conferences in 2011 and 2018, respectively.[51] With about 450 participants from all around the world, the fifth conference had a broad outreach and kicked off a cross-sectoral and multi-stakeholder dialogue involving representatives from governments, industry, academia and civil society,[52] who all committed to 'reduce waste in order to halt

referred to the GPA, with increasing emphasis, in its annual resolutions on oceans and the law of the sea. Four intergovernmental review meetings on the implementation of the GPA were held in Montreal, Canada (2001), in Beijing, China (2006), in Manila, the Philippines (2012) and in Bali, Indonesia (2018) respectively.

[50] See UNEP, *Marine Litter – Trash That Kills* (2001); *Marine Litter*, supra n. 8; *Marine Litter: A Global Challenge* (UNEP, 2009); G. Macfadyen, Tim Huntington and Rod Cappell, *Abandoned, Lost or Otherwise Discarded Fishing Gear* (UNEP/FAO, 2009); Anthony Cheshire et al., *UNEP/IOC Guidelines on Survey and Monitoring of Marine Litter* (UNEP/IOC, 2009); Ten Brink et al., supra n. 40; UNEP, *Plastic in Cosmetics: Are We Polluting the Environment through Our Personal Care?* (2015); *Biodegradable Plastics & Marine Litter: Misconceptions, Concerns and Impacts on Marine Environments* (UNEP, 2015); UNEP and GRID-Arendal, supra n. 13; UNEP, *Marine Litter Legislation: A Toolkit for Policymakers* (UNEP, 2016); 'Marine Plastic Debris and Microplastics: Global Lessons and Research to Inspire Action and Guide Policy Change' (2016) (UNEA-2 Technical Report on Marine Plastic Debris); 'Combating Marine Plastic Litter and Microplastics: An Assessment of the Effectiveness of Relevant International, Regional and Subregional Governance Strategies and Approaches – Summary for Policy Makers' (2018) UNEP/AHEG/2018/1/INF/3; 'Addressing Marine Plastics: A Systemic Approach – Stocktaking Report' (2018); 'Mapping of Global Plastics Value Chain and Plastics Losses to the Environment (with a Particular Focus on Marine Environment)' (2018); *Single-Use Plastics: A Roadmap for Sustainability* (2018); 'Legal Limits on Single-Use Plastics and Microplastics: A Global Review of National Laws and Regulations' (2018); 'Analysis of Voluntary Commitments Targeting Marine Litter and Microplastics Pursuant to Resolution 3/7 – Report of the Executive Director' (2018) UNEP/EA.4/11; 'Plastics and Shallow Water Coral Reefs: Synthesis of the Science for Policy-Makers' (2019). In 2015, UNEP also launched a Massive Open Online Course on marine litter with more than 6,500 participants. The course was relaunched in 2017 and 2019.

[51] See UNEP and NOAA, 'Summary Proceedings of the 5th International Marine Debris Conference, Held on 20–25 March 2011 in Honolulu, HI, USA' (2011), 4.

[52] Stakeholder engagement rapidly increased in the last couple of years. Several national agencies, private companies and business associations have organized a number of international conferences on the topic of marine debris and marine plastic pollution. Examples include: German Federal Environment Agency, 'International Conference on Prevention and Management of Marine Litter in European Seas' (Berlin, 10–12 Apr. 2013) www.marine-litter-conference-berlin.info/index.php (accessed 29 June 2019); nova-Institut GmbH, 'Microplastic in the Environment: Sources, Impacts & Solutions' (Cologne, 23–24 Nov. 2015) http://microplastic-conference.eu/ (accessed 29 June 2019); PlasticsEurope, 'PolyTalk 2016: Zero Plastics to the Ocean' (Brussels, 16–17 Mar. 2016) www.polytalk.eu/polytalk2016 (accessed 29 June 2019); St. John's

and reverse the occurrence of marine debris'.[53] The UN General Assembly took note of the event and encouraged states 'to further develop partnerships with industry and civil society to raise awareness of the extent of the impact of marine debris on the health and productivity of the marine environment and consequent economic loss'.[54] At about the same time, other international bodies started to pick up the topic, including, for instance, under the auspices of the Convention on Biological Diversity (CBD).[55]

In a common declaration in 2012, sixty-four governments and the European Commission recognized that

> marine litter is a problem that is global in scale and underestimated in impact; that it directly threatens coastal and marine habitats and species, economic growth, human health and safety, and social values; that a significant portion of marine litter originates from land-based activities; and that movement of litter and debris, exacerbated by storm events, has significant impacts on the marine environment.[56]

At the 2012 UN Conference on Sustainable Development (UNCSD, also known as Rio+20), states noted with concern that 'the health of oceans and marine biodiversity are negatively affected by marine pollution, including marine debris, especially plastic' and committed to 'take action to reduce the incidence and impacts of such pollution on marine ecosystems, including through the effective implementation of relevant [frameworks] as well as the adoption of coordinated strategies to this

---

Island National Marine Laboratory, 'International Conference on Plastics in the Marine Environment' (Singapore, 5–7 Dec. 2018) www.icpmesg.com/ (accessed 29 June 2019).

[53] This is one out of twelve commitments ('Honolulu Commitment' (2011) https://5imdc .files.wordpress.com/2011/03/honolulucommitment.pdf (accessed 20 Sept. 2019)).

[54] UNGA Res. 66/231 (2011), 'Oceans and the Law of the Sea', para. 141.

[55] The issue has been addressed by the CBD in reports, special workshops and in COP decisions (STAP, 'Marine Debris as a Global Environmental Problem: Introducing a Solutions Based Framework on Plastic' (GEF 2011); CBD Secretariat and STAP, 'Impacts of Marine Debris on Biodiversity: Current Status and Potential Solutions' (2012) CBD Technical Series 67; CBD COP Decision XI/18 (2012), 'Marine and Coastal Biodiversity: Sustainable Fisheries and Addressing Adverse Impacts of Human Activities, Voluntary Guidelines for Environmental Assessment, and Marine Spatial Planning' UNEP/CBD/ COP/DEC/XI/18, paras. 25–7; CBD, 'Report of the Expert Workshop to Prepare Practical Guidance on Preventing and Mitigating the Significant Adverse Impacts of Marine Debris on Marine and Coastal Biodiversity and Habitats' (2014) UNEP/CBD/MCB/ EM/2014/3/2).

[56] 'Manila Declaration on Furthering the Implementation of the Global Programme of Action for the Protection of the Marine Environment from Land-Based Activities' (2012) UNEP/GCSS.XII/INF/10, Annex preamble.

168   JUDITH SCHÄLI

end' as well as 'to take action to, by 2025 ... achieve significant reductions in marine debris to prevent harm to the coastal and marine environment'.[57] Since then, the General Assembly's annual law of the sea resolutions have referred to plastics as a source of concern for the marine environment.[58]

In 2015, the UN General Assembly adopted the 2030 Agenda on Sustainable Development and, with it, seventeen sustainable development goals and 169 targets to be achieved by 2030.[59] Goal 14 is to conserve and sustainably use the oceans, seas and marine resources. Target 14.1 is to prevent and significantly reduce marine pollution of all kinds by 2025, in particular pollution from land-based activities, including marine debris. In June 2017, a high-level conference was held under the auspices of the UN in order to identify ways and means to support the implementation of Goal 14, enhance stakeholder involvement and provide input to the High-Level Political Forum on Sustainable Development.[60] The conference produced different outcomes, including an intergovernmentally agreed Call for Action and a registry of voluntary commitments with 1,328 initial registrations and more than 150 commitments submitted to reduce plastic waste. In the Call for Action, states called on all stakeholders to accelerate actions to prevent and significantly reduce marine pollution of all kinds, particularly from land-based activities, including marine debris, plastics and microplastics; promote waste prevention and minimization; develop sustainable consumption and production patterns; and implement long-term and robust strategies to reduce the use of plastics and microplastics, in particular plastic bags and single-use plastics.[61]

At its first meeting in June 2014, the UNEA, which has universal membership, recognized 'that plastics, including microplastics, in the marine environment are a rapidly increasing problem due to their large and still increasing use combined with the inadequate management and

---

[57] UNGA Res. 66/288 (2012), Annex, 'The Future We Want', para. 163.

[58] UNGA Res. 67/78 (2012), para. 142; Res. 68/70 (2013), paras. 152 and 164; Res. 69/245 (2014), paras. 163, 181 and 298; Res. 70/235 (2015), paras. 170, 188–90 and 192; Res. 71/257 (2016), paras. 182–4 and 204–10; Res. 72/73 (2017), paras. 188 and 208; Res. 73/124 (2018), paras. 209–17; Res. 74/19 (2019), paras. 217–227; Res. 75/239 (2020), paras. 217–229.

[59] UNGA Res. 70/1 (2015), 'Transforming Our World: The 2030 Agenda for Sustainable Development'.

[60] See IISD, 'Summary of the Ocean Conference: 5–9 June 2017', *Earth Negotiations Bulletin: Ocean Conference Final*, 32 (2017).

[61] UNGA, 'Our Ocean, Our Future: Call for Action' (A/CONF230/11, Annex 2017), para. 13(g–i).

disposal of plastic waste'.[62] For this reason, the UN Environment Executive Director was requested to undertake a study on marine plastic debris and marine microplastics and to present it at the second UNEA in May 2016. In his report, the UN Environment Executive Director found that '[t]he accumulation of plastic litter in the ocean is a common concern for humankind owing to its far-reaching environmental, social and economic impacts'.[63] Based on the report and a set of policy recommendations, UNEA-2 requested the Executive Director to assess the effectiveness of international, regional and subregional governance strategies and according regulatory frameworks relevant to marine plastic litter and microplastics, and to identify possible gaps and options for addressing them.[64] In the respective report as presented at UNEA-3 in December 2017, the Executive Director judged the existing framework as insufficient and recommended the establishment of a global umbrella mechanism specific to marine plastic litter and microplastics. He moreover proposed, as an option for action, the establishment of a new international legally binding architecture as one out of several measures to effectively tackle the problem in a multilayered governance approach.[65] UNEA-3 hence established an Open-Ended Ad Hoc Working Group to make recommendations to strengthen international governance structures for combating marine plastic litter and microplastics.[66] At UNEA-4 in March 2019, the groups mandate was expanded and a multi-stakeholder platform was established to take immediate action against discharges of litter and microplastics into the oceans.[67]

---

[62] UNEA Res. 1/6 (2014), 'Marine Plastic Debris and Microplastics', para. 4.

[63] UNEP, 'UNEA-2 Technical Report on Marine Plastic Debris', *supra* n. 50, xii.

[64] UNEA Res. 2/11 (2016), 'Marine Plastic Litter and Microplastics' UNEP/EA.2/Res.11, para. 21.

[65] UNEP, 'Combating Marine Plastic Litter and Microplastics: An Assessment of the Effectiveness of Relevant International, Regional and Subregional Governance Strategies and Approaches' (2017) (UNEA-3 Legal Report) UNEP/EA.3/INF/5. See also UNEP, 'UNEA-3 Legal Report – Summary for Policy Makers', *supra* n. 50.

[66] UNEA Draft Resolution UNEP/EA.3/L.20 (2017), 'Draft Resolution on Marine Litter and Microplastics' (adopted version not yet published as of June 2018). See also UNEP, 'Report of the First Meeting of the Ad Hoc Open-Ended Expert Group on Marine Litter and Microplastics' (2018) UNEP/AHEG/2018/1/6; 'Co-Chairs' Summary of First Meeting of the Ad Hoc Open-Ended Expert Group on Marine Litter and Microplastics'.

[67] In addition, a resolution was adopted proposing various measures to combat single-use plastic products pollution (UNEA Res. 4/9 (2019), 'Addressing Single-Use Plastic Products Pollution' UNEP/EA.4/L.10).

170   JUDITH SCHÄLI

There is, thus, international recognition of the matter as a concern of global scope, as well as a prevalent willingness to enhance cooperation in this respect and take common action.

3.2.3 Core Obligations of States with regard to Marine Plastic Pollution

3.2.3.1 The General Obligation to Protect and Preserve the Marine Environment

Environmental concerns have an increasingly prominent place on today's global agenda related to ocean governance. Also, the protection and preservation of the marine environment is one of the core objectives of international law of the sea. An obligation to protect and preserve the marine environment can be derived from general international law and is reflected in various legal instruments, including the United Nations Convention on the Law of the Sea (UNCLOS).[68] UNCLOS is the most central global legal instrument with regard to the protection of the marine environment from land- and sea-based sources of pollution, including plastic pollution. Often referred to as the 'constitution for the ocean',[69] it 'sets out the legal framework within which all activities in the oceans and seas must be carried out'[70] and 'provides the legal framework for the conservation and the sustainable use of the oceans and their resources'.[71] UNCLOS entered into force in 1994 and today has 168 parties. The convention's substantive provisions, including with regard

---

[68] 1982 UNCLOS, *supra* n. 31.

[69] See remarks by Tommy T. B. Koh, President of the Third United Nations Conference on the Law of the Sea, at its final session in Montego Bay, Jamaica, 11 Dec. 1982, reprinted in *The Law of the Sea: Official Text of the United Nations Convention on the Law of the Sea* (United Nations, 1983), p. xxxiii; Shirley V. Scott, 'The LOS Convention as a Constitutional Regime for the Oceans', in Alex G. Oude Elferink (ed.), *Stability and Change in the Law of the Sea: The Role of the LOS Convention* (Leiden: Martinus Nijhoff, 2005), p. 12. See also Thomas Cottier, *Equitable Principles of Maritime Boundary Delimitation: The Quest for Distributive Justice in International Law* (Cambridge: Cambridge University Press, 2015), pp. 50ff.

[70] See preamble to the annual UNGA Resolution on oceans and the law of the sea: UNGA Res. 63/111 (2008); Res. 64/71 (2009); Res. 65/37 (2010); Res. 66/231 (2011); Res. 67/78 (2012); Res. 68/70 (2013); Res. 69/245 (2014); Res. 70/235 (2015); Res. 71/257 (2016); Res. 72/73 (2017); Res. 73/124 (2018); Res. 74/19 (2019); Res. 75/239 (2020).

[71] UNGA Res. 66/288 (2012), Annex *supra* n. 57, para. 158; Res. 69/245 (2014), 'Oceans and the Law of the Sea' 2. See also Agenda 21, *Report of the United Nations Conference on Environment and Development, Rio de Janeiro, 3–14 June 1992, Vol I., Resolutions Adopted by the Conference* (United Nations publication, Sales No E93I8 and corrigendum) res. 1, Annex II, para. 17.1. According to Agenda 21, UNCLOS 'provides the

MARINE PLASTIC POLLUTION 171

to the protection of the marine environment, are widely recognized to reflect customary international law.[72] In some of its parts, the treaty provides a framework for international cooperation in marine affairs in order to protect the common interests of the international community as a whole.[73] A sound marine environment is one of these common interests.

The general duty of states to protect and preserve the marine environment, as expressed in UNCLOS Article 192, is both the core and foundation of the global legal regime on marine plastic pollution mitigation. The duty refers to both areas under national and beyond national jurisdiction, including the high seas and the deep seabed. The normative content of this provision is informed by the subsequent provisions of UNCLOS Part XII and needs to be interpreted in light of contemporary international environmental law.[74] The content of the duty to protect and preserve the marine environment may also be informed by other international legal instruments dealing with related subject areas, such as the protection of biodiversity, the regulation of international watercourses or the regulation of chemicals and wastes.[75]

---

international basis upon which to pursue the protection and sustainable development of the marine and coastal environment and its resources'.

[72] Respective rules are, thus, also binding on non-member states. On the customary nature of rules related to the protection of the marine environment, see Patricia Birnie, Alan Boyle and Catherine Redgwell, *International Law and the Environment* (3rd ed., Oxford: Oxford University Press, 2009), p. 387; Alan E. Boyle, 'Land-Based Sources of Marine Pollution: Current Legal Regime', *Marine Policy*, 16 (1992), 20, 25; Philippe Sands and Jacqueline Peel, *Principles of International Environmental Law* (3rd ed., Cambridge: Cambridge University Press, 2012), p. 350. See also Myron H. Nordquist, Shabtai Rosenne and Alexander Yankov (eds.), *United Nations Convention on the Law of the Sea 1982: A Commentary, Vol. IV: Articles 192 to 278* (Berlin: Center for Oceans Law and Policy–Kluwer Law International, 2002), paras. 192.8 and 194.10(c). For a list of UNCLOS provisions that have been recognized as reflecting customary law, see, in general, J. Ashley Roach, 'Today's Customary International Law of the Sea', *Ocean Development & International Law*, 45 (2014), 239.

[73] See Yoshifumi Tanaka, *The International Law of the Sea* (2nd ed., Cambridge: Cambridge University Press, 2015), pp. 4 and 37.

[74] See *South China Sea Arbitration (the Philippines v. China)* [2016] Arbitral Tribunal 2016 Case No. 2013-19, PCA 373, para. 941.

[75] See Art. 31(3)(c) of the Vienna Convention on the Law of Treaties (1969 VCLT) (adopted 23 May 1969, entered into force on 27 Jan. 1980) 1155 UNTS 331, 8 ILM 679 (1969). See also the comments by the ILC in 'Fragmentation of International Law: Difficulties Arising from the Diversification and Expansion of International Law (Fragmentation Report)' (Study Group of the International Law Commission 2006) A/CN.4/L.682 212, para. 423.

The very core of the duty to protect and preserve the marine environment is outlined by the treaty itself: UNCLOS requires states to take action at every level of governance, from national to international. Specifically, it requires them to adopt laws and regulations and take other measures at the national level, to assess environmental impacts and monitor activities, to effectively cooperate at the regional level, to provide assistance to developing countries, and to establish global rules and standards to prevent marine pollution and harmonize policies in this regard. Related case law moreover suggests that due diligence, environmental impact assessment and precaution are among the core elements of the duty to protect and preserve the marine environment.[76] The normative content thus widely corresponds with what has been identified in this project as the main elements of the cooperation and homework pillars under the concept of Common Concern of Humankind.[77]

3.2.3.2 The Duty to Cooperate

Under the UNLCOS Part XII regime, the duty to cooperate primarily refers to the common formulation and elaboration of international rules, standards and recommended practices and procedures for the protection and preservation of the marine environment.[78] Such rules and standards can be formulated at the international or regional level, as appropriate. It further refers to the customary duty to consult and negotiate, as well as to policy harmonization, technical assistance and the peaceful resolution of disputes.

Common Formulation of International Rules and Standards   International rules and standards play a particular role in the implementation of the duty to protect and preserve the marine environment as stipulated under the convention. UNCLOS does not define the content of the legislative, administrative or other measures that need to be taken at the national

---

[76] See *Pulp Mills on the River Uruguay (Argentina v. Uruguay), Judgment* [2010] ICJ Rep. 2010 14, paras. 101, 164, 193, 197 and 204; *Certain Activities Carried Out by Nicaragua in the Border Area (Costa Rica v. Nicaragua) and Construction of a Road in Costa Rica Along the San Juan River (Nicaragua v. Costa Rica)* [2015] ICJ General List Nos. 150 and 152, para. 104; *Responsibilities and Obligations of States Sponsoring Persons and Entities with Respect to Activities in the Area (Advisory Opinion)* [2011] ITLOS (Seabed Disputes Chamber) case No. 17 paras. 13, 110, 131, 135 and 145; *South China Sea Arbitration, supra* n. 74, para. 944.

[77] See Section 3.3.1.

[78] See 1982 UNCLOS, Arts. 194 and 197.

level in order to prevent, reduce or control marine pollution, nor does it define the exact level of protection to be achieved in this regard. Instead, UNCLOS uses a mechanism of reference to international standards that are set in other forums, and thus works as a framework convention with regard to these standards.

UNCLOS explicitly distinguishes between five sources of marine pollution: (1) land-based sources; (2) seabed activities;[79] (3) dumping; (4) vessels and (5) the atmosphere. For most of these sources, including seabed activities, dumping and vessel-based pollution, the mechanism of reference has a relatively strong effect, as preference is given to internationally agreed rules and standards over national law:[80]

1 States have to *establish* global and regional rules and standards to prevent, reduce and control pollution of the marine environment from seabed activities or vessels.[81]
2 States have to *adhere to the international rules and standards* in the adoption of national legislation and other measures.[82]
3 States have to adopt laws and regulations and take other measures necessary to *implement* applicable international rules and standards established through competent international organizations or diplomatic conference to prevent, reduce and control pollution of the marine environment from these sources.[83]

The mechanism of reference allows incorporating standards that were agreed under the auspices of international organizations competent in a specific field related to the protection and preservation of the marine environment. Examples of such organizations include the International

---

[79] UNCLOS distinguishes between seabed activities subject to national jurisdiction and activities in the Area.

[80] See Alan E. Boyle, 'Marine Pollution under the Law of the Sea Convention', *American Journal of International Law*, 79 (1985), 347, 352.

[81] 1982 UNCLOS, Arts. 208(5) and 211(1).

[82] With regard to seabed activities, such laws, regulations and measures 'shall be no less effective than international rules, standards and recommended practices and procedures' (ibid., Arts. 208(3) (pollution from seabed activities subject to national jurisdiction) and 209(2) (pollution from seabed activities in the Area)). With regard to dumping, they 'shall be no less effective in preventing, reducing and controlling such pollution than the global rules and standards' (ibid., Art. 210(6)). Regulation of pollution from vessels by the flag state 'shall at least have the same effect as that of generally accepted international rules and standards established through the competent international organization or general diplomatic conference' (ibid., Art. 211(2)).

[83] Ibid., Art. 214; cf. Arts. 216(1) and 217(1).

174   JUDITH SCHÄLI

Maritime Organization (IMO)[84] and the UN Food and Agriculture Organization (FAO).[85] With regard to marine plastics, relevant incorporated standards are contained in the Convention on the Prevention of Marine Pollution by Dumping of Wastes and Other Matter (1972 London Dumping Convention),[86] which strictly prohibits dumping of wastes at sea from vessels, aircraft or offshore installations, as well as in Annex V of the International Convention for the Prevention of Pollution from Ships and its 1978 protocol (MARPOL),[87] generally prohibiting the disposal of plastics from vessels. Through the UNCLOS mechanism of reference, such standards can possibly become binding on states that have never ratified these conventions. If applied by parties to UNCLOS in a consistent way, they may develop into customary rules of international law.[88]

The situation is different with respect to land-based pollution sources, which are highly significant with regard to plastics. On the one hand, standard-setting instruments specifically dealing with land-based pollution sources are either regional in scope or non-binding in character. UNLCOS does not oblige its parties to strictly adhere to these standards, but merely requires states to take such standards into account.[89] Also, states do not have a strict obligation under UNCLOS to adopt the measures necessary to implement non-binding standards.[90] With regard to land-based pollution sources, states thus have much wider discretion in national implementation when compared with other pollution

---

[84] The IMO (originally called the Inter-Governmental Maritime Consultative Organization) was created in 1948 by the UN Maritime Conference in Geneva. IMO is a specialized agency of the UN responsible for global standard-setting in the field of maritime safety and security, and of environmental performance of international shipping. In 1975, the IMO Marine Environment Protection Committee (MEPC) was formed.

[85] As a standard-setting organization with regard to fisheries.

[86] Convention on the Prevention of Marine Pollution by Dumping of Wastes and Other Matter (1972 London Dumping Convention) (adopted 13 Nov. 1972, entered into force on 40 Aug. 1975).

[87] International Convention for the Prevention of Pollution from Ships (signed on 2 Nov. 1973) 12 ILM 1319 (1973), 1340 UNTS 184 and Protocol relating to the International Convention for the Prevention of Pollution from Ships (adopted 17 Feb. 1978) 17 ILM 546 (1978), 1340 UNTS 61, both entered into force on 2 Oct. 1983 (1973/78 MARPOL).

[88] See IMO, 'Implications of the United Nations Convention on the Law of the Sea for the International Maritime Organization' (2014) LEG/MISC/8, 10–12. See also Birnie *et al.*, *supra* n. 72, pp. 150 and 404; Boyle, 'Marine Pollution under the Law of the Sea Convention', *supra* n. 80, 356; Donald R. Rothwell and Tim Stephens, *The International Law of the Sea* (2nd ed., Oxford: Hart, 2016), p. 372; Tanaka, *supra* n. 73, 277.

[89] 1982 UNCLOS, Art. 207(1).

[90] See ibid Art. 213.

sources, except for atmospheric pollution.[91] On the other hand, wording is also weaker with regard to the formulation of international rules and standards. With respect to land-based pollution sources, states only have to *endeavour* to establish them.

The absence of global legally binding rules and standards on pollution prevention from land-based sources might be the very cause for the weaker form of the mechanism of reference under UNCLOS in this field. However, it results in a regime in which there is little international control, although land-based sources are the most problematic type of pollution sources, especially with regard to plastics.[92] The convention therefore does not provide sufficient guidance, whether directly or by reference, on the content of the measures to be taken or the level of protection to be applied.

Global and Regional Cooperation The protection and preservation of the marine environment is a concern that is regional and global in scope. It cannot be achieved by individual states alone but has to be based on common efforts. UNCLOS Part XII therefore has a specific section on global and regional cooperation. Its significance has been emphasized in case law. In a case decided in 2001, the International Tribunal on the Law of the Sea held that 'the duty to cooperate is a fundamental principle in the prevention of pollution of the marine environment under Part XII of the [Law of the Sea] Convention and general international law'.[93]

Under UNCLOS, states have a duty to cooperate on a global basis and, as appropriate, on a regional basis in developing international rules, standards and recommended practices and procedures for the protection and preservation of the marine environment. They may do so directly or through competent international organizations. With respect to plastics and marine debris, UNEA (through UN Environment) would seem a suitable forum for international legal standards to be set. The UN Environment's Regional Seas Programme and related programmes are

---

[91] See Nordquist *et al.*, *supra* n. 72, para. 132.

[92] See Boyle, 'Marine Pollution under the Law of the Sea Convention', *supra* n. 80, 354.

[93] *The MOX Plant Case (Ireland v. United Kingdom), Provisional Measures* [2001] ITLOS case No. 10, para. 82. See also *Case Concerning Land Reclamation by Singapore in and around the Straits of Johor (Malaysia v. Singapore), Provisional Measures* [2003] ITLOS case No. 12, para. 92; *Lac Lanoux Arbitration (Spain v. France)* (1957) 7 UN Rep. Int'l Arb Awards 281, para. 22; *North Sea Continental Shelf, Judgment* [1969] ICJ Rep. 1969 3 47, para. 85; *Gabčíkovo–Nagymaros Project (Hungary v. Slovakia), Judgment* [1997] ICJ Rep. 1997 7 78, para. 141; *Southern Bluefin Tuna Cases (New Zealand v. Japan; Australia v. Japan), Provisional Measures* [1999] ITLOS cases Nos. 3 and 4, para. 78.

the main forums for regional cooperation to take place. Some of the programmes are based on regional conventions with specific protocols on land-based pollution sources. Some programmes have adopted specific action plans on marine litter. Others, however, do not have any legally binding foundation, do not specifically address land-based pollution sources and plastics, or are very poorly resourced and thus ineffective. Especially some of the most polluting regions are not covered by a legal instrument or by any programme at all. There are no regional legal instruments on the protection of the marine environment applying to the South Asian Seas, the South-East Asian Seas, the North-West Pacific region and the South-West Atlantic region. Fourteen of the twenty most polluting countries are located in these areas.[94]

UNCLOS further provides that in case of imminent or actual damage to the marine environment, states have an obligation to immediately notify the states 'likely to be affected by such damage, as well as the competent international organizations'.[95] The obligation to notify is a rule of customary international law.[96] States in areas affected by imminent or actual damage and the competent international organizations have to cooperate 'in eliminating the effects of pollution and preventing or minimizing the damage'. To this end, states 'shall jointly develop and promote contingency plans for responding to pollution incidents in the marine environment'.[97] States bordering an enclosed or semi-enclosed sea are required to endeavour to coordinate management, conservation efforts and research.[98] A duty to cooperate is also expressed with regard to studies, research programmes and exchange of information and data acquired about pollution of the marine environment.[99] Finally, cooperation is required for the establishment of 'appropriate scientific criteria for the formulation and elaboration of rules, standards and recommended practices and procedures for the prevention, reduction and control of pollution of the marine environment'.[100]

Burden Sharing and Capacity Building A main source of marine plastic debris is mismanaged waste. A study published in 2015 suggests

---

[94] The assumption is based on a study by Jenna R. Jambeck *et al.*, 'Plastic Waste Inputs from Land into the Ocean', *Science*, 347 (2015), 768, 769.

[95] 1982 UNCLOS, Art. 198; Rio Principles 18 and 19.

[96] See Nordquist *et al.*, *supra* n. 72, para. 83.

[97] 1982 UNCLOS, Art. 199.

[98] Ibid., Art. 123.

[99] Ibid., Art. 200.

[100] Ibid., Art. 201.

that a more adequate waste disposal by the twenty most polluting countries could have significant positive impacts.[101] Most of the countries figuring in the list of the main contributors to marine plastic pollution from land-based sources are low- or lower-middle income countries. A minority is classified by the World Bank as upper-middle-income countries. The only high-income country in the list is the United States, ranking twentieth.[102] Waste management improvement in low- and middle-income countries is, therefore, essential to reduce global plastic input into the marine environment. Waste collection and the establishment of respective infrastructure are, however, extremely expensive, which is why the development of sound waste management procedures and infrastructure often happens slowly and lags behind the development of unsustainable consumption patterns. Lack of financial resources, technologies and know-how is a major problem in this regard. At the same time, low- and lower-middle income countries often are extremely vulnerable to the negative impacts of marine plastic pollution.

In order to achieve a timely reduction of global plastic waste input into the ocean through waste management improvement in the main polluting countries, support by high-income countries is urgently needed. Support might also be needed to mitigate the consequences of marine plastic pollution, for instance in small island developing states. Without such support, the ability of developing countries to effectively participate in global mitigation efforts is very limited, even if they are willing to do so.

In its general and more specific provisions, UNCLOS takes account of the limited capacities of some countries. Obligations are formulated in a due diligence manner, allowing for a graduation in the standard of care according to the capabilities of states. Hence, high-income countries generally will have to meet a much stricter standard for measures preventing, reducing or controlling pollution than low-income countries. At the same time, UNCLOS requires states to provide scientific and

---

[101] Jambeck *et al.*, *supra* n. 94, 770.

[102] The list is based on World Bank 2010 classification, according to which low-income economies included those with a gross national income (GNI) per capita of US$1,005 or less; lower middle-income economies were those with a GNI per capita between US$1,006 and US$3,975; upper-middle-income economies were those with a GNI per capita between US$3,976 and US$12,275; and high-income economies were those with a GNI per capita of US$12,275 or more (World Bank, 'World Bank Historical Classification by Income' (2018) http://databank.worldbank.org/data/download/site-con tent/OGHIST.xls (accessed 1 Oct. 2018)). For current definitions, see World Bank, 'World Bank Country and Lending Groups – Data' (2018) https://datahelpdesk .worldbank.org/knowledgebase/articles/906519 (accessed 1 Oct. 2018).

technical assistance to developing states and international organizations to grant them preferential treatment in the allocation of funds.[103]

The duty to provide technical assistance to developing states may be considered as an extraterritorial component of the duty to protect and preserve the marine environment. It is closely related to the notion of intragenerational equity and points out that the interest in a sound marine environment goes beyond national borders and is global in scope. In this sense, the duty to protect and preserve the marine environment is incumbent upon the international community as a whole. The duty of a state to protect the marine environment therefore includes a duty to support less-developed countries in the fulfilment of their obligation. The duty to provide technical assistance does not affect the obligations of developing states as contained in the substantive rules of Part XII.[104]

Yet, the obligations to provide technical assistance under UNCLOS are deliberately open worded. States have a considerable discretionary space in their decision on the type and degree of assistance they provide. UNCLOS does not prescribe financial support or refer to any financial mechanism such as the Global Environment Facility (GEF), nor does it provide the institutional basis for concerted action in this regard. While it provides for the necessary flexibility in the standard of care, it does not counterbalance this flexibility with a sufficiently strong capacity-building scheme.

3.2.3.3   Obligation to Do Homework

The formulation of domestic policies and laws, as well as domestic marine resource management lies at the very heart of the obligation to protect and preserve the marine environment. While the sovereign right of states to exploit their resources is confirmed in UNCLOS, it is explicitly qualified by the duty to protect and preserve the marine

---

[103]   1982 UNCLOS, Arts. 202 and 203.

[104]   See Nordquist *et al.*, *supra* n. 72, paras. 107–8. The general obligation to protect and preserve the marine environment, and obligations related to pollution prevention and the prevention of transboundary harm are not subject to the principle of common but differentiated responsibility (CBDR) in the sense that implementation by developing states is conditional on the provision of financial assistance and transfer of technology by developed states. Unlike climate change, domestic and transboundary pollution – plastic or other – is not attributable to developed states in particular, not even from a historical perspective, but to the state that caused the pollution or harm by its activities and failed to prevent it. With regard to marine plastic pollution, including in areas beyond national jurisdiction, main contributors are mostly not developed countries in the traditional sense, but include China, Indonesia, the Philippines, Vietnam, Sri Lanka and other middle- and low-income countries with limited capacities with respect to waste collection and management. CBDR therefore does not apply.

MARINE PLASTIC POLLUTION 179

environment.[105] Also, in the exercise of their right, states need to weigh up purely economic interests against environmental concerns. UNCLOS Article 193 implicitly refers to a balancing of interests as suggested by the concept of sustainable development and requests states to include environmental considerations in their marine resource management.[106]

A core component of the duty to protect and preserve the marine environment is the duty of states to 'take ... all measures ... necessary to prevent, reduce and control pollution of the marine environment from any source, using for this purpose the best practicable means at their disposal and in accordance with their capabilities'.[107] States moreover have to 'endeavour to harmonize their policies in this connection'.[108] The provision primarily aims at protecting the marine environment as such, independently from its social or economic value or any human uses. It therefore includes in its scope purely domestic pollution, as well as pollution caused to the global commons.[109] Interstate interests are addressed in paragraph 2 of the provision, which requires states to 'take all measures necessary to ensure that activities under their jurisdiction or control are so conducted as not to cause damage by pollution to other States and their environment, and that pollution arising from incidents or activities under their jurisdiction or control does not spread beyond the areas where they exercise sovereign rights'.[110] The norm is mainly bilateral in scope with regard to damages caused to other states. Yet, in cases of damage caused to the environment of the high seas or the deep seabed, the provision is *erga omnes* in character.[111] Remedy must thus be open to all states.[112]

---

[105] 1982 UNCLOS, Art. 193.

[106] See also Rio Principle 4 (1992); *Gabčíkovo–Nagymaros, supra* n. 93, 78 para. 140; *The Iron Rhine Arbitration (Belgium v. the Netherlands)* [2005] 27 UN Rep. Int'l Arb Awards 35, 66–67, para. 59; *Pulp Mills on the River Uruguay (Argentina v. Uruguay), Provisional Measures, Order of 13 July 2006* [2006] ICJ Rep. 2006 113 133, para. 80.

[107] 1982 UNCLOS, Art. 194(1).

[108] Ibid., Art. 194(1).

[109] Birnie *et al., supra* n. 72, p. 129; Nicolas de Sadeleer, *Environmental Principles: From Political Slogans to Legal Rules* (Oxford: Oxford University Press, 2002), p. 64; Sands and Peel, *supra* n. 72, p. 201.

[110] 1982 UNCLOS, Art. 194(2).

[111] On *erga omnes* obligations, see *Barcelona Traction, Light and Power Company, Limited (Belgium v. Spain) Judgment* [1970] ICJ Rep. 1970 3 32, para. 33. See also *East Timor (Portugal v. Australia)* [1995] ICJ Rep. 1995 90 102, para. 29; *Application of the Convention on the Prevention and Punishment of the Crime of Genocide, Preliminary Objections, Judgment* [1996] ICJ Rep. 1996 595 616, para. 31.

[112] See Jonathan I. Charney, 'Third State Remedies for Environmental Damage to the World's Common Spaces', in Francesco Francioni and Tullio Scovazzi (eds.),

The prescribed measures have to deal with all sources of pollution of the marine environment. In terms of the convention, these include land-based sources, seabed activities within or beyond national jurisdiction, vessels, dumping and pollution from or through the atmosphere.[113] Measures have to be designed to minimize to the fullest possible extent the release of toxic or harmful substances from land-based sources and pollution from other sources.[114] They must not unjustifiably interfere with other lawful activities in the marine environment.[115] A particular focus lies on the protection and preservation of 'rare or fragile ecosystems as well as the habitat of depleted, threatened or endangered species and other forms of marine life'.[116] In taking measures to prevent, reduce and control pollution of the marine environment, states have to make sure 'not to transfer ... damage or hazards from one area to another or transform one type of pollution into another'.[117] Also, states have to prevent, reduce and control pollution resulting from the use of technology or the introduction of new or alien species into parts of the marine environment.[118]

Part XII Section 5 (international rules and national legislation)[119] and Section 6 (enforcement)[120] specify the obligation of states to take and enforce measures (especially laws and regulations) to prevent, reduce and control pollution of the marine environment from all different sources, including land-based. The provisions can be seen as a substantiation of the duty of states to enact effective environmental legislation as reflected in Rio Principle 11. They are complemented by the provisions on monitoring and assessment (Section 4), liability (Section 9) and compliance with other rules of international law (Section 11).

International Responsibility for Environmental Harm (Leiden: Graham & Trotman–Martinus Nijhoff, 1991), pp. 165–6.

[113] 1982 UNCLOS, Arts. 194 and 207–12.

[114] Ibid., Art. 194(3).

[115] Ibid., Art. 194(4).

[116] Ibid., Art. 194(5). A recent ruling by the International Tribunal on the Law of the Sea (ITLOS) clearly depicts the importance of ecosystem protection, conservation of endangered species and sustainable use of living resources of the sea in the protection and preservation of the marine environment (*South China Sea Arbitration, supra* n. 74, 380, para. 956, citing *Southern Bluefin Tuna Cases, supra* n. 93, 295 para. 70).

[117] 1982 UNCLOS, Art. 195.

[118] Ibid., Art. 196.

[119] Ibid., Arts. 207–12.

[120] Ibid., Arts. 213–22.

MARINE PLASTIC POLLUTION 181

Several non-binding instruments and documents,[121] as well as regional legal instruments[122] and marine litter action plans[123] provide valuable

[121] See, among others, UNEP, 'GPA', *supra* n. 49; UNEP and NOAA, 'The Honolulu Strategy: A Global Framework for Prevention and Management of Marine Debris' (2011); UNEP, *Marine Litter Legislation: A Toolkit for Policymakers*, *supra* n. 50; CBD Secretariat, *supra* n. 12; Patrick ten Brink *et al.*, 'Plastics Marine Litter and the Circular Economy: A Briefing by IEEP for the MAVA Foundation' (IEEP, 2016); UNEP, 'UNEA-2 Technical Report on Marine Plastic Debris', *supra* n. 50, chs. 8 and 9; UNGA Res. 70/1 (2015), *supra* n. 59; A. Arroyo Schnell *et al.*, 'National Marine Plastic Litter Policies in EU Member States: An Overview' (IUCN, 2017); European Commission, 'A European Strategy for Plastics in a Circular Economy' (2018) COM(2018) 28 final, with annexes.
[122] Especially those on land-based sources: Caspian Sea Region: Protocol for the Protection of the Caspian Sea against Pollution from Land-Based Sources and Activities to the 2003 Tehran Convention (2012 Moscow Protocol) (adopted 12 Dec. 2012, not yet entered into force). Mediterranean Region: Protocol for the Protection of the Mediterranean sea against Pollution from Land-Based Sources (1980 Athens Protocol) (signed on 17 May 1980, entered into force on 17 June 1983) 19 ILM 869 (1980); Protocol for the Protection of the Mediterranean Sea against Pollution from Land-Based Sources and Activities (1996 Syracuse Protocol) (originally adopted in 1980 in Athens, amended on 7 Mar. 1996, entered into force on 11 May 2008). West and Central Africa Region: Additional Protocol to the Abidjan Convention Concerning Cooperation in the Protection and Development of Marine and Coastal Environment from Land-Based Sources and Activities in the Western, Central and Southern African Region (2012 Abidjan Protocol) (adopted on 22 June 2012, not entered into force yet). Western Indian Ocean Region: Protocol for the Protection of the Marine and Coastal Environment of the Western Indian Ocean from Land-Based Sources and Activities (2010 Nairobi Protocol) (adopted 31 Mar. 2010; not yet entered into force). Wider Caribbean Region: Protocol Concerning Pollution from Land-Based Sources and Activities to the Convention for the Protection and Development of the Marine Environment of the Wider Caribbean Region (Aruba Protocol) (adopted 6 Oct. 1999, entered into force on 13 Aug. 2010). Black Sea Region: Protocol on Protection of the Black Sea Marine Environment Against Pollution from Land Based Sources (1992 Bucharest Protocol) (adopted 21 Apr. 1992, entered into force on 15 Jan. 1994) 32 ILM 1122 (1993); Protocol on the Protection of the Marine Environment of the Black Sea from Land-Based Sources and Activities (2009 Sofia Protocol) (originally adopted in Bucharest in 1992, fully revised in 2009, revised version not entered into force yet). Red Sea and Gulf of Aden: Protocol concerning the Protection of the Marine Environment from Land-Based Activities in the Red Sea and Gulf of Aden (2005 Jeddah Protocol) (adopted 25 Sept. 2005, not yet entered into force). ROPME Sea Area (Kuwait): Protocol for the Protection of the Marine Environment against Pollution from Land-Based Sources (1990 Kuwait Protocol) (adopted in 1990, entered into force on 2 Jan. 1993). South East Pacific Region: Protocol for the Protection of the South-East Pacific against Pollution from Land-based Sources (1983 Quito Protocol) (signed on 22 July 1983, entered into force in 1986).
[123] See UNEP–NOWPAP, 'NOWPAP Regional Action Plan on Marine Litter' (2008); HELCOM, 'Regional Action Plan for Marine Litter in the Baltic Sea' (2015); OSPAR Commission, 'Regional Action Plan for Prevention and Management of Marine Litter in the North-East Atlantic' (2014); UNEP–CAR/RCU, 'Regional Action Plan on Marine

guidance to policymakers on how to implement the duty to protect and preserve the marine environment with regard to plastic pollution. Effective implementation takes place at different levels of governance, from subregional to local. It is highly versatile and uneven. With regard to land-based pollution sources, implementing measures usually touch on *consumer responsibility*, aiming at a change in consumption habits, including through more reasonable, needs-based consumption and a decrease in the consumption of disposable plastics and microbeads. They further promote *producer responsibility* with regard to green product design, chemical safety, transparency, life-cycle thinking and cost internalization. *Sustainable resource management* is another pillar of national implementation and includes endeavours towards a circular economy (that is, the reintroduction of resources into the production and consumption cycles through reuse, recycling and composting) and integrative waste management, which is based on the so-called waste hierarchy, preferring waste prevention and minimization over reuse, recycling and waste incineration with energy recovery, while other disposal methods are the least preferable option. Improvement of waste management infrastructure in developing countries is of particular importance in this regard, but goes beyond purely domestic obligations to the extent that it depends on the support by other countries, including through technology transfer and financial assistance.

It was already held in 1992 – and still holds true – that in order to prevent, reduce and control degradation of the marine environment so as to maintain and improve its life-support and productive capacities,

> states should apply preventive, precautionary and anticipatory approaches; ensure prior assessment of activities that may have significant adverse impacts upon the marine environment; integrate protection of the marine environment into relevant general environmental, social and economic development policies; develop economic incentives consistent with the internalisation of environmental costs and the polluter pays principle; and take into account equity concerns.[124]

A specific category of possible measures are market-based instruments (MBIs). They can have a legal foundation or be based on voluntary industry agreements. MBIs influence product demand and individual

---

Litter Management (RAPMali) for the Wider Caribbean Region 2014' (2014); UNEP–MAP, 'Regional Plan for the Marine Litter Management in the Mediterranean' (2013) UNEP (DEPI)/MED WG.379/5.

[124] Agenda 21, *supra* n. 71, para. 17.22.

and corporate choices by setting economic incentives or disincentives. They allow for the internalization of environmental costs associated with the production or use of a product and otherwise paid by affected people or the public at large. MBIs include, for instance, taxes or levies on products (such as single-use plastic items) or materials (such as polystyrene) at the production or retail level; standards and labels containing information on the environmental performance of a product; subsidization of green business models, or green public procurement. Revenues generated by taxes and levies can be invested in awareness-raising campaigns or similar mitigation measures. Regulatory measures include bans of specific products or materials, as well as technical regulations, for instance with regard to packaging or the use of certain chemicals in products. Regulatory measures and, as the case may be, MBIs can have extraterritorial effects, especially with regard to international trade in goods.

In the past, environmental measures, for instance in form of import bans on environmentally destructive goods, have given rise to a number of disputes under World Trade Organization (WTO) law. In the past, the WTO Appellate Body has underscored the autonomy of member states 'to determine their own policies on the environment (including its relationship with trade), their environmental objectives and the environmental legislation they enact and implement'.[125] Accordingly, it accepted different measures related to the protection of the environment as provisionally justified under the General Agreement on Tariffs and Trade (GATT)[126] exception clauses. Yet, parties to the disputes that invoked the exception clauses lost their cases due to the flanking conditions for their use, which are very restrictive. However, whenever states are able to base their measures on an international obligation, such as imposed by multilateral environmental agreements, the measures are usually not challenged by other WTO member states.[127] Also, WTO dispute settlement bodies basically respect environmental obligations of parties arising

---

[125] *United States – Standards for Reformulated and Conventional Gasoline (US Gasoline)* [1996] Appellate Body Report WT/DS2/AB/R 30.

[126] General Agreement on Tariffs and Trade (GATT 1994) Marrakesh Agreement Establishing the World Trade Organization, Annex 1A, 1867 UNTS 190, 33 ILM 1153 (1994) 1994.

[127] No measures have been challenged that have been adopted in implementation of: Convention on International Trade in Endangered Species of Wild Fauna and Flora (CITES) (adopted 3 Mar. 1973, entered into force on 1 July 1975, as amended in 1979 and 1983) 993 UNTS 243; Basel Convention on the Control of Transboundary

184   JUDITH SCHÄLI

from international treaties. By contrast, unilateral trade measures that do
not find a direct basis in an international treaty have a much more
difficult stand: although the GATT provides for environmental exceptions, none of the members that resorted to such measures has been able
to actually justify them in a WTO case.[128] The requirements of the
chapeau of GATT Article XX are a major stumbling block for unilateral
measures with coercive, extraterritorial effects when these measures are
not based on prior consultation and cooperative efforts.[129]

The debate on process and production methods (PPMs), as outlined in
the introductory chapter, may also be of relevance to plastics and plastic
pollution mitigation.[130] Possible non-product-related PPMs include criteria related to the use of different energy sources or raw materials
(renewable or non-renewable) for the production of the same plastic
material, the use of different technologies (such as filters) and chemicals
in the production process, pellet leakages and dissimilar management of
production wastes, and different transportation modes. As of today,
measures that treat products differently based on such criteria will
possibly not be justifiable under WTO law. While in *US Shrimp*, the
Appellate Body considered a US measure protecting marine turtles as

---

Movements of Hazardous Wastes and Their Disposal (1989 Basel Convention) (adopted
22 Mar. 1989, entered into force on 5 May 1992) 1673 UNTS 126, 28 ILM 657 (1989).

[128] Examples include *United States – Restrictions on Imports of Tuna (US Tuna I)* [1991]
GATT Panel Report (unadopted) DS21/R, BISD 39S/55; *United States – Import
Prohibition of Certain Shrimp and Shrimp Products (US Shrimp)* [1998] Appellate
Body Report WT/DS58/AB/R. Also in *US Gasoline, supra* n. 125 the US measure, which
was found in violation of GATT, Art. III, did not meet the requirements for an environmental exception. However, the Appellate Body accepted a French measure prohibiting
the manufacture, processing, sale and import of asbestos and asbestos-containing products to be 'necessary to protect human life or health' and thus to be justifiable as an
exception under GATT.

[129] See, for instance, *US Shrimp, supra* n. 128, 63–72, paras. 161–76.

[130] On PPMs, see, for instance, Christiane R. Conrad, *Processes and Production Methods
(PPMs) in WTO Law: Interfacing Trade and Social Goals* (Cambridge: Cambridge
University Press, 2011); OECD, 'Processes and Production Methods (PPMs):
Conceptual Framework and Considerations on Use of PPM-Based Trade Measures'
(OECD 1997) OCDE/GD(97)137; Robert Read, 'Process and Production Methods and
the Regulation of International Trade', in Nicolas Perdikis and Robert Read (eds.), *The
WTO and the Regulation of International Trade: Recent Trade Disputes between the
European Union and the United States* (Cheltenham, UK: Edward Elgar, 2005); Erich
Vranes, *Trade and the Environment: Fundamental Issues in International Law, WTO
Law, and Legal Theory* (Oxford: Oxford University Press, 2009), pt III, ch. 3; Jochem
Wiers, 'WTO Rules and Environmental Production and Processing Methods (PPMs)',
ERA-Forum, 2 (2001), 101.

MARINE PLASTIC POLLUTION

provisionally justified under the GATT exception clauses in spite of its extraterritorial effects,[131] a 'sufficient nexus' between the objective of protection and the country applying the measure is still required.[132] Hence, a landlocked country may currently have a difficult stand before a WTO dispute settlement body to justify a measure in favour of zero pellet-loss plastics in order to protect and preserve albatrosses of Midway Island when these birds do not spend any stage of their life in the respective country.

Packaging regulations present another interesting case from a WTO law perspective. As considerable parts of marine plastic debris stem from packaging, qualitative and quantitative packaging regulations[133] may be an interesting option for preventing marine plastic debris. Mandatory packaging regulations fall under the Agreement on Technical Barriers to Trade (TBT) and have to meet the restrictive requirements of its Article 2.2.[134] They shall not be more trade-restrictive than necessary to fulfil a legitimate objective, such as the protection of the environment. The TBT also demands the use of relevant international standards as a basis for the regulations if such standards exist, unless their use is ineffective or inappropriate.[135]

3.3 Implications of the Concept of Common Concern

3.3.1 Outline of the Concept

The concept, or principle,[136] of Common Concern, as suggested by the authors of this book and described in the introductory chapter, is based on the observation that some of the most challenging problems of our time demand for common responses that are based on cooperation and mutual support. It is also linked to the idea of shared responsibilities of

---

[131] *US Shrimp, supra* n. 128, 53–4 paras. 141–2.

[132] Ibid., 51, para. 133.

[133] Qualitative regulations promote the use of less harmful materials and packaging designs, better recyclability or degradability of packaging materials, as well as lower rates of chemical contamination. Quantitative regulations aim to limit the use of plastic packaging where this is compatible with sanitary standards.

[134] Agreement on Technical Barriers to Trade (TBT) Marrakesh Agreement Establishing the World Trade Organization, Annex 1A, 1868 UNTS 120 1998 5.

[135] Ibid., Art. 2.4.

[136] The authors of this book argue that the concept of Common Concern of Humankind may evolve as a legal principle in the process of claims and responses (Chapter 1, p. 55).

states or the international community to commonly resolve grave problems, especially when they are human-made. In this sense, common concerns usually correspond to collective action problems that are related to the lack of appropriate and effective (global) institutions that ensure the sustainable production of (global) public goods.[137]

The concept defines a range of legal responses – in form of rights and obligations – to shared problems within different spheres of action. From an international law point of view and when speaking of a common concern of humankind, which corresponds to global concerns beyond a certain degree of severity, these spheres include responses within states, among states in a cooperative environment, and against free-riders. The concept, however, can also be transposed to the substate level and may require action at different levels of government, as appropriate. The three areas of action are the principal frame of the concept and are referred to as its very pillars:

- *The duty to cooperate*:[138] Acceptance by the international community of a grave and shared problem as a common concern of humankind triggers an enhanced duty to negotiate and cooperate in the first place. Enhanced cooperative duties also refer to transparency, burden sharing and differentiated responsibility.
- *Obligation to do homework*:[139] Cooperative duties are complemented by a duty of states to take action in their domestic area. Domestic measures usually include regulatory measures but are not limited to these. The concept may legitimize extraterritorial effects of domestic law to the extent that they effectively serve the internationally agreed goal of addressing an issue of common concern.
- *Compliance and unilateral actions*:[140] Assumingly, international organizations are the prime actors or decision forums in the enforcement of duties related to common concerns. Subsidiarily, states may take unilateral actions, especially in the form of economic or trade sanctions against states that refuse to take part in common efforts in addressing a common concern. The concept suggests allowing for unilateral actions by states or the European Union in addressing free-riding, provided that these actions respect the principle of proportionality.

---

[137] Ibid., pp. 3–11.
[138] Ibid., pp. 59–63.
[139] Ibid., pp. 63–8.
[140] Ibid., pp. 68–78.

The concept suggests that for a problem to be qualified as a Common Concern of Humankind, it needs to meet a certain threshold of severity, below which some responses may be unjustified and thus inadmissible. Common Concerns of Humankind are inherently transboundary and potentially affect all of humanity or the international system as a whole in terms of stability and viability. Common Concerns may bear the risk of threatening international stability, peace and welfare. This threshold is intended to catch the seriousness of a problem in a long-term perspective. With regard to inherently environmental problems, it needs to be understood in a broad sense, such as covering severe threats to broad and essential ecosystems and their services, including, for instance, food supplies, the lack of which may lead to social unrest in an indirect way. Because of the potentially grave and wide impact of an issue of Common Concern, states are entitled, but also obliged to act in a certain way at home and – perhaps in a more limited way – abroad.

With regard to international law, the concept of Common Concern of Humankind has the potential to influence the interpretation of existing agreements, rights and obligations in that common concerns are to be taken into account in the interpretation of norms. Moreover, the concept may reinforce third party standing with respect to the violation of norms owed to the international community as a whole (such as specific environmental duties).

3.3.2 Promises and Opportunities with regard to Marine Plastic Pollution

In its current form, the duty to protect and preserve the marine environment is hardly enforceable with regard to marine plastic pollution due to the diffuse, dispersed and cumulative character of this form of pollution. UNCLOS dispute settlement and liability provisions are not well tailored to this particular form of pollution. The absence of internationally agreed standards on land-based pollution sources of plastics possibly also has negative implications with regard to the policy space of states to adopt mitigation measures within the WTO regime, as states are not able to base their measures on specific international obligations when there are extraterritorial effects. Overall, the current regime lacks both carrots and sticks to reach the main polluting countries, which have enormous waste problems and limited capacities to deal with them. This shortcoming limits the effectiveness of the current regime and results in continuing massive plastic waste input into the world's oceans.

188   JUDITH SCHÄLI

The concept of Common Concern as defined and described in the introductory chapter brings about a set of chances and valuable responses to the issue at stake. It implies an enhanced commitment of states and obligations to international cooperation. In doing so, it backs states when applying their domestic law in implementation of these obligations, and thus may contribute to the justification of extraterritorial effects of such law. Finally, it arguably also influences questions related to the enforceability of the UNCLOS obligation to protect and preserve the marine environment against plastic pollution.

3.3.2.1 The Duty to Cooperate

A principle of Common Concern would considerably strengthen and reinforce the duty of states to commonly formulate rules and standards on marine plastic pollution, especially from land-based sources. When identified as a Common Concern of Humankind, marine plastic pollution, most of which stems from land, has to be addressed with the necessary resoluteness and effectiveness through the formulation, implementation and enforcement of specific, well-tailored global and regional rules binding on – and practically implementable for – the most polluting countries in particular. Many of these countries do not, as for now, participate in a legally binding regime addressing land-based pollution sources beyond UNCLOS. This being, recognizing marine plastic pollution as a Common Concern would make a difference, as UNCLOS does not sufficiently take into account the particularities of marine plastic pollution as a diffuse form of pollution. An enhanced duty to cooperate would go beyond the obligation of states under UNCLOS to '*endeavour* to establish global and regional rules ... to prevent, reduce and control pollution of the marine environment from land-based sources'.[141] It would make a strong case for a convention to be adopted under the auspices of UN Environment. Such a convention would, among other things, inform the obligation to protect and preserve the marine environment with regard to plastics. It would specify the applicable standard of care and could provide a platform for states to formulate national targets and commitments. With regard to applicable environmental principles, institutional mechanisms and substantive obligations, the convention could build upon experiences gained under the regional instruments on marine pollution and under other multilateral environmental agreements,

---

[141] 1982 UNCLOS, Art. 207(4), emphasis added.

including, for instance, the Montreal Protocol on Substances that Deplete the Ozone Layer or the Paris Agreement on Climate Change.[142] Along with clear standards and the institutional setting, important building blocks of a global instrument on marine plastic pollution would include provisions on funding, compliance facilitation, reporting, implementation review and a strong capacity-building scheme, including with regard to technology and knowledge transfer and financial assistance.

Especially the obligation to provide support to countries with limited resources to contribute to the global efforts in solving the problem can be derived from the concept or principle of Common Concern.[143] With regard to plastics, technology and knowledge transfer can be important with respect to waste collection and disposal systems (with due regard to regional differences in waste composition), sewage and wastewater treatment, chemical safety, green design (which is often protected by trademarks), recycling, biodegradable materials, monitoring methods and methodology, and valuable clean-up technologies, as far as they exist. Financial assistance is important for education and awareness campaigns and for covering administrative and institutional costs related to plastic pollution mitigation and prevention, as well as costs related to the infrastructure for and the operation of waste collection and disposal (which is often the single largest budget item for municipalities)[144] and coastal clean-ups. Support to governance structures and exchange on policies and law can be another form of assistance that is important both at the national and the regional level. Regional Seas secretariats or offices in developing country regions are often not equipped with enough resources and staff to effectively fulfil their tasks. Funding schemes would thus have to be reconsidered.

3.3.2.2 Obligation to Do Homework

In order to avoid free-riding and counter the tragedy of the global commons, the concept of Common Concern of Humankind calls for action in domestic law and policy. In the case of marine plastic pollution, at least two levels of implications of the concept of Common Concern, when established as a principle, can be identified in the homework pillar.

---

[142] Montreal Protocol on Substances that Deplete the Ozone Layer (Montreal Protocol) (adopted 16 Sept. 1987, entered into force on 1 Jan. 1989, last amended in 1999) 1522 UNTS 3, 26 ILM 1550 (1987); Paris Agreement (adopted by UNFCCC COP decision on 12 Dec. 2015) in Report of the COP 21, FCCC /CP/2015/10/Add.1, Annex.

[143] See Chapter 1 in this volume, pp. 61–3.

[144] Hoornweg and Bhata-Tata, *supra* n. 3, 1.

190   JUDITH SCHÄLI

The first level concerns the obligation to adopt autonomous measures. While the duty to adopt regulatory and other measures to protect and preserve the marine environment already exists as a customary rule of international law that is reflected in UNLCOS, this duty would be specified and reinforced with regard to marine plastic pollution. The second level concerns the question of extraterritorial effects of domestic measures and potential tensions with rights and obligations of states as stipulated under WTO covered agreements. The second level of implications is strongly related to the adoption of international rules and standards as required under the cooperation pillar.

International trade regulation plays a restraining role with regard to the adoption of measures with extraterritorial trade effects. This is even more true with regard to trade measures[145] that aim at influencing the behaviour of actors abroad and enforcing self-set standards in other countries, including in protection of the global commons. Such measures have been used by states for addressing environmental problems caused outside their own jurisdiction. Trade law disciplines states in the adoption of measures, particularly with regard to arbitrariness and discriminatory treatment. It curtails the states' freedom to take unilateral actions and gives preference to concerted action instead.[146] States thus have an obligation to seek compatible solutions through cooperation, which is an obligation of conduct.[147]

The concept of common concern does not at all negate the importance of cooperation and the preference accorded to concerted action. With regard to collective action problems, however, cooperation and the exhaustion of diplomatic means through serious international negotiations with potentially affected states may be a too time-consuming means for a timely reaction to an urgent concern. By contrast, trade measures allow for immediate reaction. Also, cooperative efforts may be impaired by the problem of free-riding. Trade measures may provide an effective response to free-riding.[148] For this reason, a principle of Common Concern would back states in the adoption of appropriate

---

[145] Unilateral trade measures can be defined as 'regulations that serve to protect the environment, but incur trade impacts and are adopted by one or more states without the consent of the affected state' (Vranes, *supra* n. 130, p. 174).

[146] The same preference can be derived from Art. 1 of the UN Charter. It is also reflected in Rio Principle 12 and Agenda 21, *supra* n. 71, para. 17.118.

[147] See Vranes, *supra* n. 130, pp. 176–7.

[148] See Brian K. Myers, 'Trade Measures and the Environment: Can the WTO and UNCLOS Be Reconciled?', *UCLA Journal of Environmental Law & Policy*, 23 (2005), 37, 68–9.

MARINE PLASTIC POLLUTION 191

measures where cooperation, due to a lack of time or to poor participation by others, does not lead to a sufficient result.

Multilateral environmental treaties have a potential to strengthen the member states' regulatory authority to enact environmental legislation under the WTO regime. Specifically, the adoption of a global convention on the protection of the marine environment from plastic pollution would considerably strengthen the policy space of states under WTO law with regard to the measures taken in implementation of the duty to protect and preserve the marine environment. Due to the general presumption of mutual supportiveness between such instruments and WTO-covered agreements,[149] a measure is presumed to be consistent with WTO obligations whenever a state is required to adopt it by an international treaty. In case of a true conflict of norms which cannot be avoided by means of treaty interpretation, multilateral environmental obligations tend to prevail over trade obligations to the extent that they are of an integral character and not, as most obligations under trade law, reciprocal in scope.[150] Also, whenever relevant and applicable, environmental agreements form part of the interpretive background of the legal provisions under WTO law.[151] The increasingly integrative approach taken by the Appellate Body towards multilateral environmental agreements arguably reflects the growing importance of the concept of global commons in international law.[152]

The case of UNCLOS is peculiar in that its Part XII does not directly require trade measures to be taken. It merely sets out principles and leaves to its parties a wide room to manoeuvre in the implementation of

---

[149] See, for instance, IISD and UNEP, *Environment and Trade: A Handbook* (IISD, 2005) 65.

[150] If the multilateral environmental rule comes later in time, it prevails as the *lex posterior* under VCLT, Art. 30(4)(a). If it is the earlier in time, it cannot, as an integral obligation, be validly deviated from *inter se* by the later WTO rule pursuant to VCLT, Arts. 41 and 58 (Joost Pauwelyn, *Conflict of Norms in Public International Law: How WTO Law Relates to Other Rules of International Law* (Cambridge: Cambridge University Press, 2003), pp. 315–24). See also Alan E. Boyle, 'Relationship between International Environmental Law and Other Branches of International Law', in Daniel Bodansky, Jutta Brunnée and Ellen Hey (eds.), *The Oxford Handbook of International Environmental Law* (Oxford: Oxford University Press, 2007), pp. 136–8; ILC, *supra* n. 75, 83, para. 154.

[151] See ILC, *supra* n. 75, 88–9, para. 167. For more information on potential conflicts between WTO law and other rules of international law, see Vranes, *supra* n. 130, pp. 68–92.

[152] Marion Panizzon, Luca Arnold and Thomas Cottier, 'Handel und Umwelt in der WTO: Entwicklungen und Perspektiven', *Umweltrecht in der Praxis* [2010], 210–12.

192   JUDITH SCHÄLI

the general obligations. When challenged before a WTO Panel, states thus may have a difficult stand to prove the necessity of their measures in the fulfilment of their obligations. However, while the need to take trade-restrictive measures is not spelled out in UNCLOS, such measures may be an efficient and effective means to achieve the objectives of the treaty. An example includes bans of microbeads in products and of other non-recoverable plastics destined to end up in waterways. Technical regulations, such as quantitative or qualitative packaging regulations, are another type of potentially effective measures in addressing marine plastic pollution. Such bans or technical regulations, or other trade-related measures, may prove necessary in order to effectively protect the marine environment from microplastics, taking into account the specific level of protection pursued by a state. In an international convention addressing marine plastic pollution, a strict standard could be set, giving states the opportunity to directly base their measures, including bans, on a concrete obligation. Such a convention could explicitly allow or require trade measures and address its relation to WTO-covered agreements with a rule of conflict.

The question of whether domestic measures are consistent with WTO law strongly depends on their exact design. It has to be examined on a case-by-case basis. Consistency has been denied due to the measure's 'intended and actual coercive effect on other governments' to 'adopt essentially the same policy' as the state adopting the measure, as well as the failure of that state to have 'prior consistent recourse to diplomacy'.[153] Specific international standards would thus alleviate conflicts in that they are the result of international cooperation and guide countries in the formulation and adoption of mutually acceptable measures. They would enhance policy harmonization and the creation of a level playing field, while the minimal level of protection would rise considerably.

As pointed out in the introductory chapter, a principle of Common Concern of Humankind would also have an effect on the territorial link as required under WTO law. While WTO dispute settlement bodies currently demand that there be a 'sufficient nexus' between a state's territory and the object to be protected (such as an endangered species)

---

[153] *US Shrimp, supra* n. 128, 63–76, paras. 161–86; cf. *United States – Measures Concerning the Importation, Marketing and Sale of Tuna and Tuna Products (Tuna II (Mexico))* [2012] Appellate Body Report WT/DS381/AB/R 324–31, paras. 124–8.

for purposes of the environmental exception clause,[154] this would no longer be a relevant factor. Under a principle of Common Concern of Humankind, the core question is whether a measure is appropriate to contribute to the abatement of a problem considered as a common concern or to the creation of a respective global public good. Preventive measures that effectively reduce the risk of plastic accumulation in the marine environment would therefore be admissible whether or not a state has access to the sea, if such measures are consistent with treaty obligations and designed in the least trade-distorting way.

3.3.2.3 Compliance and Unilateral Actions

Plastics bring about a set of particular challenges with regard to enforcement of UNCLOS provisions, be it through invocation of state responsibility or by resort to the dispute settlement procedures as provided by the convention. One of the main hurdles is its continuous, dispersed and diffuse character due to which it can seldom be traced back to a specific polluter. Moreover, nearly all the states contribute to the problem. In this constellation, bringing a case against another state is not obvious. This is particularly true with regard to purely domestic pollution or pollution to common spaces, including the high seas and the deep seabed. The lack of binding standards on land-based pollution sources, the lack of capacities in a context of due diligence obligations, and the lack of reporting obligations and compliance assessment procedures are further obstacles to the enforcement of UNCLOS obligations with respect to plastic pollution. In a plastic-related context, traditional dispute settlement seems more of a theoretical option than of a way to give the provisions real effect.

Against this backdrop, an argument can be made that the concept of Common Concern may step in and allow for unilateral actions, such as economic sanctions against free-riders. However, with regard to marine plastic pollution, especially from land-based sources, economic sanctions have an ambiguous stand. Intervention against gross domestic plastic pollution is potentially justified, as plastic pollution easily spreads to areas beyond a country's jurisdiction and threatens various marine species, including species migrating between various countries. It is thus an inherently transboundary problem. Economic sanctions and other unilateral actions may be essential to leverage mitigation action and the

---

[154] See *US Shrimp, supra* n. 128, 51, para. 133.

194 JUDITH SCHÄLI

development of sufficient standards on the international level. On the other hand, economic sanctions arguably have limited or undesirable effects with regard to environmental problems that are not caused by a lack of commitment and willingness in the first place, but to a lack of necessary means and capacities. As main contributors to marine plastic pollution mostly include low and lower-middle income countries, awareness-raising activities and capacity building seem the more effective means to encourage global commitment.

With regard to the issue of third-party standing, the International Law Commission's (ILC) Draft Articles on State Responsibility allow non-injured states to invoke the responsibility of a state for an internationally wrongful act under restrictive conditions.[155] They may do so in the collective public interest in protection of shared fundamental values.[156] The indirect reference in UNCLOS Article 194(2) to areas beyond national jurisdiction strongly suggests that there is a third party standing with regard to the pollution of such areas.[157] In theory, the same argument can be made with regard to UNCLOS Article 194(1) and activities with purely domestic effects.[158] Yet, states are extremely reluctant to resort to the possibility of invoking state responsibility with regard to damage caused to domestic areas or the global commons. Only in about two cases decided by arbitral tribunals, public interest standing has been granted in contexts related to the protection of the marine

[155] ILC, 'Draft Articles on Responsibility of States for Internationally Wrongful Acts', *Report of the International Law Commission 53rd session* (UN Doc. A/56/10 ch IVE1 2001), Art. 48(1).

[156] See Antonio Cassese, *International Law* (Oxford: Oxford University Press, 2005), p. 263; James Crawford, 'Overview of Part Three of the Articles on State Responsibility', in James Crawford, Alain Pellet and Simon Olleson (eds.), *The Law of International Responsibility* (Oxford: Oxford University Press, 2010), p. 934.

[157] See *Responsibilities of States in the Area, supra* n. 76, 54, para. 180. The question of standing is closely related to the one of the level of threshold environmental damage must have in order to be actionable in these different constellations. Legal practice and doctrine suggest some vague criteria, especially applying to transboundary damage. Similar criteria have not, however, been elaborated for domestic damage or damage to common spaces.

[158] On the suggestion that a coastal state is obliged towards the world at large to prevent pollution of its territorial sea, see Louis Cavaré, 'Les problèmes juridiques posés par la pollution des eaux maritimes au point de vue interne et international', *Revue générale de droit international public* [1964], 617, 631; Daniel P. O'Connell, *The International Law of the Sea*, vol. 2 (Ivan Anthony Shearer ed., Oxford: Clarendon Press, 1984), pp. 987–8.

environment.[159] Due to the reciprocity in interstate relations, states usually prefer solving problems by diplomatic channels, including through cooperation and negotiation. Also, domestic pollution is most often treated as an internal affair of the polluting state even when there is an international obligation at stake.

Even a consolidation of public interest standing under a principle of Common Concern would probably not significantly alleviate the identified difficulties with regard to the enforceability of the general provisions under UNCLOS. Again, the main impact of such a principle is directly linked to enhanced cooperation and the adoption of common standards within a specific convention on marine plastic pollution mitigation. Enforceability of agreed standards depends on flanking procedural obligations related to reporting, monitoring and compliance facilitation, as well as on the institutional setup (possibly including a scientific committee and supervisory powers of the governing body) and effective capacity building. Also, with regard to the law regulating specific aspects of marine pollution, states often fall back on special liability regimes focusing on the polluter, including private operators. Such liability regimes can provide a valuable alternative to state responsibility claims.[160]

3.4 Conclusions

Marine plastic pollution has been repeatedly recognized in different international forums as a matter of global concern and a problem of utmost urgency with a wide range of serious economic, social and environmental impacts. It raises concerns of intragenerational and intergenerational equity and affects the environment and biodiversity in common areas, including the high seas and the deep seabed, the latter of which has been defined as the common heritage of mankind.[161] To date, regulation is flawed, as the general duty to protect and preserve the marine environment is not sufficiently substantiated by internationally agreed legally binding standards on land-based sources of pollution

---

[159] *Whaling in the Antarctic (Australia v. Japan: New Zealand intervening), Judgment* [2014] ICJ Rep. 2014 226; *South China Sea Arbitration, supra* n. 74. It follows from the tribunal's considerations in the *South China Sea* case that harm to the marine environment 'as such' may be sufficient for constituting a breach of the obligations under Part XII, regardless of whether any country suffered a measurable loss (ibid., 380–2, paras. 956–60).

[160] See Birnie *et al.*, *supra* n. 72, p. 431.

[161] 1982 UNCLOS, Pts VII and XI.

(especially including the main polluting countries) and backed by a strong and effective capacity-building scheme, allowing developing countries to effectively participate in global mitigation efforts. With regard to sea-based sources, effective implementation of existing legal instruments seems the main challenge today.

There is full acknowledgement by the international community of the harm caused by marine plastic pollution, as well as of its severity and its global character. In line with the concept of Common Concern, this acknowledgement may serve as the foundation for enhanced obligations with regard to international cooperation and domestic action in addressing plastic pollution. Enhanced cooperation would potentially include the establishment of a specific legal framework on land-based pollution sources in which standards can be set regarding national implementation. The concept of Common Concern further suggests that all countries be requested to 'engage in making contributions and commitments commensurate with their levels of social and economic development'.[162] This is only possible if, on the one hand, there is a solid capacity-building scheme allowing developing countries to effectively engage in marine litter mitigation efforts; and, on the other hand, effective technical and regulatory solutions are developed and promoted by a number of countries, especially big economies. WTO law should not hamper domestic application of regulatory solutions that (in spite or because of their extraterritorial effects) proof successful in addressing marine litter, even if they precede an international agreement on the matter in time. Also, in view of the transboundary nature of the problem and the global commons that are affected, admissibility of measures in protection of the marine environment should not depend on a territorial link.

Implications in the third pillar seem less obvious. According to the theory as outlined in the introductory chapter, states that have a solution at hand should be able to push it, especially vis-à-vis free-riders. With regard to marine plastic pollution, a lack of capacity seems to be at the core of the issue; a problem that is more sensitive to carrots than to sticks. Also, in a plastic-specific context, strict packaging and product standards as applied by the European Union and an increasing number of states and applying to both imported and domestic goods seem a more suitable answer to the problem than targeted action against a single state. Through its implications on cooperation and homework, the concept of

---

[162] Chapter 1 in this volume, p. 9.

Common Concern may at least have indirect positive implications on the enforceability of UNCLOS provisions on the protection and preservation of marine environment with regard to plastic pollution.

* * *

Select Bibliography

Andrady, A. L. (ed.) (2003). *Plastics and the Environment* (Hoboken, NJ: Wiley-Interscience).

Arroyo, Schnell A. *et al.* (2017). 'National Marine Plastic Litter Policies in EU Member States: An Overview' (IUCN).

Bergmann, M., Gutow, L. and Klages, M. (2015). *Marine Anthropogenic Litter* (New York: Springer).

Boucher, J. and Friot, D. (2017). 'Primary Microplastics in the Oceans: A Global Evaluation of Sources' (IUCN).

CBD Secretariat, (2016). 'Marine Debris: Understanding, Preventing and Mitigating the Significant Adverse Impacts on Marine and Coastal Biodiversity' (New York: McGraw-Hill Education) CBD Technical Series No. 83.

Cottier, T. (2015). *Equitable Principles of Maritime Boundary Delimitation: The Quest for Distributive Justice in International Law* (Cambridge: Cambridge University Press).

de Sadeleer, N. (2002). *Environmental Principles: From Political Slogans to Legal Rules* (Oxford: Oxford University Press).

Earle, S. A. (2010). *The World Is Blue: How Our Fate and the Ocean's Are One* (Washington, DC: National Geographic).

Eriksen, M. *et al.* (2014). 'Plastic Pollution in the World's Oceans: More than 5 Trillion Plastic Pieces Weighing over 250,000 Tons Afloat at Sea', 9 *PLoS ONE* e111913.

Geyer, R., Jambeck, J. R. and Law, K. L. (2017). 'Production, Use, and Fate of All Plastics Ever Made', 3 *Science Advances* e1700782.

Jambeck, J. R. *et al.* (2015). 'Plastic Waste Inputs from Land into the Ocean' (2015) 347*Science* 768.

Lebreton, L. *et al.* (2018). 'Evidence That the Great Pacific Garbage Patch Is Rapidly Accumulating Plastic' (2018) 8 *Scientific Reports* www.nature.com/articles/s41598-018-22939-w (accessed 20 Sept. 2019).

McIlgorm, A., Campbell, H. F. and Rule, M. J. (2011). 'The Economic Cost and Control of Marine Debris Damage in the Asia-Pacific Region', 54 *Ocean & Coastal Management* 643.

Myers, B. K. (2005). 'Trade Measures and the Environment: Can the WTO and UNCLOS Be Reconciled?', 23 *UCLA Journal of Environmental Law & Policy* 37.

Pauwelyn, J. (2003). *Conflict of Norms in Public International Law: How WTO Law Relates to Other Rules of International Law* (Cambridge: Cambridge University Press).

Rochman, C. M. (2016). 'The Ecological Impacts of Marine Debris: Unraveling the Demonstrated Evidence from What Is Perceived', 97 *Ecology* 302.

UNEP (2016). 'Marine Plastic Debris and Microplastics: Global Lessons and Research to Inspire Action and Guide Policy Change' (UNEA-2 Technical Report on Marine Plastic Debris).

(2018). 'Combating Marine Plastic Litter and Microplastics: An Assessment of the Effectiveness of Relevant International, Regional and Subregional Governance Strategies and Approaches – Summary for Policy Makers', UNEP/AHEG/2018/1/INF/3.

Vranes, E. (2009). *Trade and the Environment: Fundamental Issues in International Law, WTO Law, and Legal Theory* (Oxford: Oxford University Press).

4

Exploring the Recognition of New Common Concerns of Humankind

The Example of the Distribution of Income and Wealth within States

ALEXANDER BEYLEVELD

[M]uch of the world has entered what could become the next long stretch – a return to persistent capital accumulation and income concentration. If history is anything to go by, peaceful policy reform may well prove unequal to the growing challenges ahead. But what of the alternatives? All of us who prize greater economic equality would do well to remember that with the rarest exceptions, it was only ever brought forth in sorrow. Be careful what you wish for.

Walter Scheidel, *The Great Leveler*[1]

4.1 Introduction

The 'sorrow' that Walter Scheidel writes of at the end of his popular book is a reference to what he has termed 'the four horsemen'; that is, the four factors that have led to the reduction of inequalities of income and wealth within societies throughout the course of known history: mass mobilization warfare, transformative revolution, state collapse and plague.[2] While his hypothesis appears rather tragic, it is worth emphasizing that it is a factual proposition that is capable – given proper data – of being

This chapter is a partial summary of the author's PhD monograph, which is titled 'Economic Inequality within States as a Common Concern of Humankind: The Impact of Cooperative Sovereignty on Transnational Corporate Taxation'. An earlier version of it was presented in June 2018 at the WTI conference 'Towards a Principle of Common Concern in Global Law' held in Bern. The ideas expressed in this chapter benefited from the comments received during the course of the conference. The author is especially grateful to Oisin Suttle, Frances Stewart, Michael Hahn and Thomas Cottier whose comments greatly strengthened the arguments presented here. Any shortcomings in the text, however, are to be attributed to the author alone.

[1] W. Scheidel, *The Great Leveler: Violence and the History of Inequality from the Stone Age to the Twenty-First Century* (Princeton, NJ: Princeton University Press, 2017), p. 444.
[2] See generally ibid.

199

objectively verified. Scheidel's hypothesis does not reflect his (or anyone else's) preferences; it merely amounts to a description of certain parts of humankind's history. As we approach the start of a fifth decade of the near-global trend towards greater inequalities of income and wealth within states,[3] then, we should perhaps begin to ask ourselves whether the four horsemen are again approaching, and, if so, what can be done to avoid their wrath. What we should *undoubtedly* ask ourselves, is how we can do better in respect of handling one of humankind's oldest concerns: that of the distribution of economic resources within our societies.

Against this backdrop, this chapter examines the possibility of better addressing changes in economic distributions within states over time from the vantage point of international law.[4] The aim of this chapter is not to make definitive assertions, but rather to start a conversation on a topic, which, for the most part, has not formed part of our post-war discourse.[5] It was a conversation that appeared largely unnecessary during the several decades immediately following the Second World War, but which should have been taken up to a greater extent in more recent times, especially since the 1990s. While there are myriad ways in which this endeavour might be undertaken, this chapter examines only one potential route without attempting to suggest that it is preferable to others: that of recognizing the changing distribution of income and wealth within states over time, and the adverse effects that flow therefrom, as a 'common concern of humankind'.

With much of the theory and practice surrounding the concept of common concern of humankind having been discussed in other chapters of this book,[6] the focus here will be on the recognition of new common concerns of humankind by looking at the economic distributions within states and the adverse effects that result as these distributions change as a

---

[3] On these trends, see generally F. Alvaredo *et al.* (eds.), *World Inequality Report 2018* (Cambridge, MA: Harvard University Press, 2018).

[4] This chapter is a condensed version of the second and third chapters of my PhD monograph with additions as presented at the SNF conference 'Towards a Principle of Common Concern in Global Law', World Trade Institute, University of Bern, 22–23 June 2018. I would like to thank all the participants of the conference for their input, but in particular I would like to express my profound gratitude to Frances Stewart, Oisin Suttle and Michael Hahn whose comments and insights have greatly helped to shape the thoughts I have expressed in this chapter. My thanks also to the two anonymous reviewers for their input. Any errors contained in the text are, of course, my own.

[5] There are, of course, some notable exceptions to this general assertion. See, for example, G. Shaffer, 'Retooling Trade Agreements for Social Inclusion', *Illinois Law Review* (2019), 1–44.

[6] See particularly Chapter 1 in this volume.

DISTRIBUTION OF INCOME AND WEALTH

potential future common concern of humankind.[7] More specifically, this chapter aims to engage the recognition discussion by expanding on an under-discussed theme in the common concern literature: that of the relationship between the common concern of humankind concept and state sovereignty.[8] To be sure, this relationship has been addressed before.[9] The consensus among scholars appears to be that common concerns require a 'balancing' of the interests of humankind, or at least those of the international community broadly construed, with the concept of sovereignty; an implication being that, at least to some degree, the two concepts are at odds with one another.[10] The approach adopted in this chapter differs from this consensus. Rather than suggest that the common concern of humankind concept is antithetical to sovereignty in some way or another, it is submitted that the recognition of common concerns of humankind is a manner in which states do, could and/or should act to 'enhance' or revisit and 'update' their perceptions of sovereignty in the light of certain changed factual circumstances in order to address certain pressing global concerns.

The basis for this argument stems from the simple idea captured by the Latin maxim *ex post facto ius oritur*; that is, that law arises out of, or is

---

[7] An interesting, not unimportant side note: scholars of this concept rarely do distinguish between the different ways in which the word 'concern' is linguistically deployed. The phrase 'common concern of humankind' as used here is, of course, legal jargon. In a looser sense, it is fairly clear to me that the distribution of income and wealth within countries is something that in a very literal sense concerns – affects – each human being. Something which I am less sure about – although I feel quite certain about it – is that most of humankind is concerned about – made anxious by, perturbed by, worried about – how economic distributions are changing within their own countries and those of others. On the manner in which the word is used in different languages in different treaties – which I think clarifies a fair deal about how the word is meant to be understood – see ibid., pp. 11–7, 37–9.

[8] The aim here being to expand on and apply what has been expressed earlier in this book by Thomas Cottier (see ibid., pp. 54–9).

[9] See generally, for example, F. Biermann, '"Common Concerns of Humankind" and National Sovereignty', in D. Hiscox and J. Levasseur (eds.), *Globalism: People, Profits, and Progress: Proceedings of the 30th Annual Conference of the Canadian Council on International Law* (London: Kluwer, 2002); L. S. Horn, 'The Common Concern of Humankind and Legal Protection of the Global Environment', PhD thesis (University of Sydney, 2000), pp. 135–45; S. Stec, 'Humanitarian Limits to Sovereignty: Common Concern and Common Heritage Approaches to Natural Resources and Environment', *International Community Law Review*, 12(3) (2010), 361–89, at 368.

[10] See N. S. Castillo-Winckels, 'Why "Common Concern of Humankind" Should Return to the Work of the International Law Commission on the Atmosphere', *Georgetown International Environmental Law Review*, 29(1) (2016), 131–52, at 135 and the sources cited there. See also F. Biermann, '"Common Concern of Humankind": The Emergence of a New Concept of International Environmental Law', *Archiv des Völkerrechts*, 34(4) (1996), 426–81, at 465 and 481; Horn, *supra* n. 10, pp. 135–45; Stec, *supra* n. 10, p. 368.

developed in response to, fact.[11] In the context of climate change, for example, the common concern of humankind concept has already been employed for more than two and a half decades, largely as a response to factual changes – the discovery of which was enabled by scientific progress – concerning the rate at which the climate has been changing and the resultant adverse effects.[12] Upon becoming aware of these factual changes, certain aspects of sovereignty had to be asserted in a new way in order for sovereigns to continue being sovereign. Recognizing climate change and its adverse effects as a common concern of humankind, therefore, is in large part simply sovereignty reconstituted; it is representative of an agreement between states, at least in large part, to define certain aspects of sovereignty in a particular way so as to maintain and preferably enhance the sovereignty of each individual state in order to more effectively address the pressing global problem of climate change *within their own territory or sovereign space.*

The recognition of a particular problem as a common concern of humankind therefore acts as a definitional instantiation of particular aspects of sovereignty such that certain global challenges may be overcome; with respect to the case in point, it would serve to clarify that sovereigns can only retain distributive autonomy individually through engaging in collective action together with other sovereigns. Without cooperation between states, the ability of each state to effect distributional change within its sovereign space is severely constrained. The retention of this ability does not only not run contrary to the notion of sovereignty but is manifestly necessary for the continued existence of states properly so called. Seen this way, the need for the legal reconstitution of sovereignty in light of particular factual changes over time is an

---

[11] For a different application of the maxim, see C. D. Zimmermann, *A Contemporary Concept of Monetary Sovereignty* (Oxford: Oxford University Press, 2013), pp. 9–16.

[12] For a brief overview of the history and development of climate change science, see S. Weart, 'The Development of the Concept of Dangerous Anthropogenic Climate Change', in J. S. Dryzek, R. B. Norgaard and D. Schlosberg, *Oxford Handbook of Climate Change and Society* (New York: Oxford University Press, 2011), pp. 67–81. For a detailed review of the physical science basis of climate change assertions, see generally T. F. Stocker *et al.* (eds.), *Climate Change 2013: The Physical Science Basis, Working Group I Contribution to the Fifth Assessment Report of the Intergovernmental Panel on Climate Change* (New York: Cambridge University Press, 2014). On the impact and effects of climate change over time, see, for example, C. B. Field *et al.* (eds.), *Managing the Risks of Extreme Events and Disasters to Advance Climate Change Adaption: Special Report of the Intergovernmental Panel on Climate Change* (New York: Cambridge University Press, 2012), pp. 109–290.

DISTRIBUTION OF INCOME AND WEALTH   203

obvious – and often overlooked – constitutive element of any common concern of humankind.

The set of changed facts contemplated in this chapter are the shifts in economic globalization that began in the late 1980s: the world saw major advances in information and communications technology (ICT) which are often described as having had – and continuing to have – a 'revolutionary' or 'transformative' impact on the global economy.[13] Most of the states in the world have also seen income and wealth within their respective territories become increasingly unequally distributed.[14] The large majority of this trend has occurred alongside the described shifts in technological change and economic globalization.[15] With this factual context sketched, the main thrust of the arguments presented here is that sovereignty-based objections to the recognition of the adverse effects stemming from the distribution of income and wealth as a common concern of humankind are premised on an inappropriate understanding of contemporary sovereignty. Once this much is accepted, the only valid objections that remain to the potential recognition of a distributional common concern of humankind revolve around the perceived severity – or lack thereof – of a substantial loss of distributive autonomy. Objections of this nature, in turn, are becoming increasingly difficult to sustain as our understanding of the empirical effects of distributional changes improve with time.[16] As a result, sovereignty not only does not constitute an impediment to the

---

[13] See, for example, R. Baldwin, *The Great Convergence: Information Technology and the New Globalization* (Cambridge, MA: Harvard University Press, 2016), pp. 81–2.

[14] See generally Alvaredo *et al.*, *supra* n. 3.

[15] See Section 4.2.1 in this chapter, pp. 205–12.

[16] Thus far I have yet to come across one source that is capable of acting as a self-standing and complete reference work for all the effects of changing distributions of income. The same is true for wealth distributions, save to say that we currently have less empirical work on wealth than we do on income. Given the enormous breadth of these topics, the lack of an all-encompassing reference work is probably understandable. Handbooks tend to be a good starting point and give one a sense of the types of things economic distributions might affect. Handbooks I have found helpful, for example, include B. Nolan, W. Salverda and T. M. Smeeding (eds.), *The Oxford Handbook of Economic Inequality* (New York: Oxford University Press, 2011); A. B. Atkinson and F. Bourguignon (eds.), *Handbook of Income Distribution (Volume 2)* (Amsterdam: Elsevier, 2015). They, however, tend to be fairly insufficient insofar as particular topics are concerned. For example, neither handbook satisfactorily addresses the relationship between changing economic distributions and some of the various forms of societal conflict, nor does either handbook explore the relationship between changing economic distributions and climate change. For these supposedly 'niche' topics, additional sources need to be consulted. In my PhD monograph, which at the time of writing was yet to be published, I have tried to point readers to a substantial number of topics in a large

recognition of a potential distributional common concern of humankind, it becomes one of the chief arguments in favour of its recognition.

In light of the above, the chapter is structured as follows: having provided a contemporary conceptualization of what will be referred to as 'distributive autonomy' in light of the changing nature of economic globalization since the late 1980s (Section 4.2), this chapter proceeds to examine the recognition of common concerns of humankind – the moment of recognition acting as a point at which the application of the Doctrine (and potential future principle) of Common Concern of Humankind, as discussed earlier in this volume,[17] is triggered – with a focus on sovereignty as a constitutive element (Section 4.3). Building on the preliminary discussions in Sections 4.2 and 4.3 – and before offering concluding remarks (Section 4.5) – the next part of this chapter contemplates the potential and utility of recognizing the distribution of income and wealth within states and the adverse effects that flow therefrom as a common concern of humankind (Section 4.4), the argument being made in the process, from the viewpoint of economic distributions, that sovereignty be viewed not only as standing for the right of peoples to self-determination and the resulting idea that they should be entitled to the creation of independent states, but also that the *raison d'être* for sovereignty is the marshalling of a conceptual device – the state – as a means to enhancing the welfare of the individuals in a given society through the provision of peace and stability. The utility of recognizing a distributional common concern of humankind, at least in large part, would be in its rebalancing of sovereignty – as practiced – in a manner that would place greater emphasis on effectively ensuring the welfare of the human beings that live within states, something which can be better – or perhaps only – accomplished through international coordination and cooperation, actions which in and of themselves are less likely to occur under conditions of growing economic inequality within states.

4.2 Sovereign 'Distributive Autonomy' and the Distribution of Income and Wealth since 'Globalization's Second Unbundling'

This part of the chapter is part contextual; using Richard Baldwin's framework for explaining technological change and economic globalization,[18] it

---

number of different fields. To the extent necessary, I have tried to do the same at various points below (see in particular pp. 232–7).

[17] See generally Chapter 1 in this volume.

[18] See generally Baldwin, *supra* n. 13.

DISTRIBUTION OF INCOME AND WEALTH   205

sketches the background – that is, the emergence of 'globalization's second unbundling' – against which the distribution of income and wealth should be evaluated in order to determine to what extent it could be considered a common concern of humankind (Section 4.2.1). It is also part conceptual development; the concept of 'distributive autonomy' is discussed and developed conceptually in light of the preceding discussion of contemporary economic globalization (Section 4.2.2).

4.2.1   The Distribution of Income and Wealth within States since 'Globalization's Second Unbundling'

In his book, *The Great Convergence*, Richard Baldwin essentially sketches a history of economic globalization, presenting as he does a 'three-cascading-constraints' view of the often discussed phenomenon.[19] He distils the history of globalization into three more or less distinct stages: the pre-globalization era; globalization's first 'acceleration' or 'unbundling'; and globalization's second 'acceleration' or 'unbundling'.[20] Others have written similar histories about globalization, but Baldwin's characterization provides a helpful framework for the purposes of this work; it provides a simple but convincing set of guidelines for understanding the contemporary global economy and how it has over time come to be what it is today.[21]

Baldwin's simplification is essentially that globalization mainly hinges on three factors – or 'cascading constraints' – trade costs (the costs of moving goods); communication costs (the costs of moving ideas); and face-to-face costs (the costs of moving people).[22] In the pre-globalized world, an era that for Baldwin came to an end in around 1820, production and consumption generally occurred in the same geographical location.[23] This came as a result of all three factors being costly – trade costs were high, communication costs were high and face-to-face costs were high; trade was mostly limited to trade within particular communities

---

[19] See Baldwin, *supra* n. 13, pp. 113–41.

[20] Ibid., pp. 4-6.

[21] See also, however, J. H. Dunning and S. M. Lundan, *Multinational Enterprises and the Global Economy* (2nd ed., Cheltenham, UK: Edward Elgar, 2008), pt I, pp. 3–200; R. Findlay and K. H. O'Rourke, *Power and Plenty: Trade, War, and the World Economy in the Second Millennium* (Princeton, NJ: Princeton University Press, 2008).

[22] See Baldwin, *supra* n. 13, pp. 8–10.

[23] On the pre-globalized era, see Baldwin, *supra* n. 13, pp. 21–46.

ALEXANDER BEYLEVELD

that were geographically close to one another and the same could be said of communication and the movement of people, with both these activities predominantly occurring between people in close proximity.[24]

Globalization's first unbundling took place in three phases. The first of these started in around 1820 with the 'steam revolution' and ended with the First World War, the second phase was the interwar period and the third phase lasted from the end of the Second World War until the late 1980s.[25] Briefly, the consequences of this unbundling as a whole were a substantial reduction in trade costs and a widening income gap between developed and developing countries.[26] Importantly, only the nature of one of the three cascading constraints changed significantly: trade costs dropped, but communication costs and face-to-face costs remained high.[27] Importantly, it was with this reality in mind that the foundation of the current international economic law regime was designed: the post-war economic order – which began to be formed in the 1940s and continues to underpin contemporary economic globalization – was accordingly developed to deal with the circumstances associated with globalization's first unbundling.

Globalization's second unbundling got underway in the late 1980s with the start of the so-called ICT revolution.[28] What made this globalization's second unbundling was the fact that the nature of the second cascading constraint began to change – communication costs fell and it progressively, but very rapidly, became virtually costless to move ideas around the globe.[29] Baldwin calls this state of affairs – where trade and communication costs are low, but the costs associated with moving people remain high – the 'New Globalization'.[30] We remain is this era today and central questions for the purposes of this chapter relate to how the

---

[24] Ibid., pp. 114–20.

[25] Ibid., pp. 47–9.

[26] See ibid., pp. 57–62; B. Milanović, *Global Inequality: A New Approach for the Age of Globalization* (Cambridge, MA: Harvard University Press, 2016), pp. 118–55.

[27] See Baldwin, *supra* n. 13, pp. 75–6.

[28] Ibid., pp. 81–5.

[29] See ibid., pp. 130–2. There had, of course, been prior technological advances that had reduced the costs of moving information across borders. See further, for example, C. Steinwender, 'Real Effects of Information Frictions: "When the States and the Kingdom Became United"', *American Economic Review*, 108(3) (2018), 657–96. Baldwin's argument does not ignore such advances; it simply stands for the proposition that earlier technological advances were substantially different from the changes observed since globalization's second unbundling.

[30] See generally Baldwin, *supra* n. 13.

New Globalization is different from what preceded it and what this means for sovereignty and the distribution of income and wealth within states.

Most important for current purposes is Baldwin's chapter entitled 'What's Really New?'.[31] In that chapter, Baldwin illustrates how globalization has changed since the second unbundling began in the late 1980s. At the beginning of the chapter he writes that '[t]he newness of the New Globalization' can be found in two integral parts of the second unbundling: (1) fragmentation and offshoring in the manufacturing and service sectors; and (2) the technology flows that 'follow the jobs sent offshore'.[32] Importantly, the New Globalization was mostly made possible by rapid technological change in ICT; but this had a clear knock-on effect on trade – the costs associated with which continued to fall – predominantly due to the new configurations it made available for the organization of production.[33]

A lot of attention has been paid to the topic of how the organization of production has changed.[34] Gerald F. Davis, for example, in his aptly entitled book *The Vanishing American Corporation*, writes of the 'Nikefication' of American industry.[35] Davis describes the process as follows:

> The new model for the corporation was to be like Nike. Nike designs and markets sneakers from its headquarters in Oregon, but hires contractors in East Asia to produce them. Its 'core' involves developing intellectual property, not manufacturing physical goods, and it has become one of the most valuable brands in history. Pressed by investors and enabled by the growth of generic suppliers, firms in industry after industry followed a path of Nikefication. Businesses like Sara Lee and Apple jettisoned production to focus on design and brand management. Computers, pet food, pharmaceuticals, shoes, and even government services are increasingly produced by contractors, not the company whose name is on the label.[36]

In essence, as Baldwin points out, whereas the frontline of competition used to be national borders they are today better thought of as

---

[31] See ibid., pp. 1–15.

[32] Baldwin, *supra* n. 13, p. 142.

[33] See ibid., pp. 149–54.

[34] See, for example, G. F. Davis, *The Vanishing American Corporation: Navigating the Hazards of a New Economy* (Oakland, CA: Berrett-Koehler, 2016).

[35] See ibid., pp. 69–80. Albeit to a lesser extent for the most part, the same applies in much of the rest of richer states.

[36] Ibid., p. 69.

'cross-national production networks' or, as they are more often referred to, as 'global value chains' (GVCs or GVC in the singular).[37] The implications of GVC proliferation have been far-reaching.[38] Comparative advantage – in the David Ricardo sense – essentially underpinned globalization for the entirety of its first unbundling.[39] This traditional conception of comparative advantage is based on the idea that goods are made in one state, relying on inputs that are from that same state.[40] Where the GVC-era is different, is in how it has led to a situation where goods are no longer made in one state; trade in part and components – in intermediate goods – has risen extensively since globalization's second unbundling.[41]

Additionally, capital has become increasingly mobile over time and there has been a drastic rise in the amount of foreign direct investment (FDI) between countries. This is indicative of production facilities, personnel and know-how moving across borders.[42] As production continued to become more dispersed, related services also gained in relative importance, as there was suddenly a need for a greater focus on the coordination of networks spanning far larger geographical areas than before.[43] The upshot of all these changes is that comparative advantage became progressively 'de-nationalized'.[44] What this means, in essence, is that the traditional comparative advantage – whereby production all occurs within one state – no longer holds in the same way it did before.[45] Commercial competition is no longer between national corporations; instead, multinational GVCs compete with other multinational GVCs,

---

[37] Baldwin, *supra* n. 13, p. 145.

[38] For a better sense of how GVCs have changed the global economy, see generally any (or all) of the following: G. Gereffi, *Global Value Chains and Development: Redefining the Contours of 21st Century Capitalism* (Cambridge: Cambridge University Press, 2018); D. Dollar, J. G. Reis and Z. Wang (eds.), *Global Value Chain Development Report 2017: Measuring and Analyzing the Impact of GVCs on Economic Development* (Washington, DC: World Bank, 2017); D. K. Elms and P. Low, *Global Value Chains in a Changing World* (Geneva: WTO Publications, 2013).

[39] See D. Ricardo, *On the Principles of Political Economy and Taxation* (London: John Murray, 1817), ch. VII.

[40] See Baldwin, *supra* n. 13, pp. 145–53.

[41] Ibid., p. 150.

[42] Ibid.

[43] Ibid.

[44] Ibid., p. 145.

[45] Ibid.

DISTRIBUTION OF INCOME AND WEALTH 209

with each GVC comprising workers and firms from a multitude of different states.[46]

As Baldwin puts it, 'international commerce became more *multifaceted* – involving flows of goods, services, intellectual property, capital and people – and . . . those flows became more *entangled* in the sense that they are generated by the same cause (production unbundling)'.[47] This makes the tasks of all actors involved in an economy more complicated because national progress is not prioritized by all actors from a particular state in a world of denationalized comparative advantage.[48] Labour unions, for example, have a more difficult time organizing because in the event that – as is the case in a large number of countries – unions are organized by sector, it could be that union members have conflicting interests vis-à-vis other members of their own union.[49] It also means that the interests of states and firms are increasingly less aligned with one another.[50] Often, firm and national interests even directly conflict with one another.[51]

Related to the organization of production are multiple other changes that have surfaced since globalization's second unbundling. Most of these find their origin in the ICT revolution in the sense that new technology ushered in, among many other things, an era of greater capital mobility. For example, the ICT revolution and other factors further enabled financial services to be provided more efficiently across borders and at greater scale. One result of this has been a proliferation of tax havens. Up until the 1980s, the lone offshore financial centre appears to have been Switzerland.[52] Since then, a majority of capital flows offshore have been to new centres, predominantly located in Europe, Asia and the Caribbean.[53] This raises an array of additional tax complications that cannot easily be resolved within a particular state's borders. As with the organization of production, this often brings the interests of firms (and,

---

[46] Ibid.
[47] Ibid., p. 150 (emphasis original).
[48] Ibid., p. 145.
[49] Ibid., p. 169.
[50] Ibid., p. 170.
[51] Ibid.
[52] For a succinct overview of the history of offshore finance, see G. Zucman, *The Hidden Wealth of Nations: The Scourge of Tax Havens* (Chicago: University of Chicago Press, 2015), ch. 1.
[53] Ibid., p. 24.

in this case, those of wealthy individuals as well) into stark contrast with those of its (or their) home state.

While there are a number of other changes perhaps worth discussing, the point is ultimately that the development of ICT has resulted in an economic system that is far more global in reach than the system that preceded it and that the nature of the relationship between states and firms has changed accordingly. The manner in which goods and increasingly services are produced, combined with the various other corollaries of the uptake of ICT has left the world with a novel set of governance challenges. One such challenge is the manner in which income and wealth are distributed within states in a world where firms, their income and their capital are increasingly decoupled from those same states.

The post–Second World War economic system was fashioned during the latter stages of globalization's first unbundling. It was premised on the traditional conception of comparative advantage, the understanding being that economic interdependence would promote mutual prosperity – and thereby peace – with international trade playing a central role. In essence, at the international level the goal was to make the global economic 'pie' as large as possible whilst trying to provide a level playing field for states and *their* firms. The distribution of income and wealth *between* states was accordingly increasingly subjected to international legal rules, first through the General Agreement on Tariffs and Trade (GATT) and later through the World Trade Organization (WTO) and its various covered agreements, among other instruments and institutions.

Distributive matters within states, however, were left entirely to the states themselves to deal with as a domestic issue.[54] This meant the development of various forms of the welfare state.[55] Governments around the world also took on more and more distributive functions, especially after human rights gained traction as a concept after the war.

---

[54] See generally E. B. Kapstein, 'Distributive Justice as an International Public Good', in I. Kaul, I. Grunberg and M. A. Stern (eds.), *Global Public Goods: International Cooperation in the 21st Century* (New York: Oxford University Press, 1999), pp. 88–115.

[55] See ibid., pp. 94–7. See also generally A. Briggs, 'The Welfare State in Historical Perspective', *European Journal of Sociology*, 2(2) (1961), 221–58; F. Nullmeier and F. X. Kaufmann, 'Post-War Welfare State Development', in F. G. Castles *et al.* (eds.), *The Oxford Handbook of the Welfare State* (Oxford, Oxford University Press, 2012), pp. 81–104; C. Pierson, *Beyond the Welfare State? The New Political Economy of Welfare* (University Park, PA: Penn State University Press, 1991), pp. 99–166.

Healthcare became something governments were involved in,[56] as did housing,[57] and the provision of trade adjustment assistance among various other functions with distributive impacts.[58] Moreover, until the 1980s the post-war globe was characterized by steady or declining levels of inequality of income and wealth within states, at least in (relatively) rich democracies, but also in countries such as India, China and Russia.

Since globalization's second unbundling, however, the distribution of income and wealth has changed dramatically within states, with a large majority of the world's citizens now living in countries where distributions have become increasingly more unequal since the 1980s. In the ICT world of denationalized comparative advantage and increasing capital mobility, the post–Second World War economic framework is unable to deliver what it was intended to deliver. This is predominantly because it was not designed with globalization's second unbundling in mind. It was not developed to deal with competition between GVCs, but rather with competition between nations. From a distributive point of view (and perhaps other viewpoints as well), what remains are global governance mechanisms that are no longer fit for purpose.

Moreover, as Baldwin notes, globalization also became 'wilder' during its second unbundling: the shocks associated with globalization grew substantially in size and they occurred a lot faster than ever before.[59] This meant – and still means – that the distributive and redistributive issues that states were required to deal with increased in importance, became more demanding and also became more complicated to resolve. At the same time, functions that were previously carried out by states could now only be carried out by states in cooperation with other states. The idea that distributive issues within states can be competently

---

[56] See, for example, P. Greengross, K. Grant and E. Collini, *Helpdesk Report: The History and Development of the UK National Health Service 1948–1999* (London: DFID Health Systems Resource Centre, 1999) for a history of the development of the National Health Service in the UK.

[57] For an overview of public housing provisioning covering a large number of states in historical and contemporary perspective, see J. Chen, M. Stephens and Y. Man (eds.), *The Future of Public Housing: Ongoing Trends in the East and the West* (Heidelberg: Springer, 2013).

[58] On trade adjustment assistance, see for example J. F. Hornbeck, *Trade Adjustment Assistance (TAA) and Its Role in U.S. Trade Policy* (Washington, DC: Congressional Research Service, 2013) for an overview of the historical development of trade adjustment assistance in the United States.

[59] See Baldwin, *supra* n. 13, pp. 165–75.

handled – as a matter of *fact* – as a purely national concern is accordingly losing traction rather quickly.[60]

4.2.2 Conceptualizing Distributive Autonomy as a Corollary of Sovereignty

The term 'sovereignty' has a certain notoriety to it; often invoked as between nations but rarely with a common understanding as to the meaning of the word or its implications, 'sovereignty' has been a contested concept for most – if not all – of its existence. For current purposes, it would be of little worth to engage in the larger sovereignty debate. Rather, it suffices to say that the view taken here is that state sovereignty is an 'essentially contestable concept' as this term was understood by Walter Bryce Gallie.[61] That is to say that sovereignty as a concept is normative in nature, intrinsically complex and a-criterial.[62] Among other things, this implies – as Samantha Besson has put it – that 'sovereignty is as once a state of affairs, a question pertaining to the nature and justification of that state of affairs and a justification of it'.[63] With this in mind, the aim here is to conceptualize a corollary notion, referred to in this chapter as the 'distributive autonomy' of a state.

4.2.2.1 An Outline of 'Distributive Autonomy': A Public Goods Perspective

In a 1985 article, Vaughan Lowe presented an outline of what he termed 'economic sovereignty'.[64] He further described methods that might be

---

[60] See Y. N. Harari, *Sapiens: A Brief History of Humankind* (London: Vintage, 2014), pp. 231–2, for example, for a similar argument.

[61] See generally W. B. Gallie 'Essentially Contested Concepts', *Proceedings of the Aristotelian Society*, 56(1) (1956), 167–98.

[62] See S. Besson, 'Sovereignty in Conflict', *European Integration Online Papers (EIoP)*, 8(15) (2004), 1–23, at 7; D. Sarooshi, 'The Essentially Contested Nature of the Concept of Sovereignty: Implications for the Exercise by International Organizations of Delegated Powers of Government', *Michigan Journal of International Law,* 25(4) (2004), 1107–39, at 1108–9; D. Sarooshi, *International Organizations and Their Exercise of Sovereign Powers* (New York: Oxford University Press, 2005), pp. 3–5; Zimmermann, *supra* n. 11, pp. 19–20.

[63] Besson, *supra* n. 62, 22; see Zimmermann, *supra* n. 11, pp. 19–24, for a detailed analysis of contemporary monetary sovereignty as an 'essentially contested concept'.

[64] See A. V. Lowe, 'The Problems of Extraterritorial Jurisdiction: Economic Sovereignty and the Search for a Solution', *International and Comparative Law Quarterly*, 34(4) (1985), 724–46.

DISTRIBUTION OF INCOME AND WEALTH

adopted in order to define the concept in greater detail.[65] For each of these methods Lowe asserted that 'the essential argument is that, if it can be shown that there are certain rights or powers which are considered to be essential components of a State's sovereignty, then other States ought not to exercise their own powers so as to undermine those rights or powers'.[66] Lowe was quick to add that:

> [i]t must be admitted at once that in the case of most, if not all, of the components of economic sovereignty this requirement of restraint imposed on third States is not the direct and logically necessary consequence of the very existence of the first State's economic rights. Rather, it will be necessary to base the duty of restraint on the more general principles of self-determination and of non-intervention in the domestic affairs of another State – themselves corollaries of the sovereign equality and independence of States which is a fundamental datum of contemporary international law.[67]

The first method Lowe refers to in order to give some content to the term 'economic sovereignty' is the 'recognition approach'.[68] This approach is based on the presumption that 'certain economic powers' are considered to be 'conditions upon which the recognition of States or governments can depend'; Lowe consequently asserts that 'it would be reasonable to regard these powers as components of a State's economic sovereignty'.[69] The second method is the 'responsibility approach'.[70] Under this approach, it is assumed that states 'have the right, free from the deliberate interference of third States, to control persons and companies within their territory in relation to matters which they are generally regarded as being entitled to bind themselves by treaty to regulate in a certain way and in respect of which they may therefore become internationally responsible'.[71]

Having set out both theories and provided examples as evidence of the exercise of economic sovereignty, Lowe reaches the following conclusion:

> [A]t the heart of the concept of economic sovereignty is *the right of a State to regulate the structure of its own economy.* There may be *ancillary rights,* such as the right to regulate the activities of all businesses within its

---

[65] Ibid.
[66] Ibid., 740.
[67] Ibid.
[68] Ibid., 741.
[69] Ibid.
[70] Ibid., 742.
[71] Ibid.

territory and the terms of trade within its territory: inevitably, its precise scope will be a matter for debate.[72]

As part of the right to regulate the structure of its own economy, one of the ancillary rights a state has is clearly the right to provide certain public goods.[73] This holds in terms of Lowe's recognition approach in the sense that the capacity to provide public goods and their actual provision is one of the *raisons d'être* of states, which exist precisely because public goods are undersupplied or not supplied at all in their absence. The right to supply public goods also holds under Lowe's responsibility approach because states are entitled to bind themselves by treaty as part of public goods provision, for example by agreeing to cooperate with other states, including in the provision of funding for example, such that public goods may be produced in each of the states that are party to the agreement.

Max Huber's often cited statement from his award in the *Island of Palmas* case perhaps makes this point more lucidly. The professor and judge wrote there that '[s]overeignty in the relations between States signifies independence. Independence in regard to a portion of the globe is the right to exercise therein, to the exclusion of any other State, the functions of a State'.[74] With respect to public goods, the assertion here is that their supply is a, if not *the*, quintessential practical function of a state. This implies that sovereignty has long included the right of a state to regulate its own economy in order to influence how income and wealth are distributed within its borders. This flows logically from Lester Thurow's persuasive argument that the distribution of income within a society – a state for current purposes – is a pure public good.[75] A brief rehearsal of his argument is warranted here. Thurow introduces his article with the following:

> Although the social welfare function – in other words, some value judgment – must ultimately be invoked to determine society's optimum distribution of income, there is a subsidiary problem. Is every initial distribution of income a Pareto optimum, or is some redistribution necessary to achieve a Pareto optimum?[76]

---

[72] Ibid., 744 (emphasis added).

[73] The concept 'public good' is used here as Paul Samuelson used it in his famous 1954 article (P. A. Samuelson, 'A Pure Theory of Public Expenditure', *Review of Economics and Statistics*, 36(4) (1954), 387–9).

[74] *Island of Palmas Case (Netherland v. USA)* [1928] 2 UNRIAA 829.

[75] L. C. Thurow, 'The Income Distribution as a Pure Public Good', *Quarterly Journal of Economics*, 85(2) (1971), 327–36.

[76] Ibid., 327.

He subsequently suggests that there are a variety of reasons to come to the conclusion that arbitrary initial distributions are not Pareto optimal and proceeds to an explanation. Among other reasons, Thurow posits that '[t]he distribution of income itself may be an argument in an individual's utility function [and that t]his may come about because there are externalities associated with the distribution of income'.[77] On the assumption that both parts of this statement are true, Thurow categorizes the distribution of income as a pure public good.[78] This is because everyone in a given society faces the same aggregate income distribution – exclusion is impossible – consumption is non-rivalrous in that no person can be excluded of any benefits that result from a particular income distribution and each person must consume the same quantity.[79] In light of the conclusion of his argument, Thurow in part concludes as follows:

> To the extent that individuals are interested in the income distribution because of externalities rather than simple tastes for equality or inequality, the public good approach focuses attention on the need for research in an area that is between economics and sociology. What are the empirical effects of the income distribution on crime, social stability, political stability, or any other characteristic of society? Perhaps the impact is significant; perhaps it is insignificant. We just do not know.[80]

With five decades having since passed, we now have a better sense of the empirical effects Thurow referred to in the above excerpt.[81] Similarly, we also have a better sense of the consequences that flow from the distribution of wealth, which can be treated as a public good in the same way as the distribution of income.[82] To be sure, there is much left to learn about the consequences of income and wealth distributions. It is also fairly clear, however, that there is sufficient evidence for us to conclude that the distribution of income and the distribution of wealth both constitute pure public goods.[83] It also follows, therefore, that, as a

---

[77] Ibid.

[78] Ibid., 328.

[79] Ibid., 328–9.

[80] Ibid., 335–6.

[81] See *supra*, n. 16.

[82] Ibid.

[83] The distribution of income and wealth has also been shown to affect the provision of other public goods. See, for example, J. M. Rao, 'Equity in a Global Public Goods Framework', in Kaul *et al.*, *supra* n. 54, 68–87, at 79–85. For experimental evidence in this regard, see, for example, L. R. Anderson, J. M. Mellor and J. Milyo, 'Inequality and

216 ALEXANDER BEYLEVELD

corollary of being sovereigns, states have the right to exercise their respective powers to effectuate changes to the distribution of income and wealth within their respective territories and to do so independent of external interference. In so doing, states exercise 'distributive autonomy'.

4.2.2.2 Towards a Contemporary Concept of Distributive Autonomy

A discussion on what contemporary distributive autonomy should look like conceptually entails addressing some of the positive or functional aspects of sovereignty, that is, those that relate to the competences exercised by states and how effectively they are able to exercise them. The view of sovereignty adopted here, however, is that the concept also has a normative component that warrants some discussion: that of distributive justice. It also serves the discussion well to distinguish at this point between internal and external sovereignty. The former refers to sovereignty over the internal affairs of a state, while the latter refers to sovereignty as it operates vis-à-vis other sovereigns.[84] These notions align well conceptually with Lowe's 'recognition' and 'responsibility' approaches as described earlier; with the 'recognition' approach seeking to define what is essentially the internal economic sovereignty of a state and the 'responsibility' approach more or less capturing the essence of external economic sovereignty.[85] It is, of course, fairly clear to most scholars that the two concepts cannot be kept distinct from one another in practice: internal and external sovereignty are basically different sides of the same coin.[86]

Public Good Provision: An Experimental Analysis', *Journal of Socio-Economics*, 37(3) (2008), 1010–28; A. Colasante and A. Russo, 'Voting for the Distribution Rule in a Public Good Game with Heterogeneous Endowments' *Journal of Economic Interaction and Coordination*, 12(3) (2017), 443–67; S. M. Rosenbaum *et al.*, 'Income Inequality and Cooperative Propensities in Developing Economies: Summarizing the Preliminary Experimental Evidence', *International Journal of Social Economics*, 43(12) (2016), 1460–80. It accordingly follows that states have the right to act in order to ensure the alteration of the distribution of income and wealth within their own territory not only because certain distributions constitute public goods as such, but also because it may be necessary to do so to ensure better provision of other public goods.

[84] See Besson, *supra* n. 62, 9; V. Lowe, 'Sovereignty and International Economic Law', in W. Shan, P. Simons and D. Singh (eds.), *Redefining Sovereignty in International Economic Law* (Portland: Hart, 2008), pp. 79–80.

[85] See Section 4.2.2.1 in this chapter, pp. 212–6.

[86] See, for example, Besson, *supra* n. 62, 9–10; Zimmermann, *supra* n. 11, p. 25, for a brief illustration of the manner in which internal and external sovereignty overlap and come

DISTRIBUTION OF INCOME AND WEALTH

At present there is no agreed upon set of competences entailed by the concept of sovereignty, even less so with respect to its distributive aspects. Some competences – capacities or powers – are beyond contestation: it can hardly be doubted, for example, that as part of its sovereignty a state has the right to make and enforce rules relating to taxation within its own sovereign space. The very existence of a state clearly depends on its ability to raise taxes.[87] To return to Huber's construction of sovereignty in the *Island of Palmas* case, taxation is clearly a function of a state which it must be allowed to pursue independently, not only as an end in of itself but also such that it can fulfil its other sovereign functions independently. The sovereign right of taxation clearly entails distributive aspects too: deciding who should be taxed, what should be taxed and deciding how the revenues derived through taxation should be spent carry clear implications for the distribution of income and wealth within a state.

Beyond taxation, there are other economic functions of a state that have distributive effects. The manner in which a state exercises its sovereignty over its currency, for example, affects the supply of money in an economy and, ultimately, inflation.[88] Inflation has historically had substantial impacts on the distribution of aggregate income and wealth.[89] Similarly, labour market regulation also has distributional impacts, most directly on the distribution of income. An obvious example is when a state makes a law imposing a minimum wage.[90] The implementation of

---

into conflict in the context of the monetary stability competence encompassed by a state's monetary sovereignty.

[87] See, for example, A. Christians, 'Sovereignty, Taxation and Social Contract', *Minnesota Journal of International Law*, 18(1) (2009), 99–153, at 104–14.

[88] On monetary sovereignty as a concept, see Zimmermann, *supra* n. 11, pp. 7–36.

[89] See, for example, T. Piketty, *Capital in the Twenty-First Century* (Cambridge, MA: Harvard University Press, 2014), pp. 133–4; A. Erosa and G. Ventura, 'On Inflation as a Regressive Consumption Tax', *Journal of Monetary Economics*, 49(4) (2002), 761–95, wherein the authors posit that inflation is effectively a regressive consumption tax and that the distributional consequences of inflation should accordingly be taken into account in setting monetary policy. A wide range of additional channels has also been identified whereby monetary policy – that is the exercise of monetary sovereignty – has distributive effects. See, for example, A. Auclert, *Monetary Policy and the Redistribution Channel* (Cambridge, MA: NBER, 2017).

[90] While it seems fairly obvious that the imposition of a minimum wage law will have distributional consequences, the precise effects, however, remain less clear. For two examples of attempts at clarifying these effects, see A. Dube, 'Minimum Wages and the Distribution of Family Incomes' (IZA Institute of Labor Economics Discussion Paper 10572, Feb. 2017), http://ftp.iza.org/dp10572.pdf (accessed 13 May 2018); K. Rinz and

competition or antitrust laws also have distributive effects; these laws are after all, at least in part, concerned with avoiding abuses of market power and the existence of – and increase in – market power has been shown to have significant distributive effects in respect of both income and wealth.[91] Various other activities – state functions – that may properly be linked with economic sovereignty have been shown to have distributive impacts. Examples include allowing FDI to flow in or out of a state,[92] and formulating corporate laws in a particular way.[93]

Ultimately there are also many possible normative components of sovereignty from an economic standpoint. Traditionally, most states have sought to prioritize economic growth – that is to say aggregate economic growth without due consideration for distributions – as the predominant normative goal in their exercise of economic sovereignty.[94] Growth, in

J. Voorheis, 'The Distributional Effects of Minimum Wages: Evidence from Linked Survey and Administrative Data' (Center for Administrative Records Research and Applications (CARRA) Working Paper 2018), www.census.gov/content/dam/Census/library/working-papers/2018/adrm/carra-wp-2018-02.pdf (accessed 13 May 2018).

[91] See A. B. Atkinson, *Inequality: What Can Be Done?* (London: Harvard University Press, 2015), pp. 123–7; S. Ennis, P. Gonzaga and C. Pike, 'Inequality: A Hidden Cost of Market Power' (OECD Discussion Paper, 2017), www.oecd.org/daf/competition/Inequality-hidden-cost-market-power-2017.pdf (accessed 13 May 2018); J. Furman and P. Orszag, 'A Firm-Level Perspective on the Role of Rents in the Rise in Inequality' (presentation at conference 'A Just Society' Centennial Event in Honor of Joseph Stiglitz, 16 Oct. 2016), https://obamawhitehouse.archives.gov/sites/default/files/page/files/20151016_firm_level_perspective_on_role_of_rents_in_inequality.pdf (accessed 13 May 2018); J. Stiglitz, *The Price of Inequality: How Today's Divided Society Endangers Our Future* (New York: Norton, 2012), pp. 28–51.

[92] See, for example, C. Choi, 'Does Foreign Direct Investment Affect Domestic Income Inequality?', *Applied Economics Letters*, 13(12) (2006), 811–14; T. Kaulihowa and C. Adjasi, 'FDI and Income Inequality in Africa', *Oxford Development Studies (online)* (2017), https://doi.org/10.1080/13600818.2017.1381233, (accessed 13 May 2018); J. S. Mah, 'Foreign Direct Investment, Labour Unionization and Income Inequality of Korea', *Applied Economics Letters*, 19(15) (2012), 1521–4; X. Wu, 'Foreign Direct Investment and Income Inequality', in H. G. Fung, P. Changhong and K. H. Zhang, *China and the Challenge of Economic Globalization: The Impact of WTO Membership* (Routledge: New York, 2006), pp. 61–82.

[93] See, for example, M. T. Bodie, 'Income Inequality and Corporate Structure', *Stetson Law Review*, 45(1) (2015), 69–90; J. A. Cobb and F. G. Stevens, 'These Unequal States: Corporate Organization and Income Inequality in the United States', *Administrative Science Quarterly*, 62(2) (2017), 304–40; G. F. Davis and J. A. Cobb, 'Corporations and Economic Inequality around the World: The Paradox of Hierarchy', *Research in Organizational Behaviour*, 30 (2010) 35–53.

[94] On the normative underpinnings of economic growth, see L. Herzog, 'The Normative Stakes of Economic Growth; Or, Why Adam Smith Does Not Rely on "Trickle Down"', *Journal of Politics*, 78(1) (2016), 50–62.

turn, hinges in part on the manner in which states exercise the various competences their respective economic sovereignty is comprised of. The rate of growth also has an impact – it feeds back in a way – on how states exercise their sovereignty. Growth acts as 'regulatory guideline' and 'legitimacy benchmark' for most, if not all, states;[95] but it is not the only normative component of economic sovereignty.

Since the start of the ICT revolution, calls for distributive justice around the globe have intensified. To be sure, 'distributive justice' here is intended to be a normative term, but its contents are intended to be variable.[96] At the same time, even if the content of different conceptions of distributive justice are more or less the same, proposed approaches for its attainment yield as much disagreement as its contents do; it may even be the case that the approach forms a part of the content itself. To further complicate matters, distributive justice and economic growth may have perceived conflicting prescriptions for how economic sovereignty should be exercised, but the international community has recently turned to 'sustainable development' and the Sustainable Development Goals (SDGs) as part of an attempt at reconciling the two supposedly conflicting goals or possible even showing that, despite established perceptions, there is in fact no need for reconciliation because there is no conflict.[97]

Accordingly, SDG 10 indicates that the international community seeks to 'progressively achieve and sustain income growth of the bottom 40 per cent of the population at a rate higher than the national average' by 2030.[98] What this indicates is that distributive aims have not supplanted growth as a normative goal but should be considered as developing the notion of growth in a different direction, with distributive justice beginning to act as a 'regulatory guideline' and 'legitimacy benchmark' alongside economic growth insofar as the exercise of economic sovereignty is concerned. SDG 10 is perhaps the most general among many reflections of this steadily changing reality, a reality which need not pose any great difficulty because a growing body of literature now suggests that, broadly

---

[95] These phrases here are used as they are by Zimmermann (*supra* n. 11, pp. 24–7).

[96] As an illustration of the variability of distributive justice as a normative concept, see generally F. Feldman, *Distributive Justice: Getting What We Deserve from Our Country* (Oxford: Oxford University Press, 2016); J. E. Roemer, *Theories of Distributive Justice* (Cambridge, MA: Harvard University Press, 1996).

[97] UN General Assembly, 'Transforming Our World: The 2030 Agenda for Sustainable Development', UNGA Resolution A/RES/70/1 (21 Oct. 2015).

[98] Ibid., 21.

220   ALEXANDER BEYLEVELD

speaking, there is in fact no trade-off between economic growth and more equal distributions of income and wealth.[99]

Within this context, the argument here is that sovereignty, at least insofar as it pertains to distributive autonomy, should be seen as cooperative sovereignty. 'Cooperative sovereignty' for the purposes of this work follows the conception adopted by Samantha Besson, among others.[100] As Besson puts it:

> [G]radually the exercize [*sic*] of sovereignty has turned from an individual exercize [*sic*] into a *cooperative* enterprise. This corresponds to the more general development of multilevel governance in a post-national constellation; sovereign political entities can no longer exercize [*sic*] their traditional competences and functions alone, especially, but not only, when these overlap within the same territory and apply to the same legal political community ... In these conditions, sovereign authorities need to collaborate with other sovereign political and legal entities when applying the same rules and principles in this pluralist constitutional order and this gives rise to a ... *cooperative form of sovereignty*. This form of sovereignty triggers duties of cooperation on the part of entities which cannot ensure the protection of all the values they should protect, as much as on the part of the entities which can help the former protect those values they share ... Only when understood in this *cooperative* way, can sovereignty be the *reflexive* and *dynamic* concept it is, stimulating constant challenging of the allocation of power, thus putting into question others' sovereignty as well as one's own. This common exercize [*sic*] of political sovereignty is then reflected in the structure of the relationship between the different legal orders at stake; none of them is ultimately and entirely submitted to another. This kind of legal cooperation reveals the possibility of a non-hierarchically organized plurality of legal orders, which may individually remain hierarchical in their internal structure or in their relationship to international law, but which relate to one another in a heterarchical way.[101]

Economic sovereignty as conceptualized here includes fiscal sovereignty, monetary sovereignty and the other parts of state sovereignty relevant to

---

[99] See, for example, A. G. Berg and J. D. Ostry, 'Inequality and Unsustainable Growth: Two Sides of the Same Coin?', *IMF Economic Review*, 65(4) (2017), 792–815; F. Grigoli and A. Robles, 'Inequality Overhang', IMF Working Paper (28 Mar. 2017), www.imf.org/en/Publications/WP/Issues/2017/03/28/Inequality-Overhang-44774 (accessed 17 Aug. 2018).

[100] See Besson, *supra* n. 62, 13; F. X. Perrez, *Cooperative Sovereignty: From Independence to Interdependence in the Structure of International Environmental Law* (Kluwer: The Hague, 2000); Zimmermann, *supra* n. 11, pp. 31–5.

[101] Besson, *supra* n. 62, 13 (emphasis original, original fn. omitted).

the distribution of income and wealth, particularly – but not limited to – those relating to the regulation of a 'national' economy. Seen this way, sovereignty – and the related idea of distributive autonomy – is only effective as a concept in the event that there operates alongside it a functioning principle of subsidiarity; that is to say a principle of power allocation. In this regard, Besson writes that 'the principle of subsidiarity implies a *test of efficiency* in power allocation. In each case, the sovereign authority will be that authority which can realize the objective in the most efficient way'.[102]

The view taken here is that the competence of states to effect changes to the distribution of income and wealth within their own territories is tied to their exercising their economic sovereignty in accordance with the normative concept of distributive justice. It is this tie that leads to a call for understanding economic sovereignty as a cooperative enterprise: to the extent that cooperation is necessary to affect the actual distribution of income and wealth in order to attain distributive justice within a state, economic sovereignty can only be made meaningful through cooperation. Moreover, ensuring a certain distribution of income or wealth can, as described above, be viewed as a public good.[103] It does not necessarily follow, however, that in doing so a state also ensures the attainment of distributive justice. The distributive justice and public goods components should accordingly be thought of as existing alongside one another, with each aspect requiring different albeit overlapping types of cooperation which, of course, should occur with the other aims of economic sovereignty, such as economic growth, as well as monetary and financial stability, in mind.

It is only through these types of cooperation that states can retain the maximum – or even an appropriate – level of distributive autonomy. While states still retain a sense of distributive autonomy in the absence of cooperation, such autonomy is becoming increasingly constrained to the point that, at least in some areas, it no longer really exists in a meaningful sense. It is precisely within this diverse set of areas that the recognition of a distributional common concern of humankind may be warranted.[104]

---

[102] Ibid., 12 (emphasis original).

[103] See Section 4.2.2.1 in this chapter, pp. 214–6.

[104] As discussed further in my PhD, these areas include the regulation of corporate taxation, cross-border investment flows and competition between firms or value chains among possible others.

To be sure, such recognition would be a new development in international law, but one of its core purposes would also be to seek to partially preserve sovereignty as envisioned – at least in terms of purpose – hundreds of years ago by the likes of Jean Bodin and Thomas Hobbes. As Thomas Cottier points out in this volume, in reference to the work of Bodin and Hobbes, in the beginning 'sovereignty ... was about enabling and preserving peace and security within states' and 'not motivated by independence and self-determination, but to enhance welfare in society'.[105] The recognition of a distributional common concern of humankind, then, would seek to rebalance sovereignty as a concept; a concept that espouses not only independence and self-determination, but also the idea that human beings should flourish as much as possible within the societies in which they live.

4.3 The Recognition of New Common Concerns of Humankind

As identified by others in this volume, common concerns of humankind are already recognized (or close to being recognized) in several fields of law. This section examines these existing common concerns of humankind insofar as it is necessary to explore the key question of how new common concerns of humankind are *recognized* in international law.[106] The discussion accordingly begins by highlighting certain common elements of currently recognized common concerns of humankind (Section 4.3.1) such that a general theory or process for the recognition of new common concerns of humankind in international law may be proposed (Section 4.3.2). The constructed theory is then applied to the distribution of income and wealth within states in the next section.

---

[105] See Chapter 1 in this volume, pp. 54–9.

[106] On the legal implications of recognition, see ibid. (pp. 59–68). Naturally, the recognition of common concerns of humankind in practice will be closely related to the understood legal implications that such recognition will bring about. Recognition, however, is a conceptually distinct notion and should – in my view at least – be discussed separately, because recognition should take place with attention being paid predominantly to the particular global problem at hand *itself*. Simply put, a common concern of humankind should not be recognized as such or not on the basis of certain legal consequences attaching themselves to recognition but rather because the issue in question truly is – in quite a literal sense – a common concern of humankind.

DISTRIBUTION OF INCOME AND WEALTH 223

4.3.1 How New Common Concerns of Humankind Have Been Recognized

Only two common concerns of humankind have thus far been explicitly recognized as such in treaty law, one in the field of climate change and one in the field of biodiversity. It thus becomes a worthwhile exercise looking as precisely as possible at their subject matter. In the area of climate change, it is the 'change in the Earth's climate and its adverse effects' that are recognized as a common concern of humankind by the United Nations Framework Convention on Climate Change (UNFCCC).[107] As for in the realm of biodiversity, it is the 'conservation of biological diversity' that has been affirmed as a common concern of humankind in the text of the Convention on Biological Diversity.[108] Understanding fully what is being protected in these conventions is helpful for understanding what can in fact be recognized as a common concern of humankind and how recognition might come about.[109]

As Jutta Brunnée points out with respect to the UNFCCC, it is not the earth's climate per se that is afforded common concern of humankind status, but rather the *change* in the earth's climate and its *adverse effects*.[110] The second paragraph of the preamble to the UNFCCC also goes on to state that the parties to the Convention are – or at the very least were at the time of the UNFCCC's enactment – '[c]oncerned that human activities have been substantially increasing the atmospheric concentrations of greenhouse gases, that these increases enhance the natural greenhouse effect, and that this will result on average in an additional warming of the Earth's surface and atmosphere and may adversely affect natural ecosystems and humankind'. This pronouncement gives additional meaning to 'change' and 'adverse effects' contained in the first paragraph of the preamble. It is human activity that has been

---

[107] Preamble, United Nations Framework Convention on Climate Change (UNFCCC), New York, 9 May 1992, entered into force 21 Mar. 1994, 1771 UNTS 107, at 165.

[108] Preamble, Convention on Biological Diversity (CBD), Rio de Janeiro, 5 June 1992, entered into force 29 Dec. 1993, 1760 UNTS 79, at 143.

[109] See Cottier, Chapter 1 in this volume (pp. 11–6), where he discusses existing common concerns of humankind in greater depth. The aim here is not to repeat or supplant that discussion but merely to draw attention to certain points pertaining to the recognition of common concerns of humankind that have not thus far been discussed with a view to describing the process of recognizing new common concerns of humankind.

[110] J. Brunnée, 'Common Areas, Common Heritage, and Common Concern', in D. Bodansky, J. Brunnée and E. Hey (eds.), *The Oxford Handbook of International Environmental Law* (New York: Oxford University Press, 2007), pp. 550–73, at p. 565.

increasing the atmospheric concentrations of greenhouse gases and driving the *particular change* in the earth's climate with which humankind has become concerned. The *additional* warming of the earth's surface and atmosphere that will result from this *change* may result in *adverse effects* to natural ecosystems and to humankind.

As Brunnée has further observed with respect to the CBD, it is the *conservation* of biological diversity that is afforded common concern status in the third paragraph of the preamble to the CBD and not biological diversity itself.[111] This distinction is clear from context given that the first paragraph of the preamble indicates that the parties to the Convention are – or at least were – '[c]onscious of the intrinsic value of biological diversity and of the ecological, genetic, social, economic, scientific, educational, cultural, recreational and aesthetic values of biological diversity and its components'. The second paragraph reinforces the distinction, illustrating that the parties were '[c]onscious also of the importance of biological diversity for evolution and for maintaining life sustaining systems of the biosphere'. Finally, the sixth paragraph spells out that the parties were '[c]oncerned that biological diversity is being significantly reduced by certain human activities'.

As with climate change, then, it appears clear that common concern of humankind status is afforded in respect of a particular *change* and the *adverse effects* flowing from it. In the biodiversity context, it is significant reduction in biological diversity caused by certain human activities that amounts to a change; the adverse effects of this change are the losses of the intrinsic value of biological diversity as described in the first two paragraphs to the preamble of the CBD. Together, the change and the adverse effects make up the common concern of humankind that is the 'conservation of biological diversity'.

From this, some constitutive elements of common concerns of humankind can start to be gleaned, but a fuller discussion is warranted. In order to guide and structure this next part of the discussion, the following conceptual characterization of Antônio Augusto Cançado Trindade is a helpful starting point. In his tome, *International Law for Humankind: Towards a New* Jus Gentium, Cançado Trindade writes as follows:

> Six constitutive elements of the concept of common concern of mankind have been identified, namely: first, the concentration of the concept – devoid of proprietary connotations – in truly fundamental questions for

---

[111] Ibid., p. 565.

all humankind, pursuant to the notion of commonness; second, the necessary engagement, in the treatment of such questions of common interest, of all countries, all societies and all the social segments within the countries and the societies; third, – as already pointed out ... the long-term temporal dimension (underlying the term humanity), to encompass both the present and the future generations; fourth, the emphasis on the element of protection, on the basis of considerations of humanity and of *ordre public*, transcending reciprocity; fifth, the attention primarily to the causes of the problems (both for their prevention and for the responses to be given); and sixth, the equitable sharing of responsibilities as an instrumental principle in the application of the concept of common concern of mankind.[112]

Writing in the *Oxford Handbook of International Climate Change Law*, Friedrich Soltau distils common concerns of humankind into the following 'fundamental characteristics':

(a) the interests concerned extend beyond those of individual states and touch on values or ethics of global significance;
(b) threats to the interests concerned are marked by their gravity and potential irreversibility of impacts; and
(c) safeguarding the interests involved requires collective action and entails collective responsibility.[113]

Moreover, in note to the Group of Legal Experts that met prior to the 1992 conclusion of the UNFCCC and the CBD, the UNEP Secretariat provided the following information:

'Common concern' concept has at least two important facets: spatial and temporal. Spatial aspect means the common concern implies co-operation of all states on matters being similarly important to all nations, to the whole international community. Temporal aspect arises from long term implications of major environmental challenges which affect the rights and obligations not only of present but also future generations ... One more aspect of the 'common concern' is a social dimension. Common concern presumes involvement of all structures and sectors of the society into the process of combatting global environmental threats. i.e.

---

[112] A. A. Cançado Trindade, *International Law for Humankind: Towards a New* Jus Gentium (Leiden: Martinus Nijhoff, 2010), p. 351.

[113] F. Soltau, 'Common Concern of Humankind', in C. P. Carlane, K. R. Gray and R. G. Tarasofsky (eds.), *The Oxford Handbook of International Climate Change Law* (New York: Oxford University Press, 2016), pp. 202–13, at pp. 207–8.

legislative, judicial and governmental bodies together with private business, non-governmental organizations, citizen groups.[114]

While there is much to quibble about when it comes to the constitutive or definitional elements – the common concern of humankind concept is after all still subject to much debate and no definitive understanding of the terms has yet to be settled on, whether in treaty practice, treaty application or by scholars of the concept – these passages can be distilled into a general theory for the recognition of common concerns of humankind in international law.

4.3.2 Towards a General Theory for the Recognition of Common Concerns of Humankind in International Law

The rationale that underlies the need for a general theory for the recognition of common concerns of humankind has been captured well by Duncan French in the CBD context:

> [W]hat we are looking for here is whether one can identify reasons that support its [that is, biodiversity's] inclusion in the panoply of issues that justify the nomenclature of common concern. If one cannot do this, and it is therefore not possible to provide normative coherence as to why certain issues are of common concern and others are not, there is a real risk that the discussion descends into little more than retrospective realpolitik.[115]

The most obvious commonality between common concerns of humankind, both existing and potential, is the implications that their recognition entails for sovereignty.[116] The position taken here is accordingly that a central element – or perhaps even *the* central element – for the recognition of common concerns of humankind is the need for a conceptual development of sovereignty. Identifying areas where current conceptions of sovereignty have become outdated or where a reconstitution of the term is required in order to enhance sovereignty such that global problems of particular significance can be solved is therefore

---

[114] M. K. Tolba, 'The Implications of the "Common Concern of Mankind Concept" on Global Environmental Issues', *Revista IIDH*, 13 (1991), 237–46, at 239.

[115] D. French, 'Common Concern, Common Heritage and Other Global(-ising) Concepts: Rhetorical Devices, Legal Principles or a Fundamental Challenge', in M. Bowman, P. Davies and E. Goodwin (eds.), *Research Handbook on Biodiversity and Law* (Cheltenham, UK: Edward Elgar, 2016), pp. 334–59, at p. 344.

[116] See Section 4.1 in this chapter, pp. 201–2.

DISTRIBUTION OF INCOME AND WEALTH 227

a good starting point for identifying potential common concerns of humankind.

To understand the recognition of common concerns of humankind in this way is one manner in which to give the concept a normative coherence that it would otherwise lack. As discussed earlier in this volume, however, the need for reconstituting sovereignty is not the only potential constitutive element related to common concern of humankind recognition.[117] The need for redefinition must also stem from a problem that affects, or has the capacity to affect, all – or at least a very large part – of humankind; the relevant problem should generally concern a rate, a change in which results in effects that are deemed 'adverse' by the entire international community (or at least the largest possible part of it). With this context sketched, the aim here is to posit a general theory of a process for the recognition of common concerns of humankind in international law.

There is currently no general process by which common concerns of humankind are recognized. The process described here is a proposal, the purpose of which is to provide a pathway for the common concern of humankind concept to find wider application in international law. It is by no means meant to stand in opposition to existing lists of constitutive elements of common concerns of humankind, but rather to complement and refine existing accounts in as simple a manner possible. As a general proposition, then, common concern of humankind recognition should entail three steps: (1) an identification process that will be referred to here as 'framing'; (2) once 'framed', the potential common concern of humankind should be tested against the threshold question of whether current constructions of state sovereignty in the area(s) related to the potential common concern of humankind need to be reconstituted in order for the 'framed' common concern of humankind to be successfully addressed and (3) if the threshold question is answered in the affirmative, the common concern of humankind must be recognized through a process of law. Each of these three steps will be examined in greater detail in turn below.

4.3.2.1 Framing a Common Concern of Humankind

'Framing' as used in this context denotes the following two-step process: (1) identifying a rate 'problem' that affects humankind, or a large part

---

[117] See Chapter 1 in this volume, pp. 26–43.

thereof; and (2) identifying the effects and potential effects that stem from the identified rate problem. 'Framing' in this sense should – as far as possible – be a purely factual exercise undertaken without any sort of normative judgement. For the purposes of this inquiry, a 'rate' is simply '[a]n amount, quantity, or value, considered relative to another; the relationship between two values'.[118] In essence, a 'rate' refers to a *change* in the nature of a particular object, whether tangible or intangible, over the course of time. A simple example is 'climate change', which is seen – in ordinary terms – as 'an *alteration* in the regional or global climate; [especially] ... the *change* in global climate patterns increasingly apparent *from the mid to late 20th [century]* ... *onwards* and attributed largely to the increased levels of atmospheric carbon dioxide produced by the use of fossil fuels'.[119]

The latter part of the above definition of 'climate change' – relating to what climate change can be attributed to – is unimportant for identifying it as a rate problem. In other words, while the cause of climate change is important in deciding whether it constitutes a common concern of humankind – and is an issue that is addressed at a later stage of the recognition analysis – it does not matter for this stage what causes climate change, it simply matters that it is an identifiable rate with particular consequences that can be objectively established as fact as a change in the identified rate occurs. Put differently, certain effects can be determined as a matter of fact. Naturally, perhaps, there will be a temptation even at this stage to begin to classify the rate change and its effects in normative terms. Such efforts should be kept for the normative stage of the identification process; that is, it should be saved for the recognition phase.

In the context of climate change, for example, 'framing' would entail (1) identifying that the climate has the capacity to change in nature, does in fact change in nature over time and that these changes have certain effects on humankind or a large part of humankind; and (2) identifying as precisely as possible what the effects of a changing climate are. Similarly, in the context of biodiversity, 'framing' would involve (1) identifying that the level of biodiversity in the world has the capacity to change over time, does in fact change over time and that changes in the

---

[118] See 'rate, *n.1*', in *Oxford English Dictionary Online* (Oxford University Press online, May 2018), http://0-www.oed.com.innopac.wits.ac.za/view/Entry/158412?rskey=Ul7VvI& result=2&isAdvanced=false#eid (accessed 12 May 2018).

[119] See 'climate, *n.1*', ibid., http://0-www.oed.com.innopac.wits.ac.za/view/Entry/34319? redirectedFrom=climate+change#eid119694526 (accessed 12 May 2018) (emphasis added).

DISTRIBUTION OF INCOME AND WEALTH 229

level of biodiversity has certain effects; and (2) identifying as precisely as possible what the effects of a changing level of biodiversity are. In both of the above-described cases, potential common concerns of humankind have now been framed and we can proceed to ask the threshold question: does state sovereignty in these areas need to be redefined in order to manage the rate changes and effects identified?

4.3.2.2 The Threshold Question: Does State Sovereignty Need Reconstitution?

'Cooperative sovereignty' and the related concept of subsidiarity have been discussed above.[120] This second stage of the recognition of common concerns of humankind entails asking whether a cooperative conception of state sovereignty is necessary in order to effectively address the framed potential common concern of humankind. Put differently, the question is simply whether the current construction of state sovereignty in a particular field allows states to affect – at a factual level – the rate change identified and accordingly the effects (including those with normative implications) that flow from the change in that rate. Turning again to the climate change context, the question becomes whether a more traditional form of sovereignty – one that does not entail cooperation as part of sovereignty itself – allows for states to alter the rate at which the climate is changing and thereby alter the effects that stem from the rate at which the climate is changing.

In the event that cooperative sovereignty is unnecessary, there is clearly far less need for the recognition of a common concern of humankind because states will already possess the necessary tools to address the rate change and its effects. For example, states are competent on current constructions of sovereignty to adequately fund a wide range of public goods. States can, for example, affect the rate at which many different crimes are committed (leaving aside certain forms of transnational crimes); they can alter the rate at which their respective populations are educated; they can build roads, railways and airports; they can establish and run a military (but they may need to cooperate with other states to attain certain shared military aims); they can provide systems for the adequate settlement of a broad array of disputes – all of this, and much more, can be achieved without reconstituting sovereignty as a cooperative enterprise.

---

[120] See Section 4.2.2.2 in this chapter, pp. 220–2.

4.3.2.3 Recognition of the Common Concern of Humankind through a Process of Law

For this part of the inquiry, it is necessary, finally, to make certain normative judgements. The normative work of the common concern of humankind concept is done – almost entirely – by the word 'adverse'. The last real hurdle – and certainly the most difficult to overcome – is reaching agreement among actors in the international law arena that the effects identified at the framing stage are of sufficient concern to a large part of humanity in order for them to be deemed 'adverse'. Once there is agreement on this point, common concern of humankind designation should necessarily follow unless states are unconcerned with addressing a particular set of adverse effects. It is also at this stage that the underlying causes of the rate change and its effects enters the fray; the causes and the ability of the international community to address them do, after all, affect perceptions as to what effects are and are not 'adverse' in nature.

Returning to climate change again, it is clear from the UNFCCC that the effects of climate change are deemed 'adverse', at least in part, because they are caused by reversible human activity.[121] This does not mean that the effects themselves are reversible; in the common concern of humankind context it is potentially irreversible effects that are more likely to be deemed 'adverse'.[122] For example, in the biodiversity context, permanent losses of biological diversity – which is in of itself considered to be intrinsically valuable – are more likely to be considered 'adverse'. Similarly, in the climate change context, damage done to natural ecosystems may be irreversible inasmuch as once particular ecosystems have been destroyed, they cannot be subsequently reproduced.

This does not mean, however, that the effects need necessarily be irreversible in order to be considered 'adverse'. Equally adverse in the climate change context, perhaps, is the threat that changes in the climate pose for natural water sources, food security and human security, among others. Ultimately, the process of recognizing that certain effects are 'adverse' leaves the international community with wide discretion to recognize common concerns of humankind. While one might propose a set of factors to guide contemplation in this regard – such as the irreversibility and scale of the effects – what is and is not deemed

---

[121] For a discussion on point, see generally D. Jamieson, 'The Nature of the Problem', in J. S. Dryzek, R. B. Norgaard and D. Schlosberg, *Oxford Handbook of Climate Change and Society* (New York: Oxford University Press, 2011), pp. 38–54.

[122] See Soltau, *supra* n. 113, 208.

DISTRIBUTION OF INCOME AND WEALTH 231

'adverse' is up to the collective will of the international community and is capable of being shaped through a process of claims and responses.[123]

The view explored here is the one that holds that the effects of a potential common concern of humankind should, at a minimum, be labelled 'adverse' when they pertain to threats to international peace and security. As Thomas Cottier argues in this volume, '[i]n assessing serious problems of major magnitude, we need to turn to the very essence of public international law, in fact of all law, which seeks to allow for and preserve peaceful relations among humans and support and promote [the] welfare of humanity'.[124] He then continues to assert as follows:

> The benchmark ... should be problems threatening and undermining this very basic function of the law. To the extent that a shared problem threatens these goals, it becomes a matter of common concern and should be addressed accordingly. At the same time, the threshold limits the principle of Common Concern to problems of utmost importance. They avoid minor problems to be exposed to the enhanced legal obligations incurred under the principle.
>
> It is therefore submitted that the principle of Common Concern of Humankind is limited to problems in the various fields of public international law which could potentially threaten international stability, peace and welfare.[125]

Seen in this light, the common concern of humankind concept is less easily capable of being 'watered down' or being dismissed as fanciful cosmopolitanism.[126] Moreover, it would allow for the advancement of the international law of peace and security as it currently stands, that is, as a framework and set of legal rules that were essentially designed – based on the principle of equality of states – to prevent wars *between* states, but which has proved fairly ineffective at preventing and ending the type of intrastate wars that have predominated the global landscape since the end of the Second World War.[127] It would additionally, as Cottier points out, allow for peace and security to be considered beyond the traditional confines of aggression and warfare.[128] It should also be

---

[123] See Chapter 1 in this volume, pp. 26–9.
[124] Ibid., p. 39.
[125] Ibid., p. 40.
[126] Ibid., pp. 39–42.
[127] On the rise of intrastate conflict vis-à-vis interstate conflicts since 1945, see generally B. Kissane, *Nations Torn Asunder: The Challenge of Civil War* (Oxford: Oxford University Press, 2016), pp. 66–107.
[128] See Chapter 1 in this volume, pp. 68–70.

232   ALEXANDER BEYLEVELD

added that many threats to peace and security come from long-term structural problems that do not pose immediate and proximate threats but instead build up over a longer period of time and are therefore often not viewed as peace and security threats in the short or medium term.

4.4   Changes in the Distribution of Income and Wealth within States: A Common Concern of Humankind?

This part of the chapter brings together the two parts that precede it. This exercise is structured into three sections. First, building on the general process for the recognition of common concerns of humankind elucidated in Section 4.3, the increasingly unequal distribution of income and wealth within states is framed as a potential common concern of humankind with due reference to the adverse effects of this phenomenon over time and across space (Section 4.4.1). In the second section, the threshold issue – as identified in Section 4.3 – of the need for 'cooperative sovereignty' is applied to the potential common concern of humankind framed in Section 4.4.1 (Section 4.4.2). Finally, having come to the conclusion that the threshold requirement is currently being met, at least within certain areas of sovereign competences and responsibilities, the potential modes of recognizing changes in the distribution of income and wealth within states as a common concern of humankind are explored with particular reference to global peace, stability and security as a factor that may drive the normative debate that the recognition of such a common concern of humankind may entail (Section 4.4.3).

4.4.1   *Framing Changes in the Distribution of Income and Wealth within States as a Common Concern of Humankind*

For the UNFCCC parties, 'change in the Earth's climate and its adverse effects are a common concern of humankind'.[129] For the parties to the CBD, 'the conservation of biological diversity is a common concern of humankind'.[130] For the purposes of this section, it will be argued, along similar lines, that 'the change, over time, in the distribution of income and wealth within states and the adverse effects stemming therefrom' could conceivably be considered a common concern of humankind. In an analogous way that the concern expressed through the CBD is 'that

---

[129]   Preamble, UNFCCC.
[130]   Preamble, CBD.

DISTRIBUTION OF INCOME AND WEALTH   233

biological diversity is being significantly reduced by certain human activities' and that concern is voiced in the UNFCCC 'that human activities have been substantially increasing the atmospheric concentrations of greenhouse gases, that these increases enhance the natural greenhouse effect, and that this will result on average in an additional warming of the Earth's surface and atmosphere and may adversely affect natural ecosystems and humankind', the concern here expressed would be that 'income and wealth within states are becoming increasingly unequally distributed'.

The distribution of income and wealth are both self-evidently rates that constantly change over time. At this point of the inquiry, the question of whether the effects stemming from the changes in the distribution of income and wealth are deleterious or adverse is irrelevant: the point at this stage is simply to ascertain the facts of the matter. The areas where changes in the distribution of income and/or wealth conceivably plays a causal role has become increasingly lengthy: climate change,[131] crime,[132] population health,[133] economic growth and its effect on poverty reduction,[134] intergenerational mobility,[135] societal cooperation, collective action and public goods provisioning,[136] and financial crises make up what is a truncated list of these areas.[137] In this chapter

[131] See, for example, N. Grunewald *et al.*, 'The Trade-off between Income Inequality and Carbon Dioxide Emissions', *Ecological Economics*, 142 (2017), 249–56; A. K. Jorgenson *et al.*, 'Domestic Inequality and Carbon Emissions in Comparative Perspective', *Sociological Forum*, 31(S1) (2016), 770–86.

[132] See, for example, P. Fajnzylber, D. Lederman and N. Loayza, 'Inequality and Violent Crime', *Journal of Law and Economics*, 45(1) (2002) 1–40; N. Metz and M. Burdina, 'Neighbourhood Income Inequality and Property Crime', *Urban Studies*, 55(1) (2018), 133–50.

[133] See, for example, A. Deaton 'Health, Inequality, and Economic Development', *Journal of Economic Literature*, 41(1) (2003), 113–58; K. E. Pickett and R. G. Wilkinson, 'Income Inequality and Health: A Causal Review', *Social Science & Medicine*, 128 (2015), 316–26.

[134] See, for example, Research Department, Agence Française de Développement (ed.), *Poverty, Inequality and Growth: Proceedings of the AFD-EUDN Conference*, 2003 (Paris: Maggelan, 2004); G. A. Cornia (ed.), *Inequality, Growth, and Poverty in an Era of Liberalization and Globalization* (Oxford: Oxford University Press, 2004).

[135] See, for example, R. Chetty *et al.*, 'The Fading American Dream: Trends in Absolute Income Mobility since 1940', *Science*, 356(6336) (2017), 398–406; M. Corak, 'Income Inequality, Equality of Opportunity, and Intergenerational Mobility', *Journal of Economic Perspectives*, 27(3) (2013), 79–102.

[136] See, for example, Anderson *et al.*, *supra* n. 83; Rosenbaum *et al.*, *supra* n. 83.

[137] On financial crises, see for example M. D. Bordo and C. M. Meissner, 'Does Inequality Lead to a Financial Crisis?', *Journal of International Money and Finance*, 31(8) (2012), 2147–61; R. Rajan, *Fault Lines* (Princeton, NJ: Princeton University Press, 2010).

234 ALEXANDER BEYLEVELD

the focus will be limited to what we might term 'threats to global peace, security and stability', which overlaps with, but is conceptually distinct from, some of the aforementioned thematic areas. It additionally serves the discussion well to bear in mind that there exists a vast range of additional effects – only some of which are mentioned above – that stem from distributional changes and that these, too, may play a role in the discussion on recognition.

Returning to Walter Scheidel's 'four horsemen',[138] it is fairly clear that two of them have become almost completely obsolete in contemporary times: ever since the Industrial Revolution, plagues akin to the Black Death experienced in the Middle Ages have not arisen, nor has there, beyond a few examples such as the case of Somalia,[139] been much state collapse of which we might speak. Since the start of the twentieth century, the two main sources for reducing the inequality of economic distributions have been mass mobilization warfare and transformative revolution.[140] As Scheidel notes, however, it is not clear – at an empirical level – that distributional changes over time in fact cause large wars or violent revolutions.[141] It accordingly serves us well to traverse briefly some of the literature on the relationship between changing economic distributions within states or societies and events that may threaten the maintenance of global peace, security and stability.

It is worth recalling that the very first listed purpose of the United Nations, under its Charter, is to 'maintain international peace and security'.[142] Under this mandate, the United Nations has concluded a variety of other agreements. For example, the United Nations Office on Counter-Terrorism notes that '[s]ince 1963 the international community has elaborated 19 international legal instruments to prevent terrorist acts' and that '[t]hose instruments were developed under the auspices of the United Nations and the International Atomic Energy Agency . . . and are open to participation by all [United Nations] Member States'.[143]

---

[138] See Section 4.1 in this chapter, pp. 199–200.

[139] See Scheidel, *supra* n. 1, p. 8.

[140] See ibid., pp. 8–9.

[141] See ibid., p. 10.

[142] Article 1.1, United Nations, Charter of the United Nations (UN Charter), San Francisco, 26 June 1945, entered into force 24 Oct. 1945, 1 UNTS XVI.

[143] See further generally United Nations Office on Counter-Terrorism, 'International Legal Instruments', www.un.org/en/counterterrorism/legal-instruments.shtml (accessed 31 May 2018).

It suffices to say that terrorism, loosely defined, is something that is at least notionally dear to the international community; one might accordingly ask whether there is some kind of relationship between distributional changes and changes in the observed level of terrorism.

In a blog post for the *Le Monde* newspaper in 2015, Thomas Piketty made what was widely seen as a controversial argument in the following terms:

> Confronted with terrorism, the response must involve security measures. We must hit Daech [the French word for 'Daesh', or as they are better known 'the Islamic State of Iraq and the Levant'] and arrest those who are members. But we must also consider the political conditions of this violence, the humiliation and the injustices which result in this movement receiving considerable support in the Middle East and today gives rise to murderous vocations in Europe. In the long run, the real issue is the establishment of an equitable model for social development both there and here ... One thing is obvious: terrorism thrives on the inequality in the Middle-East which is a powder keg we have largely contributed to creating.[144]

In this area, systematic empirical research – of which Piketty is an enthusiastic supporter generally speaking – is sparse. The little available work that exists, however, does tend to suggest – with admittedly little certainty as to how precisely the causal mechanisms operate – that increased levels of income inequality within a state leads to a greater amount of terrorist activities.[145] As one might expect in such a nascent area of research, however, the existing research leaves much to be desired: it does not, as yet, account properly for different definitions of terrorism or for different types of distributions.[146] Given that there is some

---

[144] See T. Piketty, 'Clamping down with Law and Order Will Not Be Enough' (*Le Monde* blog, 24 Nov. 2015), http://piketty.blog.lemonde.fr/2015/11/24/clamping-down-with-law-and-order-will-not-be-enough/ (accessed 31 May 2018).

[145] See, for example, Tim Krieger and Daniel Meierrieks, 'Income Inequality, Redistribution and Domestic Terrorism', *World Development*, 116 (2019), 125. Economic distributions, of course, do not operate in a vacuum, and other factors – such as a history of colonial domination or resentment related to prior military intervention – should be considered alongside the distribution of income and wealth. For a broader discussion on the causes of terrorism, see 'Part Four: Causes and Motivations', in E. Chenoweth *et al.* (eds.), *The Oxford Handbook of Terrorism* (Oxford University Press, 2019).

[146] Some studies are, however, careful to make some distinctions in this regard. See, for example, R. Ezcurra and D. Palacios, 'Terrorism and Spatial Disparities: Does Interregional Inequality Matter?', *European Journal of Political Economy*, 42 (2016), 60–74, where the authors are careful to limit the scope of their definition of terrorism

preliminary evidence for concern, this is an area of research that should be monitored carefully as it develops in precision with time; especially so given that there is a fairly well established theoretical basis for the hypothesized linkages and that interest in data of this sort as well as its collection is continually increasing.[147]

A relationship that has, however, been studied more systematically is that between distributional variables and the onset of conflict, violence and civil war.[148] It suffices to say that any summary of what has become a dense literature over time is likely to oversimplify findings in a field where there is much scope for nuance. For example, much of the literature distinguishes between what are often labelled 'vertical inequalities' (VIs) – that is to say the difference in income or wealth as measured or as estimated between *individuals* within a defined area – and 'horizontal inequalities' (HIs), which refer to differences in income or wealth between *groups*.[149] There are various questions here to which one could – and should where possible – dedicate much time to unpack. For example, with respect to HIs, how are 'groups' defined?[150] Methodological questions such as this are important – and a great deal has been done to answer them – but much of what follows will be simplified to make the broader point that changing economic distributions within countries have the capacity to contribute – to varying degrees – to events that threaten and/or harm international peace and security.

As a general proposition, VIs have not been found to contribute to the onset of civil conflict or to civil war. To simplify a lengthy discussion, following Ted Robert Gurr's 'relative depravation', which he first appears to have posited in the late 1960s, empirical techniques have been applied over and over again with the aim of proving (or disproving) Gurr's theoretical construct.[151] Different theories have, of course, appeared over

to one that only includes 'domestic' terrorist acts and examine interregional income inequality.

[147] On the theoretical basis, see, for example, the discussions in Krieger and Meierrieks, *supra* n. 145; Ezcurra and Palacios, *supra* n. 146, 61–2.

[148] See, for example, F. Stewart (ed.), *Horizontal Inequalities and Conflict: Understanding Group Violence in Multiethnic Societies* (Basingstoke, UK: Palgrave Macmillan, 2008).

[149] See F. Stewart, 'Horizontal Inequalities and Conflict: An Introduction and Some Hypotheses', ibid., pp. 3–24, at pp. 12–13.

[150] On this question, see for example the discussion in Stewart, ibid., 7–12.

[151] On Gurr's 'relative deprivation' hypothesis, see T. R. Gurr, *Why Men Rebel* (Princeton, NJ: Princeton University Press, 1970), pp. 22–56.

DISTRIBUTION OF INCOME AND WEALTH 237

time,[152] with empirical studies and various critiques of both theory and measurement following soon after. Even with respects to VIs, the debate continued – and to an extent still does – to flare. An influential study undertaken by Paul Collier and Anke Hoeffler in 2004, using a VI-style measure – that is, the Gini coefficient of either income or land ownership – came to the conclusion, among other things, that the change in economic distributions over time do not contribute to the onset of civil war.[153] Some studies have come to similar conclusions.[154] Yet, other studies have come to the conclusion that VIs do have a contributory impact on the onset of civil war.[155]

More recently, and specifically in light of the work done by Frances Stewart,[156] the focus has shifted away from VIs towards HIs. At their simplest, HIs can be defined as 'inequalities in economic, social or political dimensions or cultural status between culturally defined groups'.[157] While an array of results has come from work on HIs,[158] perhaps the most important of these is that, simplistically put, the probability of conflict, including the onset of civil war, rises when socio-economic – which of course includes an economic distribution component – HIs grow higher over time.[159] Understanding what causes a complex event such as a civil war naturally remains a difficult task, especially given that the data used in the relevant studies, although they have improved in quantity and quality over time, still remains inadequate

---

[152] See, for example, T. Boswell and W. J. Dixon, 'Marx's Theory of Rebellion: A Cross-Nation Analysis of Class Exploitation, Economic Development, and Violent Conflict', *American Sociological Review*, 58(5) (1993), 681–702.

[153] See generally P. Collier and A. Hoeffler, 'Greed and Grievance in Civil War', *Oxford Economic Papers*, 56 (2004), 563–95.

[154] See, for example, H. Buhaug, L. E. Cederman and K. S. Gleditsch, 'Square Pegs in Round Holes: Inequalities, Grievances and Civil War', *International Studies Quarterly*, 58(2) (2014), 418–31.

[155] See, for example, C. Boix, 'Economic Roots of Civil Wars and Revolutions in the Contemporary World', *World Politics*, 60(3) (2008), 390–437; L. E. Cederman, N. B. Weidmann and K. S. Gleditsch, 'Horizontal Inequalities and Ethnonationalist Civil War: A Global Comparison', *American Political Science Review*, 105(3) (2011), 478–95; G. Østby, 'Polarization, Horizontal Inequalities and Violent Civil Conflict', *Journal of Peace Research*, 45(2) (2008), 143–62.

[156] See especially Stewart, *supra* n. 148. See also F. Stewart, 'Crisis Prevention: Tackling Horizontal Inequalities', *Oxford Development Studies*, 28(3) (2000), 245–62.

[157] Stewart, *supra* n. 149, p. 3. For examples of HIs in conflict situations, see ibid., p. 15.

[158] See further F. Stewart, G. K. Brown and A. Langer, 'Major Findings and Conclusions on the Relationship Between Horizontal Inequalities and Conflict', in Stewart, *supra* n. 148, pp. 285–300.

[159] Ibid., p. 287.

at times.[160] The fact remains, however, that there is a growing body of literature that comes to the conclusion that HIs have a strong contributory effect when it comes to the causes of civil war and other similar forms of violence.[161]

It should additionally be pointed out that researchers in this area tend to focus either on VIs *or* HIs. That there exists a relationship between these different types of inequalities is self-evident. HIs do, after all, have a clear vertical component to them. While the exact contours of the overlap have not been determined with great precision, it is an area where more work is clearly warranted. Where a state starts from a position where initial economic distributions are highly inegalitarian in a horizontal sense for systemic reasons, such as in apartheid South Africa or as a result of slavery in the United States, increased vertical inequality may also exacerbate existing HIs. Indeed, the distributional trends in each of these countries tend to suggest that this is exactly what has been happening.[162]

Increasingly unequal economic distributions pose additional, far subtler, threats to global peace, stability and security as well. Increasing economic inequality contributes significantly to political polarization.[163] As already alluded to, more unequal distributions of income and wealth accordingly lead to a breakdown in social cohesion and the propensities of the constituent members of states to cooperate for the collective – and also individual – benefit of those members. During times of (relatively) high economic inequality, international cooperation consequently takes a hit as well, with states that are incapable of functionally cooperating internally being highly unlikely to successfully – and *effectively* – cooperate with other states. This is almost an inevitable consequence of political polarization in a world that is highly interdependent but is split into states.

---

[160] For an overview of attempts to overcome data-related difficulties, see, for example, L. E. Cederman, N. B. Weidmann and N. C. Bormann 'Triangulating Horizontal Inequality: Toward Improved Conflict Analysis', *Journal of Peace Research*, 52(6) (2015), 806–21.

[161] See, for example, Buhaug *et al.*, *supra* n. 154; Cederman *et al.*, *supra* n. 155; Cederman *et al.*, *supra* n. 160; Østby, *supra* n. 155.

[162] See, for example, in this regard V. Wilson and W. M. Rodgers, *Black–White Wage Gaps Expand with Rising Wage Inequality* (Washington, DC: Economic Policy Institute, 2016), www.epi.org/files/pdf/101972.pdf (accessed 31 Dec. 2018).

[163] See in this regard, for example, J. Voorheis, N. McCarty and B. Shor, 'Unequal Incomes, Ideology and Gridlock: How Rising Inequality Increases Political Polarization' (21 Aug. 2015), https://ssrn.com/abstract=2649215 (accessed 31 Dec. 2018).

DISTRIBUTION OF INCOME AND WEALTH 239

It is also a significant threat to global peace, stability and security in contemporary times because – as documented in this volume – increasingly many of the challenges faced by the world concern humankind as a whole or at least substantial parts of it. As such, a functional world which solves the problems of its time is one wherein there is more cooperation. As a general matter, then, lower cooperative propensities accordingly threaten our ability as a species to cooperate effectively to solve problems other than the distribution of income and wealth, problems that in and of themselves greatly threaten global peace, stability and security – and therefore human welfare – such as climate change, or the availability of fresh water or food security, or any of the other common concerns of humankind discussed in this volume. As a result, there is a good argument to be made that a system of global economic governance that results in levels of economic inequality that are optimal for international cooperation is an example of a global public good, something which the common concern of humankind concept and the related Doctrine (and potential principle) of Common Concern of Humankind seeks to produce.[164]

4.4.2 The Distribution of Income and Wealth within States and Cooperative Sovereignty

Plato had already taken what is a highly pointed stance on economic distributions by today's standards in his *Laws*.[165] Writing in the fourth century BC, Plato poignantly demonstrated the unparalleled power of law as a discipline to alter the distribution of income and wealth in a society in a deliberate and systematic fashion. His *Laws* is made up of twelve different books and consists of a dialogue between three fictional characters: one dubbed the 'Athenian Stranger', an ordinary Spartan citizen named Megillos and a lawmaker from Crete called Clinias.[166] Through the Athenian Stranger, Plato initiates the dialogue by questioning the other men whether a god or a man should be credited as the author of their laws.[167] What follows during the rest of the dialogue is essentially an

---

[164] On the relationship between common concerns of humankind and the concept of global public goods, see Chapter 1 in this volume, pp. 44–6. See also T. Cottier *et al*, 'The Principle of Common Concern and Climate Change', *Archiv des Völkerrechts* 52 (2014) 293–324, at 308–10.

[165] Plato, *Laws, Volume I: Books 1–6* (London: Heinemann, 1926).

[166] See ibid., pp. vii–xvii.

[167] See ibid., pp. vii–xvii.

240 ALEXANDER BEYLEVELD

attempt at answering this question, but the dialogue additionally allows the Athenian Stranger to contemplate the design of his ideal political order in practical terms. In Book V, the dialogue turns to contemplate an array of issues, including how many people an ideal society should be made up of and who should own how much property and wealth.[168] The answers are incredibly concrete.

Taking from Book V only that which is necessary to make this point, the following (admittedly simplified ideas) can be gleaned about Plato's notion of an ideal society: (1) out of what appears to essentially amount to mathematical convenience, it would be made up of no more than 5,040 citizens;[169] (2) equality of material possessions (wealth) is desirable in theory, but considered impossible as a practical matter;[170] (3) acquisition of wealth is constructed so as to be based on merit, at least to the extent possible;[171] (4) honours and offices are determined in proportion to a man's wealth;[172] (5) there will be four classes based on wealth alone;[173] (6) there will be level of wealth that each person should be allotted at a minimum, based on the limit of poverty;[174] and (7) no person will be allowed more to acquire more than four times the minimum allotment in wealth.[175] Most importantly of all, all of these characteristics are to be backed by the coercive power of law: any wealth acquired in excess of the limit, for example, would in one way or another be handed over to the state and 'the gods who keep [it]'.[176]

As illustrated earlier in this chapter, pursuing and attaining these sorts of results – whether its attainment is in fact desirable is of little moment – is not realistically possible. The contemporary realities of ascertaining which distributions of income and/or wealth would constitute ones which are distributively just within a state are far more complex than those imagined by Plato. The modern state, of course, is vastly different from any state Plato could imagine. The fact remains that contemporary sovereigns cannot secure certain distributions of income or wealth as

---

[168] See ibid., pp. 323–92.
[169] Ibid., pp. 356–9.
[170] Ibid., pp. 360–5, 378–9.
[171] Ibid., pp. 378–9.
[172] Ibid.
[173] Ibid., pp. 378–9.
[174] Ibid., pp. 378–81.
[175] Ibid., pp. 380–1.
[176] Ibid. Plato also spoke to additional rules relating, for example, to the coining of money, foreign aid and immigration. See generally ibid., pp. 323–93.

DISTRIBUTION OF INCOME AND WEALTH 241

public goods, nor can they secure distributive justice, without cooperation. This remains the case regardless of one's conception of distributive justice. Whether one takes a similar approach to the one of Plato as described above, whether one prefers a more Rawlsian understanding of distributive justice,[177] or whether one takes the view that an economic system can be considered as providing for distributive justice only when government interference with the free market is at a minimum,[178] the fact remains that in contemporary times distributive justice can only realistically be achieved through cooperation between sovereign entities.

4.4.3 The Distribution of Income and Wealth within States as a Common Concern of Humankind: Examining the Causal and Normative Debates

The distribution of income and wealth within a state depends on a very large number of factors, ranging from technology, to labour regulation to taxation, among myriad other factors.[179] Making one single normative claim about the distribution of income and wealth within a state is accordingly a highly complex task. Consider for a moment the international rules relating to the protection of foreign investment. Even within this one field of international law, it is a complex exercise to cover all the potential normative aspects relating to the distributive aspects of foreign investments. The normative claims relating to taxation are, of course, a different set of claims entirely. What these differing sets of normative claims have in common, however, is that they are all related – albeit it to differing degrees – to any given state's pursuit of a particular distribution of income and/or wealth as public goods or that state's pursuit of distributive justice.

Matters are further complicated by the vast plurality of sovereigns, especially given that the actions of one state are likely to affect the

---

[177] See generally J. Rawls, *A Theory of Justice (Revised Edition)* (Cambridge, MA: Harvard University Press, 1999); more specifically, see ibid., pp. 228–335.

[178] For a defence of such a view, see generally, for example, M. Friedman, *Capitalism and Freedom* (Chicago: University of Chicago Press, 1962); more specifically, see ibid., pp. 161–76.

[179] For an overview and an interesting attempt at determining the relative importance of some of these causes in respect of income distribution, see M. F. Förster and I. György Tóth, 'Cross-Country Evidence of the Multiple Causes of Inequality Changes in the OECD Area', in A. B. Atkinson and F. Bourguignon (eds.), *Handbook of Income Distribution (Volume 2B)* (Amsterdam: Elsevier, 2015), pp. 1729–843.

pursuits of other states. There are currently clear political impediments to reaching agreement on the distribution of income and wealth as a common concern of humankind. One of the more pertinent examples, perhaps, is the issue of China's economy and how it operates. Ongoing discussions at the WTO as to China's 'market-economy status' illustrate this well. The two largest economies in the world, in the form of the United States and China, maintain economies that are highly interdependent and wherein income and wealth is distributed in vastly different ways. Belabouring this point is unnecessary for present purposes. It suffices to say that agreement on all distributive issues at a bilateral level, let alone a global level, is unlikely to be forthcoming any time soon.

To recall, however, this stage of the proposed common concern of humankind recognition process entails terming certain effects that stem from changes in the distribution of income and wealth within countries 'adverse'.[180] Those recognized could conceivably be limited, perhaps on a temporary basis, to narrowly tailored 'adverse' effects. For example, the effects recognized as 'adverse' could be limited to civil war or large-scale civil violence based on the likely causal link between changing distributions and the onset of intrastate violence as discussed above. A broader notion of 'adverse effects' could, of course, be taken up. On the assumption that the broader international community at large were to get past the two earlier steps in the proposed recognition process, the normative underpinning for recognition could be tied back to international peace, stability and security.

To avoid setting a precise threshold of when economic distributions begin to be an imminent threat to peace and security, a longer-term view of threats to international peace and security – such as the one taken in the climate change context – could be taken much in the way that it has been taken in the context of international trade legal frameworks. The WTO and the EU trade regimes are both premised on the idea that, in the long run, wars between nations are far less likely in the event that nations are closely economically integrated. Empirical evidence indeed suggests that states with more trading partners are less likely to go to war with other states.[181] In a similar way, it could be asserted that a world

---

[180] See Section 4.3.2.3 in this chapter, pp. 230–2.

[181] Or, as Harry Hopkins put it, '[t]rade conflict breeds noncooperation, suspicion, bitterness. Nations which are economic enemies are not likely to remain political friends for long' (quoted in T. Cottier, 'John H. Jackson, the Law and the Economics', *World Trade Review*, 15(3) (2016), 412–14). See M. O. Jackson and S. Nei, 'Networks of Military

DISTRIBUTION OF INCOME AND WEALTH 243

where economic distributions within states are more equal is a world where interstate and intrastate war is less likely. This assertion is clearly consistent with distributional trends over time.[182]

From this longer-term viewpoint, the recognition of a distributional common concern of humankind would complement and build on long-term economic cooperation obligations that seek to ensure peace and stability and which stem from existing legal frameworks. As internal distributional matters are not currently recognized, recognition could expand on the Article 55 UN Charter imperative of promoting certain types of economic cooperation '[w]ith a view to the creation of conditions of stability and well-being which are necessary for peaceful *and* friendly relations among nations based on the equal rights and self-determination of peoples' to include the cooperation necessary in order to ensure the retention of the distributional autonomy of states.[183] Such an expansion could, in turn, form the basis for more specific actions in discrete areas of international law.[184]

Additionally, as discussed above, recognition of a distributional common concern of humankind as envisioned would aim to refocus sovereignty.[185] In contemporary times, there is, in the face of rapid economic globalization, often an overly strong focus on 'control' when it comes to the perceived sovereignty of various nation states. There is a desire for a return to a time of self-determination based on the perception that peoples' capacity to chart their own paths as nations has been eroding – and continues to do so – at a frightening pace. What is often lost in all the noise, however, at least as sovereignty is discussed as a concept that involves nations vis-à-vis nations, is a discussion on the welfare *raison d'être* of sovereignty of states vis-à-vis *themselves*. It is high time that international law rethinks the balance between

---

Alliances, Wars and International Trade', *National Academy of Sciences*, 112(50) (2015), 15277–84, for an empirical take on the matter.

[182] Branko Milanović has even gone so far, for example, as to argue that high levels of income inequality played a central causal role in bringing about the First World War (B. Milanović, 'Inequality, Imperialism and the Outbreak of World War I', in S. Broadberry and M. Harrison (eds.), *The Economics of the Great War: A Centennial Perspective* (Washington, DC: CEPR Press, 2018)).

[183] See Art. 55, UN Charter (emphasis added).

[184] As mentioned above, these areas could include the regulation of corporate taxation, cross-border investment flows and competition between firms or value chains among possible others. One could also imagine its being applied in connection to the laws that govern multilateral development institutions such as the World Bank.

[185] See Section 4.2.2.2 in this chapter, pp. 221–2.

self-determination and effectively ensuring the welfare of people. In order to do so, we must look more carefully *within states themselves* as we begin to construct new foundational principles in international law.

4.5 Concluding Remarks

This chapter has made an argument for recognizing changes in the distribution of income and wealth within states and the adverse effects flowing therefrom as a common concern of humankind. Central to this argument has been the idea that states increasingly need to cooperate with one another in order to retain their individual distributional autonomy under conditions of contemporary economic globalization, with such a loss resulting in deleterious consequences for a substantial majority of humankind. While this point has been made in broad terms during the course of the chapter, it should not be read as an argument that states no longer have *any* distributional autonomy. Rather, the assertion has in essence been that states have lost – and continue to lose – substantial amounts of distributional autonomy to the extent that a principle of subsidiarity in some form or another, whether termed as such or not, is necessary in order to ascertain who is responsible for ensuring economic distributions are appropriately dealt with within states.

This state of affairs has come to be largely as a function of techno-logical change with existing international laws being accepted as part of the pre-existing factual matrix within which these changes have taken – and continue to take – place. In other words, as a combination of factual changes and existing legal arrangements, an existing precept connected to international law – the idea that 'internal' distributive concerns are to be treated as resoluble within a purely domestic framework of laws and regulations – no longer holds. The recognition of a distributive common concern of humankind as conceived of above is a possible response to this state of affairs that would seek to reconfigure the foundations of international (economic) law – mainly through adopting a different understanding of sovereignty – such that distributional matters within states can continue to be dealt with effectively.

Returning to Scheidel's warning as quoted at the outset of the chapter, it should also be clarified that the underlying motivation for the recogni-tion of a distributional common concern of humankind is one that recognizes the violent history of economic levelling as a historical fact but urges *against* fatalism. The history of the reduction of economic inequality is indeed a tragic one, but the salience of economic inequality

DISTRIBUTION OF INCOME AND WEALTH 245

also rises as inequality becomes ever more extreme. This easily looks bleak: as inequality rises, the desire for less inequality increases and the only way in which inequality can meaningfully be decreased, historically, is through mass violence or events that are to a large degree beyond human control and are intrinsically violent (disease, or perhaps climate change in future). The recognition of a distributional common concern of humankind would be an attempt by the international community, through what would essentially be a dialogue about subsidiarity with respect to economic distributions within states, at constructing an alternative, non-violent way to level things out where necessary. In fashioning such an alternative, however, it would be foolish not to note humanity's poor track record in respect of economic levelling to date.

* * *

Select Bibliography

Alvaredo, F. *et al.* (eds.). (2018). *World Inequality Report 2018* (Cambridge, MA: Harvard University Press).

Atkinson, A. B. (2015). *Inequality: What Can Be Done?* (London: Harvard University Press).

Baldwin, R. (2016). *The Great Convergence: Information Technology and the New Globalization* (Cambridge, MA: Harvard University Press).

Besson, S. (2004). 'Sovereignty in Conflict', *European Integration Online Papers (EIoP)*, 8(15), 1–23.

Buhaug, H., Cederman, L. E. and Gleditsch, K. S. (2014). 'Square Pegs in Round Holes: Inequalities, Grievances and Civil War', *International Studies Quarterly*, 58(2), 418–31.

Cederman, L. E., Weidmann, N. B. and Bormann, N. C. (2015). 'Triangulating Horizontal Inequality: Toward Improved Conflict Analysis', *Journal of Peace Research*, 52(6), 806–21.

Cederman, L. E., Weidmann, N. B. and Gleditsch, K. S. (2011). 'Horizontal Inequalities and Ethnonationalist Civil War: A Global Comparison', *American Political Science Review*, 105(3), 478–95.

Gallie, W. B. (1956). 'Essentially Contested Concepts', *Proceedings of the Aristotelian Society*, 56(1), 167–98.

Gurr, T. R. (1970). *Why Men Rebel* (Princeton, NJ: Princeton University Press).

Harari, Y. N. (2014). *Sapiens: A Brief History of Humankind* (London: Vintage).

Lowe, A. V. (1985). 'The Problems of Extraterritorial Jurisdiction: Economic Sovereignty and the Search for a Solution', *International and Comparative Law Quarterly*, 34(4), 724–46.

(2008). 'Sovereignty and International Economic Law', in W. Shan, P. Simons and D. Singh (eds.), *Redefining Sovereignty in International Economic Law* (Portland: Hart), pp. 79–80.

Perrez, F. X. (2000). *Cooperative Sovereignty: From Independence to Interdependence in the Structure of International Environmental Law* (Kluwer: The Hague).

Piketty, T. (2014). *Capital in the Twenty-First Century* (Cambridge, MA: Harvard University Press).

Sarooshi, D. (2004). 'The Essentially Contested Nature of the Concept of Sovereignty: Implications for the Exercise by International Organizations of Delegated Powers of Government', *Michigan Journal of International Law*, 25(4), 1107–39.

(2005). *International Organizations and Their Exercise of Sovereign Powers* (New York: Oxford University Press).

Scheidel, W. (2017). *The Great Leveler: Violence and the History of Inequality from the Stone Age to the Twenty-First Century* (Princeton, NJ: Princeton University Press).

Stewart, F. (2000). 'Crisis Prevention: Tackling Horizontal Inequalities', *Oxford Development Studies*, 28(3), 245–62.

(ed.). (2008). *Horizontal Inequalities and Conflict: Understanding Group Violence in Multiethnic Societies* (Basingstoke: Palgrave Macmillan).

Thurow, L. C. (1971). 'The Income Distribution as a Pure Public Good', *Quarterly Journal of Economics*, 85(2), 327–36.

Zimmermann, C. D. (2013). *A Contemporary Concept of Monetary Sovereignty* (Oxford: Oxford University Press).

5

Reshaping the Law of Economic Sanctions for Human Rights Enforcement

The Potential of Common Concern of Humankind

IRYNA BOGDANOVA

5.1 Introduction

International human rights law evolved from the promising aspiration to put an end to appalling atrocities. Yet the discernible deficiencies of the human rights regime seriously undermine the achievement of this goal. These shortcomings also pose a difficult dilemma for individual states – when and how to respond to egregious human rights violations abroad. Among the strictly limited alternatives, economic sanctions have been playing an increasingly significant role. Notwithstanding their considerably expanded implementation, the legitimacy of such measures, as well as their compatibility with WTO law remains unsettled. This chapter explores the potential of the emerging doctrine of Common Concern of Humankind to legitimize such unilateral actions of states and to provide a legal framework for their application. Furthermore, the doctrine of Common Concern puts forward the idea of improved international cooperation between the states aimed at redressing instances of grave human rights violations.

At the outset, the deficiencies of the international human rights enforcement are revealed and the underlying reasons are discussed. The subsequent sections focus on coercive economic measures. The unilateral economic sanctions and their compatibility with public international law and WTO law are discussed. The last section describes the theoretical

This chapter is a partial summary of the author's doctoral thesis "Unilateral Sanctions in International Law and the Enforcement of Human Rights: The Impact of the Principle of Common Concern of Humankind". It was presented at the conference 'Towards a Principle of Common Concern in Global Law' held at the World Trade Institute, University of Bern, 22–23 June 2018. I would like to thank all the participants of the conference for their input. In particular, I am grateful to Professor Thomas Cottier and the members of our research team for their valuable comments on the earlier drafts. Any errors that remain are my sole responsibility.

248 IRYNA BOGDANOVA

framework of the doctrine of Common Concern and its potential implications. We argue that the emerging doctrine of Common Concern of Humankind, set out in the introductory chapter of this volume, offers a suitable framework to address the problem of non-reciprocal interests and to redefine rights and obligations in the human rights field.

5.2 Enforcement of International Human Rights: between Promise and Practice

5.2.1 Unveiled Deficiencies of Human Rights Enforcement

The number of international human rights treaties, as well as the number of states participating in such treaties, increased exponentially after the Second World War. Notwithstanding this, grave violations of human rights are still epidemic. Such inconsistency has been vividly described as 'the paradox of empty promises', implying that a higher number of human rights treaties does not entail improved human rights record.[1]

In order to explain this paradox, scholars relied upon statistical methods to determine the impact of treaty ratification on human rights protection. A number of studies demonstrated a lack of causality between treaty ratification and enhanced respect for human rights.[2] In a similar vein, Adam S. Chilton and Eric A. Posner, while acknowledging that the compliance with human rights treaties slightly improved over time, emphasized that 'it is possible that this improvement in human rights has coincided with the adoption of human rights treaties rather than been caused by it'.[3]

Not all scholars are so sceptical about the impact of treaties on human rights protection though. Beth Simmons, Daniel Hill, and Christopher Fariss have found a positive correlation between the ratification of human rights treaties and enhanced respect for human rights.[4] While

---

[1] E. M. Hafner-Burton and K. Tsutsui, 'Human Rights in a Globalizing World: The Paradox of Empty Promises', *American Journal of Sociology*, 110 (2005), 1373.

[2] L. C. Keith, 'The United Nations International Covenant on Civil and Political Rights: Does It Make a Difference in Human Rights Behavior?', *Journal of Peace Research*, 36 (1999), 95–118; O. A. Hathaway, 'Do Human Rights Treaties Make a Difference?', *Yale Law Journal*, 111 (2002), 1935–2042; Hafner-Burton and Tsutsui, *supra* n. 1; E. Neumayer, 'Do International Human Rights Treaties Improve Respect for Human Rights?', *Journal of Conflict Resolution*, 49 (2005), 925–53.

[3] A. S. Chilton and E. A. Posner, 'Respect for Human Rights: Law and History', Coase-Sandor Working Paper Series in Law and Economics No. 770 (2016), at 4.

[4] B. A. Simmons, *Mobilizing for Human Rights: International Law in Domestic Politics* (Cambridge: Cambridge University Press, 2009); D. W. Hill, 'Estimating the Effects of

appearing optimistic, these positive results are observed either in democratic states or with respect to a narrowly defined group of human rights.[5] The overall conclusion is that ratification of human rights treaties may potentially improve awareness and human rights protection, yet it does not inevitably induce compliance with human rights standards, especially among autocratic and repressive states.

In the subsequent paragraphs, we will unravel the multiple reasons behind the current state of play.

First and foremost, the Achilles heel of international human rights law is the lack of incentives to comply with the undertaken obligations. There is a profound lack of reciprocity, which primarily determines attitudes and conduct of the governments and politicians. In this regard, Oona A. Hathaway has accurately pointed out:

> After all, the major engines of compliance that exist in other areas of international law are for the most part absent in the area of human rights. Unlike the public international law of money, there are no 'competitive market forces' that press for compliance. And, unlike in the case of trade agreements, the costs of retaliatory noncompliance are low to nonexistent, because a nation's actions against its own citizens do not directly threaten or harm other states. Human rights law thus stands out as an area of international law in which countries have little incentive to police noncompliance with treaties or norms. As Henkin remarked, 'The forces that induce compliance with other law ... do not pertain equally to the law of human rights'.[6]

Additionally, the lack of reciprocity is further augmented by the weak enforcement mechanisms that dominate the field. The analysis of the core human rights treaties unveils that all of them prescribe a three-prong enforcement mechanism.[7] The constitutive elements of the

Human Rights Treaties on State Behavior', *Journal of Politics*, 72 (2010), 1161–74; C. J. Fariss, 'Respect for Human Rights Has Improved over Time: Modeling the Changing Standard of Accountability', *American Political Science Review*, 108 (2014), 297–318.

[5] Beth A. Simmons has found that ratification of human rights treaties improve respect for human rights in transitional democracies, and not so much in autocracies or stable democracies. Simmons, *supra* n. 4; Daniel W. Hill concludes that 'while the Convention on the Elimination of All Forms of Discrimination against Women (CEDAW) shows promise for improving state behaviour the Convention against Torture and other Cruel, Inhuman or Degrading Treatment or Punishment (CAT) and, to a lesser extent, the International Covenant on Civil and Political Rights (CCPR) seem to actually be associated with worse practices' (Hill, *supra* n. 4).

[6] Hathaway, *supra* n. 2, at 1938.

[7] International Convention on the Elimination of All Forms of Racial Discrimination; International Covenant on Civil and Political Rights; International Covenant on Economic, Social and Cultural Rights; Convention on the Elimination of All Forms of

enforcement are: an obligation to submit regular reports on measures taken to fulfil treaty obligations, interstate and/or individual complaints mechanism and dispute settlement provisions.

Despite the alleged ability to induce compliance with human rights obligations, these instruments suffer from the following shortcomings. First, states ignore their duty to report.[8] Even when states submit their reports, the authority of a committee established to consider such reports is severely constrained.[9] Second, the complaints mechanisms require explicit consent from a state to be bound. Furthermore, the ultimate result of a complaints procedure is a summary report prepared for the parties.[10] Other remedies are not available. Finally, dispute settlement provisions refer any dispute between the parties to the ICJ. The analysis of the court practice demonstrates that such disputes are not frequent.[11] Moreover, all these disputes were initiated by the states willing to protect their nationals from the unlawful conduct of other states.[12]

Discrimination against Women; Convention against Torture and Other Cruel, Inhuman or Degrading Treatment or Punishment; Convention on the Rights of the Child; International Convention on the Protection of the Rights of All Migrant Workers and Members of Their Families; International Convention for the Protection of All Persons from Enforced Disappearance; Convention on the Rights of Persons with Disabilities; Optional Protocol to the Covenant on Economic, Social and Cultural Rights; Optional Protocol to the International Covenant on Civil and Political Rights; Second Optional Protocol to the International Covenant on Civil and Political Rights, aiming at the abolition of the death penalty; Optional Protocol to the Convention on the Elimination of Discrimination against Women; Optional Protocol to the Convention on the Rights of the Child on the involvement of children in armed conflict; Optional Protocol to the Convention on the Rights of the Child on the sale of children, child prostitution and child pornography; Optional Protocol to the Convention on the Rights of the Child on a communications procedure; Optional Protocol to the Convention against Torture and Other Cruel, Inhuman or Degrading Treatment or Punishment; Optional Protocol to the Convention on the Rights of Persons with Disabilities.

[8] E. A. Posner, *The Twilight of Human Rights Law* (Oxford: Oxford University Press, 2014).

[9] Each of the eighteen core human rights conventions establishes a committee to consider submitted reports and prepare general recommendations to states.

[10] The eighteen core human rights conventions prescribe similar procedures and outcomes.

[11] The parties invoked provisions of the five international human rights conventions in the disputes before the ICJ. There are only eight disputes in which these conventions were relied upon.

[12] For example, Georgia relied upon the relevant provision of International Convention on the Elimination of All Forms of Racial Discrimination in the proceedings against the Russian Federation (*Application of the International Convention on the Elimination of All Forms of Racial Discrimination (Georgia v. Russian Federation)*, Preliminary Objections, Judgment, ICJ Reports, 2011, p. 70); in a similar vein, Ukraine invoked the same convention in the dispute filed after the Russian Federation annexed Crimea (*Application of the International Convention for the Suppression of the Financing of*

RESHAPING THE LAW OF ECONOMIC SANCTIONS   251

Apart from the treaty law, fundamental human rights gained a status of *jus cogens norms* (peremptory norms)[13] or might be recognized as obligations *erga omnes*.[14] Beyond contestation, such recognition entails, at least in theory, enhanced protection of such norms. Despite this, the practice has demonstrated that the categories *jus cogens* and obligations *erga omnes* have remained ambiguous[15] and have not been properly enforced.[16]

Due to the deficiencies of international human rights law, individual states redress instances of severe or continuous human rights violations by relying upon unilateral measures, including coercive economic measures (economic sanctions). A recent example is legislation adopted by a number of states modelled after the United States statutes, which allows

---

Terrorism and of the International Convention on the Elimination of All Forms of Racial Discrimination (Ukraine v. Russian Federation), Provisional Measures, Order of 19 Apr. 2017, ICJ Reports, 2017, p. 104).

[13] The concept of *jus cogens* was recognized in positive international law through Article 53 of the Vienna Convention on the Law of Treaties of 1969. According to the United Nations International Law Commission the most frequently cited candidates for the status of *jus cogens* include: (a) the prohibition of aggressive use of force; (b) the right to self-defence; (c) the prohibition of genocide; (d) the prohibition of torture; (e) crimes against humanity; (f) the prohibition of slavery and slave trade; (g) the prohibition of piracy; (h) the prohibition of racial discrimination and apartheid; (i) the prohibition of hostilities directed at civilian population ('basic rules of international humanitarian law'). 'Fragmentation of International Law: Difficulties arising from the Diversification and Expansion of International Law: Report of the Study Group of the International Law Commission – Finalized by Martti Koskenniemi' (2006), para. 374.

[14] The ICJ introduced the concept of obligations *erga omnes* in 1970 (*Barcelona Traction, Light and Power Company, Limited*, Judgment, ICJ Reports, 1970, p. 3).

[15] 'The scope and boundaries of jus cogens, however, remain controversial and contested in a decentralized legal order, in particular in relation to core labour standards and humanitarian law' (T. Cottier, 'Improving Compliance: *Jus Cogens* and International Economic Law', *Netherlands Yearbook of International Law 2015* (The Hague: TMC Asser Press, 2016), pp. 329–56, at pp. 330–1); Maurizio Ragazzi has expressed a similar view: 'obscurities still surround the concept of jus cogens' (M. Ragazzi, *The Concept of International Obligations erga omnes* (Oxford: Clarendon Press, 1997)); Christian J. Tams has acknowledged the existence of different views on the concept of obligations *erga omnes* (C. J. Tams, *Enforcing Obligations 'erga omnes' in International Law* (Cambridge: Cambridge University Press, 2005)).

[16] 'In terms of enforcement and compliance, it [*jus cogens*] has remained an idealist construct' (Cottier, *supra* n. 15 at 331); Christian J. Tams has concluded that 'It must be conceded that there is at present no universal support for a provision expressly enshrining a right to take countermeasures in response to serious erga omnes breaches' (*supra* n. 15 at 311).

imposing 'targeted sanctions' against human rights perpetrators responsible for human rights violations abroad.[17]

The next part of this chapter discusses state practice in applying such restrictive measures.

5.2.2 Coercive Economic Measures to Induce Compliance with Human Rights

States routinely employ unilateral measures to enforce public international law.[18] In the last decades, coercive economic measures have been used more frequently than before.[19] This tendency can be explained by a number of reasons. W. Michael Reisman argues that economic coercion is 'politically cheap' and this explains its substantially increased deployment.[20] According to him, society is more willing to accept economic than a military intervention in the affairs of other states and domestic costs of such economic intervention are hardly noticeable, except for the industries that bear these costs.[21] Another possible

---

[17] The Magnitsky Bill was initially introduced by the United States in 2012 (the Magnitsky Rule of Law Accountability Act 2012) and targeted only Russian officials, in 2016 the Global Magnitsky Human Rights Accountability Act was enacted, which is an expansion of the original act and applies globally. In 2017 Canada passed Justice for Victims of Corrupt Foreign Officials Act (Sergei Magnitsky Law) with the objective 'to provide for the taking of restrictive measures in respect of foreign nationals responsible for gross violations of internationally recognized human rights'. The UK government passed the Criminal Finances Act 2017 (Commencement No. 4) Regulations 2018 (SI 2018/78), which, among other things, brings section 13 of the Criminal Finances Act 2017 into force on 31 Jan. 2018. Section 13 deals with the UK's 'Magnitsky-style' sanctions provisions by expanding the definition of 'unlawful conduct' under Part 5 of the Proceeds of Crime Act 2002 (POCA) to include conduct (occurring outside of the UK) which 'constitutes, or is connected with, the commission of a gross human rights abuse or violation'. Estonia adopted similar sanctions by amending its Obligation to Leave and Prohibition on Entry Act. Lithuania introduced Magnitsky sanctions by amending the Law on the Legal Status of Aliens.

[18] Part II of the article provides a literature review on the unilateral coercive measure, their lawfulness, and their role in international law. M. Hakimi, 'Unfriendly Unilateralism', *Harvard International Law Journal*, 55 (2014), 105.

[19] G. C. Hufbauer, *Economic Sanctions Reconsidered* (3rd ed., Washington, DC: Peterson Institute for International Economics, 2007).

[20] W. M. Reisman, 'Sanctions and International Law', *Intercultural Human Rights Law Review*, 4 (2009), 13.

[21] Ibid.

RESHAPING THE LAW OF ECONOMIC SANCTIONS 253

explanation is the complete prohibition on the use of force enshrined in the UN Charter,[22] and as a result the increased significance of the alternatives.

Historically, the United States heavily relied upon the instruments of economic pressure for achieving its foreign policy objectives.[23] According to some estimates, the United States implemented five times more unilateral sanctions than the United Nations adopted multilateral sanctions since the end of the Second World War.[24] More recently the European Union has also been increasingly using these instruments. According to a study, the European Union accounts for 36 per cent of coercive economic measures worldwide since 1980.[25] Other states also engage in efforts to pursue their foreign policy objectives by counting on coercive economic measures. In 2017 Qatar was subjected to economic pressure exercised by Saudi Arabia, the United Arab Emirates, Bahrain, and Egypt.[26] Despite the fact that the Russian Federation questions the legality of unilateral coercive economic measures,[27] it repeatedly relied upon these measures to advance its political agenda in the neighbouring countries.[28]

Economic coercion may pursue many various goals, including remedying instances of grave human rights violations abroad. For instance, the Office of Foreign Assets Control, the US agency that administers and enforces economic and trade sanctions, currently administers nineteen

---

[22] Art. 2, United Nations, Charter of the United Nations, 24 Oct. 1945, 1 UNTS XVI.

[23] The database compiled by Hufbauer, Schott, and Elliot and used in their analysis of the sanctions' effectiveness covers more than 200 sanctions episodes imposed between 1914 and 2000 and according to it, the United States is the most frequent user of economic coercive measures. Hufbauer, *supra* n. 19.

[24] S. Egle, 'The Learning Curve of Sanctions – Have Three Decades of Sanctions Reform Taught Us Anything?', *Currents – International Trade Law Journal*, 19 (2010), 34–50.

[25] C. Portela, 'Targeted Sanctions against Individuals on Grounds of Grave Human Rights Violations – Impact, Trends and Prospects at EU Level' (2018).

[26] D. D. Roberts, 'Qatar row: What's caused the fall-out between Gulf neighbours?', BBC News, www.bbc.com/news/world-middle-east-40159080 (2017); S. Atkinson, 'Qatar Row: Economic Impact Threatens Food, Flights and Football', BBC News, www.bbc.com/news/business-40156029 (2017).

[27] For a detailed overview of the Russian arguments in this regard, see M. Doraev, 'The "Memory Effect" of Economic Sanctions against Russia: Opposing Approaches to the Legality of Unilateral Sanctions Clash Again', *University of Pennsylvania Journal of International Law*, 37 (2015), 355.

[28] Mergen Doraev summarized the unilateral sanctions imposed by the Russian Federation against neighbouring states in 2000–2014 (*supra* n. 27).

country-specific sanctions programmes, twelve of which pursue the objective of remedying human rights violations abroad.[29] The European Union's active engagement in human rights protection has resulted in forty-two ongoing sanctions regimes, among which thirty-two are unilateral coercive measures (not authorized by the UNSC) and more than a half of these restrictive measures are imposed on human rights grounds.[30] Furthermore, the European Union encourages other states to introduce similar restrictive measures against the states engaged in appalling human rights violations.

This state practice poses a challenging question: what instigates states to remedy human rights violations occurring abroad? Eric Posner in his sharply critical book *The Twilight of Human Rights Law* raises a similar question: why would democracies care about how foreign governments treat their foreign populations? In answering his own question, Posner has drawn inferences from the two possible hypotheses explaining such an outcome.[31]

The first hypothesis emanates from the belief that liberal democracies are the societies that care about the well-being of both foreigners and their own citizens.[32] The research conducted by political scientists has reassured that demands of the electorate can influence policymakers to respond to grave human rights violations taking place elsewhere in the world.[33] For example, scholars have demonstrated a positive correlation between the coverage of human suffering in the US media and a government's response in the form of economic sanctions.[34]

---

[29] This calculation is made based on the information about sanctions programs available at the official website of the Office of Foreign Assets Control, accessed at: www.treasury.gov/resource-center/sanctions/Programs/Pages/Programs.aspx, the objectives of each country-specific sanctions program were reviewed based on the presidential executive orders by which each program was established. In twelve instances the presidential executive orders explicitly mentioned 'human rights' as one of the objectives of the sanctions program.

[30] Information about the European Union restrictive measures is available at: http://ec.europa.eu/dgs/fpi/documents/Restrictive_measures-2017-08-04-clean_en.pdf

[31] Posner, *supra* n. 8, at 60–1.

[32] Ibid.

[33] T. Whang, 'Playing to the Home Crowd? Symbolic Use of Economic Sanctions in the United States', *International Studies Quarterly*, 55 (2011), 787–801; E. V. McLean and T. Whang, 'Designing Foreign Policy: Voters, Special Interest Groups, and Economic Sanctions', *Journal of Peace Research*, 51 (2014), 589–602; S. Chan, 'Principle versus Profit: Debating Human Rights Sanctions', *Human Rights Review*, 19 (2018), 45–71.

[34] D. Peksen, T. M. Peterson, and A. C. Drury, 'Media-driven Humanitarianism? News Media Coverage of Human Rights Abuses and the Use of Economic Sanctions',

The second explanation is more rational-based and is centred on the idea that the regimes that violate human rights are prone to cause other distresses as well. Posner observed that these regimes 'quarrel with their neighbours, drive refugees into foreign countries, export revolution, battle with insurgents who cross border in order to regroup, shelter terrorists, and collapse into civil war'.[35] As a matter of fact, numerous historical examples attest to the accuracy of this assumption.

5.3 Human Rights Economic Sanctions and Public International Law

The abundance of state practice in applying unilateral economic sanctions might lead us astray and give an illusion that their application is well regulated by the disciplines of public international law. This part of the chapter is aimed at dispelling this illusion.

First and foremost, the definition of unilateral economic sanctions evades precision. More specifically, there is a number of legal categories in public international law that cover certain unilateral economic sanctions, but not all of them. These legal categories are: retorsions, reprisals, countermeasures, third-party countermeasures, and sanctions (implying UN-authorized sanctions).[36] Unilateral economic sanctions imposed on human rights grounds do not fall squarely within one legal category.

The majority of unilateral human rights sanctions can be defined either as retorsions[37] or third-party countermeasures.[38] The reason behind the impossibility of defining human rights economic sanctions as countermeasures has been well captured by James Crawford: 'Human

---

International Studies Quarterly, 58 (2014), 855–66. Similar views have been expressed by legal scholars: for example, Sarabeth Egle has noted that 'the growth of media outlets and technology has led to an increased public knowledge of foreign policy. This attenuation to news has forced politicians to turn toward sanctions in order to appease public demand for a U.S. response' (*supra* n. 24).

[35] Posner, *supra* n. 8, at 61.

[36] For more, see T. Ruys, 'Sanctions, Retorsions and Countermeasures: Concepts and International Legal Framework', in *Research Handbook on UN Sanctions and International Law* (Cheltenham, UK: Edward Elgar, 2017), pp. 19–51.

[37] We rely upon the following definition of retorsion: 'acts which are wrongful not in the legal but only in the political or moral sense, or a simple discourtesy' (Thomas Giegerich, 'Retorsion', in *Max Planck Encyclopedia of Public International Law* (2011), https://opil .ouplaw.com/view/10.1093/law:epil/9780199231690/law-9780199231690-e983 (accessed 3 Oct. 2019)).

[38] Third-party countermeasures (solidarity measures) are countermeasures imposed by a non-injured state or a group of states.

rights obligations are not, in the first instance at least, owed to particular states, and it is accordingly difficult to see how a human rights obligation could itself be the subject of legitimate countermeasures.'[39]

Withdrawal of humanitarian aid is a classic example of retorsion. Import or export restrictions on goods or services targeting the state that is responsible for gross human rights violations exemplify conventional third-party countermeasures. While retorsions do not raise any questions regarding their legality, it is not the case with third-party countermeasures. Indeed, the legality of the third-party countermeasures was debated at length within the international community.[40]

In light of the above, unilateral economic sanctions imposed on human rights grounds are particularly vulnerable to a legal challenge. Thus, below we attempt to forge a path through the thicket that has grown around this area and outline the main legal challenges for unilateral human rights sanctions.

5.3.1 Human Rights Economic Sanctions and the Charter of the United Nations (UN Charter)

Since the early 1970s, the United Nations has become a battlefield for the supporters of unilateral economic sanctions and their opponents. This legal debate was a mere reflection of the political rift between the Western democracies and the communist bloc states backed up by the developing countries, mainly former colonies. The latter group of states opposed the idea that states can rely upon the measures of economic coercion irrespective of the motives for such measures. As the recent research by Alexandra Hofer demonstrates half a century later this sharp divide has not been settled.[41]

In a nutshell, the opponents of the unilateral economic sanctions advance two principal arguments. The first of them is that the use of economic coercion, channelled through the unilateral economic

---

[39] J. Crawford, *State Responsibility: The General Part* (Cambridge: Cambridge University Press, 2013), p. 692.

[40] For more details, see E. Katselli Proukaki, *The Problem of Enforcement in International Law: Countermeasures, the Non-Injured State and the Idea of International Community* (paperback ed., New York: Routledge, 2011); M. Dawidowicz, *Third-Party Countermeasures in International Law* (Cambridge: Cambridge University Press, 2017).

[41] A. Hofer, 'The Developed/Developing Divide on Unilateral Coercive Measures: Legitimate Enforcement or Illegitimate Intervention?', *Chinese Journal of International Law*, 16 (2017), 175–214.

sanctions, violates the prohibition on the use of force enshrined in Article 2(4) of the UN Charter.[42] The second argument is that economic coercion encroaches on the principle of non-intervention, which is embedded in the UN Charter.[43] Each of these arguments deserves more detailed consideration.

The term 'force' is not defined in the UN Charter. Notwithstanding this, the historical context provides evidence that the prohibition on the use of force should be narrowly defined.[44] Furthermore, the interpretations developed by the ICJ in the Nicaragua dispute buttress this conclusion.[45] Overall, the balance seems to tilt in favour of a narrow definition and as Krista Schefer has accurately pointed out: 'it is unlikely that anything less than an armed blockade will be deemed to reach the severity of a "use of force" deserving condemnation under Article 2(4) (and even that is likely to depend on the military enforcement of the blockade than the economic effects of it)'.[46]

The second argument that economic coercion encroaches on the principle of non-intervention seems more plausible, yet it is still subject to controversy. To start with, Maziar Jamnejad and Michael Wood vividly described the principle of non-intervention as: 'One of the most potent and elusive of all international principles'.[47] That is to say, the exact contours of the principle have not been determined with great precision in the UN Charter. Against this backdrop, the literature has abounded in claims when economic coercion impedes the principle of non-intervention.[48] Despite this scholarly attention, the relations between unilateral economic sanctions and the principle of non-intervention

---

[42] James Delanis, writing on the subject after the notorious Arab oil embargo, provided a comprehensive summary of the legal claims advanced by both sides of the debate (J. A. Delanis, '"Force" under Article 2(4) of the United Nations Charter: The Question of Economic and Political Coercion', *Vanderbilt Journal of Transnational Law* 12 (1979), 103–14).

[43] A. Tzanakopoulos, 'The Right to Be Free from Economic Coercion', *Cambridge International Law Journal*, 4 (2015), 616–33.

[44] The Brazilian proposal to include economic coercion in the definition of 'force' in Article 2(4) of the UN Charter was explicitly denied.

[45] *Military and Paramilitary Activities in and against Nicaragua (Nicaragua v. United States of America)*. Merits, Judgment, ICJ Reports, 1986, p. 14.

[46] K. Nadakavukaren Schefer, *Social Regulation in the WTO: Trade Policy and International Legal Development* (Cheltenham, UK: Edward Elgar, 2010) p. 39.

[47] M. Jamnejad and M. Wood, 'The Principle of Non-intervention', *Leiden Journal of International Law*, 22 (2009), 345–81.

[48] Y. Z. Blum, 'Economic Boycotts in International Law', *Texas International Law Journal*, 12 (1977), 5; O. Y. Elagab, *The Legality of Non-Forcible Counter-Measures in*

remain undefined. In this regard, Tom Ruys succinctly concluded: 'In the end, it remains altogether unclear to what exact extent the principle of non-intervention prohibits certain economic sanctions.'[49]

Against this background, we must admit that unilateral economic sanctions imposed on human rights grounds are not exempted from the aforesaid legal challenges.

5.3.2 Human Rights Economic Sanctions and the Draft Articles on Responsibility of States for Internationally Wrongful Acts (Draft Articles)

As has been discussed, unilateral economic sanctions imposed on human rights grounds face a significant risk of being recognized as third-party countermeasures, the legal status of which is ambiguous.

The abundance of the relevant state practice in applying third-party countermeasures encouraged some legal scholars to question the conclusions of the ILC embedded in the Draft Articles.[50] Martin Dawidowicz in his numerous publications on the subject has argued that third-party countermeasures are permitted as a matter of customary international law and that the abundance of the pertinent state practice is supported by the required *opinio juris*.[51] Criticizing the Draft Articles for the lack of legal certainty with respect to third-party countermeasures, Andreas Paulus argued that: 'if countermeasures are permitted in cases of simple breach of a bilateral obligation, it is

---

International Law (Oxford: Clarendon Press, 1988); Tzanakopoulos, *supra* n. 43; Hofer, *supra* n. 41.

[49] Ruys, *supra* n. 36.

[50] The right to impose countermeasures by a non-injured state is not explicitly embedded in the text of the Draft Articles on Responsibility of States for International Wrongful Acts. The commentary to the Draft Articles explains this outcome by the following: 'Occasions have arisen in practice of countermeasures being taken by other States, in particular those identified in article 48, where no State is injured or else on behalf of and at the request of an injured State. Such cases are controversial and the practice is embryonic' (International Law Commission, Draft Articles on Responsibility of States for Internationally Wrongful Acts, Nov. 2001, Supplement No. 10 (A/56/10), chp.IV.E.1). This conclusion has been questioned by a number of legal scholars.

[51] M. Dawidowicz, 'Public Law Enforcement without Public Law Safeguards? An Analysis of State Practice on Third-party Countermeasures and Their Relationship to the UN Security Council', *British Yearbook of International Law*, 77 (2007), 333–418; M. Dawidowicz, 'Third-Party Countermeasures: A Progressive Development of International Law?', *Questions of International Law* 29 (2016), 3–15; Dawidowicz, *supra* n. 40.

inconceivable to provide a lower threshold of protection to those obligations considered erga omnes or even jus cogens'.[52] Christian Hillgruber goes much further and argues that the inefficiency of the enforcement mechanisms embedded in the human rights treaties implies that the states implicitly agreed to rely upon third-party countermeasures.[53]

While various objections against acknowledging the legality of the third-party countermeasures, at least in instances of grave human rights violations, are becoming difficult to sustain, the legal status of such countermeasures is far from being settled.

5.3.3 Human Rights Economic Sanctions and Immunities in International Law

The negative impact on civilian populations of the targeted states has undermined the legitimacy of comprehensive economic sanctions.[54] Therefore 'smart' or 'targeted' sanctions – sanctions directed against named individuals, groups, or entities – have replaced comprehensive measures.

One example of note is the restrictive measures against the Central Bank of Syria imposed by the European Union.[55] These measures were imposed as economic sanctions and pursued policies related to human rights protection. The EU relied upon them to protect human rights of the civilian population, who are victims of the war in Syria.

It is a well-settled principle in public international law that states and their constituencies benefit from the special set of rules – immunities, which emanate from customary international law. In this regard, one

---

[52] A. Paulus, 'Whether Universal Values Can Prevail over Bilateralism and Reciprocity', in Antonio Cassese (ed.), *Realizing Utopia: The Future of International Law* (Oxford: Oxford University Press, 2012), p. 101.

[53] C. Hillgruber, 'Chapter XII. The Right of Third States to Take Countermeasures', in Christian Tomuschat and Jean-Marc Thouvenin (eds.), *The Fundamental Rules of the International Legal Order* (Leiden: Brill–Nijhoff, 2006), pp. 265–93, at pp. 273–8.

[54] An example that was extensively discussed is comprehensive economic sanctions against Iraq established pursuant to the Security Council's Resolution 661 (1990). 'No one knows with any precision how many Iraqi civilians have died as a result, but various agencies of the United Nations, which oversees the sanctions, have estimated that they have contributed to hundreds of thousands of deaths' (J. Mueller and K. Mueller, 'Sanctions of Mass Destruction', *Foreign Affairs*, 78 (1999), 43–53).

[55] Council Regulation (EU) No. 168/2012 of 27 Feb. 2012 amending Regulation (EU) No. 36/2012 concerning restrictive measures in view of the situation in Syria, OJ 28 Feb. 2012, L-51/1.

should be aware that the immunity of states has to be carefully distinguished from diplomatic immunity or the immunity of a head of a state.[56] For our subsequent analysis, we rely upon the subset of rules, which constitute immunity entitlements of states. Immunity of states entails jurisdictional immunity as well as enforcement immunity.[57]

The analysis of whether states are prohibited from freezing the assets of the central banks of the other states or imposing other types of economic restrictions requires further discussion. At the outset, we discuss whether central banks are entitled to the protection guaranteed under state immunity.

It is debatable whether central banks belong to those domestic constituencies that are entitled to the protection granted under the state immunity. In this regard, Peter-Tobias Stoll has pointed out: 'the protection of the property of central banks from execution appears to be stronger than that afforded to other entities'.[58] In a similar vein, Jean-Marc Thouvenin and Victor Grandaubert argue in favour of such protection.[59] To the contrary, Ingrid Wuerth has noted: 'During the middle of the 20th century, central banks became more independent from the state, making it more difficult to characterize central banks as foreign states or other entities entitled to immunity.'[60]

Notwithstanding the status of the central banks, we claim that the protection from economic sanctions under the state immunity is highly problematic. In this regard, we tend to agree with the view expressed by Tom Ruys. The crux of his argument is that the immunity rules apply in the course of court proceedings, yet the majority of economic sanctions (e.g. in the form of asset freezes) are measures imposed by the executive branch and thus, as a rule, such measures could not violate the state immunity.[61]

---

[56] P.-T. Stoll, 'State Immunity', in *Max Planck Encyclopedia of Public International Law* (2011), https://opil.ouplaw.com/view/10.1093/law:epil/9780199231690/law-9780199231690-e1106 (accessed 3 Oct. 2019).

[57] Ibid.

[58] Ibid.

[59] J.-M. Thouvenin and V. Grandaubert, 'The Material Scope of State Immunity from Execution', in Tom Ruys and Nicolas Angelet (eds.), *The Cambridge Handbook of Immunities and International Law* (Cambridge: Cambridge University Press, 2019), pp. 245–65.

[60] I. Wuerth, 'Immunity from Execution of Central Bank Assets', ibid., p. 269.

[61] T. Ruys, 'Immunity, Inviolability and Countermeasures – A Closer Look at Non-UN Targeted Sanctions', ibid., pp. 670–710.

RESHAPING THE LAW OF ECONOMIC SANCTIONS   261

To conclude this section, it has to be acknowledged that the legality of unilateral economic sanctions under public international law remains unsettled.

5.4   Human Rights Economic Sanctions and WTO Law

Coercive economic measures imposed on human rights grounds face a significant risk of being WTO-inconsistent. Notably, the WTO dispute settlement system permits imposition of retaliatory measures in instances of non-compliance with the undertaken obligations.[62] Such a strong enforcement mechanism provides incentives for the WTO members to comply with their commitments.

Below we discuss whether WTO commitments might be infringed by human rights economic sanctions and whether under WTO law such measures might be justified. For the purposes of this chapter, we analyse the possibility of justifying such measures under the public morals exception and the national security exception.[63] The analytical framework for further analysis is based on the text of the relevant exceptions as well as the existing jurisprudence and the treaty interpretation practices of the WTO adjudicators.

The discussion of the potential conflicts between international human rights law and WTO law is intentionally avoided. The rationale behind this decision is that the core international human rights treaties do not authorize states to remedy human rights violations by coercive economic measures,[64] hence there is no explicit conflict between these treaties and WTO law.

---

[62] This right is conditional and the necessary preconditions are prescribed in Article 22, DSU, Dispute Settlement Rules: Understanding on Rules and Procedures Governing the Settlement of Disputes, Marrakesh Agreement Establishing the World Trade Organization, Annex 2, 1869 UNTS 401, 33 ILM 1226 (1994).

[63] The analysis focuses on the possibility to justify coercive economic measures imposed on human rights grounds based on the exception clauses of the GATT 1994 and the GATS. Both agreements stipulate the public morals exception and the security exception. Article XX(a) of the GATT 1994 and Article XIV(a) of the GATS prescribe the public morals exception. Article XXI of the GATT 1994 and Article XIV *bis* of the GATS prescribe the security exception.

[64] 'none of the major human rights treaties mandate the imposition of unilateral trade sanctions to advance their goals' (S. H. Cleveland, 'Human Rights Sanctions and International Trade: A Theory of Compatibility', *Journal of International Economic Law*, 5 (2002), 133, at 153).

5.4.1 Human Rights Economic Sanctions and Their Potential Inconsistency with WTO Law

Frequently coercive economic measures take the form of import or export restrictions on goods and/or services originated in or destined for a targeted state. Sarah Cleveland classifies such measures into the following categories: 'tailored', 'semi-tailored', and 'general' sanctions depending on the relation between a particular trade-restrictive measure and human rights violations.[65] In this chapter, we focus on 'general' sanctions – sanctions that target economic sectors unrelated to human rights violations, which according to Cleveland are 'the most common form of human rights trade measures'.[66]

5.4.1.1 Import Restrictions on Goods

Complete or partial import bans are frequently used to put an end to massive atrocities and to induce compliance with human rights law. Complete import ban imposed on human rights grounds can be formulated such as that imposed by the United States against the Sudanese government: 'The following are prohibited ... (a) the importation into the United States of any goods or services of Sudanese origin, other than information or informational materials'.[67] Partial import restrictions, as a rule, impact commodities, goods or services that are of paramount importance for a certain state. For instance, the United States in the furtherance of the sanctions against the Syrian government introduced the following partial import ban: 'The following are prohibited ... (c) the importation into the United States of petroleum or petroleum products of Syrian origin'.[68]

Import restrictions on goods fall foul of the most-favoured-nation obligation enshrined in Article I:1 of the GATT 1994.[69] Furthermore,

---

[65] Cleveland uses the term 'unilateral human rights sanctions' (*supra* n. 64).

[66] Ibid., at 142.

[67] The President, Executive Order 13067, 5 Nov. 1997, Blocking Sudanese Government Property and Prohibiting Transactions with Sudan.

[68] The President, Executive Order 13582, 17 Aug. 2011, Blocking Property of the Government of Syria and Prohibiting Certain Transactions with Respect to Syria.

[69] Article I:1 reads as follows: 'With respect to customs duties and charges of any kind imposed on or in connection with importation or exportation or imposed on the international transfer of payments for imports or exports, and with respect to the method of levying such duties and charges, and with respect to all rules and formalities in connection with importation and exportation, and with respect to all matters referred to in paragraphs 2 and 4 of Article III,* any advantage, favour, privilege or immunity

RESHAPING THE LAW OF ECONOMIC SANCTIONS   263

according to the well-established WTO jurisprudence complete or partial import bans are incompatible with Article XI:1 of the GATT 1994.[70]

5.4.1.2   Export Restrictions on Goods

States routinely introduce human rights export restrictions such as complete or partial prohibitions on the export of weapons, technology, or strategic goods.[71] A historical example worth noting is the US embargo on aeroplanes and aviation gasoline destined for the countries that were engaged in bombing civilians.[72]

The WTO adjudicators have interpreted Article XI:1 as broadly as to encompass a wide range of measures[73] and therefore export bans that

---

granted by any contracting party to any product originating in or destined for any other country shall be accorded immediately and unconditionally to the like product originating in or destined for the territories of all other contracting parties.'

[70] Article XI:1 reads as follows: 'No prohibitions or restrictions other than duties, taxes or other charges, whether made effective through quotas, import or export licences or other measures, shall be instituted or maintained by any contracting party on the importation of any product of the territory of any other contracting party or on the exportation or sale for export of any product destined for the territory of any other contracting party.' The Panel in *Canada – Periodicals* pronounced that 'since the importation of certain foreign products into Canada is completely denied under Tariff Code 9958, it appears that this provision by its terms is inconsistent with Article XI:1 of GATT 1994.' This conclusion was not appealed. Panel Report, *Canada – Certain Measures Concerning Periodicals*, WT/DS31/R and Corr.1, adopted 30 July 1997, as modified by Appellate Body Report WT/DS31/AB/R, DSR 1997:I, p. 481 para. 5.5; the Panel in *Brazil – Retreaded Tyres* noted: 'There is no ambiguity as to what "prohibitions" on importation means: Members shall not forbid the importation of any product of any other Member into their markets.' Panel Report, *Brazil – Measures Affecting Imports of Retreaded Tyres*, WT/DS332/R, adopted 17 Dec. 2007, as modified by Appellate Body Report WT/DS332/AB/R, DSR 2007:V, p. 1649 para. 7.11.

[71] For instance, the prohibition on the export of certain goods to Syria. President Executive Order 13338, 11 May 2004, Blocking Property of Certain Persons and Prohibiting the Export of Certain Goods to Syria.

[72] S. Charnovitz, 'The Moral Exception in Trade Policy', *Virginia Journal of International Law*, 38 (1998), 689, at 715.

[73] Panel Report, *India – Quantitative Restrictions on Imports of Agricultural, Textile and Industrial Products*, WT/DS90/R, adopted 22 Sept. 1999, upheld by Appellate Body Report WT/DS90/AB/R, DSR 1999:V, p. 1799, para. 5.128; Panel Report, *India – Measures Affecting the Automotive Sector*, WT/DS146/R, WT/DS175/R, and Corr.1, adopted 5 Apr. 2002, DSR 2002:V, p. 1827, para. 7.265; Panel Report, *Colombia – Indicative Prices and Restrictions on Ports of Entry*, WT/DS366/R and Corr.1, adopted 20 May 2009, DSR 2009:VI, p. 2535, para. 7.240; Panel Reports, *China – Measures Related to the Exportation of Various Raw Materials*, WT/DS394/R, Add.1 and Corr.1/WT/DS395/R, Add.1 and Corr.1/WT/DS398/R, Add.1 and Corr.1, adopted 22 Feb. 2012, as modified by Appellate Body Reports WT/DS394/AB/R/WT/DS395/AB/R/WT/DS398/AB/R, DSR 2012:VII, p. 3501, para. 7.1081.

264   IRYNA BOGDANOVA

constitute quantitative restrictions violate Article XI:1 of the GATT 1994. Moreover, they violate Article I:1.

5.4.1.3   Import Restrictions on Services

Restrictive measures imposed on human rights grounds may prevent domestic constituencies from receiving services from foreign services suppliers or prohibit foreign services suppliers from establishing their branches inside the country.

These restrictions discriminate between services and services suppliers based on their origin and thus might potentially benefit from the presumption of 'likeness' that has been developed in the WTO jurisprudence.[74] Such measures, as a matter of principle, violate Article II:1 of the GATS (MFN treatment), if a WTO member undertook commitments in a particular services sector and mode of supply and then introduced origin-based import restrictions that impede its commitments.[75] Furthermore, they might potentially infringe Article XVI:1 of the GATS, if a WTO member imposing them has inscribed the relevant commitments in its schedule.[76]

---

[74] The Appellate Body has stated the following: 'In our view, where a measure provides for a distinction based exclusively on origin, there will or can be services and service suppliers that are the same in all respects except for origin and, accordingly, "likeness" can be presumed and the complainant is not required to establish "likeness" on the basis of the relevant criteria set out above. Accordingly, we consider that, under Articles II:1 and XVII:1 of the GATS, a complainant is not required in all cases to establish "likeness" of services and service suppliers on the basis of the relevant criteria for establishing "likeness". Rather, in principle, a complainant may establish "likeness" by demonstrating that the measure at issue makes a distinction between services and service suppliers based exclusively on origin.' Appellate Body Report, *Argentina – Measures Relating to Trade in Goods and Services*, WT/DS453/AB/R and Add.1, adopted 9 May 2016, DSR 2016:II, p. 431, para. 6.38; Panel Report, *European Union and Its Member States – Certain Measures relating to the Energy Sector*, WT/DS476/R and Add.1, circulated to WTO members, 10 Aug. 2018, para. 7.741.

[75] Article II:1 reads as follows: 'With respect to any measure covered by this Agreement, each Member shall accord immediately and unconditionally to services and service suppliers of any other Member treatment no less favourable than that it accords to like services and service suppliers of any other country.'

[76] Article XVI reads as follows: 'With respect to market access through the modes of supply identified in Article I, each Member shall accord services and service suppliers of any other Member treatment no less favourable than that provided for under the terms, limitations and conditions agreed and specified in its Schedule.'

RESHAPING THE LAW OF ECONOMIC SANCTIONS 265

5.4.1.4 Export Restrictions on Services

Restrictive measures may include prohibitions on the provision of services to citizens or legal entities from a targeted state or even prohibitions on the provision of services to any entity that is/was in business relations with the targeted individuals or entities (secondary sanctions).[77]

These export restrictions might be WTO consistent. The discussion of this conclusion is warranted here. At the outset, we must emphasize that the GATS does not prescribe a general prohibition on quantitative restrictions similar to Article XI of the GATT. Furthermore, export restrictions on services fall outside the scope of the GATS most-favoured-nation obligation. Finally, the market access commitments do not prevent WTO members from relying upon export restrictions on services. In this regard, Rudolf Adlung has accurately pointed out: 'Members remain free to impose export restrictions (a) on their own services or service suppliers – even in the event of full commitments under Article XVI – as well as (b) on any services or service suppliers, whether foreign or national, in sectors not subject to specific commitments.'[78] However, this conclusion must be qualified in the following way: a WTO member might prohibit the export of services from its territory, yet such prohibition cannot apply to a foreign legal entity established under its laws.[79] To put it differently, such prohibition shall not impede the right to the commercial presence (mode 3) if the relevant commitments were made.

5.4.2 Possible Justifications for Inconsistent Human Rights Economic Sanctions

5.4.2.1 Justification under the Public Morals Exception

The public morals exception reads as follows: 'Subject to the requirement that such measures are not applied in a manner which would constitute a

---

[77] For more on the secondary sanctions and the debate on their legality, see J. A. Meyer, 'Second Thoughts on Secondary Sanctions', *University of Pennsylvania Journal of International Law*, 30 (2009), 905.

[78] R. Adlung, 'Export Policies and the General Agreement on Trade in Services', *Journal of International Economic Law*, 18 (2015), 487–510, at 498.

[79] This conclusion was reached by the Panels in the following disputes: Panel Report, *Mexico – Measures Affecting Telecommunications Services*, WT/DS204/R, adopted 1 June 2004, DSR 2004:IV, p. 1537, para. 7.375; Panel Report, *China – Certain Measures Affecting Electronic Payment Services*, WT/DS413/R and Add.1, adopted 31 Aug. 2012, DSR 2012:X, p. 5305, para. 7.618.

means of arbitrary or unjustifiable discrimination between countries where the same conditions prevail, or a disguised restriction on international trade, nothing in this Agreement shall be construed to prevent the adoption or enforcement by any contracting party of measures: (a) necessary to protect public morals.'[80]

According to the well-established WTO jurisprudence, a WTO-inconsistent measure can be justified if such measure falls under one of the listed exceptions and meets the requirements of the *chapeau*. Thus, our analysis proceeds in the following way. At the outset, the definition of 'public morals' is provided. Subsequently, the prerequisites required for a measure to be 'necessary to protect public morals' are enumerated and the possibility of human rights economic sanctions to comply with these prerequisites is discussed. Finally, the requirements of the *chapeau* and compliance with these requirements are examined.

Before we proceed with the analysis, the question of whether the public morals exception can be relied upon to justify outwardly directed measures calls for further clarification.[81] The wording of the exception and the WTO jurisprudence do not provide a straightforward answer. The WTO tribunals examined the public morals clause in a number of disputes, such as *US–Gambling* and *China–Publications and Audiovisual Products*, and the regulations scrutinized in those disputes intended to protect morals of persons residing inside the state that introduced them. To the contrary, in *EC–Seal Products* the challenged measure also impacted the protection of animal welfare outside the European Union. In this dispute, parties agreed that there was a 'sufficient nexus' between the import ban, the public moral concerns, and the activities addressed by the measure and thus the AB did not elaborate on the issue.[82]

In spite of the apparent significance of the question at hand, we argue that similarly to the import ban in *EC–Seal Products* unilateral economic

---

[80] Article XX(a) of the GATT 1994 and Article XIV(a) of the GATS prescribe the public morals exception.

[81] Definitions of inwardly directed and outwardly directed trade measures are arbitrary and imprecise. For instance, Steve Charnovitz framed these definitions in the following way: 'This Article will employ the term "outwardly-directed" in order to describe trade measures used to protect the morals of foreigners residing outside one's own country. Conversely, trade measures used to protect morals of persons in one's own country will be described as "inwardly-directed"' (*supra* n. 72, at 695–6).

[82] Appellate Body Reports, *European Communities – Measures Prohibiting the Importation and Marketing of Seal Products*, WT/DS400/AB/R/WT/DS401/AB/R, adopted 18 June 2014, DSR 2014:I, p. 7, para. 5.173.

RESHAPING THE LAW OF ECONOMIC SANCTIONS   267

measures imposed on human rights grounds might be implemented to protect public morals of a WTO member that imposes such restrictive measures.

The Definition of 'Public Morals'

Standard Developed by the WTO Tribunals   The majority of bilateral trade agreements signed after 1927 incorporated public morals exception, which was commonly drafted as 'prohibitions or restrictions imposed on moral or humanitarian grounds'.[83] Hence it is not a coincidence that the public morals exception was incorporated in the GATT 1947. Discussing the negotiating history, Steve Charnovitz provides numerous examples of state practice,[84] and acknowledges: 'the moral exception was a response to the fact that many governments were banning imports and exports for moral or humanitarian reasons'.[85]

The negotiating history sheds little light on the meaning of the ambiguous term 'public morals'.[86] In order to offset this deficiency and strike a balance between the members' trade and moral interests, the WTO adjudicators adopted an all-embracing and amorphous definition of 'public morals'. The Panel in *US–Gambling* asserted that 'the term "public morals" denotes standards of right and wrong conduct maintained by or on behalf of a community or nation'.[87] Furthermore, the Panel observed that various factors may be taken into consideration when the exact scope of 'public morals' is defined. In other words, the notion of public morals 'can vary in time and space, depending upon a range of factors, including prevailing social, cultural, ethical and religious values'.[88]

The Panel recognized the member's right to determine 'public morals' within its territory. It was noted that: 'Members should be given some scope to define and apply for themselves the concepts of "public morals"

---

[83] Charnovitz, *supra* n. 72, at 708–9.

[84] The examples include anti-slavery treaties, the narcotics regime, international regime regulating trade in liquor, and regime regulating traffic in obscene publications (ibid., at 710–16).

[85] Ibid., at 710.

[86] Charnovitz, *supra* n. 72; M. Wu, 'Free Trade and the Protection of Public Morals: An Analysis of the Newly Emerging Public Morals Clause Doctrine', *Yale Journal of International Law*, 33 (2008), 215.

[87] Panel Report, *United States – Measures Affecting the Cross-Border Supply of Gambling and Betting Services*, WT/DS285/R, adopted 20 Apr. 2005, as modified by Appellate Body Report WT/DS285/AB/R, DSR 2005:XII, p. 5797, para. 6.465.

[88] Ibid., at para. 6.461.

and "public order" in their respective territories, according to their own systems and scales of values'.[89] This approach has been further reiterated in *EC–Seal Products*, when the AB in response to Canada's argument that similar moral concerns should be addressed in the same way, pronounced that: 'Members may set different levels of protection even when responding to similar interests of moral concern'.[90] The WTO tribunals sustained these conclusions in the subsequent jurisprudence.[91]

Whether the Objectives Pursued by Human Rights Economic Sanctions Might Constitute 'Public Morals'? The member that invokes the public morals exception is obliged to prove that a challenged measure was introduced to address prevailing 'public morals'. To prove this, a WTO member can demonstrate that the objective of a challenged measure reflects 'standards of right and wrong conduct' in a particular society and that a challenged measure is, in fact, implemented to achieve such 'public morals' objective.

A WTO member can demonstrate that its domestic legal system condemns certain behaviour, as it was the case in *Colombia–Textiles*. In this dispute, Colombia relied upon the Colombian Criminal Code to prove that money laundering constitutes 'public morals'.[92] Additionally, Colombia pointed out its international anti-money-laundering obligations.[93]

Presumably, a WTO member can rely upon its obligations under human rights treaties and domestic human rights standards to prove

---

[89] Ibid.

[90] Appellate Body Reports, *supra* n. 82, at para. 5.200.

[91] Panel Report, *China – Measures Affecting Trading Rights and Distribution Services for Certain Publications and Audiovisual Entertainment Products*, WT/DS363/R and Corr.1, adopted 19 Jan. 2010, as modified by Appellate Body Report WT/DS363/AB/R, DSR 2010:II, p. 261; Panel Reports, *European Communities – Measures Prohibiting the Importation and Marketing of Seal Products*, WT/DS400/R and Add.1/WT/DS401/R and Add.1, adopted 18 June 2014, as modified by Appellate Body Reports WT/DS400/AB/R/WT/DS401/AB/R, DSR 2014:II, p. 365; Panel Report, *Colombia – Measures Relating to the Importation of Textiles, Apparel and Footwear*, WT/DS461/R and Add.1, adopted 22 June 2016, as modified by Appellate Body Report WT/DS461/AB/R, DSR 2016:III, p. 1227; Panel Reports, *Brazil – Certain Measures Concerning Taxation and Charges*, WT/DS472/R, Add.1 and Corr.1/WT/DS497/R, Add.1 and Corr.1, circulated to WTO members 30 Aug. 2017 [appealed by Brazil 28 Sept. 2017].

[92] Appellate Body Report, *Colombia – Measures Relating to the Importation of Textiles, Apparel and Footwear*, WT/DS461/AB/R and Add.1, adopted 22 June 2016, DSR 2016:III, p. 1131.

[93] Ibid.

that human rights measures are implemented for 'public morals' reasons. In this regard, Gabrielle Marceau suggests that if a WTO member justifies its human rights measures under the public morals clause, a Panel can examine this member's participation in the relevant human rights treaties.[94] Other scholars buttress this conclusion.[95]

Thus, the all-embracing interpretation of 'public morals' allows a WTO member the possibility to argue that human rights measures pursue 'public morals' objectives.

The Requirement for a Measure to Be 'Necessary to Protect' Public Morals   The AB developed an analytical framework to assess whether a disputed measure is 'necessary to protect public morals'. This analytical framework consists of two steps: a member must demonstrate that a measure is adopted 'to protect public morals' and that a measure is 'necessary' to protect such morals.[96]

The First Analytical Step: Whether a Measure Is Adopted 'to Protect Public Morals'   The Panel in *Colombia–Textiles* had to examine whether the measure was adopted 'to protect public morals'. At first, the Panel assessed whether the pursued policy objective is covered by the policies to protect 'public morals'.[97] The subsequent analysis focused on whether the measure itself is designed to achieve the declared public policy goal. In this regard, the Panel analysed the measure's 'design, architecture and revealing structure' to decide whether it is designed 'to protect public morals'.[98]

On appeal, the AB agreed with the sequence of the analytical steps, yet clarified that the requirement 'to protect' should not be excessively restrictive.[99]

---

[94] G. Marceau, 'WTO Dispute Settlement and Human Rights', *European Journal of International Law*, 13 (2002), 753.

[95] 'Human rights law is most likely to be raised by a party to a dispute as evidence supporting an assertion of fact' (R. Harris and G. Moon, '"GATT" Article XX and Human Rights: What Do We Know from the First 20 years?', *Melbourne Journal of International Law*, 16 (2015), 432–83).

[96] Appellate Body Reports, *supra* n. 82, at para. 5.169; Panel Report, *Colombia - Measures Relating to the Importation of Textiles, Apparel and Footwear, supra* n. 91, at para. 7.293.

[97] Panel Report, *Colombia - Measures relating to the Importation of Textiles, Apparel and Footwear, supra* n. 91, at para. 7.297.

[98] Ibid., at para. 7.343.

[99] Appellate Body Report, *supra* n. 92, at para. 5.68.

The Second Analytical Step: Whether a Measure Is 'Necessary' to Protect Public Morals   The AB explicitly emphasized that the assessment of a measure's necessity imposes a stricter standard than the evaluation of a measure's ability to protect public morals.[100] The previous jurisprudence introduced the following standard of 'necessity': 'a necessity analysis involves a process of "weighing and balancing" a series of factors, including the importance of the objective, the contribution of the measure to that objective, and the trade-restrictiveness of the measure'.[101] Moreover, a challenged measure and possible alternatives ought to be compared.[102]

The final determination of whether a WTO-inconsistent measure is 'necessary' to protect public morals requires not only the review of the above four criteria, but also entails a holistic weighing and balancing exercise.[103]

The First Analytical Step: Whether Human Rights Economic Sanctions Can Be Designed 'to Protect' Public Morals?   The WTO adjudicators pronounced that the assessment of whether a measure is capable to 'protect public morals' is an initial, threshold examination. Thus, we argue that unilateral human rights sanctions may be 'designed to' or 'capable of' protecting public morals if certain prerequisites are met. More specifically, a WTO member can demonstrate that human rights protection is a matter of significant concern for its domestic constituencies. Furthermore, a WTO member can explain how its domestic regulation, which introduces human rights economic sanctions, contributes to achieving declared public morals goals. For instance, a complete import ban imposed against a state that commits grave human rights violations can protect citizens of a sending state from being exposed to buying goods from the rogue state. Similar arguments might be relied upon to justify a partial import ban. If export restrictions are imposed,

---

[100] 'We do not see the examination of the "design" of the measure as a particularly demanding step of the Article XX(a) analysis. By contrast, the assessment of the 'necessity' of a measure entails a more in-depth, holistic analysis of the relationship between the measure and the protection of public morals' (ibid., at para. 5.70).

[101] Appellate Body Report, *Brazil – Measures Affecting Imports of Retreaded Tyres*, WT/DS332/AB/R, adopted 17 Dec. 2007, DSR 2007:IV, p. 1527, para. 5.169.

[102] Ibid., at para. 5.169.

[103] In this respect, the weighing and balancing exercise can be understood as 'a holistic operation that involves putting all the variables of the equation together and evaluating them in relation to each other after having examined them individually, in order to reach an overall judgment' (Panel Reports, *Brazil – Certain Measures Concerning Taxation and Charges*, *supra* n. 91, at para. 7.534).

a responding state can argue that such exports contribute to an ongoing violation and a measure addresses concerns of its own population in respect of grave human rights violations abroad.

The Second Analytical Step: Whether Human Rights Economic Sanctions Can Be 'Necessary' to Protect Public Morals? Coercive economic measures imposed to remedy grave human rights violations, apparently, pursue an important objective – to redress appalling atrocities. However, a WTO member that introduces such measures must demonstrate that their objective is to protect a member's residents from being exposed to goods or services originated in a country where grave human rights violations happen or from contributing to such violations by exporting goods or services. This line of argument sounds similar to the legal reasoning advanced by the European Union in *EC–Seal Products*[104] and accepted by the AB.[105] For this reason, we recognize the protection of residents from being exposed to the goods and/or services originated in a country where massive atrocities happen or from contributing to such violations by exporting as a valid and vital objective.

Yet we must admit that this line of argument has discernible flaws. First, human rights violations, the ones we are referring to, are not inherently related to goods or services as it was the case with the import prohibition on the seal products in *EC–Seal Products*. Second, this lack of

---

[104] 'The General Ban responds to the moral concerns of the EU public in two different manners. First, because of the way in which seals are killed, the EU public regards seal products from commercial hunts as morally objectionable and is repelled by their availability in the EU market. The General Ban addresses directly this concern by prohibiting the placing on the EU market of seal products, so that the members of EU public do not have to confront those products. Second, the EU public does not wish to be accomplice to the killing of seals in a manner which causes them excessive suffering. By prohibiting the placing on the EU market of seal products, the General Ban reduces the global demand for those products. By doing so the General Ban contributes to limit the overall number of seals which are killed every year and, consequently, also the number of seals which are killed in a manner that causes them excessive suffering. Thus, while the EU Seal Regime prescribes no killing methods, it does make a substantial contribution to the welfare of seals' (*European Communities – Measures Prohibiting the Importation and Marketing of Seal Products*, First Written Submission by the European Union, Geneva, 21 Dec. 2012).

[105] 'Having reviewed the Panel's findings and the participants' arguments on appeal, we consider that the principal objective of the EU Seal Regime is to address EU public moral concerns regarding seal welfare, while accommodating IC and other interests so as to mitigate the impact of the measure on those interests' (Appellate Body Reports, *supra* n. 82, at para. 5.167).

connection between human rights violations and goods and/or services undermines the strength of the negative consumer attitudes and moral objections in relation to such goods and services. This makes it more complicated to argue that the mere fact of being exposed to any type of goods and/or services, even not related to human rights violations, responds to societal moral concerns.

The measure's contribution to the pursued objective is the next step of the 'necessity' analysis. Although Panels enjoy certain latitude in choosing an appropriate framework for the contribution analysis, a measure's contribution must demonstrate a relationship between a particular measure and an outcome.[106] Unilateral human rights sanctions might be imposed to restrict market access and to guarantee that the country's residents are not exposed to buying goods and/or services and contributing to massive atrocities. However, a WTO member might find it burdensome to demonstrate that the goods and/or services that do not have any connection with human rights violations are 'morally objectionable' goods and/or services for the majority of its citizenry. Export restrictions that cover goods and/or services that cannot be used for human rights violations stand even less chance of demonstrating that they contribute to the protection of public morals inside the particular society. Hence, we argue that a WTO member might be unable to prove that human rights economic sanctions make a contribution to the pursued objective.

The trade-restrictiveness of unilateral human rights sanctions depends on whether it is a complete or partial ban. It is reasonable to assume that a complete ban, being the most trade-restrictive measure available to the WTO members, requires a significant level of contribution to achieving the pursued objectives, in order to be justified. Therefore, unilateral human rights restrictions ought to contribute to the pursued objectives in a way that balances out their trade-restrictiveness.

An examination of alternative measures is the last step of the analysis. A complaining party bears the burden of proof that alternative measures, which guarantee the same level of protection and are less trade restrictive, were available. Possible alternatives might include labelling schemes or international negotiations with a state that is engaged in grave human rights violations.

---

[106] Ibid., at paras. 5.210.–5.211.

RESHAPING THE LAW OF ECONOMIC SANCTIONS   273

The preliminary analysis has demonstrated that unilateral human rights sanctions have a significant chance of not meeting the standard of 'necessity' under the public morals exception.

Test under the *Chapeau*   The test under the *chapeau* consists of the three subsequent analytical steps.[107] An initial step is an identification whether the conditions are the same in the countries between which a measure allegedly discriminates. The AB emphasized that "'conditions" relating to the particular policy objective under the applicable subparagraph are relevant for the analysis under the chapeau'.[108] Determination of whether there is discrimination follows. Finally, the WTO tribunals have to decide whether discrimination is arbitrary or unjustifiable. The analysis of whether discrimination is arbitrary or unjustifiable 'should focus on the cause of the discrimination, or the rationale put forward to explain its existence'.[109]

Whether Human Rights Economic Sanctions Can Meet the Requirements of the Chapeau?   If human rights restrictions are imposed against a state, which persistently violates human rights, then the situation prevailing in this particular state might be unprecedented. That is to say, a WTO member might prove that human rights violations occurring in other states do not meet the same threshold of severity and therefore the conditions are not the same. Even so, the respondent state is obligated to demonstrate that it applies similar restrictions to all the countries, where the same conditions prevail.

Conclusion   Various types of unilateral human rights sanctions face a significant risk of being WTO-inconsistent. According to our preliminary conclusions, such measures cannot be justified under the public morals exception. The stringent requirements of the 'necessity' test, as they have been developed in the WTO jurisprudence, preclude human rights measures from being justified.

5.4.2.2   Justification under the National Security Exception

Grave violations of human rights may raise security concerns for neighbouring countries and even for the international community. The

---

[107] Appellate Body Reports, *supra* n. 82.
[108] Ibid., at para. 5.300.
[109] Appellate Body Report, *supra* n. 101, at para. 226.

objective of the following section is to analyse whether a WTO member can justify WTO-inconsistent human rights sanctions under the national security exception.[110]

The national security clause is comprised of a number of security exceptions. Despite this, the exception enshrined in Article XXI(b)(iii) of the GATT 1994 is the most frequently invoked.[111] Article XXI(b)(iii) reads as follows: 'Nothing in this Agreement shall be construed (b) to prevent any contracting party from taking any action which it considers necessary for the protection of its essential security interests (iii) taken in time of war or other emergency in international relations.'

Jurisdiction over the National Security Clause and Its Justiciability
The recent disputes unveiled that there was no unanimity between the members as to whether the WTO tribunals have jurisdiction over the security clause and whether the security clause is justiciable.[112]

In light of the above, the Panel in *Russia–Traffic in Transit* started its analysis from ascertaining its own jurisdiction to entertain the legal claims before it. The starting point of the Panel's analysis was the reiteration of the principle that international courts and tribunals 'possess inherent jurisdiction which derives from the exercise of their adjudicative function'.[113] As a result, the Panels are entitled to decide their own substantive jurisdiction.[114] In line with this preliminary assertion, the Panel delved into the relevant provisions of the DSU just to conclude that the invocation of the security clause falls squarely within its terms of reference.[115]

The next question is whether the national security clause is justiciable. The Russian Federation by emphasizing the 'self-judging' nature of the

---

[110] The GATT 1994 and the GATS stipulate the security exception clause – Article XXI of the GATT 1994 and Article XIV *bis* of the GATS respectively.

[111] 'While theoretically every subparagraph of Article XXI could be invoked; surprisingly, only subparagraph (b) was often utilised.' The article contains a good summary of disputes, in which the security exception was invoked (J. Y. Yoo and D. Ahn, 'Security Exceptions in the WTO System: Bridge or Bottle-Neck for Trade and Security?', *Journal of International Economic Law*, 19 (2016), 417–44).

[112] I. Bogdanova, 'Adjudication of the GATT Security Clause: To Be or Not to Be, this Is the Question', *WTI Working Paper 01/2019* (2019).

[113] Panel Report, *Russia – Measures Concerning Traffic in Transit*, WT/DS512/R and Add.1, adopted 26 Apr. 2019, para. 7.53.

[114] Ibid.

[115] Panel Report, *supra* n. 113, at para. 7.56.

clause maintained that the Panel is deprived of its jurisdiction *ratione materiae* over the trade measures justified by this exception.[116] The Panel engaged in an interpretive exercise, which confirmed that some elements of the national security clause are susceptible to judicial review.[117] To buttress this interpretive outcome, the Panel has made ample use of the negotiating history of the International Trade Organization.[118]

In order to assess whether WTO-inconsistent unilateral human rights sanctions can be justified under the national security exception a number of questions need to be addressed. At the outset, the ambit of the 'self-judging' nature of the national security clause is determined. Following this, the element 'taken in time of war or other emergency in international relations' is defined. Subsequently, the interpretation of the language 'which it considers necessary' and the term 'essential security interests' are briefly discussed.

The Ambit of the 'Self-Judging' Nature of the National Security Clause   In the majority of the ongoing disputes that involve the national security clause, the crux of the discussion is the scope of latitude granted to the WTO members under Article XXI(b)(iii). Determination of such scope inevitably includes discussion of the self-judging nature of the clause. The Panel report in *Russia–Traffic in Transit* sheds some light on the matter. The Panel has distinguished between objective and subjective elements of the national security clause as well as identified the scope of the reviewability of the subjective elements. Below we identify the objective and subjective elements of the clause and proceed with the standards of their reviewability.

Objective Element – 'Taken in Time of War or Other Emergency in International Relations'   By relying upon the general rule of interpretation along with the negotiating history of the Charter of the International Trade Organization, the Panel concluded that subparagraphs (i)–(iii) of Article XXI of the GATT 1994 establish objective elements, amenable to objective determination.[119] To put it differently, the existence of such circumstances as 'war' and 'emergency in international relations' is an objective fact amenable to objective

---

[116] Ibid., at para. 7.57.
[117] Ibid., at para. 7.102.
[118] Ibid., at paras. 7.83–7.100.
[119] Ibid., at para. 7.101.

276   IRYNA BOGDANOVA

determination.[120] Besides that, the chronological concurrence 'taken in time of' is also an objective fact.[121]

The Panel equated the term 'war' with an armed conflict,[122] while defined 'emergency in international relations' as 'a situation of armed conflict, or of latent armed conflict, or of heightened tension or crisis, or of general instability engulfing or surrounding a state'.[123]

The Subjective Standard of Necessity – 'Which It Considers Necessary' The Panel has interpreted the wording 'which it [WTO member] considers necessary' as granting unfettered discretion to the WTO members to decide the necessity of the measures imposed to protect essential security interests.[124]

The Subjective Standard of 'Essential Security Interests' The Panel defined interests that might fall under the definition of 'essential security interests' as 'interests relating to the quintessential functions of the state, namely, the protection of its territory and its population from external threats, and the maintenance of law and public order internally'.[125] Yet this definition should not lead us astray: the panel left the right to define what might constitute 'essential security interests' to the WTO members.[126] It has been pointed out that such determination 'will depend on the particular situation and perceptions of the state in question, and can be expected to vary with changing circumstances'.[127]

Since the exercise of this discretion is prone to politicization and abuse, the Panel emphasized that it is subject to the principle of good faith.[128] It implies an obligation to articulate such essential security interests sufficiently enough in order to demonstrate their veracity.[129]

Furthermore, the Panel set out the standard of 'a minimum requirement of plausibility' between the essential security interests defined by

---

[120] Ibid., at para. 7.71, reiterated para. 7.77.
[121] Ibid., at para. 7.70, reiterated para. 7.77.
[122] Ibid., at para. 7.72.
[123] Ibid., at para. 7.76.
[124] Ibid., at paras. 7.146–7.147.
[125] Ibid., at para. 7.130.
[126] Ibid., at para. 7.131.
[127] Ibid.
[128] Panel Report, *supra* n. 113, at paras. 7.132–7.133.
[129] Ibid., at para. 7.134.

RESHAPING THE LAW OF ECONOMIC SANCTIONS   277

the WTO member and the implemented measures.[130] To put it differently, the measure should not be 'implausible as measures protective of these interests'.[131]

Whether WTO-Inconsistent Human Rights Economic Sanctions Can Be Justified under the National Security Clause?   This chapter focuses on coercive economic measures imposed to redress grave human rights violations and we are keen on exploring whether the wording 'other emergency in international relations' can be interpreted as to include instances of grave human rights violations.

The Panel in *Russia–Traffic in Transit* pronounced that the only objective criterion of the national security clause is a determination whether the measure was taken 'in time of war or other emergency in international relations'. As has been stated, in the Panel's view the 'other emergency in international relations' entails 'a situation of armed conflict, or of latent armed conflict, or of heightened tension or crisis, or of general instability engulfing or surrounding a state'. While this definition might be prudent, taking into account the political nature of the national security exception, it might be too stringent to allow human rights economic sanctions to be justified under this exception. That is to say, that such measures may be justified if grave human rights violations occur in the neighbouring state, yet not in any other circumstances. Moreover, the standard of what constitutes essential security interests prioritizes rather narrow application of the national security exception.

Conclusion   Justification under the national security exception raises a number of crucial interpretive questions that were resolved by the Panel in *Russia–Traffic in Transit*. Our analysis revealed that human rights economic sanctions, which are imposed to remedy grave human rights violations, can be justified under the national security clause only in limited circumstances.

5.5   The Doctrine of Common Concern of Humankind and Its Potential Implications

Given all the legal uncertainties in enforcing human rights through economic sanctions and their undefined legal status in international

---

[130] Ibid., at para. 7.138.
[131] Ibid.

278   IRYNA BOGDANOVA

law, we now explore the idea to what extent the doctrine and principle of Common Concern of Humankind, expounded in the introductory chapter of this volume, can assist in framing more appropriate responses to the problem of inefficient human rights enforcement. Below we explore to what extent the doctrine of Common Concern of Humankind assists in defining the threshold of intervention, rights, and obligations in responding to grave human rights violations that might threaten international peace and security.

5.5.1 The Proposed Theoretical Framework

The doctrine of Common Concern of Humankind emerged in the field of international environmental law as a response to the inadequacy of international cooperation. The preamble to the United Nations Framework Convention on Climate Change acknowledges that 'change in the Earth's climate and its adverse effects are a common concern of humankind'.[132] Both the Convention on Biodiversity[133] and the recently concluded Paris Agreement[134] make reference to it as well.

Although the idea of common concern is well established in international law, its legal content and normative implications remain undefined.[135] Indeed, the Special Rapporteur of the International Law Commission, Shinya Murase, recognized that 'the main benefit of employing the term "common concern" in prior relevant environmental treaty practice has been to encourage participation, collaboration and action rather than discord'.[136] In light of the above, the theoretical framework of the doctrine of Common Concern of Humankind as

---

[132] United Nations Framework Convention on Climate Change, 9 May 1992, S. Treaty Doc. No. 102–38 (1992), 1771 UNTS 107.

[133] Convention on Biological Diversity, 1760 UNTS 79; 31 ILM 818 (1992).

[134] Paris Agreement (13 Dec. 2015), in UNFCCC, COP Report No. 21, Addendum, at 21, UN Doc. FCCC/CP/2015/10/Add, 1 (29 Jan. 2016).

[135] Frank Biermann in his article published in 1996 recognized broad acceptance of the concept of 'common concern', yet emphasized that 'its specific legal content and its implications for the international community and for individual States has yet to be developed more clearly'. F. Biermann, '"Common Concern of Humankind": The Emergence of a New Concept of International Environmental Law', *Archiv des Völkerrechts*, 34 (1996), 426–481.

[136] S. Murase, *Second Report on the Protection of Atmosphere - 67th Session of the International Law Commission* (2015), p. 20.

suggested by Thomas Cottier and others may provide a sound basis for a coordinated response to instances of grave human rights violations.[137]

At the outset, it is essential to clarify that the suggested theoretical framework applies to a problem that due to its nature and potentially negative consequences requires a response from the international community. The rationale behind the need to designate a problem as a common concern has been captured well by Thomas Cottier: 'Recourse to common concern both in literature and in treaty language suggests that it stands for the proposition of an important shared problem and shared responsibility, and for an issue which reaches beyond the bounds of a single community and state as a subject of international law.'[138] Hence, the doctrine of Common Concern of Humankind is of particular importance to the areas of international law, in which natural interests in cooperation are absent due to the deficient reciprocity and the option to free ride. These areas include not only environmental issues,[139] but also the field of human rights for the reasons discussed at the outset of this chapter.

The framework, expounded in the introductory chapter of this volume, prescribes the following normative implications.

5.5.1.1 The Duty to Cooperate

International cooperation lies at the heart of the suggested framework of Common Concern.[140] The general duty to cooperate is not embedded in public international law. In this regard, Cottier notes: 'Overall, duties to cooperate have remained specific and limited to particular areas. They do not establish general obligations across the board of international law.'[141] The recognition of a problem as of Common Concern implies a duty to

---

[137] See Chapter 1 in this volume. Also T. Cottier, P. Aerni, B. Karapinar, S. Matteotti, J. de Sépibus, and A. Shingal, 'The Principle of Common Concern and Climate Change', *Archiv des Völkerrechts*, 52 (2014), 293–324; T. Cottier and S. Matteotti, 'International Environmental Law and the Evolving Concept of "Common Concern of Mankind"', in T. Cottier, O. Nartova, and S. Z. Bigdeli (eds.), *International Trade Regulation and the Mitigation of Climate Change: World Trade Forum* (Cambridge: Cambridge University Press, 2009), pp. 21–47; K. N. Schefer and T. Cottier, 'Responsibility to Protect (R2P) and the Emerging Principle of Common Concern', in P. Hilpold (ed.), *The Responsibility to Protect (R2P): A New Paradigm of International Law?* (Leiden: Brill Nijhoff, 2014), pp. 123–42.

[138] See Chapter 1 in this volume, p. 36.

[139] For more, see Chapter 3 in this volume.

[140] See Chapter 1, pp. 59–60.

[141] Ibid., at p. 59.

280 IRYNA BOGDANOVA

cooperate in good faith and obligations of transparency, burden sharing, and cooperation in implementation.[142]

5.5.1.2 Obligation to Do Homework

The international community consists of sovereign states and thus each state is required to respond to instances of common concern independently. This obligation entails an effective implementation of international obligations as well as a need to introduce domestic measures conducive to safeguarding positive outcomes.[143]

5.5.1.3 Securing Compliance

In order to secure compliance, every state has a legal right to resort to unilateral measures to enforce common concern. The fully-fledged doctrine of Common Concern might even prescribe an obligation to act.[144]

As set out earlier, the idea of common concern emerged in international environmental law and its evolution was instigated by the shared understanding of the pressing need to find an acceptable solution for climate change and its adverse effects. Within this context, the framework of Common Concern, which is suggested in this book, strictly follows the logic of effectiveness in solving environmental problems. The underlying principles for mutual efforts include cooperation between all the parties involved, allocation of the duties between these parties, and, finally, enforcement in the instances of non-compliance. Against this backdrop, this section focuses on exploring the potential of the doctrine of Common Concern in addressing the deficiencies of international human rights enforcement. In essence, the purpose of this exercise is to 'transpose' the idea of common concern along with the suggested normative implications into the reality of human rights law.

We start with an identification of the grave human rights violations that might trigger adverse ramifications for several states or even for the international community as a whole, and thus might be recognized as a matter of common concern.

---

[142] For more, see ibid., at pp. 60–3.
[143] Ibid., at pp. 63–5.
[144] Ibid., at pp. 73–8.

5.5.2 Prerequisites for Human Rights Violations to Constitute a 'Common Concern'

Two conceptions of human rights can be found in philosophical thought.[145] The nonpartisan or restricted conception focuses on the common element in the views on social justice and political legitimacy in various cultures.[146] To the contrary, the liberal or full conception stands for distinguishing human rights from social justice and political legitimacy. The crux of the liberal conception can be illustrated as follows: 'human rights identify conditions that society's institutions should meet if we are to consider them legitimate.'[147] We find this distinction instrumental in explaining the diverging stances on the scope of international human rights, which range from the idea that only a subset of human rights shall benefit from international protection to the view that the ambit of international human rights shall transcendent political and cultural differences between the states. However, an extensive discussion of this matter falls outside of the scope of this chapter.

Having said that, we argue that the doctrine of Common Concern of Humankind should apply only to a narrowly defined subset of human rights violations, which due to their nature and potentially negative implications for neighbouring countries or the international community can neither be justified by the claims of 'cultural relativism' nor ignored. In line with this view, we suggest that three criteria must be considered cumulatively to recognize a particular human rights violation as a matter of common concern. Notably, these criteria are generally accepted by the international community as valid justifications for actions to redress human rights violations abroad.

The first criterion is the gravity or severity of a violation. The next requirement is systematicity. Along with these two preconditions, the potential to threaten international peace and security is the final benchmark. It must be noted that an actual or potential threat to international peace and security is the essential threshold. Thus, human rights violations fall under the definition of common concern only to the extent that they potentially deploy such effects.

---

[145] C. R. Beitz, 'Human Rights as a Common Concern', *American Political Science Review*, 95 (2001), 269–82.
[146] Beitz, *supra* n. 145.
[147] Ibid., at 270.

A determination as to whether a particular human rights violation meets the threshold of being a common concern should be decided on a case-by-case basis. Notwithstanding this, the violation of *jus cogens* norms as the most severe violation is recognized as a common concern irrespective of the presence of other criteria.

5.5.2.1 Gravity or Severity of Violation

As a rule, human rights guarantees are subject to restrictions. To put it differently, international instruments and constitutional laws allow restrictions on the exercise of human rights in the pursuit of the other legitimate policy goals. International courts, for example the European Court of Human Rights, as well as national constitutional courts carefully define the boundaries of these restrictions. The gravity of human rights violation for the purposes of constituting a matter of common concern ought to relate to the protection of the essence of human rights (known as *Kerngehalt* in the German legal tradition),[148] which is inalienable and cannot be restricted. This concept is closely related to the idea of *jus cogens*, but it enlarges the scope of rights beyond the few core standards of *jus cogens*.[149] Thus the gravity of violation is defined by the essence of the right at stake. Every human right potentially might qualify as a matter of common concern under the doctrine of Common Concern of Humankind.

5.5.2.2 Systematicity of Violation

Human rights violations do not require any quantitative threshold to warrant an appropriate response. Every human rights violation committed vis-à-vis an individual or a group deserves protection by law. In the context of Common Concern of Humankind, however, bearing in mind that such violations should threaten peace and stability, violations need to be systematic and persistent and not limited to rare occasions. This threshold is also crucial in relation to economic sanctions. Economic coercive measures can be potentially effective if they address a persistent pattern of conduct, the change of which is the ultimate goal of such measures.

---

[148] Art. 36(4) of the Federal Constitution of the Swiss Confederation and Art. 19(2) of the Basic Law for the Federal Republic of Germany.

[149] Cottier, *supra* n. 15.

5.5.2.3 Grave Human Rights Violations and a Threat to Peace and Security

Grave and systematic human rights violations not only provoke philosophical debates, but also cause negative externalities or spill-over effects, such as refugees, a slowdown in the economic development of neighbouring countries, security threats. International human rights scholars emphasize the moral side of the debate when they argue in favour of the enhanced protection of human rights. Yet, empirical research conducted by social scientists proves that human rights violations may have negative externalities for other states or even the whole international community.

The civil conflicts characterized by grave human rights violations negatively impact different groups of the population. In particular, the research on the impact of Guatemala's civil war confirms that 'internal armed conflict reinforces poverty and social exclusion among the most vulnerable groups'.[150] Furthermore, such events negatively influence access to education, expected returns from such education, and discourage investment in human capital.[151] Similar results have been reported in the other regions affected by atrocities and egregious human rights violations. As the recent research shows, children in conflict regions, not only experience suffering, but also encounter 'a human capital loss due to time away from schooling and work experience and higher levels of psychological distress'.[152] Other research demonstrates that early life exposure to civil war and human rights violations is closely related to loss in adult earning.[153] Health problems, along with the school deficits and the negative shocks in household wealth, explain the relationship between early life exposures to civil war atrocities and decreased adult earnings.[154] To sum it all up, the reported consequences of grave human rights violations include negative effects on human capital, economic development, and long-term stability of the countries or regions where such adverse events occur. As a matter of fact, such negative developments threaten regional and international peace and security.

---

[150] R. Chamarbagwala and H. E. Morán, 'The Human Capital Consequences of Civil War: Evidence from Guatemala', *Journal of Development Economics*, 94 (2011), 41–61.

[151] Ibid.

[152] C. Blattman and J. Annan, 'The Consequences of Child Soldiering', *Review of Economics and Statistics*, 92 (2010), 882.

[153] J. Galdo, 'The Long-Run Labor-Market Consequences of Civil War: Evidence from the Shining Path in Peru', *Economic Development & Cultural Change*, 61 (2013), 789.

[154] Ibid.

The end of the Cold War coincided with the period when the UN Security Council started to recognize non-military sources as a threat to international peace and security. A number of the Security Council's resolutions explicitly stipulate that human rights violations, which led to massive cross-border refugee flows, threaten international peace and security.[155] For example, condemning the ongoing repression of the Iraqi civilian population in parts of Iraq the Security Council declared it was: 'Gravely concerned by the repression of the Iraqi civilian population in many parts of Iraq, including most recently in Kurdish populated areas, which led to a massive flow of refugees towards and across international frontiers and to cross-border incursions, which threaten international peace and security in the region'.[156] In a similar vein, the Security Council expressed concern in respect of the Haitian crisis in the following statement: 'the incidence of humanitarian crises, including mass displacements of population, becoming or aggravating threats to international peace and security'.[157]

The situation in Kosovo was on the Security Council's agenda for a long time. During the heated debate on Kosovo, the representative of Canada admitted the causal nexus between human rights violations and peace and security and put it as follows:

> From Rwanda to Kosovo, there is mounting historical evidence which shows how internal conflicts which threaten human security spill over borders and destabilize entire regions. We have learned in Kosovo and from other conflicts that humanitarian and human rights concerns are not just internal matters. Therefore, unlike the delegation of China, Canada considers that such issues can and must be given new weight in the Council's definition of security and in its calculus as to when and how the Council must engage.[158]

In 2017 the Security Council held a special meeting devoted to the discussion of the interlinkages between human rights violations and a threat to peace and security. The President of the Council Mrs Haley in her opening speech stated:

---

[155] UN Security Council, Security Council Resolution 688 (1991) [Iraq], 5 Apr. 1991, S/RES/688 (1991).

[156] Ibid.

[157] UN Security Council, Security Council Resolution 841 (1993) [Haiti], 16 June 1993, S/RES/841 (1993).

[158] UN Security Council, 4011th Meeting, 10 June 1999, Document S/PV.4011, p. 13.

RESHAPING THE LAW OF ECONOMIC SANCTIONS 285

I am here today to assert that the protection of human rights is often deeply intertwined with peace and security. The two things often cannot be separated. In case after case, human rights violations and abuses are not merely the incidental by-products of conflict, but the trigger of conflict. When a State begins to systematically violate human rights, it is a sign; it is a red flag; it is a blaring siren – one of the clearest possible indicators that instability and violence may follow and spill across borders. It is no surprise that the world's most brutal regimes are also the most ruthless violators of human rights.[159]

As has been demonstrated above, human rights violations might threaten international peace and security. International peace and security is the weakest-link global public good and its provision depends on the efforts of the least capable states.[160] Therefore, international peace and security can be guaranteed only if all states cooperate, including the one that can contribute the least.[161] In this regard, Scott Barrett claims that provision of such global public good 'may thus require some combination of sticks and carrots.'[162]

Discussing the interaction between global public goods and international law, Daniel Bodansky suggests that various responses exist to address the inability or unwillingness of a state to provide a global public good of international peace and security.[163] Assistance and capacity-building initiatives can resolve deficiencies in the ability to provide peace and security; while coercive measures, such as economic sanctions or military actions, can remedy unwillingness. Bodansky points out that international law can legitimize coercive measures either by establishing norms that require actions from the international community or by authorizing coercive measures of individual states.[164] This view is reminiscent of the normative implications offered by the doctrine of Common Concern discussed in this book.

[159] UN Security Council 7926th meeting, 18 Apr. 2017, Document S/PV.7926.
[160] S. Barrett, *Why Cooperate? The Incentive to Supply Global Public Goods* (paperback ed., Oxford: Oxford University Press, 2010).
[161] Ibid., at 47–73.
[162] Barrett, *supra* n. 160.
[163] D. Bodansky, 'What's in a Concept? Global Public Goods, International Law, and legitimacy', *European Journal of International Law/Journal européen de droit international*, 23 (2012), 651–68.
[164] Ibid., at 662–3.

5.5.3 The Potential Contribution of the Doctrine of Common Concern

There are several ways in which the emerging doctrine of Common Concern can contribute to improving human rights enforcement.

5.5.3.1 Duty to Cooperate under the Doctrine of Common Concern

At present, international cooperation in the human rights field can be divided into two modalities: *ex ante* and *ex post* cooperation. By *ex ante* cooperation we mean ratification of the human rights treaties, as well as the establishment of international human rights bodies authorized to exercise their competence over sovereign states, such as regional human rights courts. The *ex ante* modes of cooperation may overlap, though not always. The *ex post* cooperation can either be an institutionalized response to appalling atrocities by the UN Security Council or ad hoc tribunals established for the prosecution of persons responsible for serious violations.

Despite the diversity of the avenues for international cooperation, the majority of the ongoing grave human rights violations do not receive an appropriate response. This lack of response can be partially explained by the absence of the responsibilities for human rights protection imposed on the international community as a whole, and not only on individual states. This deficiency has received some attention in the literature on the subject.[165]

In light of the above, the doctrine of Common Concern suggests a framework that might enhance international cooperation between sovereign states if such cooperation is essentially required. In fact, the doctrine of Common Concern obligates the international community to cooperate effectively to resolve international emergencies. Furthermore, if recognized, this doctrine may encourage non-state actors to petition their governments and demand compliance with their obligations, including demands to respond to grave human rights violations abroad. As the historical record has demonstrated, domestic constituencies may be empowered by the existence of the recognized international obligations imposed on a state.[166]

---

[165] More on the problem of the allocation of human rights responsibilities, please, see S. Besson, 'The Bearers of Human Rights' Duties and Responsibilities for Human Rights: A Quite (R)evolution?', *Social Philosophy and Policy*, 32 (2015), 244–68.

[166] Susanne Zwingel, discussing the impact of the Convention on the Elimination of All Forms of Discrimination against Women, noted: 'we have seen that CEDAW is created

RESHAPING THE LAW OF ECONOMIC SANCTIONS 287

In the human rights field, the duty to cooperate might include the duty to prevent grave human rights violations as well as the duty to cooperate in addressing such violations. The duty to prevent grave human rights violations has been already recognized as one of the obligations prescribed by the doctrine of Responsibility to Protect (R2P).[167] The doctrine of Common Concern thus reinforces and expands this obligation.

The doctrine of Common Concern introduces a framework that allows allocating duties to different levels of government, which implies that not only sovereign states will bear human rights responsibilities, but also the international community as a whole.[168] Indeed, as Thomas Cottier has argued: 'It is a fallacy to believe that labour standards and human rights are best protected by domestic law and thus by reducing the impact and scope of public international law. To the contrary, effective protection is mainly secured by appropriate disciplines within public international law and its institutions.'[169]

To an extent, this doctrine fills an existing gap between a moral obligation to react to instances of grave human rights violations and a lack of the legally binding obligation imposed on the international community. Indeed, core international human rights treaties do not oblige states to engage in effective cooperation pursuing the goal of effective human rights enforcement, including instances of prevention grave human rights violations. Similar attempts have been undertaken by the recently emerged doctrine of R2P.[170] However, the implementation of the R2P still remains embryonic and controversial. Partially this outcome can be attributed to a narrow definition of the human rights violations that warrant the application of the doctrine.[171] Besides this, the

---

within a broader, in itself evolving, global discourse on gender equality and that a variety of women's rights proponents have used it to influence domestic practices' (S. Zwingel, *Translating International Women's Rights: The CEDAW Convention in Context* (New York: Palgrave Macmillan, 2016), p. 7).

[167] R2P consists of a number of obligations: 'responsibility to prevent', 'responsibility to react', and 'responsibility to rebuild' (William W. Burke-White, 'Adoption of the Responsibility to Protect', in J. Genser and I. Cotler (eds.), *The Responsibility to Protect: The Promise of Stopping Mass Atrocities in Our Time* (Oxford: Oxford University Press, 2012), pp. 17–36).

[168] Besson, *supra* n. 165.

[169] Thomas Cottier, 'International trade, human rights and policy space', in L. Biukovic and P. B. Potter (eds.), *Local Engagement with International Economic Law and Human Rights* (Cheltenham, UK: Edward Elgar, 2017), pp. 3–25.

[170] Genser and Cotler, *supra* n. 167.

[171] The 2005 World Summit Outcome Document narrowed the application of the R2P only to four types of human rights violations. Paragraph 139 of the Outcome Document, in

288   IRYNA BOGDANOVA

ultimate remedy proposed by the R2P is a humanitarian intervention, which some states, as well as their domestic constituencies, may find morally objectionable.[172]

5.5.3.2 Obligation to Do Homework under the Doctrine of Common Concern

As mentioned at the outset, the majority of states signed and ratified the core human rights treaties. Despite this, states do not always comply with the undertaken international obligations in the human rights field. The weak enforcement mechanisms and lack of reciprocity are to blame.

The obligation to do homework under the doctrine of Common Concern requires that states implement their international obligations at the domestic level. Such implementation might entail not only recognition of human rights in domestic legal instruments, but also establishment of unbiased and uncorrupted courts of law to enforce such rights and introduce legitimate and justified boundaries in the exercise of the protected rights.

5.5.3.3 Securing Compliance: Human Rights Economic Sanctions

Human rights economic sanctions are prone to politicization and abuse. Furthermore, as our thorough analysis has indicated, unilateral economic sanctions remain one of the murky legal terrains in public international law. Against this backdrop, the doctrine of Common Concern has the potential to discipline the use of such unilateral coercive instruments by establishing grounds for their use and by requiring cooperation efforts to precede any enforcement action.

Apart from this, the doctrine of Common Concern might legitimize unilateral economic sanctions imposed on human rights grounds, if they apply as a measure of last resort. The legality of such coercive measures was debated at length within the international community, including a heated debate at the United Nations. Yet as of today there is no unanimity between the members on whether unilateral economic sanctions are

---

the relevant part, reads as follows: 'We stress the need for the General Assembly to continue consideration of the responsibility to protect populations from genocide, war crimes, ethnic cleansing and crimes against humanity and its implications, bearing in mind the principles of the Charter and international law.'

[172] The Responsibility to Protect: Report of the International Commission on Intervention and State Sovereignty (2001).

legal. The doctrine of Common Concern has considerable potential to allow coercive economic measures once there is a pressing need in such actions and preclude states from imposing them if they are politically motivated.

It is worth noting that the initial report on the R2P prepared by the International Commission on Intervention and State Sovereignty acknowledged that economic sanctions imposed on human rights grounds may be an efficient response to redress grave human rights violations.[173] This proposition was qualified in several ways. At the outset, it was noted that comprehensive economic sanctions disproportionately impact the civilian population.[174] Thus, such coercive measures should be properly devised to carry negative implications for the targeted groups, mainly political elites. In line with this proposal, the following types of economic sanctions were identified as particularly potent:[175]

- financial sanctions that target the foreign assets of a country, or a rebel movement or terrorist organization, or the foreign assets of particular leaders;
- restrictions on income-generating activities such as oil, diamonds, logging, and drugs;
- restrictions on access to petroleum products;
- aviation bans.

The recognition of grave human rights violations as a common concern might inform the interpretation of WTO law. As our analysis has revealed WTO-inconsistent human rights economic sanctions face a significant risk of failing the 'necessity test' under the public morals exception. Recognition of grave human rights violations as a common concern may inform 'the necessity analysis' under the public morals exception and as a result, allow such measures to be justified under WTO law. Alternatively, the incidents of human rights violations that meet the thresholds of a common concern can be acknowledged as circumstances that constitute 'other emergency in international relations' for the purposes of the national security exception. The Panel in *Russia–*

---

[173] Ibid., at 29–30.

[174] It was pointed out: 'Blanket economic sanctions in particular have been increasingly discredited in recent years as many have noted that the hardships exacted upon the civilian population by such sanctions tend to be greatly disproportionate to the likely impact of the sanctions on the behaviour of the principal players' (ibid., at 29).

[175] Ibid., at 30.

Traffic in Transit interpreted the prerequisite 'other emergency in international relations' in a way that forestalls the majority of grave human rights violations from being justified under the national security clause. Thus, the doctrine of Common Concern can expand the notion of 'other emergency in international relations' as to include instances of grave human rights violations.

In light of the above, we envision that the doctrine has considerable potential to make a valuable contribution to enhanced enforcement of human rights.

5.6   Concluding Remarks

This chapter explored the potential of the emerging doctrine of Common Concern of Humankind to provide a new legal framework for improving enforcement of human rights. The doctrine puts forward the idea of improved international cooperation between the states aimed at redressing instances of grave human rights violations. This idea reinforces the previous attempts to promote enhanced cooperation for efficient human rights enforcement, in particular, duty to prevent gross human rights violations embedded in the R2P. Furthermore, the doctrine and its normative implications can legitimize human rights economic sanctions as well as restrict their use if such coercive measures are politically motivated. At the time when human rights enforcement suffers from a number of deficiencies and economic coercion has been playing an increasingly significant role, there is a pressing need to employ human rights economic sanctions for the benefit of humanity.

* * *

Select Bibliography

A. Delanis, J. (1979). '"Force" under Article 2(4) of the United Nations Charter: The Question of Economic and Political Coercion', 12 *Vanderbilt Journal of Transnational Law* 103–14

Adlung, R. (2015). 'Export Policies and the General Agreement on Trade in Services', 18 *Journal of International Economic Law* 487–510.

Barrett, S. (2010). *Why Cooperate? The Incentive to Supply Global Public Goods* (paperback ed., Oxford: Oxford University Press).

Beitz, C. R. (2001). 'Human Rights as a Common Concern', 95 *American Political Science Review* 269–82.

Besson, S. (2015). 'The Bearers of Human Rights' Duties and Responsibilities for Human Rights: A Quite (R)evolution?', 32 *Social Philosophy and Policy* 244–68.

Bodansky, D. (2012). 'What's in a Concept? Global Public Goods, International Law, and Legitimacy', 23 *European Journal of International Law/Journal européen de droit international* 651–68.

Charnovitz, S. (1998). 'The Moral Exception in Trade Policy', 38 *Virginia Journal of International Law* 689–745.

Chilton, A. S. and Posner, E. A. (2016). 'Respect for Human Rights: Law and History', Coase-Sandor Working Paper Series in Law and Economics No. 770 1–22.

Cleveland, S. H. (2002). 'Human Rights Sanctions and International Trade: A Theory of Compatibility', 5 *Journal of International Economic Law* 133–189.

Schefer, K. N. and Cottier, T. (2014). 'Responsibility to Protect (R2P) and the Emerging Principle of Common Concern', in P. Hilpold (ed.), *The Responsibility to Protect (R2P): A New Paradigm of International Law?* (Leiden: Brill Nijhoff), pp. 123–42.

Dawidowicz, M. (2017). *Third-Party Countermeasures in International Law* (Cambridge: Cambridge University Press).

Elagab, O. Y. (1988). *The Legality of Non-Forcible Counter-Measures in International Law* (Oxford: Clarendon Press).

Genser, J. and Cotler, I. (2012). *The Responsibility to Protect: The Promise of Stopping Mass Atrocities in Our Time* (Oxford: Oxford University Press).

Hofer, A. (2017). 'The Developed/Developing Divide on Unilateral Coercive Measures: Legitimate Enforcement or Illegitimate Intervention?' 16 *Chinese Journal of International Law* 175–214.

Paulus, A. (2012*)*. ''Whether Universal Values Can Prevail over Bilateralism and Reciprocity', in Antonio Cassese (ed.), *Realizing Utopia: The Future of International Law* (Oxford: Oxford University Press), pp. 89–104.

Portela, C. (2018). 'Targeted Sanctions against Individuals on Grounds of Grave Human Rights Violations – Impact, Trends and Prospects at EU Level' 1–35.

Posner, E. A. (2014). *The Twilight of Human Rights Law* (Oxford: Oxford University Press).

Ruys, T. (2017). 'Sanctions, Retorsions and Countermeasures: Concepts and International Legal Framework' *Research Handbook on UN Sanctions and International Law* (Cheltenham, UK: Edward Elgar), pp. 19–51.

(2019). 'Immunity, Inviolability and Countermeasures – A Closer Look at Non-UN Targeted Sanctions', in Tom Ruys and Nicolas Angelet (eds.), *The Cambridge Handbook of Immunities and International Law* (Cambridge: Cambridge University Press), pp. 670–710.

Tzanakopoulos, A. (2015). 'The Right to be Free from Economic Coercion' 4 *Cambridge International Law Journal* 616–33.

6

Migration as a Common Concern of Humankind

THOMAS COTTIER AND ROSA MARIA LOSADA

Working from the bottom up, by solving practical problems related to migration, will eventually enable broader normative action. Smaller groups of states, banding together in a kind of mini-multilateralism, can trail-blaze solutions to common challenges that might eventually become global standards. This will only speed the way to a normative future.

The bottom-up practical approach and the top-down normative one share a common cause: To improve outcomes for migrants and our societies. The pursuit of grander goals should not undermine more incremental efforts; polarization between these two approaches would jeopardize all progress. States must eschew the short-term satisfaction of scoring political points in favor of working hard at cooperation. We are on the threshold of a new era of international cooperation on migration. Let's make sure we cross over it.

Peter Sutherland[1]

6.1 Migration: A Fact of International Life

Throughout the history of humankind, migration has been a constant companion. Before and after the first settlements some twelve thousand years ago and the evolution of agriculture, people migrated within tribal territories, later within states and nations, and subsequently internationally.[2]

The chaper is partly based upon work by Thomas Cottier, Aniriudh Shingal, 'Migration, Trade and Investment: Towards a New Common Concern of Humankind', 55 *Journal of World Trade* 51–76 (2021), originally commissioned by the International Organization for Migration, Geneva. The authors are indebted to Shalom Cook for his edits and valuable suggestions.

[1] Peter D. Sutherland, former special Representative of the UN Secretary-General for Migration, 'Migration 2.0: A Time for Action at the UN Summit on Migration and Development', www.un.org/en/development/desa/population/migration/partners/docs/Time_for_Action_UN%20Summit_by_PSutherland_RMAD.pdf (accessed Sept. 2019).

[2] E. G. Ravenstein, 'The Laws of Migration', *Journal of the Statistical Society of London*, 48 (1885), 167–235.

The scope and breadth of human history is to a large extent a history of migration. Civilisation, progress and deprivation accompanied migration over this time; there is hardly a more complex web of causes and effects than the drive of people to seek better grounds for making a living and building a future for their families. There are numerous and varied reasons to migrate: displacement, conquest and war, death, deprivation, poverty, economic prosperity and hope, political and religious persecution, fear, climatic changes and desertification. Destitution rarely allows for migration due to lack of resources. It is only when societies have reached a certain level of development that people are given the resources and opportunity to migrate.[3] Humans rarely migrate and travel on their own. With the exception of political persecution mainly of intellectuals, people migrate in groups and settle in the diaspora, carrying along their heritage and culture. In 2017, some 258 million people lived outside their country of origin,[4] with women comprising slightly less than 50 per cent, and refugees and asylum seekers amounting to 25.9 million in 2016. The overall numbers of migrants have been increasing from 173 million in 2000, at a growth rate of 2 per cent every year with industrialised countries absorbing 64 million out of 85 million people.[5] Remittances flowing back to countries of origin are of key importance to families back home and by far exceed the levels of official development assistance (ODA).[6] They reached about $USD529 billion in 2018.[7] Countries today thus show increasing levels of the population with a migratory background.[8] Developed societies have a tendency to be more

---

[3] W. Zelinsky, 'The Hypothesis of the Mobility Transition', *Geographical Review*, 61 (1971), 219–49; P. L. Martin and J. E. Taylor, 'The Anatomy of a Migration Hump', in J. E. Taylor (ed.), *Development Strategy, Employment and Migration: Insights from Models* (Paris: Organisation for Economic Co-operation and Development, 1996), pp. 43–62; R. Skeldon, 'Migration and Development', UN/POP/EGM-MIG/2008/4, 9 Sept. 2008, www.un.org/en/development/desa/population/events/pdf/expert/14/P04_Skeldon.pdf (accessed July 2019).

[4] According to the UN, 258 million people or 3.4 per cent of the world's inhabitants today are international migrants, www.un.org/development/desa/publications/international-migration-report-2017.html (accessed July 2019).

[5] For a detailed account, see United Nations, *International Migration Report 2017* (highlights), at 4, www.un.org/en/development/desa/population/migration/publications/migra tionreport/docs/MigrationReport2017_Highlights.pdf (accessed July 2019).

[6] International Organization for Migration, Migration Data Portal, 'The Bigger Picture' (key trends): remittances to low- and middle-income countries are more than three times higher than the amount of Official Development Aid to these countries, https://migrationdataportal.org/themes/remittances (accessed July 2019).

[7] Ibid., at 5.

[8] Ibid., at 4 (highlights), 5–6.

294   THOMAS COTTIER AND ROSA MARIA LOSADA

mobile.[9] For example in Switzerland, a country among those with the highest percentage of migrants, today some 25 per cent of the population bears foreign passports, albeit partly due to restrictive naturalisation.[10]

Today, migration has become a major policy issue in the wake of globalisation, enhanced international trade in goods and services and capital flows. A gradual decline in this process ('slowbalisation') will not fundamentally alter the challenges. It rather will make them more difficult, focusing more on regions.[11] Divergences in social and economic development and income disparities increased migration flows mainly of economic migrants for which, unlike political refugees, established multilateral disciplines and rules that do not properly exist in international law and relations.[12]

The concepts of migrants and refugees are often confused within a context of mixed migration flows. Mixed migration flows refer to cross-border movements of people including all types of migrants such as climate-induced migrants, refugees, economic migrants and asylum seekers.[13] According to the United Nations (UN) an 'international migrant is someone who changes his or her country of usual residence, irrespective of the reason for migration or legal status for a short period of time (from three to twelve months) or for a longer (one year or more) or permanent change of country of residence'.[14] A refugee is primarily defined in the 1951 Refugee Convention.[15] Bringing together, or confusing, the terms 'refugees' and 'migrants' can undermine public support for refugees and the establishment of asylum at a time when more refugees need such protection than ever before. Recently, in a context of mixed migration flows, this confusion was one of the main causes for enhanced

---

[9] Ibid., at 2.

[10] N. Q. Nguyen, 'Defining the 25% Foreign Population in Switzerland', 19 Nov. 2017, www.swissinfo.ch/eng/society/migration-series-part-1-_who-are-the-25-foreign-population-in-switzerland/42412156 (accessed July 2019).

[11] *The Economist*, 26 Jan. 2019, 9, 17–20.

[12] According to the UN an international migrant is someone who changes his or her country of usual residence, irrespective of the reason for migration or legal status for a short period of time (from three to twelve months) or for a longer (one year or more) or permanent change of country of residence, https://refugeesmigrants.un.org/definitions (accessed July 2019); while a refugee is primarily defined in the 1951 Convention Relating to the Status of Refugees, signed 28 July 1951, entered into force 22 Apr. 1954, 189 UNTS 150; www.unhcr.org/1951-refugee-convention.html (accessed July 2019).

[13] Glossary of the European Commission, 'Migration and Home Affairs', https://ec.europa.eu/home-affairs/content/mixed-migration-flow_en (accessed July 2019).

[14] https://refugeesmigrants.un.org/definitions (accessed July 2019).

[15] See *supra* n. 12.

MIGRATION 295

populism and the exploitation of the challenges for ideological political ends, often way beyond existing facts. Not all countries are equally affected. But in Europe and the United States, since the global refugee crisis in 2015,[16] the polarised political and public discourse on the incoming mixed migration flows strongly contributed and still contributes to increased tensions within society and the political process. It undermines commitments to international obligations and breeds nationalism well beyond migration.[17] It opens Pandora's box by questioning the *jus cogens* principle of non-refoulement.[18] These developments may eventually pose a threat to peace and stability within societies and well beyond.[19]

As a result, it is imperative to foster parameters and arguments which allow for more rational debate and to bring about an appropriate multilateral legal framework addressing the challenges of migration and 'the conjunction of convergent expectations and patterns of behaviour or practice'[20] of national governments within an international cooperation framework. This by definition incorporates the preservation of the interests and entitlements of all concerned, including the migrants themselves that have become an important factor in future development.

This chapter examines to what extent the doctrine and principle of Common Concern of Humankind can offer guidance in law and the policy debate. It can also offer a narrative to jointly work on solutions

[16] Amnesty International, 'The Global Refugee Crisis in 2015', www.amnesty.org/en/latest/news/2015/12/global-refugee-crisis-2015-gallery/ (accessed July 2019).

[17] On the tension of international law between the traditions of sovereignty of nation states and universal norms and aspirations, see Thomas Cottier, 'Das Völkerrecht im Spannungsfeld von Nationalstaatlichkeit und Universalität, *Zeitschrift für Politik (ZfP)* 57, 156–69 (Munich, 2/2010).

[18] The non-refoulement principle has been questioned in the application of the pushback praxis of the Spanish authorities on the border to Morocco: *ECtHR N.D. and N.T. v. Spain* (Nos. 8675/15 and 8697/15) [Art. 4 Protocol 4, Art. 13 ECHR], 3 Oct. 2017, submission for the interveners, 5 Apr. 2018, www.icj.org/wp-content/uploads/2018/04/Spain-ICJothers-AmicusBrief-NDNT-ECtHR-GC-legalsubmission-2018-.pdf (accessed July 2019). Swiss Parliament wants to deport jihadists to countries where they face torture and the death penalty: www.nzz.ch/meinung/die-ausschaffung-von-terroristen-in-folterstaaten-bringt-wenig-und-ist-der-schweiz-nicht-wuerdig-ld.1468367 (accessed July 2019).

[19] GFMD, 'Third and Final Thematic Workshop on Migration for Peace, Stability and Growth', New York, 19 July 2016, www.gfmd.org/news/migration-peace-stability-and-growth (accessed July 2019).

[20] O. Young, 'Regime Dynamics: The Rise and Fall of International Regimes', *International Organization*, 36(2) (1982), 277–97, www.cambridge.org/core/journals/international-organization/article/regime-dynamics-the-rise-and-fall-of-international-regimes/6885F64E8C0166 4F4B7EA48C556AB5E8 (accessed July 2019).

and to assist in bringing about conditions of stability in fairness to migrants, sending, transit and host communities alike by structuring it in accordance with the conceptual chapter in this volume.[21] We first expound the current state of play in international migration law and policy and then discuss and apply the normative implications of the principle of Common Concern of Humankind.

6.2 Beggar-thy-neighbour: The Legacy of Sovereignty and the Lack of Multilateral Cooperation

Given the history of growing interdependence and mobility, it is noteworthy that migration flows still are essentially and almost exclusively controlled by domestic law and what was called the 'emerging migration state'.[22] Countries largely on their own and independently define the extent to which they wish to unilaterally welcome or reject migrants in accordance with domestic needs and prevailing ideologies. Given this history, it is not at all astonishing that strong general disciplines are lacking in international law and international cooperation, despite the fact that current reality proves the failure of unilateral actions: whereas populist leaders in Europe plead for a unilateral and self-determined approach – in the traditions of the Westphalian idea of sovereignty – and have resisted a collective approach to migration, the number of deaths in the Mediterranean proves that unilateral action – and foremost the lack of it – produces devastating and depressing results.[23]

While international environmental law developed a comprehensive Convention on Migratory Species of Wild Animals,[24] no equivalently comprehensive agreement and code exist in relation to human migrants and labour standards for migrants. Principles and rules, to the extent they exist, are scattered in different fields and instruments mainly limited

---

[21] See Chapter 1.

[22] J. Hollifield, 'The Emerging Migration State', *International Migration Review*, 38 (2004), 885–912.

[23] The same goes for US foreign policy on immigration, see T. L. Friedman, 'Trump Is Wasting Our Immigration Crisis: The System Needs to Be Fixed, But "the Wall" Is Only Part of the Solution', *New York Times*, 24 Apr. 2019, www.nytimes.com/2019/04/23/opinion/trump-immigration-border-wall.html (accessed July 2019).

[24] Convention on Migratory Species of Wild Animals, www.cms.int/en/node/3916 (accessed July 2019).

MIGRATION 297

to bilateral relations, resulting in a fragmented legal landscape.[25] Multilateral disciplines are essentially limited to the law of refugees, labour standards and shared aspects of security.

6.2.1 A Brief History

The period after the First World War brought the first efforts to address the problem of minorities and refugees.[26] The 1938 Conference on Refugees in Evian failed to anticipate the Holocaust, partly due to insistence on domestic restrictions by the United States.[27] After the Second World War, disciplines emerged as a matter of refugee law, limited to politically persecuted persons. The office of the UN Commissioner for Refugees was established in 1950.[28] It brought about the 1951 Convention Relating to the Status of Refugees.[29] It was complemented by important guarantees to asylum seekers by the 1951 European Convention for the Protection of Human Rights and Fundamental Freedoms.[30] The principle of non-refoulement amounts to the cornerstone of international refugee law. It is one of the very few core standards of *jus cogens* and peremptory international law which states must respect and cannot restrict by domestic law. Nobody must be sent back to territories where the life and physical and mental integrity of the person is jeopardised. Within the European Union (EU), including European Free Trade Association (EFTA) states (Iceland, Liechtenstein, Norway and Switzerland as associated states), the Dublin system applies common standards on refugee law, rendering the country of the first application

---

[25] See T. Cottier and Ch. Sieber Gasser, 'Labour Migrations, Trade and Investment: From Fragmentation to Coherence', in M. Panizzon. G. Zürcher and E. Fornalé (eds.), *The Palgrave Handbook of International Labour Migration* (Basingstoke, UK: Macmillan, 2015), pp. 41–60; for clarification of the scope of legal norms in the field of migration, see T. A. Aleinikoff, 'International Legal Norms and Migration: A Report', in T. A. Aleinikoff and V. Chetail (eds.), *Migration and International Legal Norms* (The Hague: TCM Asser Press, 2003), pp. 41–60.

[26] For a survey, see D. Kugelmann, 'Migration', *Max Planck Encyclopedia of Public International Law* (Oxford: Oxford University Press 2012), vol. II, 149–60.

[27] See United States Holocaust Museum, www.ushmm.org/outreach/en/article.php?ModuleId=10007698 (accessed July 2019).

[28] History of the UNHCR, www.unhcr.org/history-of-unhcr.html (accessed July 2019).

[29] See *supra* n. 12.

[30] Signed 4 Nov. 1950, entered into force 3 Sept. 1953, 213 UNTS 221; see N. Mole and C. Meredith, *Asylum and the European Convention on Human Rights* (Council of Europe, 2010).

responsible for asylum seekers.[31] The Schengen *acquis*[32] works towards the abolishment of internal borders within the Schengen area and a reinforced control of external borders.[33] It represents the implementation of enhanced cooperation around an inner space of common concerns being the readmission agreements and their security component to facilitate the return of irregular migrants to non-European countries an essential part of these common concerns within the EU area.[34]

Less attention was paid to labour mobility and migration in international law and relations. Migrants enjoy the protection of relevant human rights, in particular, the International Covenant on Civil and Political Rights,[35] the International Covenant on Economic, Social and Cultural Rights[36] and the International Convention on the Protection of the Rights of All Migrant Workers and Members of Their Families (ICMW).[37] Migrant workers benefit from international labour standards, in particular, the Convention No. 97 concerning Migration for

---

[31] Regulation (EU) No. 604/2013 of the European Parliament and of the Council of 26 July 2013 establishing the criteria and mechanisms for determining member states responsible for examining an application for international protection lodged in one of the member states by a third-country national or a stateless person, OJ L 180, 29.6.2013, pp. 31–59; http://eur-lex.europa.eu/legal-content/en/TXT/?uri=CELEX:32013R0604 (accessed July 2019).

[32] The Schengen *acquis* comprises the Schengen Agreement signed 14 June 1985, the Convention implementing the Schengen Agreement of 14 June 1985 between the Governments of the States of the Benelux Economic Union, the Federal Republic of Germany and the French Republic on the gradual abolition of checks at their common borders, the Accession Agreements to the Schengen Convention by Italy, Spain, Portugal, Greece, Austria, Denmark, Finland and Sweden, the Association Agreements by Norway, Iceland and Switzerland, the decisions of the Executive Committee and the Central Group and further regulations, directives and decisions adopted by the European Parliament and the Council. After the Treaty of Amsterdam, the Schengen Agreement was brought into the institutional framework of the EU, a protocol attached to it.

[33] Regulation (EC) No. 562/2006 of the European Parliament and of the Council of 15 Mar. 2006 establishing a Community Code on the rules governing the movement of persons across borders (Schengen Borders Code) OJ L 105/1 of 13.4.2006.

[34] Council of the European Union, Council Conclusions defining the European Union strategy on readmission, Doc. 11260/11 MIGR 118, 8 June 2011, 2.

[35] Adopted by UN General Assembly 16 Dec. 1966, entered into force 23 Mar. 1966, Annex to GA Res. 2200, 21 GAOR Supp. 16, UN Doc. A/6316, at 52 (1966); www.ohchr.org/en/professionalinterest/pages/ccpr.aspx (accessed July 2019).

[36] Adopted by the UN General Assembly 16 Dec. 1966, entered into force 3 Jan. 1973, Annex to GA Res. 2200, 21 GAOR, Supp. 16, UN Doc. A/6316, at 49 (1966); www.ohchr.org/EN/ProfessionalInterest/Pages/CESCR.aspx (accessed July 2019).

[37] Adopted by the UN General Assembly 18 Dec. 1990; www.ohchr.org/EN/ProfessionalInterest/Pages/CMW.aspx (accessed Sept. 2019).

Employment[38] and Convention No. 143 concerning Migrations in Abusive Conditions and the Promotion of Equality of Opportunity and Treatment of Migrant Workers.[39] In 1999, the UN Commission on Human Rights (now the Human Rights Council) instituted the office of the Special Rapporteur on the human rights of migrants, with a view to improving the realisation and enforcement of related human rights of migrants.[40] The work of successive commissioners has been of great importance in creating awareness and addressing deficiencies of legal protection in the different regions of the world. But migration as such has not been recognised as a service in international economic law and does not benefit from general market access guarantees.[41] These are only modestly and partly addressed in multilateral disciplines of Mode 4 under Article I(2)(d) of the General Agreement on Services of the World Trade Organization (WTO) for key personnel.[42] More recently, migration relating to skilled labour movement and recognition of professional qualifications also form part of economic cooperation agreements, jointly addressed with trade and investment, for example in CETA.[43] Of significant and increasing importance are more than 580 bilateral labour

---

[38] Adopted 8 June 1949, entered into force 22 Jan. 1952; www.ilo.org/dyn/normlex/en/f?p= NORMLEXPUB:12100:0::NO::P12100_INSTRUMENT_ID:312242 (accessed July 2019).

[39] Adopted 24 June 1975, entered into force 9 Dec. 1978; www.ilo.org/dyn/normlex/en/f?p= NORMLEXPUB:12100:0::NO::P12100_ILO_CODE:C143 (accessed July 2019).

[40] See *supra* n. 36.

[41] WTO, General Agreement on Trade in Services (hereafter GATS), Annex on Movement of Natural Persons Supplying Services under the Agreement; www.wto.org/english/tra top_e/serv_e/8-anmvnt_e.htm (accessed July 2019).

[42] For the two-way interaction between international migration and agreements for enhanced cross-border trade and investment, see J. Poot and A. Strutt, 'International Trade Agreements and International Migration', *World Economy*, 33 (2010); T. Cottier, A. Shingal, 'Migration Trade and Investment: Towards a New Common Concern of Humankind', *Journal of World Trade* 55(1) 2021, 51–76; M. Panizzon, 'Migration: GATS Mode 4 and Migration Agreements' (Dialogue on Globalization, Occasional Paper No. 47, Jan. 2010), *American Society of International Law: Proceedings of the Annual Meeting* (2011), 407–22; M. Panizzon ,'Temporary Movement of Workers and Human Rights Protection: Interfacing the "Mode 4" of GATS with Non-Trade Bilateral Migration Agreements', *Proceedings 104th Annual Meeting* 104 (2010), 131–9.

[43] Comprehensive Economic and Trade Agreement, OJ L11/23 14.1.2017, chs. 10 and 11; http://ec.europa.eu/trade/policy/in-focus/ceta/; https://eur-lex.europa.eu/legal-content/ EN/TXT/?uri=CELEX:22017A (accessed July 2019).

migration agreements facilitating market access for labour.[44] These agreements mainly relate to unskilled labour.

Free movement of labour is generally recognised, albeit with exceptions and subject to conditions, within the federate states and unions, including the EU and EFTA, guaranteeing free movement of persons, freedom of services and the right to establishment.[45] The EU established the right of freedom of movement for all workers as a fundamental principle of its Treaty. Article 45 TFEU[46] provides for free movement of employed workers which was eventually extended to EFTA countries in the EEA Agreement and a bilateral agreement with Switzerland. Article 49 TFEU[47] comprises freedom of establishment. It extends to self-employed natural persons. Mainly based on the Union's citizenship, migration rights were eventually extended to non-commercial residents. The scope of transnational migration rights within Europe is exceptional. It is close to federacy and for such reasons also triggers much resistance which led to populism and the Brexit movement in the UK.

Multilateral agreements exist on certain single security aspects related to the mobility of people, such as terrorism, drug trafficking, transnational organised crime, migrant smuggling and trafficking in human beings. These aspects are regulated in international conventions such as the United Nations Convention against Transnational Organized Crime and the Protocols thereto[48] and the Protocol to Prevent, Suppress and Punish Trafficking in Persons, Especially Women and Children.[49] A significant number of signatory states have shown their willingness

---

[44] See University of Chicago, 'Bilateral Labor Agreements Data Set', www.law.uchicago.edu/bilateral-labor-agreements-dataset (accessed July 2019); A. S. Chilton and E. Posner, 'Why Countries Sign Bilateral Labor Agreements' (2017), https://ssm.com/abstract_2926994 (accessed July 2019). 2019). Philippines is the country of origin with the most bilateral labour agreements according to ILO, www.ilo.org/asia/areas/labour-migration/WCMS_226300/lang–en/index.htm (accessed July 2019).

[45] For example, Article 27(2) Federal Constitution of Switzerland; Articles 45–62 Treaty of the functioning of the European Union (hereafter TFEU), 2012/C 326/1, https://eur-lex.europa.eu/legal-content/EN/TXT/PDF/?uri=OJ:C:2012:326:FULL&from=EN (accessed July 2019).

[46] Ibid., at 40.

[47] Ibid., at 43.

[48] GA Res. A/RES/55/25 of 15 Nov. 2000.

[49] GA Res. A/RES/55/25 of 15 Nov. 2000, Text Doc. A/55/383 , supplementing the United Nations Convention against Transnational Organized Crime.

MIGRATION

to cooperate on various security aspects through these conventions to reinforce their sovereignty, effective control and law enforcement.[50]

Overall, states have been extremely reluctant to enter into legally binding commitments in international law allowing for the influx of migrants outside of political and economic unions. Refugee law marks the exception and proves the point. There are currently no legally binding multilateral instruments or formal structures at the international level to regulate economic or climate-induced migration, nor are such in view. However, a certain convergence in practice related to certain aspects of migration governance can be observed in single areas, which over time and in the long term could lead to legally binding international instruments, structures and/or forums:

On a regional level, the state-led, informal and non-binding Regional Consultative Processes on Migration (RCPs) build confidence among the participant states and foster thus common understanding on specific migration issues in a cooperative manner. They are composed by states and observer organisations such as the IOM, the Centre for Migration Policy Development (ICMPD), the Office of the United Nations High Commissioner for Refugees (UNHCR) and the Economic Community of West African States (ECOWAS).[51] These RCPs feed the discourse at a higher level of governance and are fed by it, such as in the Global Forum on Migration and Development (GFMD). At the same time, the RCPs interact with the nation states, which defend their domestic interests in a regional context as they do at the same time shape the national debates on migration. A good example of this interplay was the discussion on the whole-of-governance approach within different international and regional processes and finally operationalised by Switzerland through its Interdepartmental Structure for International Cooperation on Migration (ICM Structure).[52] It was adopted by the Philippines and

---

[50] For an overview of the international conventions addressing crimes frequently associated with migration, see D. Fischer, S. Martin and A. Schoenholtz, 'Migration and Security in International Law', in Aleinikoff and Chetail, *supra* n. 25, pp. 87–120.

[51] For an exhaustive list, see IOM, 'Regional Consultative Processes on Migration', www .iom.int/regional-consultative-processes-migration (accessed July 2019).

[52] Swiss Government, 'Swiss Interdepartmental Structure for International Cooperation on Migration (ICM Structure)', www.sem.admin.ch/sem/en/home/internationales/internat-zusarbeit/imz-struktur.html (accessed July 2019). See Section 6.4.

influences similar governmental structures in Peru, Salvador, Spain and Haiti.[53]

Finally, at the international level, the resettlement programmes of the states in cooperation with the UN Refugee Agency (UNHCR) are an expression of international cooperation, solidarity and responsibility on a voluntary basis.[54] These programmes relieve the burden on first refugee states that have already taken in a large number of refugees. They are an expression of enhanced international cooperation and fulfil positively the Migration Governance Indicators developed by the International Organization for Migration (IOM)[55] (to assess national migration governance frameworks).[56] The GFMD is a further expression of deep international cooperation on a voluntary basis. It paved the way for the adoption of the Global Compact for Safe, Orderly and Regular Migration (GCM) discussed below.[57]

6.2.2 The Legacy of Pervasive National Sovereignty

Compared to international trade regulation for goods and services on the basis of WTO law and preferential trade agreements,[58] international regulation of migration and migration law enforcement thus has remained embryonic. Governments invoke national sovereignty, mainly perceived to grant independence and self-determination.[59] They wish to regulate and control migration on their own terms. In addition, populist movements around the world, in particular, emphasise the importance of national sovereignty and self-regulation of migration flows, abhorring

---

[53] See OECD/KNOMAD, opinion notes, 'Workshop: Strengthening the Migration–Development Nexus through Improved Policy and Institutional Coherence', www.oecd .org/dev/migration-development/2013%2012%2010%20opinion%20notes%20-%20with %20cover.pdf (accessed July 2019).

[54] See UNHCR Schweiz/Staatssekretariat für Migration, 'Ressetlement-Programm Schweiz', www.sem.admin.ch/dam/data/sem/asyl/syrien/booklet-resettlement-d.pdf and UNHCR Deutschland, www.uno-fluechtlingshilfe.de/fluechtlinge/zukunft/resettlement/ (accessed July 2019).

[55] IOM, 'Migration Governance Indicators', https://gmdac.iom.int/migration-governance-indicators (accessed July 2019).

[56] IOM, 'Migration Governance Framework', www.iom.int/sites/default/files/about-iom/ migof_brochure_a4_en.pdf (accessed July 2019).

[57] Section 6.2.3.5.

[58] See generally T. Cottier and M. Oesch, *International Trade Regulation: Law and Policy in the WTO, the European Union and Switzerland* (London Cameron May & Staempfli, 2005).

[59] On sovereignty, see Chapters 1 and 4 in this volume

MIGRATION 303

multilateral agreements as anathema to proud self-determination, even democracy and self-governance.

As a result, states seek to keep out as many foreigners and return as many irregular migrants as possible while inviting and expelling the amount of (guest) workers[60] they need on their own terms. They do not care if other states and neighbours run into problems, for example by brain drains[61] or in the allocation of refugees. This holds true even within higher levels of integration, including the EU or within confederacies. Relating to refugees, burden-sharing agreements have been difficult to achieve and are not always implemented.[62] Hungary and Poland categorically refuse to accept a quota system; and the EU failed to support Italy in the operation *Mare Nostrum*, saving shipwrecked refugees in the Mediterranean Sea. This is impossible to square with the EU's commitment to human rights and human dignity. Rather, it is easily squared with outdated perceptions of national sovereignty of the member states and related countries. Even within federacy, different cantons and communes in Switzerland, for example, quarrel about the burden-sharing of refugees, the geographical placement of federal centres and the allocation of work permits for foreign workers in pursuit of their own economic and financial interests. Some of these cantons and communes support the idea of an automatic deportation of convicted terrorists even in those cases where the non-refoulement principle applies contravening though the *jus cogens* precept.[63]

[60] These programmes were designed to meet the short-term shortage in European and US labour markets, and created unexpected problems when the workers did not usually return, but evolved into residents or overstayed enlarging the numbers of irregular migrants (P. L. Martin and M. J. Miller, 'Guestworkers: Lessons from Western Europe', *ILR Review*, 33(1980), 315–30).

[61] Ibid., at 37. For example health personnel in search of better quality of life, see S. Dodani and R. E. LaPorte, 'Brain Drain from Developing Countries: How Can Brain Drain Be Converted into Wisdom Gain?', *Journal of the Royal Society of Medicine*, 98 (2005), 487–91, www.ncbi.nlm.nih.gov/pmc/articles/PMC1275994/ (accessed July 2019).

[62] Only a limited number of countries participate in the UNHCR's resettlement programme, www.unhcr.org/resettlement.html (accessed July 2019) although the UNHCR projected global resettlement needs from more than sixty countries of asylum: 'Africa remains the region with the highest projected resettlement needs with an estimated 629,744 refugees in need of resettlement from 31 different countries of asylum', 10, www.unhcr.org/protection/resettlement/5b28a7df4/projected-global-resettlement-needs-2019.html (accessed July 2019).

[63] Swissinfo, 'Swiss Parliament's Move to Deport Terrorists Draws Criticism', www .swissinfo.ch/eng/basic-rights_swiss-parliament-wants-to-deport-terrorists/44836866 (accessed July 2019).

All these reflect one-sided perceptions of sovereignty. Since the Westphalian Peace of 1648, the American Revolution and the process of decolonisation in nineteenth-century Latin America and after the Second World War in the twentieth century, national sovereignty stands for the proposition of liberty, independence and self-determination. Principles of non-intervention and the prohibition of war and aggression are essentially built on this trait and tradition. It is on this foundation that migration laws are currently built.

The attitude has led into migration what in the field of international trade we call beggar-thy-neighbour policies.[64] Mercantilist policies seek to maximise benefits at the cost of partners and neighbours, letting alone individuals to be affected. They are perceived as a zero-sum game. For example, countries such as Spain 'import' Moroccan tomato pickers. Or it outsources tomato production to Morocco, depending on the season, to lower the production costs irrespective of implications for social and economic development.[65] As a result, restrictive policies often lead to large numbers of illegal migration. The number of undocumented migrants (*sin papeles*) in Spain is estimated to be around 500,000.[66] Or, the lack of coordination with trade and investment policies results in unexpected migration flows.[67] In the case of the North American Free Trade Agreement (NAFTA), the relationship between trade liberalisation and migration data indicates that increasing trade flows cause larger illegal migration from Mexico to the United States.[68] In reaction to this, some countries try to reverse the flows with fences and walls, but:

---

[64] Beggar-thy-neighbour policies aim at addressing domestic problems at the expenses of other states; according to the *Business Dictionary* it 'attempts to cure a country's balance of trade, inflation, and unemployment problems by practices that harm the economic interests of its trading partners', www.businessdictionary.com/definition/beggar-thy-neighbor-policy.html (accessed 24 July 2019). Similarly the former UN Special Representative of the Secretary-General on Migration, Peter Sutherland defines the standoff in the negotiations to readmission agreements as an exercise of 'mutual blackmail', in Report of the Special Representative of the Secretary-General on Migration (A/71/728), United Nations, 14, para. 39.

[65] See www.theguardian.com/business/2011/feb/07/spain-salad-growers-slaves-charities.

[66] W. G. White, 'Sovereignty and International Labor Migration: The "Security Mentality" in Spanish–Moroccan Relations as an Assertion of Sovereignty', *Review of International Political Economy*, 14 (2007), 690–718.

[67] Ibid., at 17.

[68] A. Melchor del Río and S. Thorwarth, 'Tomatoes or Tomato Pickers? Free Trade and Migration in the NAFTA Case', *SSRN Electronic Journal* (2007), http://dx.doi.org/10.2139/ssrn.1102031.

MIGRATION   305

The stricken aspect about the fences is that they have not slowed the flow
of contraband/cambia into the Moroccan 'hinterland'. They have also has
not slowed the flow of day laborers. They may, however, have diverted
flow of migrants to taking more perilous crossing in pateras, rickety boats,
across the Strait of Gibraltar and increasingly the Atlantic Ocean passage
to the Canary Islands.[69]

There is an agreement in the literature as well as in domestic policy that
improving economic perspectives in source countries is the most promising long-term strategy for real development.[70] Yet, restrictive policies
are not sufficiently coordinated with such long-term goals, entailing
education and training, and often operate with an isolated logic of
their own.

6.2.3   Towards International Cooperation

The shortcomings of the situation in light of increasing and complex
migration flows are increasingly recognised on the international level.
Since the inception of the Berne Initiative by the Swiss government
important efforts are underway to address legal fragmentation and to
bring about better coordination among states and of different policies
with an influence on migration.

6.2.3.1   The Berne Initiative

The Berne Initiative, intellectually led by Jean Daniel Gerber, the then
Director of the Federal Office of Refugees in 2001,[71] was a state-led
consultative process composed by source, transit and destination countries with the goal to converge expectations on the governance (conceptual and strategic level) and the management (operationalisation level
defining variables into measurable factors) of migration. It aimed at
enhancing cooperation between states with a holistic or comprehensive
approach to international migration and related issues, such as economic
growth. As a result of the informal debates during the time of this
Initiative, irregular migration was identified as the major common concern for developed and developing countries alike, undermining state

---

[69] Ibid., at 58, 705.
[70] M. Susan, 'Toward a Global Migration Regime', *Georgetown Journal of International
Affairs*, 1 (2000), 119–27.
[71] M. Susan, *International Migration: Evolving Trends from the Early Twentieth Century to
the Present* (Cambridge: Cambridge University Press 2014), pp. 270–5.

sovereignty and representing a potential risk to state security and welfare and thus representing a risk to peace and stability.

The Berne Initiative developed as its major outcome an International Agenda for Migration Management, creating a process of non-binding, voluntary consultations among states from all regions for a 'common understanding for the management of international migration' in a comprehensive approach including effective practices.[72] This agenda set the road map to all further steps leading to the adoption of the GCM in 2019 (discussed later in the chapter).

6.2.3.2 The United Nations Dialogue on International Migration and Development

The legacy of sovereignty and the long-standing focus on security aspects of migration and on administrative and penal law for a long time retarded the creation of appropriate international forums and organisations dealing with migration in a comprehensive manner. The United Nations started a process in 1994 with the Programme of Action at the International Conference on Population (CPD). Since 2001, IOM hosts the annual International Dialogue on Migration, addressing a wide range of topics.[73]

The work of the special rapporteurs on the right to migration has increasingly contributed to the debate. In 2005, the Global Migration Group (GMG) was founded on a recommendation by the Commission on International Migration. Today, it provides a network of twenty-two UN organisations addressing issues of migration in their respective fields with a view to achieving transparency and greater policy coherence.[74] The United Nations held a first high-level dialogue on international migration and development in 2006 which initiated the GFDM. This forum started work in 2007 as an active platform for governments and civil society in the field.[75] Since its inception, it held annual conferences producing topical reports and recommendation on migration policies.[76] A second high-level dialogue on international migration and development was held at the United Nations in October 2013. It paved the way to

---

[72] Ibid., at pp. 71, 273; Federal Office for Migration (FOM)/IOM, 'International Agenda for Migration Management', https://publications.iom.int/system/files/pdf/iamm.pdf (accessed July 2019).

[73] www.iom.int/international-dialogue-migration (accessed July 2019).

[74] www.globalmigrationgroup.org/ (accessed July 2019).

[75] https://gfmd.org/ (accessed July 2019).

[76] https://gfmd.org/meetings (accessed July 2019).

MIGRATION

including migration in the 2030 Sustainable Development Goals (SDGs), adopted in 2015. It laid the groundwork towards the 2018 Global Compact for Migration. The Report of the Special Representative of the Secretary-General on Migration, issued in 2017, amounts to an important landmark in this process.[77]

6.2.3.3   2030 SDGs

The 2030 Agenda for Sustainable Development provides an important framework to improve global governance of international migration.[78] It acknowledges the contribution of migrants to development. The call to facilitate safe and regular migration marks a change of paradigm, which began with the report of the Global Commission on International Migration in 2005. This commission was composed of nineteen members to promote a comprehensive debate on international migration to reach a broader understanding of it by reviewing migration policy approaches and best practice, by conducting research on the interlinkages of migration to other areas such as trade and international cooperation, by collecting and diffusing migration-related information and by focusing on the international governance of migration.[79] It finished its work on 31 December 2005. As a result of its recommendations, the GMG was established by the United Nations Secretary-General in early 2006.[80] By sustaining the inter-agency cooperation, it contributed to the establishment of the intergovernmental consultative process, the GFMD. The GMG was replaced on 23 May 2018 by the UN Network on Migration based on the decision of the Executive Committee.[81] António Guterres, UN Secretary-General 'commends the Network . . . as a visible sign of the United Nations system's commitment to working . . . in the implementation of this historic Global Compact for Migration'.[82]

---

[77] www.un.org/en/ga/search/view_doc.asp?symbol=A/71/728&=E%20%20 (accessed July 2019).

[78] https://sustainabledevelopment.un.org/?menu=1300 (accessed July 2019).

[79] IOM, Global Commission on International Migration, and related documents, such as its mandate, in www.iom.int/global-commission-international-migration (accessed July 2019).

[80] On the GMG and related documents, see https://globalmigrationgroup.org/what-is-the-gmg (accessed July 2019).

[81] UN, Terms of Reference for the UN Network on Migration, www.un.org/en/conf/migration/assets/pdf/UN-Network-on-Migration_TOR.pdf (accessed July 2019).

[82] António Guterres, 'Remarks on UN Network on Migration', 9 Dec. 2018, United Nations, www.un.org/sg/en/content/sg/speeches/2018-12-09/remarks-un-network-migration (accessed July 2019).

The seventeen SDGs, with their 169 targets,[83] form the core of the 2030 Agenda. The SDGs recognise for the first time in history the contribution of migration to sustainable development – particularly in its target 10.7 to facilitate orderly, safe, regular and responsible migration and mobility of people, including the implementation of planned and well-managed migration policies, which appears under Goal 10 to reduce inequality within and among countries.[84]

Eleven out of its seventeen goals are related directly or indirectly to migration and contain targets and indicators that are relevant to migration or mobility, such as: Goal 3 on health, because migrants are particularly vulnerable to health issues; Goal 4 on education, for instance to facilitate mobility to students from developing countries to study abroad, Goal 5 on gender equality to support migrant women in its different gender-based aspects such as gender-based violence; Goal 8 on decent work for an ethical recruitment or to protect human working conditions; Goal 11 on sustainable cities as the centre of the lives of migrants; Goal 13 on climate action to tackle with climate-related displacement; Goal 16 on peaceful societies to prevent trafficking in persons and to eliminate all form of violence against migrants; and finally Goal 17 on partnerships to meet the specific needs on migration and to pursue better data for improved evidence-based migration policies.[85]

For the first time, the SDGs were developed as a blueprint and pledged to leave no one behind to achieve a better and more sustainable future for all. The goals balance the economic, social and ecological dimensions of sustainable development by interconnecting all the challenges in a comprehensive 360-degree perspective. They place the struggle against poverty and sustainable development on the same agenda with migration and provide an important foundation towards developing better concentration and concertation of different policy areas, including migration to reach the goals.

---

[83] UNSTAT, Global Indicator Framework for the Sustainable Development Goals and Targets of the 2030 Agenda for Sustainable Development, https://unstats.un.org/sdgs/indicators/Global%20Indicator%20Framework%20after%20refinement_Eng.pdf (accessed July 2019).

[84] KNOMAD, Statistics for SDG indicator 10.7.1, Draft Guidelines for their Collection, www.knomad.org/sites/default/files/2018-10/Guidelines%20for%20statistics%20for%20SDG%20indicator%2010.7.1%20-%20%20September%2019.2018.pdf (accessed July 2019).

[85] Migration Data Portal; see the SDG wheel migration-related goals, https://migrationdataportal.org/sdgs#0 (accessed July 2019).

6.2.3.4   The Sutherland Report

Peter Sutherland, the UN Special Representative on Migration (and former Director-General of the WTO) developed in his 2017 Report to the UN General Assembly a forward-looking agenda for action and sixteen recommendations for improving management of international migration through international cooperation.[86] In this report, the Special Representative shares his views in a road map for improving the governance of international migration.

His report makes sixteen recommendations for better managing migration through enhanced international cooperation by means of facts-based migration policies. It postulates a multi-actor engagement in migration policy planning and implementation, including the relevant actors of all layers of the multilayered governance approach such as civil society, especially including migrants and diaspora. His report was used as a basis for all interested stakeholders to inform the Global Compact which the UN member states negotiated in 2017 and 2018 and was understood as commitments forming a road map and had to be embedded in a wider social contract between government and their citizens,[87] creating thus a new fact-based narrative on migration enhancing its positive effects and managing its adverse ones.

Peter Sutherland understood migration as an enduring fact and a contribution to foster development – in the same way as migration is understood by other relevant UN bodies.[88] He highlights in his report the contributions of migrants to GDP – bringing into the migration discourse a new interrelationship beyond the migration–development nexus, such as the triangle between trade, investment and migration to foster development.[89] He highlighted the important role of migrants as catalysers or engines for development.

---

[86] UN, Report of the Special Representative of the Secretary-General on Migration, GA 71st Session Doc. A/71/728 (3 Feb. 2017); https://refugeesmigrants.un.org/sites/default/files/sg_report_en.pdf (accessed July 2019) (hereafter A/71/728); see also United Nations, *Making Migration Work for All*, Report of the Secretary General, GA A/72/643 (12 Dec. 2017); https://refugeesmigrants.un.org/sites/default/files/sg_report_en.pdf (accessed July 2019).

[87] A/71/728, *supra* n. 86, paras. 15 and 88.

[88] See IOM, 'The Contribution of Migrants and Migration to Development – Strengthening the Linkages', Global Compact Thematic Paper, www.iom.int/sites/default/files/our_work/ODG/GCM/IOM-Thematic-Paper-Contributions-of-Migrants-and-Migration-to-Developm.pdf (accessed July 2019).

[89] A/71/728, *supra* n. 86, para. 35, fn. 16; *e contrario* para. 39 blackmailing states by conditioning trade and development aid to cooperation in return policies; para. 42 'aid

His thoughts have influenced the GCM to the effect that the GCM indeed took up the triangle of migration, trade and investment as a new dimension to explore in the global discourse.[90]

Peter Sutherland intended to develop instruments for an evidence-based narrative to change the fundamentally negative perception of migration into a better one to support more positive attitudes towards migrants.[91] Based on his experience as a the founding director-general of the WTO, he tried to overcome the dual policy paradox[92] between trade and immigration policies tackling the challenges of migration at the lowest level where they can be solved, usually at the local level (cities as first point of contact of migrants and refugees) – sometimes at the national level and by trying to neutralise narratives on migration[93] by tackling the issue with facts and figures,[94] as it is done in trade policy.

Peter Sutherland postulated in his report a global and comprehensive partnership approach among all actors concerned to tackle migration together with other relevant policies such as trade, investment, education and agriculture among others in order 'to strengthen the social contract between host countries and communities, and refugees and migrants'.[95]

---

for trade'; para. 59 (a) including health and agriculture. On the migration–trade–investment nexus, see T. Cottier and C. Sieber-Gasser, 'Labour Migration, Trade and Investment: From Fragmentation to Coherence', in Panizzon et al., supra n. 25, pp. 41–60.

[90] A/71/728, supra n. 86, at 75.

[91] Ibid., para. 88, the UN TOGETHER campaign was launched at the UN Summit for Refugees and Migrants in 2016 and has been implemented in partnership with member states, the private sector and civil society running until 2018 when the two global compacts were adopted. See https://refugeesmigrants.un.org/ (accessed July 2019).

[92] T. J. Hatton and J. G. Williamson 'A Dual Policy Paradox: Why Have Trade and Immigration Policies Always Differed in Labor-Scarce Economies', IZA Discussion Papers, No. 2146, Nov. 2005, www.nber.org/papers/w11866 (accessed July 2019).

[93] This goal has been reflected in objective 17 of the GCM, A/RES/73/195, p. 7, www.un.org/en/ga/search/view_doc.asp?symbol=A/RES/73/195 (accessed July 2019).

[94] This goal has been reflected in objective 1 of the Global Compact for Migration (GCM), A/RES/73/195, p. 6, www.un.org/en/ga/search/view_doc.asp?symbol=A/RES/73/195 (accessed 19 July 2019). G. Lemaitre and OECD, The Comparability of International Migration Statistics, Problems and Prospects, www.oecd.org/migration/49215740.pdf (accessed 19 July 2019): Data available on international migration flows lack compatibility due to the different survey methods and therefore do not provide a clear idea on the real scale of international migration flows.

[95] A/71/728, supra n. 86, para. 88, fn. 50.

6.2.3.5 The GCM: A New Social Contract

Over the years, states as well as many overburdened governments in other parts of the world drew the conclusion that migration movements can no longer be controlled nationally alone, but that this requires lasting cooperation based on trust between the countries of origin, transit and receiving.[96] In 2016, the UN states therefore agreed in the New York Declaration to initiate a process to ensure better cooperation.

Given the political sensitivities, the effort to develop a Global Compact for Migration (GCM) and on Refugees (GCR) does not entail the creation of a rule-based system, but rather serves as a forum of discussion and soft-law standard making. The main purpose of these instruments is to create the foundations for international cooperation and to build mutual trust.

The GCM was approved by 192 countries in June 2018. It was adopted by the Intergovernmental Conference to Adopt the Global Compact for Safe, Orderly and Regular Migration which took place in Marrakech, Morocco, from 10 to 11 December 2018 by 164 countries with the United States, Austria, Hungary and Switzerland abstaining.[97] It was eventually endorsed during a plenary meeting of the UNGA on 19 December 2018, at UN headquarters in New York by 152 states.[98] Six countries, including the United States, Hungary, Israel, Czech Republic and Poland voted against it. Twelve countries, including Algeria, Australia, Austria, Bulgaria, Chile, Italy, Latvia, Libya, Liechtenstein, Romania, Singapore and Switzerland as a co-facilitator abstained from the vote. Such conduct was mainly motivated by national conservative pressures and misunderstandings on the purpose and content of the instrument. The Swiss government postponed on motion of parliament despite its role as an active and successful co-coordinator of the effort. (It did not wish to indirectly support a concurrent impending constitutional amendment seeking to challenge the primacy of international law under the federal

---

[96] IOM, *World Migration Report 2018*, pp. 145–7, www.iom.int/sites/default/files/country/docs/china/r5_world_migration_report_2018_en.pdf (accessed July 2019).

[97] United Nations Blog, *Historic Global Compact for Migration Adopted*, 10 Dec. 2018, https://blogs.un.org/blog/2018/12/10/historic-global-compact-for-migration-adopted/ (accessed July 2019).

[98] Global Compact for Safe, Orderly and Regular Migration, Res. A/73/195, UNGA 73rd Session (19 Dec. 2018) (hereafter A/RES/73/195), www.un.org/en/ga/search/view_doc.asp?symbol=A/RES/73/195 (accessed July 2019).

constitution which was eventually defeated in November 2018.)[99] The United States voted against the GCM based on its 'America first' policy. The Trump administration understands the GCM as 'simply not compatible with US sovereignty'.[100]

The Global Pact on Migration is the result of intense global dialogue and cooperation within the framework of the GFMD. In this dialogue on migration, insights and instruments have been developed which, due to their soft-law character, often have not been implemented by states. Examples include migration partnerships or the holistic and comprehensive whole-of-government approach, as well as improved intragovernmental cooperation structures in the field of migration.[101] Also, in this forum, the connection between migration and trade and investment for more development in the countries of origin was discussed for the first time in 2011 during the Swiss presidency.[102]

In addition to the desire for effective migration management, there is a well-documented realisation that safe, regulated and legal migration is in the interest of all involved – the countries of origin, the countries of destination and the migrants themselves. In recent years, it has become increasingly clear how much industrialised countries are dependent on immigration to maintain their productivity and prosperity. On the other hand, the importance of remittances and safe money transfers and investments by migrants became prominent, both for their home countries and for improving the lives of families and thus for social and economic development in general.[103]

These findings have been incorporated into the twenty-three objectives of the Pact. It explicitly includes the objective of reducing irregular

---

[99] Swissinfo, '"Swiss Law First" Initiative Given Short Shrift at Polls', Nov. 2018, www.swissinfo.ch/eng/vote-november-25-2018_hotly-debated-swiss-law-first-initiative-awaits-public-verdict/44559238 (accessed July 2019).

[100] 'Donald Trump Pulls US Out of UN Global Compact on Migration', *The Guardian*, 3 Dec. 2107, www.theguardian.com/world/2017/dec/03/donald-trump-pulls-us-out-of-un-global-compact-on-migration (accessed July 2019).

[101] OECD, *supra* n. 53. New forms of cooperation such as cooperatives in migration in the case of economic migrants are explored by M. Osterloh and B. S. Frey, 'Cooperatives Instead of Migration Partnerships', *Analyse & Kritik*, 40 (2018), 201–25; www.business.uzh.ch/dam/jcr:d7516072-358d-4976-a032-8005bb891e2d/Analyse__Kritik__Cooperatives_Instead_of_Migration_Partnerships.pdf (accessed July 2019).

[102] GFMD 2011, 'Markets for Migration and Development, Trade and Labour Mobility Linkages – Prospects for Development?' (thematic meeting), https://gfmd.org/files/documents/m4md_meeting_report_draft_10112011.pdf (accessed July 2019).

[103] A/RES/73/195, *supra* n. 98, objectives 15–16 and 18–20.

migration and its negative effects on all participants.[104] The objectives include issuing documents and forgery-proof passports,[105] combating human smuggling and trafficking,[106] improving cooperation between states on border controls and on the readmission and reintegration of migrants who have to leave the host country.[107]

The GCM is not a binding treaty under international law, but a declaration of intent, the implementation of which is decided solely by the signatory states. It is therefore no more and no less than a framework for more effective migration policy. To this end, the Pact reaffirms legal principles that the UN states must follow anyway because they are laid down in international treaties. These include human rights, but also the promotion of the rule of law and good governance. The Pact is important because it offers the signatory states practical support in cooperation, especially in setting up administrative structures to better manage migration. At no point, however, does the Pact interfere with the right of states to determine to whom they grant access to their territory. Even though it is repeatedly asserted, the Pact does not call for an expansion of migration.[108] The Pact expressly points out that states will continue to establish their own rules for entry, settlement and access to the labour market and to decide on them independently.

6.2.3.6 Challenges Ahead

The support of the GCM by the vast majority of the UN member states proves the need for a new social contract entailing the twenty-three objectives of the Pact. While recognising national prerogatives, the document expresses, on the basis of a process dating back to 2006, that migration as a fact can only be successfully managed and regulation in international cooperation with a view to securing global peace and stability. In a sense, migration has been established with the Pact as a common concern of all states and societies affected.

Today, the main international challenges relate to the process of implementation and of funding of migration policies.[109] How can the

---

[104] Ibid., objective 2 as well as indirect in objectives 10–11 and 21.

[105] Ibid., objective 4.

[106] Ibid., objective 9–10.

[107] Ibid., 11–12, 21 and 23.

[108] This is despite there being the misleading and unfortunate 'for' in the title Global Compact 'for' Migration.

[109] RES A/71/728, *supra* n. 86, Recommendation 9 calls for a more concerted effort (e.g. through a coordinated campaign led by the International Fund for Agricultural

problem of free-riding, the lack of reciprocity and failure to cooperate be addressed? How can policies of beggar-thy-neighbour be overcome in the field of international migration? What legal obligations at cooperation should states eventually incur with a view to jointly and orderly managing international migration flows? How could compliance with commitments made be secured?

In terms of instruments, and following the advice of Sutherland, one has to mainly rely on tools available and to be developed in international economic law and those available in domestic constitutional law and rules in regulating migration flows. These approaches need to be developed and supported on the basis of empirical evidence on the efficiency of the policy. They recognise that states have the power to deny entry and to expel foreigners who do not have adequate immigration status and their security agencies have a legitimate mandate to investigate security risks related to the presence of foreigners within their jurisdiction. At the same time, these approaches also recognise the need for international cooperation and the need to assume international responsibilities beyond own borders.

Finally, if migration is commonly perceived as part of the present reality and is accompanied by a new evidence-based narrative defining it as such, it could indeed be possible to harness the dynamics of migration and manage its negative consequences more efficiently than has been the case to date. At the same time, this new narrative may potentially influence the public outlook to accept migration in an objective manner, opening the opportunity to develop a symbiotic relationship with it, in turn influencing the narrative in the long term.[110]

In this context, the question arises as to what the emerging doctrine and principle of Common Concern of Humankind, developed in other areas of public international law, offers guidance in shaping future rights and obligations of international cooperation in the field of migration. Much of the recent process observed in migration discussions resemble the underlying ideas of common concern as a focus to strengthen international cooperation. We submit that the doctrine and emerging

---

Development and the World Bank) to forge operational partnerships among government policymakers and regulators, financial industry representatives and technology entrepreneurs (p. 23).

[110] C. Betsch, N. Haase, F. Renkewitz and P. Schmid, 'The Narrative Bias Revisited: What Drives the Biasing Influence of Narrative Information on Risk Perception', *Judgment and Decision Making*, 10 (2015), 241–64.

principle can make an important contribution to offer guidance in fostering awareness of interdependence and working towards a different narrative of migration for which common concern could emerge as a foundation and symbol. It may lead the field towards the perception of cooperative sovereignty.[111]

We thus briefly recall the emergence of the doctrine of Common Concern of Humankind in international law. Based on the principle and its implications outlined, we examine its potential in the field of international migration law in the following sections.

6.3 The Emerging Doctrine and Principle of Common Concern of Humankind

The 1992 United Nations Framework Convention on Climate Change[112] and the 2015 Paris Agreement[113] recognise that climate change amounts to a common concern of humankind. The same is true for the loss of biodiversity,[114] access to genetic resources[115] and the threats to cultural heritage.[116] The notion of common concern is, at this point in time, not

---

[111] For the concept of shared sovereignty, see T. Cottier and M. Hertig, 'The Prospects of 21st Century Constitutionalism', *Max Planck Yearbook of United Nations Law*, 7 (2003), 304–13.

[112] https://unfccc.int/resource/docs/convkp/conveng.pdf (accessed July 2019) ('Acknowledging that change in the Earth's climate and its adverse effects are a common concern of humankind').

[113] United Nations Framework Convention on Climate Change, 9 May 1992, 31 ILM 849, 851; https://unfccc.int/files/essential_background/convention/application/pdf/english_paris_agreement.pdf (accessed July 2019) ('Acknowledging that climate change is a common concern of humankind, Parties should, when taking action to address climate change, respect, promote and consider their respective obligations on human rights, the right to health, the rights of indigenous peoples, local communities, migrants, children, persons with disabilities and people in vulnerable situations and the right to development, as well as gender equality, empowerment of women and intergenerational equity').

[114] Convention on Biological Diversity, 5 June 1992, 31 ILM 818, 822 ('Affirming that the conservation of biological diversity is a common concern of humankind'). www.cbd.int/doc/legal/cbd-en.pdf (accessed July 2019).

[115] International Treaty on Plant Genetic Resources for Food and Agriculture, preamble, para. 3, adopted by consensus at the 31st Session of the Conference of the FAO, 3 Nov. 2001, ftp://ftp.fao.org/docrep/fao/011/i0510e/i0510e.pdf; stating that 'plant genetic resources for food and agriculture are a common concern of all countries, in that all countries depend very largely on plant genetic resources for food and agriculture that originated elsewhere'.

[116] Convention for the Safeguarding of the Intangible Cultural Heritage, Convention for the Safeguarding of the Intangible Cultural Heritage adopted 17 Oct. 2003; http://unesdoc.unesco.org/images/0013/001325/132540e.pdf (accessed 18 Feb. 2018) ('Being aware of

further defined in these instruments, but simply evoked. The contours still need to be defined, and its implications and impact are unclear. We submit, as developed in the introductory chapter to this volume, that the emerging doctrine of Common Concern of Humankind is suitable to develop into a legal principle of international law, offering guidance in defining obligations at cooperation, homework and compliance.[117] Obviously, the state of play and law, in the tradition of the migration state, is far from meeting these goals. Common Concern, however, offers a long-term view and a compass as to how the complexities and intricacies of the field can be approached with a different narrative.

The principle of Common Concern offers the potential to rebalance international law based on territoriality, sovereignty and a reframing of international institutions to better manage global public goods. A basic premise of this chapter is that the principles of Common Concern of Humankind, as originally developed to address global climate change concerns, can be reformulated to address collective aspects of migration as well. Migration, if badly managed, entails the potential to threaten international peace and security and lead to internal strife and potentially even warfare. Moreover, it is recalled that migration is hardly addressed in international law beyond the status and treatment of refugees. We have seen that international cooperation still is in an infant stage, but a promising one. Dealing with migration as a Common Concern of Humankind offers a framework to develop responsibilities of states towards better and more successful migration governance, both at home and abroad.

6.3.1 Claims and Responses

We recall that it is not possible to define a particular Common Concern of Humankind all at once for all and in advance. Some concerns are known and were recognised in international law; new problems and challenges may yet arise in the course of globalisation and technological progress. We thus need to reiterate the mechanisms of how Common Concerns may be identified. They may be recognised in treaty law, such as in the cases of global warming and of the loss of biodiversity. They may eventually be recognised as a matter of customary international law

---

the universal will and the common concern to safeguard the intangible cultural heritage of humanity').

[117] See Chapter 1 in this volume.

MIGRATION 317

in the process of claims and responses. Civil society and governments may invoke a concern to be common, and it may be accepted, or refuted, as such based on expression and conduct by governments. Common Concerns may also be recognised by courts of law. The process is comparable to the recognition of the principles of the common heritage of humankind, or the principle of sustainable development which travelled a long way since it was introduced by the *Brundtland Report* in 1987[118] until its general acceptance in the international and business community as one of the principles guiding action and future rulemaking in all the different fields.

The long process of claims and responses from a wide range of different agents, such as governments, civil society, companies, international organisations, migrants themselves (as organised in diaspora associations) contributed, within different regional and global forums, to an ongoing and evolving international migration dialogue. This dialogue depicted above created a common understanding that a common cooperative approach to migration needs to be developed. It resulted, as a first step, in the GCM. We are confident that these processes of claims and responses may eventually qualify migration as a Common Concern of Humankind, further building on its recognition for climate migration under the 2015 Paris Agreement. Of course, the quest for enhanced international cooperation will, for the time being, be subjected to reiterated recourses to national sovereignty and the tradition of the migration state unilaterally defining its policies in the field. Increasing flows of migration, however, will support learning processes in society and politics that the topic cannot be addressed in isolation, but depends on effective international cooperation, similar to other areas such as international trade. A new doctrine or principle thus will be most welcome in this debate.

6.3.2 Addressing Shared Problems Relevant to Peace and Stability

Common concern essentially depicts shared and unresolved problems which cannot be dealt with in isolation by a particular legal entity.[119]

---

[118] Commission on Environment and Development, *Our Common Future* (1987), www.are .admin.ch/are/en/home/sustainable-development/international-cooperation/2030agenda/un- _-milestones-in-sustainable-development/1987–brundtland-report.html (accessed July 2019).

[119] See Chapter 1 in this volume. For previous works on the subject, see T. Cottier, Ph. Aerni, B. Karapinar, *et al.*, 'The Principle of Common Concern and Climate Change', *Archiv des Völkerrechts*, 52 (2014), 293–324; T. Cottier, 'Improving Compliance: *jus cogens* and International Economic Law', *Netherlands Yearbook of International Law*, 46

They are inherently transboundary. Such problems may exist on all layers of governance, from local to global levels.[120] They may be bilateral or regional in dimension and depict a common concern limited to those involved.

It is important to stress that not every unsettled transboundary problem amounts to a Common Concern in the legal sense. Common Concerns are limited to potential threats of peace and stability and challenges of comparable importance for respective communities. Such threats may develop bilaterally, regionally or globally. There can be no doubt that significant migration flows, irrespective of their legal qualifications – as legal or not, as irregular or regular flows – bear the potential to threaten international peace and security in light of the fact that migration is not dealt with casually, but often gives rise to highly emotional debates and reactions. They may lead to confrontation. Recent history in Europe, following the refugee crisis caused by the Syrian civil war, demonstrates the need for early containment and international cooperation. The principle of Common Concern of Humankind addresses such configurations. Thus, not all issues of migration are matters of common concern. Individual refugees, seeking asylum in a country, do not trigger the threshold required and will not trigger rights and obligations under the principle of Common Concern unless they show patterns of constant abuse. Large flows of refugees, including economic and climate migration, however, will trigger the operation of the principle as inaction bears the potential of threatening peace and security globally or in a particular region.

Clearly, issues of migration have remained unresolved to the detriment of millions of humans on the move; migration is one of the major problems and challenges of our time, if not the most pressing one. It could be argued that the issue of international migrants not constituting more than 2.58 per cent of the world's population[121] (not counting

---

(2015), 329–56; K. N. Schefer and T. Cottier, 'Responsibility to Protect (R2P) and the Emerging Principle of Common Concern', in Peter Hilpold (ed.), *Responsibility to Protect (R2P): A New Paradigm of International Law?* (Leiden: Brill Nijhoff, 2014), pp. 123–42.

[120] See Chapter 1 in this volume, pp. 46–7.

[121] Our World in Data, net migration chart, https://ourworldindata.org/grapher/net-migra tion?tab=chart&time=1962..2017&country=East%20Asia%20%26%20Pacific%20(exclud ing%20high%20income)+Europe%20%26%20Central%20Asia%20(excluding%20high% 20income)+High%20income+Latin%20America%20%26%20Caribbean%20(excluding %20high%20income)+Low%20%26%20middle%20income+Low%20income+Lower%

MIGRATION

domestic displacements) is not a problem of magnitude, threating global peace and security. Yet, the political sensitivity of the issue, due to legitimate concerns and fears on all sides (expounded below), bears the potential of extensive spill-over effects in creating political tensions, damaging international relations and institutions. National conservative forces exploit migration for electoral gain, which substantially fosters populism and undermines democratic institutions, including the rule of law. Such developments have consequences for migrants, including effective protection of their rights, and beyond. They may affect the fabric of society at large as it creates an environment of nationalist hostility transposed in us–they, friend-and-foe policies. If not successively handled, migration is a ticking time bomb which may trigger explosions threatening peaceful relations among nations..

6.3.3   Adjustment to Migration as a Common Concern of Humankind

Defining the topic, it is important to note that it is not migration as such which amounts to the Common Concern. In much the same way that climate or biodiversity is not the concern as such, but rather changing climatic conditions and global warming, or the loss of biodiversity, we are concerned with transitional problems caused by migration and the challenges of integration and assimilation into foreign lands and cultures. From a historical point of view, migration flows have settled in the long run, with mainly positive, but sometimes negative effects. As much as climate change is an enduring fact of life, migration is a reality. The problem addressed here as a Common Concern relates to the transitional structural and societal challenges and adjustments which migration induces by international movements of persons. Today countries often cannot resolve and manage this problem successfully on their own. Migrating populations need support both when in transit and during transitional stays in migration camps and eventually in new working environments. Decisions on stays and allocations of migrants to different countries have to be made. For the past twenty years, the regional and global processes discussed have fostered a 'common language' of migration to this effect. Its evolution has shed light on what Common Concern

20middle%20income+Middle%20East%20%26%20North%20Africa%20(excluding%
20high%20income)+Middle%20income+Sub-Saharan%20Africa%20(excluding%20high
%20income)+Upper%20middle%20income (accessed July 2019), the chart shows global
differences among regions in the net migration rate.

seeks to capture in this context: the adaptation from a destabilising, transitioning and transformative process in all countries and societies involved in the migration cycle into a more harmonious, integrated society. This long-term cycle is referred to by Phil Martin as the 'migration hump'.[122] However, the correlation between income levels and the individual decision to migrate is more complex than suggested by this model.[123] A longer time period of about thirty years is needed for broader transformation and adaptation processes leading after two or three generations to a real inclusion of migrants and particularly their progeny in host societies. This process in return regularly triggers long-term sustainable development, resulting in a wage approximation in their home countries thanks to the investment of remittances or resulting from new forms of trade and thus curbing migratory pressure.

6.3.4   Basic Legal Implications Proposed

What are the legal implications once a problem is recognised as a Common Concern of Humankind in international law and relations? Briefly summarising, we suggest that they are threefold. The doctrine and a future principle of Common Concern of Humankind (in capital letters) allow for developing appropriate structures of international cooperation, the definition of homework by states and of remedies in case of failing compliance. These components may evolve into a legal principle entailing rights and obligations.[124]

6.3.4.1   The Duty to Cooperate

First, Common Concern triggers obligations of international cooperation. So far, such obligations only exist on the basis of specific customary or treaty provisions. No state, under the doctrine of self-determination and

---

[122] P. Martin, 'The Anatomy of a Migration Hump', in Taylor, *supra* n. 3, pp. 43–62.

[123] H. de Haas, 'Migration and Development: A Theoretical Perspective', *International Migration Review*, 44 (2010), 227–64; other factors such as demographic and structural transition, obstacles to migration, lack of capitalisation possibilities to increase wealth or acquire assets because of credit restriction as well as optimism or gender inform more or less the individual decision to migrate.

[124] See R. Dworkin, *Taking Rights Seriously* (Cambridge, MA: Harvard University Press, 1978) ('It follows from the definition of a right that it cannot be outweighed by all social goals. We might, for simplicity, stipulate not to call any political aim a right unless it has a certain threshold weight against collective goals in general; unless, for example, it cannot be defeated by appeal to any of the ordinary routine goals of political administration, but only by a goal of special urgency') (p. 92).

national sovereignty is otherwise obliged to work with other states if it does not wish to do so. This is particularly true in the field of migration. Apart from specific customary or treaty provisions, states are free to act on their own. It is even doubtful whether binding rules in the field, in particular, the principle of non-refoulement and guarantees of human rights, today trigger obligations of cooperation in the field. Recognising migration and its problems as Common Concern of Humankind establishes a basic and general obligation to cooperate in addressing impending and shared problems. It also entails a duty to negotiate. This is fully in line with, and confirms, international efforts described above since the first high-level dialogue on international migration, fostering international cooperation and the need for it. The doctrine and emerging principle of Common Concern provides a framework for cooperation and renders it legally binding beyond soft law.

6.3.4.2 The Duty to Do Homework

Second, Common Concern entails responsibilities to act within a given jurisdiction. States are obliged to do their homework in addressing an identified and recognised Common Concern of Humankind. These obligations may stem from international obligations incurred, including SDGs. They, however, are not limited to those but also call for autonomous measures and action in addressing the problem. In contrast to the principle of permanent sovereignty, the principle of Common Concern not only authorises but basically obliges governments to take action in addressing the Common Concern within their own jurisdictions and territories, for example with a view to achieving pledged goals under the Paris Accord of 2015. In climate change, however, we submit that national efforts towards abatement of global warming and addressing adaptation emanate from this principle independently of specific treaty obligations. Likewise, Common Concern of Humankind may in the future oblige states to take action to facilitate the adjustment and adaptation of migrants within their jurisdiction. Other than in climate change, we, however, do not see a problem with production and process methods having extraterritorial effects. We cannot imagine a similar configuration of extraterritorial effects in migration. Measures taken with effects abroad are either agreed on or pertain to the domain of compliance and law enforcement.

6.3.4.3 The Duty to Secure Compliance

Third, the principle of Common Concern authorises taking action in relation to facts and situations produced outside the proper jurisdiction of a state but pertaining to the recognised Common Concern. This is of particular importance where free-riding states fail to act and do their homework. A government failing to comply with obligations incurred in international law is subject to state responsibility. Other countries affected are entitled to take up countermeasures; when it comes to non-refoulement as a peremptory norm of *jus cogens*, all countries are entitled to take appropriate measures irrespective of whether their own nationals are affected or not. States may be obliged to do so under R2P (responsibility to protect).[125]

Under the principle of Common Concern, compliance amounts to an obligation *erga omnes*, and all states are entitled to take action irrespective of whether they are directly affected. The principle entails a right to act. It also entails, within its scope defined by threats to international peace and security, a duty to act. There is no automaticity. Such a duty is subject to the principle of proportionality, which in many cases will rule out appropriate action but nevertheless oblige governments, in the face of crisis, to justify non-action in a transparent manner.[126]

Rights and obligations relating to Common Concerns go beyond the traditional precepts of territoriality due to the fact that the problem is recognised as a Common Concern and potential threat to peace and stability. Today, state actions that trigger mass migration into neighbouring nations are recognised as a threat to international security. For example, UN Security Council Resolution 688 (1991) authorised the establishment of safe havens in northern Iraq.[127] While today extraterritorial action can be defended if the nexus with own territory is sufficient, Common Concern would not require such linkages but would depend on examination whether the measure and action are able to support the resolution and mitigation of a Common Concern as defined by the international community.

Countermeasures in response to state failure and free-riding measures or sanctions may relate to immigration itself. Mostly, and given the asymmetry, such measures will not be effective, and sanctions need to

---

[125] See K. N. Schefer and T. Cottier, 'Responsibility to Protect (R2P) and the Emerging Principle of Common Concern', in Hilpold, *supra* n. 119, pp. 123–42.
[126] See Chapter 1 in this volume, pp. 73, 76.
[127] United Nations Security Council Res. 688(1991), 5 Apr. 1991, http://unscr.com/en/resolutions/doc/688 (accessed July 2019).

MIGRATION 323

be found in other areas of international relations, in particular, international trade and investment to the extent permissible.[128]

6.4 Structuring the Debate and Approach to Migration

The recognition of relevant aspects of migration as a Common Concern of Humankind and basic legal implications deploy normative guidance in several respects. First, the recognition that this is a shared and common problem among nations helps to design proper structures of governance in terms of international cooperation and interagency cooperation within states in addressing migration issues. Second, the very recognition of a problem as a Common Concern also calls for all pertinent interests and stakeholders involved to be taken into account. It requires working towards a well-balanced approach taking into account all legitimate concerns and interests involved. Common Concern thus may assist in organising and reducing some of the complexities dominating the field.

6.4.1 Issues of Governance

The principle of Common Concern of Humankind, as applied to migration, supports the effort to enlarge the debate from its traditional focus on the migration state to international cooperation and the need for embedding powers and regulations on appropriate levels and layers of governance within states.

6.4.1.1 International Cooperation

Conceptualising migration as a Common Concern inherently leads to cooperative sovereignty and the recognition of the need for international cooperation. States need to come to grips with the allocation of rights and domestic obligations of states and the proper role of international organisations in the field. States will benefit from mutual support and collective action if they create appropriate international forums for such cooperation. They need to define the interaction with other international organisations and forums in coordinating different policy areas. The framework thus offers the basis and potential of greater coherence. Finally, efforts at compliance often will require cooperation as obligations to act may best be assumed jointly vis-à-vis failing states.

---

[128] See Section 6.5.1.

In developing appropriate governance structures within states, the principle of Common Concern also offers an interesting foundation for supporting such efforts in developing countries with weaker structures of government and a lack of respect for the rule of law. Cooperation with partner states from developed countries supports accelerating the socialisation of their own administration and governance. A good example of this process of socialisation is the set of bilateral relations between Switzerland and countries that are part of its migration partnerships.[129] With the enlargement of the subject matter of such agreements beyond migration pertaining to the jurisdiction of other ministries (such as economic affairs or education), the partner states were reciprocally required to involve the relevant ministries or administrative units in the negotiations. This in return triggered enhanced interagency cooperation within governments, which allowed for the whole-of-government approach to be enhanced. As a direct consequence, interior ministries are increasingly participating in multilateral forums and bodies in the field of migration. The relevant different ministries contribute concrete whole-of-government experience-based knowledge to migration that not only allows migration agreements to be expanded thematically but they also indirectly promote the development of governance structures in partner states. This in return also has the potential to somewhat reduce the asymmetry in bilateral relations between countries such as Switzerland and selected African countries.[130] The whole-of-government approach promotes more effective cooperation and creates better relations, which ultimately also strengthens the area of repatriation of migrants. Functioning mutual relations between states strengthen trust among the involved states and within societies, North and South. Trust gained has usually a positive influence on public perception on migration and thus also on attitudes towards migrants.[131] As a result, states are working together on what is perceived as a common concern.

---

[129] See O. Rittener, R. Losada, L. Perriard and S. Toscano, 'Swiss Migration Partnerships: A Paradigm Shift', in R. Kunz, S. Lavenex, and M. Panizzon (eds.), *Multilayered Migration Governance: The Promise of Partnership* (New York: Routledge, 2011), pp. 249–64.

[130] Countries in the top ten of the statistics with high rates of asylum applications are usually eligible for migration partnerships.

[131] Maastricht Graduate School of Governance, 'Independent Evaluation of Swiss Migration Partnerships', table 10, www.sem.admin.ch/dam/data/sem/aktuell/news/2015/2015-07-01/mgmt-response-e.pdf (accessed July 2019).

The stumbling block here is enforcement of agreed steps in case a state remains or becomes uncooperative, particularly in the area of returns of migrants despite the partnership approach.[132] There are no, or none that are effective, international instruments available at this stage to properly address such stumbling blocks. The principle of Common Concern of Humankind could offer a key to create appropriate mechanisms.[133] The fact that several areas in a migration partnership agreement are addressed enhances incentives to improve compliance and honour commitments made. Migration dialogues may thus be a key component of future strategies and policy planning on all levels (local, regional, global) within the existing bilateral relations, as stipulated for example in the evaluation of these Swiss agreements.[134] The creation of wider interests eventually may lead to the migration being incorporated more extensively in economic partnership agreements, linking trade, investment and migration.[135]

6.4.1.2 Multilevel Governance

Migration is not only a Common Concern among states and nations but also among different communities and sub-federal entities within a state or union. The principle also bears a vertical dimension and may facilitate cooperation and allocation of powers and resources in the field of migration among different layers of governance. In allocating tasks to different levels of governance and in particular defining international obligations, international cooperation and homework tasks in the field of migration, the doctrine and principle of Common Concern can draw

---

[132] NZZ, 'Brüssel droht afrikanischen Staaten', www.nzz.ch/international/europa/eu-kommission-zur-fluechtlingskrise-bruessel-droht-afrikanischen-staaten-ld.87314 (accessed July 2019).

[133] See also M. Panizzon, 'Migrationspartnerschaften der Schweiz: Verkörperung eines sozialen internationalen Migrationsrechts?', www.wti.org/media/filer_public/7a/e0/7ae0e072-77d7-48e8-ba43-300eb269ff77/mp_der_schweiz__verkoerperung_eines_sozialen_internationalen_migrationsrecht.pdf (accessed July 2019).

[134] On 14 December 2012, at the request of the Federal Council, the National Council accepted the Amarelle postulate (12.3858; Migration partnerships. Control and evaluations) for an evaluation of Switzerland's migration partnerships: 'The results of the external evaluation confirm that migration partnerships are an appropriate instrument for intensifying our cooperation with countries of origin and transit while striking a balance between the different interests of all those involved' (Report from the Federal Swiss Government, 'Migrationspartnerschaften. Kontrolle und Evaluation', Bericht des Bundesrates in Erfüllung des Postulats 12. 3858, www.sem.admin.ch/dam/data/sem/aktuell/news/2015/2015-07-01/ber-br-po-123858-d.pdf (accessed July 2019)).

[135] Cottier and Shingal, *supra* n. 42.

from different theories of multilevel governance.[136] The doctrine of the five-storey house, an approach inspired by the constitutional structure of the Swiss Confederation and emphasising the equal importance of all levels of governance (including their taxing powers) may be particularly useful in allocating the production of appropriate public goods relating to the management of migration. All levels of government, from communes to international forums have to take up appropriate responsibilities in the field of migration in producing appropriate public goods.

At the local level, cities are the first anchor of migrants arriving in host countries, where the administrative steps are taken on arrival. Cities are also conurbations[137] for migrants. All major cities in all continents have the largest concentrations of migrants.[138]

Half of the world's population is to be found in megacities such as Tokyo, Delhi, Shanghai, Sao Paulo.[139] They are the core of innovation and productivity holding the major pool of labour market. As the processes of industrialisation, migration and urbanisation began to intertwine at the beginning and middle of the nineteenth century, national and international population dynamics began also to change considerably.[140] International migration became a key and systemic factor in globalisation in the 1990s due to the mass migration movements triggered by conflict in Eastern Europe, the war in the former Yugoslavia.[141]

---

[136] J. H. Jackson, *Sovereignty, the WTO, and Changing Fundamentals of International Law* (Cambridge: Cambridge University Press, 2006); Cottier and Hertig, *supra* n. 111, 261–322; T. Cottier, 'Towards a Five Storey House', in C. Joerges and E. U. Petersmann (eds.), *Constitutionalism, Multilevel Trade Governance and International Economic Law* (rev. ed., Oxford: Hart, 2011), pp. 495–532; T. Cottier, 'John H. Jackson, Sovereignty-Modern and the Constitutional Approach to International Law', *Journal of International Economic Law*, 19(2) (2016), 323–8. Also see Chapter 1 in this volume, pp. 46–51.

[137] The term conurbation was introduced by Sir Patrick Geddes in his book *Cities in Evolution: An Introduction to the Town Planning Movement and the Study of Civics* (London: Williams & Norgate, 1915), https://ia800302.us.archive.org/12/items/citiesine volutio00gedduoft/citiesinevolutio00gedduoft.pdf (accessed Aug. 2019). A conurbation or agglomeration is a polycentric urbanised or metropolitan area, in which transportation has developed to link areas to create a single urban labour market or travel to work area.

[138] S. Castles, 'Host Societies and the Reception of Immigrants: Institutions, Markets and Policies', *International Migration Review*, 36 (2002), 1143–68.

[139] S. Curtis (ed.), *The Power of Cities in International Relations* (New York: Routledge, 2014), p. 4.

[140] Although international migration is above all a phenomenon of migration to cities, there are hardly any studies on the link between migration and urban development.

[141] BBC, 'Balkans War: A Brief Guide', www.bbc.com/news/world-europe-17632399 (accessed Sept. 2019).

Understanding the shifts in society due to migration movements, the adaptation processes become a key element in forecasting realistic future scenarios. The empowerment of cities is a reflection of the shift in nature in global politics. Cities emerged beyond national boundaries into transnational networks and amalgamated into multilayered governance of international migration. Subnational authorities play an essential role for joint efforts to find efficient local solutions and contribute to an efficient process that creates 'a more equitable balance between the global and the local through new patterns of diplomacy',[142] so-called glocalisation.[143]

Local mayors address issues with their pertinent knowledge of local needs, which cannot be addressed by general solutions from a central national government. In local contexts, there are no 'one-size-fits-all'. Mayors play an important role not only for global governance but also to spread best practice and relevant information to essential players, such as civil society organisations. Their influence on migration and development issues plays a catalytic role in domestic and world politics and on sharing information. Mayors also play an important role in connecting mayors in other capacities and cities and contribute in this way to the dissemination of best practice and knowledge throughout the globe and in different layers of governance.

However, due to the lack of reliable statistics, especially in developing countries, it is difficult to document the actual migration flows between countries.[144] Given the current growth of cities, which are already surpassing the capacity of many local governments to provide the necessary services and infrastructure, and the projections that in the next thirty years almost all population growth will take place in the cities of the Global South, planning and managing the urban transition is probably

---

[142] M. Acuto, 'An Urban Affair, How Mayors Shape Cities for World Politics', in Curtis, *supra* n. 139, pp. 69–88.

[143] Erik Swyngedouw, 'Globalisation or 'glocalisation'? Networks, territories and rescaling', *Cambridge Review of International Affairs*, 17(1) (2004), 25–48; Roland Robertson, 'Globalisation or Glocalisation?', *Journal of International Communication*, 18(2) (2012), 191–208,

[144] R. E. B. Lucas, 'Migration in Developing Countries', www.ssc.wisc.edu/~walker/wp/wp-content/uploads/2012/04/lucas97.pdf (accessed July 2019) (the situation is complicated by the fact that not all countries collect the data in the same way or collect the same parameters. More typically a census or survey may record the place of birth as well as the place of enumeration, though occasionally a place of prior 'residence' is reported).

one of the greatest challenges of the twenty-first century to preserve peace and stability.[145]

We submit that an appropriate framework for multilevel cooperative governance may also assist in developing and bringing about better institutional coherence in the field of migration, both horizontally and vertically. As transnational migration demands international cooperation, regional measures first must be coordinated among states that are active in a specific region. As migration policy is primarily formulated at the domestic level, so it must be from there that coherence should begin. Migration is a complex problem which requires close cooperation and mutual support, particularly between different governmental institutions and layers of governance.

The complexity of migration issues is clearly reflected by a host of divergent domestic migration policy interests that coexist and compete within a given state. It requires close coordination and cooperation between the governmental institutions and offices involved. Cooperation not only promotes coherence but also secures a balancing of interests between the various mandates, priorities and objectives of the governmental institutions and offices. This, in return, contributes to curbing irregular migration yet allows for the benefits that migration can offer to the sending and receiving country as well as to the migrants themselves – a so-called triple win.[146] It is only by means of close and coherent cooperation between all governmental actors involved in migration issues that the migration-development nexus can be strengthened. This, in particular, is true for the coordination of development assistance, trade, investment and migration policies.

6.4.2 Recognising Legitimate Concerns

Second, the principle of Common Concern may assist in identifying all the pertinent and conflicting concerns, preoccupations and interests that migration law and policy need to take into account and properly balance in the process of transition and adaptation of migrants. 'Common

---

[145] K. Farrell , 'The Rapid Urban Growth Triad: A New Conceptual Framework for Examining the Urban Transition in Developing Countries', *Sustainability*, 9 (2017), 1407 ('During the 25-year period from 1950 to 1975, developing countries went from an urbanization level of 17.6 to 26.9 percent, which is very similar to today's developed countries between 1875 and 1900, which experienced an increase from 17.2 to 26.1 percent') (see data in OECD, *International Migration Outlook 2019*).

[146] See Rittener *et al.*, *supra* n. 129, pp. 249–64.

Concern' inherently stands for the proposition of an all-inclusive approach. Conflicting interests are of course complex – they compete on exist on both sides of the equation. They lead, on both sides – settled humans and migrants – to existential fears and anxieties. These fears explain the potential of disruption of peace and security in any society and explain exactly why the problem needs to be dealt with as a Common Concern. They need to be properly expressed and balanced in defining international obligations, domestic obligations and appropriate mechanism of law enforcement.

6.4.2.1 Legitimate Concerns of Migrants

Migrants worry about the protection of human dignity and fundamental rights as individuals, irrespective of status and papers, and the recognition of non-refoulement. They worry about access to labour markets which is of essential importance. They worry about discriminatory treatment in such markets. Wages gained are partly destined to be to be sent home (using the least expensive means of transfer available). They worry about participating in and becoming integrated into society, and finding appropriate recognition. They worry about their family and an appropriate education for their children, and they worry about the social and legal status of parents. They worry about arbitrary treatment at the hands of the authorities.

The capacity to attain comprehensively the potential of migration for sustainable development depends largely on the framework conditions, including the appropriate protection of human rights of those migrants.

With the evolution of international human rights standards and protection efforts after the Second World War, the basic legal status of individuals – irrespective of location – is inherently defined by recourse to human rights. No longer are states free to treat their constituents as they please and no longer are the relationships between the government and those who are governed beyond the realm of international law. The treatment of human beings, irrespective of their nationality, in fact, irrespective of whether or not they have a particular nationality, is measured according to human rights inherent to the individual, and violators of such rights held accountable.

This implies that human rights are not at the disposal of the government. They may be lawfully restricted (under strict conditions provided for by the human rights framework itself) but cannot be denied. Some human rights standards are even considered to belong to *jus cogens* or peremptory norms of customary international law, such as the prohibition of torture, the principle of non-refoulement and the principle of racial non-discrimination. Human rights are therefore of particular importance to migrants, who are by definition not strongly anchored in domestic legal orders and thus highly dependent on international and regional human rights mechanisms available to them. They, in particular, should include the right for lawful residents to have access to labour markets without any discrimination and the right to be able to send remittances home under normal financial conditions. It should be noted that these remittances boost development more effectively that ODA is able to do. Such conditions are essential for the host country to provide if the migrant is to live without existential fears, make long-term plans and thus contribute positively to the host community and country.

While the importance of human rights frameworks for migrants is well established, the scope of the rights and freedoms of migrants is constantly challenged in countries of destination, as private actors and official institutions often refuse to recognise that migrants have rights and often hamper access by migrants to recourses and remedies otherwise available to citizens.

The crucial question pertains as to how legitimate public interests may be invoked to restrict specific human rights guarantees as they apply to various categories of migrants, taking into account the rights and security needs of citizens and other categories of foreigners. The lack of a well-established corpus of law dedicated to migrants, defining their inalienable, specific rights (beyond the 1990 International Convention for the Protection of the Rights of All Migrant Workers and Members of Their Families,[147] which is ill-ratified, Global North countries having never accepted its legitimacy), leaves us with the task of identifying and interpreting relevant rights and freedoms as general instruments of human rights protection.

Many questions arise: what is the relevance of due process of law in the context of migration procedures? What is the extent, in favour of migrants, of the right to family unity or the right to privacy? What are the implications of the fact that migrants are denied political rights, often for a long period of time, often forever, and are therefore prevented from directly accessing the political stage to voice their concerns? What are the human rights implications for persons not having appropriate identification or travel documentation? What is the meaning of human dignity

---

[147] www.ohchr.org/EN/ProfessionalInterest/Pages/CMW.aspx (accessed July 2019).

MIGRATION   331

when applied to migrants, and especially to migrants who are inherently vulnerable or placed in a very precarious legal status or social position? What access should migrants, regardless of status, be permitted to have to public and private services, in implementation of the right to food and shelter, or the right to health services, or the right to education? What are the implications of general exception clauses expressing public interests and security concerns, as they should be applied to migrants? Why should all migrant workers, regardless of migration status or lack of, not benefit from labour law or health and safety protections guaranteed to all workers? What is the meaning of 'access to justice' in a context where migrants without relevant social capital are denied information, time to prepare, free and competent legal representation, free and competent interpretation and translation services, and easy access to effective recourse and remedies? Why are most countries turning a blind eye to underground labour markets, which sustain the competitiveness of many economic sectors (agriculture, care, construction, extraction, fisheries, hospitality, to name a few), but at the same time foster high levels of labour exploitation and human rights abuse by migrant smugglers, unethical recruiters, exploitative employers or greedy landlords, who actively benefit from an atmosphere of complete impunity for their crimes.

Such questions can usually be resolved when one considers the evolution of the human rights doctrine from its infancy in the post-war period to the present day. Many marginalised groups have been able to use the international and domestic human rights frameworks to advance their cause at political and judicial levels: from, say, the feminist movement, to racial minorities (the American civil rights movement),[148] to the emancipation of Indigenous peoples (especially in countries such as Australia, Canada,[149] New Zealand[150] or the United States)[151] or to the fight for the

---

[148] Library of Congress, 'Collection Civil Rights History Project, Women and Civil Rights Movement', www.loc.gov/collections/civil-rights-history-project/articles-and-essays/women-in-the-civil-rights-movement/ (accessed July 2019).

[149] A/HRC/27/52/Add.2, J. Anaya, 'The Situation of Indigenous Peoples in Canada', report of Special Rapporteur on the rights of Indigenous peoples, www.ohchr.org/EN/.../A_HRC_27_52_Add_2_ENG.doc (accessed July 2019).

[150] C. McMurchy-Pilkington, N. Pikiao and N. Rongomai, 'Indigenous People: Emancipatory Possibilities in Curriculum Development', *Canadian Journal of Education*, 3 (2008), 614–38, https://files.eric.ed.gov/fulltext/EJ809263.pdf (accessed July 2019).

[151] C. Saunt, 'The Paradox of Freedom: Tribal Sovereignty and Emancipation during the Reconstruction of Indian Territory', *Journal of Southern History*, 70 (2004), 63–94, www.jstor.org/stable/27648312?seq=1#page_scan_tab_contents (accessed July 2019).

rights of members of the LGBT communities (the 'gay marriage' issue in many countries).[152]

In a similar manner, migrants' human rights and labour rights, practically non-existent for decades, have recently been increasingly acknowledged by international, regional and national courts, tribunals and other conflict resolution mechanisms, as well as by international organisations. Inside a number of governments, some institutions have started to take migrants' rights seriously. For example, some education authorities have insisted that all children have the right and obligation to be schooled, without exception, and have prohibited school administrators from collaborating with immigration enforcement authorities in order to avoid migrant parents being afraid to school their children. Some police departments have been requested by the municipal authorities to refrain from checking immigration status and papers, in order to foster a spirit of collaboration between all communities, with the police allowing the latter to better perform their mission of serving and protecting all against crime. Some healthcare institutions have insisted on providing healthcare services to all women or children, regardless of migration status, in order to achieve their public health objectives as well as in the implementation of their professional oath, which commands them to 'do no harm'.

However, the international human rights framework still lacks adequate enforcement mechanisms. They are subject to lengthy and costly domestic legal proceedings short of effective international protection. Regional human rights treaties, in particular, the European Convention on Human Rights, are important exceptions to a generally dire situation, explaining the degree of arbitrary and capricious treatment of migrants frequently observed. Even where rights exist and the scope is well defined, many governments around the world lack appropriate governance structures to ensure compliance with the normative framework at individual levels.

Even in developed countries with sophisticated administrations, migrants are rarely actively empowered to effectively defend their rights. Unionisation is rarely encouraged, legal assistance and interpretation services are often unavailable in administrative and labour matters, complaint mechanisms are rarely used as migrants fear retaliation and especially being detected as undocumented or a troublemaking, and thus detained and expelled from the country, to take only a few examples.

---

[152] A/HRC/29/2/, Mothusi Bruce Rabasha Palai, 'Report of the Human Rights Council on Its Twenty-Ninth Session' (advance unedited version), pp. 117–18 .

MIGRATION 333

Some countries have even instituted an official policy of 'hostile environment' towards undocumented migrants, insisting that employers, landlords, banks and other service providers check the immigration status of the people with whom they interact and denounce to immigration enforcement authorities the undocumented migrants they encounter, with a view to getting migrants to leave the country and to deter potential migrants from coming.[153] There is a spill-over effect on other categories of migrants, with temporary or precarious legal status, in terms of the creation of a fear factor preventing migrants from contacting the authorities or fighting for their rights.

We submit that the recognition of migration as a Common Concern of Humankind strengthens the understanding for legitimate concerns of migrants and thus helps to improve human rights conditions of migrants and their families in due course by reinforcing international cooperation, a focus on homework, but also by additional tools to improve compliance in addressing the endemic weaknesses of international human rights protection.

6.4.2.2   Legitimate Concerns of Residents

Citizens and residents are concerned about the impact on jobs, competition and levels of remuneration. They worry about displacement by foreigners, given the history of colonialism. They worry about housing costs and density due to the growth of urban centres. They worry about the loss of cultural identity. They worry about the schooling of their children in schools predominantly frequented by migrant children. Finally, they worry about the taxes and financial costs of hosting and integrating migrants in society. These questions are rarely discussed in terms of fundamental rights and entitlement. As much as migrants, residents enjoy the protection of human rights, including economic and cultural rights, which need to be considered in the overall equation. What, for example, is the impact of the right to education in terms of

---

[153] House of Lords, Parliament UK, 'Impact of Hostile Environment, Policy Debate', 14 June 2018, https://researchbriefings.files.parliament.uk/documents/LLN-2018-0064/LLN-2018-0064.pdf (accessed Aug. 2019); 'Home Office Windrush Report Damns Hostile Environment Policy', *The Guardian*, 27 June 2019, www.theguardian.com/uk-news/2019/jun/27/home-office-windrush-report-damns-hostile-environment-policy (accessed Aug. 2019); L. Kirkaldy, 'How Hostile Environment Immigration Policy Reaches into Every Area of UK Society', 17 Jan. 2019, www.holyrood.com/inside-politics/view,how-hostile-environment-immigration-policy-reaches-into-every-area-of-uk-society_9755.htm (accessed Aug. 2019).

an appropriate cultural and linguistic environment? What are the implications of these rights for the allocation of pupils to different schools? For example, which language should be taught in kindergarten in a multilingual environment?

Problems thus are not limited to exclusion, but Paul Collier stresses the concerns of residents and finds new anxieties of those people left behind triggered by the process of globalisation. Globalisation has, in his view, built a new group of highly skilled but socially detached people. The rifts caused by ideologues and populists are not a repetition of the past but have to be understood as a new and complex phenomenon of the societal divide. The sense of belonging shifted from a provincial and national attachment to a more metropolitan and cosmopolitan way of life. The new class of highly skilled persons does not make any difference between their national peers and the rest of the world. This results in an indifference regarding the redistribution of wealth through taxation, whether it benefits provincial peers or foreigners in or outside the country. It creates a schism between the well-educated, highly skilled and those left behind (working class and nationalists).[154] It also partly explains increasing income and wealth disparities within societies for which migration serves as a scapegoat.

The Principle of Common Concern of Humankind has the potential to address the legitimate concerns of residents and realign through its implementation of the duties and responsibilities of all communities and its members including migrants. Migration as a Common Concern is not limited to migrants but equally addresses the concern of residents and homework needs to consider the impact of income and wealth distribution as society changes with and by migration and technological evolution. It has the potential to develop a new and more comprehensive perspective on migration which leaves mutual scapegoating behind. A more objective and factual data-based narrative on migration may be produced, offering new guidance by understanding migration as a Common Concern: 'Narratives not only tell us about belonging, they tell us what we ought to do – they give us the norm of our group.'[155]

6.4.2.3 Emphasising Practical Experience

Due to exploitation of migration for political purposes, these different worries and interests play out in major ideological arguments and battles,

---

[154] P. Collier, *The Future of Capitalism: Facing the New Anxieties* (London: Penguin, 2018), pp. 3–68.

[155] Ibid., p. 33.

MIGRATION 335

emphasising sovereignty and self-determination on the one hand, and non-discrimination and human rights on the other hand. The political debate and discussion often are biased as migrants by definition do not have political rights. Political decisions often are taken by those not directly affected. At the same time, labour migrants are subject to taxation and their exclusion from the political process violates the constitutional principle of no taxation without representation. Institutionally, the worries are taken care of in a biased manner and migrants largely depend on the courts of law to protect their interests.

These clashes between majority and minorities, between nationalist, or statist, versus cosmopolitan views on the level of ideologies, need to be squared with real-life experiences. These experiences provide the relevant background and inform a fact-based debate. They show a variety of different levels of integration where people meet on par and mutual respect and individual friendship. Without ignoring larger difficulties mainly due to ghettoisation, segmentation and discrimination and often dependence of first-generation migrants on welfare programmes, it is the everyday experience of migration and integration of individuals and families which provide a solid basis for hope that much progress can be achieved in the process of transition and integration. People tend to distinguish ideology from individual experience. This is of great hope. They recognise the importance of contributions that individual migrants and their families make on completion of the transition to the economy and society at large. These contributions should guide us in assessing the benefits and of costs of migration. Migration law should express them accordingly and require governments, authorities and courts of law to balance interests in taking into account practical life experience supported by sufficient evidence in accordance with principles of due process. Common Concern reiterates that a common problem needs to be solved. Ideology is no suitable guidance to balance complex and diverging interests in practical life.

6.4.2.4 Recognising the Costs, Benefits and Complexity of Migration

Framing migration as a Common Concern of Humankind requires taking into account all benefits and costs of migration in setting out appropriate rights and duties. While domestic law stresses the costs of migration, the doctrine of Common Concern allows introducing a proper balance with the benefits incurred. Common Concern is able to depict a more balanced view.

The preoccupation with self-determination, sovereignty and political rights limited to residents, amplified by underlying fears, generally depicts a negative image and impression of migration and migrants. It is perceived to be something unavoidable, something to be contained. Traditional migration in law, therefore, forms part of policing and limiting movement and migration. It is about refusing or granting permits. It is about granting a privilege for which migrants are expected to be grateful. It is about expulsions and repatriation in law enforcement. People not falling under established categories are lost. The prevailing approach to policing migration by means of administrative and penal law ignores the many contributions migrants make to society and the economy, in particular in countries with ageing populations and low levels of reproduction. It is important to recognise long-term benefits on completing the transitions of migration.

Benefits of Migration   Benefits of migration can be seen as reducing inequality when migration is from poorer countries into wealthier ones and in the long run, the host societies are strengthened through enrichment, definitely by the third and fourth generations.[156] People moving from poor areas to more prosperous areas improve their own conditions and are enabled to support those left behind at home. Migration contributes to powerful human resources to society. Migrants seek a better future for their families and children. Moving is an act of hope. Migrants provide impulses and cultural pluralism in society. Many achievements, in hindsight, have resulted from a migratory background. Migration enriches and enhances welfare beyond the initial costs of shelter and education. The next generation pays all back and more. Migration thus strengthens society in the long run and makes it more robust to meet the challenges ahead. Migration also strengthens international trade and investment as these activities often are operated by diaspora communities, opening up new channels of commerce. Migration thus contributes to job creation and welfare. As discussed, remittances exported generate more revenue and disposable income in home countries than ODA.

Costs of Migration   There are also substantial costs to migration during periods of transition and sometimes beyond. It means painful parting

---

[156] P. Martin, 'The Challenge of Population and Migration' (Copenhagen: Cambridge University Press, 2004); www.copenhagenconsensus.com/sites/default/files/cp-population finished_0.pdf (accessed July 2019).

and farewell to those leaving and to those remaining at home. It brings about brain drains, leaving those left behind poorer. Most of the costs, however, are felt by residents: it affects traditional patterns of residence, lifestyles and identity. It enhances competition in the labour market. It requires positive efforts of integration and training. It requires investment at the expense of the taxpayer's financial resources and at the expense of other policy fields. It creates ideologies, tensions and debate and risks increasing fosses, fissures, fractures and division within society. Finally, it bears the potential for the revival of racism.

There is an exaggerated perception that migration could be a threat to host countries, which is exploited by nationalist claims that all newcomers are thieves with limited available resources. This results in ideological debates which heighten the risk of racism, especially when the facts around migration are misrepresented. For this reason, migrants require appropriate integration and training as an investment to be successful.

Complexity of Migration   Migration thus, from a neutral perspective, is a highly complex area which calls for appropriate policies in supporting benefits and containing costs and negative effects. Given the transnational nature of the problem, it is essential to identify the proper level of governance in addressing migration-related problems. This may be local, for example in supporting integration in schools and sports clubs. It may be subnational or national in regulating access to labour markets. It may be regional in allocating migrants to different countries, operating a system of burden-sharing and support. It may be global in particular in addressing disaster and emergency relief to migrants on the move and to coordinate efforts undertaken by different countries and unions. In other words, it is a matter of assessing where these efforts and public goods are best produced. Today this is not limited to the level of national law or to administrative/penal measures.

What is called for is an approach combining the benefits and costs of migration and placing them within an overall framework allocating appropriately tasks to different jurisdictions in an effort to deploy cooperative or shared sovereignty in addressing a Common Concern.

6.5   The Prospects of International Migration Law

Clearly, there is a recognition that migration can no longer be aptly pursued in isolation as a matter of national sovereignty, and that higher levels of cooperation are warranted among states and within international organisations. The work undertaken so far supports governments in achieving greater policy coherence. Modern theories of sovereignty, stressing the production of public goods and welfare, are conducive to this effort. Yet, it has not produced principles and rules, and its recommendations at best may be considered a matter of soft law informing domestic policies, with some and treaty-making. The field still lacks a leading idea for encapsulating and framing international cooperation.

Recognition of migration as a Common Concern of Humankind triggers basic legal obligations in international cooperation, homework and compliance. When problems arise, states are obliged to cooperate and negotiate. They are obliged to implement existing obligations at home and undertake additional efforts in solving impending problems. Finally, they are obliged to appropriately respond to free-riding countries. This is substantial. But foremost, the principle of Common Concern of Humankind is able to inspire an agenda for further work on the basis of the Global Compact for Safe, Orderly and Regular Migration. As a philosophy, it offers direction which governments should pursue. It is therefore submitted that further work on the Global Compact should explicitly recognise migration as a Common Concern of Humankind and thus establish the foundations for fundamental obligations at international cooperation, the obligation to do the homework and measures to be taken in case of state failures. Recognising migration as a matter of Common Concern of Humankind in the GCM offers a framework by which the beggar-thy-neighbour problem could be addressed, taking into account all the pertinent interests and concerns at stake.

We suggest that the emerging doctrine and principle of Common Concern of Humankind could assume a central role in organising, informing and structuring the field of migration in coming debates and international negotiations.

6.5.1 Towards a Rule-Based System

The operation of shared or cooperative sovereignty calls for a rule-based system in international law, addressing key concerns relating to migration. There is no fundamental difference in the necessity of a rule-based system in international trade and investment, based on the WTO plurilateral and preferential trade agreements as well as bilateral investment protection agreements subject to arbitration. Labour migration, to a large extent, pertains to the realm of international economic law. Refugee law and humanitarian law are closely related to economic underpinnings.

There is a need for minimum standards and principles of non-discriminatory treatment. Similar to international economic organisations, in particular, the WTO, principles and rules are expressions of shared sovereignty, allowing states to balance market access needs and non-trade concerns. Similar to WTO law, fundamental principles of non-discrimination, due process, transparency and market access should be designed and introduced. Other than unfettered sovereignty, the framework helps governments to fend off excessive domestic pressures and maintain peaceful relations with partner countries. It is wrong to assume that nations would lose sovereignty; in fact, they would gain control in extending international cooperation in this complex migration field.

Effective dispute settlement between states needs to be developed, as much as minimal guarantees to individuals before domestic authorities and courts of law should be agreed on. There is a need to further develop the different categories of migrants, from political refugees to climate refugees, from individual refugees to groupings in particular in the case of war and natural disasters. Accordingly, procedural principles and rules should be designed, allowing different national authorities to interface. Immigration rules need to be partly approximated. Modes of enhanced cooperation should be designed when migration no longer can be dealt with on an individual, or case-by-case basis. Categories of economic migration need to be shaped more clearly and linked to opportunities and options induced at home, induced by domestic education, industries and by means of international cooperation. Training and options to return need to be developed. Financial services allowing low-cost transactions of remittances need to be agreed on. Burden-sharing and financial support systems need to be developed. Forums and procedures to share experiences that include stakeholders in the process of decision-making would need to be designed.

The standards and goals in order to avoid international threats to peace and stability that should be applied in the sense of the Common Concern can be identified or extracted from the GCM and can be understood as agreed by the UN Community and all participants within this process too. Nations have already defined in this document the common goals and the minimum standards. These standards eventually have to become part of an internationally binding agreement. Beyond the operational principle of Common Concern, additional and more detailed modalities of international cooperation, homework and compliance should be adopted in treaty law. Migration management (quotas) and funding need to be agreed on in the framework of the UN based on collected data (demography) and on labour market needs and possibilities (e.g. taking into account GPD of the signatory states). Basing migration management/governance on these collected data could transform the public narrative into a positive, more intellectual public evidence-based discourse.

6.5.2 Extending Linkages to International Economic Law

The GCM should establish the necessary interlinkages to existing and other international organisations relevant to migration. As discussed above, migration is a complex cross-sectoral field. It buys into the regulatory realm of many different institutions. The GCM should seek to develop a platform intersecting all these different pertaining areas and to coordinate work on the global level in a coherent manner. By doing so, it would also bring together different ministries and domestic agencies which often work in isolation, fragmenting policies. The current network of twenty-two UN agencies under the Global Migration Group (GMG) or its successors should involve human rights bodies, especially in the case of the Global Compact on Refugees (GCR)[157] the humanitarian organizations, and for the GCM the Bretton Woods institutions, in particular, the World Bank Group, the International Labour Organization (ILO) and the WTO. It should also extend to bilateral trade and investment agreements to the extent that they deal with market access and labour standards.[158] The two Global Compacts, the GCM and the GCR, could assume functions of transparency and debate in interlinking the different and complex areas of regulating migration flows. It could help to create public awareness, but also within different international organisations still largely operating as silos in a functionalist tradition which are no longer able to grasp the complexity and interdependency of contemporary regulatory challenges.

There are important linkages of migration not only to labour standards and human rights but also to access labour markets for goods and services. Mode 4 of the GATS Agreement essentially defines market access rights for key personnel which often are modified or extended in preferential trade agreements. So far, labour as such has not been recognised in WTO law and states reserve immigration laws across the board. The principle of non-discrimination does not generally apply. In the long

---

[157] Global Compact on Refugees as contained in A/73/12 (Part II) was adopted by the General Assembly on 17 December 2018 (A/RES/73/151)
[158] See Cottier and Sieber-Gasser, *supra* n. 89, pp. 41–60.

MIGRATION 341

run, improved and stable access in particular for developing countries to labour markets will be negotiated in return for other commitments, particularly in professional services. There are also interesting links to the promotion and protection of investment. Investors often depend on foreign and specialised personnel, and market access rights for third-party nationals are considered of importance and should be secured in investment protection agreements. Finally, the general relationship of trade and investment remains of paramount importance in long-term efforts to contain migration flows: the more open trade and investment, the fewer people are compelled to move to make a living abroad. This is of particular importance in the field of agriculture where markets in industrialised countries have remained protected, attracting workers and pickers from abroad rather than the importation of fruits and vegetables. While market liberalisation generally increases migration flows, long-term effects may contribute to an overall balance.[159] The Global Compact should oblige trade negotiators to consider the impact on migration in the process of shaping trade regulation.

However, it should be noted that the Heckscher–Ohlin–Samuelson economic model that posits that freer trade decreases the need for labour migration did not result in an expected decrease of migration pressure especially in the case of Mexico, and has accordingly been discredited. Evidence shows that trade, investment and migration are, at least in the short term, not substitutes, but that development triggers migration.[160] Rather they complement each another; despite this joint determination and a growing literature, the migration–investment–trade nexus has not yet been explored as an integrated nexus.[161] Trade, investment and migration are different economic processes. One is a two-way or multi-lateral process driven by comparative advantages. The other is a one-way phenomenon driven by absolute advantages.[162] The term 'absolute advantages' stems from an economic perspective and only applies to successful migrants, without taking into account tragedies affecting mainly low-skilled people seeking a better life abroad. Economists have come to conclude that migrants are a powerful engine for

---

[159] Cottier and Shingal, *supra* n. 42, pp. 53–4.
[160] GFMD, *supra* n. 102.
[161] Curtis, *supra* n. 139.
[162] Collier, *supra* n. 154, p. 20.

342   THOMAS COTTIER AND ROSA MARIA LOSADA

development.[163] Migrants' contributions are accepted by the UN as a factor of development.[164]

6.5.3   Homework and Compliance

Commensurate with the doctrine of Common Concern, the GCM should also further develop obligations of states at home, implementation and the scope for sanctions in case of state failure and free-riding.

6.5.3.1   Domestic Obligations

Beyond the principle of Common Concern, the international framework needs to eventually define the rights and obligations of states in a clear manner. It will define commitments which countries are supposed to undertake in terms of homework, in addition to their own initiatives and policies towards integrating migrants in accordance with national traditions. The framework thus provides the benchmark as to whether a state assumes its responsibilities in the field and complies with obligations incurred. Partly, these obligations may be binding, partly they may be voluntary and incurred on the basis of autonomous measures but creating legitimate expectations as to compliance. The recent debate on the soft-law nature of the GCM implies the recognition of such effects. The fact that it is adopted as a non-binding, soft-law instrument does not exclude legal effects in assessing homework done, or not done, within a particular state.

Most of the work, however, remains to be done within states in addressing migration law and policy and a coordinated manner with other policy areas. The tradition of the migration state looms large, and it will take a long time to develop binding international commitments beyond existing human rights. Rather, such commitments will build on the experience of national policies developed. Homework on the basis of Common Concern of Humankind goes beyond international commitments and obligations but needs to seek an appropriate and balanced regime commensurate with constitutional requirements, in particular, the protection of human rights and of minorities. Such policies may also

---

[163] Gordon Jennifer, 'People Are Not Bananas: How Immigration Differs from Trade', *Northwestern University Law Review*, 1004 (2010), 1109, https://papers.ssrn.com/sol3/papers.cfm?abstract_id=1547153 (accessed July 2019).

[164] M. A. Clemens, 'Migration Is a Form of Development: The Need for Innovation to Regulate Migration for Mutual Benefit'; www.un.org/en/development/desa/population/migration/publications/technicalpapers/docs/TP2017-8.pdf (accessed July 2019).

MIGRATION   343

develop legitimate expectations, and to the extent that they are based on unilateral commitments and policies, they may deserve the protection of good faith and estoppel in international and domestic law.

Within states, and using the model of multilevel governance, rights and obligations of federated states or the cantons, and of communes and cities will be defined accordingly. The framework of a five-storey house allows developing appropriate policies respecting the bottom-up principle of subsidiarity.[165] It will not be merely a matter of imposing duties, but of creating appropriate spacing and funding from policies on integration which mainly take place at the local level. While this chapter stresses the importance of international law, it should be reiterated that all levels of governance are of equal importance in contributing to the overall task of coping with migration flows, hopes, disappointment and challenges within an overall framework of perceiving migration as a Common Concern of Humankind.

6.5.3.2   Compliance

It will be necessary to study more closely options of linking the enforcement of minimal rights and standards on migration and the field of economic sanctions and countermeasures in case of violations. This is an area untouched as of today but will need to form part of implementing and developing the doctrine of Common Concern in the field of migration which in principle allows for unilateral countermeasures. The problem is no different from other areas of public international law, except for international trade which has spearheaded the rule of law and which continues to serve as a yardstick of aspiration in a globalising and highly interdependent world.

Except for restrictions affecting market access under Mode 4 of GATS, WTO law does not allow operating unilateral trade restrictions due to restrictions imposed on migration flows. Expect for sanctions adopted by the UN Security Council, restrictions need to have a sufficient linkage to goods and services produced, which in the case of labour may apply to child labour and other violations of ILO minimal standards. It is not established in relation to market access restrictions for labour migration. Other areas, in particular, political refugees or humanitarian actions or inactions, remain without sufficient linkages under current rules. Wider options exist in federacies. Within the EU, transfer payments may be

---

[165] Cottier, *supra* n. 126, pp. 495–532; Section 6.4.1.2.

reduced or stalled in case compliance with commitments incurred fails. The same holds true in federal states where burden-sharing among federated states or the cantons in Switzerland is of equal relevance.

The implementation of unilateral or concerted measures and policies relating to defined areas of Common Concern in particular by large powers and markets will be met with opposition, resistance and perhaps retaliation. The governments will continue to invoke traditional precepts of sovereignty and sovereignty over natural resources. Yet, taking seriously Common Concerns as a right and obligation to address these concerns beyond territorial jurisdiction has to take these tensions into account and channel them towards the establishment of a global governance able to handle these issues more effectively and based on commonly agreed rules beyond soft-law recommendations of groups or forums such as the GFMD. The principle of Common Concern of Humankind provides, therefore, the incentives to work towards agreed regimes and multilateral structures. The principle of Common Concern of Humankind allows both for bottom-up and top-down approaches: it is these two approaches within a combination of whole-of-government and a whole-of-system approaches which will bring about progress in international law and relations in addressing Common Concerns of Humankind.

For the international enforcement of the new global migration agreement, a particular forum should be created or designated. None of the existing forums or international organisations in the field of migration (e.g. IOM, ILO, UNHCR) is sufficiently prepared to cope with this task in the present international setting. For economic migration and workers as providers of services, the enforcement could in the future be partly incorporated into the WTO dispute settlement system for the protection of migrant workers and market access, excluding unilateral suspension of concessions without dispute settlement and approval by the dispute settlement body. Such would facilitate the realisation of effective migration governance in a comprehensive manner and bring more coherence into the field of migration. Labour should, therefore, be defined as a service – a novelty against which mostly industrialised countries have opposed fearing loss of control and sovereignty, mainly because of the possible pull effect on developing and least developed countries.

6.6   Conclusions

Readers may dismiss this chapter as not being sufficiently realistic. They will object that the goal of a legally binding framework on migration is at odds with the strong traditions of national sovereignty and is bound to fail accordingly. They would have a point, looking at currently prevailing attitudes. States still see their interest best defended by retreat and insistence on regulatory powers – very much as they did in the 1930s prior to the advent of the United Nations, the multilateral trading system and the Bretton Woods institutions after the Second World War. Yet, recent developments in migration policy on the level of the United Nations have made much progress with the adoption of the GCM. Moreover, it is not a matter of changing the state of play from one day to the next in a radical manner. Rather, it is a matter of defining an evolving concept and idea which shows the paths for longer-term developments. It is important to define the direction which policymaking should take in the long term in order to enable governments to cope with the challenges ahead in a world of increasing migration undertaken for different reasons. It does not matter if progress is slow, and the steps are small. What counts is that they go in the right direction and that the international community is being offered a compass and a road map in what today is an utterly foggy, messy disoriented and politically abused area.

The principle of Common Concern offers a number of legal implications, but foremost a new narrative to this effect. It is hoped that the doctrine of Common Concern one day will be recognised as an emerging principle, deploying legal effects and offering normative guidance in different regulatory fields, including the crucial one of migration. As a philosophy, it may inspire future directions in migration law. Much will be gained if it helps to convince people that migration should no longer be perceived as a negative zero-sum game, but rather as a field of shared opportunities and hopes which history in many instances proved to be a major force of transformation. Much is also gained for realism if we see migration positively as an opportunity, enriching our lives, rather than as a toxic burden imposed on society.

* * *

Select Bibliography

Clemens, M. A. (2017). 'Migration Is a Form of Development: The Need for Innovation to Regulate Migration for Mutual Benefit', UN Population Division, Technical Paper No. 2017/8 (New York: United Nations).

Cottier, T. and Shingal, A. (2021). 'Migration Trade and Investment: Towards a New Common Concern of Humankind', *Journal of World Trade*, 55 pp. 51–76.

Cottier, T. and Sieber-Gasser, C. (2015). 'Labour Migration, Trade and Investment: From Fragmentation to Coherence', in M. Panizzon, G. Zürcher and L. Fonalé (eds.), *The Palgrave Handbook of International Labour Migration, Law and Policy Perspectives* (Basingstoke, UK: Palgrave Macmillan), pp. 41–60.

de Haas, H. (2010). 'Migration and Development: A Theoretical Perspective', *International Migration Review* 44(1) 227–64.

Hollifield, J. (2004). 'The Emerging Migration State', *International Migration Review*, 38(3) 885–912.

Jennifer, G. (2010). 'People Are Not Bananas: How Immigration Differs from Trade', *Northwestern University Law Review* 104(3) 1109.

Losada, R. M. (2013). 'Strengthening the Migration–Development Nexus through Improved Policy and Institutional Coherence', Opinion Notes, 58–60, www .oecd.org/dev/migration-development/2013%2012%2010%20opinion% 20notes%20-%20with%20cover.pdf (accessed 30 Sept. 2019).

Martin, P. (1996). 'The Anatomy of a Migration Hump', in J. E. E. Taylor (ed.), *Development Strategy, Employment, and Migration: Insights from Models* (Paris: OECD Development Centre), pp. 43–62.

(2004). *The Challenge of Population and Migration* (Cambridge: Cambridge University Press).

Martin, S. (2000). 'Toward a Global Migration Regime', *Georgetown Journal of International Affairs* 1(2) 119–27.

(2014). *International Migration: Evolving Trends from the Early Twentieth Century to the Present* (Cambridge: Cambridge University Press), pp. 270–5.

Nadakavukaren Schefer K. and Cottier, T. (2014). 'Responsibility to Protect (R2P) and the Emerging Principle of Common Concern', in Peter Hilpold (ed.), *Responsibility to Protect (R2P): A New Paradigm of International Law?* (Leiden: Brill Nijhoff), pp. 123–42.

Rittener, O., Losada, R. M., Perriard, L. and Toscano, S. (2011). 'Swiss Migration Partnerships: A Paradigm Shift', in R. Kunz, S. Lavenex and M. Panizzon (eds.), *Multilayered Migration Governance: The Promise of Partnership* (New York: Routledge), pp. 249–64.

Skeldon, R. (2008). 'Migration and Development', United Nations Expert Group Meeting on International Migration and Development in Asia and the Pacific, UN/POP/EGM-MIG/2008/4, 9 Sept. 2008, www.un.org/en/develop ment/desa/population/events/pdf/expert/14/P04_Skeldon.pdf (accessed 30 Sept. 2019).

7

International Monetary Stability as a Common Concern of Humankind

LUCIA SATRAGNO

7.1 Introduction

This chapter[1] argues that international monetary stability is an under-provided global public good (GPG) under the current design of the international monetary system (IMS). It proposes to apply the emerging doctrine of Common Concern of Humankind (Common Concern) as a methodological approach to analyse this problem from an innovative perspective.[2] Common Concern refers to 'an important shared problem and shared responsibility, and for an issue which reaches beyond the bounds of a single community and state as a subject of international law'.[3] This incipient doctrine promotes Common Concern as a new principle in international law that redefines the responsibilities of states concerning the promotion and protection of GPGs by adding an extra layer of responsibility beyond their jurisdictional domains. The nature of problems associated with Common Concerns calls for a collective action response and demands cooperation among states. Hence, while

---

[1] This chapter expands and also draws partially on my previous writings: T. Cottier and L. Satragno, 'The Potential of Law and Legal Methodology in Monetary Affairs', in T. Cottier, R. M. Lastra, C. Tietje and L. Satragno (eds.), *The Rule of Law in Monetary Affairs* (Cambridge: Cambridge University Press, 2014), p. 411; L. Satragno, 'Responsibility for International Monetary Stability in the Post-Crisis Era', in S. Besson (ed.), *International Responsibility: Essays in Law, History and Philosophy* (Zurich: Schulthess, 2017), p. 77; L. Satragno, 'Monetary Stability as a Common Concern in International Law', PhD thesis (University of Bern, forthcoming). I thank Prof. Thomas Cottier and Prof. Rosa Lastra for their insightful and detailed comments.

[2] Hereafter, the term 'Common Concern' in upper case will be used to describe the doctrine and emerging principle as proposed to be applied in this volume and the term 'common concern of humankind' or 'common concern' in lower case will be used to describe the general principle as used in international instruments and most literature. Cottier develops the emerging doctrine and principle in Chapter 1 of this volume.

[3] Ibid., p. 36.

international cooperation among states remains the best outcome to solve the problems associated with Common Concerns, unilateral lawful action stands as the second best result.

International or global monetary stability refers to the stability of the whole IMS. A recent policy paper released by the International Monetary Fund (IMF, or Fund) states that the term IMS covers:

> (a) the rules governing exchange arrangements between countries and the rates at which foreign exchange is purchased and sold; (b) the rules governing the making of payments and transfers for current international transactions between countries; (c) the arrangements respecting the regulation of international capital movements; and (d) the arrangements under which international reserves are held, including official arrangements through which countries have access to liquidity through purchases from the Fund or under official currency swap arrangements.[4]

According to this interpretation, the IMS is about arrangements between countries and the rules governing such arrangements. These official arrangements are about the four elements that presently constitute the core of the IMS – exchange rates, international payments system, international capital movements, and monetary reserves and access to liquidity. The stability of the IMS relies on the smooth operation of each of these four core elements or, in other words, the stability of each country's 'balance of payments' position.

Notwithstanding the international nature of the core elements of the IMS, this chapter observes that since the collapse of the rule-based system of Bretton Woods in the 1970s[5] these elements have been mostly governed by domestic and regional policies dictated by national and regional monetary authorities aiming to achieve self-oriented objectives (based on the monetary sovereignty attributes of states). Hence, regardless

---

[4] IMF, *Modernizing the Legal Framework for Surveillance: An Integrated Surveillance Decision* (2012), www.imf.org/external/np/pp/eng/2012/071712.pdf (accessed 30 Sept. 2019).

[5] During the Bretton Woods system of 1944 the member states of the IMF committed themselves to maintaining the external value of their currencies. This system of 'fixed exchange rates' was abandoned de facto in the early 1970s and *de jure* in 1978 with the entry into force of the Second Amendment of the Articles of Agreement of the IMF. For a very interesting book on the emergence of the Bretton Woods system, see B. Steil, *The Battle of Bretton Woods: John Maynard Keynes, Harry Dexter White, and the Making of a New World Order* (Princeton, NJ: Princeton University Press, 2014).

of the existence of overlapping jurisdictions dealing with monetary stability at different levels of governance, under the current design of the IMS domestic and regional monetary systems prevail over international cooperation agreements dealing with monetary stability.

This situation created a trade-off between domestically oriented policies and the stability of the global monetary order resulting in the underprovision of the GPG of international monetary stability. As stressed by Viterbo '[c]ertainly, domestic monetary policy frameworks are essential components of the IMS: they contribute to its overall stability (or instability)'.[6] The debate on this trade-off among the different levels of governance in monetary affairs is not new but regained much relevance in the aftermath of the global financial crisis of 2007–9 (GFC).[7]

In order to address the main issues associated with this trade-off, this chapter starts by exploring the concept of monetary stability at the different levels of governance and its relationship with the sovereign power of states. It is followed by a brief description of the emerging doctrine of Common Concern as a valuable method to deal with collective action problems. It continues with an analysis of the three-dimensional approach proposed by the doctrine starting with the duty to cooperate in monetary affairs both from a *top-down* approach (international level of governance) and a *bottom-up* approach (central banking cooperation). The chapter continues by examining domestic obligations concerning monetary stability with an emphasis on the special role of the central banks and also by examining some cases of unilateral actions and issues of extraterritoriality in the pursuit of monetary stability. Lastly, it offers some remarks on the most controversial aspect of the emerging doctrine of Common Concern that relates to securing compliance with the obligations that may emerge from an accepted Common Concern of international monetary stability. To sum up, it describes the complexities that the Common Concern analysis exposes in the pursuit of monetary stability and offers some concluding remarks.

---

[6] A. Viterbo, *International Economic Law and Monetary Measures* (Cheltenham, UK: Edward Elgar, 2012), p. 25.

[7] Lastra and Wood considered that the core of the GFC was between 2007 and 2009 (R. M. Lastra and G. Wood, 'The Crisis of 2007–2009: Nature, Causes, and Reactions', *Journal of International Economic Law*, 13 (2012), 531).

7.2 International Monetary Stability: A Common Concern Approach

7.2.1 Monetary Stability at the Different Levels of Governance

International law recognises a state's sovereignty over its internal affairs within its territorial boundaries. The power to issue and regulate currency is one of the sovereign attributes of states.[8] According to Proctor the concept of monetary sovereignty presents both internal and external attributes. '"Internal" sovereignty includes the rights to define the monetary system, to devalue the currency, and to operate a monetary policy; "external" sovereignty includes the right to impose a system of exchange control.'[9] This monopoly power of states in the monetary field is no longer absolute and has been subject to some limitations. As explained by Lastra, the limitations to monetary sovereignty are both consensual and de facto, 'Consensual limitations represent a voluntary surrender of monetary sovereignty. De facto limitations are the result of globalisation, the information revolution and of economic and financial developments during the last three decades of the twentieth century.'[10]

In addition, Proctor remarks that the conduct of monetary affairs is not only limited but also assisted by the rules of public international law through specific treaty provisions and also by rules of customary international law.[11] Article 38 of the Statute of the International Court of Justice states that the primary sources of international law are international treaties, customary international law and general principles of law accepted by all nations.[12] For the purposes of this study the primary sources of international law in international monetary stability are the Articles of Agreement of the IMF,[13] the customary international law applicable and the general principles of law.

---

[8] For an extended analysis of the notion of monetary sovereignty and its evolution, see inter alia, R. M. Lastra, *International Financial and Monetary Law* (3rd ed., Oxford: Oxford University Press, 2015), pp. 3–27; C. D. Zimmermann, *A Contemporary Concept of Monetary Sovereignty* (Oxford: Oxford University Press, 2013).

[9] C. Proctor, *Mann on the Legal Aspect of Money* (7th ed., Oxford: Oxford University Press, 2012), pp. 526–8.

[10] R. M. Lastra, 'The Role of Central Banks in Monetary Affairs: A Comparative Perspective', in Cottier *et al.*, *supra* n. 1, p. 78.

[11] Proctor, *supra* n. 9, p. 587.

[12] Statute of the International Court of Justice (San Francisco, 26 June 1945), 3 Bevans 1179, 59 Stat 1055, TS No 993, entered into force 24 Oct. 1945.

[13] The Articles of Agreement of the International Monetary Fund (Articles of Agreement) were adopted as a result of the United Nations Monetary and Financial Conference,

Notwithstanding the consensual and de facto limitations to monetary sovereignty, states remain as key actors in the exercise of their own attributes of monetary sovereignty. It is in this context that Zimmermann argues that a contemporary concept of monetary sovereignty can be understood both in a direct manner by focusing only on the supreme authority of states and also in an indirect manner as a form of 'cooperative sovereignty' that can be exercised at the different layers of governance. This is done by considering 'the various sovereign powers that originally all derive from the same source, namely the capacity of independent statehood'.[14]

The concept of monetary stability is intrinsically linked to the sovereign power of states in the realm of money.[15] It is under the exercise of their attributes of monetary sovereignty that states define what is to be considered monetary stability at the domestic level. Monetary stability has been included in central bank laws and statutes as the core objective of its monetary policy since the late twentieth century. In the aftermath of the GFC some central banks also consider financial stability as the primary or concomitant objective of their monetary policy together with monetary stability. Zimmermann considers that financial stability is not a target of monetary policy, but central banks have no choice but to achieve both objectives together.[16]

This stability phenomenon is not confined to the domestic sphere. It also has a regional and an international dimension. These dimensions are not static and influence each other through spillover effects or cross-border externalities generated by policies and decisions aimed at achieving a desired level of stability in the domestic sphere. It can be argued that the main reason for the existence of those spillovers is the very

---

Bretton Woods, held in New Hampshire, United States of America, 22 July 1944 and were entered into force 27 Dec. 1945. They were amended on six occasions. IMF, Articles of Agreement of the International Monetary Fund, www.imf.org/external/pubs/ft/aa/ (accessed 30 Sept. 2019).

[14] Zimmermann, *supra* n. 8, p. 18. He argues in favour of contemporary monetary sovereignty as cooperative sovereignty by stating that '[I]n light of the increasing integration of financial markets and the interdependence of "national" economies, the effective promotion of global monetary and financial stability requires cooperation among those exercising sovereign powers in the realm of money and finance.' See also Zimmermann in this volume (Chapter 10, p. 455).

[15] F. Lupo-Pasini, 'Financial Stability in International Law', *Melbourne Journal of International Law*, 18(1) (2017), 52.

[16] C. D. Zimmermann, 'Global Benchmark Interest Rates', in Cottier *et al.*, *supra* n. 1., pp. 153–77.

nature of interconnectedness of the global financial and monetary systems. However, the IMS is different from the 'international financial system'.[17] The Fund makes this difference very clear by stating that 'the international monetary system is *not* synonymous with the international financial system. Rather, it is comprised of, and limited to, those arrangements that directly control the balance of payments of members.'[18]

Monetary stability, an indisputable national 'public good', has become increasingly globalised and also developed as a GPG for the international community. Michel Camdessus, former managing director of the IMF, argued in 1999 that both the IMS and the international financial system should be considered GPGs on the premise that:

> It is essentially the same system for everyone. If it works well, all countries have the opportunity to benefit; if it works badly, all are likely to suffer. Hence, all have an interest in reforms that will improve the system for the global public benefit. And, as is so frequently true for public goods, not many people care for, and even fewer are prepared to pay for, its improvement even if many comment about it.[19]

Accordingly, it can be argued that international monetary stability achieved the public good qualities of being non-rivalrous in its enjoyment and providing non-excludable benefits. This consideration was reinforced by events that occurred during the GFC: 'The 2007–2010 crisis demonstrated that a coordinated global response was necessary to minimize free riding and negative spillovers and that global institutions should be strengthened and supported.'[20]

The increase in the spillover effects (or negative externalities) which originated from decisions taken by the domestic monetary authorities since the beginning of the GFC is the main example on this point. As

---

[17] Because of the remarkable differences between the IMS and the international financial system, this chapter will only specifically focus on monetary stability as a Common Concern. For a consideration on international financial stability as a Common Concern, see Chapter 8 in this volume.

[18] IMF, *The Fund's Mandate: The Legal Framework* (2010), www.imf.org/external/np/pp/eng/2010/022210.pdf (accessed 30 Sept. 2019).

[19] M. Camdessus, 'International Financial and Monetary Stability: A Global Public Good?', www.imf.org/en/News/Articles/2015/09/28/04/53/sp052899 (accessed 30 Sept. 2019). On monetary and financial stability as global public goods, see, inter alia, B. Eichengreen, 'Hegemonic Stability Theories of the International Monetary System', *NBER Working Papers No. 2193* (1987); E. Dorrucci and J. McKay, 'The International Monetary System After the Financial Crisis', *ECB Occasional Paper Series No. 123* (2011); C. Tietje, 'The Role of Law in Monetary Affairs: Taking Stock', in Cottier *et al.*, *supra* n. 1.

[20] Viterbo, *supra* n. 6.

INTERNATIONAL MONETARY STABILITY 353

remarked by Dorrucci and McKay, 'this neglect of the longer-term impact of domestic policies was one of the root causes of the global financial crisis'.[21] This situation highlighted both market and government failures and the consequent underprovision of the GPG of monetary stability.

As Lastra reminds us, 'It is the existence of market failures and deficiencies that provides the economic rationale for banking regulation.' She also states 'that is why a key aim of regulation is to internalize such externalities'.[22] Hence, it can be argued that the GFC revealed not only the market imperfections with an inadequate domestic regulatory framework to internalise negative externalities but also the absence of an appropriate international regulatory framework to ensure the provision and protection of the GPG of international monetary stability. Consequently, the consideration of international monetary stability as a GPG justifies the need for collective action and international cooperation among states as the main providers of public goods.

7.2.2 Common Concern of Humankind: Emerging Doctrine

Beyond economic and political considerations, it can be stated that the main reason for the failure of cooperation at the global level is rooted in the current legal and institutionally deficient design of the multilevel system of governance. That is, as mentioned before, powerful sovereign states driven by domestic interests, and soft-law arrangements and weak institutions at the international level. In this context, Common Concern aims to work as a foundation to strengthen international cooperation and also to define and legitimise unilateral domestic measures in absence of adequate cooperation.[23] On this issue it has been argued that states should 'take domestic action as a matter of international law'.[24]

---

[21] These authors consider that monetary stability as a GPG includes two goods: international currency and external stability (Dorrucci and McKay, *supra* n. 19).

[22] Lastra, *supra* n. 8, p. 113.

[23] I present briefly in this section the emerging doctrine of Common Concern. For a detailed description on the origins and evolution of this doctrine, I rely extensively on the excellent introductory chapter to this volume (see Chapter 1).

[24] T. Cottier, P. Aerni, B. Karapinar, S. Matteotti, J. de Sépibus and A. Shingal, 'The Principle of Common Concern and Climate Change', *Archiv des Völkerrechts (AVR)*, 52 (2014), 293. On this point, Ahmad raised the debate about the coexistence of the duty to cooperate with unilateral domestic measures (Z. Ahmad, 'State Responsibility Aspects of a Common Concern Based Approach to Collective Action', in Besson, *supra* n. 1, p. 107).

As suggested by literature and treaty language, the expression 'common concern of humankind' comprises a shared problem and a shared responsibility for the international community as a subject of international law. The International Court of Justice (ICJ) in the *Barcelona Traction* case recognised that international law comprises obligations owed to the international community of states as a whole rather than to particular states. In this decision the ICJ considered that the obligations owed to the international community, 'by their very nature ... are the concern of all States'.[25] Therefore, the issues categorised as common concerns require a 'collective action' response and demand 'international cooperation' among states.[26] In this line Bodansky considers that 'One way of conceptualizing these obligations *erga omnes* is in terms of global public goods: if an obligation primarily relates to the provision of a global public good or the prohibition of a global public bad, then the obligation protects a "collective" or "common" interest and should be owed to the international community of states as a whole.'[27]

Common Concern as an emerging principle in international law aims, on the one hand, to redefine the responsibilities of states concerning the promotion and protection of GPGs. The term 'public good', on the other hand, is a key concept in economics introduced by Paul Samuelson in the 1950s and is mainly applied at the local or national level.[28] This expression contains two essential characteristics: 'non-rivalry' in consumption and 'non-excludability' in benefits.[29] The first characteristic implies that the use of the public good by one person will not diminish its availability to others. The second characteristic denotes that the public good is

---

[25] *Barcelona Traction, Light and Power Company, Limited (New Application: 1962) (Belgium v. Spain)*, Judgment, ICJ Rep 1970 (5 Feb.), p. 3, para. 33.

[26] According to Cottier *et al.*, 'The term "collective action problem" describes a situation in which multiple individuals would all benefit from a certain action, which, however, has an associated cost that makes it implausible that any one individual can or will undertake and solve it alone' (*supra* n. 24).

[27] D. Bodansky, 'What's in a Concept? Global Public Goods, International Law, and Legitimacy', *European Journal of International Law*, 23(3) (2012), 651.

[28] P. Samuelson, 'The Pure Theory of Public Expenditure', *Review of Economics and Statistics*, 36 (1954), 387.

[29] Samuelson's study focused on the first characteristic of 'non-rivalry'. The second characteristic of 'non-excludability' was introduced by Musgrave (R. A. Musgrave, 'Public Goods', in B. E. Cary and R. M. Solow (eds.), *Paul Samuelson and Modern Economic Theory* (New York: McGraw Hill, 1983), p. 141).

available to everybody, no matter if they contribute to its production or not. Both concepts are interrelated, but not identical.

It was only in the 1990s that the theory of 'public goods' was first applied at the global or international level with the expression 'global public goods' gaining interest among the work of the United Nations Development Programme (UNDP).[30] In 2003 the International Task Force on Global Public Goods was created and in 2006 it issued its final report providing a definition of the concept of 'global public goods' as 'issues that are broadly conceived as important to the international community, that for the most part cannot or will not be adequately addressed by individual countries acting alone and that are defined through a broad international consensus or a legitimate process of decision-making'.[31]

The main problems associated with the provision or underprovision of GPGs are threefold – the 'free-riding' or 'easy riders' issue, market failures and government failures. As explained by Kaul, 'GPGs tend to involve policy interdependence among countries, because in most instances no nation, however powerful, can self-provide these goods. They require international cooperation based on a blend of fairness and power politics.'[32] This failure is exacerbated by the interference of national self-interests in the production of GPGs, which happens when states put their national interests above the global interest and therefore do not make appropriate commitments at the international level. This is identified in literature as a 'jurisdictional gap', that is, the gap among nation states in charge of making policies within their territories and GPGs with transboundary benefits.[33]

---

[30] The research on GPGs pursued within the UNDP resulted in three publications: I. Kaul, I. Grunberg and M. Stern (eds.), *Global Public Goods: International Cooperation in the 21st Century* (Oxford: Oxford University Press, 1999); I. Kaul, P. Conceição, K. Le Goulven and R. U. Mendoza (eds.), *Providing Global Public Goods: Managing Globalization* (Oxford: Oxford University Press, 2003); I. Kaul and P. Conceição, *The New Public Finance: Responding to Global Challenges* (Oxford: Oxford University Press, 2006).

[31] International Task Force on Global Public Goods, *Meeting Global Challenges: International Cooperation in the National Interest* (2006), https://ycsg.yale.edu/sites/default/files/files/meeting_global_challenges_global_public_goods.pdf (accessed 30 Sept. 2019).

[32] I. Kaul, 'Global Public Goods: Explaining Their Underprovision', *Journal of International Economic Law*, 15(3) (2012), 729.

[33] See Kaul *et al.*, *supra* n. 30.

356   LUCIA SATRAGNO

Consequently, an effective international cooperation within the multi-level governance structure is needed in order to produce and operate GPGs. This requires active participation by the authorities at the different levels of governance (local, national, regional and international) in the production of GPGs. In the absence of an adequate international regulatory framework for the provision of GPGs, the role of states as the main providers of such goods becomes more relevant in a multilevel governance context.

The multilevel or multilayered governance doctrines encompass diverse constitutional theories, a human rights–based approach, sovereignty concerns and global administrative law considerations.[34] These doctrines aim to contribute to an optimal promotion and protection of public goods at the different levels of governance, which are informed not only by states and international organisations but also non-state actors.[35] Within these doctrines the 'five-storey house' doctrine in particular argues that all levels of governance are of equal relevance but recognises that the international level has a key role to play in the pursuit of GPGs, which include Common Concerns.[36] To complement these multilevel governance doctrines Cottier argues that:

> Common Concern will help refining jurisdiction in matters, which no longer can be dealt with on the basis of strict territorial application of domestic law; it will explore channels of mobilising non-state actor action to resolve Common Concern issues through participation and

[34] For multilevel governance doctrines, see on constitutional theories, A. Peters, 'Compensatory Constitutionalism: The Function and Potential of Fundamental International Norms and Structures', *Leiden Journal of International Law*, 19 (2006), 579; N. Walker, 'The Idea of Constitutional Pluralism', *Modern Law Review*, 65 (2002), 317; on human rights considerations, see E. U. Petersmann, *International Economic Law in the 21st Century: Constitutional Pluralism and Multilevel Governance of Interdependent Public Goods* (Oxford: Hart, 2012); on the administrative law-based approach, see B. Kingsbury, N. Krisch and R. B. Stewart (eds.), 'The Emergence of Global Administrative Law', *Law and Contemporary Problems*, 68 (2005), 1.

[35] E. U. Petersmann, 'Framework of Analysis: Multilevel Governance', in Cottier *et al.*, *supra* n. 1, pp. 434–61.

[36] T. Cottier, 'Challenges Ahead in International Economic Law', *Journal of International Economic Law*, 12(1) (1999), 15; T. Cottier and M. Hertig, 'The Prospects of 21st Century Constitutionalism', *Max Planck Yearbook of United Nations Law*, 7 (2003), 261; T. Cottier, 'Multilayered Governance, Pluralism and Moral Conflict', *Indiana Journal of Global Legal Studies*, 16(2) (2009), 647; T. Cottier, 'Towards a Five Storey House', in C. Joerges and E. U. Petersmann (eds.), *Constitutionalism, Multilevel Trade Governance and International Economic Law* (Oxford: Hart, 2011); see Chapter 1 in this volume, pp. 46–51.

deliberation in the broader and more transformative sense of reinvention of governance. Yet, states and government continue to play a key role. The multitude of actors does not undermine the structure of multilayered governance.[37]

Bodansky remarks that 'Although international law does not recognise the category of "global public goods", several international law concepts bear a close relationship to it.'[38] Common Concern is one of the concepts that relates intrinsically to GPGs, but they are not the same. Basically, while Common Concern refers to an unresolved international issue and proposes solutions and outcomes, the theory of public goods describes issues associated with non-rivalrous and non-excludable goods. Hence, Common Concern intervenes when there is an under-provision or deficiency in connection to a GPG, but the GPGs theory goes further.

Cottier argues in the opening chapter of this volume that Common Concern may evolve as a legal principle within a process of claims and responses that will determine its contours and normative contents.[39] In this process the differentiation between principles and rules acquires relevance.[40] While rules are specific and apply in a particular context, legal principles aim to provide guidance and directions.[41] Cottier also claims that Common Concern as an emerging principle relies on and builds upon established principles of international law such as sovereignty, non-interference and self-determination, equality of states, shared interest and public trust.[42]

It is argued that the process of claims and responses for an issue to amount to a Common Concern can be initiated both by states and non-state actors in the context of an international forum or organisation that deals with that specific area. Cottier considered that while the role of the Security Council of the United Nations is limited in this process (because

---

[37] Chapter 1 in this volume, p. 51.

[38] Bodansky, *supra* n. 27.

[39] Chapter 1 in this volume, pp. 26–9.

[40] R. M. Dworkin, 'The Model of Rules', *The University of Chicago Law Review*, 35(1) (1967), 14.

[41] R. Kolb, 'Principles as Sources of International Law (with Special Reference to Good Faith)', *Netherlands International Law Review*, 53(1) (2006), 1; J. Wouters, D. Coppens and D. Geraets, 'The Influence of General Principles of Law', in S. E. Gaines, B. E. Olsen and K. E. Sørensen (eds.), *Liberalising Trade in the EU and the WTO: A Legal Comparison* (Cambridge: Cambridge University Press, 2012).

[42] Chapter 1 in this volume, pp. 29–36.

it only deals with short-term crises), the Group of 20 (G20) should take the lead in the consideration of potential Common Concerns of horizontal nature and, in particular, when they involve economic issues.[43]

The benchmark or threshold for an issue to be considered a Common Concern is a threat to peace, stability and welfare.[44] This threshold is aimed to act as a trigger to start the process of claims and responses for an issue to be considered a Common Concern of Humankind. The considerations of peace, stability and welfare lie on the very foundations of public international law that in some scenarios legitimise limitations to the traditional notions of state sovereignty, independence and self-determination. In the context of this chapter, an unstable IMS can lead to unrest and breakdowns. This is illustrated by the historical example of the interwar period, during which the economic breakdown in the Great Depression contributed to the breakdown of international peace and stability. As very clearly remarked by Lastra, the maintenance and promotion of peace, stability and welfare is enshrined on the very foundations of the IMF:

> Drawing on the lessons of history, it was in the context of World War II that countries were ready to make the sacrifices needed in terms of sovereignty by signing a number of international treaties that gave rise to international organizations such as the United Nations, the International Monetary Fund (IMF), and the World Bank. John Maynard Keynes had wisely stated that in order to win the war we needed to 'win the peace'. It was this understanding that also inspired Henry Morgenthau (then US Treasury Secretary) to proclaim in the opening remarks of the Bretton Woods conference in New Hampshire in July 1944 that 'prosperity like peace is indivisible'. Neither Keynes nor Morgenthau were thinking only in territorial/national terms: they were thinking in international terms.[45]

Consequently, it is proposed by the emerging doctrine of Common Concern of Humankind that the process of claims and responses to determine whether a collective action problem is to be considered a Common Concern should be analysed from a three-dimensional perspective. First, enhancing the *duty to cooperate*, consult and negotiate

---

[43] Ibid., p. 42.
[44] Ibid., pp. 39–41.
[45] R. M. Lastra, 'Do We Need a World Financial Organization?', *Journal of International Economic Law*, 17 (2014), 787.

(international cooperation among states). Second, providing the basis for the *obligations at home* (responsibilities at the state level – homework) delineating not only the rights but also the duties of states to act beyond the scope of the territorial application of laws in order to comply with the international commitments made (extraterritoriality). Third, *securing compliance* with the obligations that emerge from Common Concerns. Hence, this chapter by following the three-dimensional analysis aims to demonstrate that international monetary stability is a Common Concern of Humankind.

7.3 The Duty to Cooperate: The Fund's Role and Cooperation among States

The emerging doctrine of Common Concern aims to enhance and strengthen the duty to cooperate internationally as the best solution to solve the problems associated with Common Concerns. Recognising that there is no general duty to cooperate, consult and negotiate under current international law, this duty would apply only to matters that are considered Common Concerns of Humankind. This proposed duty to cooperate would entail an improved transparency in information sharing and the timely and accurate publication of laws and regulations. It would also involve the duty to consult and negotiate to reach a consensus. The discussions will surround the issue of the burden-sharing among parties and the shared but differentiated responsibilities of the actors involved in the specific subject matter.

Concerning monetary affairs and as presented elsewhere in this chapter, since the collapse of the Bretton Woods system in the 1970s the role of international public law and international institutions is limited. Thus, international cooperation for the pursuit of monetary stability lacks an appropriate international regulatory framework and instead rests on soft governance arrangements and mostly on the goodwill of states to promote monetary policy coordination among the central banks. Consequently, Common Concern if established as a principle, aims to enhance the duty to cooperate in monetary affairs both from a *top-down approach* and a *bottom-up approach*. While the *top-down approach* relates to the duty to cooperate at the international level of governance with the IMF as the central international monetary institution, the *bottom-up approach* considers the cross-border cooperation among countries with a special emphasis on monetary policy coordination among central banks.

7.3.1 Top-down Approach: International Level of Governance

Notwithstanding the indisputable fact that monetary stability is a sovereignty issue, it also has an international dimension. This global dimension refers to the stability of the IMS as a whole. According to the Fund's view,[46] the stability of the IMS refers to the stability of the overall system of exchange rates in accordance with the purpose of the Fund as stated in Article I(iii) of the Articles of Agreement, that is, 'To promote exchange stability, to maintain orderly exchange arrangements among members, and to avoid competitive exchange depreciation.' However, as stated above in this chapter the stability of the IMS goes beyond stability of exchange rate agreements and also depends on the stability of the other key elements of the system.

7.3.1.1 The Fund's Role

The role of the IMF as the central international monetary institution has evolved since its conception, but the primary purpose to 'ensure the stability of the international monetary system – the system of exchange rates and international payments that enables countries (and their citizens) to transact with each other'[47] remains unchanged. With the entry into force of the Second Amendment the Fund shifted the centre of its activities from a rule-based system monitoring the 'par value' regime to a surveillance-based function[48] (that, coupled with the other key IMF functions, namely conditional financial assistance, provides the post Second Amendment *raison d'être* of the IMF).[49] The surveillance

---

[46] IMF, *supra* n. 4.

[47] IMF, *The IMF at a Glance* (2019), www.imf.org/About/Factsheets/IMF-at-a-Glance?pdf= 1 (accessed 30 Sept. 2019). Article I of the Articles of Agreement enumerates the objectives of the IMF in a detailed manner.

[48] According to Guitián this surveillance-based function of the IMF is discretionary and thus, judgement is of the essence. However, he also remarks that the discretion is limited by the code of conduct enshrined in the Articles of Agreement (M. Guitián, 'The Unique Nature of the Responsibilities of the International Monetary Fund', *IMF Pamphlet Series No 46* (1992), www.imf.org/external/pubs/ft/pam/pam46/pam46con.htm (accessed 30 Sept. 2019)).

[49] In 2010 the IMF published two documents entitled, 'The Fund's Role and Mandate: An Overview' (in January) and 'The Fund's Mandate: The Legal Framework' (in February) aiming to clarify the role of the IMF in the promotion of international stability. IMF, *The Fund's Role and Mandate: An Overview* (2010), www.imf.org/external/np/pp/eng/2010/ 012210a.pdf (accessed 30 Sept. 2019); IMF, *supra* n. 18.

INTERNATIONAL MONETARY STABILITY 361

function enables the IMF to monitor compliance with standards and rules[50] and to provide incentives for member states to comply with such standards and rules (through the design of conditionality policies).[51]

Since the modifications introduced by the Second Amendment the limits set by international public law on the monetary sovereignty powers of states have been general, non-specific and of a soft-law nature. The so-called soft law are rules or standards characterised as informal, voluntary and non-enforceable. Soft law usually emerges to fill regulatory 'gaps' but it cannot replace the named 'hard law' or formal law. Hard law is characterised as being formal, externally imposed and enforceable.[52] According to Tietje, 'The significance of soft law in the global financial and monetary system is not necessarily a negative phenomenon.' He also considers that 'However, a stable international monetary system cannot rely exclusively on soft law. In fact, one may argue that the entire phenomenon of soft law essentially rests on the existence of "hard" law. Soft law fills gaps and in this it depends on gaps, gaps in a legal system.'[53]

There are also other international actors that play a fundamental role in the functioning of the IMS.

> [T]he World Trade Organization focuses on the regulation of international trade. The Bank for International Settlements (BIS), aims to foster international monetary and financial stability, acting as a forum for 'cooperation among central banks and the financial community'. The Financial Stability Board (FSB) focuses on promoting international

---

[50] The surveillance of rules and standards is done via consultations in accordance with Article IV of the Articles of Agreement, the Financial Sector Assessment Program and the Reports on the Observance of Standards and Codes. For more detailed information on IMF surveillance, see N. Rendak, 'Monitoring and Surveillance of the International Monetary System: What Can Be Learnt from the Trade Field?', in Cottier *et al.*, *supra* n. 1, p. 204.

[51] Conditionality only applies to IMF member states that request financial assistance from the Fund. IMF, *IMF Conditionality* (2019), www.imf.org/en/About/Factsheets/Sheets/2016/08/02/21/28/IMF-Conditionality (accessed 30 Sept. 2019).

[52] E. Ferran and K. Alexander, 'Can Soft Law Bodies Be Effective? The Special Case of the European Systemic Risk Board', *European Law Review*, 35(6) (2010), 751; C. Brummer, 'Why Soft Law Dominates International Finance: And Not Trade', in T. Cottier, J. H. Jackson and R. M. Lastra (eds.), *International Law in Financial Regulation and Monetary Affairs* (Oxford: Oxford University Press, 2010); C. Bummer, *Soft Law and the Global Financial System: Rule Making in the 21st Century* (Cambridge: Cambridge University Press, 2011).

[53] Tietje, *supra* n. 19.

financial stability. And the World Bank's overarching goal is poverty reduction through inclusive and sustainable globalization.[54]

Besides these actors and since the onset of the GFC, the G20 assumed a fundamental role as an informal political forum for the coordination and promotion of the reforms to the international financial and monetary system.[55]

7.3.1.2   Core Elements of the IMS

The core elements of the IMS can change or evolve over time. Consequently, for the purposes of this chapter I analyse these elements in the present context and also with the challenges that emerged since the GFC.

Exchange Rates   With the Second Amendment the Fund's members can decide on their preferred exchange rate regime and the era of 'floating exchange rates' began.[56] The revised Article IV, section 2(b), reads as follows:

> [E]xchange arrangements may include (i) the maintenance by a member of a value for its currency in terms of the special drawing right or another denominator, other than gold, selected by the member, or (ii) cooperative arrangements by which members maintain the value of their currencies in relation to the value of the currency or currencies of other members, or (iii) other exchange arrangements of a member's choice.

Notwithstanding this total freedom in the choice of their exchange rate regime the new Article IV, section 1 of the IMF Code of Conduct creates obligations on the conduct of members' policies with the intention to promote exchange rate stability. This article aims to provide guidance to the Fund's members in the conduct of their exchange rate policies. In its introduction the article states that 'each member undertakes to collaborate with the Fund and other members to assure orderly exchange arrangements and to promote a stable system of exchange rates'. It is interesting to note that this provision states the duty to 'promote' exchange rate stability but not to 'maintain' exchange rate stability.

---

[54] IMF, *Strengthening the International Monetary System: A Stocktaking* (2016), www.imf .org/external/np/pp/eng/2016/022216b.pdf (accessed 30 Sept. 2019).
[55] Zimmermann, *supra* n. 8, p. 192.
[56] The Second Amendment of the Articles of Agreement eliminated the so-called gold-dollar standard that was a two-tier system of convertibility.

INTERNATIONAL MONETARY STABILITY 363

Accordingly, Proctor affirms that since the Second Amendment 'there is at present no positive treaty or other obligation on States to ensure the international stability of currencies, nor does the creation of any such obligation appear to be all likely'.[57]

This general duty to collaborate and promote exchange rate stability is followed by a non-exhaustive list of specific obligations concerning the members' domestic and external policies. The provision reads as follows:

> (i) endeavor to direct its economic and financial policies toward the objective of fostering orderly economic growth with reasonable price stability, with due regard to its circumstances; (ii) seek to promote stability by fostering orderly underlying economic and financial conditions and a monetary system that does not tend to produce erratic disruptions; (iii) avoid manipulating exchange rates or the international monetary system in order to prevent effective balance of payments adjustment or to gain an unfair competitive advantage over other members; and (iv) follow exchange policies compatible with the undertakings under this Section.

These obligations are drafted in a manner so that they are considered of a 'soft' nature and would only require the best efforts of the members, with the exception of Article IV, section 1(iii), which is considered of a 'hard' nature and requires the members to achieve results beyond their best efforts.[58]

International Payment System and International Capital Movements These two elements of the IMS are intrinsically related and have been subject to challenges imposed by the liberalisation of current international payments and increased openness of trade and capital flows.[59] Despite the interface between these two elements, the Fund took two opposite directions in the regulation of international payments and capital flows under the revised Articles of Agreement.

---

[57] Proctor, *supra* n. 9, p. 595.

[58] For an overview of the legal framework of Article IV of the Articles of Agreement, see IMF, *Article IV of the Fund's Articles of Agreement: An Overview of the Legal Framework* (2006), www.imf.org/external/np/pp/eng/2006/062806.pdf (accessed 30 Sept. 2019), para. 3.2.

[59] In the balance-of-payment position of a country the 'international payments system' is related to the 'current account' and the 'international capital movements' are related to the 'capital account'. While 'current account' restrictions are prohibited 'capital account' restrictions are permitted.

On one hand, Article VIII, section 2(a) prohibits IMF members, without the approval of the Fund, from imposing restrictions on the making of payments and transfers for current international transactions. The term 'payments for current transactions' includes transactions in goods and services and also some transfers for capital transactions.[60] The transactions must be 'international' as opposed to domestic and the prohibition reaches only to the 'making' of international payments and transfers *outwards* and not to the 'reception' of international payments and transfers *inwards*. The trend towards the liberalisation of international payments is widely accepted and the events of the GFC did not enhance restrictive measures.[61]

On the other hand, Article VI, section 3 expressly recognises the right of the Fund's members to regulate capital flows. This discretional right includes the possibility of the Fund's members regulating both *outwards* and *inwards* international capital movements as long as the measures do not affect current transactions. According to these provisions the IMF's jurisdiction reaches 'current international transactions' and not 'international capital movements'.[62] The long-standing debate about the liberalisation of international capital movements and the benefits of capital controls have been revitalised since the start of the GFC. In this context the IMF approved in 2012 the institutional view (Institutional View).[63]

Monetary Reserves and Access to Liquidity   The management of monetary reserves is part of the foreign exchange policy dictated by the governments and implemented by the monetary authorities (usually a central bank). In the case of states (members of the IMF), the Second Amendment incorporates a new provision (Article VIII, section 7) in

---

[60]   Article XXX(d) of the Articles of Agreement provides a definition of the term 'payments for current transactions'. For a detailed study of the scope of this term, see D. Siegel, 'Legal Aspects of the IMF/WTO Relationship: The Fund's Articles of Agreement and the WTO Agreement', *American Journal of International Law*, 96 (2002), 561.

[61]   This tendency is exposed by the results of IMF, *Annual Report on Exchange Arrangements and Exchange Restrictions 2016* (2016), https://imf.org/en/Publications/Annual-Report-on-Exchange-Arrangements-and-Exchange-Restrictions/Issues/2017/01/25/Annual-Report-on-Exchange-Arrangements-and-Exchange-Restrictions-2016-43741 (accessed 30 Sept. 2019).

[62]   On this issue, see Lastra, *supra* n. 8, p. 450.

[63]   This view does not alter the members' obligations under the Articles of Agreement and also states that the measures should be limited and temporary. IMF, *The Liberalization and Management of Capital Flows: An Institutional View* (2012), www.imf.org/external/np/pp/eng/2012/111412.pdf (accessed 30 Sept. 2019), pp. 29–30.

relation to this element of the IMS and establishes a new obligation that reads as follows:

> Each member undertakes to collaborate with the Fund and with other members in order to ensure that the policies of the member with respect to reserve assets shall be consistent with the objectives of promoting better international surveillance of international liquidity and making the special drawing right the principal reserve asset in the international monetary system.

At the moment that the aforementioned provision was included the main purpose was to favour the role of the special drawing rights (SDR) and diminish the role of gold as reserve assets. However, it can be stated that the course of history did not follow such purpose and that the reserve currencies, especially the US dollar, acquired a de facto central role for this element of the IMS.[64]

This element of the IMS is also about the 'access to international liquidity' as a main component of the so-called global financial safety net (GFSN). There is no international regulation on the supply of liquidity despite its being a core element for the smooth functioning of the IMS. It can be indicated that the GFSN is comprised of four classes of elements: foreign exchange reserves, bilateral currency swap lines, regional financing arrangements (RFAs) and financing through multilateral institutions.[65]

7.3.2 Bottom-up Approach: Central Banking Cooperation

It is interesting to remark that the first set of responses to the GFC generated an unprecedented level of informal cooperation among the major central banks, but this cooperation quickly vanished when the crisis started to cool down. According to Heath, 'Spontaneous coordination may occur in a global crisis because countries may face similar circumstances that overwhelm other individual country conditions, and so many nations interests align in seeking action.'[66] Some examples of cooperation during the crisis, or as a response to the crisis, were the establishment of swap lines among the US Federal Reserve System

---

[64] IMF, *supra* n. 54. For an extended analysis on monetary reserves, see Section 7.4.1.5.

[65] For more detailed information about the GFSN, see IMF, *Adequacy of the Global Safety Net* (2016), https://imf.org/external/np/pp/eng/2016/031016.pdf (accessed 30 Sept. 2019).

[66] D. Heath, 'International Coordination of Macroprudential and Monetary Policy', *Georgetown Journal of International Law*, 45 (2013–14), 1093.

(the Fed) and various central banks[67] of the considered major advanced economies, the synchronised reduction of the interest rate policy by 25 to 50 basis points by six central banks after the collapse of Lehman Brothers and the almost simultaneous start of monetary easing of the major central banks in October 2008.[68]

Notwithstanding the above-mentioned examples, most of the solutions adopted to manage the GFC were nation-oriented and uncoordinated. As remarked in a discussion paper by the Bank of England, 'The landscape for international monetary policy co-operation has not changed in any fundamental way since the crisis: with the exception of the co-ordinated monetary easing at the onset of the crisis, conventional monetary policy is still being set by individual central banks without co-ordination.'[69] For example, the setting of key interest rates is one of the main instruments (together with open market operations and reserve requirements) of the monetary policy pursued by central banks in search of monetary stability. As a response to the crisis the central banks resorted to this instrument but used it differently. As remarked by Zimmermann:

> The Fed reacted with a series of interest rate cuts aimed at saving employment while the ECB kept interest rates unchanged for much longer in order not to endanger price stability. This illustrates that the current lack of harmonization in the way interest rates policies are being conducted by central banks may lead to major differences in how similar economic problems are tackled by different countries.[70]

As a reaction to this situation, the IMF Staff Team prepared a discussion note paper about the form monetary policy should have in the aftermath of the GFC. In this discussion paper they argued that in crisis times, 'the potential gains from cooperation are significant. Cooperation reduces the risk of tail events with large international feedback effects, and in those

---

[67] The Fed started liquidity lines with the ECB and the Swiss National Bank in December 2007, with twelve more central banks in September–October 2008 (R. Mohan and M. Kapur, 'Monetary Policy Coordination and the Role of Central Banks', *IMF Working Paper 14/70* (2014), www.imf.org/external/pubs/ft/wp/2014/wp1470.pdf (accessed 30 Sept. 2019)).

[68] Ibid. The coordinated reduction of the interest rate was taken on 8 October 2008 among the Bank of Canada, the Bank of England, the ECB, the Fed, the Sveriges Riksbank and the Swiss National Bank.

[69] Bank of England, *One Bank Research Agenda Discussion Paper* (2015), www .bankofengland.co.uk/research/Documents/onebank/discussion.pdf (accessed 30 Sept. 2019).

[70] C. D. Zimmermann, 'Global Benchmark Interest Rates', in Cottier *et al.*, *supra* n. 1, p. 158.

circumstances, central banks have been willing to cooperate.' While in regular times, 'there is insufficient clarity on the size of the welfare gains from monetary policy cooperation'.[71] Moreover, the discussion note remarks that even though the welfare gains were clear during normal times there are several obstacles to cooperation. It listed the obstacles that range from the different economic situations across countries to the lack of harmonised domestic objectives for the pursuit of monetary stability.

On the obstacles to international monetary policy cooperation, Ostry and Ghosh pointed out that:

> [T]he most compelling reasons are asymmetries in country size; disagreement about the economic situation and cross-border transmission effects of policies; and often policymakers' failure to recognise that they face important trade-offs across various objectives.

To address these concerns they proposed on one hand that 'a neutral assessor may play a useful role in helping to bridge the divergent views of national policymakers' and on the other hand 'to buttress international coordination and to provide safeguards when coordination proves impossible to achieve, by implementing two guideposts to limit negative spillovers through the current account and the capital account, respectively.'[72]

7.3.3   Conclusion

The recognition of global monetary stability as a Common Concern would imply a reinforcement of the role of the IMF as the central international monetary institution from a *top-down* perspective. In spite of the fact that the regulatory function in global monetary affairs is shared by a number of formal and informal international setters, including most notably the FSB and BIS, the IMF keeps the lead as claimed in this chapter.

The main reason for this is that the Fund's key surveillance function enables it to monitor the member states' compliance with rules and standards and provide incentives for members to comply with them.

---

[71] T. Bayoumi, G. Dell-Ariccia, K. Habermeier, T. Mancini-Griffoli, F. Valencia and an IMF Staff Team, *Monetary Policy in the New Normal* (2014), www.imf.org/external/pubs/ft/sdn/2014/sdn1403.pdf (accessed 30 Sept. 2019).

[72] J. D. Ostry and A. R. Ghosh, *Obstacles to International Policy Coordination, and How to Overcome Them* (2013), www.imf.org/external/pubs/ft/sdn/2013/sdn1311.pdf (accessed 30 Sept. 2019).

Also, beyond bilateral surveillance that is performed by individual countries, the IMF performs multilateral surveillance of the global economy, thus helping to identify the impact domestic policies may have on other countries and the global economy.[73] This analysis may assist with the allocation of burden-sharing of the shared but differentiated responsibilities proposed under the principle of Common Concern.

Notwithstanding the key role of the Fund's surveillance in crisis prevention and enhanced international cooperation, all policy recommendations made in the context of IMF surveillance are of an advisory nature and non-mandatory. Therefore, the *bottom-up* perspective acquires relevance in the pursuit of a Common Concern of global monetary stability. As remarked by Gopinath, recently appointed chief economist at the IMF, cross-border cooperation efforts among countries from a domestic level approach are welcome developments to support the well-functioning of the international system:

> It is then all the more important for countries to cooperate on financial regulation, to strengthen the global safety net, and to reduce the stigma attached to the lender of last resort role of the IMF. The creation of regional monetary funds like the European Stability Mechanism (ESB) set up in 2012, the Chiang Mai Initiative Multilateralization (CMIM) in 2012, BRICS Contingent Reserve Arrangement (CRA) in 2014 and other smaller regional arrangements that taken together have committed resources of US 1.3 trillion dollars similar to that of the IMF (Denbee et al. (2016)) are welcome developments that complement the IMF in supporting a well functioning international monetary and financial system.[74]

Consequently, the enhanced duty to cooperate proposed by Common Concern would have a positive impact on the promotion of international monetary stability both from a *top-down* and *bottom-up* approach. However, the efficacy of such enhanced duty would still depend on the IMF member states' willingness to enhance the Fund's mandate on the premises of Common Concern and also on each state's readiness to engage in further cross-border cooperation under the guidance of the potential principle of Common Concern.

---

[73] IMF, *IMF Surveillance* (2018), www.imf.org/en/About/Factsheets/IMF-Surveillance (accessed 30 Sept. 2019).

[74] G. Gopinath, *Rethinking International Macroeconomic Policy* (2017), https://scholar .harvard.edu/files/gopinath/files/openeconomypolicy100317.pdf (accessed 30 Sept. 2019).

7.4 Obligation to Do Homework: The Special Role of Central Banks

As stated by Cottier, the emerging doctrine of Common Concern grants a special place to the obligation to do homework. This element encompasses two levels of commitment: the duty to promote and protect the Common Concern at the local level and the duty to implement international commitments assumed in international agreements and in customary law.[75] Cottier remarks that the doctrine is not meant to affect the existing obligations under international law but to confer them with the foundations of the emerging principle of Common Concern. That is, encouraging the timely and effective implementation of international commitments and promoting bottom-up initiatives to address the global challenges presented by the Common Concerns.

For the *first level of commitment*, the pursuit and maintenance of monetary stability as a domestic public good and a local Common Concern is a clear attribute of a state's monetary sovereignty prerogative. Under this sovereignty attribute a state defines what is to be considered as monetary stability locally and the pursuit of monetary stability is usually entrusted to an independent central bank or the relevant monetary authority as the core objective of its monetary policy.

For the *second level of commitment*, states shall comply with international commitments assumed in international agreements and in customary law. The main reason for this is that international law recognises the sovereign powers of other states in monetary affairs. However, this monopoly power of states in the monetary field is no longer absolute and has been subject to some limitations by the rules of public international law through specific treaty provisions and also by rules of customary international law. The primary sources of international law applicable to monetary stability are the Articles of Agreement of the IMF, the customary international law applicable and the general principles of law. However, as detailed in the previous section, since the modifications introduced by the Second Amendment to the Articles of Agreement of the IMF the limits set by international public law on the monetary sovereignty powers of states are general, non-specific and of a soft-law nature.

---

[75] See Chapter 1 in this volume.

7.4.1   The Special Role of Central Banks

Domestic monetary stability is both a fundamental economic goal and an essential monetary policy objective. Lastra provides a definition of monetary stability that considers both a positive and a negative perspective:

> In positive terms, monetary stability refers to the maintenance of the internal value of money (ie, price stability) as well as of the external value of the currency (ie, the stability of the currency vis-à-vis other currencies, which is, in turn, influenced by the choice of exchange rate regime). In negative terms, monetary stability refers broadly to the absence of instability.[76]

While 'internal monetary stability' refers to the stability of domestic prices and is generally measured by the consumer price index calculated by a public agency,[77] 'external monetary stability' is understood as the stability of the value of a specific currency vis-à-vis other currencies and the law refers to it in very ambiguous terms.[78]

The design of the international monetary order in the post Bretton Woods era has preferred legal and institutional arrangements at the national level in the pursuit of monetary stability. Independent central banks have been the predominant institutional arrangement since the 1990s, playing a crucial role in the promotion and protection of

---

[76] R. M. Lastra, *supra* n. 8, p. 56.

[77] The *Oxford Dictionary of Finance and Banking* states that the Consumer Price Index (CPI) is:

> 1. In the UK ... a measure of price level introduced in 1997 to enable comparisons within the EU ... 2. In the USA, the measure of price level calculated monthly by the Bureau of Labor Statistics. It is commonly known as the cost-of-living index and gives the cost of specific consumer items compared to the base year of 1967.

> (J. Law and J. Smullen (eds.), *A Dictionary of Finance and Banking* (4th rev. ed., Oxford: Oxford University Press, 2008))

[78] On this point Lastra considers that the law is ambiguous about the external dimension of domestic monetary stability because 'the issue of which is the best exchange rate arrangement for a given country (fixed, floating, or some version of managed float) remain a matter of great controversy' (*supra* n. 8, p. 60). See also F. Gianviti, 'The Objectives of Central Banks', in Mario Giovanoli and Diego Devos (eds.), *International Monetary and Financial Law: The Global Crisis* (Oxford: Oxford University Press, 2010), p. 473.

INTERNATIONAL MONETARY STABILITY

monetary stability.[79] Proctor provides a functional definition of a central bank stating that 'A central bank is an institution of a State. In the issue of money, the conduct of national monetary policy, the administration of a system of exchange control, and the management of a country's foreign reserves, it plainly discharges functions of a peculiar sovereign nature.'[80]

7.4.1.1 Institutions of a State

Central banks as *institutions of a state* are usually established by law or statute which provides legitimacy to operate under a specific mandate. The mandate of a central bank is of a peculiar nature because of its special relationship with the government. As remarked by Lastra:

> Central banks are at the centre, equidistant from the government and the financial system (they are both banker to the government and banker to the banks). Central banking is thus defined by the relationships of the central bank upwards with the government and downwards with the banking and financial system. The law must govern both relationships.[81]

Accordingly, Lastra states that central banks are both regulatory agencies and banks and consequently they carry out public functions governed by administrative law and commercial functions ruled by commercial law.[82] As regulatory agencies most central banks around the world have been granted independence in the pursuit of monetary stability.[83] This movement towards the granting of independence to central banks gained traction in the late 1980s and spread throughout the 1990s with the purpose of combating high inflation. Consequently and in pursuit of

---

[79] There are other institutional arrangements for the promotion of monetary stability such as currency boards and legislated monetary rules (Lastra, *supra* n. 8, pp. 63–4).

[80] Proctor, *supra* n. 9, p. 573. Proctor also remarks that:

> It may be added that a central bank may have other functions. In some jurisdictions the central bank is responsible for the prudential supervision of the banking sector, whilst in other countries a separate agency is established for this purpose. But these additional features do not add to (or detract from) an entity's legal status as the central bank of a given country.
>
> (Ibid., p. 571)

[81] Lastra, *supra* n. 8, p. 33.

[82] Ibid.

[83] The legal framework for the independence of central banks is explained in detail in R. M. Lastra, *Central Banking and Banking Regulation* (London: London School of Economics and Political Science, 1996).

domestic price stability, states amended central bank laws to grant independence to central banks to control inflation.

Central bank independence is not absolute but limited to the policy goals set by law, statute or treaty. Hence, central banks are granted independence from the government but at the same time they are accountable to this government. As pointed out by White: 'In a democratically ordered society, no government agency, including the central bank, can be wholly "independent" from government.'[84] Therefore, while independent central banks are entitled to exercise their delegated powers with some degree of discretion in the pursuit of their mandates, they are still accountable to the government and to the electorate on the success or failure to achieve their mandates. In the aftermath of the GFC the issue of transparency of central bank policies has also come to the forefront, accompanying accountability.[85] This new trend on greater transparency in relation to central bank policies aims to improve the success of the policies by enhancing communication mechanisms and providing clearer expectations for market participants.[86]

7.4.1.2 Issuance of Money

States exercise monetary sovereignty in the *issuance and regulation of money* according to the law of the currency (*lex monetae*), which defines what money is and the nominal value that money has in a particular jurisdiction. Hence money, as a creation of the law, is territorial and must be studied within a legal system. The 'state theory of money', adopted in most modern constitutions, claims that money is what the law of states dictate it to be and as a result falls within the jurisdiction of the issuing state.[87]

---

[84] W. R. White, 'Changing Views on How Best to Conduct Monetary Policy' (2012), www.bis.org/speeches/sp021018.htm (accessed 30 Sept. 2019).

[85] A study by Dincer and Eichengreen established a significant movement towards greater central bank transparency in the last decade and also considered that transparent monetary policies are more likely in democratic countries (N. Dincer and B. Eichengreen, 'Central Bank Transparency: Causes, Consequences and Updates', *NBER Working Paper No. 14791* (2009), www.nber.org/papers/w14791 (accessed 30 Sept. 2019)).

[86] Kaufmann and Weber also pointed out that enhanced transparency in relation to central bank policy relates to democratic accountability and thus, is a mechanism to balance central bank independence (C. Kaufmann and R. H. Weber, 'Transparency and Monetary Affairs', in Cottier *et al.*, *supra* n. 1, p. 467).

[87] For a more detailed analysis on monetary sovereignty and the 'state theory of money', see Proctor, *supra* n. 9, pp. 15–25.

The law usually entrusts the central bank with the function of issuance as a monopoly in the given jurisdiction.[88] Central banks by being a monopolist in this function can control the volume of the fiat money[89] in circulation and also its seigniorage (that is, the face value of the money minus the cost of their production). The fiat money (physical bank notes and coins) in circulation is legal tender as defined by the legislators of the specific monetary system. Proctor remarks that 'only physical money is legal tender, whilst the expression "money" embraces a much wider variety of instruments'.[90]

This note-issuance function together with the fractional reserve basis under which most commercial banks operate provide the reasons for the 'lender of last resort' function of central banks.[91] In a fractional reserve system only a portion of a bank's assets are liquid. Consequently, banks are not able to convert all of their assets into cash at the same time without losing value or selling them at fire-sale price. This characteristic of a bank's balance sheet makes it fragile to confront a massive liquidity crisis. The central banks, having monopoly of note issuance, are ultimate providers of high-powered money and are given the final responsibility to ensure the convertibility of a bank's assets into cash.

The fractional reserve banking system under which most commercial banks operate and create the so-called commercial bank money has been subject to a long-standing criticism that acquired new relevance in the aftermath of the GFC and more recently in the debate about the 'Vollgeld' or 'sovereign money' referendum held and rejected in Switzerland on 10 June 2018.[92] The advocates of this referendum proposed a radical reform aimed to prohibit commercial banks from issuing

---

[88] While the monopoly of note issuance by the central bank is the predominant arrangement, there are other arrangements with different levels of competition. Lastra provides a list of some theoretical scenarios of commercial banks competing in the issuance of money (*supra* n. 83).

[89] Fiat money is defined as 'Paper money or coins of little or no intrinsic value in themselves and not convertible into gold or silver, but made legal tender by fiat (order) of the government' (Financial Times Lexicon, 'Definition of Fiat Money', http://lexicon.ft.com/Term?term=fiat-money (accessed 30 Sept. 2019)).

[90] Proctor, *supra* n. 9, p. 74 (fn. 51).

[91] For a comprehensive description of this notion, see A. Campbell and R. M. Lastra, 'Revisiting the Lender of Last Resort', *Banking & Finance Law Review*, 24 (2009), 453.

[92] R. Atkins, 'Radical Reform: Switzerland to Vote on Banking Overhaul', *Financial Times*, Bern, Switzerland (29 May 2018); M. Sandbu, 'Treat Money as the Public Good It Is', *Financial Times* (31 May 2018); M. Wolf, 'Why the Swiss Should Vote for "Vollgeld"', *Financial Times* (6 June 2018).

commercial money through their traditional business model and to reinstate the central bank as the monopolist provider of all the money in circulation in the given jurisdiction.

7.4.1.3 Conduct of National Monetary Policy

Most central bank laws assign the central bank with the *monetary policy function* listing its objectives and instruments but do not provide a legal definition of the term. However, it can be stated that 'Monetary policy involves control over the supply of money within the economy and the cost of borrowing that money in terms of its interest rate.'[93]

The conduct of monetary policy is directed and also constrained by the objectives or goals set in central bank's mandate. According to Lastra 'In the context of the rules versus discretion monetary debate, it is interesting that the advent of central bank independence granted a substantial degree of discretion (technical, not political) to central bankers within the realm of their legal mandate to strive for monetary stability.'[94] These goals are usually determined by the central bank's statute or treaty. In some cases, such as the Fed, central banks are conferred an additional discretion in selecting the objectives to pursue.

The mandates of the central banks are generally domestic objectives to pursue the common good. As acknowledged by Gianviti, former general counsel of the IMF:

> Most countries officially recognise that preserving the value of money is a desirable objective, a 'public good', which has to be attained and preserved to achieve real growth. What this entails, however, is not uniformly understood. Between preserving the value of the currency in terms of one or more foreign currencies and preserving it in terms of domestic prices, a choice has to be made.[95]

Since the 1990s the objective of domestic price stability prevailed over others in most central bank laws. For example, for the European System of Central Banks (ESCB) its 'primary objective ... shall be to maintain price stability',[96] the Fed, to 'promote ... stable prices'[97] and the Bank of

---

[93] Proctor, *supra* n. 9, p. 94.
[94] Lastra, *supra* n. 10, p. 91.
[95] F. Gianviti, 'Relationship Between Monetary Policy and Exchange Rate Policy', in Cottier *et al.*, *supra* n. 1, p. 568.
[96] Treaty on the Functioning of the European Union [2008] OJ C115/47 Art 127; Protocol (No. 4) on the Statute of the ESCB and of the ECB [2010] OJ C326/230 Art 2.
[97] 12 US Code 226 Federal Reserve Act, s. 2 A.

England, 'to maintain price stability'.[98] Lastra explains that the price stability objective of central banks acquired relevance in the early 1990s as a response to the inflationary conditions of the 1970s and 1980s. She also explains that this objective is backed by economic theory focused on keeping inflation under control and on the empirical proof that independent central banks can control inflationary scenarios better than politicians.[99] A standard definition of inflation is: 'A general increase in prices in an economy and consequent fall in the purchasing value of money.'[100] However, domestic price instability can come both from increasing prices (inflation) and decreasing prices (deflation). Thus, White considers that 'there is a growing recognition that "price stability" as an objective of policy implies resisting both rising and falling prices'.[101]

The prevailing goal of domestic price stability on central banks mandates follows the 'Tinbergen rule'.[102] This economic rule relies on the assumption that each policy objective correlates to a policy instrument. Multiple policy objectives should be achieved with multiple instruments otherwise some of the objectives will be missed out or under achieved. That said, this rule is applied by central banks (one institution) in the implementation of monetary policy (one instrument) for the pursuit of monetary stability (one goal).

The Tinbergen rule worked very well for monetary affairs for a long period and helped successfully to contain inflation. However, the rule presented some fissures. For example, in the context of deflation increasing prices are not a concern (e.g. the case of Japan)[103] and in the context of the most recent GFC the central banks have moved their main concern from price stability to financial stability.[104] With the expanded objectives

---

[98] Bank of England Act 1998, s. 11.

[99] Lastra, *supra* n. 8, pp. 56–9.

[100] Law and Smullen, *supra* n. 77.

[101] White, *supra* n. 84.

[102] J. Tinbergen, *On the Theory of Economic Policy* (Amsterdam: North-Holland, 1952).

[103] As remarked by Samya Beidas-Strom *et al.*, 'The Japanese economy has experienced weak inflation for most of the past two decades … Continued efforts to reflate the economy have so far fallen short, highlighting the difficulty in escaping a deflation trap once expectations are anchored around a deflation equilibrium' (S. Beidas-Strom *et al.*, 'Global Disinflation in an Era of Constrained Monetary Policy', in IMF, *World Economic Outlook* (2016), www.imf.org/en/Publications/WEO/Issues/2016/12/31/Subdued-Demand-Symptoms-and-Remedies (accessed 30 Sept. 2019)).

[104] The rediscovered objective of financial stability and also the concerns about growth and employment during the GFC triggered regulatory changes for mandates of central banks.

(financial stability, growth and employment) central banks resorted to a new series of instruments to achieve them. Hence, since the beginning of the GFC central banks have resorted not only to conventional monetary policy instruments but also unconventional monetary policy instruments.[105]

The expanded goals of central banks together with the recourse to unconventional monetary policies have been subject to much debate and scrutiny since the start of the GFC. The discussion is mainly concerned with the legality of the expansion of central bank mandates and the limits of their emergency powers. In this context, the 'rules versus discretion' debate in monetary affairs regained relevance because central banks have discretionary powers within a legal framework.[106] As clearly pointed out by Goodhart and Lastra:

> Central bank discretion (a key component of independence) is the freedom to act within the limits of a legal framework. Judicial review does not extend to the 'content of the decision' (the aim of the Court is not to supplant or replace the decision taken or to second guess what central banks should have done), but it does extend to the parameters and legal framework that surround such decision in order to determine whether or not the central bank mandate has been exceeded.[107]

For example, in the USA, the Dodd–Frank Act 2010 reinforced the mandate of financial stability of the Fed. In the UK, the law governing the Bank of England was changed to include financial stability together with monetary stability as dual mandate. In the EU, despite monetary stability remaining as the primary objective in the Treaty, the mandate of the ECB has been expanded through secondary law during the GFC and a new 'banking union' is underway. For a detailed explanation of these regulatory changes and the rediscovered objective of financial stability, see Lastra, *supra* n. 8, pp. 29–110; R. M. Lastra and C. Goodhart, 'Interaction Between Monetary Policy and Bank Regulation', in European Parliament (ed.), *Interaction between Monetary Policy and Bank Regulation: Monetary Dialogue 23 September 2015*, www.europarl.europa.eu/committees/en/econ/monetary-dialogue.html?id=20150914CPU05481 (accessed 30 Sept. 2019).

[105] See Section 7.5.1.

[106] This consideration was reflected in the famous statements made by Ben Bernanke, former chairman of the Fed, 'the Federal Reserve has done, and will continue to do, everything possible within the limits of its authority to assist in restoring our nation to financial stability and economic prosperity', and by Mario Draghi, former president of the ECB, 'Within our mandate, the ECB is ready to do whatever it takes to preserve the euro. And believe me, it will be enough' (B. S Bernanke, 'Federal Reserve Policies to Ease Credit and Their Implications for the Fed's Balance Sheet' (2009), www.federalreserve.gov/newsevents/speech/bernanke20090218a.htm (accessed 30 Sept. 2019); European Central Bank, 'Verbatim of the Remarks Made by Mario Draghi' (2012), www.ecb.europa.eu/press/key/date/2012/html/sp120726.en.html (accessed 30 Sept. 2019)).

[107] C. Goodhart and R. M. Lastra, 'Populism and Central Bank Independence', *Open Economies Review*, 29(1) (2018), 49.

INTERNATIONAL MONETARY STABILITY 377

Therefore, while independent central banks are entitled to exercise their delegated powers with some degree of discretion in the pursuit of their mandates, they are still accountable to the government and to the electorate on the success or failure to achieve their mandates. Accountability can take different forms, such as parliamentary accountability, judicial review and cooperation with the executive to coordinate policy.

Up until the GFC the judicial review of acts and decisions by central banks was scarce but this situation has changed since the GFC. Goodhart and Lastra observed that most notably the Northern Rock case[108] opened in UK the debate about discretion, financial stability and the moral hazard associated with the lender-of-last-resort role of the Bank of England. Also, in the EU the *Pringle* case[109] and the *Gauweiler* case[110] dealt with the role of the Court of Justice of the European Union (CJEU) in the formation of economic and monetary policy and the *Gauweiler* case[111] also considered the legality of an unconventional monetary policy measure (the Outright Monetary Transactions (OMT) Programme).

7.4.1.4 Administration of a System of Exchange Control

Countries are free to choose from different exchange rate regimes or arrangements. Since the collapse of the 'fixed exchange rates' system promoted by the Bretton Woods system of 1944 and the subsequent enactment of the Second Amendment to the Articles of Agreement

---

[108] Northern Rock, a UK mortgage lender, received liquidity assistance from the Bank of England in September 2017 and this situation triggered a bank run that was followed by nationalisation of the entity and a series of legislative and regulatory responses in the UK (R. M. Lastra, 'Northern Rock, UK Bank Insolvency and Cross-border Bank Insolvency', *Journal of Banking Regulation*, 9(3) (2008), 165).

[109] Case C-370/12 *Thomas Pringle* v. *Government of Ireland* EU:C:2012:756.

[110] Case C-62/14 *Peter Gauweiler and Others* v. *Deutscher Bundestag* EU:C:2015:400.

[111] The technical features of the OMT were published in a press release in September 2012 but were never implemented. European Central Bank, 'Technical Features of Outright Monetary Transactions' (2012), www.ecb.int/press/pr/date/2012/html/pr120906_1.en.html (accessed 30 Sept. 2019). The legality of this programme was questioned by German citizens in the German Constitutional Court and the case was brought to the CJEU for a preliminary ruling. On 16 June 2015 the CJEU issued its final ruling that the conditional OMT programme was legal on the basis that the ECB has not exceeded its power concerning monetary policy and does not violate the prohibition against monetary financing to EU nations. Case C-62/14 *Peter Gauweiler and Others* v. *Deutscher Bundestag*.

378　　　LUCIA SATRAGNO

(Second Amendment) of the IMF[112] in 1978 the era of 'floating exchange rates' began. Countries can choose from a variety of arrangements that include free-floating and floating regimes, pegging exchange rates to one currency or to a basket of currencies, using the currency of another state, and participating in a currency bloc arrangement. Notwithstanding the choice of the exchange rate regime Lastra considers that:

> The reality of exchange markets is that exchange rates do fluctuate. Under a system of flexible exchange rates, such variations (appreciation or depreciation of the currency vis-à-vis other currencies) are triggered by market forces. Under a system of government controlled exchange rates, such variations (devaluation or revaluation) are officially imposed decisions.[113]

Although market forces – ruled by the law of offer and demand – determine the 'market rate' of a currency in relation to another currency, governments retain control over the administration of the system of exchange control and the determination of exchange rate in the given country. The administration of the system of exchange control is not an exclusive function of the central bank and, as mentioned before, usually the central bank implements an exchange rate policy that is decided by the government.[114]

A system of exchange control is usually conducted through domestic regulations that include limitations on capital transfers and/or international payments as artificial boundaries aimed at the protection of national credit markets. While capital transfers relate to the 'capital account' of a country, international payments relate to the 'current account' of a country. States are free to adopt 'capital account'

---

[112] As noted by Sir Joseph Gold in 1984:

> The outstanding characteristic of the provisions on exchange rates in the Second Amendment is that there is no insistence on a unified regime. *Each member is free to choose its exchange arrangement*, with the exception that a member may not maintain the external value of its currency in terms of gold. *A member is free also to determine the external value of its currency under the chosen exchange arrangement.*
>
> (J. Gold, 'Public International Law in the International Monetary System', *Southwestern Law Journal*, 38 (1984), 819 (emphases added))

[113] Lastra, *supra* n. 8, p. 425.

[114] For example in the UK the system of exchange control is a function of the Treasury delegated to the Bank of England. Hence, the Bank of England is independent in the conduct of monetary policy but is dependent in the conduct of exchange rate policy.

restrictions but the rules of international law pose some limitations on 'current account' restrictions.[115]

7.4.1.5 Management of a Country's Foreign Reserves

The term 'reserve assets' refers to 'external assets that are readily available to and controlled by monetary authorities for meeting balance of payments financing needs, for intervention in exchange markets to affect the currency exchange rate, and for other related purposes'.[116] This definition explains the economic foundation for countries in holding foreign reserves. That is, exchange rate stability (for both appreciation and depreciation episodes), trade financing and servicing of the country's debts.

Reserve assets can be classified into seven main categories: monetary gold (gold bullions), SDR holdings (IMF reserve assets), reserve position in the IMF, currency and deposits, securities (including debt and equity securities), financial derivatives and other claims (loans and other financial instruments).[117] These categories qualify as reserve assets because they are readily available in unconditional form to the monetary authorities. To be readily available the country's reserve assets must be liquid and denominated in a convertible currency.

The management of a country's foreign reserve assets is usually entrusted with the central bank or relevant monetary authority and is part of the foreign exchange policy dictated by the government.[118] For example, in the USA, the Exchange Stabilization Fund (ESF) of the United States Treasury was established by the Gold Reserve Act of 1934 to contribute to the US dollar exchange rate stability. The ESF operates under the Federal Reserve Bank of New York in its capacity as

---

[115] See pp. 363–4 in this chapter.

[116] IMF Statistics Department, *Balance of Payments Manual* (6th ed., 2009), www.imf.org/external/pubs/ft/bop/2007/pdf/bpm6.pdf (accessed 30 Sept. 2019), p. 111.

[117] IMF Statistics Department, *Balance of Payments Manual*, pp. 113–15. The SDR holdings and the reserve position in the IMF only apply as reserve assets for the Fund's members. The SDRs are the IMF's unit of account and an international reserve asset. IMF, *Special Drawing Right (SDR)* (2018), http://imf.org/external/np/exr/facts/sdr.htm (accessed 30 Sept. 2019).

[118] As noted by Goldberg *et al.*, 'Most often these reserves are held by central banks, although in some cases they may be held by finance ministries or sovereign wealth funds' (L. Goldberg, C. E. Hull and S. Stein, 'Do Industrialized Countries Hold the Right Foreign Exchange Reserves?', *Current Issues in Economics and Finance*, 19(1) (2013), www.newyorkfed.org/research/current_issues/ci19-1.html (accessed 30 Sept. 2019)).

fiscal agent for the Treasury.[119] In the United Kingdom (UK), the Exchange Equalisation Account (EEA) was created in 1932 to make available a fund that can be used to regulate the pound sterling exchange rate stability. The EEA is under the control of the Treasury, which appoints the Bank of England as its agent to manage the reserve assets under the EEA.[120] In Switzerland, the Governing Board of the Swiss National Bank (SNB) decides on the composition of the reserve assets and manages them in order to fulfil the SNB statutory mandate.[121]

7.4.2 Conclusion

In the post Bretton Woods era central banks have become the key players in the promotion and protection of monetary stability at the domestic (and regional EU) level. Monetary policy decisions from major central banks have played a fundamental part in the response to GFC. For this policy reaction to the GFC central banks have been called the 'only game in town'.[122] Notwithstanding the central banks' crucial role in global crisis management scenarios, as remarked in this section, they are institutions of state that are constrained by their domestic goals and mandate. Hence, when it comes to central banks assuming international commitments or engaging with enhanced monetary policy cooperation it rests on unpredictable soft-law commitments that are decided on a case-by-case situation.

Consequently, it can be argued that under the current circumstances the obligations at home concerning monetary stability are constrained to domestic and regional objectives that do not consider the global dimension. Hence, the aim of Common Concern, if it develops as a principle of law, is to reinforce the role of states as main providers of GPGs not only locally but also globally. This may involve an expansion on the mandate

---

[119] Federal Reserve Bank of New York, *Exchange Stabilization Fund* (2007), www.newyorkfed.org/aboutthefed/fedpoint/fed14.html (accessed 30 Sept. 2019).

[120] HM Treasury, *Management of the Official Reserves*, https://assets.publishing.service.gov.uk/government/uploads/system/uploads/attachment_data/file/236352/management_of_the_official_reserves_2013_14.pdf (accessed 30 Sept. 2019).

[121] Federal Act of 3 Oct. 2003 on the Swiss National Bank (National Bank Act, NBA) Arts. 5 and 46, www.admin.ch/opc/en/classified-compilation/20021117/index.html (accessed 30 Sept. 2019).

[122] R. Rajan, *The Only Game in Town* (2012), www.project-syndicate.org/commentary/the-limits-of-unconventional-monetary-policy-by-raghuram-rajan (accessed 30 Sept. 2019); M. El-Erian, *The Only Game in Town Central Banks, Instability, and Avoiding the Next Collapse* (New York: Random House, 2016).

goals of central banks to include global stability considerations while deciding domestic policy action. Also, going further, to provide central banks with the possibility to assume international commitments for special situations using as a trigger the Common Concern threshold of the threat to peace, stability and welfare applied to monetary stability. For example, in a liquidity crisis scenario states which are issuers of reserve currencies may have a commitment to establish bilateral or multilateral swap lines (through their respective central banks) with the central banks of the countries in need of liquidity. Hence, moving from a discretional attribute of central banks to a commitment activated by the principle of Common Concern (resorting to the principle of shared but differentiated responsibility). Furthermore, the emerging doctrine of Common Concern demands increased transparency and accountability. Hence, the implementation of these enhanced obligations of central banks will also involve renewed efforts on transparency, information sharing and accountability, as with more responsibility comes more accountability.

7.5 Obligation to Do Homework: Unilateral Actions and Extraterritoriality

Also, on the domestic front concerning the homework obligations, the emerging doctrine of Common Concern intends to inspire autonomous domestic policymaking aimed to address the issues underlying the Common Concerns. For example when international cooperation to safeguard a specific Common Concern is limited, *lawful domestic unilateral measures* with international effects are encouraged. The implementation of international law obligations or domestic measures may often result in an impact beyond the boundaries of the particular jurisdiction. International law does not exclude such effects, but seeks to achieve a careful balance between the interests of different jurisdictions.[123]

In monetary affairs, unilateral actions with extraterritorial effects have proved useful in the pursuit of monetary stability but are limited and temporary in nature. The main examples of this point have been brought by the GFC and its aftermath. In order to restore and promote monetary and financial stability and in the absence of appropriate global institutions and adequate international cooperation, states have been implementing a series of conventional and unconventional monetary policy

---

[123] See Chapter 1 in this volume.

measures. These measures have had and continue to have spillover effects (both positive and negative) beyond their intended borders. Consequently, states have resorted to a set of lawful unilateral measures to limit or repel the spillover effects generated both by the conventional and unconventional monetary policies in place since the beginning of the GFC. The unilateral measures are comprised mostly by capital controls and exchange restrictions. Additionally, the accumulation of reserves and regional financial agreements have been cited as examples of unilateral measures of a precautionary nature.

7.5.1 International Spillovers of Monetary Policy

As highlighted both by the 'Rapport Camdessus'[124] issued in February 2011 by a group of worldwide leading economists and the IMF paper 'Strengthening the International Monetary System: Taking Stock and Looking Ahead'[125] published almost simultaneously in March 2011, the GFC put in evidence manifold weaknesses of the IMS. These reports agreed that the weaknesses of the system are manifested in four fundamental problems which demand urgent responses to pursue the GPG and Common Concern of international monetary stability.

The *first problem* is about 'global current account imbalances'[126] and the 'inadequate global adjustment mechanisms to prevent inconsistent or imprudent policies among systemic countries'.[127] The *second problem* considers the 'financial excesses and destabilizing capital flows'[128] highlighting the absence of a 'comprehensive oversight framework for growing cross-border capital flows'.[129] The *third problem* observes the

---

[124] Palais-Royal Initiative, *Reform of the International Monetary System: A Cooperative Approach for the Twenty First Century* (2011), http://global-currencies.org/smi/gb/tele char/news/Rapport_Camdessus-integral.pdf (accessed 30 Sept. 2019). This report was written by a group of leading economists convened by Michel Camdessus, Alexandre Lamfalussy and Tommaso Padoa-Schiopa.

[125] IMF, *Strengthening the International Monetary System: Taking Stock and Looking Ahead* (2011), https://imf.org/external/np/pp/eng/2011/032311.pdf (accessed 5 June 2018).

[126] As explained by Viterbo, 'Global imbalances are characterized, on one hand, by large and persistent current account deficits in a group of systemic countries (notably the United States) and, on the other hand, by corresponding surpluses in another group of States, which includes emerging economies (like China and India) and the oil exporters' (*supra* n. 6, p. 8).

[127] IMF, *supra* n. 125.

[128] Palais-Royal Initiative, *supra* n. 124.

[129] IMF, *supra* n. 125.

INTERNATIONAL MONETARY STABILITY 383

'inadequate systemic liquidity provision mechanisms'[130] together with the 'excessive exchange rate fluctuations and deviations from fundamentals'.[131] Finally, the *fourth problem* observes the 'structural challenges in the supply of safe assets'[132] with a special focus on the 'excessive reserves accumulation and reliance on few reserve currencies'.[133]

The aforementioned problems highlighted demand a collective action response because by their very nature they cannot be solved in isolation by individual states, thus making the case for strengthening of international cooperation. Notwithstanding that, as argued elsewhere in this chapter, the GFC evidenced the lack of appropriate global institutions and the lack of adequate international cooperation to deal with these issues. This state of affairs precipitated the emergence of unilateral and domestically oriented reactions aiming to restore and maintain both monetary and financial stability.

The main examples of these unilateral reactions are the domestically oriented monetary policy decisions. The GFC triggered not only 'conventional' monetary policy responses (like changes in the interest rate policies) but also 'unconventional' monetary policy reactions. These unconventional measures comprise 'credit support, credit easing, interventions in foreign exchange and securities markets, provision of liquidity in foreign currency and quantitative easing (QE)'.[134] It can be inferred that the main reasons for resorting to unconventional instruments were the expansion of the objectives of the central banks (financial stability, growth and employment) and the lack of effectiveness of the existing instruments to tackle the problems that arose during the GFC (e.g. in a world of zero lower bound the changes in interest rate policies are no longer effective).[135]

These changes in the monetary policy stance (mostly from advanced economies in control of the leading currencies) have had and continue to

---

[130] Ibid.

[131] Palais-Royal Initiative, *supra* n. 124.

[132] IMF, *supra* n. 125.

[133] Palais-Royal Initiative, *supra* n. 124.

[134] On conventional and unconventional monetary policies, see Lastra, *supra* n. 8, pp. 41–2. For an extended analysis of the unconventional monetary policies taken since the GFC, see C. Borio and P. Disyatat, 'Unconventional Monetary Policies: An Appraisal', *BIS Working Paper No. 292* (2009), www.bis.org/publ/work292.pdf (accessed 30 Sept. 2019).

[135] Proctor pointed out that, 'The limitations on the ability of interest rates to influence economic activity have, however, become apparent as a result of the recent economic crisis' (*supra* n. 9, p. 95). See also Zimmermann, *supra* n. 8, pp. 86–7.

have spillover effects on other countries (commonly to emerging market countries).[136] In this regard, the International Finance Discussion Papers (IFDP) note published on the Fed's website in February 2016 provides a short but comprehensive analysis on the basic issues connected to the international spillovers of monetary policy.[137] In this note the authors highlighted that the discussions on the topic are not new but started in the early interwar period and recovered relevance in the aftermath of the GFC due to the use of conventional and unconventional monetary policies by central banks in order to provide monetary stimulus.

The authors of the IFDP note recognised that international spillovers can be positive or negative, mainly subject to the strength of the channels of transmission. However, they acknowledged that beyond the cost–benefit analysis of the impact of the spillovers, the key issue relates to the impact of monetary spillovers on the stability of the global economy. On this issue the authors pointed out that:

> In response to common adverse shocks such as the GFC, the positive spillovers of easing actions by the Federal Reserve and other central banks proved stabilizing for the global economy. Conversely, some years afterwards, these positive spillovers from ongoing policy accommodation were not welcomed by emerging market economies (EMEs) whose cyclical positions had much improved.[138]

Consequently, the authors concluded on this issue that international monetary policy spillovers can have both stabilising and destabilising

---

[136] On this point Janet Yellen, former chair of the Fed, recognises the international linkages of domestic monetary policy by stating that:

> [M]onetary policy actions in one country spill over to other economies through three main channels: changes in exchange rates; changes in domestic demand, which alter the economy's imports; and changes in domestic financial conditions – such as interest rates and asset prices – that, through portfolio balance and other channels, affect financial conditions abroad.
>
> (J. L. Yellen, 'Macroeconomic Research after the Crisis' (2016), www .federalreserve.gov/newsevents/speech/yellen20161014a.htm (accessed 1 June 2018))

[137] J. Ammer, M. De Pooter, C. Erceg and S. Kamin, 'International Spillovers of Monetary Policy', *IFDP Notes* (2016), https://federalreserve.gov/econresdata/notes/ifdp-notes/2016/international-spillovers-of-monetary-policy-20160208.html (accessed 30 Sept. 2019).

[138] Ibid.

INTERNATIONAL MONETARY STABILITY   385

effects on the global economy depending on the business cycle[139] situation of states globally.[140]

It can be argued that the particular business cycle of states also influences the course of monetary policy directions opted by central banks worldwide. For that reason, Benoît Cœuré, a member of the executive board of the European Central Bank (ECB), considers that 'the global economy is currently characterised by an environment of diverging monetary policy cycles'[141] and as an illustration on the point he presents the example of interest rate level disparities between the European Economic Area and the United States of America.[142] Similarly, a recent special report issued by *The Economist* remarked that:

> This divergence between America and the rest means divergent monetary policies, too. The Federal Reserve has raised interest rates eight times since December 2015. The European Central Bank (ECB) is still a long way from its first increase. In Japan rates are negative. China, the principal target of Mr Trump's trade war, relaxed monetary policy this week in response to a weakening economy. When interest rates rise in America

---

[139] The *Oxford Dictionary of Finance and Banking* provides a definition of 'business cycle' that reads as follows:

> The process by which investment, output, and employment in an economy tend to move through a recurrent cycle of upturn, prosperity, downturn, and recession. The cycle does not describe a regular pattern in either length or amplitude. Cycles in the immediate postwar period were of historically low amplitude, while those of the late 1970s and 1980s had greater amplitude and involved much deeper recessions. The reasons for the business cycle remain little understood.

> (Law and Smullen, *supra* n. 77)

[140] Accordingly, Albagli *et al.* remarked that:

> While increased financial integration has multiple benefits, it also presents important challenges. In particular, it raises the question of whether the cost of funds in non-core economies can remain independent from developments in major financial centers, possibly undermining the ability of central banks in setting appropriate monetary conditions given each country's macroeconomic stance.

> (E. Albagli, L. Ceballos, S. Claro and D. Romero, *Channels of US Monetary Policy Spillovers into International Bond Markets* (2017), https://bis.org/events/ccaconf2017/ccaconf2017_12.pdf (accessed 30 Sept. 2019))

[141] B. Cœuré, *Domestic and Cross-Border Spillovers of Unconventional Monetary Policies* (2015), www.bis.org/review/r150513a.pdf (accessed 30 Sept. 2019).

[142] Ibid.

but nowhere else, the dollar strengthens. That makes it harder for emerging markets to repay their dollar debts. A rising greenback has already helped propel Argentina and Turkey into trouble; this week Pakistan asked the IMF for a bail-out.[143]

Cœuré also remarks that this pattern of 'global monetary policy divergence' also brought with it the debate on the loss of monetary policy independence. On this point he argues that:

> [C]entral banks in large advanced economies can free themselves from the global financial cycle and regain monetary independence, provided that they show clarity in purpose and resolve in implementation.
>
> For emerging markets and smaller advanced economies, there is also evidence that while the global financial cycle has indeed been a dominant factor for the last two decades, the arrangement of open macro policies such as the exchange rate regime and financial openness still have direct influence on sensitivity to the financial cycle.[144]

Accordingly, Lastra argues that 'the ability to have a truly independent monetary policy diminishes with the growth of cross-border capital flow'.[145] The matters of monetary policy independence and the global business cycle are intrinsically related to the so-called monetary trilemma identified almost sixty years ago by the economists Mundell (1963) and Fleming (1962).[146] This trilemma considers that there is a policy trade-off among three objectives that cannot be achieved at the same time so governments must give up one of them. The conflicting objectives are: a fixed exchange rate, free capital movements and an independent monetary policy. A recent and influential study on this policy trade-off made by Hélène Rey considers that it is not a trilemma, but a dilemma between free capital movements and the control of local financial conditions.[147]

---

[143] *The Economist*, 'The Next Recession' (11 Oct. 2018).

[144] Cœuré, *supra* n. 141.

[145] Lastra, *supra* n. 8, pp. 24–5.

[146] J. M. Fleming, 'Domestic Financial Policies under Fixed and under Floating Exchange Rates', *Staff Papers (International Monetary Fund)*, 9(3) (1962), 369; R. A. Mundell, 'Capital Mobility and Stabilization Policy under Fixed and Flexible Exchange Rates', *Canadian Journal of Economics and Political Science*, 29(4) (1963), 475.

[147] Rey argues that:

> For the past few decades, international macroeconomics has postulated the 'trilemma': with free capital mobility, independent monetary policies are feasible if and only if exchange rates are floating. The global financial cycle transforms the trilemma into a 'dilemma' or an 'irreconcilable duo':

INTERNATIONAL MONETARY STABILITY 387

7.5.2   Unilateral Responses

The key channels of transmission of monetary policy spillovers are capital flows and exchange rates.[148] The main responses to repel the unwanted spillovers (or negative externalities) are typically unilateral through capital controls and exchange restrictions. Viterbo provides a clear and detailed description of the different types of exchange restrictions and capital controls and their corresponding rationales.[149]

In doing so Viterbo considers that exchange restrictions are emergency measures that respond to serious balance-of-payment imbalances. These measures can regulate both outwards and inwards international payments and, as a consequence, 'residents and non-residents cannot purchase (or sell) foreign currencies and dispose freely of them for current international transactions and transfers'.[150] On capital controls Viterbo considers that 'Governments resort to capital controls to regulate the volume, composition, or allocation of international capital flows and to restrict foreign investors' entrance or exit opportunities.'[151] She also mentions that these measures can have a precautionary purpose or an emergency nature and can target capital inflows and capital outflows. On one hand, measures to limit capital inflows are usually precautionary with the intention to prevent the entrance of non-desirable investments such as large and volatile short-term capital investments. On the other hand, the measures to limit capital outflows are usually reactions to crisis scenarios aimed to prevent capital flight and to 'protect foreign exchange reserves and the ability of the monetary authority to act as a lender of last

> independent monetary policies are possible if and only if the capital account is managed.
>
> (H. Rey, 'Dilemma Not Trilemma: The Global Financial Cycle and Monetary Policy Independence' (2013))

[148] The BIS stated in 2012 that the changes in the monetary policy in the major advanced economies 'are being transmitted to emerging economies in the form of undesirable exchange rate and capital flow volatility' (Bank for International Settlements, *BIS Annual Report 2011/2012*, www.bis.org/publ/arpdf/ar2012e4.pdf (accessed 30 Sept. 2019), ch. IV). The immediate subsequent annual reports, 2012–13, 2013–14 and 2014–15 provide an extensive and detailed examination of the spillovers (Bank for International Settlements, *Annual Reports*, www.bis.org/annualreports/index.htm (accessed 30 Sept. 2019)).

[149] Viterbo, *supra* n. 6, pp. 153–9.

[150] Ibid, p. 153.

[151] Ibid, p. 155.

388   LUCIA SATRAGNO

resort, to manage external debt problems, to prevent large sales of domestic assets as well as investors and lenders flight risk'.[152]

Acknowledging both the risks and the benefits of capital flows and in order to provide consistent advice to its members, the IMF approved in 2012 the Institutional View on the liberalisation and management of capital flows. This view states that 'Capital flow management measures (CFMs) are measures that are specifically designed to limit capital flows' and a differentiation is made between residence-based measures (capital controls) and others.[153] On this point Zimmermann makes an interesting observation by considering that:

> [T]he Fund's new institutional view on capital flows may serve as an interesting illustration of how the principle of subsidiarity frames the contemporary exercise of specific sovereign powers on the realm of money. The Fund has eventually given up its quest for shifting the jurisdiction over capital controls to the multilateral level in light of overwhelming economic evidence showing that outright liberalization of the capital account should not be a one-size-fits-all remedy.[154]

Capital flow volatility also put appreciation pressures on the currencies, and thus in order to limit this pressure the spillover-receiving countries took recourse to exchange restrictions. These interventions led to the debate on 'currency wars' or 'exchange rate misalignment' (for example in the cases of massive interventions by China[155] and Switzerland[156] to maintain the value of their currencies and avoid appreciation).

---

[152] Ibid, p. 157.

[153] IMF, *supra* n. 63.

[154] Zimmermann, *supra* n. 8, p. 44.

[155] According to Bergsten and Gagnon, it was the massive accumulation of foreign exchange reserves (mostly in US dollars) by China that resulted in a 'decade of manipulation', through its intervention in the currency market to avoid the appreciation of the renminbi, which had given it large surpluses (reaching almost 10 per cent of its GDP in 2017). Consequently, they argued that these large surpluses led to the proposals to include currency manipulation clauses in the new trade agreements to be entered into by United States (C. F. Bergsten and J. E. Gagnon, *Currency Conflict and Trade Policy: A New Strategy for the United States* (Washington, DC: Peterson Institute for International Economics, 2017)). For an extended description of the monetary dispute between US and China, see Proctor, *supra* n. 9, p. 605.

[156] In March 2009 the SNB started with a series of interventions in the foreign exchange market to prevent the appreciation of the Swiss franc. Later, in September 2011, the SNB pegged its minimum exchange rate at 1.20 Swiss franc per euro arguing that 'The current massive overvaluation of the Swiss franc poses an acute threat to the Swiss economy and carries the risk of a deflationary development.' After almost four years of maintaining the peg the SNB discontinued the minimum exchange rate and lowered the interest rate

INTERNATIONAL MONETARY STABILITY

In addition to capital controls and exchange restrictions, Villard Duran remarked that since the 2000s the accumulation of reserves in hard currencies (e.g. US dollar and euro) by emerging market economies has also been a unilateral measure of a precautionary nature in order to increase their monetary independence in times of crisis.[157] It is also interesting to note that beyond the unilateral reactions or as a consequence of the unilateral actions, there has been an emergence of regional financial agreements to manage the volatility caused by monetary spillovers. The main examples are the European Stability Mechanism, the Asian Infrastructure Bank and the BRIC's Contingent Reserve Agreement, among others.[158] However, these regional initiatives are not the panacea to confront a liquidity crisis: as pointed out by Villard Duran, 'These regional structures are contributing to the fragmentation of the global monetary system without guaranteeing certain and timely access to liquidity in an event of a crisis.'[159]

7.5.3 Conclusion

An accepted principle of Common Concern would strengthen the notion that unilateral lawful measures are a valuable tool to mitigate negative spillovers when international cooperative efforts are insufficient. It would also encourage the use of these measures on a regular basis and for long-term purposes if needed but always as a complement to cooperative

---

into negative territory considering that 'divergences between the monetary policies of the major currency areas have increased significantly ... The euro has depreciated considerably against the US dollar and this, in turn, has caused the Swiss franc to weaken against the US dollar. In these circumstances, the SNB concluded that enforcing and maintaining the minimum exchange rate for the Swiss franc against the euro is no longer justified' (Swiss National Bank, *Annual Reports* (2000–9), www.snb.ch/en/iabout/pub/annrep/id/pub_annrep (accessed 30 Sept. 2019); Swiss National Bank, 'Swiss National Bank Sets Minimum Exchange Rate at CHF 1.20 per Euro' (2011), www.snb.ch/en/mmr/reference/pre_20110906/source/pre_20110906.en.pdf (accessed 30 Sept. 2019); Swiss National Bank, 'Swiss National Bank Discontinues Minimum Exchange Rate and Lowers Interest Rate to –0.75%' (2015), www.snb.ch/en/mmr/reference/pre_20150115/source/pre_20150115.en.pdf (accessed 30 Sept. 2019)).

[157] C. V. Duran, 'The International Lender of Last Resort for Emerging Countries: A Bilateral Currency Swap?' *GEG Working Paper 2015/108* (2015), www.geg.ox.ac.uk/publication/geg-wp-2015108-international-lender-last-resort-emerging-countries-bilateral-currency (accessed 30 Sept. 2019).

[158] IMF, *supra* n. 125.

[159] C. V. Duran, *Voice and Exit: How G20 Emerging Powers are Challenging the Global Monetary Order* (2016).

solutions that remain the best option to accomplish prosperous and stable Common Concerns. For monetary affairs in particular, the principle of Common Concern would reinforce the need for states to recognise and internalise the negative externalities of their policies and to seek to achieve a careful balance between the interests of different jurisdictions (resorting to the principle of shared but differentiated responsibility). As recognised by Mario Draghi, former president of the ECB:

> We have to think not just about the composition of policies within our jurisdictions, but about the global composition that can maximise the effects of monetary policy so that our respective mandates can best be delivered without overburdening further monetary policy, and so as to limit any destabilising spillovers. This is not a preference or a choice. It is simply the new reality we face.[160]

Thus, the recognition of the spillovers inherent in domestic policies may result in a limitation on domestic law by a source of international law (that is, the potential principle of Common Concern).

7.6 Securing Compliance: Monetary Stability Considerations

Securing compliance with the obligations that emerge from the emerging doctrine and eventually principle of Common Concern is of utmost importance.[161] As remarked by Cottier, there is a fundamental difference between the discretionary right of states to act under the existing mechanism of international law of sanctions and countermeasures and the new obligation to act as suggested by Common Concern. This new obligation to act might be applicable only in the case of a fully-fledged doctrine of Common Concern and determined within the process of claims and responses that is subject to the principles of proportionality and accountability.

The process of claims and responses calls for a multilateral system and appropriate international institutions in order to secure compliance with the obligations that emerge from the collective action problems recognised as Common Concerns of Humankind. These obligations, as laid out in the doctrine of Common Concern, entail an enhanced duty to cooperate globally and the obligations to do homework both within the

---

[160] European Central Bank, *The International Dimension of Monetary Policy* (2016), www .ecb.europa.eu/press/key/date/2016/html/sp160628.en.html (accessed 1 June 2018).

[161] See Chapter 1 in this volume, p. 68.

local jurisdiction and across borders when needed through unilateral lawful measures.

7.6.1 Obligations and Sanctions under International Monetary Law

As pointed out elsewhere in this chapter the stability of the IMS depends both on domestic and international policies. As explained in the previous sections, there are clear mandates that attribute responsibility for the promotion and maintenance of monetary stability at the domestic and regional level to the central banks (as state agencies) and for the promotion of monetary stability at the international level to the IMF (a nearly universal institution). These overlapping dominions dealing with monetary stability are not static and interact with each other.

At the international level the key rules are laid down in the Articles of Agreement of the IMF. The Articles of Agreement contain rights, obligations and sanctions. The legal nature of these rights and obligations create on the one hand, a vertical relationship between each member state and the Fund and, on the other hand, eliminate any possible horizontal relationship among the Fund's members. Consequently, the obligations set forth in the treaty are owed by the Fund's members to the IMF as an institution. There is no bilateral type of obligation among the members of the IMF.[162] Accordingly, in case of breach of an obligation under the Articles of Agreement, the Managing Director of the Fund is in charge of raising a claim to the Executive Board and there is no possibility for any particular Fund member to bring claim accusing other member.[163]

The main obligations of the IMF member states are enshrined in Article IV as reformed by the Second Amendment.[164] Article IV, section 1 starts with an introduction (*chapeau*) consisting of a general obligation of the members to collaborate with the Fund and other members (IMF Code of Conduct) and is followed by a non-exhaustive list of specific

---

[162] This is the position of the IMF and it is widely accepted in the literature with some exceptions. For further detail on this issue, see Zimmermann, *supra* n. 8, p. 131.

[163] IMF, 'By-Laws Rules and Regulations' (2016), www.imf.org/external/pubs/ft/bl/blcon.htm (accessed 10 Oct. 2018), rule k-1.

[164] For an overview of the legal framework of Article IV of the Articles of Agreement, see IMF, *supra* n. 58.

obligations concerning the members' domestic and external policies.[165] These obligations are considered of a 'soft' nature and would only require the best efforts of the members, with the exception of Article IV, section 1(iii): 'avoid manipulating exchange rates or the international monetary system in order to prevent effective balance of payments adjustment or to gain an unfair competitive advantage over other members', which is considered of a 'hard' nature and requires the members to achieve results beyond their best efforts.

According to Zimmermann, the considered 'best effort' obligations under Article IV recognise the full regulatory autonomy of the Fund's members over their economic and financial policies. By contrast, Article IV, section 1(iii) highlights the international essence of the exchange rate policies and consequently the obligation contained therein is of a 'hard' law nature.[166] Hence, it can be stated that in general terms Article IV of the Articles of Agreement gives the Fund's members great regulatory autonomy to implement their domestic policies. However, it should also be noted that this Article IV ought to be read together with the principles

---

[165] The text of Article IV, Section 1. General obligations of members, reads as follows:

> Recognizing that the essential purpose of the international monetary system is to provide a framework that facilitates the exchange of goods, services, and capital among countries, and that sustains sound economic growth, and that a principal objective is the continuing development of the orderly underlying conditions that are necessary for financial and economic stability, each member undertakes to collaborate with the Fund and other members to assure orderly exchange arrangements and to promote a stable system of exchange rates. In particular, each member shall:
>
> (i) endeavor to direct its economic and financial policies toward the objective of fostering orderly economic growth with reasonable price stability, with due regard to its circumstances;
> (ii) seek to promote stability by fostering orderly underlying economic and financial conditions and a monetary system that does not tend to produce erratic disruptions;
> (iii) avoid manipulating exchange rates or the international monetary system in order to prevent effective balance of payments adjustment or to gain an unfair competitive advantage over other members; and
> (iv) follow exchange policies compatible with the undertakings under this Section.

(IMF, *supra* n. 13)

[166] Zimmermann, *supra* n. 8, p. 92.

INTERNATIONAL MONETARY STABILITY 393

adopted by the IMF concerning its reformed bilateral surveillance mechanism.[167]

The principles adopted by the Fund's Integrated Surveillance Decision of 2012 are the following:

A. A member shall avoid manipulating exchange rates or the international monetary system in order to prevent effective balance of payments adjustment or to gain an unfair competitive advantage over other members.
B. A member should intervene in the exchange market if necessary to counter disorderly conditions, which may be characterized inter alia by disruptive short-term movements in the exchange rate of its currency.
C. Members should take into account in their intervention policies the interests of other members, including those of the countries in whose currencies they intervene.
D. A member should avoid exchange rate policies that result in balance of payments instability.
E. A member should seek to avoid domestic economic and financial policies that give rise to domestic instability.

These principles, with the exception of principle A that reinstates the obligation laid down in Article IV, section 1 (iii), are merely recommendations to the Fund's members and, thus, unenforceable. The new mechanism set forth in the Fund's 2007 and 2012 reforms of bilateral surveillance exposed the current limits that the Articles of Agreement impose over the conduct of the IMF member's domestic policies (economic, financial and exchange rates).[168] As argued in Section 7.3, the surveillance function enables the IMF to monitor compliance with standards and rules and to provide incentives for member states to comply with such standards and rules.

The Articles of Agreement (Article XXVI, section 2) detailed in an exhaustive manner the three possible sanctions to which a Fund member can be subject in case of breach of its obligations. These sanctions are, ineligibility to use the Fund's resources, suspension of voting rights and expulsion from the Fund.[169] However, as pointed out by Gianviti, 'there has not been a single instance in which sanctions have been applied or

---

[167] IMF, *supra* n. 4, par. 21. For an extended analysis of these principles, see Zimmermann, *supra* n. 8, p. 94; Rendak, *supra* n. 50, p. 208.

[168] IMF, *supra* n. 4.

[169] In addition to these sanctions, Zimmermann pointed out that, 'the three pillars of the Fund's toolset – conditionality, surveillance, and technical assistance – give the Fund many subtle possibilities, combined with peer pressure, to motivate a member to change

report has been made for breach of obligation under Article IV'.[170] Neither has the IMF ever found a member in violation of the 'hard' nature provision set forth in Article IV, section 1(iii) concerning exchange rate manipulation.

The determination of whether an IMF member has committed exchange rate manipulation has become a political and economically delicate issue. Especially in recent years several countries like Brazil, India, Indonesia, Israel, Japan, Korea, Malaysia, the Philippines, Singapore, South Africa, Switzerland, Taiwan, Thailand and particularly China have been accused of exchange market intervention and issuance of capital controls to contrast local currency appreciation.[171] These accusations must be verified using the threshold imposed by Article IV, section 1(iii). The language of this article requires demonstration that the member had performed exchange rate manipulation with the *intent* to prevent effective balance-of-payments adjustment or to gain an unfair competitive advantage over other members. Hence, as remarked by Zimmermann 'the requirement of intent renders the key provision of the IMF's code of conduct essentially inoperative'.[172] In this regard Viterbo considers that the *intent* element is focused on a subjective consideration rather than on the economic impact of the measures.[173]

Consequently, it can be argued that the current design of the IMF's Code of Conduct (Article IV) and its surveillance mechanism is not sufficiently equipped to secure compliance with the Fund's members' obligations under Article IV and it is even more uncertain as to whether the sanctions in Article XXVI, section 2 will ever apply in this context. Accordingly, Viterbo stressed that 'the greater perception that IMF rules are not being enforced the greater is the likelihood that currency issues will be handled bilaterally, or even unilaterally, and outside the IMF framework'.[174] Consequently, state leaders have resorted to diplomatic bilateral discussions in different forums. In particular, since the beginning of the GFC the G20 has assumed a key role in debates concerning

---

a contested policy without even having to formally prove a breach of obligation by that member' (*supra* n. 8, p. 132).

[170] F. Gianviti, 'Evolving Role and Challenges for the International Monetary Fund', *International Lawyer*, 35(4) (2001), 1371.

[171] W. R. Cline and J. Williamson, 'Currency Wars?', *Peterson Institute for International Economics Policy Brief* (2010).

[172] Zimmermann, *supra* n. 8, p. 90.

[173] Viterbo, *supra* n. 6, p. 297.

[174] Ibid, p. 301.

international monetary and financial stability. In the USA, several legislative proposals have been submitted in order to apply antidumping measures and countervailing duties on imports from countries with undervalued currencies. Also, the possibility of bringing exchange rate issues to the WTO dispute settlement body has been intensively debated.[175]

7.6.2 Conclusions

International monetary law provides, under the premises of the IMF multilateral treaty, a detailed set of obligations for the Fund's members and a list of sanctions applicable on breach of those obligations in order to secure compliance. The obligations set forth in the Articles of Agreement are aimed at promoting a prosperous and stable IMS in concordance with the purpose of an accepted Common Concern of global monetary stability. However, as analysed in this section, the obligations laid down in the Articles of Agreement are of a 'soft' nature requiring only the discretional best efforts of the IMF's member states to comply with them, with the notable exception of the case of exchange rate manipulation that is considered of a 'hard' nature. Despite the hard nature of the rule provided by Article IV, section 1(iii) regarding exchange rate manipulation, the IMF has been severely questioned on its ability to ensure compliance with this obligation. The main reason for this is that the IMF has never found a member in violation of this provision.[176]

The lack of effectiveness of the existing mechanisms of international law to secure compliance with the obligations concerning global monetary stability bring us back to the debate about the trade-off among the different levels of governance in monetary affairs and how domestic and regional levels prevail over the international dimension. That is, as long as the Fund's members' policies pursue domestic objectives and they do not engage with *intent* on specific beggar-thy-neighbour policies the IMF will not bring them into question.[177] This uncertain scenario has pushed the delicate compliance debate to other diplomatic and political forums outside the IMF. Hence, it is under these circumstances that the new obligation to act as suggested by Common Concern acquires relevance.

---

[175] Ibid, p. 315.
[176] Gianviti, *supra* n. 170.
[177] Zimmermann, *supra* n. 8, p. 133.

396   LUCIA SATRAGNO

A fully-fledged and accepted principle of Common Concern will determine, after a process of claims and responses, whether it is necessary to move from the current 'soft' obligation of conduct concerning the existing treaty-based obligations to a 'hard' obligation to act in order to secure compliance with international monetary law. This new obligation to act in monetary affairs may demand the commitment of the international community to reform the Articles of Agreement, in particular the provisions in Article IV, so as to move from obligations of conduct to obligations of result to ensure compliance. As stated by Viterbo, 'The provisions of global public goods needs global solutions and a strengthened role of international organizations in economic regulation and supervision.'[178]

7.7 Concluding Remarks

This chapter has analysed the manifold complexities associated with the provision of the GPG of international monetary stability through the lenses of the emerging doctrine, and eventually principle, of Common Concern of Humankind and from a multilevel governance perspective. As a result, it can be argued that the promotion and maintenance of a stable international monetary order fulfils the threshold of peace, stability and welfare for an issue to be considered a Common Concern. Subsequently, the process of claims and responses guided by the three pillars of the emerging doctrine – duty to cooperate, obligations at home and securing compliance – has been examined.

This three-dimensional examination proposed under the Common Concern doctrine reveals that international cooperation is the optimal arrangement for the provision of the GPG of international monetary stability. However, in the current state of affairs legal and institutional arrangements at the national and regional levels have overtaken multilateral and international cooperative solutions. Overall, international cooperation for monetary stability is informal or soft-law based and limited to specific scenarios driven mostly by the goodwill of states. In order to address these shortcomings the Common Concern doctrine proposes an enhanced duty to cooperate internationally. This duty would encompass a reinforcement of the role of the IMF as the central international monetary institution from a *top-down* approach (international

---

[178] Viterbo, *supra* n. 6, p. 315.

level of governance) and an increased engagement of individual states in cross-border cooperation from a *bottom-up* perspective (central banking cooperation).

Concerning obligations at home, the Common Concern analysis points out that central banks and relevant monetary authorities have become the key players in the promotion and protection of monetary stability at the domestic and regional level. However, central banks as institutions of state are constrained by their domestic goals and mandate. Hence, when it comes to central banks assuming international commitments or engaging with enhanced monetary policy cooperation it rests on unpredictable soft-law commitments that are decided on a case-by-case situation. Therefore, a principle of Common Concern would entail an expansion of the mandate of central banks to include global stability considerations and going further, to provide central banks with the possibility of assuming international commitments for special situations.

Also, on the domestic front the Common Concern examination shows that in monetary affairs lawful unilateral actions with extraterritorial effects have proved useful in the pursuit of monetary stability but have been limited and temporary in nature. Consequently, an accepted principle of Common Concern would encourage the use of these measures on a regular basis and for long-term purposes. For monetary affairs in particular, the principle of Common Concern would reinforce the need for states to recognise and internalise the negative externalities of their policies and to seek to achieve a careful balance between the interests of different jurisdictions (resorting to the principle of shared but differentiated responsibility).

Lastly, the Common Concern analysis highlights that international monetary law provides, under the premises of the IMF multilateral treaty, a detailed set of obligations for the Fund's members and a list of sanctions upon breach of those obligations in order to secure compliance. Nonetheless, the analysis also demonstrates the lack of effectiveness of the existing mechanisms of international law to secure compliance with the obligations concerning global monetary stability. Therefore, a fully-fledged principle of Common Concern would determine whether it is necessary to move from the current 'soft' obligation of conduct concerning the existing treaty-based obligations to a 'hard' obligation to act in order to secure compliance with international monetary law. This new obligation to act in monetary affairs may demand the commitment of the international community to reform the Articles of Agreement, in particular the provisions in Article IV, so as to move from obligations of conduct to obligations of result.

In conclusion, the emerging doctrine and eventually the principle of Common Concern as presented and defined in the introductory chapter of this volume offers some valuable guidance and directions for the issues pointed out in this specific case study on global monetary stability. As defined by Cottier:

> CCH, as a source of inspiration, direction and eventually a legal principle of international law recognised by the international community deploys, while building upon the existing framework, significant long-term structural effect on international law. It will move it from coexistence and cooperation to integration in the long run. In reality, this blueprint is likely to materialise piecemeal in a gradual process of claims and responses, trial and error. In the long run, it will develop and foster a new understanding of sovereignty of states and the realization of multilevel governance with a view to producing appropriate public goods on appropriate levels of governance.[179]

Accordingly and despite the fact that at the moment a reform of the legal and institutional arrangements concerning monetary affairs at the international level with the new obligation to act proposed by Common Concern seems unrealistic, this chapter aims to be a source of debate and inspiration for academics and policymakers alike in the path to achieve a more prosperous and stable IMS with the guidance of the emerging doctrine of Common Concern of Humankind.

* * *

Select Bibliography

Bummer, C. (2011). *Soft Law and the Global Financial System: Rule Making in the 21st Century* (Cambridge: Cambridge University Press).

Camdessus, M. 'International Financial and Monetary Stability: A Global Public Good?', www.imf.org/en/News/Articles/2015/09/28/04/53/sp052899.

Cottier, T. (2011). 'Towards a Five Storey House', in C. Joerges and E. U. Petersmann (eds.), *Constitutionalism, Multilevel Trade Governance and International Economic Law* (Oxford: Hart).

---

[179] See Chapter 1 in this volume, p. 83.

INTERNATIONAL MONETARY STABILITY 399

Cottier, T., Aerni, P., Karapinar, B., Matteotti, S., de Sépibus, J. and Shingal, A. (2014). 'The Principle of Common Concern and Climate Change', *Archiv des Völkerrechts (AVR)*, 52.

Cottier, T., Jackson, J. H. and Lastra, R. M. (eds.) (2010). *International Law in Financial Regulation and Monetary Affairs* (Oxford: Oxford University Press).

Cottier, T., Lastra, R. M., Tietje, C. and Satragno, L. (eds.) (2014). *The Rule of Law in Monetary Affairs* (Cambridge: Cambridge University Press).

Dorrucci, E. and McKay, J. (2011). 'The International Monetary System after the Financial Crisis', *ECB Occasional Paper Series No. 123*.

Gianviti, F. (2001). 'Evolving Role and Challenges for the International Monetary Fund', *International Lawyer*, 35(4).

Giovanoli, M. and Devos, D. (eds.) (2010). *International Monetary and Financial Law: The Global Crisis* (Oxford: Oxford University Press).

IMF, *Articles of Agreement of the International Monetary Fund*, www.imf.org/external/pubs/ft/aa/.

   (2010). *The Fund's Mandate: The Legal Framework*, www.imf.org/external/np/pp/eng/2010/022210.pdf.

   (2016). *Strengthening the International Monetary System: A Stocktaking*, www.imf.org/external/np/pp/eng/2016/022216b.pdf.

Lastra, R. M. (1996). *Central Banking and Banking Regulation* (London: London School of Economics and Political Science).

   (2015). *International Financial and Monetary Law* (3rd ed., Oxford: Oxford University Press).

Palais-Royal Initiative (2011). *Reform of the International Monetary System: A Cooperative Approach for the Twenty First Century*, http://global-currencies.org/smi/gb/telechar/news/Rapport_Camdessus-integral.pdf.

Mohan, R. and Kapur, M. (2014). 'Monetary Policy Coordination and the Role of Central Banks', *IMF Working Paper 14/70*, www.imf.org/external/pubs/ft/wp/2014/wp1470.pdf.

Proctor, C. (2012). *Mann on the Legal Aspect of Money* (7th ed., Oxford: Oxford University Press).

Steil, B. (2014). *The Battle of Bretton Woods: John Maynard Keynes, Harry Dexter White, and the Making of a New World Order* (Princeton, NJ: Princeton University Press).

Viterbo, A. (2012). *International Economic Law and Monetary Measures* (Cheltenham, UK: Edward Elgar).

Zimmermann, C. D. (2013). *A Contemporary Concept of Monetary Sovereignty* (Oxford: Oxford University Press).

8

Financial Stability as a Common Concern of Humankind

FEDERICO LUPO-PASINI

8.1 Introduction

Almost fifty years have passed since in 1971 US President Richard Nixon officially ended the Bretton Woods international monetary system framed by the rules of the International Monetary Fund. While the decision to end the convertibility of the US dollar to gold and the system of fixed exchange rates had little to do with the desire to spur financial integration, it nonetheless represented its very beginning.[1] Since then, the global financial system has changed dramatically. From a situation of financial autarchy in which cross-border capital flows were very limited and financial systems purely national, it slowly morphed into a truly global financial system in which banks and capital markets operate across borders. In the meantime, however, the world had experienced a number of regional and global financial crises, from the Latin American debt crisis in the 1980s and the 1997 Asian Financial Crisis, to the very recent 2008 US subprime mortgage crisis and European sovereign debt crisis of 2009–12.[2]

Those watershed moments in recent economic history have taught us that the process of financial integration cannot be sustained without a parallel process of regulatory cooperation. Since the creation of the Basel Committee on Banking Supervision in 1974, the governance of global finance has relied on the voluntary cooperation of regulators through the

---

[1] See B. Eichengreen, *Globalizing Capital: A History of the International Monetary System* (Princeton, NJ: Princeton University Press, 2008).

[2] R. P. Buckley and D. Arner, *From Crisis to Crisis: The Global Financial System and Regulatory Failure* (Leiden: Kluwer Law International, 2011); T. Geithner, *Stress Test: Reflection on Financial Crises* (New York: Broadway Books, 2015); N. Irwin, *The Alchemists: Three Central Bankers and the World on Fire* (New York: Penguin, 2014); T. Phillips *et al.*, *Europe on the Brink: Debt Crisis and Dissent in the European Periphery* (London: Zed Books, 2014); A. Mody, *EuroTragedy: A Drama in Nine Acts* (Oxford: Oxford University Press, 2018).

FINANCIAL STABILITY 401

various transnational regulatory networks and the useful guidance of the International Monetary Fund.[3] Yet, despite the growing complexity of the global financial architecture and the positive steps towards regulatory convergence, cooperation in finance has shown various limits. Such limits were mostly evident during the 2008 global financial crisis and the 2009–12 European sovereign debt crisis. These two events demonstrated that voluntary international cooperation through soft law is often not enough as regulators face tremendous pressure from national stakeholders to protect national interests, especially during a crisis.[4]

In those circumstances, the open structure of the global financial system reveals the main weakness of the current approach to financial integration: the lack of defences against global instability. A question therefore arises as to how to reconcile the desire of states to maintain the benefits of an open financial system with their need to protect it against dangerous cross-border financial spillovers.[5] From a legal perspective, the question is how to guarantee (and not to simply encourage) states' cooperation in financial regulation, supervision, and crisis management so as to minimize the risks of future international crises.[6] International law can play a fundamental role in this regard.[7]

The theory of Common Concern of Humankind (also hereafter, the Common Concern doctrine) has emerged in the last few years as a key doctrine of international law for the protection of global commons, especially with regard to the environment. As this book demonstrates, the Common Concern doctrine has the potential to be applied to many other global common problems, from human rights to low-carbon technology.[8] This chapter will contribute to the discussion by investigating whether and to what extent this doctrine can also be applied to tackle the

---

[3] C. Brummer, *Soft Law and the Global Financial System* (Cambridge: Cambridge University Press, 2012).

[4] F. Lupo-Pasini, *The Logic of Financial Nationalism: The Challenges of International Cooperation and the Role of International Law* (Cambridge: Cambridge University Press, 2017).

[5] F. Lupo-Pasini and R. P. Buckley, 'Global Systemic Risk: Squaring Sovereignty and Financial Stability', *American University Journal of International Law*, 30(4) (2015).

[6] F. Lupo-Pasini, 'Financial Stability in International Law', *Melbourne Journal of International Law*, 18(1) (2018), 48–70.

[7] T. Cottier, J. H. Jackson, and R. M. Lastra (eds.), *International Law in Financial Regulation and Monetary Affairs* (Oxford: Oxford University Press, 2012); T. Cottier, R. M. Lastra, C. Tietje, and L. Satragno (eds.), *The Rule of Law in Monetary Affairs* (Cambridge: Cambridge University Press, 2014).

[8] See Chapters 2 and 5 in this volume.

problem of global financial stability. More specifically, it discusses the challenges faced by financial regulators in cooperating on banking, insurance, and securities regulation and supervision when it comes to tackling the cross-border systemic risks of financial crises. It complements the work on monetary stability discussed in this book, which instead covers the cooperation challenges of monetary authorities in the area of sovereign financing, exchange rates, and balance of payments.[9]

Before beginning the analysis of how the doctrine of Common Concern fits with the objective of an integrated and stable global financial system, it is worth clarifying that this chapter will deal only with international financial cooperation, thus leaving the European Union outside the scope of the analysis. While the European Union's forty-year path towards financial integration offers invaluable cues as to the problems and potential solution to cross-border financial stability, the uniqueness of the European project makes its comparison with the problems affecting the rest of the world very challenging. The chapter will be structured as follows. I will first introduce the concept of financial stability and analyse the theory of systemic risk in finance to explain the role of the law in reducing it. I will then discuss how global instability propagates across national boundaries and the challenge to square the global scope of financial markets with the national scope of financial policies. The last two sections will explain the main shortcomings of the current international law of finance, and then analyse the potential new role of international law and the principle of Common Concern of Humankind in protecting global financial stability.

8.2 Financial Stability and the Role of the Law

Financial stability has emerged over the last fifteen years as the most important objective of financial policy. Yet, despite its growing importance, it has eluded any clear definition. In its simplest interpretation, it denotes the absence of crises or economic swings affecting the financial system.[10] Banks are thus able to intermediate money without imposing any losses on their depositors or other creditors, capital markets price assets correctly and efficiently, and firms and individuals are able to

---

[9] See Chapter 7 in this volume.
[10] R. M. Lastra, *Legal Foundations of International Monetary Stability* (Oxford: Oxford University Press, 2005).

FINANCIAL STABILITY 403

tender payment in discharge of their debts without risks. However, when looked at from a closer perspective it reveals itself as fraught with complexities. Financial stability is an evolving concept, which mutates and takes different forms according to the specific economic settings. It is no surprise that academics and policymakers alike have always been struggling to find the perfect formula for stability.[11]

Garry Schinasi, one of the leading scholars on the issue of financial stability, defined it as:

> a situation in which the financial system is capable of satisfactorily performing its three key functions simultaneously. First, the financial system is efficiently and smoothly facilitating the intertemporal allocation of resources from savers to investors and the allocation of economic resources generally. Second, forward-looking financial risks are being assessed and priced reasonably accurately and are being relatively well managed. Third, the financial system is in such condition that it can comfortably if not smoothly absorb financial and real economic surprises and shocks.[12]

This, however, is a very technical definition that does not fully explain the role of the law in the protection of financial stability. In order to understand how financial instability propagates in domestic and global financial markets, it is therefore necessary to explain the concepts of interconnectedness and systemic risk, and the role of the law in addressing them.

Unlike most other economic sectors, the financial industry is structured as a constellation of private entities that invariably operate through a complex web of mutual financial relationships. In finance, we refer to this particular setting as the 'financial system' to highlight the relation of mutual dependence between the various nodes of the network.[13]

---

[11] Charles Kinderberger's account of financial crises shows how financial stability and the policies to address it change constantly from country to country and across different periods (C. P. Kindleberger and R. Z. Aliber, *Manias, Panics, and Crashes: A History of Financial Crises* 16 (5th ed., Hoboken, NJ: Wiley, 2005)); for a recent work on financial crises, see C. Reinhart and K. Rogoff, *This Time Is Different: Eight Centuries of Financial Folly* (Princeton, NJ: Princeton University Press, 2009).

[12] G. Schinasi, *Safeguarding Financial Stability: Theory and Practice* (International Monetary Fund, 2006), p. 82. In one of his papers, Schinasi collected the various alternative definitions of stability (G. Schinasi, 'Defining Financial Stability', IMF Working Paper WP/04/187 (2004), at 13–16).

[13] IMF, Understanding Financial Interconnectedness (2010); D. Acemoglu *et al.*, 'Systemic Risk and Stability in Financial Networks', *American Economic Review*, 105 (2015), 564.

Banks, investment funds, insurance companies, clearing and settlement banks, payment providers and virtually all financial firms rely on each other for the large majority of the service they offer to their clients. Banks borrow from other banks and investment funds to finance the mortgages and loans they provide to their retail clients. On the asset side of the balance sheet, the same bank might use part of their liabilities to invest in other financial institutions or to buy corporate or sovereign debt. Investment funds similarly purchase stocks and debts from a variety of sources. Even if financial institutions do not invest in each other, they are nonetheless indirectly connected by having invested in securities of the same asset class, which tend to move in synchrony. Finally, all firms rely on the same underlying payment and clearing infrastructures to move money and discharge their debts.[14]

In sum, financial systems are structured as networks in which entities are inextricably linked by millions of mutual financial relationships. In financial jargon, we define these relationships as financial interconnectedness. The reason why the financial system has evolved as a network as opposed to a standard nuclear industry made of totally independent service providers has to do with the constant need to increase efficiency and with the wave of securitization that overtook the financial industry over the last thirty years. Borrowing money from other firms is less expensive than raising through capital or retail depositors, while proprietary trading is probably more profitable than lending.

Financial interconnectedness has undoubtedly improved the efficiency of the industry but at a very high price: instability. This latter element is nothing new in finance. Financial crises are an intrinsic component of finance and the inevitable consequence of the need of financial intermediaries to take risks. They have occurred since the birth of finance in Sumerian times.[15] Before the emergence of the modern systemically important financial institutions (SIFIs), banks have routinely suffered from irrational investors' panics and runs. Yet, the unprecedentedly high level of interconnectedness now makes the problem of a single financial

---

[14] O. Burrows, K. Low, and F. Cumming, 'Mapping the UK Financial System', *Q2 Bank of England Quarterly Bulletin*, 114 (2015); V. V. Acharya and T. Yorulmazer, 'Information Contagion and Inter-Bank Correlation in a Theory of Systemic Risk', 2–3, Center for Economic Policy Research, Discussion Paper No. 3743 (2003).

[15] Kindleberger and Aliber, *supra* n. 11.

institution transcend its balance sheet to impact all other firms that are directly or indirectly involved with it. Economists call it 'systemic risk'.[16]

Financial institutions are typically unwilling to reduce their risk appetite to minimize the chances of crises – for instance by funding their investment through capital rather than debt – as this would require them to forego possible profits and increase costs. Thus, in a pure market economy, rational actors will therefore tend to ignore the costs that their action might pose on other financial intermediaries to which they are connected. At the same time, however, it is undoubted that the absence of crisis is the first condition for any financial market to function as financial institutions would not be able to make profit in a situation of financial chaos. This makes financial stability a pure public good.[17]

In a national financial system, the state exerts a fundamental function to maintain financial stability as it uses its coercive powers to force financial institutions to internalize the externalities of their actions. The protection of financial stability as a domestic public good relies on a number of policy actions and legal interventions. For instance, supervisory authorities have the power to give and revoke the licence to financial institutions, to monitor them, and to give very hefty fines if regulations are breached. Regulatory agencies design and implement prudential regulations to force financial institutions to reduce the level of risk they take in their business activities. For instance, capital adequacy requirements are a fundamental tool to reduce the overall risk in the banking system as they require shareholders to bear the losses of their institution. Finally, in the event of a crisis, bank resolution authorities, the Central Bank, and the Treasury have a variety of tools at hand to ensure that individual banks' losses are minimized, and systemic risk contained.[18]

In sum, at the national level, the state through its legislative and coercive powers is able to exert a tight grip on financial institutions and, to the extent possible, minimize the risk of instability. This does not guarantee the absence of instability, as finance is by definition based

---

[16] S. Schwarcz, 'Systemic Risk', 97 *Georgetown Law Journal*, 193 (2008); Acharya and Yorulmazer, *supra* n. 14.

[17] V. V. Acharya, 'A Theory of Systemic Risk and Design of Prudential Bank Regulation', 5 *Journal of Financial Stability*, 224 (2009); D. W. Diamond and P. H. Dybvig, 'Bank Runs, Deposit Insurance, and Liquidity', 91 *Journal of Political Economy*, 401 (1983); I. Anabtawi and S. L. Schwarcz, 'Regulating Systemic Risk: Towards an Analytical Framework', 86 *Notre Dame Law Review*, 1351 (2011).

[18] On this, see Lupo-Pasini, *supra* n. 4.

on risk and subject to cyclical downturns.[19] Yet, as long as the state through the central bank and the various agencies tasked with the supervision and regulation of financial institutions exert their role as guardians of the system, those risks are reduced. As I will explain in the next section, the fact that financial systems are now interconnected, reduces substantially the control of states on the stability of their domestic financial systems, as systemic risk can be 'imported' from foreign markets.

8.3 The Nature of Global Financial Stability

The inherently risky nature of financial intermediation is, not surprisingly, reflected also in the global financial system. However, as we will see in this section, the regulatory balance and checks present in most domestic financial systems are not as strong as one might expect when we move to the international level.

The global financial system has undergone a drastic transformation since the 1970s. It evolved from being a constellation of purely national financial systems with no capital movements between countries, into a truly integrated system in which free capital mobility is the rule.[20] The absence of capital controls spurred a wave of financial globalization that led to the emergence of cross-border banking conglomerates operating in multiple jurisdictions (the so-called global systemically important banks) and truly international capital markets open to issuers and investors from different countries.[21]

8.3.1 Global Instability

The same evolution, however, led to an extension of the perimeter of markets and the financial network on which they operate. This means that systemic risk has stopped being a purely domestic concern and has

---

[19] Fundamental in this regard is the work of Hyman Minsky, who has developed the theory whereby financial systems are inherently unstable and subject to cycles of boom and bust (L. Randall Wray, *Why Minsky Matters: An Introduction to the Work of a Maverick Economist* (Princeton, NJ: Princeton University Press, 2015)).

[20] Eichengreen, *supra* n. 1; R. Abdelal, *Capital Rules: The Construction of Global Finance* (Cambridge, MA: Harvard University Press, 2007).

[21] R. M. Lastra, 'Systemic Risk, SIFIs, and Financial Stability', *Capital Markets Law Journal*, 6(2) (2011), at 197–213.

become an international problem.[22] The literature on financial globalization has provided various examples of how global financial instability propagates across borders.[23]

For instance, given the tightly interconnected corporate and financial structures of cross-border banks, a problem in the parent bank can immediately be transmitted across the group towards its various foreign branches and subsidiaries. The classical example in this regard is the default of Lehman Brothers in the wake of the 2008 global financial crisis.[24] The US-based global conglomerate had operations across the globe in the forms of branches and subsidiaries. Due to the losses incurred by the firm in the USA during the subprime mortgage crisis, it became clear that declaring insolvency was the only viable option. In order to protect the interests of the US creditors of the banks, the US regulators forced Lehman Brothers to repatriate all possible assets located in the bank's foreign operations, which remained fully exposed to markets' pressure. The lack of cooperation between the US regulators and the European regulators in the context of the insolvency procedure of the bank meant that all foreign operations in London, Frankfurt, and Amsterdam became insolvent in a matter of a day. Given their systemic nature, their default, in turn, led to a cascade of insolvencies in other European firms exposed to Lehman Brothers.[25]

The Argentine and Greek sovereign debt crises similarly showed that sovereign defaults can transmit a wave of financial contagion across markets through the banks that hold trillions of now worthless debt contracts.[26] Similarly, given the international nature of capital markets, a crisis in Wall Street can now propagate in a matter of hours to London and Tokyo.[27]

Another good example of the interconnected nature of global finance is the payment system.[28] Like many other aspects of finance, the payment

---

[22] IMF, *Global Financial Stability Report* (2012).

[23] For an overview, see Lupo-Pasini and Buckley, *supra* n. 5.

[24] M. J. Fleming and A. Sarkar, 'The Failure Resolution of Lehman Brothers', *Federal Reserve Bank on New York Economic Policy Review*, 20(2) (2014), 193–4.

[25] S. Claessens *et al.*, *A Safer World Financial System: Improving the Resolution of Financial Institutions*, Geneva Reports on the World Economy, 12 (2012), at 42–6.

[26] Reinhart and Rogoff, *supra* n. 11; J. Caruana and S. Avdjiev, 'Sovereign Creditworthiness and Financial Stability: An International Perspective', *Financial Stability Review*, 16 (2012), 71–85, at 74.

[27] IMF, *supra* n. 13.

[28] Lastra, n. 21, at 203–4

system in both its domestic and international dimensions rests upon a very complex structure made of various layers of contractual and financial arrangements between commercial banks and various intermediaries such as clearing and settlement banks and central banks.[29] In order for an international payment transaction to reach its destination, it can indeed often necessitate the involvement of more than six private entities across two or more jurisdictions. This not only increases costs and time, but also the risk that jurisdictional and regulatory barriers in one of the countries where the payment is processed might disrupt the transaction. In the literature on international payments there are numerous examples of such problems, from the Libyan Arab Foreign Bank case to the Herstatt Bank collapse.[30]

8.3.2 The Inefficiencies of International Law in Addressing Global Instability

The previous section thus shows that the global financial system is not much different, albeit with different degrees among states, from any domestic financial system in terms of interconnectedness and financial dynamics. Yet, unlike other areas of international economic law, international finance has mostly remained exempted from the heavy regulatory interference that we see in international trade or investment law.

This might seem surprising given the number of financial standards negotiated over the years. Indeed, since 1975, the Basel Committee on Banking Supervision has issued a number of standards on banking supervision and bank prudential regulations. The various Basel Accords on the Capital Adequacy of Banks, known as Basel I, II, III, and the Basel Core Principles for Effective Banking Supervision are two fundamental pillars of the global supervisory structure for cross-border banks.[31] Undoubtedly after the global financial crisis, there has been a relatively high degree of cooperation on regulatory matters through the various transnational regulatory networks.[32] For instance, the FSB has covered a

---

[29] See J. Armour et al., Principles of Financial Regulation (Oxford: Oxford University Press, 2016), pp. 391–409.

[30] C. Bamford, Principles of International Financial Law (Oxford: Oxford University Press, 2015), pp. 58–90.

[31] C. Goodhart, The Basel Committee on Banking Supervision: A History of the Early Years 1974–1996 (Cambridge: Cambridge University Press, 2013).

[32] See P. H. Verdier, 'Transnational Regulatory Networks and Their Limits', Yale Journal of International Law, 34 (2009), 113.

FINANCIAL STABILITY

wide spectrum of financial policies from OTC derivatives to bank bonuses.[33] The Basel Committee on Banking Supervision has revamped its regulatory activities through new supervisory rules and new prudential standards under Basel III and IV.

Yet, the global financial system is far from having a proper regulatory framework. First, despite the efforts of the TRNs, there are still huge gaps in the regulatory perimeters covered by those standards.[34] For instance, as of now, there is no consensus on rules for cross-border bank insolvencies, while rules on cross-border bank resolution are yet to be implemented.[35] Moreover, there are no standards on the emerging area of fintech, while the entire shadow banking sector has remained untouched by regulation.

Second, with the exception of the OECD Financial Action Task Force on money laundering, none of the abovementioned financial standards is binding.[36] This ultimately means that policy and regulatory coordination is voluntary.[37] The absence of binding force and the lack of precision of the standards sometimes leads to a situation whereby states refuse to implement them or simply ignore them. This is especially true in the context of crises. At present, there is a worrying trend towards more financial nationalism, exemplified by the Trump administration's refusal to contribute to the work of the TRNs and their decision to scale down the scope of the Dodd–Frank Act.[38]

---

[33] S. Gadinis, 'The Financial Stability Board: The New Politics of International Financial Regulation', *Texas International Law Journal*, 48 (2013), 157; E. R. Carrasco, 'The Global Financial Crisis and the Financial Stability Forum: The Awakening and Transformation of an International Body', *Transnational Law and Contemporary Problems*, 19 (2010), 203.

[34] Atlantic Council, *The Danger of Divergence: Transatlantic Financial Reform & the G20 Agenda* (2013); Financial Markets Law Committee, 'Discussion Paper on Coordination in the Reform of International Financial Regulation', Interim Feedback Statement (Sept. 2015); Financial Stability Board, 'Implementation and Effects of the G20 Financial Regulatory Reforms', FSB 3rd Annual Report (3 July 2017).

[35] J. Vazquez and M. Boer, 'Addressing Regulatory Fragmentation to Support a Cyber-Resilient Global Financial Services Industry', Institute of International Finance (Apr. 2018).

[36] Brummer, *supra* n. 3.

[37] S. Gadinis, 'The Politics of Competition in International Financial Regulation', *Harvard International Law Journal*, 49 (2008) 447.

[38] Simon Johnson, speech at conference 'US Interest in International Financial Cooperation', Peterson Institute for International Economics, Washington (17 Mar. 2017), at 33; Clifford Chance, 'US Congress Passes Dodd–Frank Reform Legislation with a "Clarification" (and Little Else) for Foreign Banks', Client Alert (May 2018).

Thus, the global financial system suffers from an inherent asymmetry between the global scope of the markets and the national scope of policies. This translates in a global financial system in which states are very well regulated in their integration efforts and incentivized to liberalize their financial sectors but discouraged from cooperating on the policies that make the system work.[39] In the next two sections, I will discuss two main inefficiencies of the current system: the lack of incentives for states to reduce the creation and transmission of global systemic risks, and the costs of protecting against those risks for partner states.

8.3.3 The Political Economy of International Financial Regulation

In an integrated financial system, the failure of states to cooperate on the protection of global financial stability leads to the creation of global systemic risks and its transmission across borders from one financial system to the other. However, the mechanisms of those transmissions are partially different from those applied to financial institutions and markets in a domestic financial system. In the case of global systemic risk, there is an additional factor besides market failures: regulatory failures.[40] More specifically, while domestic systemic risk originates from the failure of the market to address the inherent disincentive of firms to contribute to the protection of financial stability, global systemic risk originates from the failure of states to cooperate on the protection of global financial stability.

This failure is due to the peculiar political economy of international finance whereby domestic regulators are statutorily bound to the protection of national interests rather than global concerns such as financial stability.[41] In political economy, this relationship could be modelled as a principal–agent problem, whereby regulators are acting as an agent to local firms and citizens. This means that unless regulators perceive a financial stability threat from non-cooperation with partner states or fear any other threat to the national interest however perceived, they will not cooperate. In the literature, there are multiple examples of systemic risks arising from cooperation failures.[42]

---

[39] Lupo-Pasini and Buckley, *supra* n. 5.
[40] Ibid.
[41] On this, see Lupo-Pasini, *supra* n. 4, at 44–5.
[42] K. D'Hulster, 'Cross Border Banking Supervision: Incentive Conflicts in Supervisory Information Sharing between Home and Host Supervisors', World Bank Policy Research Working Paper No. 5871 (2011).

FINANCIAL STABILITY 411

Let's imagine two countries that share a common financial system. If one of them wants to adopt more stringent regulations to protect its depositors against the solvency or liquidity risks of the banks, it must do so at a cost: its domestic banks will be required to internalize the costs of the increased protection by adopting corporate rules that make their operation more expensive and less profitable. However, in an integrated financial system, no regulator would like to put its banking system at a disadvantage against foreign competitors that operate with higher margins. This means that regulatory coordination works only to the extent that all countries level up their regulatory playing field.

The clearest example of a success is Basel I, which revolutionized global banking in 1988.[43] However, cooperation does not always work. For instance, the USA and the EU have taken more than six years to agree to a fragile compromise on the regulation of OTC derivatives.[44] At the time of writing of this chapter, news has it that the same deal has been scrapped, with the US and EU regulators turning against each other in another bitter regulatory face-off.[45] Once again, this risks to divide into two the trillion US dollars derivative market, two with traders required to choose which regime to comply with if they wanted to access the market. At present, with the focus of regulators shifting from systemic risk to growth, there is a further risk that regulatory cooperation on important topics such as cryptocurrencies could be set aside.

An interesting example of the selfish nature of national financial policies is the recent regulatory conflict between the USA and the EU concerning the US decision to reimpose sanctions on Iran.[46] The implications from a financial stability perspective arise from the critical role played by the US dollar as the leading reserve currency and, henceforth, by the USA as a key player in the global payment landscape. At present, more than 40 per cent of the overall cross-border transactions are denominated in the US dollar.

---

[43] A. Singer, *Regulating Capital: Setting Standards for the Global Financial System* (Ithaca, NY: Cornell University Press, 2007).

[44] European Commission and United States Commodity Futures Trading Commission, 'The United States Commodity Futures Trading Commission and the European Commission: Common Approach for Transatlantic CCPs' (10 Feb. 2016); Y. Yadav and D. Turing, 'The Extraterritorial Regulation of Clearinghouses', *Journal of Financial Regulation*, 2 (2016), 21.

[45] G. Tett, 'A Transatlantic Front Opens in the Brexit Battle over Derivatives', *Financial Times* (19 Mar. 2019).

[46] S. Fleming and K. Manson, 'Donald Trump Pulls US Out of Iran Nuclear Deal', *Financial Times* (8 May 2018), www.ft.com/content/fb369232-52d1-11e8-b3ee-41e0209208ec.

This has the fundamental legal implications that each of these transactions is subject to US law, even if the transaction itself does not actually involve a US bank or a customer. The USA is indeed famous for making use of the extraterritorial reach of its laws for non-financial purposes such as the combat of terrorism or tax evasion.

In May 2018, the US administration decided to withdraw from the Iran nuclear deal negotiated with the EU and Russia and to reimpose financial sanctions on Iran. This implies that any entity under the reach of US law is prohibited from doing business with Iranian entities. As a consequence of the Iran deal, the Worldwide Interbank Financial Telecommunication (SWIFT) – the world leading payment provider – will be forced to suspend any dealing with Iranian banks by November 2018.[47] This means not only that Iranian banks and their operations abroad will be prevented from executing their payments through the SWIFT network but also that, more crucially, all worldwide financial institutions dealing with Iran will be prevented from transferring money towards financial firms. In case of non-compliance, SWIFT would be subject to a barrage of countermeasures which target both the Board members and the financial institutions that employ them. Not surprisingly, SWIFT announced that it would pull out from Iran, thus making it impossible for companies – which need to use its service – to perform payments with Iranian companies.

The US decision to apply extraterritorially its laws pivoting on the exorbitant privilege of the US dollar as the world's leading reserve currency shows to what extent regulatory sovereignty and the lack of cooperation can actually produce a cascade of consequences for other countries. Even though SWIFT is a Belgian incorporated company, the threat of the US sanctions has proved to be simply too much to bear. In turn, SWIFT's decision to pull out from Iran has de facto made impossible for all European and non-European companies relying on its service to enter into any business with Iranian counterparts, thus costing billions of euros of lost revenues for European firms.

8.3.4 Protection against Global Systemic Risk

The second main inefficiency of the current system is that it forces states receiving systemic risk from partners' financial systems to sacrifice the

---

[47] M. Peel and J. Brunsden, 'SWIFT Shows Impact of Iran Dispute on International Business', *Financial Times* (6 June 2018), www.ft.com/content/9f082a96-63f4-11e8-90c2-9563a0613e56.

benefits of financial integration. More specifically, since the systemic risk is transmitted through the channels of the global financial system, states have no option but to raise barriers to capital mobility as this is the only way for them to protect themselves against global instability. This can be done in many ways. For instance, by imposing capital controls on the inflow of capital in order to prevent foreign investors from overheating the economy.[48] Another classical example is the adoption of ring-fencing techniques to isolate foreign banks' subsidiaries or branches in the context of a cross-border banking crisis.[49] In both scenarios, capital mobility is sensibly reduced with great costs to the local financial system.

This situation is inefficient in many ways. First of all, if a regulator deems it necessary to raise barriers to capital mobility, it will have to impose a fundamental cost on its domestic constituencies. For instance, borrowers will face a rise in the cost of credit as this can only be obtained from local institutions. Firms and investors will be prevented from repatriating their profits and, more generally, moving assets where they are more profitable.

Second, imposing on the receiving state the burden of dealing with global systemic risk puts on the wrong party the costs of monitoring. In law and economics, there is a theory called the 'cheapest cost avoider' which roughly states that the cost of accidents should be borne by the party that was in the best position to prevent them.[50] In the context of our analysis this translates into imposing the burden of controlling global systemic risk on the states that generate them, rather than on the states that receive them.

There are various reasons in support of this legal approach. First, the receiving states are in the impossible position of monitoring the growth of global systemic risk in their partner states' territory. Even in the most advanced supervisory cooperation framework, incentives will still remain on each side to forebear and not to disclose to the other party confidential information about the financial system or the broader economy. Second, assuming that both parties agree to contribute to the

---

[48] IMF, *Capital Flows: The Role of Controls* (2011).

[49] K. D'Hulster and I. Otker-Robe, 'Ring-Fencing Cross-Border Banks: An Effective Supervisory Response?', *Journal of Financial Perspectives*, 5 (2018).

[50] This theory was first formulated by G. Calabresi in *The Costs of Accidents: A Legal and Economic Analysis* (New Haven, CT: Yale University Press, 1970). For a recent review of the literature on the cheapest cost avoider principle, see E. Carbonara, A. Guerra, and F. Parisi, 'Sharing Residual Liability: The Cheapest Cost Avoider Revisited', *Journal of Legal Studies*, 45(1) (2016), 173.

minimization of global systemic risks, it is more sensible to impose the costs of prevention on the party that can do so more efficiently and at the least cost. In the context of global systemic risk, this would entail the adoption of state-of-the-art prudential and supervisory rules, sustainable finances, and binding cooperation on cross-border resolution regimes for banks, central counterparties, and other financial firms. Third, imposing on the receiving country the costs of global systemic risk create a dangerous moral hazard problem. Indeed, states will have no incentives to reduce the risk-taking activities that lead to cross-border systemic risk, while at the same time they will enjoy all the benefits of financial integration.

8.3.4.1 Common Concern and Global Financial Stability

In the previous sections, I have demonstrated how the integrated nature of the global financial system coupled with the weak appetite of regulators for real international cooperation inevitably increases the risks of global instability. The inefficiencies of current international law in addressing this problem are well too evident. While the political economy of international finance clearly suggests financial nationalism as the default approach of regulators, the current international legal framework relies on voluntary cooperation and very weak compliance mechanism. The very opposite of what we would need.

Global financial stability is a common problem that every state with an open capital account needs to address. Collective action is required. The emerging Common Concern doctrine could help in building a new foundation for the international law of financial stability.[51] The foundations of this doctrine can be traced to the theory of global public goods and to the need of international law to provide an adequate response to its protection.[52] The Common Concern doctrine's objective is to provide a legal template to organize states' obligations *erga omnes*: those collective responsibilities that states have with regard to the interest of the

---

[51] In general, on the Common Concern doctrine, see F. Soltau, 'Common Concern of Humankind', in Kevin R. Gray, Richard Tarasofsky, and Cinnamon Carlarne (eds.), *The Oxford Handbook of International Climate Change Law* (Oxford: Oxford University Press, 2016), pp. 202–12; Alexandre Kiss, 'Economic Globalization and the Common Concern of Humanity', in Alexandre Kiss, Dinah Shelton, and Kanami Ishibashi (eds.), *Economic Globalization and Compliance with International Environmental Agreements* (2003). Also see Chapter 1 in this volume.

[52] See I. Kaul, I. Grunberg, and M. Stern (eds.), *Global Public Goods: International Cooperation in the 21st Century* (Oxford: Oxford University Press, 1999).

global community. Its flexible and open international approach offers legal solutions to unsolved transnational issues that are aimed to be achieved by states' cooperation rather than private solutions alone.[53] This can translate into various legal strategies. For instance, norms of obligation that require states to abstain from engaging in specific actions such as polluting the environment, violating human rights, or discriminating against foreign traders. But it can also translate into positive norms that incentivize direct action such as the right to invest or trade with another country. From an institutional perspective, it can also translate into the creation of international institutions that promote cooperation or international tribunals to solve disputes.

Nadavukaren and Cottier have proposed a formulation of the Common Concern doctrine along a three-dimensional legal approach.[54] The first element is a duty to cooperate. At present, there is no international norm obliging states to cooperate on shared concerns. Thus, as the theory of global public goods shows, when collective action is voluntary, there is a risk of free-riding and the danger of a race to the bottom.[55] As the recent example of US President Trump shows with regard to climate change, states could refuse to sit at the negotiating table in order to extract better concessions or to protect short-term domestic interests. Enshrining a duty to cooperate for the protection of global public goods in international law would prevent such collective action problems. The second is the implementation of domestic policies that do not cause external harm and the right to act to minimize risks arising outside the national territorial boundaries. As I will reiterate later on with regard to global financial stability, states are reluctant to legislate laws that confer rights to non-domestic stakeholders. For instance, laws that would consider the harmful external effects of domestic actions and therefore give to those hurt by those actions the right to seek a change in policy or compensation. The political economy of domestic lawmaking is such that laws are usually made with the interest of domestic stakeholders in mind, thus ignoring the global efficiency effect of the norms. The obligation to consider the external effects of domestic policies as prescribed by the

---

[53] See Chapter 1 in this volume.

[54] K. Nadavukaren and T. Cottier, 'Responsibility to Protect (R2P) and the Emerging Principle of Common Concern' (2012), in P. Hilpold (ed.), *Die Schutzverantwortung (R2P): Ein Paradigmenwechsel in der Entwicklung des internationalen Rechts?* (Leiden: Martinus Nijhoff, 2013), pp. 123–42. For more, see Chapter 1 in this volume.

[55] I. Kaul, 'Global Public Goods: Explaining Their Underprovision', *Journal of International Economic Law*, 15(3) (2012), 729.

doctrine would guarantee the adoption of globally optimal policies in areas that are deemed global common concerns. Third, and the right to secure compliance with international law by imposing sanctions and countermeasures. As Prof. Trachtman acutely observed, only if rights can be litigated and enforced, is the law made formally binding.[56] Dispute settlement and remedial systems serve precisely this purpose: they give rightsholders the power to change the domestic political trade-offs by reducing the incentive for non-compliance. In the context of Common Concern, the threat of fines or retaliation imposed against states whose policies are impacting negatively the common goods, would force them to rethink the rationale of the policy and reset it in line with the globally optimal. As such, the doctrine of Common Concern provides a flexible regulatory and legal template in the fight against global financial instability.

As various authors have pointed out, this doctrine so far does not have a clear definition in international law.[57] Some scholars have argued that it defines the level of protection accorded to sustainable development, human rights, the environment, the high seas, and other public goods.[58] Other scholars have attempted to extend its application to monetary law[59] and exchange rates.[60] As Cottier clearly demonstrates in this book, not all public goods require the intervention of international law, even if they suffer from cooperation problems. Given the invasiveness of the Common Concern doctrine on national sovereignty, a clear threshold for its application is required. Cottier argues that such a threshold is to be found in a threat to peace, stability, and welfare, such as civil unrest, wars, mass migrations, or biological degradation.[61] However, as he

---

[56] Joel Trachtman, *The Economic Structure of International Law* (Cambridge, MA: Harvard University Press, 2008), pp. 208–71.

[57] T. Cottier, P. Aerni, B. Karapinar, S. Matteotti, J. de Sépibus, and A. Shingal, 'The Principle of Common Concern and Climate Change', *Archiv des Völkerrechts (AVR)*, 52 (2014), at 297; F. Biermann, 'Common Concern of Humankind: The Emergence of a New Concept of International Environmental Law', AVR 34 (1996), 426–81; J. Murillo, 'Common Concern of Humankind and its Implications in International Environmental Law', *Macquarie Journal of International and Comparative Environmental Law*, 5 (2008), at 133–47; E. Brown Weiss, 'The Coming Water Crisis: A Common Concern of Humankind', *Transnational Environmental Law*, 1 (2012), at 153–68.

[58] L. Horn, 'Globalisation, Sustainable Development and the Common Concern of Humankind', *Macquarie Law Journal*, 7 (2007), 53.

[59] See Chapter 7 in this volume.

[60] Z. Kontolemis, 'Exchange Rates Are a Matter of Common Concern: Policies in the Run-up to the Euro?', Directorate General Economic and Monetary Affairs Papers 191, 2003.

[61] See Chapter 1 in this volume, pp. 39–42.

FINANCIAL STABILITY 417

rightly points out, the efficacy of such a doctrine will be limited if we wait until these stages are reached. Thus, the triggering of the doctrine must be necessarily set at a prior stage, when all elements point out to a serious threat.[62]

There is no doubt in my view that global financial instability would qualify as a serious operational trigger point for application of the doctrine of Common Concern. There is a wealth of evidence showing the destructive effect of financial crises. As Reinhart and Rogoff show, financial crises are not simply about bank creditors losing their money, but they can turn into widespread economic crises.[63] The European sovereign crisis of 2009–12 demonstrates that the bank–sovereign vicious loop which forces states to intervene to bail out the banking sector can immediately lead to a sovereign debt crisis and, in turn, to economic collapse.[64] Moreover, the cycle of poverty, frustration, anger, and disillusionment that is associated with economic crises inevitably often leads to civil unrest.

8.4 The Operational Aspects of the Common Concern Doctrine in International Finance

In the following sections, I will discuss how each pillar of the doctrine of Common Concern can be applied with regard to international finance and the problems of global instability.

8.4.1 Ensuring Cooperation

The duty to cooperate is one of the key pillars of the proposed doctrine.[65] As I showed in the previous sections, cooperation is key also for a stable global financial system. Yet, under current international law, states are not obliged to cooperate on any area of financial policy. The voluntary approach to financial cooperation applies to all areas of policy, from prudential regulation, to supervision, and crisis management, although

---

[62] Ibid., pp. 39–40.

[63] Reinhart and Rogoff, *supra* n. 11

[64] See S. Merler and J. Pisani-Ferry, 'Hazardous Tango: Sovereign–Bank Interdependence and Financial Stability in the Euro Area', in 'Public Debt, Monetary Policy and Financial Stability', *Banque de France Financial Stability Review*, 16 (2012), 201; L. Reichlin and L. Garicano, 'Squaring the Eurozone's Vicious Circle', Project Syndicate, 27 Jan. 2014.

[65] Chapter 1 in this volume.

418 FEDERICO LUPO-PASINI

the problems associated to the lack of clear and binding legal obligations are more serious in certain areas than others.

The political economy and legal literature on financial standards show that the more open is a state's financial system, the higher will be the pressure from markets for that state to adopt international financial standards.[66] This explains why, when it comes to prudential policies, states tend to converge on the key pillars of financial regulation, albeit with differences in the level of implementation. Moreover, studies show that once regulators converge on a particular financial standard, they face very little incentives to deviate as this would reduce the market available for firms.[67]

The situation, however, is partially different with regard to supervision and crisis management. The regulatory framework applicable to this area of financial policy is typically made of bilateral memoranda of understanding among supervisory agencies that address basic cooperation issues such as data sharing, inspections, licences, and in the most advanced cases, recognition of resolution actions. Unlike for prudential regulation, in the event of a crisis, supervisory agencies face a tremendous pressure to protect national interests. Thus, they sometimes refuse to share data, ring-fence foreign banks' assets, or simply refuse to apply to the failing foreign banks under their supervision the same treatment accorded to local ones.[68]

The decision to structure regulatory cooperation only on soft laws is, in my view, one of the reasons behind some of the compliance problems in international finance. Even though regulatory convergence in finance is, historically, more flexible than in other areas of international economic law, it is by no mean more resilient to shocks. The need to preserve policy space for macroeconomic and financial development or innovation has been usually used as the main motivation behind the choice of soft law in finance.[69] Yet, while regulatory convergence on financial standards does not need the support of a hard regulatory framework to elicit cooperation, crisis management and supervision

---

[66] B. A. Simmons, 'The International Politics of Harmonization: The Case of Capital Market Regulation', *International Organization*, 55 (2001), 589; D. W. Drezner, 'Globalization, Harmonization, and Competition: The Different Pathways to Policy Convergence', *Journal of European Public Policy*, 12 (2005), 841.

[67] Verdier, *supra* n. 32, p. 123.

[68] D'Hulster, *supra* n. 42.

[69] C. Brummer, 'Why Soft Law Dominates International Finance and Not Trade', *Journal of International Economic Law*, 13 (2010), 623.

desperately do. Indeed, it is precisely when the refusal to cooperate is globally inefficient that international law is desperately needed.

In this light, a progressive switch from soft law to hard law in international finance, as suggested by the Common Concern doctrine, might increase the pressure of national financial authorities to stick to their legal commitments. For instance, memoranda of understanding on cross-border banking – a key legal device to structure cooperation among supervisory authorities – could be made binding and envisage a mediation mechanism to address conflicts of interpretation, and a remedial system for non-compliance.[70]

Another possible option to induce cooperation is to leverage on the existing incentive structure at the core of global financial integration. In order to understand this option is necessary to discuss briefly the current legal approach to market integration in finance. At present, international trade and investment in financial services are based on an international regulatory platform pivoted on the mutual exchange of concessions on market access but that excludes regulatory cooperation. The economic bargain of financial integration is thus structured on the reciprocal, albeit not identical, liberalization of financial services in exchange for better and more protected access to the other partner's market. We can see this approach in all international trade agreements with a financial services component, from the WTO to the CPTPP, as well as in all international investment agreements covering portfolio flows. Rules on market access, non-discrimination, national treatment, repatriation of profits, and fair and equitable treatment serve precisely to protect the investment and trade interest in the host market.

Yet, while states are incentivized to integrate further, they are not incentivized to cooperate on a common regulatory framework that would make the shared financial system more resilient. Indeed, international trade and investment agreements purposely excluded rules and policies on financial stability from the scope of the application of the agreements. The quintessential example in this regard is Article 2 of the GATS Annex on Financial Services: the prudential carve-out.[71] The ultimate outcome

---

[70] For a more comprehensive discussion on this point, see Lupo-Pasini, *supra* n. 4, at 279–83.

[71] M. Yokoi-Arai, 'GATS' Prudential Carve Out in Financial Services and Its Relation with Prudential Regulation', *International and Comparative Law Quarterly*, 57 (2018), 613; L. E. Panourgias, *Banking Regulation and World Trade Law: GATS, EU and 'Prudential' Institution Building* (Oxford: Hart, 2006); R. Bismuth, 'Financial Sector Regulation and

of this approach is that regulatory cooperation is not part of the political economy bargain of international financial integration. States can still refuse market access to foreign financial firms if they do not comply with their own rules and adopt discriminatory regulations, but this approach is purely voluntary. Moreover, a recent worrying trend – especially in international investment law – sees a surge in the use of international investment agreements by foreign firms to challenge host authorities' prudential and supervisory decisions.[72]

In order to guarantee the resilience of the financial system, it is necessary to change this incentive structure, and to reset the financial globalization bargain on regulatory cooperation.[73] At the centre of this shift lies a different regulatory approach that I call *regulatory passporting*.[74] In a nutshell, this relies on a legal platform that requires binding cooperation on key prudential and supervisory policies as a condition for mutual financial liberalization. Unlike mutual recognition, which focuses on the bilateral recognition of rules, regulatory passporting extends to other policy areas such as supervision and crisis resolution. Moreover, unlike mutual recognition, which passively accepts a different foreign regulatory standard in lieu of the local's, this new approach requires the active harmonization of key prudential rules on both sides and a binding commitment to act when it comes to supervision and crisis resolution. Only if the two partners agree on a common regulatory platform, can market access to the partner's firm be granted.

This approach has the benefit of changing the political economy's incentives in favour of cooperation. Indeed, those firms that are more interested in accessing foreign markets will have to lobby their own governments to implement domestic regulations that are in line with those required by the partner and to agree on a common supervisory and resolution approach to financial institutions. For instance, before granting market access, the members of the regulatory passport might

---

Financial Services Liberalization at the Crossroads: The Relevance of International Standards in WTO Law', *Journal of World Trade*, 44 (2010), 489.

[72] Federico Lupo-Pasini, 'Financial Disputes in International Courts', *Journal of International Economic Law*, 21(1) (2018).

[73] See also Cottier and Krajewski on combining carve-out and commitments in financial services (Thomas Cottier and Markus Krajewski, 'What Role for Non-Discrimination and Prudential Standards in International Financial Law?', *Journal of International Economic Law*, 13 (2010), 817.

[74] For a more comprehensive discussion on this point, see Lupo-Pasini, *supra* n. 4, at 227–60.

FINANCIAL STABILITY

have to agree on the rules on the recognition of foreign resolution actions as suggested by the FSB.[75] This might entail also the establishment of a dispute settlement system mechanism. In the absence of compliance with the rules, market access could be denied to the firms originating from the violating member.

8.4.2   Homework: Global Financial Stability in Domestic Law

Sound domestic laws and policies are another fundamental pillar of the doctrine of Common Concern.[76] The adoption of global Pareto-optimal domestic financial policies is a key element also for a stable global financial system. The history of international finance teaches that regulatory holes in critical areas or nodes in the system can spread system risks and concentrate exposures. In a globally integrated financial system, a weak link in the chain of financial intermediation can trigger a wave of financial contagion. The experience with Argentina, Greece, Iceland, and the history of banking crises in the 1970s–1980s demonstrate that even peripheral jurisdictions can become systemic. For this reason, levelling up the regulatory playing field in each jurisdiction with an open capital account is fundamental. This requires the adoption of key policies, including capital and liquidity regulations, rules for systemically important financial institutions and, more generally, the wide armoury of standards proposed by the FSB and all other transnational regulatory network in finance. Having said that, the situation we are now in is much better compared to that we had prior to the global financial crisis, as the work of the FSB and the BCBS in the last few years has increased greatly the regulatory perimeter of finance.

Another possible domestic policy reform entails the inclusion of global financial stability in the list of statutory objectives of central banks and supervisory authorities. One of the reasons why regulators are reluctant to cooperate with their foreign counterparts during a crisis is because they are bound to protect their national interests, even if this leads to a suboptimal global outcome. This political economy dynamic is not surprisingly reflected in the law. Indeed, with very few exceptions, none of the statutes of central banks, supervisory or prudential authorities list

---

[75] Financial Stability Board, Recognition of Resolution Action (2015).
[76] See Chapter 1 in this volume.

the protection of global financial stability as one of their statutory goals.[77] While financial stability now features as a fundamental objective of financial policymaking at the national level, it is absent when it comes to its global dimension. In practice, this means that domestic regulators do not need to factor the international effects of their domestic policies in their policymaking, and do not need to intervene in the market when global financial stability – and not domestic stability – is in jeopardy. International cooperation is conceived only as a mere recommendation to cooperate but not as a duty.

Changing the statutes of central banks and financial authorities to include global financial stability would change the attitude of regulators during a global crisis. Not only would it make explicit the nature of systemic risk in an interconnected global financial system, which is now ignored, but it would also increase the pressure on regulators to cooperate when it is demonstrated that this is necessary to reduce the risks of instability, even if this means sacrificing the national interest. This does not mean that regulators would have to accept domestic instability at home to prevent it abroad, but, more simply, that when the achievement of global financial stability does not undermine other objectives of domestic policy such as consumer protection or domestic stability, global cooperation must be pursued. Moreover, if global financial stability becomes one of the statutory objectives of domestic policy, regulators will have to run preventive impact assessments on the global effects of domestic macroeconomic and financial policies to prevent potential negative spillovers.

A core tenet of the Common Concern theory is the use of legal action with extraterritorial effect to address a failure in the protection of the public good by partner countries.[78] In international finance law, there are various examples of extraterritoriality, especially in the regulation of securities and clearing houses.[79] Given the structure of the transaction, which is often difficult to attach to a particular jurisdiction, the global

---

[77] F. Gianviti, 'The Objectives of Central Banks', in Mario Giovanoli and Diego Devos (eds.) *International Monetary and Financial Law: The Global Crisis* (Oxford: Oxford University Press, 2010), pp. 22.91–22.112.

[78] Z. Ahmad, 'State Responsibility Aspects of a Common Concern Based Approach to Collective Action', in Samantha Besson (ed.), *International Responsibility Essays in Law, History and Philosophy* (Zurich: Schulthess, 2017), p. 107.

[79] Yadav and Turing, *supra* n. 44; A. Artamonov, 'Cross-Border Application of OTC Derivatives Rules: Revisiting the Substituted Compliance Approach', *Journal of Financial Regulation*, 1 (2016), 206.

FINANCIAL STABILITY

derivatives market is at the epicentre of the war of extraterritoriality as all major financial centres are fighting to impose their own regulatory approach on those transactions.

For instance, according to the European Market Infrastructure Regulation, when two non-EU parties enter into a derivative contract that has a direct, substantial, and foreseeable effect within the EU, the transaction is considered as if it is operated by local firms and therefore subject to EU law.[80] Similarly, according to the Dodd-Frank Act, all activities that 'have a direct and significant connection with activities in, or effect on, commerce in the United States' are subject to US law.[81] In order to fall under the reach of US law, financial entities must (1) have transacted with a US counterparty, or (2) enjoyed a financial guarantee provided by a US entity, or (3) have entered into a derivative transaction with a counterparty that was guaranteed by a US entity. Being subject to the extraterritorial application of US law imposes substantial burden on the foreign firm, which has to comply with margin requirements, segregation, risk management and a plethora of complex regulation.[82]

Research on the use of extraterritoriality as a regulatory technique demonstrates that this approach to regulation is extremely dangerous as it sacrifices the benefits of cooperation with the short-term gains of unilateralism.[83] Ultimately, it will be firms that suffer the extra burden of complying with double or triple regulatory requirements.[84] Moreover, firms will try to bypass overly burdensome regulatory constraints by placing their contracts in less regulated jurisdictions or by avoiding booking them through a clearing house. In this last scenario, the potential systemic risks would be enormous. Yet, the most negative repercussion would be the breaking of the market with the consequent

---

[80] Regulation 648/2012/EU of the European Parliament and of the Council of 4 July 2012 on OTC Derivatives, Central Counterparties and Trade Repositories, 2012 OJ (L 201/1), Art. 4(1)(a)(v).

[81] Dodd–Frank Wall Street Reform and Consumer Protection Act §722(d).

[82] L. McKinstry, 'Regulating a Global Market: The Extraterritorial Challenge of Dodd–Frank's Margin Requirements for Uncleared OTC Derivatives & a Mutual Recognition Solution', *Columbia Journal of Transnational Law*, 51 (2012–13), 776; D. Vagts, 'Extraterritoriality and the Corporate Governance Law', *American Journal of International Law*, 97 (2013), 289; H. E. Jackson, 'Substituted Compliance: The Emergence, Challenges, and Evolution of a New Regulatory Paradigm', *Journal of Financial Regulation*, 1 (2015), 169.

[83] S. Choi and A. Guzman, 'The Dangerous Extraterritoriality of US American Law', *Northwestern Journal of International Law and Business*, 17 (2016), 207.

[84] Yadav and Turing, *supra* n. 44, at 24–5; Atlantic Council, *supra* n. 31.

424   FEDERICO LUPO-PASINI

reduction in global financial flows. Indeed, the core feature of extraterritoriality is the extension of domestic law to financial transactions conducted abroad or firms that are not registered in that jurisdiction. In order to avoid the higher costs of duplicative requirements firms will have to choose the market in which to transact and be regulated and drop all connections with other markets. The very opposite of free capital mobility.

8.4.3   The Quest for Compliance in International Financial Law

Another key tenet of the Common Concern doctrine is the duty to cooperate in securing compliance with international law obligations.[85] Undoubtedly, the fact that both international financial standards as well as bilateral agreements between regulators are in the form of soft laws, makes the question of compliance extremely more challenging in the financial sphere, especially if we consider the peculiar sovereignty issues and political economy dynamics attached to cooperation in finance. Indeed, there is a very long literature that demonstrates that regulators tend to bypass their soft cooperation commitments whenever the implementation costs are too high.[86] For instance, during financial crises, bank supervisors tend not to fully cooperate with their foreign counterparts, either by not disclosing data or by ring-fencing foreign assets, whenever this might put their financial institutions or local creditors in a worse position.

The absence of a hard international legal framework is a fundamental loophole in the global financial architecture. Indeed, not only are regulators disincentivized to cooperate, but they are also unable to rely on a framework to settle their potential disputes. At present, none of the standard-setting bodies in finance envisages a dispute settlement mechanism to address coordination issues or compliance problems. Indeed, while regulators do solve regulatory disputes behind closes doors, they do so only voluntarily and outside of a proper and structured mediation system. Using unilateral extraterritorial retaliatory measures to address the lack of cooperation on international standards, while in theory possible as demonstrated by the US regulations, would be extremely risky as it would affect the good relationship between regulators. At present, the use of soft law in international finance is well accepted by the

---

[85]   See Chapter 1 in this volume, pp. 62–4.
[86]   D'Hulster, *supra* n. 42.

regulatory community and there are no signs of moving into the opposite direction.[87] The only possibility to retaliate against a foreign partner is to impose on the foreign investors and financial entities an equivalence requirement for market access. In practice, foreign firms and investors will be able to trade and operate in the host market as long as foreign firms' home supervisory rules are deemed by the host authority as substantially 'equivalent' to the local. Thus, if the foreign regulator refuses to comply with established prudential standards, its firms will be denied market access. This is, for instance, the EU's approach to market access used with Japan, Canada, Singapore, and the United States.[88]

Dispute settlement mechanism for privates are more challenging. At present, creditors, firms, or investors affected by the measure of a foreign financial authority have no official avenue to channel their complaints. As I have demonstrated in a recent study, the absence of a proper dispute settlement mechanism in finance has led to a surge of international disputes in non-financial courts.[89] More specifically, investors' financial creditors use existing rights under international investment treaties, international trade agreements, or human rights conventions to challenge a regulatory measure that affect them negatively. Most of the time, this involves alleged discriminatory measures or expropriations in the context of bank insolvencies or debt restructurings. Parallel litigation, however, is very inefficient as financial regulatory issues are then litigated under an applicable law – mostly international investment and human right law – that has very little to do with finance, thereby increasing further regulatory uncertainty.

In this light, the establishment of specific dispute settlement systems for financial regulatory or supervisory disputes is a necessary and unavoidable step in rebuilding the global financial architecture. Unfortunately, the literature on dispute settlement in finance is extremely scant, and mostly focuses on international commercial dispute. Very little has been researched on which specific legal and regulatory issues are apt to be litigated in courts or simply mediated, and on the design and jurisdiction of the tribunal. For instance, while there is a compelling case

---

[87] Brummer, *supra* n. 3.

[88] Linklaters, 'Financial Services Post-Brexit: "Equivalence" Does Not Mean "Equal to"; European Parliament, Third Country Equivalence in EU Banking and Financial Regulation' (Nov. 2018).

[89] Lupo-Pasini, *supra* n. 72.

to provide a more structured dispute settlement system for cross-border supervisory disputes or for sovereign debt restructuring, it would be very difficult to subject prudential regulation to the binding force of an award. In the latter case, a mediation mechanism hosted by the FSB would probably be the most feasible option.

8.5 Concluding Remarks

The evolution of the global financial system, from a constellation of separate and independent national systems into an integrated global network of firms and investors, requires a change in the international regulatory framework. A change that forces states to cooperate on financial policies when necessary and to internalize the costs of their domestic policies on their neighbours. Only when cooperation is ensured, will markets be able to operate safely.

International law needs to be the vector driving such change. Only when rules are binding, and a dispute settlement mechanism is available, cooperation is credible. The Common Concern doctrine provides a very good regulatory framework upon which the international law of finance can evolve. Its wide-encompassing focus on the domestic policy requirements as well as the international institutional framework that make cooperation possible give a very good starting point for a serious discussion on the reform of the global financial architecture.

* * *

Select Bibliography

Abdelal, R. (2007). *Capital Rules: The Construction of Global Finance* (Cambridge, MA: Harvard University Press).

Boccuzzi, G., (2016). *The European Banking Union: Supervision and Resolution* (London: Palgrave Macmillan).

Brummer, C. (2012). *Soft Law and the Global Financial System* (Cambridge: Cambridge University Press).

Caprio, G., Evanoff, D., and Kauffman, G. G. (eds.) (2006) *Cross-Border Banking: Regulatory Challenges* (Singapore: World Scientific).

Cottier, T., Jackson, J. H., and Lastra, R. M., (eds.) (2012). *International Law in Financial Regulation and Monetary Affairs* (Oxford: Oxford University Press).

Desai, P. (2003). *Financial Crisis, Contagion, and Containment: From Asia to Argentina* (Princeton, NJ: Princeton University Press).

FINANCIAL STABILITY

Drezner, D. W. (2005). 'Globalization, Harmonization, and Competition: The Different Pathways to Policy Convergence', 12 *Journal of European Public Policy* 841.

Eichengreen, B. (2008). *Globalizing Capital: A History of the International Monetary System* (2nd ed., Princeton, NJ: Princeton University Press).

Goodhart, C. and Lastra, R. M. (2010). 'Border Problems', 13 *Journal of International Economic Law,* 705.

Hüpkes, E. (2010). 'Rivalry in Resolution: How to Reconcile Local Responsibilities and Global Interests?', 7 *European Company and Financial Law Review* 216.

IMF (2010). 'Understanding Financial Interconnectedness' (IMF, 4 Oct.).

Kindleberger, C. P. and Aliber, R. Z. (2005). *Manias, Panics and Crashes: A History of Financial Crises* (rev. ed., London: Palgrave Macmillan).

Lupo-Pasini, F. (2017). *The Logic of Financial Nationalism: The Challenges of International Cooperation and the Role of International Law* (New York: Cambridge University Press).

   (2017). 'Financial Stability in International Law', 18 *Melbourne Journal of International Law* 45.

Schoenmaker, D. (2013). *Governance of International Banking: The Financial Trilemma* (Oxford: Oxford University Press).

Schwarcz, S. (2008). 'Systemic Risk', 97 *Georgetown Law Journal* 193.

Singer, A. (2007). *Regulating Capital: Setting Standards for the Global Financial System* (Ithaca, NY: Cornell University Press).

Wyplosz, C. (1999). 'International Financial Instability', in I. Kaul, I. Grunberg, and M. A. Stern (eds.), *Global Public Goods: International Cooperation in the 21st Century* (Oxford: Oxford University Press), pp. 152–89.

PART III

Epilogue

9

Comments

The Doctrinal Approach of Common Concern

PETER-TOBIAS STOLL, DUNCAN FRENCH
AND OISIN SUTTLE

Discussants Professor Peter-Tobias Stoll, Professor Duncan French, and Dr Oisin Suttle were asked at the workshop held on 22–23 June 2018 at the World Trade Institute, Bern, Switzerland, to offer an overall assessment of the notion and potentially emerging legal principle of Common Concern of Humankind in international law. Their authorised interventions are transcribed below. They raise pertinent questions as to the novelty of the concept, the thresholds discussed, the relationship to public goods, the feasibility, and methodological implications a prospective principle of Common Concern of Humankind poses. They are encouraging and cautioning at the same time, pointing to conceptual innovation and weaknesses in the chapters of this volume, and offer guidance for further research on the topic.

9.1 Peter-Tobias Stoll

Thank you very much for your endurance to listen to my final comment. We had a very interesting seminar. I am grateful for all the presentations and discussions which I immensely enjoyed.

At the beginning of the conference, I was under the impression that the project is somehow engaged in transferring normative substance and terminology from certain international treaty regimes and applying them to other situations. I said that this is a process of generalisation and we should be careful about it. I also felt that the problem would be how to trigger and extend common concern of humankind beyond the treaty regimes where it has been recognised. Environmental advocates often apply this copy–paste technology. Much of international environmental law has developed after the Second World War using concepts from one convention to draft the next one. This was how I first saw the common concern project.

After many excellent presentations and our stimulating discussion, I now understand that the common concern, as understood here, is not only a transfer operation. As far as I can see, it is meant also, and even more importantly so, as a strengthening process for rules and norms of international law which are already in existence. The common concern approach may strengthen human rights, for instance, to allude to the presentation by Iryna Bogdanova and discussions thereon. Or, it is about plastic pollution to which the Law of the Seas Convention already applies. This aspect may possibly become even more prominent if the Responsibility to Protect would be made a core element of the whole concept. In this perspective, the common concern approach could add a new enforcement dimension to international legal regimes which are already there.

My other point is about the trigger (i.e. what constitutes particularly a common concern). That issue is even more relevant when you think about regimes and rules, which are already in place. Which element, or part of such regimes, could be identified as a common concern? Is it, for instance, grave human rights violations? This question relates to the issue of emergency and severity which I have brought into play in earlier comments. I thought that because of what has been said in various discussions, the one point is to say: 'Ah! Common concern is particularly about emergency'. I think Gabrielle Marceau earlier noted with reference to sustainable development – that it is like a goal, to which we need to speed up our journey. That is an emergency, which could be adopted as a common concern. If that would be so, I think then we will see a second line of justification of common concern, which would be something like necessity, or something comparable which could come in addition to the justifications that you already explained in your chapters. So that is why I would be interested in understanding whether you think about it in such terms as emergency. I do not say that I necessarily would see it in this way, but it could be discussed. You would then have different kinds of justifications. But you would also have different lines of thought about distributional issues. Because coming from a national legal order, if I hear emergency, I am of course thinking about police power. If I think about police power, I think about effective responses to a situation of an imminent or at least clear and concrete danger, and all measures taken are governed by the principle of effectively remedying that situation. That also has an effect on the question of distributional justice. Because if measures are directed to that person or entity that can most effectively do something about such a situation in the context of a near danger and limited time–space to react, you might pick someone different as compared to a situation, where time is available to make your selection on the basis of responsibility and justice. Simply, if there is urgency, the individual or entity has to be chosen that can most effectively solve the problem. So, I think this notion of emergency is something that you could conceptually discuss. It would add different justifications with different implications on distribution of powers, rights, and obligations under the doctrine of common concern.

And then we were also discussing about severity. We spoke about grave cases of human rights violations and I think in other areas we were discussing the distributional part with reference to potential situations, where we see millions of people close to starvation. I think severity is also something which should be kept in mind, especially in situations where international law already has a regime at hand. It is here that we come to the questions – what really constitutes a common concern, and what justifies all the measures that we have in mind when we discuss common concern? Otherwise, if we do not have a qualifier to distinguish normal treaty objectives, purposes, obligations, and concepts from the common concern, the problem would arise of how to justify stepping out of an existing treaty regime. It would be difficult to see whether we simply can refer to a common concern, and then in a way override all the shortcomings and the strengths of certain treaty regimes as they reflect kind of a consensus achieved between individual states. The related triggers of emergency and severity thus deserve further work.

We also need such triggers and thresholds when talking about equity and distributional justice. I think the concept needs a bit of a safeguard against an idealist Western approach to international law. Much of our society's concern about plastics in the oceans, or deficits in human rights enforcement and things might look pertinent and important for us, but it would be difficult to see us imposing such preferences automatically on other societies, or other parts of the world. That is an issue which came to my mind when I was writing on trade and the environment. Like many others, I was welcoming the extension of trade remedies for environmental purposes. However, when looking at it from a distance, it is quite apparent that the cases and issues at hand do match particularly well with the environmental agenda in American society (i.e. conservation of marine mammals and sea turtles for example). It is more difficult to imagine a climate change case brought to the WTO in the same way. What we address here is the luxury of the Western markets which sometimes even forget that they have this enormous power to use their markets as a policy tool in international relations. I have seen many papers and books written in the West on those wonderful new possibilities of international trade. But, it should be kept in mind that we impose our agenda on the rest of the world and we are so advanced in doing so that we do not even recognise what we are doing. So, I think there is a question of justice here. And although it is very old-fashioned, I think that in this context the consensus principle in international law has something to say. Although the common concern concept is built in a way to override the need for consensus, one should be careful in defining the conditions and in looking for means to give legitimacy to claims under the doctrine of common concern.

Otherwise, I think the concept is very interesting. Normally I am cautious about concepts of global commons and global public goods and similar ideas. But I think talking about common concern has the potential of agenda-setting and framing. In order to organise a rational debate, we need an appropriate frame. A frame can even be a terminology. So, it is important, I think – and this is a valid point – to have something like a common concern, to use it as a flag for certain issues that under certain conditions, and subject to certain procedures, are considered by some actors to have a priority status. I would be happy to see the common concern concept further emerging.

Thank you very much!

9.2 Duncan French

Thank you to all the organisers and for the presentations; I found them incredibly stimulating. I am also bemused about what common concern might mean in the future beyond its common development, its continued evolution, and whether it has some substantive merit to it. As I have sat here over the last two days, I would say my thoughts on common concern have become more complicated in light of the conversations we have had. So, I'm just going to try and rationalise or explain why my thoughts have become complicated over the last twenty-four hours or so.

I am going to start with the question: what does it signify for an issue to be classified as being of common concern, be that legally or politically? I was very taken with Judith Schäli's presentation where she quoted from UNEP about how common concern is a moral issue as well. For me, these are definitely two stages in the process and I think Tobias has indicated this perhaps by his reference to a trigger. The decision or the trigger as to whether something is to be classified of common concern, for me, is an innately political choice. Undoubtedly, law frames part of that conversation, it clarifies, and is very much going to be involved subsequently in its implementation. But the role of law in the actual classification of an issue of common concern, I'm a little bit more reticent about. So, the role of law at the classification stage – and I think Krista Schefer has put this well earlier when she said: 'to what extent is commonality imposed from above?'. And I come at this, very admittedly, from an international environmental law perspective. So, historically, undoubtedly common concern has been a gateway concept. Much more an adjective than a noun. I'm not criticising anybody, but my shoulders bristled when people started talking about CCHs as some kind of descriptive – as sort of shorthand. Because I think that that it's much more nuanced than that. It's a much more political choice than a simplistic legal principle. So, for me, the way that common concern has been used up to this point with environmental law is that it provided a justification – part political, part legal – for international action and international interest.

Also, importantly, if one compares the Climate Change Convention with the Biodiversity Convention in which both refer to their respective problems as a common concern, I think international law doesn't really prescribe what that international interest should entail. So, the Climate Change Convention comprises, in many ways, very formalised differentiation. The Biodiversity Convention is very much more open-textured, very much more programmatic. So, to just take in two very, in some ways, related conventions, there's quite large diversity in there. So, if we were to transplant it outside into other disciplines I think it starts to say that it is difficult to identify those common themes.

In some ways, I wonder, with references already about *erga omnes*, whether common concern is a little bit like the concept of *erga omnes* in the way that it has developed over time. I'm not dealing here with the detail of *erga omnes* but rather the conceptualisation of it. The International Court, while addressing an *erga omnes* based claim in the *East Timor* case, recognised it as an interest but didn't prescribe a remedy.[1] For me, common concern has something of that similarity. Now, of course, over time *erga omnes* has started to have a more substantive, remedial, enforcement effect, primarily through its inclusion by James Crawford in the State Responsibility Draft Articles, although it

---

[1] *Case Concerning East Timor (Portugal v. Australia)*, Judgement, ICJ Rep. 1995, para. 29.

was not there at the beginning. I wonder whether we are on a journey too, for common concern.

So, for me, common concern's first particular overriding impact is to further dismantle, or to further dent the exclusive domain of the state. We have another opportunity to question the absolute nature of sovereignty on a particular issue. But as a gateway concept or as a trigger, one might tend to even say principle, it has been normatively quite soft; a precursor to substantive obligation. International environmental law has always relied on soft law (i.e. soft law in form, or soft law in content). And I think common concern has been part of that trend.

But does that mean there is no possibility of the hardening of common concern over time? Will it be able to generate clear obligations as we go forward? Again, I think we need to tread carefully and distinguish between the generalised and the specific. The generalised obligation – as Thomas Cottier has rightly mentioned – is around an interested duty to negotiate, an obligation of cooperation, the right of the international community to be involved or to be interested in a subject at some level, to negotiate on the matter in good faith; and perhaps in time to hold that state to account. These rules, in one form or another, are the general obligations that we might want to see in relation to some of these issues. Whether we use the term common concern or not we can see them in most areas of law, including human rights. As regards specific obligations within particular regimes, and you can think in terms of the climate change regimes, financial regulation, or transfer of technologies – there has been a lot of talk at the workshop about peace and security, much more so than I was actually expecting. Because I never really thought about a common concern as a concept in peace and security in the way we've talked about today and it has given me some thoughts to go away and unpack a bit more. But it seems to me that specific obligations flowing from common concern really are issue-specific and it will be very much dependent on the development of express agreement and the development of practice going forward.

There's been some discussion of a dichotomy between *lex lata* and *de lege ferenda*, which I think is a genuine conversation. I also wonder if there is another dichotomy at work here. And that is between the optimal versus the aspirational. It seems to me there are some optimal situations where common concern can be used, and more tangential, aspirational ones, which need some further thought. The presentations over these two days have sort of indicated where we may be able to bring some of these issues in, but we need to think about what it is we're about to bring in.

For me, what makes an issue of common concern optimal is that it occurs within a legal regime. It's no surprise that where we have seen common concern finding its most secure roots is in the preamble at the start of a treaty, which has created a treaty regime. The treaty regime has created institutional oversight, created clear rules, provided support, also dispute settlement to some extent, as it is variable under international environmental law. So, for me, *lex lata–de lege ferenda* is one way of expressing the optimal and the possible.

Will common concern generate more substantive content over time or prompt further insights? I think yes, but especially in the areas where it is already most developed – in international environmental law and the law of the sea. I think the marine plastics presentation highlighted that just as it wasn't used in the Ozone Convention, it doesn't even get used in the Law of the Sea Convention, but the same sort of reasoning is very present. I mentioned yesterday the development, in particular, the fleshing out of many of the concepts in some recent case law in relation to the due diligence of holding states to account for how they deal with private citizens and corporations, and I think that is going to be part of this development. Equally, we have talked about *erga omnes* in its more substantive setting and what I think is interesting is probably the way that common concern has supported if not expressly referenced the sort of *erga omnes partes* adjudication that we have started to see in relation to some of the multilateral environmental agreements, perhaps most notably so far in the *Whaling in the Antarctic* case (Australia, and New Zealand against Japan).[2]

I am less convinced – or I need to go away and think about it more – as to how far common concern can be made akin to a coalescing around the responsibility to protect and similar concepts. Similarly, I have concerns about utilising common concern in relation to human rights regimes simply because we have some very strong justifications for human rights protection already – human dignity, etc. I think for me it highlights the relatively low level of action that might be forthcoming if we are reliant on common concern. You still have this huge rock that is sovereignty, and Thomas rightly said we are in an arena of realism. But I think we have to accept that. The conversation about what to do with those populations in West China, I think highlights that to a large degree.

---

[2] *Whaling in the Antarctic (Australia v. Japan: New Zealand intervening)*, Judgment, ICJ Rep. 2014.

438   PETER-TOBIAS STOLL, DUNCAN FRENCH, OISIN SUTTLE

Alan Boyle, in some of his writings, has coined a phrase 'soft general principles of law'. He uses the phrase to include legal principles that exist at a quite abstract and broad level, that guide states towards developing more specific regimes and rules over time, but without being prescriptive in themselves. I think, to some extent, that is where we are with common concern at the present time. There is a job of work. We may be able to develop it further. But I would not want to go further than we probably have got.

This is an altogether inappropriate analogy but I'm going to use it anyway. I was thinking actually of Charlesworth and Chinkin's work on feminism and international law.[3] There is a metaphor at the start of their book, where they talk about international law as archaeology – that you dig down to different periods of geology over time. I think we are still at the topsoil, if I can put it like that. In some of the areas of international law, we will hit the sand or loose soil and we will get further down. Some of the time we will hit rock. And I think that is where we are with common concern. It is a concept which has got some value, but I think we still need to do quite a lot of work as to where it's going to fit in in international legal discourse.

I think I'll leave it there. Thank you!

9.3   Oisin Suttle

Thank you very much for inviting me here and for allowing me to be involved in this project. Unlike Professor French I do not have much experience thinking about and using this concept of common concern, so my comments here are simply a response to your project, which is to date the beginning and the end of my engagement with this concept. What I would, therefore, like to do here is to raise what seem to me to be some important questions that I continue to have after reading the papers – chapters – and participating in the workshop discussions. Some of these at least are questions that I believe are worth trying to clarify in taking this work forward, whether within the terms of this current project, or in subsequent efforts. To that end, I want to raise one question about methodology, a set of interlinked questions about the boundaries of the concept of common concern and how common concerns are identified,

---

[3] H. Charlesworth and C. Chinkin, *The Boundaries of International Law: A Feminist Analysis* (Manchester: Manchester University Press, 2000).

DOCTRINAL APPROACH OF COMMON CONCERN 439

and one question about the allocation of obligations to address such concerns.

My first question, picking up somewhat on a point raised by Peter-Tobias Stoll, is what exactly is the methodology that is adopted in this project, or more accurately, in this set of projects? My impression is that the methodology probably varies across the papers (chapters) presented at the conference (in the volume). It is important to clarify this, because the methodology, in turn, has implications for the kinds of claims that the authors are making about this concept.

Thomas has been very clear that the project is not wholly one of positive law – it is developing rather than simply stating the law as it stands. Nor is it simply an exercise in trying to deduce new claims from existing law. But it's also not wholly, or at least not straightforwardly, a normative project – advancing a free-standing moral or political argument for a particular revision to the law. Cedric yesterday suggested that it stands within an optimistic Grotian tradition that sees positivism and naturalism as cohering quite closely. That may indeed be the case. However, I am not sure that we can make even that quite general claim about the volume's chapters as a whole, given what seem to be differences in the methodologies they adopt. By way of illustration, Judith Schäli's argument, as I read it, draws very heavily, and quite convincingly, on a set of existing legal obligations that quite closely parallel the sorts of implications that it has been suggested flow from something being a common concern. This provides a powerful route to arguing that her object of concern, marine plastics pollution, is in fact a common concern: we know it is a common concern because it is already implicitly recognised as such, by virtue of the obligations attaching to it. That's quite different to Iryna Bogdanova's argument, which is built much more around a normative principle. This point also came out clearly at the workshop in discussions of Thomas Cottier's and Rosa Maria Losada's joint chapter. How exactly can we categorise migration as a common concern in a situation where nobody seems to be treating it like one? It seems to me that the response offered is straightforwardly one of political morality: this is a pressing issue, of urgency for individual human persons, and treating those persons with the respect to which they are entitled requires that we take the sorts of actions that we associate with recognising a common concern.

These are different methodologies, but each grounds a claim that a particular issue should be treated as a common concern. I think it would be helpful both to see those methodologies foregrounded more in the individual chapters, and also to develop a bit more conversation between them, as to exactly what the appropriate methodology is for a project of this nature. Thomas suggests in his framing paper (i.e. Chapter 1 in this volume) that this is a developmental exercise built on a process of claim and response. That idea comes up again in a number of other chapters, and Alex Beyleveld draws on it in his discussion of how new common concerns come to be recognised. But, of course, there are many different ways that we can make claims. Claims can have very different structures, they can have very different grounds, and those structures and grounds can, in turn, affect the sorts of responses that they evoke.

A second set of questions concern how exactly the principle of common concern should be formulated. My impression on reading these chapters is that there is a tension between a unifying and a fragmenting tendency among the various authors and contributions in this project – in the sense that we all want to invoke and address the same concept, but actually the concept looks quite different across our different areas of interest, and the result is that we get slightly different formulations in the different chapters. That is not necessarily problematic. It would be surprising if our concepts fit perfectly without any modification across these very different domains. However, again, I think it would be valuable to see more conversation between the chapters, seeking to articulate why a concept that looks a particular way in the environmental regime is reconceived in the context of, for example, distributive justice across states, and how some characteristics are necessarily the same and some are different. Differences may reflect the features of a particular issue area. However, they may also reflect the extent to which the different contributors to this volume have different views, genuine disagreements rather than simply variation across contexts. Either way, I think that the overall project would be much richer if these differences in formulations were given more prominence, giving readers a clearer sense that this conversation is taking place, and of the arguments for understanding the concept in particular ways in particular contexts. While recognising, then, that there is some divergence among contributors as to precisely how this concept should be understood, I would like to try to interrogate what seem to me to be the principal criteria that you have attached to it.

My first definitional question, which came up a number of times in discussions at the workshop, is exactly what the significance of public goods is for the concept of common concern. Thomas has been very clear that the two concepts are not identical, but they are clearly adjacent, and most, if not quite all, of the chapters spend at least some time discussing

DOCTRINAL APPROACH OF COMMON CONCERN   441

whether or not public goods are involved in or connected to the particular problems with which they are concerned. My question then becomes exactly how far is the existence of a public goods problem part of the starting point in thinking about a common concern? And I guess my worry in posing that question is that public goods problems are one quite specific type of cooperation problem. There are lots of cooperation problems that are not public goods problems. Some problems are coordination problems; some are assurance problems; some are common pool resource problems. Just because something is not a public goods problem doesn't mean that it is not urgent, or that it doesn't require cooperation, including potentially cooperation through law, to resolve it. In any event I think it would be helpful to see the relationship between common concerns and public goods fleshed out and clarified a bit more, if only so that those reading your work, and attracted by the concept of common concern that you are advancing, should be able to take it up and to work out for themselves whether it applies in any particular context.

Setting aside the specific issue of public goods, it does seem clear that the concept of common concern as it is being advanced here is at least to a significant extent concerned with the problems of coordination, cooperation, and joint action. The next question I have is, therefore, whether the project is to some extent built on an assumption that there is a general duty on states and/or individuals to solve problems of cooperation. If you believe there is a moral obligation to maximise welfare, whether in classical utilitarian or other terms, then you might see cooperation problems, including public goods problems, as inherently normative in this way. However, if your goal is to speak to a broader audience, then it's important to pause and ask the question: is there really a general duty to solve problems of cooperation? Is there a general duty to contribute to the provision of public goods? Robert Nozick argues forcefully against that suggestion, denying that we can legitimately be coerced into contributing to cooperative schemes for the delivery of public goods, regardless of whether we value those goods or benefit from those schemes.[4] You might argue that those who are taking the benefits of such a scheme should contribute to it.[5] However, outside of relatively specific circumstances, it's not clear that there is anything wrong with leaving cooperation problems unsolved, or free-riding on the efforts of

---

[4] R. Nozick, *Anarchy, State and Utopia* (New York: Basic Books, 1974).

[5] See for this argument, H. L. A. Hart, 'Are There Any Natural Rights?', *Philosophical Review*, 64 (1955), 175–91; J. Rawls, 'Legal Obligation and the Duty of Fair Play', in

others to solve them. Rather – at least given the kinds of broadly liberal premises that I and many others endorse – it seems free-riding on a common provision is normatively objectionable only where – at a minimum – what is being provided is a good that I unquestionably benefit from, and that I would really be worse off without.

The argument here – like so much in political thought – goes back at least to Thomas Hobbes. Hobbes tells us that we have an obligation to submit to the authority of the state. Why? Because without the state, life is solitary, poor, nasty, brutish, and short. No matter how much you think the state is oppressing you, he argues, you would be worse off without it. The imperative of self-preservation thus motivates a duty of submission to political authority.[6] That seems plausible to me, but very few problems in the world are quite as urgent as the problem of self-preservation for individual human beings faced with the insecurity of the state of nature. There may be public goods that it is simply not in the interest of some states to see provided. The reference to 'some states' here is important – states are radically unequal, and we cannot generalise across all of them, assuming away their differences. One of the things that makes Hobbes's arguments so powerful is, as Hobbes tells us, that it applies to all human beings equally. Each of us, no matter how strong, is vulnerable, at least when we sleep. So, there is a real symmetry in the extent to which, as individuals, we have reason to submit ourselves to and to contribute towards the support of the state. That symmetry doesn't hold for states.[7] Even if we think just about problems of peace and security, these look very different from the perspectives of different states. We, therefore, need to think harder about the precise nature of the normative obligation to contribute towards the resolution of these sorts of problems, and how far that obligation really attaches to all states to a similar extent. If it is the case that the normative force of common concern is at least significantly connected with problems of cooperation, problems of the provision of public goods, or the addressing of public bads, then it is important to identify what the normative link is between the diagnosis of that problem and the obligation on any given individual or community to contribute to its remedy.

S. Hook (ed.), *Law and Philosophy* (New York: New York University Press, 1964), pp. 3–19.

[6] T. Hobbes, *Leviathan* (Cambridge: Cambridge University Press, 1996 [1651]).

[7] For this point as an objection to social contract accounts of global justice generally, see M. Nussbaum, *Frontiers of Justice* (Harvard, MA: Harvard University Press, 2007).

The most common response to that question in the chapters seems to be that the threshold for recognising a common concern is more than simply the existence of a problem of cooperation. Rather, the concept is defined in part by reference to a link between a particular issue and international peace and security, which incorporates an element of gravity or emergency to the definition. That connection to international peace and security is what allows us to pick out one particular set of issues and to say that these are problems of common concern, motivating the sorts of implications and obligations that designating something as a problem of common concern generates. That, however, poses the subsequent question of whether we can adequately distinguish a discrete class of problems that have this required normative standing, such that we can say that these are entitled to be designated as issues of common concern and others are not?

Various possible thresholds come out in the chapters presented here. A number of the chapters share a concern for negative cross-border externalities. That probably reflects the heritage of this concept in the environmental regime and thinking about physical harms crossing borders. But then I wonder, can we think about some of the non-physical impacts discussed here – concerns around economic stability, financial stability, domestic inequality – in the same sorts of ways? Physical harm can be defined reasonably straightforwardly, but talking about other forms of harm requires first defining rights and baselines against which it can be measured. This is a point that comes out clearly from Federico Lupo-Passini's analysis of financial instability as a common concern. As Federico identifies, international financial instability is not something to which states must expose themselves. They could choose to have financial systems that were entirely closed, and therefore within their sovereign control, avoiding the need to worry about international financial stability. However, this will likely impose significant costs in terms of their domestic economic development. States that have chosen to internationalise their financial systems, this line of thought runs, have also chosen to bear risk, in exchange for expected benefits. Such risk–reward trade-offs are not unusual. Part of what is at stake here is how we work out when someone has been harmed, when instead of physical injury, we are thinking about the ways the benefits and burdens of cooperation are allocated. What level of economic well-being, what degree of economic stability, or what share of the benefits of economic cooperation are we each entitled to? Those aren't questions that can be answered without recourse to a substantive account of political morality.

Another suggestion is that we might think of common concern as referring to matters that affect all, or almost all, of humanity. That seems plausible as an explanation of why 'humanity' should be concerned. However, it's also potentially a very low threshold. If we think about the ways problems cross borders in the context of the Internet, for example, almost any example of online speech at least potentially affects, if not all, then at least a very large proportion, of humanity. But that probably is not enough to give it the sort of urgency and significance that a common concern is understood to have.

We might instead try to distinguish common concerns in terms of their seriousness. I am not sure how far this suggestion comes through in the chapters, but it came out in conversations at the workshop. Given the roots of this concept in the context of climate change, we might identify problems of common concern as being all those problems of a similar magnitude to climate change. However, we might worry that the standard this implies is just too high. There are few problems of the magnitude of climate change, with the possible exception of nuclear proliferation. Humanity faces existential threats and climate change is plausibly one of them. Humanity also faces many other very serious challenges that are not existential in the same way. If we think that any of these other challenges constitute common concerns, and it is clear from the chapters presented here that we do, then looking to the climate regime for a threshold of gravity risks being too demanding.

So, then, I come to the threshold most frequently invoked in the chapters, which is that there is some link between the relevant issue and problems of international peace, security, and welfare. International peace and security is the formulation used in most of the chapters. International peace, security, and welfare is the formulation used in Thomas's framing piece.[8] I would have two questions about that as a standard. First of all, how do we justify that being a standard? Why is it this and not some other standard? Why is this not an arbitrary line to draw? Thomas tells us in his chapter that it is because the promotion of peace, security, and welfare is the essence of law. However, this is itself a contestable claim. I think many would be tempted to deny that law has an essential purpose at all, while those who do understand law in such teleological terms will disagree radically about exactly what its purpose is, from the preservation of physical security to the protection of liberty and

---

[8] See Chapter 1 in this volume (Section 1.3.2.4).

DOCTRINAL APPROACH OF COMMON CONCERN 445

property, to the maximisation of well-being or the advancement of equality or dignity. The upshot is that it's hard to see how a definite threshold for common concern can be uncontroversially derived from a claim about the essential purpose of law.

Apart entirely from its justification, there is also an important question about the determinacy of this standard. This point comes out clearly from a number of the chapters and emerged in discussions of others. Human life is complicated. Causal relations in human life are complicated. Almost anything can be a cause of almost anything. For example, Alex argued that inequality constituted a common concern in part because extreme inequality makes civil unrest more likely. However, I imagine if we trawl through the literature we will find many other things that also make civil unrest more likely. Are these all common concerns? In discussing Judith's chapter, Thomas suggested we can make the link from marine plastics pollution to international peace and security through the possibility pollution may ultimately undermine the capacity of the oceans to provide fish for food, which could, in turn, lead to issues of peace and security. Again, that is plausible, but it relies on a very long causal chain, into which we might submit many other issues in place of marine plastics. Iryna highlighted the extent to which many human rights violations have cross-border effects, but the specific cross-border effects mentioned, including things like the reduction in economic growth, are not specific to human rights abuses. Nor, I imagine, are these effects the real reason why we regard human rights abuses as pressing issues of common concern for humanity as a whole. So, merely saying there is a causal chain that I can draw which will eventually lead to a threat to international peace and security seems like a dangerously low threshold, while also potentially missing the point in particular cases. But, equally, if you require a more direct link to international peace and security, then many of the topics discussed in these chapters will likely be ruled out.

The upshot is that I think there is some serious work to do in identifying exactly what the threshold of common concern is if this is to be a sharp analytical concept. That work is needed to avoid the risk of conceptual inflation, where everything can be claimed by someone to be a matter of common concern. It is not enough to say 'here are some problems that look like they might be common concerns'. Rather, we also need to be able to say with confidence 'here are some others that *are not* common concerns'. It's only when you can do this that I think you'll reasonably be able to answer the question of how useful this concept is. It has to be possible to draw a line, and to say of some issues – perhaps with sorrow – that's a horror, that's a tragedy, that's a problem, but it is not a common concern of humanity.

The final question that I would like to raise in response to this project is who gets what obligations? This, it seems to me, is a critical question, which points towards the kinds of global distributive justice issues that have occupied me for a number of years. It is important to remember that once we identify a problem of cooperation, there will almost always be a number of different ways we can solve that problem. One of the important ways those solutions will differ is that they will place the benefits and burdens with different agents, whether different individuals, different states, different organisations, and so on. The step from saying 'this is a shared problem' to saying 'this is the particular solution we need to adopt' is a big one. A whole panoply of problems of justice and fairness arise in trying to make that step. I'm not sure that simply saying that in the first instance our obligations are obligations of cooperation and negotiation really gets us out of that difficulty because ultimately, as I understand the claim being advanced here, unilateralism has a backstop role in addressing problems of common concern. If negotiation doesn't solve the problem, then individual agents may – and presumably must – use whatever resources they have themselves to address them. But such unilateral action presupposes that we have not only a shared diagnosis of the problem, but also the legitimate authority to select a particular response to it. If you think of something like the EU's aviation emissions trading scheme, we see this very clearly. We can all get together and say: yes, climate change is a common concern, it's urgent, it poses an existential threat, aviation emissions are a significant element of the problem, and so forth. But to then move from there to the idea that we, the European Union, get to say how those burdens are allocated, that's a much more difficult move to make. I guess that goes back to a point that Duncan French touched on. Politics is central; not necessarily politics as an electoral process, but politics as the way that human societies make decisions where conflict exists. In almost all of the common concerns you've identified in the project, and in almost all common concerns we might identify, there will likely be some element of conflict, wherein interests will be only partly convergent. I think there is, therefore, an important question to be asked about how we make the distributive choices that are required to be made there, and what contribution naming something as a common concern makes to those choices. Because it is only once those distributive choices can be made, and justified, that the concept of common concern can fully come into its own.

10

Comments

Extraterritoriality and Common Concern

CEDRIC RYNGAERT, CLAUS ZIMMERMANN
AND KRISTA NADAKAVUKAREN SCHEFER

Discussants Professor Cedric Ryngaert, Dr Claus Zimmermann, and Professor Krista Nadakavukaren Schefer were asked to address at the workshop held on 22–23 June 2018 at the World Trade Institute, Bern, Switzerland, the implications of the notion, concept, and potentially emerging principle of Common Concern of Humankind on territoriality and extraterritorial effects and the critical issue of compliance and unilateral enforcement. Their authorized interventions are transcribed below. The comments place the doctrine in the context of current research on extraterritorial effects and efforts to balance interests at stake and define the scope of unilateral measures in international law. They discuss the implications of Common Concern of Humankind on sovereignty of states and how the doctrine supports the idea of cooperative or shared sovereignty. They discuss jurisdiction in the context of multilevel governance and the 'five-storey house' and show that extraterritorial effects are necessarily inherent. Finally, they address the duty to act and support the idea that this amounts to the most important aspect of an emerging principle of Common Concern of Humankind. The comments are encouraging and by and large support the findings of the chapters in this volume.

10.1   Cedric Ryngaert

Professor Cottier writes in his paper 'Think Globally, Act Locally' regarding common concerns, conveying that acting locally does not mean a state only regulates conduct within its borders. The state could extend its laws extraterritorially in order to protect global or even local (although foreign) concerns. At Utrecht University, I have headed a related project over the last five years, called UNIJURIS, an acronym which stands for unilateral jurisdiction and global values.[1] The project took a public international law perspective and was specifically focused on issues of extraterritoriality. I was the principal investigator, and seven PhD researchers were affiliated with the project.

The empirical starting point of the research was that in various fields of the law, states and the European Union (EU) have unilaterally extended the reach of their law (i.e. their 'jurisdiction') to address what looks like global governance challenges. What may immediately come to mind is the decision of the Court of Justice of the EU in *ATAA* (December 2011),[2] in which the Court validated the long arm of the amended EU Aviation Directive as compatible with international law, the territoriality principle under customary international law in particular. The Directive required all airlines whose flights departed from or landed in the EU to surrender allowances for the EU Emission Trading Scheme, in respect of all air miles, also outside EU airspace.[3] In an article which I published at the time together with Geert De Baere, we argued that the jurisdictional ground on which this decision rests is a weak version of territoriality, combined with the *nature* of the governance challenges at issue, namely the global governance challenge of climate change.[4] Because this challenge is insufficiently addressed multilaterally, states, or the EU, may act unilaterally.[5] Similar common concern-based dynamics are at play in other areas.

In this contribution, I first give a brief overview of such dynamics in the field of (1) oceans governance; (2) corporate human rights accountability and (3) cyberspace. I go on to argue that unilateral assertions to protect common concerns in these fields may be informed by parochial

---

[1] http://unijuris.sites.uu.nl (accessed 20 Sept. 2019).

[2] Court of Justice of the EU, Grand Chamber, Judgment of 21 Dec. 2011, ECLI:EU: C:2011:864, Case C-366/10, reference for a preliminary ruling under Art. 267 TFEU from the High Court of Justice of England and Wales, Queen's Bench Division (Administrative Court), *Air Transport Association of America et al.* v. *Secretary of State for Energy and Climate Change*.

[3] Directive 2008/101/EC of the European Parliament and of the Council of 19 Nov. 2008 amending Directive 2003/87/EC so as to include aviation activities in the scheme for greenhouse gas emission allowance trading within the Community (Text with EEA relevance), OJ L 8, 13.1.2009, pp. 3–21.

[4] G. De Baere and C. Ryngaert, 'The ECJ's Judgment in *Air Transport Association of America* and the International Legal Context of the EU's Climate Change Policy', *European Foreign Affairs Review*, 18(3) (2013), 389–410.

[5] N. Dobson, *Extraterritorial Climate Protection Under International Law: A Jurisdictional Analysis of EU Unilateralism*, Utrecht University, 2018.

EXTRATERRITORIALITY AND COMMON CONCERN   449

considerations, but that this need not detract from its cosmopolitan purposes and consequences (4). I conclude with formulating a number of legitimating principles that may render jurisdictional unilateralism 'reasonable' (5).

10.1.1 Port State Jurisdiction

The project studied two major oceans governance challenges: overfishing and vessel-source marine pollution. The relevant question here was whether *port states* (i.e. states where ocean-going vessels call or dock) could play a role in combating illegal, unsustainable, and unreported fishing, and marine pollution activities. We concluded that port states can rely on a vessel's territorial presence to regulate that vessel's activities on the high seas (i.e. an area beyond a state's national jurisdiction), and enforce those regulations. We should bear in mind in this respect that vessels do not have the right of entry, and that entry could thus be denied to non-compliant vessels, with the attendant deterrent consequences. If these vessels do enter, their extraterritorial activities could be captured by territorial(-ized) offences, such as having prohibited fishing gear (e.g. driftnets), or having inaccurate oil book records in port. These are however just the overlying offences. The underlying offences are extraterritorial, and amount to 'common concern violations'.[6] Thus, what is happening in reality may be a form of extraterritorial jurisdiction by bystander states with a view to protecting common concerns.

10.1.2 Corporate Accountability and Human Rights

Jurisdictional questions with respect to the accountability of multinational corporations have recently gained in prominence, as victims of human rights and environmental abuses committed by corporations (or their representatives) have brought tort cases against multinational

---

[6] See on port state jurisdiction, C. M. J. Ryngaert and H. Ringbom, 'Port State Jurisdiction: Challenges and Potential', *International Journal of Marine and Coastal Law*, 31(3) (2016), 379–94; N. Coelho, 'Unilateral Port State Jurisdiction: The Quest for Universality in the Prevention, Reduction and Control of Ship-Source Pollution', PhD (Utrecht University, 2019), 346–66. https://dspace.library.uu.nl/handle/1874/377339 (accessed 12 Nov. 2020); A. Honniball, 'Extraterritorial Port State Measures: The Basis and Limits of Unilateral Port State Jurisdiction to Combat Illegal, Unreported and Unregulated Fishing', PhD (Utrecht University, 2019), 338–42. https://dspace.library.uu.nl/handle/1874/375223 (accessed 12 Nov. 2020).

corporations in their home states, and sometimes in other states, in respect of what are in essence violations of common concerns (human rights, environmental interests).[7] This triggers the question whether these states have jurisdiction to entertain these claims.[8] At first sight, these states appear to be exercising extraterritorial jurisdiction in that the relevant abuse took place outside the territory. As such, however, the exercise of jurisdiction over parent corporations is not controversial as it is based on the domicile principle under private international law.[9] The domicile principle does however not confer jurisdiction on bystander states regarding non-domiciled corporations (e.g. a parent's foreign subsidiary which may have actually committed the wrong). There is in all likelihood no such thing as universal civil jurisdiction.[10] However, there are legal techniques in private international law that could be productively relied on to extraterritorially pursue common concerns in such situations (e.g. the connected claims doctrine),[11] or the doctrine of forum of necessity which offers an exceptional bystander state forum if the claimant faces a denial of justice elsewhere.[12] Again, what may be happening here is bystander states exercising extraterritorial jurisdiction to protect common concerns.

10.1.3   Regulation of Cyberspace

The challenges described so far are characterized by a tension between the classic territoriality of state regulation and enforcement on the one hand, and the transnational character of the governance challenges at issue. How can the state, as a territorially bounded community, address problems that are essentially transboundary? This question is brought into even starker relief when we consider the challenges posed by digital

---

[7] For example, *A. F. Akpan v. Royal Dutch Shell, plc, E. Dooh v. Royal Dutch Shell, plc, F. A. Oguru v. Royal Dutch Shell plc*, Court of Appeal of The Hague (18 Dec. 2015).

[8] L. Roorda, *Jurisdiction in Business and Human Rights Cases: Towards an Effective Right to Remedy*, forthcoming Utrecht University, 2019.

[9] Arts. 4 and 63 Regulation (EU) No. 1215/2012 of the European Parliament and of the Council of 12 Dec. 2012 on jurisdiction and the recognition and enforcement of judgments in civil and commercial matters (recast), OJ L 351/1 (2012).

[10] A. G. Jain, 'Universal Civil Jurisdiction in International Law', *Indian Journal of International Law*, 55(2) (2015), 209.

[11] As relied on in the Dutch *Akpan* case, *supra* n. 7.

[12] Note that in *Naït-Liman v. Switzerland*, the European Court of Human Rights held that there is no international obligation to offer such a forum (Case of *Naït-Liman v. Switzerland*, Application No. 51357/07, Judgment of 15 Mar. 2018).

EXTRATERRITORIALITY AND COMMON CONCERN 451

data-gathering and cybercrime. In the digital world, it may seem that there are no territorial borders at all anymore. Data are moved instantaneously from one place to another on the globe with the click of a mouse. Confronted with such a deterritorialized phenomenon, the question arises whether states can still (unilaterally) regulate it?[13] These issues are obviously quite pertinent these days, in light of the ubiquity of the Internet and the threats to privacy posed by commercial and governmental data-gathering practices. States and the EU have not hesitated to regulate unilaterally. The EU has recently enacted a General Data Protection Regulation, which also applies to non-EU-based companies offering their (electronic) services to EU citizens.[14] The USA, for its part, has enacted legislation to enable its law-enforcement agencies to obtain, from Internet intermediaries, information stored on servers outside the USA.[15]

10.1.4 Cosmopolitanism and Parochialism

Jurisdictional assertions in some of the fields discussed above may, at first sight at least, be aimed at protecting parochial concerns rather than common concerns. This applies in particular to unilateralism in the field of cyberspace regulation. Such action protects the state's *own citizens* against privacy violations or against crime, and does not strongly relate to a global common concern. However, such parochialism may go hand in hand with a push for universality (i.e. for local concerns to become a common concern). For instance, the EU's 'territorial extension' of the EU fundamental right to data protection may in due course lead to such right being recognized as a universal human right (i.e. a common concern).[16]

---

[13] See generally on the role of the state in Internet governance, Uta Kohl (ed.), *The Net and the State* (Cambridge: Cambridge University Press, 2017).

[14] Art. 3 Regulation (EU) 2016/679 of the European Parliament and of the Council of 27 Apr. 2016 on the protection of natural persons with regard to the processing of personal data and on the free movement of such data, and repealing Directive 95/46/EC (General Data Protection Regulation).

[15] Clarifying Lawful Overseas Use of Data Act or CLOUD Act (HR 4943) (2018). See on extraterritorial enforcement jurisdiction in cyberspace, Mark Zoetekouw, 'Extraterritorial Jurisdiction on the Internet: The Criminals Have Crossed the Border – Will Law-Enforcement Follow?', Utrecht University, 2019.

[16] See also M. Taylor, *Transatlantic Jurisdictional Conflicts in Data Protection Law How the Fundamental Right to Data Protection Conditions the European Union's Exercise of Extraterritorial Jurisdiction*, Utrecht University, 2018.

At the same time, jurisdictional assertions that are, at first sight, aimed at realizing common concerns may on closer inspection be informed by rather self-centred political and economic considerations. Regulation and enforcement is often not just aimed at 'saving the world', but also at levelling the playing field for a state's own corporations, a playing field which has been distorted as a result of lax foreign regulation (e.g. in the field of the environment, fisheries, corruption, or human rights). This self-interest is also borne out in enforcement practices. States tend to enforce regulations nominally serving the global interest if there is something in it for them too: law-enforcement resources are limited after all.[17] That regulation and enforcement practices protecting common concerns are partly informed by parochial considerations need however not undermine their legitimacy, as long as they are not protectionist in nature. Protectionist abuses could occur when states stop imported goods at the border, citing concerns over 'human rights abuses' committed in the supply chain, while in reality protecting the state's own industry from foreign competition.

10.1.5 Reasonable Extraterritoriality

The main question animating the project was whether jurisdictional assertions pursuing global values and common concerns were in keeping with public international law, as well as whether the foundations of the law of jurisdiction were shifting. Does the law of jurisdiction more readily accommodate states' wishes to unilaterally address common concerns, global governance challenges, or transnational problems?

The conclusion of the project is that by and large, states continue to rely on territoriality or other classic principles of jurisdiction to address global governance problems and transnational threats. Globalization has, at first sight, not undermined the jurisdictional relevance of territoriality. At the same time, however, territoriality has been pushed almost to breaking point. Territoriality seems to be such a capacious concept that 'anything may go'. This begs the question whether it can still have analytical purchase: can it serve its role as a delimiter of regulatory spheres?

---

[17] See regarding the (non-)exercise of universal jurisdiction, C. Ryngaert, 'Cosmopolitan Jurisdiction and the National Interest', in S. Allen, D. Costelloe, M. Fitzmaurice, P. Gragl, and E. Guntrip (eds.), *Oxford Handbook of Jurisdiction in International Law* (Oxford: Oxford University Press, 2019), 218–21.

Recently, Dan Svantesson, who mostly writes on cyber issues, has suggested to simply do away with territoriality, as it does no longer mean anything.[18] Our project does not go that far. Arguably, territoriality still serves as a restraining factor, in that it eliminates entirely unconnected states from the circle of regulators. Still, it is true that transnational challenges will have connections with multiple states. To bring some order in the chaos that may ensue, second-order jurisdictional principles may be necessary.

In my previous work, I have suggested 'reasonableness' as the overarching concept of jurisdictional restraint.[19] Reasonableness also informs the various case studies of the UNIJURIS project. Depending on the issue area, reasonableness may take on different guises. However, some basic principles can be listed that may apply across the board, and may boost the reasonableness of unilateral jurisdictional assertions. They mitigate the imperial overtones of cosmopolitan extraterritoriality, and legitimize unilateral assertions serving global values and common concerns.

The first principle pertains to the international proscription of, or at least the international concern regarding a specific challenge. This implies that if a problem has been considered as of international concern, and in particular if conventions have been adopted to address that concern, the lawfulness of unilateral action is enhanced. Sometimes there may even be a duty to exercise jurisdiction.[20]

The second principle is democratic legitimacy and participation. This is an issue which Eyal Benvenisti in his Global Trust project at Tel Aviv has looked at in particular.[21] It should be conceded that unilateralism with extraterritorial effects may be inherently undemocratic. Therefore, one may have to inquire whether unilateral jurisdictional assertions are sufficiently 'other-regarding', in the sense of factoring third-country interests affected by such unilateralism.

---

[18] D. J. B. Svantesson, 'A New Jurisprudential Framework for Jurisdiction: Beyond the Harvard Draft', *AJIL Unbound*, 109 (2015), 69–74.

[19] C. Ryngaert, *Jurisdiction in International Law* (2nd ed., Oxford: Oxford University Press, 2015), ch. 5.

[20] For example, Art. 11 of the Agreement on Port State Measures to Prevent, Deter and Eliminate Illegal, Unreported and Unregulated Fishing (2016) (requiring port state denial of entry to visiting foreign vessels suspected of IUU fishing); Art. 5.2 UN Torture Convention (requiring states to exercise *aut dedere aut judicare* based jurisdiction if a presumed torturer is present on its territory).

[21] http://globaltrust.tau.ac.il/ (accessed 20 Sept. 2019).

A third principle is the principle of equivalence. Arguably, states and the EU should only exercise unilateral jurisdiction if the value or issue in question is not adequately protected by foreign or international regulation and action. This means that they should defer to foreign or international norms which provide equivalent, although perhaps non-identical protection. Such deference prevents foreign operators from becoming overburdened with multiple layers of slightly different regulation.

Fourth, we should bear in mind that foreign states may find themselves at a lower level of economic development and may not be able to meet stringent Western standards imposed via unilateral jurisdiction. To enable these states and their operators to actually comply, in line with the principle of common but differentiated principles, richer states may be under an obligation to provide technical or financial assistance to poor states.

What extralegal factors influence the adoption of extraterritorial regulation, and how enforcement priorities are set, are important fields for future research on actual practices of protecting global values and common concerns. As far as enforcement practices are concerned, the relevant question is whether, assuming there is a jurisdictional grant, states also *act* on it. For instance, in what cases do they enforce global anti-corruption norms; what social dynamics inform enforcement strategies?[22] This empirical question is an important one, as in terms of international legality, many unilateral assertions are presumptively valid, within certain bounds of course.[23] An important challenge then is to move from the law on the books to the law in action. Such research requires that legal methods be combined with social science techniques.[24]

10.2 Claus Zimmermann

The serious research undertaken around the emerging doctrine of Common Concern of Humankind reflects that countries worldwide, in light of our joint responsibility towards future generations, share a number of serious problems, preoccupations and challenges that countries cannot, at least not most of the time, solve on their own.

---

[22] F. Haijer, *Minding Their Own Business: Enforcement of Anti-Foreign Corruption in the Netherlands and the USA* (Utrecht University, forthcoming 2019).

[23] See regarding corruption, K. Davis, *Regulation of Transnational Bribery: Between Impunity and Imperialism* (Oxford: Oxford University Press, forthcoming 2019).

[24] G. Shaffer and T. Ginsburg, 'The Empirical Turn in International Legal Scholarship', *American Journal of International Law*, 106 (1) (2012), 1–46.

EXTRATERRITORIALITY AND COMMON CONCERN 455

There is no denying that finding effective solutions to shared, or common, concerns depend upon the degree to which the international community, through enhanced international cooperation and effective enforcement will be able to find ways towards identifying appropriate responses to the many sizeable challenges at hand.

In an ideal world, countries worldwide would organize a major multilateral conference, to do three things: first, reach agreement, with proper involvement of civil society, as to which perceived problems or challenges are properly to be viewed as 'common concerns of humankind'; second, revise and expand the multilateral treaty framework to spell out what exactly the international community should do to address these shared concerns; and, third, set up the proper institutional framework to monitor and ensure compliance.

It is obvious, that this is a sizeable challenge and that, in reality, progress will have to be made in an incremental manner, along much less ambitious, second-best, options.

It seems safe to say that the key prerequisite for making progress towards addressing common concerns of humankind is to make state leaders and the populations electing them to public office realize that there is indeed no inherent conflict between the principle of common concerns of humankind, on the one side, and national sovereignty and self-determination, on the other.

I could not agree more with how Professor Cottier put it in his contribution: sovereignty cannot, at least not today, be reduced to self-determination and independence. The concept of sovereignty has indeed always been deeply rooted in safeguarding peace, order, and prosperity, in accordance with ultimate goals of international law. And in light of contemporary challenges, such as global climate change and the increasing integration of financial markets, these goals can best or exclusively be achieved by means of international cooperation. Cooperative, or shared, sovereignty is therefore indeed the only realistic option at hand.

The contemporary mainstream view of states being instruments at the service of their peoples as true holders of sovereignty may be regarded as a corollary of the fundamental idea of popular sovereignty or sovereignty of the people. As was first explained by Samantha Besson, this form of sovereignty triggers duties of cooperation, on the part of the entities which cannot ensure the protection of all the values they should protect, or, translated into the concept we are discussing here, which cannot ensure that the common concerns of humankind are properly addressed.

This duty to cooperate in addressing the common concerns of humankind must be strictly framed by the principle of subsidiarity. Respecting the principle of subsidiarity is fundamental to ensure that the regulatory decisions that are needed to address common concerns are taken at a decision-making level not more distant than absolutely necessary from the people to whom those in power are ultimately responsible.

Professor Cottier rightly framed this as 'responsibilities at home', explaining that Common Concern primarily entails responsibilities to act within a given jurisdiction. States are not only entitled to, but also obliged, to address Common Concerns as defined by the international community within their own boundaries.

While it is of course of vital importance that everyone does their own homework, the principle of Common Concern of Humankind indeed has the potential to shake the balance and equation of extraterritorial application of domestic law.

As discussed in the various contributions to this workshop, this emerging principle rightly questions the existing system of international sanctions considering that the Security Council of the United Nations is not properly equipped and authorized to address most of the pressing common concerns of humankind.

It indeed appears vital to find new modes within the UN system and in other international organizations. I agree that the general exception provisions of the WTO treaty framework and the introduction of WTO-compliant labels linked to certain production methods provide some limited margin of manoeuvre to address common concerns of humankind already under the existing treaty framework. This said, however, one should be very careful not to provoke the explosion of the WTO legal framework by stretching too far what the WTO treaties were meant to achieve. A proper renegotiation of the treaty framework certainly appears to be the only real long-term solution.

In the meantime, and in parallel, unilateral countermeasures by big countries with large markets addressing common concerns of humankind remain an option but one that should be treated with utter care.

From a conceptual point of view, there is no doubt that rights and obligations relating to common concerns go beyond the traditional precepts of territoriality. It is equally plausible to say that the principle of Common Concern of Humankind may be understood as providing a certain degree of authorization, or even obligation, for a state to take action in relation to facts relating to a common concern produced outside the proper jurisdiction of the state.

Thus, governments may indeed take the view that they are authorized, and even obliged, to take appropriate action against highly polluting means of production bluntly ignoring the common concern of global warming by means of adopting appropriate production and process standards. Likewise, governments are authorized to take action in response to blatant and systematic neglect of the common concern of preserving the essence of fundamental human rights and combating systematic violations thereof.

The crucial point is not whether a foreign measure negatively affects persons and resources within a given jurisdiction, but whether it affects the attainment of the solution to what amounts to a common concern of humankind. But the theoretical possibility of unilateral actions should not serve as a false excuse for delaying the urgent need to revise the global treaty framework.

Ideally, unilateral actions to address common concerns of humankind would be taken only once the international treaty framework has been revised. It then indeed becomes a realistic, and a much more appealing option to have large markets with bargaining power shoulder a larger burden of the international community's shared responsibility to address common concerns of humankind. Countries with large markets and rich economies are indeed in a better position, in purely practical terms, to take action and exert focused pressure on others to comply.

Ideally, such measures would not be imposed purely unilaterally, but as a means of collective enforcement, upon explicit authorization from the broader international community. Unless in absolutely exceptional situations, we certainly would not want to move towards a situation in which countries unilaterally decide that they need to raise trade barriers to address common concerns akin to what the United States currently does in the name of 'national security' under section 232 investigations.

Enforcement of international law may indeed not be left to powerful markets and actors, such as the EU, the United States, and China even if these actors are subject to the rule of law and to the principle of proportionality in shaping countermeasures. Shortcuts to strengthening the competent international organizations must remain an absolute exception.

In the meantime, I am convinced that, in particular as concerns large countries or markets, there is much room for fostering the promotion of common concerns of humankind even within the traditional view that extraterritorial action can be defended only if the nexus to the own territory is sufficient – precisely if and when the territory is large and the problems are blatant.

As pointed out by Dr Lupo-Pasini in his presentation, international finance law is one domain where there are various notable examples of extraterritoriality, especially in the regulation of securities and clearing houses. The European Market Infrastructure Regulation is indeed an insightful example as it illustrates that much can be achieved already under a traditional approach to extraterritoriality. Thus, when two non-EU parties enter into a derivative contract that has a direct, substantial, and foreseeable effect within the EU, the transaction is considered as if it is operated by local firms and therefore subject to EU law. The only challenge that then remains is to ensure that the domestic laws having extraterritorial effects, are apt to address the common concerns at issue, here, financial stability.

Overall, considering the daunting nature of many of the potential common concerns of humankind, it appears vital to me that the international community progresses on various levels and at different speeds towards addressing these concerns:

- First, by better addressing common concerns of humankind on the domestic level, not shying away from justifiable and justified extraterritorial effects of the domestic measures.
- Second, by making better use of the existing treaty framework, notably at the WTO and the UN Security Council.
- And, third, in a long-term perspective, by aiming to achieve the much-needed reforms of the multilateral treaty framework, by ensuring that countries are subject to the right hard rules serving to address common concerns of humankind, combined with proper mechanisms for monitoring and effective enforcement.

10.3   Krista Nadakavukaren Schefer

Thank you very much. Extraterritoriality is a topic that has long been of interest to me. Although I haven't been working on it very recently, there are some thoughts that I would like to share. In relation to extraterritoriality, there are two additional issues that I think have come up throughout the conference, which are equally important. Those would be unilateralism and the positive duties. And to me, these three things go together.

Extraterritoriality to me is similar to what Gabrielle Marceau said this morning – extraterritoriality exists and it does not seem to be a big problem when it comes down into the case law. It is sort of a fact, as she said, and I agree. What becomes interesting is, if I start to think about the Common Concern project with the 'five-storey house' idea,[25] how does extraterritoriality fit there? When you talk about acting locally, for example, may local governments or local organizations also act extraterritorially in the same way as on the national level? I think that is an interesting question. How are you going to define extraterritorial concepts within a federacy or within the EU? And, if so, at what levels is that going to be allowed? Are we going to look at extraterritorial as any effect beyond the immediate jurisdiction of the unit you are talking about? I think there you can take up some interesting theoretical ideas, but in terms of the extraterritoriality of state action, litigation, and enforcement properly speaking, I do not see this as problematic. I see it actually as inherent in the concept of common concern and that it is absolutely necessary to have this extraterritorial aspect if you want to have common concerns really addressed effectively.

That brings me to the issue of unilateralism. Do you want this extraterritoriality to be exercised unilaterally, regionally, or multilaterally? As Michael Hahn mentioned, when you have an extraterritorial action that is exercised by a group of states, you do not usually talk about extraterritorial impact. It is only if it is unilateral that you seem to care about extraterritorial issues. I think it is a difficult issue on a normative level to say in our international system that we want to allow for unilateralism. Because we are coming from a UN community angle. To what extent should a single state be able to be the representative of the international community to foster a community ideal? My particular position on this is that unilateralism in and of itself is not the problem if it is unilateral action; unilateralism is a problem if it is a unilateral goal that a unilateral actor is trying to promote, a goal purely in the interest of a particular country. If it is a common concern, I again do not have problems with unilateral action. I believe in the need for leadership, a kicker off of the ball, which might be required to get others to follow. This, of course, does have some implications in terms of who is going to be the kicker. It is usually going to take a bigger country to really generate the after effects of what you are intending to achieve. However, I do not think that unilateralism is a problem in and of itself if it is for an established and recognized common concern.

---

[25] T. Cottier, 'Towards a Five Storey House', in Christian Joerges and Ernst-Ulrich Petersmann (eds.), *Constitutionalism, Multilevel Governance and International Economic Law* (Oxford: Hart, 2011). See also Chapter 1 in this volume, pp. 49–50.

And, finally, the most interesting angle of common concern for me is the aspect of a positive duty to act. To what extent do we want to say you have an actual positive duty to do something? I think this again is absolutely critical for the success of the project of addressing common concerns and promoting common goals. Because if you do not have these duties, states are left with the *right* to act, and the right, I think, is something that is generally not used. It is unused because governments do not want to spend the resources to exercise that right: it costs something to promote a common goal, especially if you're the only one acting. If you are the only one acting, moreover, you might be at a competitive disadvantage. But a positive duty to act makes a state have to pursue this common concern even if it does not want to pursue it on cost grounds. We know from the experience in humanitarian interventions that the right to act is not sufficient and further steps, as outlined in R2P, are necessary. That is the critical element. It is the positive duty to act in the context of common concern which makes the difference. But you also need to figure out how you are going to enforce the positive aspect of it. And that is what is really hard because even if you have the possibility legally to do it, how are you going to make countries actually act on this and how are you going to enforce that if they do not act?

These are some of my thoughts. Thank you!

INDEX

Agreement on Subsidies and
  Countervailing Measures
  (ASCM), 134
benefit, conferment of
  Alternative benchmark, *137*
  New market argument, *137*
  Traditional outcome, *136*
export contingency, *de jure* or de
  facto, 140
GATT Article XX, relationship with,
  142
illustrative list, 138
  safe-haven clause, *138*
non-actionable subsidies,
  resumption of, 142
Arrangement on Officially Supported
  Export Credits, 135, 138–9
Commercial Interest Reference Rate
  (CIRR), 138
ATAA case, 10, 448

Barcelona Traction dispute, 354
Basel Committee on Banking
  Supervision: *see* Transnational
  Regulatory Networks, Basel
  Committee
Berne Initiative, 305
Bodansky, Daniel, 285, 354, 357
Brown Weiss, Edith, 19, 32–3
Brundtland Report, 17, 28
Brunnée, Jutta, 18–19, 223–4

Canada–Renewable Energy dispute,
  104, 128, 136, 141
carbon pricing, 118
  revenue recycling, 120
  tax vs. tariff approach, 119

Central Bank
  definition, by Proctor, 371
  exchange control, 378
  foreign reserve assets, management
    of, 379
  issuance of money, role of, 373
  monetary policy, conduct of, 374
    common good, pursuance of,
      374
    price stability goal, *374*
    unconventional policy
      instruments, *376*
  relation with government
    Lastra, Rosa M., 371
central banks, cooperation among
  global financial crisis, cooperation in
    response, 365–6
  obstacles, *367*
  Gopinath, Gita, 368
  key interest rates, setting of, 366
    Zimmermann, Claus D., *366*
China, market economy, 242
Climate Change Litigation Database, 81
coercive economic measures, use of
  political cheapness, 252
  Posner, Eric A., 254
  practice examples
    European Union, *253–4*
    United States, *253–4*
Common but Differentiated
  Responsibility, 62, 115, 132
Common Concern of Humankind,
  meaning of
  adverse effects, focus on, 38, 223
  basis
    community interests, *33–5*
    equity, *31–2*

461

462 INDEX

Common Concern of Humankind,
meaning of (cont.)
  peace and security, preservation
    of. see peace and security,
    meaning of
  public trust, 32–3
  etymological interpretation, 37–8
  exclusive sovereignty, challenge to, 436
  global financial stability, in the area
    of, 414
  human rights violations, in the area
    of, 281–2
  international monetary stability, in
    the area of, 359, 367
  jus cogens, relationship to: *see jus*
    cogens
  low-carbon technology diffusion, in
    the area of, 108
  migration, in the area of, 319–20
  multilevel governance, relationship
    to: *see* multilevel governance
  permanent sovereignty, relationship
    to, 58
  political choice, role of, 435
  responsibility to protect, relationship to:
    see Responsibility to Protect (R2P)
  soft general principle, 438
  threshold, threat to peace. *see* peace
    and security
    emergency, potential threshold
      function, 432
    seriousness, potential threshold
      function, 444
    severity, potential threshold
      function, 433
Common Concern of Humankind,
    the doctrine of
  claims and responses, 27–9, 42, 357,
    436, 440
  migration, in the area of, 317
  duty to act, 73
    accountability, role of, 77
    challenges, 76
    necessity, role of, 76
    proportionality, role of, 77–8
    R2P, relation with: see
      Responsibility to Protect (R2P)
    right to act, distinction with, 73, 76

duty to cooperate, 60–1, 279
  global financial stability, in the
    area of, 419
  human rights, in the area of, 286–7
  international monetary stability,
    cooperation bottom-up, 368
  international monetary stability,
    cooperation top-down, 367
  low-carbon technology, in the area
    of, 145
  marine plastic pollution, in the
    area of, 188
  migration, in the area of, 320, 323
homework obligation, 63, 280
  central banks, enhanced mandate
    of, 380
  domestic monetary stability, role
    of central banks, 369
  global financial stability, in the
    area of, 421
  human rights, in the area of, 288
  low-carbon technology, in the area
    of, 147
  marine plastic pollution, in the
    area of, 189
  migration, in the area of, 321
  monetary policy, controlling
    negative externalities, 390
public goods, relationship to,
    44–6
securing compliance, 70, 280
  human rights, in the area of, 288
  low-carbon technology, in the area
    of, 149
  marine plastic pollution, in the
    area of, 193
  migration, in the area of, 321
  monetary affairs, obligation to act,
    396
Common Heritage of Mankind, 12, 17,
    52–3
  common concern, difference with,
    18, 25, 53
Comprehensive Economic and Trade
    Agreement (CETA)
  labour movement, 299
Convention on Biological Diversity
    (CBD), 6, 15, 167

INDEX

Convention Relating to the Status of
Refugees, 297
Cottier, Thomas
Common Concern, as emerging
principle, 19
R2P, relation with: *see*
Responsibility to Protect (R2P)
WTO law, relation with, *20*
five-storey house: *see* multilevel
governance
Court of Justice of the EU, 10, 377, 448

Declaration of Ethical Principles in
relation to Climate Change, 14
Doha Ministerial Declaration, 102
domestic monetary stability, 370
Lastra, Rosa M., 370
Draft Articles on Responsibility of States
for Internationally Wrongful
Acts (ARSIWA), 71, 194
third-party countermeasures, validity
of, 258
Dublin system, 297

East Timor case, 435
economic globalization, unbundling of
Baldwin, Richard, 205–7, 209, 211
Davis, Gerald F., 207
global value chains, 207–9
equity, role of, 162
erga omnes, 19, 22, 71, 251, 354
estoppel, doctrine of, 64
Export Credit Agency (ECA), 133
export credit support, 133–4
extraterritorial effect
indirect extraterritoriality, 65–8
monetary policy: *see* monetary
policy, international spillover
effects
international finance law, examples
from, 422–3
US financial measures, 412
exorbitant privilege, *412*

financial stability, 403
as public good: *see* public goods
Schinasi, Garry, 403
global financial stability, 410

global systemic risk, 410
inefficiencies, *413*
responses, *413*
regulatory passporting, 420
financial system, 403
dispute settlement system, need for,
425
global financial system
compliance enforcement, absence
of, *424*
inherent asymmetry, *410*
transformations, *406*
instability, 404
national financial policy, selfish
aspect, 411
network structure, 404
systemic risk, 405
Fisheries Jurisdiction case, 60
floating exchange rates, 378
French, Duncan, 21
Friedmann, Wolfgang, 59

Gauweiler case, 377
General Agreement on Tariffs and
Trade (GATT), 7
discrimination analysis, legal
standard of, 126
Common Concern doctrine,
influence of, *127*
general exceptions
chapeau test, regarding carbon
pricing, *131*
chapeau test, regarding human
rights sanctions, *273*
Common Concern, influence of,
66
differentiated responsibility,
relevance of, *132*
difficulty to satisfy, *184*
exhaustibility, of climate, *129*
necessity test, regarding carbon
pricing, *130*
necessity test, regarding human
rights sanctions, *271–3*
public moral, meaning of, *267–8*
public moral, applicability of, *266*
sufficient nexus, requirement of,
72

464 INDEX

General Agreement on Tariffs and
Trade (GATT) (cont.)
likeness, test of, 123–4
Common Concern doctrine,
influence of, *124–5*
security exception: *see* human rights
economic sanction
Global Compact for Safe, Orderly and
Regular Migration (GCM), 302,
311–13
challenges, 313
international economic law, creating
linkage with, 340
global financial crisis, 352, 362, 364,
382, 407
monetary policy response, 383–4
Global Forum on Migration and
Development (GFMD), 301–2, 312
global public goods: *see* public goods

Horn, Laura, 19
human rights economic sanction
GATT security exception
ambit, *275*
applicability, *274*
Russia – Transit, Panel report:
see Russia – Traffic in Transit
market access restrictions
trade in goods, *262–3*
trade in services, *264*
human rights economic sanction,
validity of
state immunity
central banks, *260*
scope of rules, *260*
state responsibility rules: *see* Draft
Articles on Responsibility of
States
UN Charter, coverage under: *see* UN
Charter, Article 2(4)
human rights, enforcement deficiency
consent requirement, 250
duty to report, 250
infrequent disputes, 250
paradox of promises, 248
reciprocity, lack of, 249
treaty ratification, causality with,
248–9

inequality, vertical and horizontal, 236
effect, 236–8
Intergovernmental Panel on Climate
Change (IPCC), 99
International Court of Justice (ICJ),
8, 60
International Covenant on Civil and
Political Rights (ICCPR), 298
International Covenant on Economic,
Social and Cultural Rights
(ICESCR), 298
International Finance Discussion
Papers (IFDP), 384
international labour standards,
relevance for migrants, 298
Convention No. 143, 299
Convention No. 97, 298
International Law Association (ILA),
105
International Law Commission (ILC),
21, 24
Conservative mandate, 23
Murase, Shinya: *see* Murase, Shinya
International Monetary Fund (IMF)
Articles of Agreement, 350
capital flow regulation, *364*
current international transactions,
364
global financial safety net, *365*
sanctions for breach, *393*
second amendment, *360*
capital flow, management of, 388
Zimmermann, Claus D., *388*
Code of Conduct, obligations under
domestic and external policies,
363, 392
exchange rate stability, *362*
obligation to collaborate, *391*
Integrated Surveillance decision, *393*
soft-law approach, 361, 392
International Monetary System (IMS),
348
core elements, 348
exchange rate regulation, *362*
international payment and capital
flow regulation, *363*
monetary reserve management,
364

INDEX

global public goods, as: *see* global
    public goods
international monetary
    stability, 348
monetary sovereignty, linkage
    with, *351*
International Organization for
    Migration (IOM), 302, 306
International Treaty on Plant Genetic
    Resources for Food and
    Agriculture (ITPGRFA), 6, 15

jurisdiction, basis for assertion, 451
reasonableness, as restraint, 453
territoriality, 452
    extended notion, *451–2*
jus cogens, 16, 18, 20, 35, 53–4, 71, 251,
    295, 297

Kyoto Protocol, 4

low-carbon technology, 96

marine pollution
pollution by plastics
    impact, *156, 158*
    scale, *155*
response
    market-based instruments (MBIs),
    182
    UNCLOS: *see* UN Convention on
    the Law of the Sea
sources, per UNCLOS, 173
market failure, 108, 162
migration
facts, 293
international economic law, role of:
    see Global Compact
international migrant,
    notion of, 294
international migration law,
    prospects of, 337
legitimate concerns, need for
    recognition
benefit, cost and complexity,
    335
migrants, *329*
residents, *333*

monetary policy
definition, 374
global financial crisis, response to:
    see global financial crisis
international spillover effects,
    381, 383
Cœuré, Benoît, *385–6*
monetary trilemma, 386
monetary sovereignty, 350
Lastra, Rosa M., 350
lex monetae, 372
'Vollgeld' referendum, 373
multilevel governance, 47–8, 356
Cottier, Thomas, 356
five-storey house, doctrine of, 49–50,
    326, 356
migration, in the area of
    cities, *326–7*
    glocalisation, *327*
    institutional coherence, *328*
Murase, Shinya, 21

Nationally Determined Contribution
    (NDC), 100
Nolte, Georg, 18, 23–4
non-reciprocity, effect of, 8

Paris Agreement, 5, 14, 27, 81, 105
Technology Framework, 112
Peace and Security, meaning of,
    35–6
as a threshold, 41, 231, 358, 443–4
determinacy, *445*
environmental problems, with
    respect to, *187*
global financial stability, in the
    area of, *417*
human rights, in the area of,
    283–5
inequality, in the area of, *231, 239,*
    242
migration, in the area of, *318–19*
Lastra, Rosa M., peace as IMF
    foundation, 358
peace, stability and welfare: *see* peace
    and security, meaning of
Piketty, Thomas, 235
plastics, history of, 154

Plato, 239
Laws, 239
Athenian Stranger, *239*
Book V, ideal society, *240*
Pringle case, 377
Process and Production Measures
(PPM), 66–8, 116, 120
non-product related, 66–7, 184
public goods, 44, 354, 440
financial stability, as, 405
global public goods, 44–5, 163, 355
international monetary system,
352
state interest, existence of, 442
Thurow, Lester, 214–15

Regional Consultative Processes on
Migration (RCPs), 301
reserve assets, 379
Responsibility to Protect (R2P), 20, 35,
42, 54, 74–5, 287, 460
Rio Declaration on Environment and
Development, 25
Russia–Traffic in Transit dispute,
274–5, 277

Scheidel, Walter, 199, 234
Schengen *acquis*, 298
Soltau, Frederiech, 19
sovereignty, classic notion
beggar-thy-neighbour policies,
304
Bodin, Jean, 55–6
Hobbes, Thomas, 56
Rousseau, Jean-Jacques, 56–7
self-regulation, effect of, 302
sovereignty, modern notion, 455
Besson, Samantha, 58, 212
cooperative sovereignty, 57, 220–1
distributive autonomy, 221
economic sovereignty: *see* Lowe,
Vaughan
Jackson, John, 58
Lowe, Vaughan, 212–13
Zimmermann, Claus D., 57
Sustainable Development, 28, 101, 106,
111
SDGs, 16, 28, 42, 168, 219, 308

Sutherland Report, 309
Swiss National Science Foundation
(SNF), 10
Swiss State Secretariat for the Economy
(SECO), 10
systemically important financial
institution (SIFI), 404

technology diffusion, 97
barriers, market-related, 113
intellectual property rights, relation
with, 114
market formation policies, need for,
114
new narrative, 115
differentiation, need for, *115*
stakeholders, *115*
tragedy of the commons, 63, 160
transnational regulatory networks,
408
Basel Committee on Banking
Supervision, 408
Basel I, *411*
Basel III and IV, *409*
Financial Stability Board, 361
OECD Financial Action Task Force,
409
Treaty on the Functioning of the
European Union (TFEU)
Article 45, movement of workers,
300
Article 49, freedom of establishment,
300
Trindade, Cançado, 18, 224–5

UN General Assembly, 29
UN Charter, 5, 9, 35, 59, 69, 190, 234,
243, 252, 256–7
Article 2(4), 28, 40, 257
coverage of economic coercion,
257
Schefer, Krista N., *257*
Article 51, 40
Article 55, expansion of, 243
Article 56, 9
UN Conference on Sustainable
Development (UNCSD), 167
UN Convention on Desertification, 15

INDEX

UN Convention on the Law of the Sea
 (UNCLOS), 17, 170–1
 duty to assist, 178
 duty to cooperate, 172, 175
 duty to protect and preserve,
 171–2
UN Environment, 18, 165, 168–9
UN Framework Convention on
 Climate Change (UNFCCC), 4,
 13–14, 102
UN General Assembly, 165, 167
 Resolution 43/53, 11
UN High Commissioner for Refugees
 (UNHCR), 297, 301–2
UNESCO Convention for the
 Safeguarding of the Intangible
 Cultural Heritage, 6, 15
UNIJURIS project, 447

US–Gasoline dispute, 103
US–Shrimp dispute, 103, 184
US–Tuna II dispute, 104

Vienna Convention on the Law of
 Treaties (VCLT), 78
Viterbo, Annamaria, 349, 387, 394

Westphalian order, 7, 29, 54, 296
World Trade Organization (WTO), 7,
 20, 101, 183
 ASCM: *see* Agreement on Subsidies
 and Countervailing Measures
 GATT: *see* General Agreement on
 Tariffs and Trade
Worldwide Interbank Financial
 Telecommunication (SWIFT),
 412

CPSIA information can be obtained
at www.ICGtesting.com
Printed in the USA
LVHW011609030821
694401LV00006B/373